Wissenschaftliche Untersuchungen
zum Neuen Testament

Herausgeber/Editor
Jörg Frey

Mitherausgeber/Associate Editors
Friedrich Avemarie · Judith Gundry-Volf
Martin Hengel · Otfried Hofius · Hans-Josef Klauck

178

Robert H. Gundry

The Old is Better

New Testament Essays in Support of Traditional
Interpretations

Mohr Siebeck

ROBERT H. GUNDRY, born 1932; 1961 PhD University of Manchester, England, with lengthy periods of research at the Universities of Basel, Switzerland, and Edinburgh, Scotland; professor emeritus of New Testament and Greek and scholar-in-residence at Westmont College, Santa Barbara, California.

ISBN 3-16-148551-3
ISSN 0512-1604 (Wissenschaftliche Untersuchungen zum Neuen Testament)

Die Deutsche Bibliothek lists this publication in the Deutsche Nationalbibliographie; detailed bibliographic data is available in the Internet at *http://dnb.ddb.de*.

The book was typeset by Verlagsservice Selignow in Berlin, printed by Gulde-Druck in Tübingen on non-aging paper and bound by Buchbinderei Spinner in Ottersweier.

Printed in Germany.

Table of Contents

Introduction

When Mohr Siebeck agreed to publish a selection of my previously published essays plus some that had not been published before, it was urged that I weave them together under a common theme. A difficult assignment, I thought, since the essays cover NT topics ranging from the biblical theological through the historical to the exegetical and from the Gospels through the Epistles to the Apocalypse. In looking over the essays, however, I detected that they all shared, more or less, the characteristic of defending traditional interpretations, usually over against new ones. Hence the subtitle, *New Testament Essays in Support of Traditional Interpretations*. These interpretations range from those in the NT itself through those in the early postapostolic church to some that have become traditional in modern study of the NT. The main title echoes the saying of Jesus recorded in Luke 5:39: "No man also having drunk old wine straightway desireth new: for he saith, *The old is better*" (KJV).

It may be thought that I support traditional interpretations because of my social location within the historic Christian faith. Well and good, but I maintain this social location because I hold that faith to be true – universally true, not just true for the confessing community to which I belong. There is room in this community, of course, for differences of interpretation so long as fundamental beliefs are not undermined. I will not try to define the line between the fundamental and the negotiable; but some of my essays, such as those that touch on questions of canon, Christology, soteriology, and resurrection, do undergird beliefs commonly accepted as of fundamental importance from the standpoint of historical theology. Readers who do not share these beliefs have their own social locations, of course. I respect those locations and hope that such readers will judge the essays herein not on the prejudicial ground of their social locations versus mine but on the ground of perceived faithfulness to the NT text. I have tried to do the same in regard to their views.

"Hermeneutic Liberty, Theological Diversity, and Historical Occasionalism in the Biblical Canon" pays homage to the Bible as a collection of documents written in and for different occasions and argues for the importance of suiting our current interpretations of the Bible to its resultant, original diversity rather than choosing a new, sleeker canon-within-the-canon or over-systematizing biblical theology at the expense of distinctive emphases found in the various parts of Scripture. Christology presents a test case.

"The Symbiosis of Theology and Genre Criticism of the Canonical Gospels" traces the history of genre criticism of the canonical Gospels, outlines the parallels between that history and developments in modern theology, and highlights the influence of the theological developments on the history and vice versa. The essay concludes that the canonical Gospels do not fit any prior literary genre very meaningfully, not even the biographical, so that the traditional titles pinned on them ever since the early Christian centuries, "The Gospel according to . . . ," suit both their uniqueness and the diversity that distinguishes them from each other. Despite the importance of the historical Jesus, moreover, the traditional Jesuses of the Gospels are theologically more important than a modernly reconstructed historical Jesus. Two addenda assess in greater detail particular examples of genre criticism (by Philip L. Shuler) and reconstruction of the historical Jesus (by N. Thomas Wright).

"The Apostolically Johannine Pre-Papian Tradition concerning the Gospels of Mark and Matthew" argues that Papias wrote ca. A.D. 110 or slightly earlier, that the elder whom Papias quotes is none other than the Apostle John, and that therefore we should accept the traditional ascriptions of Mark to John Mark and of Matthew to the Apostle Matthew and likewise accept the Petrine origin of the materials that John Mark wrote down. Talk about early tradition and the favor it deserves!

"On the Secret Gospel of Mark" takes up Helmut Koester's and John Dominic Crossan's interpretations of the Secret Gospel of Mark discovered, it is generally but not universally accepted, by Morton Smith. Both of those interpretations date the Secret Gospel of Mark earlier than canonical Mark. My analysis disputes that dating and in accordance with tradition puts canonical Mark at the start of a timeline leading to the Secret Gospel of Mark. It also offers a little noticed interpretation of the material that the Secret Gospel of Mark adds to canonical Mark, an interpretation that links up with a known development in early Alexandrian Christianity.

"Jesus' Blasphemy according to Mark 14:61b–64 and *Mishnah Sanhedrin* 7:5" harmonizes Mark's account of Jesus' Sanhedric trial with the Mishnaic rule that capital blasphemy must include a pronunciation of the tetragrammaton. It is a false appearance, I argue, that Jesus avoided pronouncing the tetragrammaton. At this point, then, the Markan and Mishnaic traditions can stand together as equally accurate and equally early.

"Matthew: Jewish-Christian or Christian-Jewish? At an Intersection of Sociology and Theology" defends the traditional view that Matthew's Gospel represents a Jewish Christianity that has broken away from Judaism over against a new view that has recently gained some popularity, viz., that Matthew's Gospel represents a Christian sect within Judaism that considered itself Judaistic, in turn was so considered by non-Christian Jews, and was thereby engaged in a struggle for dominance over Judaism.

"Salvation in Matthew" discusses various aspects of Matthean soteriology: what salvation consists in, who saves, who are saved, how and when they are saved, and the likely circumstances that prompted Matthew to write as he did concerning salvation. The discussion extends the traditional view defended in the preceding essay by saying that Matthean soteriology arose in response to non-Christian Jews' persecution of Jewish Christians that had broken away from Judaism and were therefore considered apostate.

"The Sermon on the Mount according to H. D. Betz" criticizes in detail Betz's Hermeneia commentary on the Sermon on the Mount, including the Sermon on the Plain. In that commentary he puts forward a humanistic view of Jesus' original teaching and bases this view on the novel theory that someone earlier than the evangelist Matthew composed Q by drawing on a primitive pool of Jesus' sayings, that someone then composed the Sermon on the Mount as a free-standing entity by drawing mainly on that same pool though occasionally on Q (likewise for the Sermon on the Plain), that someone substituted the Sermon on the Mount for a protosermon already contained in Q (likewise again for the Sermon on the Plain), and that without redaction Matthew incorporated into his Gospel the version of Q containing the Sermon on the Mount (likewise yet again for Luke and the Sermon on the Plain). To the contrary I argue for what by now has become a traditional view in NT studies, viz., that redaction by Matthew himself is responsible for the present shape of the Sermon on the Mount (and similarly in regard to the Sermon on the Plain in Luke's Gospel).

"Spinning the Lilies and Unraveling the Ravens: An Alternative Reading of Q 12:22b–31 and P. Oxy. 655" defends the traditional understanding that Luke 12:22b–31 and its parallel Matt 6:25–33 represent a tradition (= Q 12:22b–31) earlier than that represented in P. Oxy. 655. The opposite understanding – in favor of the Greek *Gospel of Thomas* as represented by P. Oxy. 655 – has been strongly argued by James M. Robinson and Christoph Heil. The refutation of this latter understanding includes exegeses of both Q 12:22b–31 and P. Oxy. 655.

"The Essential Physicality of Jesus' Resurrection according to the New Testament" rejects modern attempts to dematerialize the resurrection or to make it a passing accommodation to the need of eyewitnesses to see Jesus. Notwithstanding glorification, according to this essay, the NT consistently teaches that the body of Jesus that suffered death by crucifixion was raised from the dead so as to empty his tomb, that this body belongs to his very being, and that the mention in traditional creeds of "the resurrection of the flesh" corresponds to this NT teaching.

"The Inferiority of the New Perspective on Paul" criticizes E. P. Sanders' presentation of the New Perspective, as it has come to be called. In particular the essay argues against Sanders that the Apostle Paul taught staying in the new covenant by faith alone as well as getting in by faith alone, that in this respect he differed from Jewish soteriology, according to which, I argue, staying in depends not purely on works but on a mixture of works and faith, and that for Paul good works give evidence of salvation rather than contributing to it even in part. Despite a salutary emphasis for the church on the socially unitive implications of his soteriology, then, the New Perspective looks inferior to the old one.

"The Nonimputation of Christ's Righteousness" resurrects a version of the Protestant doctrine of justification older than the one that includes an imputation of Christ's righteousness to believing sinners. The latter version arrived on the scene soon enough but not at first, and the older version has careful exegesis of the relevant Pauline texts on its side.

"The Moral Frustration of Paul before His Conversion: Sexual Lusts in Romans 7:7–25" takes the original view of Saint Augustine that that passage describes the moral frustration of a non-Christian and defends an old interpretation, viz., that Paul is describing his own (though typical) experience on coming to sexual maturity and adult responsibility in Judaism.

"Style and Substance in Philippians 2:6–11" interprets the passage more in terms of an emphasis on Jesus' crucifixion as a contrast to his exaltation than in terms of an emphasis on the incarnation as such a contrast. This emphasis on the crucifixion represents an earlier tradition in the NT than would an emphasis on the incarnation.

"The Hellenization of Dominical Tradition and Christianization of Jewish Tradition in the Eschatology of 1–2 Thessalonians" defends the traditional understanding of Jesus' return as a descent all the way to earth and rejects recent attempts to make Paul teach that Jesus will descend only part of the way, turn around in midair, and take Christians back to heaven with him.

"Is John's Gospel Sectarian?" treats the Fourth Gospel as sectarian in the sense most commonly accepted by modern sociologists. Such a treatment has become traditional in Johannine studies but is now encountering some criticisms, or is at least undergoing considerable qualifications. (Sectarianism makes "mainline" and "worldly" Christians uneasy.) My essay counters those criticisms and qualifications.[1]

"How the Word in John's Prologue Pervades the Rest of the Fourth Gospel" opposes the view that Word-Christology disappears from this Gospel after 1:18. On the contrary, the enormous emphasis that then falls on Jesus' words – an emphasis using a wide vocabulary referring to them – shows that in line with the traditionally accepted unity of 1:1–21:25 (or at least 20:31) John carries the Christology throughout his Gospel.

---

[1] In large part this essay responds to a forthcoming essay by Miroslav Volf, who criticizes my earlier work on this topic but for whose abilities and work I have immense admiration. In friendly fashion he and I have discussed this topic and other matters in face-to-face conversations that at least for me have proved invaluable even when disagreements persist. Thanks to him for graciously sending me a copy of his essay prior to its publication.

"The Sense and Syntax of John 3:14–17 with Special Reference to the Use of οὕτως... ὥστε in John 3:16" examines the meaning of this locution in ancient Greek literature and concludes that in accord with its traditional meaning the Fourth Evangelist and his original audience would have understood the locution not in terms of degree (here, of God's love for the world) but in terms of an aforementioned manner (οὕτως) and a parallelistic addition (ὥστε). Thus the passage as a whole divides into a complex sentence of two main clauses or a pair of independent sentences, with the division between them occurring in the middle of John 3:16.

"Angelomorphic Christology in the Book of Revelation" argues in the first place that such a Christology crops up repeatedly in the book of Revelation, most clearly in ch. 10, and secondly that it represents an early christological tradition rather than a Christology that blossomed not till later than the NT.

"The New Jerusalem: People as Place, Not Place for People" adopts an interpretation of the city as its people rather than their place of residence just as the OT often uses place names for people rather than for geographical locations. This interpretation relates to the mutual indwelling of Christ and believers as taught in John 14–15.

These essays vary in length. Some are heavily documented, others only lightly. Without regard to length or documentation I have selected each of them according to what seems to me their value. Thus some review essays have made it into the collection, and here and there an addendum has been attached to enhance value. Never before published are the essays on hermeneutic liberty, theological diversity, and historical occasionalism and on the sectarianism of the Fourth Gospel, though the latter defends against criticism a position taken in an earlier publication. Most of the essays have undergone updating and other revision, sometimes very extensively, as in the essays on Rom 7:7–25 and the eschatology of 1–2 Thessalonians. The essay on the pre-Papian tradition represents a combination of arguments presented in my commentaries on Mark and Matthew (see below for bibliographical information) plus a new account-taking of some criticisms recently lodged against those arguments. The critique of Koester's and Crossan's treatments of the Secret Gospel of Mark likewise appeared in my commentary on Mark but, I am afraid, lies buried there in such a welter of other discussions as to have escaped the notice of even some specialists in the field. Material in the essay on Jesus' blasphemy appeared in somewhat scattered fashion in my commentary on Mark but has its true origin in a carefully concatenated paper delivered orally at an annual meeting of the SBL, and the present version contains a large amount of new material related especially to recent discussions of the same topic by Darrell Bock, Adela Yarbro Collins, and D. Moody Smith. The discussion of Matthew as Jewish-Christian or Christian-Jewish melds together previously published critiques of presentations by Anthony Saldarini and others, and the discussion of angelomorphic

Christology similarly melds together previously published and unpublished materials. The essay on salvation in Matthew includes a controversial aside on what I take to be Matthew's very uncomplimentary portrayal of the Apostle Peter. Following the defense of Jesus' resurrection as physical, and essentially so, is an addendum in which I ask Christian philosophers and scientists as well as theologians and biblical scholars who are advocating "nonreductive physicalism" what I think to be questions damaging to their view. The addendum has had no prior publication. Given the vast amount of literature recently published for and against the New Perspective on Paul, I had expected to do major revisions of the essay on that topic. But rereading the essay led me to believe that apart from some additional remarks it has retained its viability pretty much as is. The essay on the nonimputation of Christ's righteousness contains new material answering objections lodged by D. A. Carson against the original presentation. The addendum on "Abiding in the New Jerusalem" likewise contains material never published before.

Material in ch. 2 comes from *New Dimensions in New Testament Study*, ed. R. N. Longenecker and M. C. Tenney, copyright 1974 by The Zondervan Corporation, 97–114; in ch. 3 from *Mark: A Commentary on His Apology for the Cross*, copyright 1993 by Wm. B. Eerdmans, 1026–45, and from *Matthew: A Commentary on His Handbook for a Mixed Church under Persecution*, 2d ed., copyright 1994 by Wm. B. Eerdmans, 609–22, 673 n. 225; in ch. 4 from *Mark: A Commentary on His Apology for the Cross*, copyright 1993 by Wm B. Eerdmans, 603–23; in ch. 6 from *Cross Currents: Religion & Intellectual Life* 44 (1994–95): 509–11, copyright 1994–95 by The Association for Religion and Intellectual Life, and from *The Social History of the Matthean Community in Roman Syria*, ed. David Balch, copyright 1991 by Augsburg Fortress, 62–67; in ch. 7 from *SBLSP, 2000*: 402–14; in ch. 8 from *CRBR 1997* 10 (1997): 39–57; in ch. 9 from *NTS* 48 (2002): 159–80, copyright 2002 by Cambridge University Press; in ch. 10 from *Jesus of Nazareth: Lord and Christ: Essays on the Historical Jesus and New Testament Christology*, ed. J. B. Green and M. Turner, copyright 1994 by Wm. B. Eerdmans, 204–19; in ch. 11 from *Bib* 66 (1985): 1–38, copyright 1985 by The Pontifical Biblical Institute; in ch. 12 from *Justification: What's at Stake in the Current Debates?* ed. M. Husbands and D. J. Treier, copyright 2004 by InterVarsity Press, 17–45; in ch. 13 from *Pauline Studies*, ed. D. A. Hagner and M. J. Harris, copyright 1980 by Paternoster Press, 228–45; in ch. 14 from *Crossing the Boundaries*, ed. D. E. Orton and S. E. Porter, copyright 1994 by E. J. Brill, 273–93; in ch. 15 from *NTS* 33 (1987): 161–78, copyright 1987 by Cambridge University Press, in ch. 17 from *Jesus the Word according to John the Sectarian*, copyright 2001 by Wm. B. Eerdmans, 1–50; in ch. 18 from *NovT* 41 (1999): 24–39, copyright 1999 by E. J. Brill; in ch. 19 from *SBLSP, 1994*: 662–78; and in ch. 20 from *NovT* 29 (1987): 254–64, copyright 1987 by E. J. Brill. Permissions were granted for all the foregoing except for chs. 1, 7, 8,

16, and 19, for which permissions were unnecessary. Permissions included the right of revision. Translations are my own unless otherwise indicated.

The SBL Handbook of Style (ed. P. H. Alexander et al.; Peabody, Mass.: Hendrickson, 1999) has guided me in most matters of abbreviation, format, and such like though I have made sparing use of ibid. and loc. cit. and rejected as ugly the use of an em-dash to indicate a transition from one biblical chapter to another. Also, to a significant extent I have adopted the style of "open punctuation," have occasionally used ff. for an indefinite number of following pages, and to conserve space have usually omitted the subtitles of books.

Finally, my thanks to Mohr Siebeck for undertaking the publication of these essays in WUNT, and in particular to Prof. Dr. Jörg Frey, Dr. Henning Ziebritzki, and Mr. Matthias Spitzner. I take great delight in dedicating this volume to my wife, Lois Anne Gundry, to whose initial and ongoing encouragement and to whose constant help and love I owe whatever scholarly success the contents of the volume may represent (dedication written on the occasion of our Fiftieth Wedding Anniversary).

1. Hermeneutic Liberty, Theological Diversity, and Historical Occasionalism in the Biblical Canon

The topic of hermeneutics in the biblical canon offers a cornucopia of possible discussions not only concerning the interpretation of the OT in the NT (which interpretation itself offers multiple possibilities ranging from quotations through allusions to imagery and theological, ethical, and literary echoes) but also concerning biblical interpretation of originally noncanonical material, such as oral traditions and written sources (e.g., the Book of Jasher [Josh 10:13; 2 Sam 1:18], the Book of the Wars of the Lord [Num 21:14], the Edict of Cyrus [Ezra 1:1–4], a putative Q [cf. Luke 1:1–4], the *Assumption of Moses* [Jude 9], and *1 Enoch* [Jude 14–15]), later OT interpretation of earlier OT material (e.g., of Samuel-Kings by the Chronicler and of Jeremiah by Daniel), and later NT interpretation of earlier NT material (e.g., of Mark by Matthew and Luke and probably of Jude by 2 Peter). Thoroughness of discussion would require volumes, of course, so that the confines of an essay combine with current concerns to produce a stress on the element of liberty as characteristic of hermeneutics in the biblical canon, especially the NT canon.

Not only when it is artistic but also when it is argumentive and even polemic, hermeneutics in the biblical canon often exhibits – perhaps exhibits more often than not – a freedom that pays little or no attention to what seems by context to have made up the originally intended meaning of used materials.[1] One might say that artistry counts as argument. For example, in his polemically forged argument against Judaizers the Apostle Paul interprets the singular of "seed" in the Abrahamic covenant individualistically of Jesus the Christ ("It does not say, 'And to the seeds,' as concerning many, but as concerning one: 'And to your seed,' who is Christ" [Gal 3:16]) whereas contextual references in the OT to making Abraham's seed as innumerable as the dust of the earth (Gen 13:15–16), the stars in heaven (Gen 15:5; 22:17), and sand on the seashore (Gen 22:17) and to his becoming the father of kings and of a multitude of nations, so that his seed consists of "their generations" (Gen 17:4–7), guarantee an originally intended collective rather than individualistic singular. Paul himself reverts to the collec-

---

[1] So long as those who argue for the illegitimacy or impossibility of ascertaining an originally intended meaning expect me to understand their position and arguments, I will speak shamelessly of such meaning.

tive a few verses later ("then you [pl.] are Abraham's seed, heirs according to promise" [Gal 3:29b]), but even there with an interpretation strange to the OT. For the promise to Abraham originally had to do with his physical seed; but Paul interprets that promise in terms of being "in Christ Jesus" and "of Christ," and this "through faith in Christ Jesus" regardless of physical ancestry (Gal 3:26–29).[2]

Again, Paul identifies "the word" that "is near you, in your mouth and in your heart" (Rom 10:8b, quoting Deut 30:14) with "the word of faith which we preach, that if you confess with your mouth Jesus as Lord,,," (Rom 10:8c–9) in contradistinction to "the righteousness [that comes] from the law" and rests on "doing" (Rom 10:5). Yet in Deut 30:8–20 the word that is so near as to be in your mouth and heart is nothing else than the very "book of the law" made up of Yahweh's "commandments" and "statutes" that require to be "done" and "obeyed." Paul even applies to Gentile Christians ("whom also he ['God'] called... from among Gentiles") passages from Hosea ("as also it says in Hosea, 'I will call "Not My People" [Gentiles as well as Jews in Paul] "My People," and [I will call] "Not Beloved" [again Gentiles as well as Jews in Paul] "Beloved"...'" [Rom 9:25–26]) which in Hosea refer solely to Israel (Hos 2:23; 1:10), and he immediately follows up with a quotation from Isaiah concerning the remnant of Jewish Christians that are to be distinguished from the Gentile Christians to whom he has applied the passages from Hosea ("But Isaiah cries out concerning Israel, '... the remnant will be saved'" [Rom 9:27–29, quoting Isa 1:9]).

Biblical examples of such free interpretation could be multiplied indefinitely. In Jesus' genealogy, Matthew changes the royal name "Asa" to the levitical name "Asaph" (1 Chron 3:10; Matt 1:8 according to the best textual tradition), apparently by anticipation of quoting a psalm of Asaph (Ps 78:2; Matt 13:35 – though with reference to Jesus' parables instead of Israel's history, as in the psalm); changes the royal name "Amon" to the prophetic name "Amos" (1 Chron 3:14; Matt 1:10 according to the best textual tradition), perhaps by anticipation of an allusion to Amos 3:5 in Matt 10:29; and – despite writing about *"all* the generations" from Abraham to David, from David to the Babylonian deportation, and from that deportation to the Christ – omits four generations between King David and the deportation to Babylon, probably to get a triple emphasis on fourteen as the numerical value of David's name written with three Hebrew consonants since Matthew has just identified "Jesus Christ" as "David's son" (1:1, 6–11, 17; cf. Matthew's listing eight fewer generations than

---

[2] C. J. Collins argues that Paul cites Gen 22:18 and that because of the singular of the pronoun "its" referring to "seed" in the preceding verse and because of an individualistic allusion in Ps 72:17 Paul's individualistic interpretation matches the original meaning of Gen 22:18 ("Galatians 3:16: What Kind of Exegete Was Paul?" *TynBul* 54 [2003]: 75–86). But Collins' view requires an unannounced shift from an admittedly collective seed in Gen 22:17a–b to a strictly individual seed in Gen 22:17c–18.

Luke does – never mind the vast differences in names – from the Babylonian deportation to Jesus). Similarly, in quoting Mic 5:2, Matthew denies Bethlehem's smallness ("you are by no means least" [2:6]) where Micah affirms or implies it ("which are little" or "Are you little? Yet ..."). For Micah's demographic estimate of Bethlehem as small in population this reversal substitutes a theological estimate of Bethlehem as large in importance: Jesus the Messiah was born there. Yet Matthew has put this christianly inspired reinterpretation of Mic 5:2 on the lips of "all the chief priests and scribes of the people" (2:4), who elsewhere in Matthew function as Jesus' bitter enemies!

If we take the majority view that Matthew used Mark, Matthew turns the Sanhedrin's *dismissal* of witnesses against Jesus because their testimony proved false (Mark 14:55–56) into the Sanhedrin's *seeking* false testimony (Matt 26:59). This change forms part of Matthew's general program of heightening the guilt of Jewish leaders. By contrast, Chronicles paints King David much more flatteringly than Samuel-Kings does. In Samuel and Kings, which appear among the Former Prophets in the HB, David's faults stand out as objects of prophetic critique. But in Chronicles, written later from a priestly and levitical standpoint, the faults of David fade in favor of his preparations for the building of God's temple, where priests and levites served.

Likewise, Joshua 1–12 presents a theologically idealized picture of the conquest of Canaan by Israel, a conquest in which all Israel conquered all Palestine from the Lebanon to the southern desert and ruthlessly exterminated the entire population of Canaanites in accordance with God's command (see esp. 10:40–43; 11:16–23), so that in chs. 13 ff. the Israelites have merely to settle in their tribal allotments. But the historical reality appears in Judges, which emphatically describes the conquest as only partial (see esp. 1:1–2:5). A united body of Israel does not seize the land through a single series of major campaigns, as in Joshua; rather, we read about a variety of campaigns conducted by solitary tribes, sometimes by a pair of tribes, with mixed success and failure. Not only do these tribes fail to exterminate all the Canaanites, but also some tribes live peacefully with them. The large cities (with a few exceptions), the fertile valleys, the seaboard plain, and scattered enclaves stay in Canaanite hands. The silences and hints of less-than-total success in Josh 11:13, 22; 13:2–6 are hardly recognizable apart from a knowledge of the historical reality described in Judges and reflected elsewhere in the OT.

Whole books could be written, *have* been written, on the phenomenon of such interpretive liberty in the biblical canon. Of course, attempts have been made to minimize the phenomenon, as though it characterizes only a few passages in the Bible, and to provide benign explanations of various sorts: literary (a mere allusion may be more evocative or decorative than interpretive), typological (a symbolic interpretation does not deny an originally intended nonsymbolic meaning), theological (Jewish rejection of Jesus reorientated the meaning of the OT toward the church), and other. But none of these explanations have succeeded in hiding from those who read without blinders that biblical writers often interpret their material with a liberty that goes far beyond original intention, distorts that material, and sometimes contradicts it, i.e., distorts and contradicts it *if* we assume a limitation of legitimate interpretation to the accurate recounting of originally intended meaning and to the application of that meaning to circumstances such as those that were originally addressed.

For Christians concerned to maintain a historically and scripturally reliable basis for their faith, the canonical phenomenon of playing fast and loose with factual data and authorial intention becomes most critical in the NT interpretation of Christ, or of what has traditionally been called his "person and work" and has more recently been called the "Christ-event." Here, then, let us spell out some theological diversity that emerges from this hermeneutic liberty.

Most Christians think that the NT teaches the heavenly preexistence of Jesus as the second person of the Trinity, his coming down to earth by way of the incarnation, virgin birth as the means of incarnation, his holy life, atoning death, and bodily resurrection, his ascension back to heaven from where he had come in the first place, his present session at the right hand of God the Father, and his future coming to raise the dead and judge the world in righteousness. The creeds of the church illustrate and fortify this understanding of NT teaching about Jesus. Take for example the old Roman Creed, forerunner of the Apostles' Creed: "I believe in God the Father Almighty and in Christ Jesus, his only Son, our Lord, who was born of the Holy Spirit and Mary the Virgin, who under Pontius Pilate was crucified and buried; the third day he rose from the dead, ascended to the heavens, [and] sat down at God's right hand, from where he will come to judge the living and the dead …." Other creeds follow suit and add details.

But Christians have put together this creedal portrait of Jesus with bits and pieces gathered from different parts of the NT. It is a composite portrait never found at one location in the NT. Jesus' preexistence comes from here, his virgin birth from there, his ascension from elsewhere, and so on.

The canonical Gospels provide an example. Mark starts with Jesus' baptism and ends with Jesus' resurrection. Matthew starts with the genealogy and birth of Jesus and ends with his appearances after the resurrection. Luke starts with the birth of John the Baptist as well as with that of Jesus and, following appearances of the risen Jesus, ends with the ascension. John the evangelist starts with Jesus' eternal preexistence and ends with appearances of the risen Jesus following his ascension.

If we had only the Gospel of Mark we would never know about Jesus' preexistence, incarnation, or virgin birth; and we would know about his ascension only by the implication of his statement that he was going to sit at God's right hand and then return with clouds and great glory. We would know that Jesus was God's Son at his baptism but we would not know of any earlier divine sonship. If we had the Gospels of Matthew and Luke as well as of Mark we would know that the divine sonship of Jesus dated back to his conception and birth, and we would know that his conception and birth were virginal. But we would not know that he came down from heaven as preexistent deity to be conceived and born of the Virgin Mary. For all we would know, he started to exist at his virginal conception and birth. In fact, we would naturally assume so.

If we had the Gospel of Mark alone we would think that Jesus was God's Son only because the Holy Spirit entered him at his baptism. If we had the Gospel of Matthew alone we would think that Jesus was God's Son because of a unique action taken by the Holy Spirit on the Virgin Mary, and this in fulfillment of OT prophecy (Matt 1:20–23; cf. Isa 7:14). If we had only the Gospel of Luke and its companion volume the Acts of the Apostles we would think of Jesus as God's Son because the virgin birth represents not a unique work of the Holy Spirit but a divine generation like that of Adam, father of the human race. For Luke traces the genealogy of Jesus God's son back to Adam, whom he also calls God's son (Luke 3:38), and quotes Paul as saying on Mars' Hill that God made every nation of human beings from this one (apparently Adam, God's son), so that all of us human beings are God's offspring, God's generation (N.B.: generation, not creation) in accordance with the statement of Greek poets such as Aratus of Soli, whom Paul quotes: "as also some of your own poets have said, 'For also we are his offspring [Greek: γένος, from which we get the English word "generation"]'" (Acts 17:26, 28–29; Aratus *Phaenomena* 5; cf. Cleanthes' *Hymn to Zeus*).

Aratus, a Cilician, lived ca. 315–240 B.C. Before him, Plato had alluded ironically to earlier human beings who, doubtless knowing well their own ancestors (προγόνους, "progenitors"), declared themselves the descendants (ἐκγόνοις) of gods (*Tim.* 40D). And Dio Chrysostom of Prusa, a youth during Paul's apostolic ministry, referred to the universally recognized and innately known truth of God's kinship (ξυγγένειαν, "family relationship" or, more literally, "cogeneration") with the human race, so that we are "filled with the divine nature" and God is our "forefather" (προπάτορος [*Discourse* 12.27–28]), "our first and immortal parent" (γονέως), called "paternal (πατρῷον) Zeus" (*Discourse* 12.42). Conversely, Dio also speaks of the kinship (συγγένειαν) of human beings with the gods (*Discourse* 12.61). Furthermore, Zeus and the other gods love human beings as being the gods' relatives (ξυγγενεῖς) inasmuch as human beings are the offspring (γένος) of the gods, not of the Titans or of the Giants (other figures in Greek mythology – *Discourse* 30.26). At some expense to the doctrine of creation, in other words, Luke-Acts assimilates the Christology of divine sonship to the old, continuing, and widespread Greek notion of the divine generation of the whole human race, so that Jesus' divine sonship becomes the example par excellence of all our divine sonship.

Of the four canonical Gospels, only that of John would give us reason to believe in Jesus as God's Son because he preexisted as divine. But John would give us no reason to believe that the preexistent Son of God became incarnate through the Virgin Mary. For not only does John omit the virgin birth. He also lets stand two references to Jesus as the son of Joseph (1:45; 6:42). Even though those references may represent characteristically Johannine irony, the irony does not need to imply the virgin birth, only that unbelievers knew Jesus as the son of Joseph without knowing him as much more importantly the Son of God.

Spatially, the narratives in Mark and Matthew start and end with Jesus on earth, though there is a reference to his being in heaven later on and coming back from heaven. The narrative in Luke likewise starts with Jesus on earth but ends with his ascension to heaven. Only John speaks about a down-and-up: Jesus comes down from heaven, lives on earth for a while, and goes back up to heaven, though in John he goes back up on the first Easter Sunday, not forty days later as in Luke-Acts, and then commutes back from heaven to earth to make two or three further appearances on earth whereas in Luke-Acts the risen Jesus stays on earth forty days to make his appearances before ascending to heaven.[3]

We find the down-and-up of preexistence, incarnation, and exaltation back to heaven also in Paul's Epistles (see esp. Phil 2:6–11). But like John, he says nothing about a virgin birth as the means of incarnation. If we had only his letters we would assume that God united his deity with a Jesus born naturally of two human parents, not supernaturally by an action of the Holy Spirit on the Virgin Mary. The author of Hebrews says that all things came into being both for Christ and through Christ and that Christ partook of our blood and flesh (Heb 1:2; 2:14). So Hebrews too teaches the preexistence and incarnation of

---

[3] I have made an inference here, but hardly a greater one than the inferring of Jesus' ascension in Matthew and Mark from the prediction of his second coming: (1) John 7:37–39 says that the Spirit was not yet [*sc.* given] because Jesus was not yet glorified. (2) His glorification included his heavenly exaltation following the earthly ministry (see, e.g., John 17:5: "And now you, Father, glorify me alongside yourself with the glory that I had alongside you before the world existed"). (3) But Jesus bestowed the Spirit already on the evening of the first Easter Sunday (John 20:22). (4) Furthermore, on the first Easter Sunday morning Jesus told Mary Magdalene to stop touching him because he had not yet ascended to the Father, and he ordered her to go tell his disciples that he was ascending to his and their Father and God (John 20:17). (5) Only a week later Jesus invited Thomas to touch him (John 20:26–27). (6) So according to John, Jesus must have ascended in the meantime – more exactly, between his command in the morning that Mary stop touching him and his bestowal of the Spirit during the evening of the same day. Luke 24:50–51 is sometimes taken to put the ascension on the first Easter; but there is no chronological marker in that account itself. Moreover, going after nightfall from Jerusalem to Bethany and back seems unlikely (cf. Luke 24:29, 33); and Acts 1:1–11, referring back to Luke's first volume, adds many more details about the ascension, including forty days of preceding ministry by the risen Jesus. Cf. Cornelis Bennema, "The Giving of the Spirit in John's Gospel – A New Proposal?" *EvQ* 74 (2002): 201–11; idem, *The Power of Saving Wisdom* (WUNT 2/148; Tübingen: Mohr Siebeck, 2002), 17, 30, 144, 153, 158, 205, 210–12, 253–54. Bennema is concerned to show that Jesus "gave over the Spirit" symbolically in John 19:30 and actually in 20:22 but that the Spirit was active in a limited way earlier.

Jesus but not his virgin birth. To note this omission is not to say that John, Paul, and the author of Hebrews denied the virgin birth or would have denied it had they known about it; only that they did not know about it or, if they did know about it, that they ignored it despite their speaking about the incarnation. And in this connection Hebrews' development of the incarnation into an interpretation of Jesus as our great high priest has nothing quite like it in the rest of the NT.

But there is diversity not only in *what* the NT says about Jesus. There is diversity also in the *chronology* of what it says about Jesus. For example, the preexistent Christ appears already in Hebrews and the Epistles of Paul, written at least mostly before the Gospels were written – and even earlier if in the famous passage Phil 2:6–11 Paul is quoting a Christian hymn (a popular though not undisputed hypothesis[4]). Yet the preexistent Christ fades from Mark, Matthew, and Luke to reappear not until the Gospel of John, most probably the last of the canonical Gospels to have been written.

And right among the Gospels we should note this difference, a huge one: In Mark, Matthew, and Luke Jesus proclaims the kingdom of God. He does not proclaim himself. Except for the more mystifying than clarifying phrase, "Son of Man," he does not even identify himself, at least not till Passion Week. When he calls himself the Son in relation to God his Father he appears to be praying to God or meditating to himself, not identifying himself to his disciples, much less to the multitudes ("At that time Jesus answered and said, 'I praise you, Father, Lord of heaven and earth …. Yes, Father …. All things have been given over to me by my Father; and no one knows the Son except the Father; neither does anyone know the Father except the Son and the one to whom the Son wishes to reveal him" [Matt 11:27–28; cf. Luke 10:21–22]). When in Mark and Luke Peter identifies Jesus as the Christ, Jesus does not even acknowledge the identification, but merely tells the disciples (who alone are present) not to speak about him. Then he goes on to predict his death and resurrection as the Son of Man, not as the Christ (Mark 8:27–31; Luke 9:18–22). Later he delivers a glancing reference to the disciples' belonging to Christ (Mark 9:41), but he does not acknowledge his christhood and divine sonship outright till standing trial before the Sanhedrin in Jerusalem the eve of his crucifixion (Mark 14:61–62).

In Matt 16:13–20 Jesus describes Peter's confession as deriving from a divine revelation to Peter. But Jesus still commands the disciples not to tell anyone that he is the Christ, nor does he himself tell anyone. And when standing trial before the Sanhedrin in Matthew he does not say, "I am," to the high priest's question whether he is the Christ, the Son of God, as he does say in Mark. Instead, he answers, "*You* have said [that I am]" (Matt 26:63–64). Why does he not say, "I am," as in Mark? Because the high priest has put Jesus under oath ("I adjure you," the high priest has said), as he has *not* done in Mark's account; and Mat-

---

[4] I myself doubt this hypothesis; see below, p. 286.

thew will not let Jesus violate his own teaching against oaths by making an oathful self-declaration of his christhood and divine sonship. We find Jesus' teaching against oaths not in Mark but in Matt 5:33–37 (cf. Jas 5:12). So ethics swallows up Christology by making Jesus say less about himself in Matthew than he does in Mark. In Luke 22:66–71 he refuses to tell the Sanhedrin whether he is the Christ and says that the identification of him as the Son of God belongs to their question, not to anything he has said.[5]

In John, however, this proclaimer of God's kingdom turns into a proclaimer of himself. Jesus does not merely acknowledge his special identity. He advertises it. He does not limit the audience of this advertisement to his disciples. He advertises his identity to the multitudes. He does not wait till late in his ministry to launch his campaign of self-advertisement. He starts right away. Though he uses the standard terms "Christ" and "Son of God," by no means does he confine his self-identification to these terms.[6] Rather, the Jesus of John heaps on himself one high-sounding designation after another: the one on whom the angels of God ascend and descend to and from the open heaven, i.e., Jacob's ladder (1:51), the one who himself has descended from heaven and ascended to it (3:13), the giver of eternal life (5:21), judge of the whole human race (5:22, 27), bread of life (6:35), light of the world (8:12), I AM (8:58), good shepherd (10:11), he who is one with the Father, making himself equal with God (10:30–33), the one who raises himself as well as everybody else from the dead (10:17–18 with 5:25–26), the resurrection and the life (11:25), the way, the truth, and the life (14:6).

And in addition to all these self-advertisements by Jesus, John has others recognize and advertise Jesus' identity, again from the very start, beginning with the Baptist's double declaration, "Behold, the Lamb of God" (1:29, 36). The Baptist even testifies to Jesus' preexistence: "The one who is coming after me ranks ahead of me because he existed before me" (1:15). This advertisement of Jesus' identity by others continues with the first disciples' declarations, already on the occasion of their becoming disciples, that Jesus is not only a rabbi, a teacher, but also the Messiah, the one about whom Moses wrote in the law, and also the prophets, the Son of God, and the King of Israel – a veritable laundry list of honorific designations straightaway in the first chapter of John's Gospel. No waiting till the middle of Jesus' ministry as in Mark, Matthew, and Luke. In fact, from the very first sign which Jesus performs in John, the turning of water to wine at Cana of Galilee – from that very first sign onward he is making public revelation of his glory as the incarnate Word who was with God in the beginning and was God (2:11: "This beginning of signs Jesus performed in Cana of Gali-

---

[5] See further below, pp. 98–110.

[6] In Jewish usage, of course, a messianic application of the phrase "Son of God" did not connote deity.

lee and manifested his glory, and his disciples believed in him"; cf. 1:1, 14; 9:3; 11:4, 40).

Since Jesus does not proclaim himself in Mark, Matthew, and Luke he does not tell anybody to believe in him. Instead, he tells people to believe in the gospel of God, i.e., in the good news that God's rule has come near (Mark 1:14–15: "Jesus came into Galilee preaching the gospel of God and saying, 'The time is fulfilled and the rule of God has come near; believe in the gospel"). Jesus does refer in Mark 9:42 par. Matt 18:6 to little ones who believe in him, but even that reference does not constitute a "call" to believe in him. On the other hand, since he proclaims himself all over the map in John's Gospel, there Jesus repeatedly tells people of the necessity to believe in him if they are to have eternal life: "[The crowd] said to him, 'What should we do that we might work the works of God?' Jesus answered and said to them, 'This is the work of God, that you believe in him whom that one has sent" (6:29); "for this is the will of my Father, that everyone who sees the Son and believes in him should have eternal life" (6:40); "for if you do not believe that I AM [N.B. the divine title; cf. Exod 3:14 and John 8:58], you will die in your sins" (8:24); "the one who believes in me will live even though that one dies, and everyone who is living and believes in me will never die" (11:25–26); "you believe in God, believe also in me" (14:1; see also 6:35; 7:38; 9:35–38; 10:38; 11:28; 12:44, 46; 13:19; 14:10–11; 16:30–31).

So a close look at NT interpretation of Jesus' person and work exposes a liberty that issues in striking diversity. Paul said that he became all things to all people that by all means he might save some (1 Cor 9:19–23). We might say that the authors of the NT made Jesus all things to all people that by all means he might save some. And this tailoring, if we may call it such, was prompted by the various and shifting circumstances of audiences that those authors had in view.

Because of persecution coming from the Roman Caesars or about to come from them on Christians living in the province of Asia the book of Revelation portrays Jesus as a conquering hero, riding a warhorse, the lion of Judah, and also a lamb, but one with seven horns with which at his return he will gore the persecutors of his people (Rev 5:1–7; 19:11–16). Matthew's church too is suffering persecution, but not from the Roman Caesars; rather, from Jewish synagogues. So he portrays Jesus as meek and mild, riding humbly on a donkey, a model of nonretaliation in accordance with his own teaching in the Sermon on the Mount (Matt 5:5, 38–48; 21:1–5). The superpower of the Caesars made it useless to attempt retaliation against them; so Revelation could only give hope for the future. But retaliation against the synagogues might seem feasible right now; so Matthew portrays Jesus, not in the way of Revelation, which might incite retaliation, but quite oppositely in a way designed to counteract the temptation to retaliate.

The particular circumstances in and for which Paul wrote differ from one epistle to another, but in general he wrote as the apostle to Gentiles to predominantly Gentile Christians, whose background included pagan cults such as the mystery religions that featured a divine lord. So Paul presents Jesus as Lord of the Christian cult ("cult" in its technical sense of a system for worshiping a deity). To this end, Paul concentrates on Jesus' death, resurrection, and exaltation and pays almost no attention to the Christology of Jesus' earthly ministry and very little to that of Jesus' preexistence and incarnation. After all, the lords of the pagan cults, over against whom Paul puts Jesus (1 Cor 8:5–6: "For… just as there are… many lords, yet for us there is… one Lord, Jesus Christ") – these lords of the pagan cults did not become human beings and lead earthly lives that could have elicited very much interest from Paul in Jesus' preexistence, incarnation and earthly ministry. But the mythology concerning those pagan lords did include their death and revival in the underworld. The Jesus of Paul goes one better by rising bodily from the dead and enjoying exaltation in heaven.

On the other hand, Luke writes for an audience of sophisticated Gentiles like the "most excellent Theophilus" whom he addresses (1:1–4), apparently God-fearers, high-minded people distrustful of polytheism and more interested in human beings than in cultic deities, in humanity than in divinity. So Luke humanizes the divinity of Jesus by drawing a parallel between the divine sonship of Jesus and the divine sonship of Adam and thus derivatively the divine sonship of the whole human race. He ascribes to Jesus an ideal human development: "Jesus advanced in wisdom and stature and in favor with God and human beings" (Luke 2:52). That is to say, he grew intellectually, physically, spiritually, and socially – a full-orbed human development such as would have drawn admiration even in the gymnasium at Athens. He displayed precocity at the age of twelve when in the temple he amazed scholars with his understanding and answers (2:46–47). A child prodigy! As an adult, he embodied the loftiest ideals of human being. He exhibited great breadth of human sympathy – for tax collectors and sinners, Samaritans, women, widows – yet moved easily among the high and mighty and wealthy. The Jesus of Luke is cosmopolitan, attractive, approachable, convivial, the kind you would like to eat dinner with and then tarry at table for conversation and drinks till midnight, as in fact people do with Luke's Jesus in accordance with the symposiums characteristic of Greek culture.

The circumstances of John's writing differed radically. He wrote – I think it has been established well enough, though some entertain reservations – during the rising tide of Gnosticism, which denied the humanity of Jesus Christ either by making the incarnation only apparent (docetism)[7] or by distinguishing a divine spirit, Christ, from a human being, Jesus, and saying that the divine spirit came on the human being not till the latter's baptism and left before the crucifixion (Cerinthianism).[8] Yet other Gnostics said that Simon of Cyrene not only carried Jesus' cross but also died on it in place of Jesus.[9]

---

[7] Ign., *Trall* 10:1

[8] Irenaeus, *Adv. haer.* 1.26.1.

[9] See esp. Irenaeus, *Adv. haer.* 1.24.4–6; 3.11.1; *Treat. Seth* VII.2 56. The argument that un-

So John emphasizes the deity of the human Jesus. The Word who was God became flesh (1:14). The glory of the human Jesus was that of the only, the *unique* Son of God (N.B. the difference from Luke's Christology of *shared* divinity). There is only one person Jesus Christ, not Jesus and Christ; and that one person came in water and in blood according to 1 John 5:6, not in water only (baptism by John the Baptist, who according to John the evangelist testified that the Spirit who came on Jesus at his baptism stayed on him [1:33], did not leave him later as taught by the Cerinthians, so that his death is described neither as an expiration as in Mark 15:37 and Luke 23:46 [ἐξέπνευσεν] nor as a relinquishment of his human spirit as in Matt 27:50 [ἀφῆκεν τὸ πνεῦμα] but as a giving over of the Spirit [παρέδωκεν τὸ πνεῦμα (John 19:30)] – now that he had been glorified by being lifted up on the cross [John 13:31] he could give over the Spirit in accordance with John 7:37–39 – with the result that right after his death, resurrection, and ascension Jesus breathed on the disciples and said, "Receive the Holy Spirit" [John 20:22]). He came not in water only but in water and in blood: he really died, as shown in John's Gospel by the outflow of blood and water at the piercing of Jesus' side (John 19:33–35). And he carried his cross "by himself" (John 19:17). Simon did not carry it for him as in Mark 15:21; Matt 27:32; Luke 23:26. Much less did Simon die on the cross in Jesus' place.[10]

Like John the author of Hebrews stresses incarnation in his interpretation of the Christ-event. But he does so under different circumstances and therefore with a different twist. Not Gnosticism, with its intellectual snobbery, but Judaism, with its sacerdotal tradition, offers the backdrop against which to understand the Christology of Hebrews. Jewish priests officiated at the offering of animals in blood-sacrifice to atone for sins. But Jesus could not have officiated

---

like 1 John, the Gospel of John contains no explicit polemic against gnostic false teaching neglects several considerations: (1) the difference between a letter dealing with church life (1 John), in which a direct attack on current false teaching is at home, and a gospel dealing with Jesus' life (John), in which such an attack would be anachronistic; (2) the suitability to an indirect, narratival polemic against Gnosticism in "the Word became flesh" (John 1:14), in the staying of the Spirit on Jesus (John 1:33), in Jesus' carrying the cross "by himself" (John 19:17), in the outflow of blood and water from his pierced side as emphasized by the testimony of an eyewitness (John 19:34–37), and in the stress on the physicality of the risen Jesus (John 20:17, 20, 24–29); and (3) the apostasy of many of his disciples in John 6:60–71 after he had talked in very contrary-to-gnostic terms of eating his flesh and drinking his blood, those apostates standing for the Gnostics of John's day. These considerations favor that what later sources report about various forms of Gnosticism had its origins already in the first century. Cf. U. Schnelle, *Antidocetic Christology in the Gospel of John* (Minneapolis: Fortress, 1992), 228–36 et passim; but the recognition of antidocetism in John does not depend on his dating of this Gospel before 1 John or on his attributing sacramentalism to John.

[10] R. E. Brown argues that "a much more likely reason for the omission of Simon is John's desire to continue the theme that Jesus went to his death as sole master of his own destiny" (*The Gospel according to John (XIII–XXI)* [AB 29A; New York: Doubleday, 1970], 917). But for that theme "by himself" is unnecessary. "Bearing the cross" would have sufficed. The addition of "by himself" emphatically excludes Simon of Cyrene.

at such sacrifices if he had wanted to. He belonged to the wrong tribe and family, the tribe of Judah and the family of David within that tribe. Jewish priests had to belong to the tribe of Levi and the family of Aaron within it. So the author of Hebrews has Jesus officiate over a better sacrifice, that of himself (9:23–28). But to officiate thus, Jesus has to have a body of blood and flesh (2:14–17). Hence the emphasis on incarnation, but not incarnation as a means of divine revelation as in the Gospel of John so much as incarnation as a means toward human sacrifice.

Let us tease out this difference a little more. Through the incarnation in John deity *reveals* itself to humanity by taking the form of a human being (1:14 again; similarly Heb 1:1–4). But through the incarnation in Hebrews deity also *learns* humanity by taking the form of a human being: "he learned obedience through what he suffered" (Heb 5:8b); "in every respect he was tempted as we are" (Heb 4:15); "and having been perfected [we never find a phrase like that in John, where it is the disciples, not the divine Word, who need to be perfected (John 17:23)], he became the source of eternal salvation for all who obey him, having been designated by God a high priest according to the order of Melchizedek" (Heb 5:9–10). The Jesus of John is not tempted. The stories of Jesus' temptation appear only in Mark, Matthew, and Luke.

Nor does the Jesus of John have to learn obedience through suffering. He does not even suffer, at least not as a victim. He prays self-composedly for his disciples (John 17) instead of throwing himself on the ground in a sweat of emotional turmoil and praying about his own fate (Mark 14:32–42 par. Matt 26:36–46 par. Luke 22:39–46). How else would we expect God in the flesh to behave than with self-composure? Not only is there no agony in Gethsemane. On the cross there is no cry of dereliction ("My God, my God, why have you forsaken me?" [Mark 15:34 par. Matt 27:46]), for in John the Word who *is* God can hardly be *forsaken* by God.

There is no prayer on behalf of Jesus' crucifiers, "Father, forgive them; for they know not what they do" (Luke 23:34), because although Pontius Pilate gives Jesus over to the Jews and they crucify him (John 19:16–18; contrast Jesus' crucifixion by Roman soldiers in the Synoptics, most clearly in Matt 27:27), at a profounder level the Jesus of John puts *himself* on the cross ("No one takes my life from me; rather, I lay it down of my own accord" [10:18]). He practically insists on his arrest. He goes out to meet the band who would take him and has to ask them twice whom they seek. He identifies himself twice as the object of their search and even imposes a condition for the taking of him: "If then you are looking for me, let these [disciples] go away" (18:2–8).

John quotes Jesus as saying on the cross, "I thirst," but introduces the statement as a fulfillment of Scripture, not as a sign of suffering. And so, ever in control, the incarnate Word of God dies by his own volition after calmly taking care of his personal affairs ("Woman, look! Your son.... Look! Your mother" [19:26–27]) and triumphantly announcing that his works, signs, and words are finished ("knowing that all things [which things presumably refer to the works, signs, and words the Father had given him to do and say] were already finished.... he said, 'They are finished' [not '*It* is finished,' but the 'all things']" [19:28, 30]).[11]

New Testament interpretations of Jesus' person and work exhibit diversity, then, a diversity prompted by varying circumstances – political, social, economic, ethnic, educational, religious. To be sure, NT Christologies were not wholly determined by such circumstances, as though the figure of Jesus were made of Silly Putty which the NT authors molded into whatever shape they thought was required by their varying circumstances. Certain brute facts and accepted traditions about him provided both a skeleton with which to work and parameters within which to work. Nevertheless, my emphasis has fallen on diversity so much that a few lines ago the plural slipped in: NT Christologies. Different parts of the NT give us different Christologies – not completely different from one another but clearly different, sometimes disconcertingly different, and certainly far more different from one another than has usually been thought in the church or world at large.

But, someone might say, we now have all the NT. So what does it matter whether Paul, Mark, and Hebrews say nothing about the virgin birth, whether Mark, Matthew, and Luke say nothing about Jesus' preexistence, whether Luke's and John's notions of Jesus' divine sonship differ from each other as broadly humanistic and narrowly sectarian, respectively, and so on. It matters because the diversity in NT interpretation of Jesus raises important questions concerning our interpretation: Should we systematize the Christologies of Matthew, Mark, Luke, and John, of Paul, Hebrews, James, Peter, and Jude, so as to produce an overarching, comprehensive, single NT Christology? Should we homogenize these Christologies? Or should we let the NT authors speak individually about Jesus as they originally did? To use hackneyed metaphors, is NT interpretation of Jesus a melting pot or a mixing bowl? A soup in which everything is blended together or a salad into which different items are put without losing their individual identity. Does the canonization of books called the NT mean that we should interpret them by each other so as to get a unified view of Jesus? Or does the NT canon present a range of different Christologies any one of which is acceptable by itself?

Are Paul and Mark and John less Christian because they seem not to know about and therefore not to believe in the virgin birth? Are Mark, Matthew, and Luke less Christian because they seem not to know about and therefore not to believe in the divine preexistence of Jesus? Or did those evangelists know about and believe in his divine preexistence and virgin birth but omit to mention them

---

[11] In Greek, neuter plural subjects (here πάντα, "all things") regularly take singular verbs (here τετέλεσται).

because these matters seemed irrelevant to their authorial purposes? Nowadays is a true Christian bound to accept all the Christologies of the NT even though it was once possible to be truly Christian on the acceptance of only a single, incomprehensive Christology? Or might a contemporary person turn and stay Christian by accepting, say, Luke's Christology without accepting, perhaps even while rejecting, the Christologies of Paul, Mark and John? Do NT Christologies complement each other or compete with each other? For example, does Luke's upwardly mobile humanistic Christology, a man rising to the level of God, undermine John's downwardly mobile theological Christology, God descending to the level of a human being? Or do they fill out a harmonious picture?

Larger questions loom on the horizon, questions less antiquarian and more contemporary. Does the NT canon limit the range of acceptable Christologies or provide paradigms for the development of new Christologies better suited than old ones to modern concerns? Does the NT tell us *what* to do or *how* to do it? Should the culture of modern psychology affect contemporary Christian interpretation of Jesus? The culture of modern sociology? Of sociobiology? Should the human genome project affect our current understanding and presentation of Jesus? Should we be developing different Christologies for blacks? For whites? For Asians? For Hispanics? For the urban poor? For the rural poor? For the suburban middle class? For Wall Street? For Main Street? For men? For women? For children? Where do we stop? Can we stop? Should we start? Or have we been developing such Christologies all along, more or less unaware of what we were doing?

How would new interpretations of Jesus differ from one another? What thread might connect them together – and to the NT? How thick a thread would be required to keep them from unraveling into different religions? Or would it be wrongheaded to suit different Christologies to diverse needs in a polymorphous society? Should Christology provide common ground on which to stand? Should it erase our cultural and otherwise circumstantial differences, or at least overarch them, rather than catering to them?

Would the development of new Christologies contribute to the spread of the gospel? Or would it expose the gospel to heresy, the NT having presented models with which to be satisfied, not models to be imitated? Are NT Christologies sufficient or seminal? Should we consider the diversity in NT interpretations of Jesus and the fundamental questions generated by that diversity as off-limits, troubling, unsettling, unspeakable, and dangerous to the life and limb of Christian faith? Or as inviting, urgent, and essential to the revitalization of Christian faith in an ever-changing world?

Earlier I made a crude reference to Silly Putty. I now wish to atone for that reference with a cultivated yet otherwise similar reference to an ancient but well-known Greek myth. In his *Odyssey* 4.382–569 Homer tells about the old man of the sea, Proteus, an Egyptian god who knows the depths and paths of every sea, so that he can give unerring advice to any seafarer facing the untold dangers of a voyage. The trouble is, Proteus does not like to give such advice. You have to grab him, hold him tight, and then force it out of him with questions. But it is hard to hold him tight, because when you do grab him, he tries to slip out of your grasp by changing from one shape to another, as when in the *Odyssey* Menelaus and his men grabbed him. At first Proteus turned into a bearded lion, then into a serpent, then into a leopard, then into a huge boar, then into flowing water, and finally into a tall and leafy tree. Try as he would, however, Proteus could not slip from the grasp of Menelaus and his men. And so, having grown tired and weary from the effort, he answered the questions of Menelaus concerning a homeward voyage.

We might say that like Proteus the Christ of the NT takes many shapes and forms. There is a difference, of course: Proteus assumed many shapes and forms to avoid answering people's questions whereas the Christ of the NT assumes many shapes and forms to answer questions. But that difference only calls attention to the initiative of divine grace. The issue remains: Does Christ still take many shapes and forms? Or does the closing of the NT canon mean that like Proteus, Christ is tired of assuming different shapes and forms, that he has assumed all the shapes and forms he needs to have assumed for answering our questions? In his canonical diversity is he able without further hermeneutic metamorphoses to ask and answer the fundamental questions that grow out of modern psychology, sociology, sociobiology, the human genome project, the black experience, the white experience, Hispanic and Asian experiences, women's experiences, men's experiences? Or do these disciplines and experiences call for new interpretations patterned after but not limited to the old Christologies of the NT?

To these questions must be added an observation, a feature of the Protean myth thus far omitted. Before the weary old man of the sea would finally answer the questions of Menelaus, he subjected Menelaus to some questioning of his own. Likewise the Christ of the NT insists on questioning us before answering us. Here as elsewhere in the Bible the text interprets us before we interpret it.

An Historical and Thetic Postscript

The biblical theology movement of the mid-twentieth century emphasized the unity of the Bible, as in the OT scholar H. H. Rowley's book titled with that very phrase[12] and in A. M. Hunter's *The Unity of the New Testament*.[13] A disintegration of the biblical theology movement and its emphasis went hand in hand

---

[12] H. H. Rowley, *The Unity of the Bible* (Philadelphia: Westminster, 1953).
[13] A. M. Hunter, *The Unity of the New Testament* (3d ed.; London: SCM, 1946).

with the rise of postmodernism and its emphasis on diversity among communities of faith. Strenuous efforts have been mounted here and there, if not always to recapture unity, at least to trace a common thread running through the Bible or NT and tying it together above all with regard to the doctrine of Christ. One thinks, for example, of J. D. G. Dunn's *Unity and Diversity in the New Testament*.[14] By and large, however, traditionalists rush so quickly to the side of unity that the benefits of diversity tend to get lost. The motive of traditionalists may be pure: to defend the faith once for all delivered to the saints – a theological benefit. But the effect can be deleterious too: a praxeological loss. I mean that it is not enough to know what the Scriptures teach; we also need to discern what is appropriate and inappropriate to be said from them in any given situation. Do not preach eternal security to careless Christians; preach the danger of apostasy by false and deceived professors of the faith. And vice versa to conscientious Christians suffering for the faith and tempted to doubt. Given my own *Sitz im Leben*, then, I have shifted ballast by stressing diversity over unity in biblical hermeneutics.

But a more than historical and autobiographical rationale may be in order. The very fact that our biblical canon is a collection of different books, each written for a different occasion, not a single book written for all occasions, argues that in general the exposition and application of biblical hermeneutics should highlight diversity. Moreover, the absence from the Bible of an explicitly unifying theme argues that the ferreting out of an underlying unity belongs to a second order of business, that purported discoveries of a unifying theme are to be invested with less confidence than are the purported discoveries of diversity, as in the foregoing survey of NT Christologies. Both kinds of discovery entail a noncanonical interpretation of the biblical canon; but the discovery of a unifying theme requires two steps of interpretation, the first one consisting in various abstractions taken from books making up the Bible and the second one in a consolidating abstraction taken from those initial abstractions. It is the secondness of remove from the Bible itself that inspires less confidence in a unifying interpretation than in the interpretation of books as they stand individually in the Bible.

Not that the search for unity is useless or improper. On the contrary, the collection of individual books into one canonical list encourages a search for unity, but more in the field of systematic theology than in that of biblical hermeneutics. Given the diverse character of the biblical canon – its books were written by a number of different authors at different times, in different places, for different audiences, and with different purposes – claims to have discovered the unity will always carry less weight and be subject to greater dispute than

---

[14] J. D. G. Dunn, *Unity and Diversity in the New Testament* (2d ed.; London: SCM/Philadelphia: Trinity, 1990).

claims to have discovered the meaning of this or that book within the Bible. And given the variety of circumstances in which the church has found itself from time to time and place to place, claims to have discovered the meaning of this or that book within the Bible also seem to offer greater and more immediate usefulness for the life and witness of the church (or should we say churches – plural?) than do claims to have discovered a theme that overarches the entire Bible. For postcanonical churches find themselves in circumstances similar to those for which biblical books were variously tailored, and tailored not for the sake of suprahistorical comprehensiveness (producing a unifiedly systematic theology) but for the sake of intrahistorical pertinence (producing diversely particularized theologies).[15] Maybe systematicians should not even be looking for a unifying center so much as for boundaries beyond which the biblical canon forbids us go and within which should take place a further search for pertinence to current circumstances.

To put the point another way and perhaps to sharpen and advance it, the demand for unity, for systematization, may itself have arisen out of a particular historical circumstance in the life and witness of the church, may therefore be just as historically conditioned and, despite appearances or claims, just as limited as was the diversity that appears in the raw materials of the Bible. Correspondingly, postmodernism may be creating, or have already created, a new historical circumstance that lessens the need to search for unity, to reach for system. One might even argue that such searching and reaching prove counterproductive in the postmodern situation. One could also argue to the contrary, however, that in a countercultural fashion we need to emphasize unity as an antidote to postmodern fragmentation, though that argument too presupposes the need for tailoring interpretation to current need.

As to the interpretation of Jesus on which this essay has concentrated, I propose the following thesis for a partial answer to some of the questions raised in the body of discussion: As canonical, the NT limits the range of authoritative Christologies but invites the development of new Christologies inasmuch as canonicity does not imply exhaustiveness in the sorts of circumstances in and for which the books of the Bible were written. Neither does the doctrine of scriptural sufficiency, which leaves open the possibility of indirect application to new and different circumstances in addition to direct application to circumstances identical with those held in view by biblical authors. Yet the development of new Christologies requires their constant testing not only negatively to insure their noncontradiction of canonical Christologies but also positively to insure their carrying forward something of what we find in canonical interpretations of Jesus. Then, but only then, will the old prove better.

---

[15] Here it is important to include in theology affection as well as understanding, practice as well as belief, worship as well as confession.

2. The Symbiosis of Theology and Genre Criticism of the Canonical Gospels

In 1882 F. Overbeck stated that a literature has its history in its forms, so that every true history of literature will be a history of form.[1] This statement sparked interest in the question, What kind of book are those commonly called "Gospels"? The republication in 1970 of C. W. Votaw's old articles on that question signaled a renewal of interest.[2]

Writing in 1915, Votaw correlated the canonical Gospels in their portrayals of Jesus with Greco-Roman biographies. According to Votaw all the biographers, canonical as well as extracanonical, purposed to eulogize and idealize their heroes by selecting the heroes' best sayings and most dramatic acts, often heightened, for hortatory rather than antiquarian aims. And all the biographers shared a lack of concern for completeness, of investigation into their heroes' genetic relations to the environment, of interest in the personal development of their heroes, and of their heroes' impact on the times. In other words, the canonical Gospels belong to the genre of popular biography well known to the Greco-Roman world.[3]

Yet despite certain concessions in the direction of Votaw's views the classicist E. Norden had at the close of the nineteenth century declared the canonical Gospels a literary novelty.[4] Also writing before Votaw, P. Wendland had undermined any significantly positive correlation between these Gospels and Greco-

---

[1] F. Overbeck, "Über die Anfänge der patristischen Literatur," *Historische Zeitschrift* 48 (1882): 423 ff.

[2] C. W. Votaw, *The Gospels and Contemporary Biographies in the Greco-Roman World* (Philadelphia: Fortress, 1970 repr. of articles in *American Journal of Theology* 19 [1915]: 45–73, 217–49).

[3] Genre has to do with different strains of literary tradition in which compositions as wholes share distinctive sets of traits, both obvious and subtle, and consequently mediate certain holistic meanings. Within a literary genre the necessity of continuity and the allowance of some variation balance each other. We study genre to determine holistic meanings of documents. See N. R. Petersen Jr., "A Note on the Notion of Genre in Via's 'Parable and Example Story: A Literary-Structuralist Approach'" (paper presented to the SBL Seminar on Parables, November 1973). In the present discussion, then, the early connotation of the term "gospel" as a message (on which see the well-known works of J. Schniewind, G. Friedrich et al.) usually gives way to the later connotation of the term "Gospel" as a kind of book.

[4] E. Norden, *Die antike Kunstprosa* (Stuttgart: B. G. Teubner, 1974 repr. of 1898 ed.), 2:480–81.

Roman biographies. Wendland drew sharp contrasts by playing up more than Votaw did the popular style of the evangelists and the literary artistry of Greco-Roman biographers. He estimated as rather high the interest of these biographers in preserving the historical truth concerning their subjects and as rather low their practical purposes related to their audiences – and reversed these estimations in the case of the evangelists. Where Greco-Roman biographical tradition came down more or less whole, Wendland posited isolated units of popular traditions prior to the writing of the Gospels. Except for the miraculous, Votaw tended to trust in the basic historicity of dominical (as well as Greco-Roman biographical) tradition; but Wendland made the precanonical units of dominical tradition, including the nonmiraculous, subject to a high degree of change through popular use and imagination. According to him the first evangelist Mark simply collected the bits and pieces of tradition, provided them with a literary framework, and prefixed them to the narrative of Jesus' passion. As a popular storyteller, "Er [Mark] hat keinen ausgeprägten theologischen Standpunkt." Therefore redaction included little more than the provision of chronological and geographical settings for the sake of a story line.[5]

It remained for K. L. Schmidt, however, to bring the basic tenets of form criticism fully into relation with the question of the Gospels' literary genre. This Schmidt did in a lengthy contribution to the *Festschrift* for H. Gunkel.[6] Here we need also to bring in the similar views of Schmidt's colleagues in form criticism, M. Dibelius and R. Bultmann.[7] Schmidt began with a severe criticism of Votaw's facile paralleling of the evangelists and Greco-Roman biographers. Whatever the similarities, Schmidt argued, they are superficial in that the biographers show themselves self-conscious litterateurs whereas the evangelists do not. True biographers describe the extraction, descent, rearing, education, and development of their heroes. They paint a portrait that includes outward appearance, character, and personality. They attempt to penetrate their heroes' motives, emotions, and private thoughts. Mark makes none of these attempts, and the remaining evangelists almost none.

Votaw had recognized many of these lacks in the Gospels, but he saw similar lacks in the popular biographies of the Greco-Roman sphere. Despite such similar lacks, however, Schmidt stood firmly against an estimation of the Greco-Roman biographies as "popular," because in *The Life of Apollonius of Tyana*, for example, Philostratus displays his literary designs. He aims to give the pub-

---

[5] P. Wendland, *Die Urchristliche Literaturformen* (2d ed.; Tübingen: Mohr [Siebeck], 1912). See p. 201 for the quotation. Wrede's *The Messianic Secret* had not yet make its mark!

[6] K. L. Schmidt, "Die Stellung der Evangelien in der allgemeinen Literaturgeschichte," in ΕΥΧΑΡΙΣΤΗΡΙΟΝ: *Studien zur Religion und Literatur des Alten und Neuen Testaments* (ed. H. Schmidt; Göttingen: Vandenhoeck & Ruprecht, 1923), 2:50–134.

[7] M. Dibelius, *From Tradition to Gospel* (Cambridge: James Clarke, 1971 repr. of 1935 ed.); idem, "The Structure and Literary character of the Gospels," *HTR* 20 (1927): 151–70; R. Bultmann, *The History of the Synoptic Tradition* (2d ed.; Oxford: 1968), 321–74, esp. 368–74.

lic a well-written book. His "I" permeates the book. At the start he advances his overall plan, explains the nature of his book, and identifies his sources. Philostratus strives for both completeness of information and good style. Not so the evangelists.

Having criticized other proposed parallels to the Gospels in pre- and non-Christian literature, Schmidt concluded that the Gospels may have analogies (such as early tales about monks, Saint Francis of Assisi, the great Maggid of the Hasidim in Poland, and Doctor Faustus in Germany). But they had no literary genealogy. Sociologically they belonged to *Kleinliteratur* rather than *Hochliteratur*. With little interest in the past either for its own sake or for the benefit of posterity the evangelists acted mainly as collectors of small units and short collections of small units and of a tradition deeply affected by imagination, exaggeration, and other historical distortions common among ill-educated and uncritical people. The fervor of eschatological expectations and the consequent renunciation of this-worldliness did not allow a flowering of literary art in the church. Dibelius hypothesized that evangelistic preaching provided the evangelists with short anecdotes which they collected into Gospels.[8] Because of the large amounts of unevangelistic material in the Gospels, however, that hypothesis struck Schmidt and Bultmann as too simplistic. They convincingly pointed to apologetics and polemics too – as well as to wisdom and catechetical instruction, exhortation, prophecy, apocalyptic, rules for church discipline, and so on.

Thus the kerygmatic hypothesis came to birth: the Gospels enshrine the kerygma (proclamation) of the early church in an expanded, illustrated, and written form. This kerygma had to do not merely with a highly admired man but with the Christ of faith, and not merely with evangelism but with the entire life of the church. Hence the Gospels were not historical and literary, but dogmatic and cultic – "expanded cult legends" in which the Hellenistic mythological interpretation of Christ had been superimposed on the story of Jesus. This hypothesis explains the lack of specifically biographical interests on the part of the evangelists, and it means that the similarities between the Gospels and certain pre- and non-Christian books are superficial. In the final analysis, so too are the similarities with the tales of the early monks, Saint Francis, the Maggid, and Doctor Faustus. For despite external similarities as to popular origins, loose-knit mixture of episodes and dialogues, and the like, such tales lack a kerygma answering to the Christian kerygma which makes these canonical books "Gospels." The novelty of that kerygma implies a literary parthenogenesis for the Gospels. And their canonization left them without true offspring in the history of literature.

---

[8] For Bultmann even the passion narrative came from originally isolated bits of tradition.

In his book, *The Apostolic Preaching and Its Development*,[9] C. H. Dodd presented a variation on the kerygmatic hypothesis. The German form critics had Mark begin with largely isolated bits and pieces on which he imposed an outline. Dodd turned that schema upside down, so that Mark began with an outline into which he (and his successors) fit the bits and pieces. And rather than emphasizing popular cultic and dogmatic origins Dodd pointed to the delay of the Parousia as causing in "finer minds" an upward valuation of the theological significance of Jesus' earthly ministry – hence the writing of the Gospels as various expansions of the kerygmatic outline.

Dodd's version of the kerygmatic hypothesis fell on hard days. Increasingly, scholars tended to take the speeches in Acts as compositions reflecting Lukan theology rather than as the reportage of kerygmatic sermons. Schmidt's analysis of the Markan framework as Markan rather than traditional held sway over majority opinion despite Dodd's counter proposal.[10] The kerygmatic outline did not seem sufficiently or consistently apparent in the sermons in Acts, and the points in the outline seemed so general as to provide little help in an attempt to understand the structure of the Gospels. The absence outside the Gospels of many details concerning Jesus' life cast doubt on the notion that the evangelists used such details to fill out the kerygma. Conversely, Jesus' death and resurrection so dominated the kerygma elsewhere that the large space devoted in the Gospels to the public ministry of Jesus remained unexplained.

Some criticisms of Dodd's hypothesis seem less than compelling. The traditional character of the sermons in Acts continues to receive repeated defenses. We may wonder whether the details of the debate between Schmidt and Dodd on the Markan chronological and geographical framework really affect the general issues concerning the impetus behind the writing of the Gospels and concerning the macrostructure of the Gospels.[11] After all, in Dodd's kerygmatic outline the phrases concerning Jesus' career are couched in the broadest possible terms. The six-point kerygmatic outline that Dodd proposed may not appear consistently enough to be considered a sufficient redefinition of the early kerygma, but it does serve as a compendium of themes variously used by early Christian heralds as occasion demanded and personal preference dictated.[12] Far from being a liability, the generality of the kerygmatic themes enabled the evangelists to develop them freely with the traditions of Jesus at their disposal. Outside the Gospels we may have more allusions to the ministry of Jesus than form

---

[9] 2d ed.; London: Hodder and Stoughton, 1936.

[10] K. L. Schmidt, *Der Rahmen der Geschichte Jesu* (Berlin: Trowitzsch, 1919); C. H. Dodd, *New Testament Studies* (Manchester: Manchester University Press, 1967), 1–11.

[11] Against J. M. Robinson, *A New Quest of the Historical Jesus* (SBT 25; London: SCM, 1959), 48–58.

[12] Cf. R. H. Mounce, *The Essential Nature of New Testament Preaching* (Grand Rapids: Eerdmans, 1960), 64–65, 76–79, 82–84.

critics have admitted. But the absence of explicit references to Jesus' ministry, limited as it was by a provincial setting in Jewish Palestine, indicates that the early church kept information regarding Jesus largely free from admixture with later teaching suited to the needs of an international body of believers scattered across the Roman Empire. Besides, the evangelistically oriented kerygma did not provide a very good handle on the churchly matters discussed in the Epistles. And in addressing Christians epistolary writers could take for granted a knowledge of the message by which those addressees had been converted.

But for the literary problem of the Gospels the real rub comes in the fact that they contain large amounts of unevangelistic material. Just as it quickly became apparent that Dibelius's catch-all explanation, mission-preaching, was far too simplistic because of the variety of subject matter in the Gospels, so also Dodd's hypothesis falls over the same stumbling block. We might make the kerygma a compendium not just of evangelistic themes but of the διδαχή, "teaching," too – i.e., of the entire theology of the early church. But then its generality would leave it helpless to solve the literary problem of "Gospels." Why Gospels instead of more Epistles?

At first blush we might suppose that Dodd answered that question by making the Gospels a response to the delay in the Parousia: the public ministry of Jesus, in all its variety, gained theological significance on account of its didactic and exemplary value to the ever-extending age of the church. In that case, however, the kerygma did not in and of itself call forth the Gospels. Rather, only after preachers had been proclaiming the kerygma for a long time – without the writing of Gospels – did delay of the Parousia create a vacuum that needed filling. When for one decade after another futuristic eschatology failed to materialize, the history of Jesus stepped in to fill the vacuum. So Dodd's appeal to a delayed Parousia sets aside his beloved kerygma as the true explanation of the Gospels and leaves the question whether the Gospels evince enough concern over the delay for us to posit it as the decisive reason behind their writing. At least Dodd did not attempt to draw out such evidence.

The kerygmatic hypothesis received another twist in Scandinavia. Where the Germans had posited a popular setting for the oral traditions H. Riesenfeld and B. Gerhardsson posited a semi-rabbinic setting in which Jesus made his closest disciples memorize his teaching, so that they became "eyewitnesses and ministers of the word." They rather than the masses in the church stood behind the dominical tradition. With the expansion of the church there developed a need for written versions of the "holy word" for the sake of widespread availability. Therefore the Gospels came into being.[13]

---

[13] H. Riesenfeld, "The Gospel Tradition and its Beginnings," *SE I* (1959), 43–65; B. Gerhardsson, *Memory and Manuscript* (Lund: Gleerup, 1961); idem, *Tradition and Transmission in Early Christianity* (Lund: Gleerup, 1964). T. Boman also stressed memory (*Die Jesus-Über-*

Despite a salutary emphasis on the role of memory in ancient pedagogics and aside from other considerations the inadequacy of this theory to explain the emergence of the Gospels comes to light in the question, Where is a gospel concerning a rabbi other than Jesus? To be sure, we can read sayings from rabbis and short anecdotes concerning them. But such traditions appear only as fragments nearly lost in the vast continent of rabbinic literature. Their sparsity for the period before A.D. 70 – i.e., for the period of Jesus' lifetime – is notorious. And we do not have any discrete books dealing with a single rabbi and containing a narrative of his ministry interspersed with more or less teaching material, to say nothing of the huge emphasis the evangelists devoted to Jesus' passion and resurrection.

Furthermore, the large amounts of narrative in the Gospels (here we think above all of Mark, usually considered the first one) do not fit very well the model of the memorized holy word of a teacher. Of course, as Gerhardsson points out, pupils in ancient times learned not only their teacher's words but also their teacher's way of life, anecdotes concerning which they carried in memory. An anecdote here and there, however, does not correspond to the continuous story line in a Gospel. And although the deeds of Jesus in many instances provided examples for emulation, the evangelists stressed the salvific character of Jesus' activity far more than its exemplary character. By contrast, the deeds of other rabbis were not portrayed as salvific.

Among the versions of the kerygmatic explanation of the Gospels, then, that which bases itself on rabbinic pedagogics has not very many adherents. Dodd's kerygmatic outline exercised a certain attraction for a short time. And the classical form critical view that the Gospels consist in collections of individual traditions and shorter collections thereof, though it lasted longest, finally collapsed. Above all, E. Güttgemanns incisively exposed the failure of the form critical version of the kerygma to explain the Gospels as wholes:[14]

---

lieferung im Lichte der neueren Volkskunde [Göttingen: Vandenhoeck & Ruprecht, 1967]). But he assigned the tradition in the Gospels to a special class of narrators instead of Jesus' closest disciples. Thus the semi-rabbinic, semi-academic setting was exchanged for that of catechetical classes in which subordinates to the apostles performed the menial task of instructing new converts. Having drawn their information from Jesus' closest disciples, these narrators arranged it into the sources of the Gospels and into the Gospels themselves. Insofar as Boman orients his hypothesis to studies of Scandinavian folklore rather than Jewish pedagogics his presentation lacks some of the cogency of Riesenfeld's and Gerhardsson's hypothesis. The distinction between apostolic eyewitnesses, who did not rehearse dominical information, and subordinate narrators, who did – a distinction crucial to Boman's hypothesis – seems doubtful.

[14] E. Güttgemanns, *Offene Fragen zur Formgeschichte des Evangeliums* (2d ed.; Munich: Chr. Kaiser, 1970); idem, *studia linguistica neotestamentica* (Munich: Chr. Kaiser, 1971); idem, various articles in *Linguistica Biblica* 1 (1970). English summaries of Güttgemanns' thought are provided by W. G. Doty, "Fundamental Questions about Literary-Critical Methodology: A Review Article," *JAAR* 40 (1972): 521–27; idem, "Linguistics and Biblical Criticism," *JAAR* 41 (1973): 114–21; but readers should not miss the richness of Güttgemanns own discussion.

First, form critics utilized the romantical notions of folklore that go back to J. G. Herder (1744–1803). Not only are those notions outdated but also they have to do with oral tradition. To use them in explanation of the Gospels fails to take account of the Gospels' writtenness.

Second, form critics failed to see the significance of the passage of oral tradition into a written state. For them the writing of the oral traditions came about almost by accident. But why were those traditions *written* rather than carried on endlessly in an oral fashion?[15]

Third, form critics wrongly assumed a graduality in the collection of bits and pieces of tradition, with the result that our present Gospels grew like Topsy with little rhyme or reason. Modern studies of folklore, on the contrary, disprove the theory of graduality in the association of small units. Such association takes place suddenly and on a large scale.[16]

Fourth, by treating a Gospel simply as the sum of its parts, form critics failed to see the significance of the whole. But modern structural linguistics and *Gestalt*-thinking in general have taught us that just as a melody is more than the aggregate of its notes (the same notes might be scored differently!), so also a piece of writing is more than an aggregate. In large measure its meaning consists in the whole *as* a whole.

Fifth, form critics wrongly attributed an active role of creativity to the community and a passive role to the scribe satisfied to put down traditions largely as they came to him. Modern studies of folklore indicate, however, that passivity characterizes the community, which wants to hear her traditions told and retold with little change. Creativity belongs on the side of the storyteller, who will exercise his creativity to the limits imposed by the community's conservatism.[17] This conservatism puts the onus of responsibility for the writing of Gospels on the evangelists rather than on the community and her traditional kerygma. Consequently, in more recent redaction and composition criticism the center of gravity shifted to the *Gestalt* of the Gospels and the authorial intent evident in the way an evangelist created that *Gestalt* by means of selection, revision, arrangement, and connection.

---

[15] See esp. W. H. Kelber, *The Oral and Written Gospel* (Philadelphia: Fortress, 1983); idem, "Jesus and Tradition: Words in Time, Words in Space," *Semeia* 65 (1994): 139–67, though Kelber overdraws the difference between writtenness and orality.

[16] Despite wide differences on other matters Güttgemanns and Boman agree on this point in their estimate of the lesson to be learned from modern studies of folklore.

[17] See esp. the firsthand observations of K. E. Bailey, "Informal Controlled Oral Tradition and the Synoptic Gospels," *Asia Journal of Theology* 5 (1991): 34–54; idem, "Middle Eastern Oral Tradition and the Synoptic Gospels," *ExpTim* 106 (1995): 563–67; also J. D. G. Dunn, *Jesus Remembered* (vol. 1 of *Christianity in the Making*; Grand Rapids: Eerdmans, 2003), 192–210, and other literature cited there. In my opinion Dunn jumps too quickly to oral performances (N.B. the plural) as an explanation of variations among the Gospels. For the pattern-like quality of most differences among them favors authorial redaction concentrated in a book over oral performances scattered willy-nilly across various occasions.

But authors are more or less bound by literary conventions. To discover the intention lying behind the evangelists' writing of Gospels instead of books belonging to some other literary genre the search for literary precedents to the Gospels revived. J. M. Robinson and H. Koester took the lead in a new effort to classify the Gospels in terms of literary precedents or, as they like to put it, to plot the "trajectories" of ancient Jewish and Greco-Roman literature along which the Gospels may be located.[18] Colleagues and students at Claremont and Harvard, along with members of the now disbanded Gospels Seminar of the Society of Biblical Literature, joined in the effort.

Robinson began by plotting the trajectory of the genre *logoi sophōn* – λόγοι σοφῶν, "sayings of [the] sages" or "words of [the] wise" – from Jewish wisdom literature (e.g., Proverbs) to Gnostic literature, especially the *Gospel of Thomas*, where the collection of dominical sayings with its *incipit* portrays Jesus as a wise man whose words convey life. Q lay along this trajectory. And Paul's opponents in 1 Corinthians had imbibed the Spirit-Wisdom Christology of Q, a dehistoricizing Christology that reached even fuller development in the *Gospel of Thomas*. Thus, Koester went on to propose, the *Gospel of Thomas* did not derive from later Gnostic spiritualizing of the teaching of Jesus found in the canonical Gospels, but from Jesus' "most original proclamation" concerning the secret coming of the kingdom – and this by way of a stream of tradition independent from the canonical Gospels and also independent from the Q used by Matthew and Luke. For that Q domesticated the earlier sayings of the sage Jesus by injecting a traditional apocalypticism which identified Jesus with the future Son of Man. Since therefore the authentic teaching of Jesus lacked such notions "the Gnosticism of the *Gospel of Thomas* appears to be a direct continuation of the eschatological sayings of Jesus."[19]

Besides Jewish wisdom literature Robinson and Koester also saw Hellenistic aretalogies lying behind the canonical Gospels.[20] Taking their cue from pagan recitals of the supernatural deeds performed by "divine men" (philosophers, he-

---

[18] J. M. Robinson and H. Koester, *Trajectories through Early Christianity* (Philadelphia: Fortress, 1971). This volume consists of a collection of articles that appeared earlier in various locations. Besides these articles see also J. M. Robinson, "Basic Shifts in German Theology," *Int* 16 (1962): 80–86; idem, "The Problem of History in Mark, Reconsidered," *USQR* 20 (1965): 130–47; idem, "On the *Gattung* of Mark (and John)," in *Jesus and Man's Hope I* (Pittsburgh: Pittsburgh Theological Seminary, 1970), 101; N. R. Petersen Jr., "So-Called Gnostic Type Gospels and the Question of the Genre 'Gospel,'" SBL Annual Meeting Papers, 1970, for Task Group on Gospel Genre, Gospels Seminar; M. J. Suggs, *Wisdom, Christology, and Law in Matthew's Gospel* (Cambridge, Mass.: Harvard University Press, 1970). In addition to what follows below see my review of Suggs' book in *Int* 27 (1973): 369.

[19] Koester, *Trajectories*, 175.

[20] For a survey with copious bibliographical references to earlier studies see M. Smith, "Prolegomena to a Discussion of Aretalogies, Divine Men, the Gospels and Jesus," *JBL* 90 (1971): 174–99. See also H. Koester, "Romance, Biography, and Gospel," in *The Genre of the Gospels* (Missoula: SBL, 1972), 136–48; D. Georgi, "The Records of Jesus in the Light of Ancient Accounts of Revered Men," *SBL 1972 Proceedings*, 2:527–42.

roes, kings, and the like), Christian aretalogists produced collections of miracles done by Jesus.[21] The resultant Christology of Jesus as a divine man informed and affected the opponents of Paul in 2 Corinthians.[22] In such circles, accordingly, brute miracles constituted proof of Christianity and faith consisted in belief in Jesus as a worker of miracles.[23] The NT apocrypha provide examples of further developments along this line.

Mark and John responded by correcting the Christology of the miracle-collections. Mark did so by means of the messianic secret, an attempt to play down the glory of Jesus' ministry in the tradition of miracles,[24] and by means the ignominy of the cross.[25] John corrected the aretalogy of his signs-source by spiritualizing the mighty works of Jesus, and did so primarily through interspersing interpretive discourses and exposing the inadequacy of faith in miracles alone. Under this view Mark and John take on the nature of aretalogies in parody. Losing uniqueness they find their literary genealogy in the biographical aretalogies of the Hellenistic world.[26] Not even as parodies do Mark and John regain a measure of uniqueness; for the aretalogical parody appears elsewhere, specifically in Lucian of Samosata's writings against Alexander and Peregrinus.

The Pauline theology of the cross, by which Mark makes his aretalogy a parody, receives the designation "kerygma." But how the meaning of the term has changed! Once it referred to communal tradition drawn and developed from the whole of Jesus' ministry. Now it refers to an individual author's correction of the tradition by means of an anti-aretalogical interpretation of the crucifixion.[27]

Matthew and Luke historicized the Spirit-Wisdom Christology of Q by framing Q within the narrative of Mark. This framework had the effect of blocking a Gnostic development of Q within the canon (but not outside the canon, as the

---

[21] See further Smith, "Prolegomena," 197–98; P. Achtemeier, "Toward the Isolation of Pre-Markan Miracle Catenae," *JBL* 89 (1970): 265–91; and R. T. Fortna, *The Gospel of Signs* (London: Cambridge University Press, 1970); idem, *The Fourth Gospel and Its Predecessor* (Philadelphia: Fortress, 1988); and other literature cited in these sources.

[22] D. Georgi, *The Opponents of Paul in Second Corinthians* (Philadelphia: Fortress, 1986).

[23] Because of its minor role we may by-pass Koester's discussion of "revelation discourses" (*Trajectories*, 193–98).

[24] H. Conzelmann, "Present and Future in the Synoptic Tradition," *JTC* 5 (1968): 41–44.

[25] Besides literature previously cited see H. D. Betz, "Jesus as Divine Man," in *Jesus and the Historian* (ed. F. T. Trotter; Philadelphia: Westminster, 1968), 114–33; T. J. Weeden, *Mark – Traditions in Conflict* (Philadelphia: Fortress, 1971); idem, "The Heresy That Necessitated Mark's Gospel," *ZNW* 59 (1968): 145–58.

[26] Or aretalogical biographies. The stress varies from scholar to scholar. In paralleling Mark with popular lives of philosophers "still close enough to the aretalogical *vita* to compete with it," Georgi forgets Schmidt's effective critique of that parallel (Georgi, "The Records of Jesus," 527–42). Still, Georgi's proposal boils down to aretalogy corrected or parodied by means of a philosopher's *vita*.

[27] Even though the messianic secret may already have existed in the tradition, apparently (according to the view under discussion) Mark was the first to use the secret as a corrective to divine-man Christology.

Gospel of Thomas gives witness). Matthean redaction of the sources resulted in a manual of church order along the lines, or trajectory, of OT law, *Jubilees*, the *Manual of Discipline* (1QS), and the *Didache*. Luke's redaction resulted in a kind of Hellenistic memoirs of Jesus and, more significantly, in a revival of the aretalogy that Luke's source Mark had taken over only to criticize. The tragedy of Jesus' passion became a triumphal exodus. Luke's second and associated volume portrayed the apostles as wonder-working divine men like their Master. Ironically, in Luke-Acts Paul's opponents in 2 Corinthians won canonicity for their views.

In summary, the historical Jesus ministered as a dispenser of wisdom and died a martyr. Oral tradition "expanded" the "facts." The conventional genres – sayings of the wise and aretalogies – led to the isolation, extraction, and writing of suitable parts of the dominical tradition. At the same time there occurred further expansion of the tradition according to the expectations within those genres. Mark and John did their correcting, Matthew and Luke their combining. We are left, then, without a literary genre "Gospel." Mark and John fall into the genre of biographical aretalogy, Matthew into that of rules for life in a community, and Luke-Acts into that of "history"[28] heavily laden with aretalogy. Properly, the term "gospel" carries no meaning as to literary genre. It can refer only to a motif, the theology of the cross.

We need, however, to examine this construct critically. Robinson's regular use of the transliteration *logoi sophōn* leaves a questionable and possibly false impression that *logoi* was largely a technical term for written collections of sayings. The term may rather have referred to sayings in their original spokenness rather than later writtenness and, very generally, to a number of words en masse or to individual words within a single saying. Robinson's documentation provides many examples of such possibilities to anyone who refuses to read the texts woodenly.[29] Greater attention to these possibilities would diminish the evidence adduced for what appears in the discussion as a nearly ubiquitous and formalistically conceived genre *logoi sophōn* in late Judaism, early Christianity, and Gnosticism. Furthermore, not everywhere does *sophōn* go with *logoi* either explicitly or implicitly. Some *logoi* have little or no connection with wisdom.[30] Although these considerations do not destroy all the evidence for a genre "sayings of the sages," the pervasiveness – and therefore influence – of such a genre shrinks.

---

[28] In the Hellenistic and Jewish sense, of course, not in a von Rankean sense.

[29] Robinson admits and discusses wide variations of connotation in *logos/logoi* (*Trajectories*, 73–74 n. 9, 75 n. 11) but proceeds to discuss passages with little or no consideration given to possible (and more probable) connotations other than the connotation of written collections.

[30] See, e.g., the references in *Trajectories*, 111–12 n. 92. More detailed work needs to be done along the above lines with reference to the data on *logoi* as set out and interpreted by Robinson.

Should we grant a trajectory of "sayings of the sages" and its importance in the milieu of the NT, the question of Q arises. Should we further grant not only the existence of Q but also its writtenness as a single document (with the possibility of different editions left open),[31] a question remains. Even though the *Gospel of Thomas* be put on the trajectory "sayings of the sages," does Q belong there? A look at the section "Logia (Jesus as the Teacher of Wisdom)" in Bultmann's *The History of the Synoptic Tradition* will reveal a surprisingly large amount of material not necessarily to be characterized as wisdom, and the remainder very often appears in the Markan tradition rather than Q.[32] Since Q and prior collections of sayings admittedly contained not only wisdom sayings but also "legal statements…, prophetic sayings (including I-words, beatitudes, and woes), and parables,"[33] why limit ourselves to the single possibility that the wisdom sayings, by no means dominant, cast the aura of "Wisdom" over the whole? Why not rather call Q, say, a book of laws or rules because of the legal statements? Or a prophetical book because of Jesus' prophetic statements? We surely have literary precedents for those kinds of book. Therefore the *structure* of Q and the *proportion* of wisdom-sayings in it would have to favor our taking Q as a member of the genre "sayings of the sages." Yet such evidence has not come to light.

But should we grant even further that along with the *Gospel of Thomas*, Q belonged to a genre "sayings of the sages," it remains possible – and perhaps probable – that Q derived from early tradition and that the *Gospel of Thomas* took sayings into that genre out of the canonical Gospels rather than out of an early edition of Q.[34] Favoring this possibility is the presence in the *Gospel of Thomas* of features commonly accepted as redactional in those Gospels. If we can think that the writer of Q and/or his predecessors extracted sayings from a mixture of words and deeds in the precanonical tradition concerning Jesus' ministry, we can just as easily think that the writer of the *Gospel of Thomas* and/or his predecessors extracted sayings from the mixture of words and deeds in the canoni-

---

[31] In view of its "loss" despite its importance, did Q (we need an earlier version than the *Gospel of Thomas*!) ever exist? If it did, to what extent did the evangelists borrow from it? Was it a single document? A gathered set of short documents or notes? Scattered oral traditions? Concatenated oral tradition? A mixture of oral and written traditions? Further questions concerning its language or languages and possible translations thereof complicate matters. The work of J. S. Kloppenborg Verbin (most recently, *Excavating Q* [Minneapolis: Fortress, 2000]) and many others has added the complexity of hypothesized successive editions to the complexity of different kinds of material.

[32] Bultmann, *History of Synoptic Tradition*, 69–108. Again, more detailed work needs doing, especially on the proportions of material necessarily wisdomlike, material necessarily prophetic and/or apocalyptic, and neutral material – and this in comparison with such materials in Mark, Q, and special sources.

[33] Koester, *Trajectories*, 138.

[34] Of course, such a view does not rule out Gnostic production of additional sayings or some borrowings from extracanonical traditions.

cal Gospels. Indeed, many students of the *Gospel of Thomas* see in it a conspicuous dependence on the canonical Gospels.[35] The *Gospel of Thomas* then loses its value as a handle on Q and the development of the canonical Gospels.[36]

Since the *Gospel of Thomas* lacks apocalyptic expectations, emphasizes a radically realized eschatology of the kingdom, and offers the revelation of divine wisdom in Jesus' words, Koester said that the source of the *Gospel of Thomas* did the same.[37] But the form(s) of Q used by Matthew and Luke in western Syria contained those elements. Therefore, concluded Koester, the *Gospel of Thomas* depended on an earlier, eastern edition of Q lacking them. But we should expect the absence of apocalyptic and the like in a Gnostic document *whatever its source(s)*. Such absence favors derivation from an independent and more original stream of dominical tradition no more than it favors purgation of canonical tradition. The later date of the *Gospel of Thomas* and the undeniable wholesale interpolation of Gnostic ideas and sayings tip the scales in favor of a Gnostic editing of mostly canonical sources. That editing included purgation as well as distortion, amplification, and sheer addition. The necessity of positing a different Q, and one much further distant in time from its representative (the *Gospel of Thomas*) than the usual Q from its representatives (Matthew and Luke), exposes the weakness of Koester's hypothesis.

The collections of miracles that hypothetically stand behind Mark and John also come into question. Supposing for the moment the actuality of such collections we still do not necessarily have aretalogies in them. Not only does the expression "divine man" fail to appear in the Gospels (or anywhere else in the NT), but also – false distinctions aside[38] – in Jesus' miracles we note an absence of self-serving and self-glorification, the failure to perform sometimes just for the sake of making an impression, the lack of curiosities, burlesque, and fantasy.[39] These differences from comparable pagan literature leave us doubtful about the aretalogical character of whatever precanonical collections might have supplied stories to the evangelists. Jesus' miracles look more like salvific miracles such as we meet in the OT.[40]

---

[35] Koester himself provided the beginnings of a bibliography in this respect (*Trajectories*, 130–31 n. 45).

[36] For further objections to taking Q as a book of wisdom see D. Zeller, "Eine weisheitliche Grundschrift in der Logienquelle?" in *The Four Gospels 1992* (ed. F. Van Segbroeck et al.; BETL 100; Leuven: Leuven University Press, 1992), 1:389–401. I by-pass the classifying of Q as a Cynic biography or as a prophetic book. Those classifications have received adequate criticism elsewhere.

[37] Koester might have said that the writer of the *Gospel of Thomas* purged those elements from his precanonical source, but then someone might ask why the writer of the *Gospel of Thomas* could not have purged the *canonical* sources.

[38] Smith justifiably complains of false distinctions ("Prolegomena," 178–79).

[39] Cf. A. Deissmann, *Light from the Ancient East* (New York: George H. Doran, 1927), 386. See also L. Sabourin, "Hellenistic and Rabbinic 'Miracles,'" *BTB* 2 (1972): 305–7.

[40] Of course, they are epiphanic too, but only insofar as they are salvific, a point unappreci-

But did collections of miracles in fact stand behind parts of Mark and John? The differences in recent reconstructions engender doubt concerning our ability to verify such collections or to rule out Mark himself as the first to put some of Jesus' miracles together.[41] The stylistic unity of John will always haunt those who argue for a signs-source behind John. The argument from Johannine aporias, put forward in lieu of stylistic dissimilarities, lapses into a hypercriticism that would find similar aporias in material known certainly to be unmediated.[42] Even appeal to the "second sign" in John 4:54 will not carry conviction so long as the verse may be taken to mean – quite naturally and harmoniously with 2:23; 3.2, and 4.45 – that Jesus once again performed a miracle after coming into Galilee from Judea.

More broadly, H. C. Kee showed that we do wrong to speak of aretalogies as an ancient form of biographical writing in which the author divinized the hero by ascribing miracles to him. So-called aretalogies have a diversity of materials that precludes our lumping the writings together into "aretalogy." We may speak of precanonical collections of miracles, Kee thinks, but we ought not to draw the inference that they represented divine-man Christology. Pagan parallels do not support apotheosis by ascription of miracles.[43] Much less did the ascription of miracles to human beings result in apotheosis in the culturally closer parallels of Jewish literature from the OT through the Talmud.

Yet more damagingly, D. L. Tiede demonstrated the erroneousness of thinking that as the tradition concerning Jesus moved out into the wider Hellenistic world, aretalogists spun miracle stories around him to portray him as a wonder-working divine man. For in literary circles of the first century, Hellenistic divine men gained authentication from their exemplification of moral virtue. Only in the literature of the late second and the third centuries of our era did miracles successfully encroach on the sphere of divine men. (This development holds

---

ated by P. J. Achtemeier, "The Origin and Function of the Pre-Marcan Miracle Catenae," *JBL* 91 (1972): 198–221. For the OT and un-Hellenistic Jewish features of Jesus' miracles, see O. Betz, "The Concept of the So-called 'Divine Man' in Mark's Christology," in *Studies in New Testament and Early Christian Literature* (ed. D. E. Aune; Leiden: E. J. Brill, 1972), 234–39.

[41] See J.-M. van Cangh, "Les sources de l'Évangile: les collections pré-marciennes de miracles," *RTL* 3 (1972): 76–85, and literature cited there. See also D. L. Tiede, *The Charismatic Figure as Miracle Worker* (SBLDS 1; Missoula: SBL, 1972), 255–69, for both discussion and further literature, and 269–85 for the same on John.

[42] Cf. the satire on H. Conzelmann's hypercriticism of Acts 27 by R. P. C. Hanson, "The Journey of Paul and the Journey of Nikias," *SE IV* (1968), 315–18.

[43] H. C. Kee, "Aretalogy and Gospel," *JBL* 92 (1973): 402–22. Kee's own stress on apocalypticism behind and in Mark admittedly fails to solve the riddle of the genre "gospel": "For the overall pattern of a gospel, Mark had no literary precedent" (ibid., 422). Apocalytpic books had nothing like the story line in Mark (inauguration, ministry of miracles and teaching, passion, resurrection), and Mark lacks apocalyptic stocks in trade such as celestial journeys, visions, and bizarre figures of speech.

true also with reference to the rabbis.) Up to that time writers took pains to play down traditions of the miraculous in portrayals of men as divine.[44]

The less authenticity we see in the canonical Gospels, the more "pull" we require on the part of the literary genres – "sayings of the sages" and apotheosizing aretalogies in our present discussion – to account for the inauthentic material. The enormity of the amounts of material attributed by trajectory critics to the "pull" of the genres almost necessitates a reification of the genres. But close inspection fails to disclose the required strength of momentum for those genres during the period of the NT.

In turning from backgrounds to the canonical texts themselves, for the sake of discussion let us suppose the establishment of apotheosizing aretalogy as a pre-canonical genre of writing. Could we say even then that by means of parody Mark produced an aretalogy in reverse? Essential to an affirmative answer is Conzelmann's topsy-turvy view that Mark imposed the messianic secret on super-christological material as a corrective drawn from his theology of the cross. But Mark did not develop and apply the messianic secret with any consistency. That fact, which led Wrede to attribute the secret to pre-Markan tradition, exposes the fundamental weakness that only on the assumption of a unified and pervasive messianic secret could we suppose that Mark focused the commands to secrecy sharply against the miracles. The assumption, however, is false.[45] Moreover, the blatancy and savagery of the attacks on Alexander and Peregrinus by Lucian of Samosata (in contrast to his equally eulogistic praise of Demonax) make Mark's messianic secret seem too subtle for a generic subclassification of Mark with Lucian's attacks. Besides, Lucian wrote not until the latter half of the second century A.D. It is therefore doubtful that we have any literary tradition of aretalogy in reverse.

Similarly, we cannot deny John's insistence on a faith that penetrates more deeply than a mere recognition of power. But the statement of purpose in John 20:30–31, "these [signs] are written that you might believe that the Christ, the Son of God, is Jesus and that by believing you may have life in his name," comes at the very close of the Gospel proper – strangely if John had as a primary purpose the correction of aretalogical Christology. Its position disagrees with

---

[44] Tiede, *Charismatic Figure*, with references to well-known treatments of the topic by Reitzenstein, Bieler, Windisch, Georgi, H. D. Betz, Hadas and Smith, Weeden, and others. The pre-Christian association of miracles and divine men in *nonliterary* circles does not help the aretalogical hypothesis, for that hypothesis needs a pre-Christian *literary* tradition to justify the hypothesizing of collections of Jesus' miracles which, it is further thought, gave rise to Mark and John.

[45] W. C. Robinson Jr., "The Quest for Wrede's Secret Messiah," *Int* 27 (1973): 10–30, esp. 26–27. Cf. E. C. Hobbs, "Norman Perrin on Methodology in the Interpretation of Mark: A Critique of 'The Christology of Mark' and 'Toward an Interpretation of the Gospel of Mark,'" in *Christology and a Modern Pilgrimage* (ed. H. D. Betz; Claremont: New Testament Colloquium, 1971), 87–90.

such a purpose even though we assign it to the signs-source, for John would hardly have let his Gospel end (except for its epilogue in ch. 21) with a statement needing correction if not outright refutation (cf. 14:11).

The accounts of Jesus' resurrection – told by Mark in terms of its awe-inspiringness and in John reaching its climax in Thomas's "My Lord and my God!" – do not read like corrections of a divine-man Christology. Nor does the exclamation of Mark's centurion at the foot of the cross, "Truly this man was God's Son!" Just as John's prologue indicates agreement with Thomas's confession, the textually probable introduction to Mark's Gospel, "The beginning of the gospel of Jesus Christ, God's Son," shows that Mark delighted in the high Christology of the centurion's exclamation (cf. 14:61–62). Not the ignominy but, as with the resurrection, the awesomeness of the manner and circumstances of Jesus' death – the darkness, the loudness of Jesus' last outcry, and the rending of the veil from top to bottom – provides Mark's point of emphasis. And these comments merely skim the surface of what might be said along such lines.[46]

We may agree that Luke-Acts belongs to the category of historical writing. But did Matthew write a Christian manual of discipline? The designation is too narrow. What of Matthew's interest in proof from prophecy? And we should have to regard as unimportant to Matthew the large amounts of historical narrative that he included all around the five dominical "discourses." Significantly, N. R. Petersen Jr. qualified his description of Matthew as a manual of discipline with the joker "historicized." But for a manual of discipline there appears in Matthew too much historical narrative, including some that the evangelist himself has added to Markan tradition. The story of the nativity is a good example. Also, Petersen has to deny that Matthew had "any particular interest" in the passion narrative "at all."[47] Why then did Matthew punctuate that narrative with a fulfillment-quotation (27:9–10), conform phraseology in it to the OT (26:3, 4, 15, 28, 52; 27:24, 34, 43, 57[48]), and add eschatological signs to the rending of the veil (27:51–54)? As Matthew's own contributions, these items do not look like excess baggage forced on him by his sources. We dare not assume that the intent of an evangelist and thereby the genre of his book come to light only in his distinctive emphases or, here, in only one of his distinctive emphases. Matthew's undoubted emphasis on the rules of the kingdom should not afflict us with tunnel vision.

We may conclude that sayings of sages, aretalogies, and manuals of discipline have proved to be generic disappointments. The genre criticism fostered by redaction and composition criticism and traced in trajectories fails. Most re-

---

[46] See R. H. Gundry, *Mark* (Grand Rapids: Eerdmans, 1993), 1–15, 1024–26, 1049–51; idem, "A Rejoinder to Joel F. Williams' 'Is Mark's Gospel an Apology for the Cross?'" *BBR* 12 (2002): 123–39.

[47] Petersen, "So-Called Gnostic Type Gospels," 26.

[48] See R. H. Gundry, *The Use of the Old Testament in St. Matthew's Gospel with Special Reference to the Messianic Hope* (NovTSup 18; Leiden: Brill, 1967), ad loc.

cently, then, Votaw's classification of the canonical Gospels as biographies has made a comeback.[49] But the arguments for and against this classification largely duplicate what the earlier part of the present essay outlined in the debate between Votaw and his critics. We do not need to go over the same ground.

One more line of enquiry remains, the theological. Votaw's attempt to set the Gospels inside the framework of ancient biographical writing aimed at the presentation of Jesus as primarily a teacher of ethics *à la* theological liberalism in the early twentieth century; for ancient biographers purposed "to eulogize their subjects, or to affect political opinion and action, or to teach uprightness and usefulness by example" and "to exhibit and perpetuate their [the biographees'] teaching."[50] On the other hand, the literary uniqueness of the Gospels as assessed by Schmidt served neo-orthodoxy. The kerygma ruled out the parallelomania of the history-of-religions school. *Sui generis*, the Gospels dropped into the history of literature as foreign bodies in the manner in which the Word of God comes into the world. Moreover, their folkloristic character went along with the separation of faith from the academic quest of the historical Jesus in favor of an existential (we might almost say "folkloristic") faith.[51]

Unhappy with a large-scale divorce of Christian faith from knowledge of the historical Jesus, Dodd tried to bring back a fair measure of historical content by means of the kerygmatic outline of Jesus' ministry. In a toned-down neo-orthodoxy the main facts about Jesus gained assurance; the details remained existentially negotiable. According to the Continental version of the kerygma, early Christians strayed from the historical Jesus. According to Dodd's British version, early Christians returned to the historical Jesus through a failure of the Parousia to materialize.

The Continental kerygma grew into Bultmann's program of demythologization. With the exposure of form criticism's inability to explain the phenomenon of the Gospels as wholes Güttgemanns undertook to continue demythologization by means of "Generative Poetics." Existentialist analysis gave way to discovery of the "deep structure" of the documents. Thus, when we have stripped away specifics concerning the miraculous, the eschatological and

---

[49] See, above all, C. H. Talbert, *What is a Gospel?* (Philadelphia: Fortress, 1977), and R. A. Burridge, *What are the Gospels?* (SNTSMS 70; Cambridge: Cambridge University Press, 1992). For a well-balanced critique see L. Hartman, "Das Markusevangelium, 'für die lectio sollemnis im Gottesdienst abgefasst'?" in *Frühes Christentum* (vol. 3 of *Geschichte – Tradition – Reflexion*; ed. H. Lichtenberger; Tübingen: J. C. B. Mohr [Paul Siebeck], 1996), 147–71. Hartman also provides an extensive bibliography (pp. 168–71). By stressing both the flexibility of Greco-Roman biography and differences from it in the canonical Gospels L. W. Hurtado has more recently come to describe those Gospels as "quasi"-biographical (*Lord Jesus Christ* [Grand Rapids: Eerdmans, 2003], 270–82; cf. M Reiser, "Die Stellung der Evangelien in der antiken Literaturgeschichte," *ZNW* 90 [1999]: 1–27).

[50] Votaw, *Gospels and Contemporary Biographies*, 7, 9 et passim.

[51] See Schmidt, "Die Stellung," 130–34.

apocalyptic, and so on, the Gospels stand before us as, say, tragedies with comic endings. This kind of demythologizing produced no theological returns.

Wanting to go further in altering Bultmannian theology, E. Käsemann called for a new quest of the historical Jesus to avoid docetism and *Enthusiasmus*.[52] Hand in hand with redaction criticism the new quest brought back genre criticism, i.e., the correlating of the Gospels and other ancient literature in a manner reminiscent of the old quest. Once again the Gospels appeared as part of the history of literature but this time not in the cubbyhole of biographical literature pure and simple – rather, in turbulent cross currents of genres such as sayings of the sages and aretalogies. Robinson and Koester brought these supposed literary movements under the aegis of process theology for the sake of creative reinterpretation in changing situations.

Taking a cue from W. Bauer's diagnosis of early Christian theology as consisting in competitive theologies rather than orthodoxy embattled by heresies,[53] Robinson and Koester evaluated the theologies of the literary trajectories related to the Gospels. In the trajectory from (early) Q to the *Gospel of Thomas* and onward, the teaching of Jesus appears as revealed eternal truth by virtue of its disengagement from the historical circumstances of Jesus' life. Matthew's and Luke's checking that docetic tendency through the insertion of (later) Q into a framework of historical narrative puts a ban on any theology which professes revealed eternal truth. Likewise, Mark's and John's critiques of aretalogy illegitimize all supernaturalistic theology from precanonical collections of miracles through Luke-Acts and the apocryphal Gospels and the apocryphal Acts up to modern day evangelicalism and fundamentalism.[54]

What then is true orthodoxy? The radical historicizing – i.e., humanizing – of Jesus by means of the theology of the cross. Because of the cross, incarnation comes to mean demythologization. All else merits being branded as heresy, for "the criterion is the humanness and radical revelation in Jesus, which makes it impossible even to speak about Jesus' divine qualities." That in turn "renders impossible the attainment of transhistorical, supernatural, and otherworldly qualities as a part of man's existence." Nothing remains "but to be humanly responsible to an existing visible community: *agapē* (Gal. 5:6, 22; cf. 6:2 ff.)."[55] And so by a devious route we have returned to early liberalism's ethic of love as the sum and substance of the gospel and test of orthodoxy.

---

[52] E. Käsemann, "The Problem of the Historical Jesus," *Essays on New Testament Themes* (London: SCM, 1964), 15–47. Cf. J. M. Robinson, *New Quest*.

[53] W. Bauer, *Orthodoxy and Heresy in Earliest Christianity* (ed. R. A. Kraft and G. Krodel; Philadelphia: Fortress, 1971).

[54] N. B. the mixed estimate of Luke (-Acts) as rightly blocking a docetic possibility in Q and wrongly reviving the aretalogy of collections of miracles.

[55] Quotations come from Koester, *Trajectories*, 146–52.

The humanity of Jesus rather than accurate information about his ministry now provides our touchstone. Therefore the historicizing of him does not imply any large measure of historicity in the Gospels. Taking the next and logical step, N. Perrin dissolved the historicizing of Jesus into present religious experience: "The voice of the Jesus of the Gospels is the voice of living Christian experience ... the evangelists and the tradition they represent are indifferent as to whether this experience is ultimately related to anything said or done in Galilee or Judea before the crucifixion." The Gospels reflect "a situation in which distinctions between past, present, and future tended to be lost as the present experience of Jesus as risen led to a new understanding of the future and of the past."[56] Thus in a backwards trajectory we were hurled back through the ethics of Harnack and Ritschl to a *Schleiermacherlich* emphasis on experience.

We have to ask, however, why a conviction that the Lord spoke presently to the church should have resulted in the antedating of his present utterances. Belief in the resurrection of Jesus and in the gift of his Spirit would seem rather to have eliminated the requirement and reduced the desire to practice antedating. Only if Jesus were thought still to lie in the grave awaiting resurrection at the last day would the early Christians have had compelling reason to assign later "revelations" to the earthly Jesus. A living Lord did not need to speak in the past tense – or be made to do so – as the messages to the seven churches in Revelation 2–3 give evidence.

Just because they are not antedated to the earthly Jesus, Perrin – in a *petitio principii* – denied that those seven messages are characteristically Christian. But we ought to overlook neither the claim of Paul to have the Spirit on matters not covered by the earthly Jesus (1 Cor 7:40) nor his careful separation of Jesus' past teaching from his own (Paul's) present teaching (1 Corinthians 7 passim). Nor should we forget either the failure of the Jesus of the Gospels to discuss such burning issues in the early church as circumcision or the practically complete limitation of Son-of-Man Christology to the Gospels. The Gospels differ in form from Revelation 2–3, then, not because present religious experience has made the tenses "flow together" but precisely because early Christians knew the difference between past statements of the earthly Jesus and present statements of the exalted Christ.

As for orthodoxy and heresy, both Bauer's denial of that antithesis and the slipperiness of truth in process thought forestall the fixing of any standard such as humanitarian *agapē* over against other theologies. Koester made it triply hard for himself to distinguish orthodoxy and heresy, for he has adjudged the trajectory from (early) Q to the *Gospel of Thomas* as closest to Jesus' original proclamation of the secret presence of God's kingdom yet regards that trajectory as

---

[56] N. Perrin, *What is Redaction Criticism?* (Philadelphia: Fortress, 1969), 74, 76–77. See also idem, "The Literary Gattung 'Gospel' – Some Observations," *ExpTim* 82 (1970): 4–7.

docetically heretical. Of course, if only the humanizing fact of the death of Jesus matters and not the content of his teaching, closeness to the original proclamation loses its virtue. But why then choose the death *of Jesus* as our touchstone? On the other hand, if theological value does inhere in Jesus' teaching and if (as Koester thinks) Jesus taught an unapocalyptic, radically realized eschatology, Paul's opponents in 1 Corinthians were right. Koester makes us decide between the theology of the cross and realized eschatology, i.e., between Paul, reflected in Mark and John, and the historical Jesus, sage of eternal truth. Koester chooses Paul. Such a choice would be unnecessary, however, if we were to take seriously Paul's other emphases on the resurrection and exaltation of Christ, the gift of the Spirit, the union of believers with Christ, and the Parousia with attendant events – and if we were to allow that Jesus too made theological expressions concerning his suffering and death (as, e.g., in the Words of Institution) and spoke in terms of futuristic eschatology as well as realized eschatology.[57]

The so-called third quest of the historical Jesus has gone hand in glove with the comeback of biography as the putative genre of the canonical Gospels. This quest arose out of a felt theological need to establish stronger links between Christian faith and the facts of history – and also to atone for the Holocaust by recapturing the Jewishness of a historically pre-Christian Jesus.

Miracle stories in the Gospels still present the biggest bugaboo. Some have attributed them to the folkloristic habits of *hoi polloi*, uneducated and imaginative as they were. Others have attributed them to the "pull" of a literary genre on self-conscious authors. (In fact, recent genre criticism of the Gospels has stemmed in part from the desire for a naturalistic literary explanation of the stories of Jesus' miracles.) But if aretalogists did not yet apotheosize human beings by attributing miracles to them and if the study of folklore has discovered conservatism on the part of communities, the problem of the shortness of time between the ministry of Jesus and the evangelists' narratives of the miraculous becomes more acute than ever. As we have seen, the Gospels resist easy categorization in terms of prior and contemporary genres of literature. But why? The more we deny or doubt the historicity of the materials (including miracle stories) in the Gospels, the more that question becomes difficult to answer. We leave the Gospels' literary distinctives without an adequate historical cause.

On the other hand, a high estimation of historicity would supply the missing cause. We could then say that the configuration and particulars of Jesus' career shattered some literary conventions (with the partial exception of Luke-Acts).[58]

---

[57] Somewhere in his *Jesus Remembered* Dunn observes that the recent de-apocalypticizing of Jesus' message coincided with the end of the Cold War, which had threatened an apocalyptic annihilation of the world as we know it.

[58] By failing to include enough particulars Dodd did not go far enough. Of course, the general conclusion above demands a thorough, detailed redoing of gospel criticism.

The diversity of the dominical material then arose out of the complexities of real life. Being early, the canonical Gospels reflected those complexities. The literary separation of materials according to types began and increased with the passage of time. We can see its beginning already in the canonical Gospels with the separation of narrative and discourse by Matthew and John. In a later document such as the *Gospel of Thomas* we have discourse (properly, sayings) purged of narrative almost entirely. The mixture in the canonical Gospels, however, shows that the facts still dominated the writing.[59] Otherwise we should have expected purer materials. The greater the disparity between literary contents and historical actualities, the greater the likelihood of conformity to established conventions of writing. Conversely, the less conformity to established conventions of writing, the greater the likelihood of agreement between literary contents and historical actualities. The unsuccessfully denied distinctives of the Gospels' literary form therefore derived from the uniqueness of Jesus' life and ministry.[60] Admittedly it remains a matter of judgment how we ought to assess the difficulty of believing in the miraculous over against the weight of data such as that considered here. In view of that data, however, we might do well to take W. Pannenberg's limitation of the principle of analogy with full seriousness in our thinking about the miraculous.[61]

---

[59] Some of the apocryphal Gospels contain a mixture of narrative and discourse. But their authors sought to conform to a convention of writing by then established in Christian circles, viz., the canonical Gospels. According to the axiom, those writers' desire to conform led them to fantasize. J. A. Baird comes to some of the above conclusions in his "Genre Analysis," in *The Genre of the Gospels* (Missoula: SBL, 1972), 1–28, and other material in manuscript kindly shared by Baird with me (see also idem, *Holy Word* [JSNTSup 224; Sheffield: Sheffield Academic Press, 2002]). Yet the "synoptic modes" from which he argues are limited largely to dominical sayings. Thus Baird does not adequately come to grips with the Gospels as wholes. For example, what are we to make of the modal analysis in which Lucian's *Demonax* appears as the most closely parallel of all Greco-Roman parallels to the Synoptics even though *Demonax* lacks miracle stories, a birth narrative, a passion narrative, and a resurrection narrative? The parallel rests primarily on teaching material and secondarily on travel narratives, analyzed modally. Apparently a predisposition in favor of teaching material has entered the very construction of the "modes" and to some degree has predetermined the outcome of the analysis. Nevertheless, Baird makes positive points worth considerably more attention than his computer/audience criticism has received.

[60] On the other hand, had the evangelists written conventional books, historicity would only have lost an argument in its favor. Inauthenticity would not necessarily have gained an argument for itself, since facts can be written up in conventional as well as unconventional ways. The element of historicity provides only slight justification for Justin Martyr's designation of the Gospels as "memoirs," for the structure of the Gospels and the sorts of information included remain unexplained.

[61] See, e.g., W. Pannenberg, *Jesus – God and Man* (London: Westminster, 1968), 98–99; idem, *Basic Questions in Theology* (Philadelphia: Fortress, 1970), 1:40–50. Naturally, a limitation of the principle of analogy applies to all questions of history, not just to Jesus' resurrection (Pannenberg's special concern).

With the philosophical question up for grabs, what finally ought we to say about the Gospels and genre? The less specific the meaning of "genre," the easier a placement of the Gospels in a prior literary tradition. But then the concept of genre regressively loses its usefulness in our attempt to discover authorial intention. To maintain the usefulness of the concept of genre and also to keep in line with ordinary usage we need to insist on a modicum of specificity. But then it becomes hard to classify the Gospels.

We might say that the Gospels arose out of an ancient practice of writing down biographical material concerning admired men. But saying so helps very little and falls short of genre criticism by failure to include very much about shared sorts of information, their structural arrangement, and the intended purpose of the resultant medium of communication. When we delve into such specifics of the Gospels, differences from precanonical and biographical literature of the period often loom large. Where are the parallels to the shared structure and information apparent in all four Gospels – an account of Jesus' introduction into public activity, a record of his authoritative teaching and miraculous deeds, a report of his trial and death, and indications of his resurrection – all with the purpose of edifying and/or converting audiences religiously?

Genre criticism allows variation, of course. We see variation in the Gospels: Matthew and Luke prefix birth stories and genealogies; John prefixes a statement concerning preexistence and incarnation; Matthew and John separate narrative and discourse; Luke adds an ascension and a second volume to show the ongoing activity of the hero through his followers, and also Hellenizes the whole by dedicating the two volumes to Theophilus, by setting the story in a larger historical context, and by playing on the motifs of symposium, travel, and shipwreck. The portraits of Jesus differ too: Mark portrays the Son of God who defeats the power of Satan and demons; Matthew portrays the Messiah who fulfills prophecies and teaches a higher law; Luke portrays the righteous innocent who does good deeds (cf. Acts 10:38–39a); John portrays the Word who interprets God his Father. But these redactional differences do not obliterate those outstanding features common to the Gospels, and they fall within the limits allowed a genre.

For two reasons, however, we probably ought not to speak of a genre known as "gospel." First, to speak of gospel as a "genre" implies a literary tradition of that kind prior to our Gospels. As we have seen, however, the canonical Gospels stand too far removed to be associated with any earlier literary tradition very meaningfully or helpfully. Second, the features common to the Gospels may have derived largely from documentary relationships among them rather than from a generic tradition preceding them.[62]

---

[62] Disputes of detail do not eliminate the point. John presents a special problem if he did not know the Synoptics. But if he wrote to supplement the Synoptics, as some of the early fathers held, we have a negative kind of documentary relationship with the other Gospels.

Consequently, from the standpoint of the first century we may speak legitimately of "Gospels" as a group of similar books in the NT but not of a genre "gospel."[63] At best, ancient literary tradition provided some precedent to the evangelists for writing documents concerning a personage. But the special characteristics of the Gospels require more of an answer to the question, Why were the Gospels written? A high estimate of historical authenticity deriving from the literary distinctives of the Gospels leads to a further, old answer. The spread of the church far from its place of origin and the dying off of Jesus' original disciples created a felt need for records. Since Christians had not divorced theology from history, those records turned out to be both theological and historical. Theological concerns for the present prompted redactional activity and resulted in differences among the Gospels. Historical concerns for the past checked fantasizing and resulted in commonalities among the Gospels. This old answer is better than other answers and conforms to early Christians' assigning to these books the title εὐαγγέλιον κατά..., "The Gospel according to...," rather than περὶ τοῦ βίου Ἰησοῦ, "Concerning the Life of Jesus."[64]

Addendum I: The Gospels as Encomia?

The preceding survey of genre criticism as it relates to the canonical Gospels leads naturally to a book that argues for classifying those Gospels very specifically. Such a book is *A Genre for the Gospels: The Biographical Character of Matthew* by P. L. Shuler.[65] It takes up the question, Did Matthew, Mark, Luke, and John follow an already established literary pattern in writing about Jesus? Allowing for variety because of differences in traditions used, occasions addressed, and authors' idiosyncrasies, Shuler answers that the evangelists did follow such a pattern: that of Greco-Roman encomiastic – i.e., laudatory – biography.

One must not think of biography in a modern sense that includes fairly full information about chronology, character, appearance, and environment. Rather, Greco-Roman authors used biographical data selectively to laud their subjects. So also the evangelists did not write as fully as possible. Neither did they simply write down the content of early Christian preaching. The Gospels have too much of a biographical look, Shuler argues, to be explained sermonically. Fur-

---

[63] It remains possible that from a *later* standpoint we may speak of a genre "gospel" beginning with the canonical Gospels and carried forward subsequently.

[64] F. Watson, *Text and Truth* (Grand Rapids: Eerdmans, 1997), 74–75, 89 n. 7. Cf. Marcion's use of εὐαγγέλιον for his expurgated edition of Luke according to reports collated by A. von Harnack in his *Marcion: Das Evangelium vom fremden Gott* (2d ed.; Neue Studien zu Marcion; Leipzig: Hinrichs, 1924), 184*; also Justin Martyr, *1 Apol.* 66; idem, *Dial.* 10.2; 100.1.

[65] Philadelphia: Fortress, 1982.

thermore, redaction criticism has done away with the form critical notion that the evangelists merely collected originally isolated traditions about Jesus and has cast the evangelists in the larger role of genuine authors working over their materials to make their own points. (We might add composition and literary criticisms to redaction criticism.)

The biographical interest of the evangelists insures a fair amount of historical data at the base of the Gospels but does not guarantee historicity even by ancient standards (which were looser than ours). On the contrary, the laudatory aim of encomiastic biographers led them to omit damaging materials quite deliberately and to make up complimentary ones, to minimize their heroes' faults, and to maximize their virtues. Thus the dreams, star, earthquakes, and other supernatural phenomena in Matthew's version of Jesus' birth, death, and resurrection are the very sorts of things Greco-Roman encomiastic biographers added by way of laudatory exaggeration. (We may note, however, that birth *from a virgin*, death *by crucifixion*, and resurrection *of the body* are not the things one reads in Greco-Roman encomiastic biographies.)

To establish his thesis Shuler surveys past genre criticism of the Gospels in the works of C. W. Votaw, K. L. Schmidt, M. Hadas and M. Smith, and C. H. Talbert. His own work carries forward, with some corrections, that of Votaw (according to whom the Gospels were popular biographies) and Talbert (who argues that ancient biographies and the Gospels shared mythical and cultic interests in large amounts). Then Shuler identifies laudatory biography as a literary genre in the Greco-Roman world and cites ancient authors' distinguishing it from history-writing. Finally, he discusses several examples of Greco-Roman encomiastic biography and correlates Matthew as an example of the NT Gospels with its Greco-Roman counterparts. Jesus' miraculous birth, escape from premature death, superiority to John the Baptist, successful resistance of Satan, and so on through the resurrection are all designed to play up the greatness of Jesus as the biographical subject.

Shuler seems to enjoy some success in applying his thesis to the Gospels, particularly to Matthew. But a sign or two suggest a reservation even in his mind: "We are not trying to claim that there are direct affinities between the gospels and the encomium per se" (p. 46); "the gospels and their writers may fall short of 'high' literary endeavors. They may, indeed, be less educated as authors, and their work less self-conscious" (p. 92). Exactly so. The Greco-Roman authors cited by Shuler state their laudatory aim outright, and their literary "I" protrudes from the text for all to see. But almost without exception the evangelists hide in the shadows and do not state their aims. To the extent that this difference forces Shuler to posit only indirect influence from encomiastic biographies, those biographies seem less likely to have prompted the evangelists to write as they did. Moreover, a reading of the Greco-Roman literature to which Shuler compares the Gospels shows that it pays far more attention to family background, edu-

2. The Symbiosis of Theology and Genre Criticism of the Canonical Gospels 41

cation, appearance, personality, physical and historical environment, moral virtues, and nonreligious exploits than the Gospels do, and little or no attention to theology, which dominates the textual landscape of the Gospels. The partial exception, Isocrates's *Helen*, is only apparent; for the divinizing of Helen serves the stress on her beauty rather than vice versa, and the orator wants to offer an example of a true encomium over against Gorgias's failed attempt more than to foster a worship of her. In other words, rhetoric triumphs over theology. The true exception, Philo's *Life of Moses*, owes its theological content to the biblical origin of the primary data and therefore does not help Shuler's thesis.

A further reservation deserves notice. All four evangelists devote a disproportionately large amount of space to Jesus' passion, including the embarrassingly shameful mode of his death – crucifixion. They labor mightily to overcome this scandal, as Shuler notes for Matthew. But if the Gospels *originated* on the pattern of laudatory biography we would have expected the evangelists to make their task easier by devoting far less space to the passion, especially since laudatory biography "meant minimizing the negative to the point of omission" (p. 50). For example, "Isocrates is silent with respect to the manner of the death of his hero Evagoras" because "murder … would not be a proper ending to so illustrious a portrait" (p. 67).

With respect to Matthew's Gospel in particular, further reservations deserve notice. Matthew certainly has his Hellenistic side. But it would be wrong to identify Greco-Roman biographers' lauding the family origins of their subjects as the mainspring of his genealogy of Jesus. We should rather see Jewish genealogical concerns – rooted in the OT, on which Matthew repeatedly draws – as the mainspring. Similarly, it throws the picture out of focus to draw a parallel between Matthew's fulfillment-quotations and Plutarch's "quotations from ancient poets to support the praiseworthiness of his subjects" (p. 99). Jewish literature provides much closer parallels. The miracles stories are better related to the cycles of miracle stories concerning Elijah and Elisha in the OT than to Philostratus's *The Life of Apollonius of Tyana*, which postdates the NT. Resurrection is a Jewish doctrine, not a Greco-Roman one; and we might well think that the utterly astounding character of Jesus' resurrection does away with any need to explain its inclusion in the Gospels through influence from laudatory biography. After all, the evidence for Jesus' resurrection begins showing up in the Epistles, before the Gospels were written. In general, Shuler's appeal to redaction criticism as justifying the search for authorial intent in the world of literary genre boomerangs, for redaction criticism highlights ecclesiastical and evangelistic concerns that resist correlation with Greco-Roman encomiastic biography. We read some significant admissions in this direction (especially on p. 106), but apparently Shuler does not see what inroads they make on his thesis. Either that or he does not intend his thesis to explain the literary origin of the Gospels, only some of their formal characteristics – a much less interesting thesis (but then why does he hitch it to

Talbert's thesis that Greco-Roman biographical myth provides the matrix for the Gospels?).

Finally, there is a hidden problem. To his credit, Shuler does not make his task too easy by choosing Luke as his parade example, though Luke's literary "I," outright statement of purpose, and laudation of Jesus' boyhood and personal virtues – plus other generally recognized Hellenistic features – make for a closer comparison with encomiastic biography. (But Acts' being the second part of Luke's work makes it doubtful that we should separate off the first part as an encomiastic biography pure and simple.) Shuler did, however, choose Matthew rather than Mark. Yet if Mark wrote first among the synoptists and if Matthew and Luke followed his lead, as most scholars hold, Shuler's thesis suffers because Mark's Gospel is least like an encomiastic biography. For example, it pays no attention whatever to Jesus' birth and, as noted in the early church, reads too much like an unliterary collection of anecdotes. The thesis suffers all the more if we are to believe the very old tradition passed on by Papias that Mark wrote down Peter's reminiscences of Jesus in a random but accurate manner.[66] It would then appear that the Gospels did not grow out of a literary genre of encomiastic biography but that to some extent the later Synoptics edged toward that genre in a process called "literaturization."[67]

Addendum II: Reconstructing Jesus

Assigning the canonical Gospels to the genre of Greco-Roman popular biography and reviving the quest of the historical Jesus enjoy a symbiotic relationship. In the foregoing, I have analyzed the generic side of this relationship, with special attention going to one proposal in Addendum I. It is now time to analyze the side of this relationship devoted to reconstructing the historical Jesus, with special attention going to one such reconstruction – an extremely popular one among conservative Christians, that of N. T. Wright in *Jesus and the Victory of God*.[68]

Wright's book makes up volume 2 in a series titled *Christian Origins and the Question of God*, ambitiously projected to run to five volumes. Volume 1, *The New Testament and the People of God*, occupied itself mainly with background and method. Volume 3, *The Resurrection of the Son of God*, has now appeared and offers a stout, convincing defense of Jesus' bodily resurrection.[69] Later vol-

---

[66] Eusebius, *Hist. eccl.* 3.39.15, on which see the next essay here.

[67] See D. E. Aune, "The Problem of the Genre of the Gospels: A Critique of C. H. Talbert's *What is a Gospel?*" in *Studies of History and Tradition in the Four Gospels* (vol. 2 of *Gospel Perspectives*; ed. R. T. France and D. Wenham; Sheffield: JSOT Press, 1981), 9–60, esp. 45–46.

[68] Minneapolis: Fortress, 1996.

[69] Minneapolis: Fortress, 2003.

umes will take up the Gospel of John through the book of Revelation – above all, the Epistles of Paul. But it is the aforementioned volume 2 that offers Wright's detailed reconstruction of the historical Jesus. In assessing this volume I will take some account of Wright's earlier published work.

With a sweeping and imaginative proposal *Jesus and the Victory of God* treats the figure of Jesus as portrayed in the Synoptic Gospels of Matthew, Mark, and Luke. Arguably, nevertheless, and despite some self-description to the contrary, the treatment does not represent biblical theology in a strict sense. For Wright is not interested in the synoptic portrayals of Jesus for their own sake so much as for what they can tell us about the Jesus of history who stands behind them. As already implied, Wright sees little difference between those portrayals and the historical Jesus, so that for the most part biblical theology and history merge into each other. But this merger prompts, in turn, another merger, that of the plural Jesuses of Matthew, Mark, and Luke into one synoptic Jesus. Thus the distinctive lineaments of the various portrayals are blurred almost to the vanishing point. Wright's main interest remains historical rather than biblical, and historicity is insulated against the doubts that differences between the Synoptics often raise (to say nothing about greater differences between these Gospels and the Gospel of John).

To some the insulation will seem facile insofar as the neglected differences fall into patterns suggesting that other-than-historical concerns led the evangelists to write unhistorically more often than Wright concedes. Repeatedly, for instance, he explains differences between parallel sayings of Jesus as due to Jesus' own variations, spoken on more than one occasion, and neglects the significant fact that – throughout – the sayings in Matthew tend toward rigorism, those in Luke toward humanitarianism, and so on.

Given his main interest, though, Wright starts appropriately with the nineteenth-century quest of the historical Jesus and moves next to the new quest inaugurated in 1953 by E. Käsemann and revived more recently in North America by the Jesus Seminar. Wright's skewering of that seminar and its construction of a nonapocalyptic, almost non-Jewish Jesus occupies considerable space and shows Wright at his jousting best. Lastly, he associates himself with the third quest, represented also by E. P. Sanders and others who on the whole value synoptic historicity higher than does the Jesus Seminar and see the historical Jesus as solidly Jewish in outlook. The rest of Wright's book is devoted to spelling out the details of that outlook. What are they?

They are, Wright proposes, that whereas the Jews regarded themselves as still living in exile because of Roman domination Jesus announced that the divinely promised and long-awaited restoration was under way. So he appeared less a teacher of wisdom than a prophet. According to him, moreover, the restoration was taking place in and through his ministry. How so, given that he was not throwing off the Roman yoke?

Well, Jesus had redefined the problem of Jewish exile and its solution. The problem lay not in Roman domination but in the Jews' satanically inspired zeal to free themselves from it by armed rebellion instead of carrying out their divinely appointed task of leading Gentiles to worship the one true God. The solution lay in repentance from that nationalistic sin and in belief in Jesus as the focal point of a renewed people of God that included Jewish outcasts and Gentiles. As such a focal point Jesus spoke and acted messianically as well as prophetically, though neither for him nor for the Jews did messiahship entail deity.

To renew God's people more inclusively Jesus also redefined the Torah along lines of mercy and forgiveness as opposed to Israelite ancestry, food laws, and such like. The temple he redefined in terms of himself and his followers. And so it became unnecessary to obtain forgiveness through offering a sacrifice at the temple in Jerusalem, to observe Mosaic restrictions on diet, or to observe other practices demarcating Jews from Gentiles.

No wonder that the leaders – Torah-centered Pharisees and temple-centered chief priests alike – opposed Jesus. He was dismantling the main symbols of Jewish national identity! It did not take omniscience for him to see the opposition mounting; so he made his last journey to Jerusalem under the conviction that there he would be put to death and thus suffer the great tribulation that was expected to befall Israel just before God ushered in his kingdom.

Then Jesus did something that galvanized his opponents, especially the chief priests. He physically assaulted the sacrificial system of worship that took place in the temple. The assault was no mere attempt at reformation. No, it was an acted-out prophecy of judgment, of coming destruction. And reports came that Jesus had predicted such destruction verbally too.

In fact, he had. Earlier warnings of coming wrath had dealt not with the eternal judgment of individual sinners hereafter but with God's using the Romans to judge the Jewish nation here and now for their insurrectionism. More recently and specifically Jesus had cleared the ground for a redefined temple by predicting that the old, corrupt one would be destroyed within a generation. Furthermore, this destruction would make obvious that he and the renewed people of God now constituted the true temple, that God had returned to it, and that for his renewed people the exile, the real one, had ended.

What to do with Jesus? Get rid of him, naturally, and use the Romans to do so. His constant talk of God's kingdom and his own kinglike deeds and words could be misrepresented as insurrectionary. The Romans crucified Jesus as King of the Jews, then. Only it was not so easy to get rid of him. He rose from the dead. That event too Wright treats as historical, not as fictional or eschatologically excluded from critical investigation.[70]

---

[70] Wright's *The Resurrection of the Son of God* elaborates this point greatly, of course.

Finally, Jesus came again at the destruction of Jerusalem and the temple in A.D. 70. Not in the way a traditional view of the second coming has it, of course. All that language about the sun's darkening, the moon's turning to blood, the stars' falling, and the Son of Man's coming in clouds derives from the OT, where it is used metaphorically not to describe an end to the space-time universe but to invest human events with theological significance.

Thus talk of celestial disasters painted the destruction of Jerusalem and the temple in colors of divine judgment, and seeing the Son of Man coming in clouds meant a recognition that the destruction both demonstrated Jesus' having already ascended to God's right hand, as distinct from descending to earth in the future, and vindicated God's renewed people still living on earth. So Jesus did not make a chronological mistake when he said that everything would happen before the contemporary generation passed away.[71] Everything did happen, right on schedule. For the events of A.D. 70 – the destructions of Jerusalem and the temple – were all that Jesus was predicting, and they took place within a generation of his prediction. Furthermore, those events marked the victory of God over those who had engineered the death of his Son Jesus (hence the title of Wright's book).

There is much to learn from this reconstruction of the historical Jesus, and we may laud Wright for some sterling contributions: his maintaining Jesus' Jewishness; his defending Jesus' messianic self-consciousness (though self-consciousness of a uniquely divine sonship gets shortchanged); his resisting the separation of faith from history; his enlarging the historical base of our knowledge concerning Jesus; and his sharpening our tools of historiography, especially his developing a criterion of double similarity-cum-double dissimilarity: what is credible in first-century Judaism and as a starting point for Christianity but sufficiently unlike both to be a mere reflection is likely historical.

But there is also much to question. Most of it has to do with the likelihood that Wright presses his thesis too far, makes it all-encompassing. In other words, does he give the theme of exile and return a prominence unjustified by the records we have of Jesus' teaching and of Jewish consciousness at the time?[72] Can all the synoptic and related texts tolerate the controlling story of reinterpreted exile and restoration that Wright places on them? For example, can the prodigal son, who wanted distance from his home and wasted his substance in riotous living, represent Israel, who did not want to go into exile and had no substance to waste there?[73] Or can the sower's sowing of good seed stand for

---

[71] Mark 13:30 parr.

[72] Cf. E. S. Gruen, *Diaspora: Jews amidst Greeks and Romans* (Cambridge, Mass.: Harvard University Press, 2002).

[73] Luke 15:11–32, esp. 13.

God's causing true Israel to return from exile, even though Jesus describes as good, not any seed, but *soil*?[74]

Why are Jesus' sheep scattered when he is struck?[75] In Wright's view is not the striking of the shepherd supposed to effect the opposite, the sheep's being *gathered* from exile? How is it that the elect are not gathered till after the great tribulation – i.e., till after the Jewish War of A.D. 66–74, again in Wright's view – if Jesus was already gathering them from their exile forty years earlier?[76] How is it that Paul put "our gathering together to him" not till a future "coming of our Lord Jesus Christ"?[77] How is it that James and Peter addressed the recipients of their epistles as exiles in the Diaspora rather than as returnees from it?[78]

According to Wright, Jesus thought that in his passion he would suffer the great tribulation vicariously and thereby enable his followers living in Judea to escape the coming Roman slaughter, as they later did by fleeing Jerusalem before its destruction.[79] Is not this restriction of the benefits of his suffering to Judean disciples too severe? Does not his expanding to "all" the addressees of his command, "Watch," imply a larger group?[80] The destruction benefited disciples outside Judea by putting a stop to persecution emanating from there, yet this benefit did not derive from *Jesus'* suffering but from that of *unbelieving Jews*. And the benefit was erased by a shift to Roman persecution.

If Jesus thought he would suffer the great tribulation for his disciples, why did he put it after the abomination of desolation and link it with their later experience rather than with his own immediate experience?[81] And how is it that he called on them to take up their crosses and follow him?[82] In what did their restoration from exile consist if they were not only going to continue living under Roman domination but also endure persecution for Jesus' sake? Does not answering that their restoration consisted in deliverance from the sin of insurrectionism spiritualize the restoration in a way analogous to the doctrine of "abstract atonement" on which Wright repeatedly pours scorn? Does not most of Jesus' pacifistic teaching have to do with nonretaliation against Jewish persecutors rather than with nonrebellion against Roman overlords?

Does it not turn a scriptural emphasis upside down to interpret the plural "sins" that people repentantly confessed as primarily the singular sin of nationalistic insurrectionism, only secondarily of individuals' sinning in vari-

---

[74] Mark 4:8, 20 parr.
[75] Mark 14:27 parr.
[76] Mark 13:24–27 parr.
[77] 2 Thess 2:1.
[78] Jas 1:1; 1 Pet 1:1.
[79] Cf. Mark 13:14 parr.
[80] Mark 13:37.
[81] Mark 13:14–20 parr.
[82] Mark 8:34–38 parr.

ous ways that Jesus discusses at length in his moral teaching?[83] And has not Wright's fixation on redefined exile and restoration likewise led him to ignore and even deny Pharisaic legalism as an object of Jesus' critique?[84]

If Jesus' charge that the temple had become "a den of robbers" meant that it had become "a den of revolutionaries," why did Jesus drive out the buyers and sellers of sacrificial animals and birds?[85] In what way did their activity represent insurrectionism? And if Jesus meant to do away with the temple and its sacrificial worship, why did he tell a cleansed leper to go show himself to the priest and offer the things commanded by Moses?[86] Why did Jesus say to offer your gift at the altar after reconciliation with your brother?[87] Why did Jesus clear the outer court of the temple to enable Gentiles to pray there?[88]

Why should we regard the mountain being cast into the sea as Mount Zion, where the temple was located, when that mountain has not been mentioned in the context, when the Mount of Olives *has* been mentioned recently, when "this mountain" refers more naturally to the Mount of Olives right where Jesus and his disciples were located than to Mount Zion in the distance and when he hardly meant that the destruction of the temple would happen because some disciple of his was actually going to tell Mount Zion to be thrown into the sea?[89]

If in speaking of judgment to come Jesus did not refer to the Last Judgment but to the destruction in A.D. 70, what are we to make of the Ninevites' and queen of the south's being raised "in the judgment with the men of this generation"?[90] Did he think the Ninevites and queen would rise from the dead at the destruction in A.D. 70? And in what sense did the destruction fulfill the judgment of "all the nations," a judgment issuing in "eternal life" for "the sheep" and "eternal punishment" for "the goats," not in temporal survival and death, as in A.D. 70?[91] Did the destruction of Jerusalem and the temple really exhaust Jesus' warnings of judgment?

Does the accusation that Jesus said he would destroy the temple and in three days build another one form "the rock of history" on which "ironically enough" we may stand? Is not the irony rather that Wright takes as rock solid a testimony whose wording differs seriously from passage to passage and whose canonical description as "false" he freely admits?[92] Solid but slippery? How can the house built on the rock be "a clear allusion to the temple," i.e., "the true temple" built

---

[83] Mark 1:5 parr.
[84] Mark 7:1–23 parr. et passim.
[85] Mark 11:15–17 parr.
[86] Mark 1:44 parr.
[87] Matt 5:23–24.
[88] Mark 11:15–17 parr.
[89] Mark 11:23 parr.
[90] Matt 12:41–42 parr.
[91] Matt 25:31–46.
[92] Mark 14:56–59 par.

by Jesus, when the wise man who builds that house is a person who "hears and does" Jesus' words, not Jesus himself?[93]

Can it be that no first-century Jew would take Dan 7:13 as the Son of Man's descent from heaven? What of John 3:13, "And no one has ascended into heaven except the one who descended from heaven, the Son of Man"? Does not Wright's way of saving Jesus from making a mistake about the occurrence of "all these things" within a generation come at the price of subverting the natural meaning of Jesus' other eschatological pronouncements?[94] If Paul agreed with Jesus by referring the Day of the Lord to the destruction of Jerusalem rather than to the end, as Wright avers, how is it that Paul made that day an object of watchfulness and source of comfort for Christians living far off in Greece and described the day as one in which the Lord himself will descend from heaven, the dead in Christ will rise, and living Christians will be caught up together with them to meet the Lord in the air?[95] How can Wright allow that Paul was describing Jesus' return to earth yet affirm that Paul thought of the Day of the Lord as entailing intermediate destruction rather than the final return?

Wright also avers that later Christians invented the doctrine of Jesus' return because they could not conceive that he was resurrected if not to join those who will yet be resurrected to populate the coming new earth. But where is the evidence for any puzzling over the problem of Jesus' absence from the new earth – till someone hit on the solution of a return? For that matter, why could not Jesus himself have followed the line of reasoning that Wright ascribes to later Christians?

Readers understandably eager to celebrate Wright's demolition of the Jesus Seminar and its anemic Jesus would do well to think twice before accepting the Jesus that Wright has reconstructed as an alternative.[96] They would do even better to put the canonical Jesuses on a higher pedestal than a putatively historical Jesus, whether Wright's or someone else's. The older Jesuses of the NT are superior to any Jesus reconstructed by modern scholars.

---

[93] Matt 7:24–27 par.
[94] Mark 13:30 parr.
[95] 1 Thess 4:13–5:11.
[96] See also R. H. Stein, "N. T. Wright's *Jesus and the Victory of God*: A Review Article," *JETS* 44 (2001): 207–18.

3. The Apostolically Johannine Pre-Papian Tradition concerning the Gospels of Mark and Matthew

The earliest tradition concerning the Gospels of Mark and Matthew is found in Eusebius, *Hist. eccl.* 3.39.3–4, 15–16, where he quotes Papias as follows:

οὐκ ὀκνήσω δέ σοι καὶ ὅσα ποτὲ παρὰ τῶν πρεσβυτέρων καλῶς ἔμαθον καὶ καλῶς ἐμνημόνευσα, συγκατατάξαι ταῖς ἑρμηνείαις, διαβεβαιούμενος ὑπὲρ αὐτῶν ἀλήθειαν. οὐ γὰρ τοῖς τὰ πολλὰ λέγουσιν ἔχαιρον ὥσπερ οἱ πολλοί, ἀλλὰ τοῖς τἀληθῆ διδάσκουσιν, οὐδὲ τοῖς τὰς ἀλλοτρίας ἐντολὰς μνημονεύουσιν, ἀλλὰ τοῖς τὰς παρὰ τοῦ κυρίου τῇ πίστει δεδομένας καὶ ἀπ' αὐτῆς παραγινομένας τῆς ἀληθείας· εἰ δέ που καὶ παρηκολουθηκώς τις τοῖς πρεσβυτέροις ἔλθοι, τοὺς τῶν πρεσβυτέρων ἀνέκρινον λόγους, τί Ἀνδρέας ἢ τί Πέτρος εἶπεν ἢ τί Φίλιππος ἢ τί Θωμᾶς ἢ Ἰάκωβος ἢ τί Ἰωάννης ἢ Ματθαῖος ἢ τις ἕτερος τῶν τοῦ κυρίου μαθητῶν ἅ τε Ἀριστίων καὶ ὁ πρεσβύτερος Ἰωάννης, τοῦ κυρίου μαθηταί, λέγουσιν. οὐ γὰρ τὰ ἐκ τῶν βιβλίων τοσοῦτόν με ὠφελεῖν ὑπελάμβανον ὅσον τὰ παρὰ ζώσης φωνῆς καὶ μενούσης.... καὶ τοῦθ' ὁ πρεσβύτερος ἔλεγεν· "Μάρκος μὲν ἑρμηνευτὴς Πέτρου γενόμενος, ὅσα ἐμνημόνευσεν, ἀκριβῶς ἔγραψεν, οὐ μέντοι τάξει τὰ ὑπὸ τοῦ κυρίου ἢ λεχθέντα ἢ πραχθέντα. οὔτε γὰρ ἤκουσεν τοῦ κυρίου οὔτε παρηκολούθησεν αὐτῷ, ὕστερον δέ, ὡς ἔφην, Πέτρῳ· ὃς πρὸς τὰς χρείας ἐποιεῖτο τὰς διδασκαλίας, ἀλλ' οὐχ ὥσπερ σύνταξιν τῶν κυριακῶν ποιούμενος λογίων, ὥστε οὐδὲν ἥμαρτεν Μάρκος οὕτως ἔνια γράψας ὡς ἀπεμνημόνευσεν. ἑνὸς γὰρ ἐποιήσατο πρόνοιαν, τοῦ μηδὲν ὧν ἤκουσεν παραλιπεῖν ἢ ψεύσασθαί τι ἐν αὐτοῖς." ταῦτα μὲν οὖν ἱστόρηται τῷ Παπίᾳ περὶ τοῦ Μάρκου· περὶ δὲ τοῦ Ματθαίου ταυτ' εἴρηται· "Ματθαῖος μὲν οὖν Ἑβραΐδι διαλέκτῳ τὰ λόγια συνετάξατο, ἡρμήνευσεν δ' αὐτὰ ὡς ἦν δυνατὸς ἕκαστος."

And by way of guaranteeing their truth for you [sg.] I will not hesitate to concatenate for the Expositions [of the Lord's Oracles] both as many things as I once learned well from the elders and [as many things as] I remembered [or 'noted down'] well. For I was not delighting in those who were saying many things, as the majority [of people were delighting in them]. Rather, [I was delighting in] those who were teaching the truth. Nor [was I delighting in] those who were remembering the commandments of anyone else. Rather, [I was delighting in] those [who were remembering] the commandments given to the faith by the Lord and deriving from the truth itself. And if somewhere anyone who had followed the elders happened to come, I was examining the words of the elders, what Andrew or what Peter had said, or what Philip or what Thomas or James or what John or Matthew or any other one of the Lord's disciples [had said], and what things Aristion and the elder John, the Lord's disciples, are saying [with reference to the time when Papias was examining these reports]. For I was not assuming that the things from books would benefit me so much as the things from a living and surviving voice.... And the elder was saying this: "On the one hand, Mark, becoming Peter's interpreter, wrote accurately as many things as he remembered. On the other hand, [he did] not [write] in order the things either said or done by the Lord. For he had neither heard the Lord nor followed him. But later, as I said, [he had followed] Peter, who was teaching in accord with the anecdotes yet not as it were arranging the Lord's oracles, so that Mark did nothing wrong by writing some things as he related [them] from memory. For he was thinking beforehand of one thing, [i.e.,] to omit not a single one of the things that he had heard or to falsify anything in them." Therefore, on the one hand, these things are related by Papias [or "to Papias" as the one who heard the tradition] concerning Mark. Concerning Matthew, on the other hand, these things were said: "On the one hand, therefore, Matthew did arrange the oracles in Hebrew 'dialect.' On the other hand, each one interpreted them as he was able."

I will take up the date, meaning, and reliability of this tradition point by point.

The date of the tradition depends on the date of Papias's writing and on the identity of the elder whom he quotes regarding Mark and Matthew. Modern handbooks used to put the date at ca. A.D. 130 or later, but a consensus seems to be developing that Papias wrote earlier by a quarter century or more, i.e., in the first decade of the second century.[1] Eusebius leads us to the earlier date by saying that Papias became famous during the time of Polycarp and Ignatius, with whom he associates Clement of Rome (*Hist. eccl.* 3.36.1–2; 3.39.1). Polycarp did not die till the middle of the second century, but Ignatius died ca. A.D. 107 and Clement ca. A.D. 100. Eusebius's discussion of Papias's writings comes right at this point, i.e., before Trajan's persecution, which started ca. A.D. 110 and which Eusebius does not describe till Book 4 of his *Ecclesiastical History* whereas these fragments of Papias appear in Book 3.

Furthermore, as pointed out by Yarbrough, Eusebius's *Chronicon* puts together and in order the Apostle John, Papias, Polycarp, and Ignatius and assigns the date A.D. 100 to this entry; and J.B. Orchard shows that Eusebius is following a chronological order according to which all the events recorded in *Hist. eccl.* 3.34–39 take place during the bishopric of Evarestus at Rome (A.D. 101–108).[2] Irenaeus, writing ca. A.D. 180, describes Papias as an "ancient man" and as "the hearer of the Apostle John" (*Adv. haer.* 5.33.4; cf. Eusebius, *Hist. eccl.* 3.39.1, 13). The failure of Irenaeus and Eusebius to quote Papias against Gnosticism is best explained by Papias's having said nothing against Gnosticism because he wrote before it became a widespread threat, i.e., before A.D. 110.[3] And the Papian fragments exhibit a general similarity to the epistles of Ignatius and Polycarp, written early.[4]

---

[1] See the survey by R. W. Yarbrough, "The Date of Papias: A Reassessment," *JETS* 26 (1983): 181–82.

[2] Yarbrough, "The Date of Papias," 186–90; R. Helm, *Die Chronik des Hieronymus* (2d. ed.; GCS 7; Berlin: Akademie-Verlag, 1956), 193–94; J.B. Orchard, "Some Guidelines for the Interpretation of Eusebius' Hist. Eccl. 3. 34–39," in *The New Testament Age* (ed. W.C. Weinrich; Macon, Ga.: Mercer University Press, 1984), 393–403.

[3] Cf. also M. Hengel, *Studies in the Gospel of Mark* (Philadelphia: Fortress, 1985), 152 n.61.

[4] For details see Yarbrough, "The Date of Papias," 188–90.

U. H. J. Körtner agrees that Papias's polemics fit the earlier rather than later date and adds that it is easier to think of the earlier date for Papias's making inquiry of those who had heard "the elders" (Eusebius, *Hist. eccl.* 3.39.3–4), but it is hard to think of the Elder John and Aristion as still alive toward the middle of the second century.[5] The present tense of λέγουσιν, "are saying" (Eusebius, *Hist. eccl.* 3.39.4), implies that they are still alive when Papias writes, however. It is also hard to believe that Papias lived so long as to have both had personal acquaintance with the daughters of "Philip the apostle" in the middle of the first century (Eusebius, *Hist. eccl.* 3.39.9; cf. Acts 21:8–9) and written toward the middle of the second century. Papias's use of "the Lord's disciples" and of "the elders" instead of "the apostles" for the guarantors of orthodoxy further favors an early date, i.e., a date before "the apostles" developed such a connotation; and Papias's lack of great attention to John's writings favors an early date, i.e., a date so soon after John had written that those writings did not yet command very much attention. Finally, E. Stauffer and H. H. Schmidt have noted a large number of Semitisms in the Papian fragment on Mark. These Semitisms favor that the tradition of the Elder John had a very early and therefore likely reliable origin.[6]

The only hard evidence favoring a late date consists in a statement by Philip of Side, who makes Papias refer to the reign of Hadrian (A.D. 117–138).[7] But we have good reasons to distrust Philip's statement. He is notoriously unreliable and wrote approximately a century later than Eusebius did (Philip – ca. A.D. 430; Eusebius – ca. A.D. 324). Comparison of Philip's statement with Eusebius's favors that Philip depended on Eusebius but garbled the information he got. Eusebius mentions a Christian writer named Quadratus, who addressed an apology to Hadrian, the very emperor during whose reign Philip puts Papias's writings. The claim of Quadratus that some of the people whom Jesus healed and raised from the dead have lived up to his own day sounds something like the claim of Papias to have gotten information about the Lord's commands "from the living and abiding voice" of the elders and other disciples of the Lord (see Eusebius, *Hist. eccl.* 3.39.1–4 with 4.3.1–2). More strikingly, however, when Philip quotes Papias the phraseology sounds more like Eusebius's quotations of Quadratus than of Papias. In other words it looks as though Philip transferred what Quadratus wrote over to Papias. Thus, just as Eusebius associates Quadratus with Hadrian's reign and quotes Quadratus as referring to people raised from the dead by Jesus and still living, so Philip associates Papias with

---

[5] U. H. J. Körtner, *Papias von Hierapolis* (FRLANT 133; Göttingen: Vandenhoeck & Ruprecht, 1983), 225–26.

[6] E. Stauffer, "Der Methurgeman des Petrus," in *Neutestamentliche Aufsätze* (ed. J. Blinzler et al.; Regensburg: Pustet, 1963), 283–93; H. H. Schmidt, "Semitismen bei Papias," *TZ* 44 (1988): 135–46.

[7] See the citation in K. Aland, *Synopsis Quattuor Evangeliorum* (2d ed.; Stuttgart: Württembergische Bibelanstalt, 1964), 531.

Hadrian's reign and writes that Papias referred to people raised from the dead by Jesus and still living. Furthermore, there appears to have been another Quadratus, who was a prophet, not an apologist. Eusebius discusses him in association with Jesus' original disciples and their immediate successors (*Hist. eccl.* 3.37.1). Philip probably confuses Quadratus the apologist with Quadratus the prophet. It was easy for him to do so, because he found Eusebius's similar discussion of Papias bounded by references to the name "Quadratus." A final cause of Philip's confusing Papias's writings with an apology by a Quadratus is Eusebius's associating this Quadratus with the daughters of Philip the evangelist (*Hist. eccl.* 3.37.1) just as Eusebius also associates Papias with them (*Hist. eccl.* 3.39.9). Poor Philip fell into a trap.

In summary, a large number of considerations unite to disfavor a date of A.D. 130 or later in accordance with Philip of Side and to favor a date of A.D. 101–108 for Papias's report concerning Mark and Matthew: (1) the late date of Philip of Side; (2) his generally acknowledged unreliability; (3) the ease with which he might have confused Papias's writing with the apology by Quadratus; (4) the earlier date and greater reliability of Eusebius, who had in his hands the writings of both Papias and Quadratus; (5) Eusebius's associating Papias with Ignatius and, through Ignatius, with Clement of Rome; and (6) Eusebius's discussing the fragments of Papias prior to his description of Trajan's persecution.[8]

Now by his own testimony Papias is not surmising. He is passing on an earlier report by a certain elder. Properly speaking, the tradition does not go back merely to Papias, as many discussions leave the impression it does, but behind Papias to an elder – hence the phrase "Pre-Papian Tradition" in the title of this essay. If Papias writes during A.D. 101–108, then, the tradition that he passes on reaches back into the first century. We can say even more. It is usually thought that Papias stands twice removed from the apostles, whom he calls "the Lord's disciples"; i.e., he is separated from them both by supposedly nonapostolic elders and by those who heard such elders and told him what they had heard. But certain data in the text indicate that he claims to have listened often to those who had themselves heard some of the disciples speak. In other words, Papias stands only once removed from Jesus' original disciples (Eusebius, *Hist. eccl.* 3.39.3–4). We have, then, only three links, not four, in the chain of tradition: (1) the apostles; (2) those who heard the apostles; and (3) Papias. What are the data supporting this view?

First, Papias equates "the words of the elders" with "what Andrew or Peter or Philip or Thomas or James or John or Matthew or any other of the Lord's disciples had said." Why this equation? There are two possible but mutually ex-

---

[8] See Yarbrough, "The Date of Papias," 182–86, against arguments even less substantial than the one from Philip.

clusive reasons. One is that the elders are identical with the original disciples of Jesus, i.e., with the apostles. Another is that the elders are different from them but faithfully handed down their teaching. Against the view which sees a difference the passage quoted by Eusebius from Papias contains no apparent indication that Papias means to distinguish the elders from the disciples. The listing of the apostolic names under the designation "the Lord's disciples" certainly does not imply such a distinction, for Papias immediately identifies John "the elder" as one of "the Lord's disciples." Here he is using the two designations as synonyms. Their interchange so far as John is concerned points to their being synonymous so far as Andrew, Peter, Philip, Thomas, James, Matthew, and other disciples too are concerned.

Second, taking the two designations as synonymous conforms to the natural understanding of Papias's text. For if they are not synonymous, Papias jumps backward from second-generation "elders" to first-generation "disciples" without any warning only to turn around and use "elder" and "Lord's disciple" for one and the same man. This use of "elder" and "Lord's disciple" for John shows that we are not to regard the repeated τί as an accusative of general reference (the accusative of "last resort"), meaning "the words of the elders *concerning* what Andrew or Peter ... had said," but as an appositive: "the words of the elders, *i.e.*, what Andrew or Peter... had said."[9] This use also shows that the expressions do not stand in apposition to each other because later elders *repeated* what earlier disciples had said. Rather, what the Lord's disciples had said is

---

[9] Instead of resorting to an accusative of general reference R. Bauckham inserts an interpretive phrase to deny an equation of the elders and the Lord's disciples: "I inquired about the words of the elders – [that is,] what [*according to the elders*] Andrew or Peter said..." ("The Eyewitnesses and the Gospel Tradition," *Journal for the Study of the Historical Jesus* 1 [2003]: 31–33 [italics added]). This insertion comes out to the same meaning as that of an accusative of general reference. Bauckham argues that under an equation "it is hard to understand why Papias uses the word 'elders' (πρεσβύτεροι) so emphatically and does not simply label this group 'the Lord's disciples' (οἱ τοῦ κυρίου μαθηταί)" and cites in support Irenaeus, *Adv. haer.* 2.22.5; 4.28.1; 5.5.1; 5.30.1; 5.36.1, 2; 6.33.3 yet admits that Eusebius sees an equation (see the third point below). But emphasis on the word "elders" makes eminently good sense if the elders are apostles. Apostles deserve more emphasis than those who handed on their testimony. And the use of "elders" as well as "the Lord's disciples" adds the authority of age to that of original discipleship. It is harder to understand, under Bauckham's view, why Papias did not call Aristion an elder as well as a disciple of the Lord, as he called John an elder as well as a disciple of the Lord. Does Bauckham slip in writing that as "prominent Christian teachers in the province of Asia," Aristion as well as the Elder John "deserved ... both the epithet 'elder' and the epithet 'disciple of the Lord'"? Papias does not call Aristion an elder. Writing some eighty years later than Papias wrote it natural for Irenaeus to use "elders" for disciples of the apostles, for those disciples already belonged to a bygone age. But for Papias "elders" more naturally referred to bygone apostles (with the noted exception of John; cf. *PGL*, s.v. πρεσβύτερος I4: "*antecedent in time*" [italics original]; also IIB: "[πρεσβύτερος] may be applied to an apostle" and the citation of Irenaeus's contemporary, Clement of Alexandria, frg. 22, for an application of the term to Saint John; see also Clement, *Q.d.s.* 42). The manifold uses of πρεσβύτερος made easy a transference of the term by Irenaeus from the apostles to their disciples.

identical with the words of the elders because the elders *were* the disciples Andrew, Peter, and the rest.

Third, though Eusebius distinguishes between John the disciple and John the elder for a tendentious reason yet to be exposed, the truth slips out in *Hist. eccl.* 3.39.7, where he writes that Papias "confesses that he had received the words of the apostles from those who had followed them." Here we find only one generation between the apostles and Papias. In a lapse, then, Eusebius himself shows that Papias used both of the terms "elders" and "Lord's disciples" to mean "apostles."

Fourth, Papias emphasizes the elders' truthfulness in repeating the commandments given by the Lord. A supposedly earlier generation of disciples do not step in as obvious go-betweens to pass the commandments from Jesus to the elders. If Papias were distinguishing later elders from original disciples we would have expected him to say outright that the elders got the Lord's commandments from the disciples. We might also have expected some emphasis on the truthfulness of the disciples as well as on that of the elders. The absence of such items means that we have no good reason to think that the elders differed from the disciples. On the other hand, Papias implies that he has not heard the elders. It is others who have heard them: "but if ever anyone came who had followed the elders, I inquired about the words of the elders." So it is easy to think that he did not hear the elders because they were the apostles and all of them except John had already died (cf. the use of "elder" for an apostle as well as for nonapostles in 1 Pet 5:1, and N.B. the close linkage of "apostles" and "elders" by the use of one definite article for them both in Acts 15:2; 16:4, though a second definite article in 15:4, 6, 22, 23 makes clear a distinction, perhaps because the apostles were not yet old enough to make "elders" a suitable designation for them).[10]

An elder named John was still speaking. Since "elder" is being used as a synonym for "Lord's disciple" and "apostle," the Elder John is none other than the Apostle John; and Papias heard others who had heard his voice. To be sure, Eusebius distinguishes between the Apostle John and the Elder John (*Hist. eccl.* 3.39.6). But the distinction is tendentious. Eusebius does not like the book of Revelation – the millenarianism that Papias, Irenaeus, and others have drawn from it seems crassly materialistic to him (*Hist. eccl.* 3.39.12–13) – so he wants to belittle the book by making it unapostolic, i.e., written by an elder named John as opposed to the apostle named John. Papias, however, not only pins the designation "the elders" on the apostles who had spoken in past times. He also repeats the term "elder" with John yet not with Aristion. Why? The reason is that al-

---

[10] These third and fourth arguments undermine the view of L. Abramowski that the second occurrence of "Lord's disciples" in *Hist. eccl.* 3.39.4 is unoriginal, a view which if true would evacuate the first and second arguments above ("Die 'Erinnerungen der Apostel' bei Justin," in *Das Evangelium und die Evangelien* [ed. P. Stuhlmacher; WUNT 28; Tübingen: Mohr, 1983], 348–49 n. 28).

though Aristion was one of Jesus' original disciples he was not an elder, i.e., not an apostle. Like John, however, Aristion was still speaking because he was still living. Papias did not mention him earlier because not till after all the apostles except John had died did what Aristion had to say attain great significance. Why go to Aristion when most of the apostles were still available? But after they had died, the fact that Aristion was an original disciple thrust him into prominence despite his not having been an apostle. Thus it appears that Papias repeats John's name because John is the last surviving elder and therefore one whose current statements Papias has been hearing by firsthand report.[11] Since Papias uses the present tense concerning the elder's speaking and since the Apostle John, who is the elder, died at least by the end of the first century or the first few years of the second, Papias must have acquired this tradition before that time.[12]

Papias delivers the statements about Mark and Matthew not as his own but as those of "the elder," apparently "the Elder John" since he has just designated John by that title (Eusebius, *Hist. eccl.* 3.39.14–16). There is no reason to take the phrase "as I said" in the statement concerning Mark as an intrusion by Papias into the elder's words. Rather, the elder is referring to his own immediately preceding statement that Mark wrote as Peter's interpreter. Prior to the phrase nothing indicates that Papias has stopped quoting the elder and started giving his own comments. Moreover, the verb that Eusebius uses to introduce Papias's account, "sets out" (ἐκτέθειται), and the one that he uses to refer back to it, "are related" (ἱστόρηται, which has the connotation of narrating what one has learned by inquiry), appear to make Papias responsible only for relaying information from the elder, not for interpreting it as well. What we have, then, is a quotation by Papias from the elder clear to the end of the paragraph in Eusebius, *Hist. eccl.* 3.39.15.

A slight disjunction exists at the beginning of the statement concerning Matthew: "Therefore, on the one hand, these things are related by Papias [or 'to Papias'] concerning Mark. Concerning Matthew, on the other hand, these things were said." Eusebius, however, is merely making an editorial transition. Consequently, Papias's quoting the elder not only extends throughout the statement concerning Mark but also carries over to the one concerning Mat-

---

[11] Here is the solution to the difficulty Bauckham feels in "believ[ing] that Papias would have included the same John in both categories [of elders and disciples of the Lord]" ("The Eyewitnesses," 33 n. 24).

[12] Some regard the change from the aorist εἶπεν, "said" or "had said," to the present λέγουσιν, "say" or "were saying," as awkward if the same John is in view. But how else could it be expressed in Greek that somebody has spoken and is still speaking? In English the perfect tense may indicate past action that continues in the present, as when a laborer says, "I have been working at this job for twenty years." But in Greek the perfect tense indicates action completed in the past, and Greek offers no other tense that covers both past and present action. Even in English we often juxtapose the past and present tenses, as in statements beginning, "She was, and is …."

thew. That no need was felt in the statement concerning Matthew to redescribe "the oracles" as "the Lord's" (as in the statement concerning Mark) confirms the original continuity in Papias's quotation from the elder which Eusebius takes over. This continuity is also confirmed by Eusebius's εἴρηται, "were said." If Eusebius meant to distinguish Papias as the speaker concerning Matthew from the elder quoted by Papias concerning Mark, instead of εἴρηται he would almost certainly have written φησί, "he [Papias] said." For this is the verb that he uses three times in the preceding context for Papias's speaking (Eusebius, *Hist. eccl.* 3.39.2, 7, 12). Furthermore, the perfect tense of εἴρηται suits especially well a speaking on the elder's part prior to the time of Papias's writing. A final confirmation of original continuity in Papias's quotation from the elder lies in οὖν at the beginning of the statement concerning Matthew, for this word links that statement to the one about Mark by nicely introducing the contrast between Matthew's orderliness and the previously mentioned disorderliness of Mark.

When recognized as referring back to the statement about Mark, οὖν contains an immensely important implication for synoptic studies. The word normally carries the inferential meaning "therefore." Nothing in the present context indicates that the unseen hand of divine providence is under consideration. Rather, Matthew's reason for writing is in view. *So the elder, i.e., the Apostle John, is saying that Matthew wrote his Gospel for the purpose of correcting Mark's lack of order. Thus we have astonishingly early external evidence that Mark wrote first and that Matthew knew Mark's Gospel and wrote his own in view of it.* This evidence would be only slightly less impressive if the statement with οὖν came originally from Papias rather than from the elder. Later patristic reversal of the order of writing was probably due to the emerging canonical order, which in turn depended on Matthew's greater suitability to liturgical reading, perhaps also on its beginning with a genealogy forming a link with the OT (cf. Clement of Alexandria's dating both Matthew and Luke before Mark expressly because of Jesus' genealogies in the first two [Eusebius, *Hist. eccl.* 6.14.5]).

Papias does not give any further or different identification of "the elder" who spoke concerning Mark. This fact suggests that in quoting Papias, Eusebius is following the order of a text which flows directly not only from the section on Mark to that on Matthew but also from the section where Papias identifies "the elder" as John to the section on Mark. If not, why the lack of further or different identification? If such an identification appeared in a different preceding context unknown to us but known to Eusebius because he had in his possession all Papias's "Exposition of the Lord's Oracles," Eusebius would surely have indicated a shift from the Elder John, who has just occupied his attention, to another elder. Since the Elder John seems to be none other than one of the Lord's disciples, i.e., the Apostle John, both the statements about Mark and Matthew come from an apostolic source. At the very least, they come from the generation before Papias's; and that is still so early as to fall within or right at the close of the apostolic period.[13]

In the 180s Irenaeus designated Papias "the hearer of John" (*Adv. haer.* 5.33.4; quoted by Eusebius, *Hist. eccl.* 3.39.1). From his own standpoint Eusebius can accept this designation only because he distinguishes between the Apostle John and the Elder John (*Hist. eccl.* 3.39.5–7). Otherwise, he could not heap scorn on Papias as a nonhearer of any apostle and on the book of Revelation as an unapostolic document (*Hist. eccl.* 3.39.2, 8–14). But how should we evaluate his affirmation that Papias heard the Elder John? Papias himself does not say so in the statement which Eusebius quotes. That Papias often quotes the Elder John by name presents us with a non sequitur, for Eusebius quotes Papias as saying that he got the traditions of the elders by listening to *others* who had heard the elders and were still hearing the Elder John (and Aristion). Nowhere in the quotation does Papias claim to have heard any of them himself. Nevertheless, Irenaeus's designation and Eusebius's agreement with it suggest that Eusebius found in parts of Papias's "Exposition of the Lord's Oracles" no longer available to us indications that Papias had heard John.[14] His hearing John could only strengthen the case for taking his quotation of the elder's statements about Mark and Matthew very seriously.

On the other hand, we need not take seriously Eusebius's inferring a distinction between the Apostle John and an Elder John from the story of two Ephesian tombs (as μνήματα is usually understood), both identified as John's. We might think that rival burial sites came into existence (cf. the ancient rivalry between the *Memoria Apostolorum ad Catacumbas* and the monuments on the Vatican Hill and the Ostian Way for the burial sites of Peter and Paul; also the modern rivalry between the Garden Tomb and the Church of the Holy Sepulchre as the place of Jesus' burial) and that the rival sites led to a distinguishing of persons in the story to which Eusebius appeals. Or it is possible that a second tomb may have belonged to a later Christian named John but quite unrelated to anyone Papias had in mind; for V. Schultze notes the frequency of ancient Christian graves in honor of elders who had NT names, such as John, Paul, Stephen et al.[15] Better yet, T. Zahn notes that μνήματα may mean memorials or monuments of any kind, not only burial sites, and is able to cite church tradition to the effect that both of the two memorials in Ephesus related to the Apostle John, one being the house where he had lived and a church had met, the other being the place where he was buried.[16]

---

[13] So Bauckham, "The Eyewitnesses," 28–60.

[14] Cf. Bauckham, "The Eyewitnesses," 33: "It is conceivable that Papias went on, following the words Eusebius quoted from the Prologue [of Papias], to say that at a later date he was able to travel and to hear Aristion and John the Elder for himself." But Bauckham is doubtful.

[15] V. Schultze, *Altchristliche Städte und Landschaften II: Kleinasien* (Gütersloh: Bertelsmann, 1926), 1:120.

[16] T. Zahn, *Acta Joannis* (Erlangen: Deichert, 1880), CLIV–CLXXII; also Schultze, *Altchristliche Städte und Landschaften II*, 2:106 n. 4.

We need to keep in mind that Eusebius had an axe to grind concerning the book of Revelation. He speaks vaguely concerning "the story of the ones who have said" and makes no claim that these storytellers linked the supposedly different men named John to Papias's text (*Hist. eccl.* 3.39.6). Finally and most damagingly he quotes Dionysius of Alexandria as saying in the mid-third century, "But I think that there was a certain other [John] of those who came to be in Asia, since they say that there also came to be two memorials in Ephesus and that each is called John's" (*Hist. eccl.* 7.25.16). Dionysius's οἶμαι, "I think," is remarkably weak. And the vague "they say" anticipates Eusebius's expression, "the ones who have said." In fact, almost all Eusebius's phraseology echoes that of Dionysius exactly:

... τῶν ἐν Ἀσίᾳ γενομένων, ἐπεὶ καὶ δύο φασὶν
ἐν Ἐφέσῳ γενέσθαι μνήματα καὶ ἑκάτερον Ἰωάννου
λέγεσθαι (Dionysius).
... τῶν δύο κατὰ τὴν Ἀσίαν ὁμωνυμία κεχρῆσθαι εἰρηκότων δύο τε
ἐν Ἐφέσῳ γενέσθαι μνήματα καὶ ἑκάτερον Ἰωάννου ἔτι νῦν
λέγεσθαι (Eusebius).

To debunk the book of Revelation, then, Eusebius apparently turns Dionysius's cautious inference, "I think there was another John," into a confident assertion, "there were two Johns." He then adds ἔτι νῦν, "still now," to strengthen the argument from two memorials and uses Dionysius's statement as a whole to distinguish an Elder John from the Apostle John in Papias's statement.[17] But Dionysius himself would not have recognized this use of his statement; for in his own context he has just identified the elder who wrote 2–3 John with the Apostle John, and he has made no mention of the tradition passed on by Papias. In all likelihood, then, Eusebius gains the dubious honor of being first to make a false distinction between the Apostle John and the Elder John. Since the distinction is not only false but also rests on an unnecessary inference from two memorials, the argument is doubly weak. Papias means to ascribe his information concerning Mark and Matthew to one and the same John, who was a disciple and elder, i.e., the famous apostle.[18]

J. Marcus lodges several main arguments against the reliability of the pre-Papian tradition:[19]

1) "It is impossible to know to what extent it ['the information Eusebius transmits'] really comes from 'the Elder,' to what extent it comes from Papias, and to what extent it comes from Eusebius himself." But Eusebius claims to be quoting directly from Papias, and Papias from the Elder John. Because he regarded Papias as "a man of very

---

[17] Cf. Orchard, "Some Guidelines," 400 n. 7, for another use by Eusebius of Dionysius's vocabulary.
[18] For further discussion see E. Gutwenger, "Papias: Eine chronologische Studie," *ZKT* 69 (1947): 385–416.
[19] J. Marcus, *Mark 1–8* (AB 27; New York: Doubleday, 1999), 21–24.

little intelligence" Eusebius is unlikely to have dressed up a tradition that Papias passed on, and because Papias valued "a living and surviving voice" above "information from books" he is unlikely to have dressed up a tradition concerning a book like Mark's Gospel. (It is Bauckham's great contribution to have shown that such a voice means that of surviving eyewitnesses, not a merely metaphorical voice of oral tradition.[20])

2) "The very vehemence of Papias' [*sic*, the Elder John's] insistence upon the connection with Peter creates suspicion." This argument misconstrues the words of John the Elder. They do not defend Mark's Gospel against a criticism "that Mark himself was not an eyewitness to Jesus' ministry" by "stoutly maintain[ing]" the Petrine origin of Mark's material (so Marcus), but against the criticism that Mark is lacking in literary art – specifically, in σύνταξις/τάξις, "syntax, arrangement, organization" – by explaining the lack as due to disjunctions in the oral ministry of Peter because he "used to give teaching as necessity demanded" on various occasions (see below).

3) Mark's Gospel is not "particularly apostolic or Petrine." But Marcus's statement that "Mark does not give the impression of being any *closer* to the events he describes than are Matthew and Luke" (italics original) disagrees with Marcus's immediately following statement that Matthew and Luke "appropriated his [Mark's] work." For a main reason to say that Matthew and Luke appropriated Mark's work is that they give the impression of having redacted it so as to set it more distant from the described events. The associated, narrower argument that a Gospel whose material stemmed ultimately from Peter would feature him more prominently and favorably, as Matthew does but Mark does not, neglects that Peter taught about Jesus and therefore spoke about himself only incidentally. The argument also neglects Matthew's derogation of Peter. Uniquely, Matthew describes Peter as a person of "little faith" (14:31); adds "you are my stumbling block" to Jesus' rebuke of Peter (16:23; contrast Mark 8:33; Luke 9:22); inserts "before all" into Peter's denial of Jesus at 26:70, so that the denial falls into the category of denials before others that issue in a denial by Jesus before his Father in heaven (10:33); pairs the bitterness of Peter's weeping (26:75; mentioned also in Luke 22:62 but not in Mark 14:72) with Judas Iscariot's hanging himself (27:1–10); and omits Peter's name from the account of Jesus' resurrection (contrast 28:7 with Mark 16:7). Correspondingly, "this bedrock" on which Jesus will build his church (Matt 16:17–19) is not Peter, "a stone," but "the bedrock" of Jesus' "words," to which – not as in Luke 6:47, 49 – Matt 7:24, 26 attached "these," corresponding to "this" with "bedrock" in Matt 16:18.[21]

If Papias were setting Mark as an authoritative Gospel over against Luke, which was captured and truncated by Marcion,[22] we would have expected a comparison between Mark and Luke. As it is, we have a comparison between Mark and

---

[20] Bauckham, "The Eyewitnesses," 28–60, esp. 41–42.

[21] For a fuller and more radical presentation of this point, see below, pp. 118, 124. I desist from discussing Marcus's lesser arguments against the reliability of the pre-Papian tradition, though it should be noted that "the supposition that between Jesus and Mark there was a lengthy course of development with many tradents" (so Marcus) pays insufficient attention to the possibility of Peter's and Mark's shaping of Jesuanic materials and – beyond that possibility – assumes the point to be proved, viz., that many more tradents and much more time are required to explain the textual phenomena in Mark.

[22] So R. P. Martin, *Mark: Evangelist and Theologian* (Contemporary Evangelical Perspectives; Grand Rapids: Zondervan, 1973), 80–83.

Matthew. To be sure, there are some similarities between the statement of Papias's elder concerning Mark and certain terms in Luke 1:1–4, viz., ἀνατά-ξασθαι, παρέδοσαν, παρηκολουθηκότι, ἀκριβῶς, and καθέξης. But there is no reason why the elder could not have known the Gospel of Luke and been influenced by the terminology of its prologue when making a defense of Mark over against Matthew, as he does. Apart from the possibility of such influence, any statement concerning the way tradition was written down is likely to contain the terms common to Luke 1:1–4 and Papias's elder. The elder's saying that Mark did not leave out anything that he had heard from Peter may defend Mark against the attractions of Matthew's greater fullness as easily as it might argue for Mark against Marcion's truncated Luke. Indeed, since the elder compares Mark with Matthew his purpose may be to save Mark from being eclipsed by Matthew. Matthew gained greater favor in the early church but the elder achieved his purpose (if such it was) to the extent that the canonization of Mark saved it from total eclipse. Against the insinuation that Papias has put his own words in the elder's mouth stand Papias's preoccupation with and devotion to "the living and abiding voice" of surviving eyewitnesses (as noted above) and his emphasizing that he "learned well and remembered well" the things that came from the elders (Eusebius, *Hist. eccl.* 3.39.3). The possibility that Papias and Marcion confronted each other face-to-face (cf. the so-called Anti-Marcionite Prologue to John) need not have anything to do with the date of the elder's comparing Mark and Matthew, for the date of such a confrontation would remain uncertain and the elder's statement is better understood against the rising popularity of Matthew than against Marcion's truncating of Luke.

Now that we have established the date of Papias's writing as during the period A.D. 101–108 and the identity of his elder as the Apostle John, the tradition that Mark wrote the Gospel which bears his name looks as early and authoritative as one could wish. But since Mark was a very common name in the Roman Empire, perhaps the most common, we must ask whether the Mark of Papias's elder is John Mark of the NT. According to Eusebius, *Hist. eccl.* 3.39.16, Papias knew 1 Peter. Since 1 Pet 5:13 describes Mark as Peter's "son," it is hard to think that Papias would have quoted the elder about another Mark as Peter's "interpreter" without making a distinction between the two. Moreover, Acts 12:11–17 puts Peter in John Mark's home on one occasion. That this same John Mark acted as a helper to the pair Barnabas and Paul (Acts 12:25; 13:13), to Barnabas alone (Acts 15:36–41), and to Paul alone (Col 4:10; 2 Tim 4:11; Phlm 24) favors that he passed into the service of Peter too, so that the NT speaks of only one Mark. According to Eusebius, *Hist. eccl.* 6.25.5, Origen identified Mark the evangelist with the Mark of 1 Pet 5:13; and Jerome (*Comm.* on Phlm 24 [PL 26:618a]) identifies Mark the evangelist with the Mark of Phlm 24. We know of no other Mark with credentials such as these that would qualify him to be the referent of Papias's elder.

But what does the elder mean by calling this Mark an interpreter of Peter? One might answer that Peter preached in Aramaic because he did not know Greek, or did not know it very well, so that Mark followed Peter in Peter's itineration outside Palestine (for which see Gal 2:11 ff.; 1 Cor 1:12 with 9:5; and above all 1 Pet 5:13, which puts the two men together in Rome) and translated Peter's Aramaic, incomprehensible to most people in the Roman Empire, into Greek, the lingua franca of the empire. Alternatively, in Italy he translated Peter's Aramaic into Latin (again see 1 Pet 5:13 and cf. the numerous Latinisms in the Gospel of Mark).[23] But Greek as well as Latin was spoken in Italy. Paul wrote his Epistle to the Romans in Greek, not in Latin. Clement of Rome wrote an epistle in Greek. The Roman emperor Marcus Aurelius wrote his *Meditations* in Greek. In Rome, Plutarch of Chaeronaea found his knowledge of Greek adequate. He did not know Latin.[24] And early tradition says that Mark wrote his Gospel, a Greek one, in Rome for Romans.[25] The presence of numerous Latinisms in a Greek gospel implies a Latin substratum only to the extent that Mark used his supposed Latin translations of Peter's teachings as a basis for the Gospel rather than going back to the supposed Aramaic original of Peter's teachings. No need exists, however, to say anything more than that a Roman provenance of the Gospel led to the use of numerous Latinisms.[26]

One might combine Latin translation in Italy or Rome with Greek translation elsewhere outside Palestine, but the more common theory of translation into Greek has its own problems. The greater the Hellenization of Palestine, more particularly of Galilee and most particularly of Capernaum, located as it was next door to the major trade route known as the Via Maris, the less likely it seems that Peter, who came from Capernaum, would have needed anyone to translate his teachings into Greek. What we know of this Hellenization would lead us to believe that Peter knew Greek well enough to speak it for himself.

We might think, then, that before writing his Gospel, Mark had become an oral expositor of Peter's teachings as he followed Peter about (cf. Paul's and Barnabas's regular use of subordinates, including Mark himself, in itinerant evangelism and subsequent pastoral ministry). Under this view the aorist tense of γενόμενος indicates an action prior to that of the main verb ἔγραψεν, "having become [an interpreter of Peter]… he wrote," and the Gospel of Mark turns into a written version of Mark's earlier oral expositions. We cannot quarrel with the use of an aorist participle for prior action. This use is normal. And though representing the usage of Papias rather than that of the elder, Eusebius's *Hist.*

---

[23] Schmidt, "Semitismen bei Papias," 137.

[24] W. Barclay, *Introduction to the First Three Gospels* (2d ed.; Philadelphia: Westminster, 1975), 122–23.

[25] See R. H. Gundry, *Mark* (Grand Rapids: Eerdmans, 1993), 1041–45.

[26] Gundry, *Mark*, 1043–45.

eccl. 3.39.1, 3 equates ταῖς ἑρμηνείαις, "the interpretations," with ἐξηγήσεως, "exposition." This equation favors that Mark became Peter's expositor rather than translator. Otherwise, a shift from exposition to translation needs to have been noted (see below for the nontranslational meaning of "interpreted" in Eusebius, *Hist. eccl.* 3.39.16).

On the other hand, "the things that he had heard" points to the author Mark as a former listener rather than as a former expositor. Thus he became Peter's interpreter *in writing the Gospel* as an exposition of Peter's oral teachings. The aorist participle γενόμενος then indicates action in conjunction with or, indeed, the same as that of the main verb ἔγραψεν (also a normal usage); and the elder's "as I said," which in the other views of his meaning makes Mark's following of Peter the background for his simultaneously becoming an oral interpreter of Peter *before* writing the Gospel, now makes Mark's following of Peter the background for his later becoming an interpreter of Peter *in* the writing of the Gospel.[27]

"As many things as he remembered" and "as he related [them] from memory" (taking the prefix ἀπ- before -εμνημόνευσεν as adding to memory the idea of telling) allude to Peter's memory and telling, not to Mark's memory and telling (cf. Justin, *Dial.* 106.3, under the view that ἐν τοῖς ἀπομνημονεύμασιν αὐτοῦ refers to reminiscences concerning Jesus as told by Peter and written by Mark; also the reference in Clement of Alexandria, *Adumbr.* to 1 Pet 5:13, to Peter's many testimonies concerning Christ, though according to Eusebius, *Hist. eccl.* 6.14.6, Clement wrote that Mark remembered Peter's sayings). Otherwise the elder would be contradicting himself when saying that Mark "was thinking beforehand of one thing, [i.e.,] to omit not a single one of the things that he had heard." Were Mark's memory in view, that statement would read that he "was thinking beforehand of one thing, [i.e.,] to omit not a single one of the things that he *remembered*." The placement of the clause ὅσα ἐμνημόνευσεν, "as many things as he remembered," before the verbal phrase of which it is the direct object – viz., ἀκριβῶς ἔγραψεν, "he wrote accurately" – draws the remembering close to the just-mentioned Peter so as to facilitate an identification of the rememberer as Peter rather than Mark. And ἔνια, "some things," agrees with the incompleteness implied by "as many things as he remembered" and by "as he related [them] from memory" just as these two clauses disagree with Mark's single-minded concern "to omit not a single one of the things that he had heard." Thus Peter remembered and related some but not all of Jesus' words and deeds, and Mark wrote accurately everything that he had heard in Peter's incomplete teachings (cf. the non-Markan materials in Matthew, Luke, and John).

---

[27] Against Schmidt, whose argument that this meaning would require the present participle ὑπάρχων, "being," instead of γενόμενος, "becoming," neglects the historical bent of the elder's statement as well as the frequent use of an aorist participle for action in conjunction with or the same as that of the main verb ("Semitismen bei Papias," 136–37).

The elder describes Mark's writing as οὐ ... τάξει, "not in order." Here it is important to observe that this description does not refer to chronological or topical disorder, but to interrupted order, i.e., to gaps. τάξις is commonly used for a list, an inventory, a detailed enumeration.[28] But that is what Mark is not. Mark is a small sampling because it rests on the hit-and-miss of Peter's oral presentations. This lack of order as lack of fullness tallies both with the incompleteness of Peter's memory as seen in the clause "as many things as he remembered," in the expression "some things," and in the further clause "as he remembered [them]" and with the elder's drawing a contrast between Mark, a short gospel, and Matthew, a long one. This lack of order as lack of fullness also results in what Aristotle calls an episodic narrative of loose-knit anecdotes whose progression from one to another is ungoverned by the laws of inevitability or even of probability (*Poet.* 9.11–13; contrast the elder's going on to say that differently from Mark, Matthew "arranged [συνετάξατο] the oracles" [N.B. the prefixing of συν- to add close-knittedness to the fullness indicated by ταξ-] – Eusebius, *Hist. eccl.* 3.39.16, and the foregoing discussion that the elder puts Mark in contrast with Matthew rather than with Luke or John). The elder excuses Mark's lack of order on the ground that Mark, having neither heard Jesus nor followed him, was dependent on Peter. Subsidiarily Peter is excused on the ground that he used anecdotes (as appropriate to oral teachings) rather than producing a full, close-knit arrangement. And to counteract the vice of Mark's gappiness the elder stresses the virtue of Mark's writing all that Peter remembered, taking care not to omit any of it, writing accurately, and falsifying nothing.[29]

The use of ποιέω in the middle voice with a direct object produces the verbal meaning of the direct object. Thus ἐποιεῖτο τὰς διδασκαλίας means "he was teaching on various occasions" (N.B. the plural), οὐχ ὥσπερ σύνταξιν ... ποιούμενος means "not as it were arranging," and ἑνός ... ἐποιήσατο πρόνοιαν means "he was thinking beforehand of one thing." The teaching was πρὸς τὰς χρείας, says the elder. Does this phrase mean that Peter suited his teachings "to the needs" of various occasions? Probably not, for three reasons: (1) no needs or needy people are identified by the elder; (2) the contents of Mark, which according to the elder reflect Peter's teachings, look apologetic of the cross rather than helpful of audiences;[30] and (3) the translation of χρείας by

---

[28] J. A. Kleist, *The Memoirs of St. Peter* (Science and Culture Series; Milwaukee: Bruce, 1932), 19–22; M. S. Enslin, "Luke and Matthew: Compilers or Authors?" in *ANRW* II 25.3:2361–62).

[29] The interpretation of B. H. M. G. M. Standaert (*L'Évangile selon Marc* [Nijmegen: Stichting Studentenpers, 1978], 448–51) starts off on the wrong foot by treating "not in order" as antithetical to "accurately" whereas these descriptions merely distinguish between Mark's not writing everything that Matthew wrote and the accuracy with which Mark wrote what he did write.

[30] See Gundry, *Mark*, passim; idem, "A Rejoinder to Joel F. Williams' 'Is Mark's Gospel an Apology for the Cross?'" *BBR* 12 (2002): 123–39.

"needs" does not suit the rhetorical tenor of the passage as established especially by τάξει, "order," and σύνταξιν, "arrangement."[31] This tenor favors
the rhetorical meaning "anecdotes" for χρείας. It is sometimes argued that
πρός makes this meaning difficult to accept. But Luke 12:47 falsifies this argument with a use of πρός in the sense required here: "acting in accord with his
will" (Luke 12:47). Thus, "teaching in accord with the anecdotes" (Eusebius,
Hist. eccl. 3.39.15). "The anecdotes" refers back to "the things either said or
done by the Lord."[32] The strong adversative ἀλλ', "yet," the adverb ὥσπερ, "as
it were," and the prefix σύν- before -ταξιν, "arrangement," emphasize that in
his teachings Peter did not even come close to providing a close-knit and comprehensive narrative of "the Lord's oracles," which are "the things either said or
done by the Lord"[33] and thus not the Gospel of Mark itself but the Jesuanic subject matter of Peter's teachings that Mark wrote down in his Gospel. The possibility that Papias added to the elder's statement Greek rhetorical terms in τάξει,
χρείας, and σύνταξιν[34] does not affect the argument from early, apostolic tradition for the Petrine origin of Mark's materials (though we should not discount
the alternative possibility that John knew, or had come to know during his time
in the province of Asia, Greek rhetorical terms and mixed them with Semitisms).[35] The elder does not deny that Mark drew from sources other than Peter's
teachings. One may even regard as deliberate the absence of a statement that
Mark added nothing to Peter's teachings (contrast Deut 4:2; 13:1[12:32];
Prov 30:6; Rev 22:18–19) and infer an implication on the elder's part that Mark
did add non-Petrine materials to Peter's teachings. Nonetheless, it is hard to escape the impression that the elder is describing as Petrine the whole, or at least
the bulk, of Mark's Gospel.

Those who for reasons such as the foregoing feel compelled to take seriously
the elder's statement quoted by Papias understand it in different ways when it
comes to Matthew. If considerations that go against authorship of the First
Gospel by the Apostle Matthew seem strong to them, they interpret the statement in a way that avoids authorship by this apostle. Some suggest that he drew
up a collection of Hebrew OT passages to be used as proof texts showing fulfillment through Christ, that the unknown, later author of the Gospel incorporated some or all of these proof texts (see 1:22–23; 2:15, 17–18, 23; 4:14–16;

---

[31] J. Kürzinger, *Papias von Hierapolis und die Evangelien des Neuen Testaments* (Eich-
stätter Materialien 4; Regensburg: Pustet, 1983), passim.

[32] See G. W. Buchanan, *Jesus, the King and His Kingdom* (Macon, Ga.: Mercer University
Press, 1984), 43 ff., that χρεία, "anecdote," carried its rhetorical meaning into the first and second centuries and could include deeds in addition to words, as here (against Körtner, *Papias* 158).

[33] Schmidt, "Semitismen bei Papias," 140–42.

[34] On the rhetorical use of these terms see Kürzinger, *Papias*, passim, with significant argumentive support from Schmidt, "Semitismen bei Papias," 138 n. 12.

[35] Against Schmidt, "Semitismen bei Papias," 144.

8:17; 12:18–21; 13:14–15, 35; 21:4–5; 27:9–10; cf. 2:5–6), and that this incorporation led to a transfer of Matthew's name from the earlier collection to the
Gospel.

But the unlikelihood of such a transfer from what became a few bits and
pieces in the Gospel to the whole of the Gospel militates against this hypothesis.
Furthermore, if Papias's elder was referring to OT passages collected before
their incorporation in the Gospel and therefore before the transfer of Matthew's
name, the parallel between Matthew and Mark in his statement breaks down; for
Mark wrote a Gospel, not anything comparable to a collection of OT proof
texts. But if the elder was referring to our Greek Gospel of Matthew after the
collection had been incorporated and after Matthew's name had been transferred, why the need for each person to translate as he was able? Under this hypothesis, the OT passages had already been translated into Greek, which is the
language of the Gospel and which nearly everybody knew.

Others suggest that the Apostle Matthew compiled a collection of Jesus' sayings (usually designated Q) no longer extant, that the unknown, later author of
the First Gospel incorporated it (as Luke also did in his Gospel), and that a
transfer of Matthew's name took place. We may cast doubt on the likelihood
that Matthew's name was transferred at a stage so early that people who knew
the apostles were still living. Again, if the elder quoted by Papias was referring
to Q, the parallel with the Gospel of Mark, which is a different kind of book,
breaks down. But if he was referring to our Greek Gospel of Matthew after the
incorporation of Q and after the transfer of the apostle's name, why (again) the
need for translation? Furthermore, the term λόγοι, "sayings," would have described Q better than the elder's term did. That term is λόγια, "oracles."[36] Some
of these objections spoil the similar suggestions that behind the elder's statement lies a loose body of materials concerning Jesus' deeds as well as sayings,
stemming from the Apostle Matthew, taken up by the later, unknown author of
the Gospel, and giving to the Gospel Matthew's name by transfer.

More traditionally and conservatively some have thought that Papias's elder
refers to a Gospel written by the Apostle Matthew in the Aramaic language (the
usual interpretation of Ἑβραΐδι διαλέκτῳ, literally, "a Hebrew dialect"; thus
possibly but not necessarily Irenaeus, *Adv. haer.* 3.1.1, cited by Eusebius, *Hist.
eccl.* 5.10.3; and Origen, cited by Eusebius, *Hist. eccl.* 6.25.3–4). This view has
the advantages of agreeing with the early ascription "According to Matthew"
and of treating "the oracles" in terms of Matthew's gospel book just as the elder
uses "the Lord's oracles" for Mark's gospel book. That is, the literary parallel

---

[36] According to H. Koester, Papias speaks only about Jesus' sayings in connection with Matthew whereas Papias speaks about the deeds as well as the sayings of Jesus in connection with
Mark (*Ancient Christian Gospels* [Philadelphia: Trinity Press International, 1990], 316). But if
λόγια covers deeds as well as sayings in Mark, as it does, the term will naturally cover both in
Matthew as well.

between Mark and Matthew is preserved whereas it is damaged in the preceding hypotheses.

We might account for the loss of an Aramaic Gospel of Matthew by noting the limited appeal of the Aramaic language and the dominance of Greek in the Hellenistic world. But our present Gospel of Matthew does not bear the marks of translation from Aramaic to Greek; and Matthew often shows familiarity with the LXX. Once in a while this Greek form of the OT seems necessary to his meaning where the Hebrew text differs (see, e.g., 12:21; 13:14–15). Besides, it is the currently prevalent and well-substantiated opinion that our Greek Matthew shows many signs of drawing in large part on the Gospel of Mark, also written in Greek. Therefore those who believe in an Aramaic Gospel of Matthew usually say that because people had difficulty translating it Matthew wrote another Gospel as well, viz., the Greek Gospel we now have, not translated from the earlier Aramaic Gospel but probably incorporating materials from it. Or such scholars qualify their belief in the words of Papias's elder by saying that he spoke accurately in ascribing a Gospel to Matthew but erred in confusing that Gospel, which is really our Greek Gospel of Matthew, with some other and perhaps similar Hebrew or Aramaic document, such as the *Gospel according to the Hebrews*, which was not written by Matthew. Against this explanation, since Papias is not giving his own opinion but relating a tradition derived from the elder of an earlier Christian generation the supposed confusion seems improbable. Possibilities of confusion decrease the closer we approach the time of writing. It is especially hard to think that one of the twelve apostles, John himself, fell into such an error.

Now it is extremely odd that Papias's elder should have talked about a collection of OT passages fulfilled by Jesus, or a collection of Jesus' sayings, or a loose body of materials concerning Jesus' deeds and sayings, or an Aramaic Gospel, yet not about our Greek Gospel, the only one of these to survive, let alone achieve canonicity. Or if the elder also talked about our Greek Gospel but somewhere else, it is extremely odd that Papias and then Eusebius do not quote what he said about it rather than what he said about a collection of OT passages, a collection of Jesus' sayings, or one of the other possibilities. This oddity arises out of the high degree of interest we should expect to have been shown toward the only one of the documents (if we assume the existence of the hypothesized ones) treasured enough to become canonical. Also, Eusebius, Papias, and the elder himself, whom they quote, are making a comparison between what Matthew wrote and the Gospel of Mark. Since the latter was written in Greek and quickly canonized, our Greek Gospel of Matthew provides by far the best comparison.

As we have seen, the elder shows concern over Mark's style, particularly over the disorderly way the single points concerning Jesus' ministry appear in the Gospel of Mark. This concern favors a similar frame of reference in the statement about Matthew, whose writing by contrast exhibits orderliness (a description especially damaging to the hypothesis that the elder refers to a loose body of Matthean materials). This contrast comes out clearly in the elder's parallelistic use of the verb συνετάξατο, "arranged," to describe what Matthew *did* do with the Lord's oracles, and of the cognate noun σύνταξιν, "arrangement," to describe what Mark, following Peter, did *not* do with the Lord's oracles. Thus far the contrast has to do with the structuring of materials, not with languages. This structural contrast is supported by the technical rhetorical meaning of χρείας, which the elder uses properly for Mark's loose, anecdotal style. Furthermore, the elder says nothing at all about the language of Mark, which he ought to mention if it is his intention to introduce by way of contrast a different language in Matthew. Apparently Matthew was not written in a language different from Mark's Greek.

But what of Matthew's "Hebrew dialect," which "each person interpreted as he was able"? The elder's and Papias's own earlier usage gives us guidance. In *Hist. eccl.* 3.39.3 Eusebius mentions that Papias describes his "Exposition of the Lord's Oracles" as "the interpretations" (ταῖς ἑρμηνείαις). Out of context an interpretation may be either a translation or an explanation. But here the associated word "Exposition" (ἐξηγήσεως) in the title shows that "the interpretations" can hardly be taken in the sense "the translations"; on the contrary, "the explanations." Furthermore, the elder quoted by Papias calls Mark an "interpreter" (ἑρμηνευτής) of Peter (Eusebius, *Hist. eccl.* 3.39.15). But the context says nothing about Mark's translating for Peter. Rather, we are told that Mark remembered and recorded what Peter had said. By the same token, when the elder compares Matthew with Mark and says that each person "interpreted" (ἡρμήνευσεν) Matthew, we should think of explanation rather than translation. The phrase "as he [each person] was able" refers, then, to expository rather than translational ability. Moreover, the phrase does not imply a greater difficulty in comparison with Mark. Just the opposite! Matthew's orderly arrangement of the Lord's oracles makes them easier to understand than those in Mark, where disorder prevails. (The elder excuses Mark's disorder, however.)[37]

"A Hebrew dialect," then, does not imply that Matthew wrote in the Aramaic language. In other connections we should expect the conjunction of "Hebrew" and "dialect" to form a reference to language. But the stylistic contrast between Mark and Matthew cancels such an expectation here. And the lack of a definite article in Ἑβραΐδι διαλέκτῳ facilitates (though it does not prove) a different

---

[37] It might be thought that the last clause in Eusebius, *Hist. eccl.* 3.39.16, means that each of the two evangelists Mark and Matthew interpreted the dominical oracles as he was able. But the μέν ... δέ construction in the sentence as a whole sets up a comparison between Matthew's Hebrew style and each person's exposition of the dominical oracles written in that style. Hence ἕκαστος means "each reader of Matthew." The exposition may have to do with private understanding rather than public dissemination.

reference since διάλεκτος always has the definite article in its six occurrences for languages in Acts, including three for the Hebrew or Aramaic language (1:19; 2:6, 8; 21:40; 22:2; 26:14). Besides, the generality of each person's interpreting as he was able fits better the exercise of reading and understanding a Gospel written in the lingua franca, Greek; for comparatively few people had the knowledge of Aramaic that would have enabled them to translate an Aramaic Gospel into Greek or into whatever other language was native to them. διάλεκτος commonly carried a stylistic meaning, especially when referring to debate (cf. the English word "dialectic"). In describing Matthew, then, "a Hebrew dialect" means a Hebrew way of presenting Jesus' messiahship. Immediately we think of all those Jewish features of Matthew – the stress on Jesus as the Son of David and Messiah, the tracing of his genealogy back to Abraham, the frequent and unique citations of OT passages as fulfilled by Jesus, and so on – that capture a large amount of attention in modern introductions to this Gospel.

What understandings have we reached? (1) That Papias wrote his book containing information about Mark and Matthew before A.D. 110. (2) That Philip of Side does not provide good support for a later date. (3) That the fragments from Papias scattered in Eusebius, *Hist. eccl.* 3.39.1–16, formed a continuous text in Papias's book. (4) That Papias quotes the elder concerning Matthew as well as concerning Mark. (5) That the elder makes Matthew write after Mark and in view of Mark. (6) That the contrast between Mark and Matthew has to do with literary style, not with different languages. (7) That Matthew's literary artistry made his Gospel easier to understand than Mark's Gospel was. (8) That Eusebius misuses a statement by Dionysius of Alexandria to distinguish the Elder John from the Apostle John. (9) That the elder who passed on this information was the Apostle John. (10) That John the elder and apostle makes the Apostle Peter the source of Mark's material and ascribes the First Gospel to the Apostle Matthew.[38]

But how can we believe that Matthew, an apostle, used the Gospel of a non-apostle, Mark? Well, the elder quoted by Papias as saying that Matthew wrote the First Gospel also indicates that Mark wrote down the reminiscences of Peter concerning Jesus' ministry (Eusebius, *Hist. eccl.* 3.39.15). According to extremely early tradition, then, the Gospel of Mark is essentially apostolic. Therefore we should put the question as follows: Is it too hard to think that one apostle took material that came from a fellow apostle? Of course not, especially since the apostle borrowed from was none other than the foremost among the Twelve. Furthermore, Matthew did not merely copy the Petrine tradition set forth by Mark. He used it in ways we have come to appreciate for their originality.[39]

---

[38] See A. F. J. Klijn and G. J. Reinink, *Patristic Evidence for Jewish-Christian Sects* (NovTSup 36; Leiden: Brill, 1973), 46–50, on the confusion and contradictions in Jerome's statements about a Hebrew or Aramaic Gospel of Matthew.

[39] In this connection we may think that Matthew borrowed from the Petrine Mark in part to criticize Peter (see below, pp. 118, 124).

More importantly, doubt that he would have used the Gospel of Mark rests on modern antipathy toward literary borrowing. Moderns regard such borrowing as plagiarism or, at best, unworthy dependency. Ancients did not share this antipathy. On the contrary, they strongly believed in literary borrowing as a way of preserving tradition.[40]

We might ask another question concerning the First Gospel. Would the Apostle Matthew, an eyewitness, have edited Mark and other materials so extensively as the author of the First Gospel did? Even under the supposition of unhistorical writing at a number of points, authorship by an eyewitness is far from inconceivable. Plato not only rehearsed the teachings of Socrates but also used Socrates as a vehicle of Platonic thought growing out of those teachings.[41] We should therefore broaden our horizons with respect to the authorial possibilities immediate disciples took advantage of when they presented and developed the thought of their masters – and that right within the lifetime of others who had heard their masters. There is a difference between Plato and Matthew, to be sure. The one belonged to classical Greek culture, the other to Jewish culture. But Matthew's Jewish culture had been hellenized. What cultural difference there was makes it easier to think that an immediate disciple of Jesus did what has been done in the Gospel of Matthew. For if even an exacting Greek philosopher could purvey as his master's teachings his own highly advanced development of them, how much more might a haggadically oriented Jew do something similar (cf. the development by R. Jonathan of a parable told by his teacher R. Hama b. R. Ḥanina [*Gen. Rab.* 9.4] and the teaching of R. Joshua of Sichnin in the name of R. Levi [*Gen. Rab.* 16.3]).[42] In the Jewish sphere we find haggadic freedom alongside careful memorization and passing on of both the written law and the oral law.

For several reasons, however, the elder's report on the composition of Mark is widely regarded as at least overly simplistic and perhaps historically worthless:[43] (1) Form criticism and redaction criticism have shown that Markan ma-

---

[40] Cf. the exhortation of classicist G. Kennedy that NT scholars give more credence to external testimony such as that of Papias's elder ("Classical and Christian Source Criticism," in *The Relationships among the Gospels* [ed. W. O. Walker Jr.; Trinity University Monograph Series in Religion 5; San Antonio, Tex.: Trinity University Press, 1978], 125–92). On the other hand, Eusebius is probably right to take Mark's "memorandum" (ὑπόμνημα) as a finished Gospel (cf. Eusebius, *Hist. eccl.* 2.15.1 with 6:14.6; also the use of ὑπομνήματα for the finished Gospels of Matthew and John in 3.24.5) and Kennedy wrong to take Mark's memorandum as a preliminary set of notes.

[41] Opinions differ concerning the degree to which Plato put his own development of Socratic thought in the mouth of Socrates. It is generally agreed, however, that he did so fairly extensively at least in the later dialogues. For a survey see A. R. Lacey, "Our Knowledge of Socrates," in *The Philosophy of Socrates* (ed. G. Vlastos; Modern Studies in Philosophy; Garden City, N.Y.: Doubleday, 1971), 22–49.

[42] I owe these citations to M. Goulder, *Midrash and Lection in Matthew* (The Speaker's Lectures in Biblical Studies, 1969–71; London: SPCK, 1974), 53, 64.

[43] See esp. K. Niederwimmer, "Johannes Markus und die Frage nach dem Verfasser des zweiten Evangeliums," *ZNW* 58 (1967): 172–88.

terials went through more stages of growth and change than allowed by the straight, short line from Jesus through Peter to Mark. The needs of church life and evangelism shaped the materials; and the supernatural elements in stories such as those of Jesus' baptism, raising of Jairus's daughter, transfiguration, and resurrection are too fantastic to have come from someone so close to what really happened as Peter was. The narrative of Jesus' long day in Capernaum arises out of artistic manipulation of originally unrelated traditions, not out of the actuality of concatenated events as narrated by someone who was there; and Mark drew on earlier collections of controversy stories, miracle stories, sayings, and parables, and on an earlier passion narrative. (2) Mark commits several errors concerning Palestinian and Syrian topography that neither Peter nor Mark, both natives of the region, would have committed. (3) The Gospel of Mark betrays an ignorance of doublets in 6:35–44 with 8:1–9; 6:45–56 with 8:10; 7:31–37 with 8:22–26, betrays an equal ignorance of Palestinian Jewish customs, and reflects a non-Jewish standpoint. (4) Mark's stories about Peter do not differ in character from other stories in the Gospel as would be expected that they differ if Peter stands behind them. They include stories severely critical of Peter and exclude both the Aramaic form of his name – viz., "Cephas" – and the specially Petrine materials in Matt 14:28–31; 16:17–19; 17:24–27; Luke 8:45; 12:41; 22:8, 31; 24:12–35, as would not be expected if Peter stands behind Mark. (5) 1 Pet 5:13 provides a connection between Mark and Peter that Papias or his elder could have used to make Mark derivatively apostolic and thus more useful in a fight against Gnostics, who had their own Gospels.

These reasons do not stand up under scrutiny. Both Peter and Mark could have shaped and developed Jesuanic materials. After all, Peter was a preacher as well as an eyewitness to most of what the Gospel of Mark contains; and the increasingly recognized homogeneity of style that characterizes Mark makes it difficult and probably impossible to prove the passage of Markan materials through pre-Markan non-Petrine stages. The supernatural element is a point at issue, i.e., a point to be argued *about*, not one to be argued *from*. Even otherwise, a greater openness to the supernatural than some moderns entertain would naturally affect the reporting of an eyewitness.[44] Markan materials are far less ecclesiastically relevant than is often claimed. Mark himself (if not Peter before him) might have drawn together similar materials, and a historical conjunction of some Markanly conjoined events, sayings, etc., is not to be ruled out of court. Some have cogently pointed out that topographical notations grow denser in materials set in and around Jerusalem, where Mark had lived, and that the worst supposed topographical error has to do with reaches far to the north, as might be expected of a Jerusalemite who like Mark had left Jerusalem long before and

---

[44] Cf. Hengel, *Studies*, 11.

apparently never traveled to those northern reaches.[45] But topographical errors are more apparent than real.[46] The argument that a Palestinian would not have had occasion to distinguish a Syrophoenician from a Libophoenician, as is done in 7:23,[47] overlooks that writing in Rome, as early tradition says Mark did, would have provided an occasion to make that distinction whatever his own geographical origin. For Libophoenicia, located on the coast of North Africa, lay closer to Rome than Syrophoenicia did; and the oldest evidence for the substantive "Syrophoenician" is to be found in Latin writers.[48]

The supposed doublets may not be doublets at all.[49] Even if they are, it is within the bounds of possibility – given the frequent looseness of ancient reportorial standards – that Mark or Peter doubled a single event for emphasis or multiple application. Mark's ignorance of Jewish customs has been much exaggerated.[50] What seems to reflect the standpoint of a non-Jewish author may equally well reflect the standpoint of a non-Jewish audience to which a Jewish author like Mark shows sensitivity (again see 7:3–4). The Jewishness of the author and his sensitivity to the non-Jewishness of his audience are much favored by his frequent citations of Aramaic and by his frequent translations of that same Aramaic into Greek.[51] If in accordance with early tradition Mark wrote in Rome for Romans and Peter had ministered in Rome and if in accordance with probability Peter had come to be known in Rome by that Greek form of his name rather than by its Aramaic form Cephas, no wonder this Aramaic form does not appear in Mark's Gospel. We would expect stories not about Peter to be similar to stories about him if both kinds of stories rested on his eyewitnessing, came from his lips, and passed through the sieve of Mark's com-

---

[45] Cf. F. G. Lang, "'Über Sidon mitten ins Gebiet der Dekapolis': Geographie und Theologie in Markus 7,31," *ZDPV* 94 (1978): 145–60; J. Lambrecht, *Die Redaktion der Markus-Apokalypse* (AnBib 28; Rome: Pontifical Biblical Institute, 1967), 20; G. Lüderitz, "Rhetorik, Poetik, Kompositionstechnik im Markusevangelium," in *Markus-Philologie* (ed. H. Cancik; WUNT 33; Tübingen: Mohr, 1984), 192 n. 67; Hengel, *Studies*, 46; C. Breytenbach, *Nachfolge und Zukunftserwartung nach Markus* (ATANT 71; Zurich: Theologischer Verlag, 1984), 322–23.

[46] See the comments and notes on 7:31 in Gundry, *Mark*, 382–83, 386–88; and for a list of supposed errors, some of them egregiously manufactured by hypercriticism, see P. Parker, "The Posteriority of Mark," in *New Synoptic Studies* (ed. W. R. Farmer; Macon, Ga.: Mercer University Press, 1983), 68–70.

[47] See Niederwimmer, "Johannes Markus," 182.

[48] Hengel, *Studies*, 29, 137–38 n. 164; G. Theissen, "Lokal- und Sozialkolorit in der Geschichte von der syrophönikischen Frau (Mk 7 24–30)," *ZNW* 75 (1984): 222.

[49] See the comments and notes in Gundry, *Mark*, ad loc.

[50] See esp. the comments and notes on 7:3–4 by Gundry, *Mark*, 348–49, 357–61, but also the notes on temporal and calendrical indicators scattered throughout Mark – e.g., on 14:12 (ibid., 823–24).

[51] 3:17–19; 5:41; 7:11, 34; 10:46; 11:9–10; 14:1, 32, 36, 45; 15:22, 34; cf. H. P. Rüger, "Die lexikalischen Aramaismen im Markusevangelium," in *Markus-Philologie* (ed. H. Cancik; WUNT 33; Tübingen: Mohr, 1984), 73–84.

position. On the one hand, anybody who has heard the testimonies of former sinners and backsliders will not find it hard to believe that Peter told on himself the stories uncomplimentary to him. On the other hand, those same stories lessen the likelihood of Papias's, the elder's, or anyone else's guessing or inferring from 1 Pet 5:13 that Mark got his materials from Peter. The presence of good as well as bad concerning Peter supports the historical connection of Mark with Peter, for a redactional program would probably have produced a more consistently good or bad portrait of him.[52] The specially Petrine notes and episodes to be found in Matthew and Luke but not in Mark may derive almost entirely from creative redaction, not from historical actuality, and therefore need not damage the case for Mark's writing of Peter's reminiscences.[53] Besides, we should not expect that in Mark's hearing, Peter told everything about his own special involvement with Jesus; and the amount of this kind of involvement that does appear in 1:16–17, 29–31, 36; 3:16; 5:37; 8:29, 32–33; 9:2, 5; 10:28; 11:21; 13:3; 14:29–31, 33–42, 54, 66–72; 16:7 agrees well enough with a Petrine origin of Mark's materials to support such an origin[54]

We have already noted the lack of evidence for an anti-Gnostic thrust in the pre-Papian tradition. The Gospel of Mark does not seem especially suitable to anti-Gnostic use anyway. Tending in the opposite direction are the supernatural powers of Mark's Jesus, the transfiguration, Jesus' dying in a manner which evokes the declaration that he is God's Son, the emptiness of the tomb, and more generally the element of secrecy. Moreover, Papias's elder defends Mark against attack rather than using Mark as a weapon of attack. Nor does Papias shift the elder's tone from defensive to offensive. In fact, Papias's stated preference for a living and surviving voice over books (Eusebius, *Hist. eccl.* 3.39.3–4) makes doubtful that he would have had any interest in elevating the Gospel of Mark from a nonapostolic book to a derivatively apostolic one. We do better, then, to regard 1 Pet 5:13 as supporting the Petrine and Roman traditions about Mark rather than as the foundation on which those traditions were fabricated. Further support for the Petrine side of the pre-Papian tradition, i.e., for Mark's writing down the reminiscences of Peter, derives from the unlikelihood that the Gospel of Mark, having been incorporated into the Gospels of Matthew and Luke,

---

[52] R. Feldmeier in M. Hengel's *Studies*, 59–60. For the good, see 1:16–17; 5:37; 8:29; 9:2 with 9:1; 10:28 with 10:29–31; 11:21; 13:3–4 with 13:5–37, esp. 9–13, 21–23, 37; 14:72; 16:7.

[53] See R. H. Gundry, *Matthew* (2d ed.; Grand Rapids: Eerdmans, 1994), 299–300, 330–36, 355–57, and the standard commentaries on Luke, ad loc.

[54] Cf. the ease with which C. H. Turner is able to turn Mark's "they" into a Petrine "we" (in *JTS* os 25 [1923–24]: 377–86; 26 [1924–25]: 225–40 and in *A New Commentary on Holy Scripture: New Testament* [ed. C. Gore et al.; New York: Macmillan, 1929], 48–49, 54; also J. K. Elliott, *The Language and Style of the Gospel of Mark: An Edition of C. H. Turner's "Notes on Marcan Usage" Together with Other Comparable Studies* [NovTSup 71; Leiden: E. J. Brill, 1993], 36–52; cf. T. W. Manson, *Studies in the Gospels and Epistles* [ed. M. Black; Manchester: Manchester University Press, 1962], 40–43).

would have survived independently except for a primitive knowledge of its Petrine background. For Q, likewise incorporated into Matthew and Luke but apparently lacking a Petrine background, did not survive independently. Nor is anyone likely to have deduced from Mark that Peter stands behind this Gospel.[55]

All in all, then, the pre-Papian tradition looks very early and apostolically Johannine. You cannot get very much older and better than that.

---

[55] F. C. Grant, *The Earliest Gospel* (New York: Abingdon, 1943), 36–37.

4. On The Secret Gospel of Mark

In 1973 Morton Smith published and discussed what he argued to be an authentic letter written to one Theodore by Clement of Alexandria (*flor.* A.D. 180–20).[1] Theodore wants to know whether all the materials in a Carpocratian version of Mark are truly present in a secret version of Mark (from here on referred to as *SGM* for the Secret Gospel of Mark) used in the church at Alexandria, Egypt. The Carpocratians were a Gnostic sect reputed to engage in sexual immorality.[2] According to the putative letter of Clement, Mark wrote a public Gospel, probably canonical Mark, during Peter's stay in Rome, but after Peter's martyrdom took his own notes and Peter's to Alexandria, where he wrote an expanded, secret Gospel (*SGM*). The letter goes on to quote two sections of *SGM*, the first (*SGM* 1) a story of Jesus' raising from the dead a rich young man who then pleads to be with Jesus, keeps Jesus in his house for six days, receives a command from him, comes to Jesus in the evening wearing a linen cloth on his naked body, and throughout that night listens to Jesus teach the mystery of God's kingdom. The letter locates this section between Mark 10:34 and 35 and denies that it includes the Carpocratian phrase "naked [man] with naked [man]" and other, unquoted Carpocratian materials that Theodore has asked about. The second, shorter section (*SGM* 2) is said to follow Mark 10:46a and to record Jesus' nonwelcome in Jericho of the rich young man's sister and mother plus Salome.

Questions have been raised about the authenticity of Clement's letter; and Smith's interpretation of the putative letter, including a dating of canonical Mark after SGM, has received extensive review.[3] Still needed, however, is scrutiny of

---

[1] M. Smith, *Clement of Alexandria and a Secret Gospel of Mark* (Cambridge, Mass.: Harvard University Press, 1973).

[2] See F. F. Bruce, *The "Secret" Gospel of Mark* (Ethel M. Wood Lecture; London: Athlone, 1974), 16–18, for the accuracy of the Carpocratians' reputation.

[3] See the bibliography in *Protocol of the Center for Hermeneutical Studies in Hellenistic and Modern Culture* (Colloquy 18; Berkeley, Calif.: The Center for Hermeneutical Studies in Hellenistic and Modern Culture, 1976): 72–73, and the whole of Colloquy 18. For a more up-to-date bibliography see S. G. Brown, "On the Composition History of the Longer ("Secret") Gospel of Mark," *JBL* 122 (2003): 89–90 nn. 2–3, to which add R. M. Price, "Second Thoughts on the Secret Gospel," *BBR* 14 (2004): 127–32. Price's own view is so highly speculative as to be untestable. Notable in favor of authenticity are C. W. Hedrick with N. Olympiou, "Secret Mark: New Photographs, New Witnesses," *The Fourth R: An Advocate for Religious Literacy* 13 (2000): 3–17; C. W. Hedrick, "The Secret Gospel of Mark: Stalemate in the Academy," *JECS* 11 (2003): 133–45; G. G. Strousma, "Comments on Charles Hedrick's Article: A Testi-

two attempts besides Smith's to make canonical Mark postdate *SGM*, one by
H. Koester[4] and another by J. D. Crossan, both of whom assume authenticity.[5] I
leave aside a further attempt by H.-M. Schenke as largely dependent on
Koester's work, though with some revision.[6] Koester argues not only that *SGM*
predates canonical Mark but also that a proto-Mark predates even *SGM* and that
Matthew and Luke redacted different versions of proto-Mark, Luke the original
version, Matthew a longer version containing the material we find in
Mark 6:45–8:26. Thus we should speak of Matthew's great addition rather than
of Luke's great omission and even then only in terms of Matthew's fidelity to his
source. *SGM* represents a less thorough redaction of proto-Mark in its longer
version. The Carpocratians then redacted *SGM*. Canonical Mark came through
another, later redaction of *SGM*, mainly by way of omitting the story of the rich
young man whom Jesus raised from the dead and the sequel to that story in
Jesus' nonwelcome of the women. Carpocratian use of *SGM* prompted these
omissions. Finally, canonical Mark was expanded by the various additions of the
short ending, the long ending, and the Freer Logion. For the lateness of canonical Mark and its nonuse by Matthew and Luke, Koester argues from the failure of
canonical Mark to be certainly quoted till the second half of the first century;
from the nonappearance of canonical Mark in the papyri till the mid-third century; from textual instability at the end of canonical Mark; from Luke's apparent
noninclusion of Mark 6:45–8:26 as against Matthew's including all of it except
Mark 8:22–26; from sentences and small pericopes in canonical Mark that have
no parallels in Matthew and Luke; from apparent remnants in canonical Mark of
an expansion of proto-Mark in *SGM*, i.e., from remnants of the story about the
rich young man; from canonical Markan phrases and terms that differ from Matthew and Luke; and from other links connecting canonical Mark to *SGM* but distinguishing it from Matthew and Luke.

---

mony," *JECS* 11 (2003): 147–53; and, in some doubt of authenticity, B. D. Ehrman, "Response
to Charles Hedrick's Stalemate," *JECS* 11 (2003): 155–63.

[4] H. Koester, "History and Development of Mark's Gospel (From Mark to *Secret Mark* and
'Canonical' Mark)," in *Colloquy on New Testament Studies* (ed. B. C. Corley; Macon, Ga.:
Mercer University Press, 1983), 35–57; idem, "The Text of the Synoptic Gospels in the Second
Century," in *Gospel Traditions in the Second Century* (ed. W. L. Petersen; Christianity and Ju-
daism in Antiquity 3; Notre Dame: University of Notre Dame, 1989), 19–37, esp. 34–36; idem,
Ancient Christian Gospels (London: SCM, 1990), 275–86 and esp. 293–303.

[5] J. D. Crossan, *Four Other Gospels* (Minneapolis: Winston, 1985), 91–121; idem, *The Cross
That Spoke* (San Francisco: Harper & Row, 1988), 283–84; idem, "Thoughts on Two Extra-
canonical Gospels," *Semeia* 49 (1990): 155–68; idem, *The Historical Jesus* (San Francisco:
Harper, 1991), 328–32, 411–16, 429–30.

[6] H.-M. Schenke, "The Mystery of the Gospel of Mark," *SecCent* 4 (1984): 65–82. See also
M. Meyer, "The Youth in the Secret Gospel of Mark," *Semeia* 49 (1990): 129–53 with criticism
by J. D. Crossan in the same issue, pp. 161–65; Meyer, "The Youth in Secret Mark and the Beloved Disciple in John," in *Gospel Origins and Christian Beginnings* (ed. James E. Goehring et
al.; Sonoma, Calif.: Polebridge, 1990), 94–105.

D. Peabody has criticized Koester's arguments from the standpoint of Mark's dependence on Matthew and Luke, i.e., from the standpoint of the Griesbach or two-Gospel hypothesis.[7] Those arguments also need criticism from the standpoint of the Mark-Q hypothesis. Though some pieces of evidence that Luke used Matthew as a secondary source will surface in the following discussion, limitation of space does not allow a full detailing of such evidence.[8] Thus many of the criticisms will leave Luke out of account and concentrate on Mark and Matthew.

Koester's theory requires a very late date for canonical Mark. Carpocrates flourished during Hadrian's reign (A.D. 117–138); so according to the theory, canonical Mark has to postdate the time within or after this period that the Carpocratians began to use *SGM* for their own purposes. That canonical Mark is not certainly quoted till the second half of the first century and not represented in the papyri till the mid-third century does not necessitate or favor such a late date, however. These phenomena are just as well explained by Mark's rough style, which Papias's elder felt obliged to defend (Eusebius, *Hist. eccl.* 3.39.15), and comparative brevity, which made Mark a poor relative of Matthew, Luke, and John. Nor does the later, known textual evolution of canonical Mark necessitate or favor an earlier, unknown textual evolution. For canonical Mark may provide the starting point of textual evolution as easily as lie along its path, especially since the abruptness of the ending at 16:8 (if that verse does mark the original ending of the Gospel) or the loss of the original ending (if at first the Gospel went beyond 16:8) explains the subsequent textual evolution so adequately that no recourse to a tradition of earlier textual evolution is needed.[9] So far as the earlier material in Mark 6:54–8:26 is concerned, it is just as easy to think that its repetitiveness, to which Koester himself points, led Luke to omit it as to think that a revised version of a proto-Mark added it to an original version of proto-Mark. The word-statistics offered to support such an addition are unimpressive.

Koester seems to step on firmer ground when he comes to sentences, small pericopes, and various remnants of *SGM* that appear in canonical Mark but have no parallels in Matthew and Luke. But these largely omissive agreements of Mat-

---

[7] D. Peabody, "The Late Secondary Redaction of Mark's Gospel and the Griesbach Hypothesis: A Response to Helmut Koester," in *Colloquy on New Testament Studies* (ed. B. C. Corley; Macon, Ga.: Mercer University Press, 1983), 87–132.

[8] But see R. H. Gundry, *Matthew* (2d ed.; Grand Rapids: Eerdmans, 1994), 682, s.v. "Luke's being influenced by Matthew"; idem, "Matthean Foreign Bodies in Agreements of Luke with Matthew against Mark: Evidence That Luke Used Matthew," in *The Four Gospels 1992* (ed. F. Van Segbroeck et al.; BETL 100; Leuven: Leuven University Press, 1992), 2:1467–95; idem, "A Rejoinder on Matthean Foreign Bodies in Luke 10,25–28," *ETL* 71 (1995): 139–50; idem, "The Refusal of Matthean Foreign Bodies to be Exorcised from Luke 9,22; 10,25–28," *ETL* 75 (1999): 104–22.

[9] For a loss of Mark's original ending see R. H. Gundry, *Mark* (Grand Rapids: Eerdmans, 1993), 1009–21, esp. 1009–12, and N. C. Croy, *The Mutilation of Mark's Gospel* (Nashville, Ky.: Abingdon, 2003), who argues also (and less convincingly) for "frontal damage" to Mark's text.

thew and Luke against canonical Mark are better explained as redactions of canonical Mark. For however one explains the agreements of Matthew and Luke
against canonical Mark, these agreements fall into patterns traceable elsewhere
in Matthew, most of the time without Luke's agreement against Mark and often
in Q-materials and materials peculiar to Matthew as well. So unless proto-Mark
exercised so overpowering an influence on Matthew that he redacted Q and materials peculiar to his Gospel in servile imitation of an already revised proto-
Mark, his and Luke's dependence on successive versions of a proto-Mark does
not provide an explanation of all the phenomena that require explanation. By
casting our net more widely than Koester has done we will see how Matthean redaction of canonical Mark better explains all those phenomena. To follow the
order of Koester's discussion will make for easier comparison with his treatment.

Both Matthew and Luke omit the saying about the humanitarian purpose of
the Sabbath (Mark 2:27a) but reproduce the one about the Son of Man's lordship over the Sabbath (Mark 2:27b) and do so in a word order that disagrees
with Mark yet not with each other. But Matthew constantly pares down non-
christological materials, expands christological materials, and does so without
Luke's agreement against Mark (see, e.g., the unique expansions in Matt 3:14–
15; 11:28–30; the unique omissions in 9:1–8, omissions that let Jesus' authority
to forgive sins stand out the more; and in 21:9 the unique addressing of hosanna
to Jesus as "the Son of David"). On the other hand, Luke elsewhere adds rather
than subtracts humanitarianism (see, e.g., Luke 7:11–17; 13:10–17; 17:11–19).
So we do better to think that here Matthew is redacting canonical Mark and influencing Luke than to think that Matthew and Luke depend on different versions of a proto-Mark that happen to agree at this point.

Mark's parable of the growing seed (4:26–29) is not omitted by Matthew as
well as Luke, as Koester argues to support dependence on proto-Mark; nor in
the strict sense is it replaced by the parable of the tares (Matt 13:24–30). Rather,
Matthew uses the parable of the growing seed to help create the parable of the
tares, which is his conflation of the parables of the sower and of the growing
seed plus a reminiscence of John the Baptist's preaching (cf. Matt 3:12). The
reason for this conflation is simple: "by itself" and "how, he does not know" in
the parable of the growing seed do not fit Matthew's stressing human responsibility and the necessity of understanding, or knowledge, for true discipleship
(13:13–15 et passim). So his concern over the mixed multitude in the professing
church of his day takes over to produce a new parable.

In the pericope about the great commandments (Mark 12:28–34; Matt 22:34–
40; Luke 10:25–28) Matthew and Luke agree against Mark in omitting the
Shema, the scribe's compliment of Jesus, and the repetition of the commandments. On the other hand, Luke's "lawyer" agrees with canonical Mark's
"scribe" against Matthew's "Pharisees"; and Luke agrees with canonical Mark

against Matthew also in having the scribe, or lawyer, recite the commandments and in having Jesus compliment him. Matthew omits the Shema to arrive as quickly as possible at the commandments. His battle against antinomianism often leads him to stress commandments, as in the Q-section at 5:17–20 but without the agreement of Luke 16:16–17 and as in his unique form of the Great Commission (28:18–20). Furthermore, he is more interested in trinitarianism, again as in his unique form of the Great Commission, than in the monotheism of "Hear, O Israel, the Lord our God is one Lord"; and he cuts the story short to leave the stress on obeying the whole of the Law, not just part of it (again as in 5:17–20 but not the present Lukan parallel), and to put the Pharisees, whom he has characteristically imported into the passage, in a bad light (as often elsewhere in his Gospel, including both Q-passages and unique passages in chs. 3, 5, 23, and 27). Should we expect the evangelist who constructs a sevenfold woe against the scribes and Pharisees (ch. 23) to take over a scribe's complimenting Jesus and Jesus' reciprocal compliment even though this evangelist's copy of Mark had both compliments? Hardly!

Koester argues that *SGM* 2 provides an original link between Mark 10:46a and b, the expurgation of which link produced an awkward text in canonical Mark. The link consists in an incident that happens in Jericho, whereas canonical Mark mentions entrance into Jericho only to have Jesus leave without having done anything there. But since the healing of blind Bartimaeus takes place on the road from Jericho the mention of arrival in Jericho looks suitable, especially if Jesus and the Twelve spent the Sabbath there, having arrived on Friday and leaving on Palm Sunday morning so as to arrive in Jerusalem late that Sunday afternoon. Besides, this is not the only passage in which Mark has Jesus going somewhere but not doing anything while there. In 7:31 he goes to Sidon and the Sea of Galilee and in 11:11b to Bethany but Mark associates no incident with either of these visits – and we do not hypothesize an expurgation of earlier materials. To double the blind man, Matthew omits Bartimaeus's name. Luke's concurrence with the omission shows Matthean influence because he writes of only one blind man and therefore has no reason to omit the name.[10] Recourse to a proto-Mark is otiose.

Mark's "the gospel of God" (1:15) drops out of Matt 4:17 because of the following substitute regarding repentance and the nearness of the kingdom. This substitute has the purpose of drawing Jesus and John the Baptist together as co-preachers of repentance and the kingdom (cf. Matt 3:1–2 with 4:17 and Matthew's correlating Jesus and John the Baptist in a number of passages).[11] Concerning Mark 8:35 and Matt 16:25, Matthew omits "and the gospel" to concentrate attention on Jesus, as often, and to make "on account of me" correspond exactly to Matt 5:11; 10:18, 39. Luke's agreeing with the omission despite his

---

[10] Gundry, *Matthew*, 176–77.
[11] Gundry, *Matthew*, 649, s.v. "John the Baptist parallel Jesus."

lacking parallels to the phrase "on account of me" in Matthew's earlier passages argues for Matthew's influencing him here. In Matt 19:29 as compared with Mark 10:29, Matthew's exchanging "the gospel" for "my name" is to be expected since he inserts ὄνομα, "name," five times in shared pericopes and uses the word five more times in unique pericopes.

In Mark 1:21–28 it is easier to think that the story, complete with the reference to "a new teaching with authority" (v. 27), is meant by Mark to illustrate Jesus' "teaching as one having authority" (v. 22), the repetitiveness in v. 27 being designed to keep Mark's audience from missing the illustrative connection, than to see a post-Matthean addition in v. 27. Luke does *not* agree with Matthew's omission of "a new teaching with authority" (see Luke 4:36); and Matthew's omission is part of a far larger omission of the whole story, which he omits in favor of an editorial emphasis on Jesus' didactic authority in the Sermon on the Mount (Matt 7:28–29 par. Mark 1:22).

Jesus' teaching a crowd by the sea in Mark 2:13 may seem "entirely gratuitous between the story of the healing of the paralytic (Mk 2:1–12) and the account of the call of Levi (Mk 2:14)" (so Koester), but it does not follow that the lack of this teaching in Matt 9:9; Luke 5:27 implies its redactional addition in a later version of Mark. Again, Matthew's omission is part of a larger omission; for Matthew omits the entirety of Mark 2:13, not just Jesus' teaching a crowd by the sea; and Matthew does so because he has inserted "the crowds" into the immediately preceding verse (contrast Matt 9:8 with Mark 2:12; Luke 5:26) and will yet introduce other elements of Mark 2:13 into Matt 13:1–2 to compensate for the present omission.[12] Compensations for earlier omissions are a regular feature of his style.[13] Luke 5:27 disagrees with Matthew in taking over part of Mark 2:13 and omits the rest of it without having Matthew's reasons for omission. All in all, then, the evidence does not point to Matthean and Lukan dependence on a proto-Mark, but to Matthean and Lukan dependence on canonical Mark and secondary, partial dependence of Luke on Matthew.

At Matt 13:1 "was sitting" replaces Jesus' teaching in Mark 4:1–2 because as yet no audience has appeared. Nevertheless, sitting – the posture of a Jewish teacher – connotes didactic authority, indirectly reflects Jesus' teaching in Mark's version, and thus eliminates the need to posit a proto-Mark that lacked the element of teaching. "Beside the sea" appears in Matthew as well as in canonical Mark; so its absence from Luke 8:4 cannot argue for a proto-Mark lacking it. Furthermore, Luke's agreement with canonical Mark's singular "a crowd" against Matthew's plural "crowds" argues for dependence on canonical Mark rather than for codependence with Matthew on a proto-Mark; and Jesus' teaching while seated in a boat at Luke 5:1–3, which has no other synoptic par-

---

[12] Gundry, *Matthew*, 165–66, 251–52.
[13] Gundry, *Matthew*, 649, s.v. "Compensation."

allel, suggests that Luke does not really agree with Matthew against Mark in this respect. That is to say, Luke 8:4 drops Jesus' teaching while seated in a boat beside the sea because Luke 5:1–3 has already included this element, not because Luke 8:4 depends with Matt 13:1 on a proto-Mark. Matthew 13:1 and Luke 8:4 have different reasons to omit the teaching in Mark 4:1–2. The teaching in Mark 6:30 looks like an original corrolary to the proclamation in Mark 6:12, not like a redactional addition to a proto Mark. Yet again, the omission of the teaching just after Matt 14:12 and in Luke 9:10a hardly counts as an agreement against Mark 6:30 that would argue in favor of common dependence on a proto-Mark; for Luke takes over the rest of Mark 6:30 but Matthew omits the entirety of Mark 6:30–31 except for transmuting Mark 6:30 into an announcement by the disciples of John the Baptist that John has been executed.[14]

Matthew 16:21 exchanges διδάσκειν, "to teach," in Mark 8:31 for δεικ-νύειν, "to show," to keep the former for public teaching and the latter for private instruction (cf. the private audiences in Matt 4:8; 8:4). In Luke 9:22 εἰπών, "saying," disagrees with Matthew as much as with Mark and therefore does not support common dependence of Matthew and Luke on a proto-Mark (cf. Luke 24:7). Matthew 17:22 and Luke 9:43 do agree against Mark 9:31 in not saying that Jesus "was teaching"; but the unique command in Luke 9:44a, "You – put these words in your ears," looks like compensation for an omission rather than like codependence with Matthew on a proto-Mark that lacked Jesus' teaching here. Against such codependence we have the several agreements of Luke 9:43b–45 with Mark 9:30–32 against Matt 17:22–23 in having "his disciples," their failure to understand Jesus' prediction of the passion and resurrection, and the disciples' fearing to ask him about it, all of which Matthew lacks. The agreement of Luke 18:33 with Mark 10:34 in ἀναστήσεται, "will rise up" (see also Luke 24:7), over against ἐγερθήσεται, "will be raised," in Matt 20:19 favors that the earlier agreement of Matt 16:21 with Luke 9:22 in having ἐγερθῆναι instead of the ἀναστῆναι of Mark 8:31 came by way of conforming canonical Mark's verb to other traditions (see 1 Cor 15:4 for an example earlier than Mark), including Mark's own account of the passion (14:28) and resurrection (16:6), not from a proto-Mark having the other verb, especially since Matthew writes the other verb eleven times where synoptic parallels lack it and eight more times in pericopes peculiar to his Gospel. The agreement of Matt 16:21; 20:19 and Luke 9:22; 18:33 in "on the third day" (see also Matt 17:23; Luke 24:7) against "after three days" in Mark 8:31; 10:34 (see also 9:31) is explained much more easily and economically as an elimination of the apparent discrepancy between "after three days" and the discovery of the empty tomb on the Sunday morning following the Friday of Jesus' death than as code-

---

[14] Gundry, *Matthew*, 289.

pendence on a proto-Mark.[15] How unlikely that canonical Mark would change an original, easy, and widespread "on the third day" (again see esp. 1 Cor 15:4) to a problematic "after three days"! Both Matt 16:21–22 and Luke 9:20 lack the plainness of Jesus' speech that Mark 8:32 mentions. But Matthew omits it because it makes Peter's obtuseness inexcusable. This omission lightens the onus on Peter. As is well known, Matthew often ameliorates or erases the misunderstanding of disciples.[16] Here Luke goes even further by erasing also Peter's rebuke of Jesus and Jesus' counter rebuke. No need to hypothesize a proto-Mark to account for these developments.

Matthew 19:2 omits Jesus' teaching in Mark 10:1 because Matthew has just devoted to Jesus' instructions the whole of his ch. 18, about the latter three quarters of it unparalleled in Mark. Now Matthew wants authentication of those instructions (cf. the sequence of instructions and miracles in chs. 5–7 and 8–9); so he substitutes ἐθεράπευσεν, "he healed," a favorite of his that he inserts ten times into paralleled pericopes. The same substitution of healing for teaching takes place in Matt 14:14 despite the underlying agreement of Luke 9:11 ("he was speaking to them about the kingdom of God") with Mark 6:34 ("he began to teach them much"). The fact that Luke 9:11 also agrees with Matt 14:14 in the mention of healing favors a drawing on Matthew as well as on canonical Mark, but codependence with Matthew on a proto-Mark that mentioned only the healing would not explain Luke's underlying agreement with Mark on Jesus' verbal ministry. The absence of a Lukan parallel to Mark 10:1; Matt 19:2 deprives Koester of a possible argument from agreement against Mark at that point.

In Mark 6:34 Jesus' compassion leads to a comparison of the crowd with shepherdless sheep and a statement about his teaching. But Matthew has already used this comparison in 9:36 and has devoted most of ch. 13 to parables. He did mention the healing as well as teaching ministry of Jesus in 9:35, however. So in 14:14 (par. Mark 6:34) Matthew omits the already used comparison of the crowd to shepherdless sheep and exchanges teaching for healing (cf. 19:2 with Mark 10:1). Luke's similarity to Matthew in these respects, along with agreements of Matthew and Luke against Mark earlier in the passage, suggests some secondary influence of Matthew on Luke; for a comparison between the crowds and shepherdless sheep failed to appear in Luke's parallel to Matthew 9:36, i.e., in Luke 8:1. Hence Luke does not have Matthew's reason to omit the comparison here and seems to have no reason of his own. Similarly the lack of a reference to Jesus' healing people in Luke's parallel to Matt 9:35 – again in Luke 8:1 – takes away the association which in Matthew triggers the

---

[15] On the apparent discrepancy, see Gundry, *Mark*, , 430, 447–48.

[16] Elsewhere Matthew increases the onus on Peter (see below, pp. 118, 124), but in this passage Peter represents the rest of the disciples, so that Matthew does the opposite.

exchange of teaching for healing. That Jesus' speaking about the kingdom of
God in Luke 9:11 looks much more like Jesus' teaching in Mark 6:34 than like
his healing in Matt 14:14 disfavors Matthean and Lukan use of a proto-Mark
which lacked teaching at this point.

Matthew 21:13 subtracts Jesus' teaching from Mark 11:17 to emphasize the
following quotations of the OT (which Matthew likes more than any of the other
evangelists do) and to make those quotations entirely accusatory, not at all didactic (cf. Matthew's intensifying the guilt of Jewish leaders throughout his
Gospel and esp. in this its last part). That Luke 19:46 agrees with Matthew's subtraction of Jesus' teaching favors Matthean influence, for elsewhere Luke does
not exhibit so much as Matthew does the tendencies which have led to the present subtraction. Matthew 22:41 subtracts Jesus' teaching from Mark 12:35 because Matthew has shifted the audience from a large crowd (cf. Mark 12:38), for
whom teaching is appropriate, to Pharisees, for whom in view of his ubiquitous
anti-Pharisaic tendency a confrontal question designed to embarrass is more appropriate: "What seems correct *to you*" (Matt 21:42). Luke 20:41 joins Matthew
in the subtraction of Jesus' teaching and does so for the similar reason that Luke
has turned the scribes into the addressees (cf. Luke 20:39 and contrast "How
come *the scribes* say ...?" in Mark 12:35 with the question to the scribes in
Luke 20:41, "How come *they* [people in general] say ...?"). But Luke's retention
of the scribes, though in another capacity, shows that he is working with Mark as
well as with Matthew rather than drawing independently from Matthew on a
proto-Mark; for the scribes make no appearance at all in Matthew's version. The
agreement of Matt 23:1–2 with Luke 20:45 in subtracting "the teaching" of
Jesus from Mark 12:38 derives from the immediately foregoing circumstances
that we have just noted for the passages. Similarly, Matt 23:1–2 subtracts "the
teaching" from Mark 12:38 to prepare for substitution of a description of and
woes to the scribes and Pharisees (Matt 23:2–36) instead of a warning against
them (Mark 12:38b–40). Furthermore, Matthew will compensate for the subtraction by introducing designations of Jesus as "teacher" and "instructor" in
23:8, 10; and the substitution in Matt 23:1 of ἐλάλησεν, "talked," which
Luke 20:45 does not share, displays a favorite verb of Matthew, one that he inserts into paralleled pericopes thirteen times and uses once in a pericope peculiar
to his Gospel. The added participle λέγων, "saying," contrasts with finite forms
of λέγω in Mark 12:38; Luke 20:45 and occurs as an insertion sixty-one times in
Matthew, as part of unique pericopes twenty-three times. Thus we have Matthean redaction, not dependence on a proto-Mark.

In Mark 4:11–12 Koester claims to detect an awkwardness that betrays earlier
textual evolution. The awkwardness consists in a disparity between the plural of
parables and the singular of mystery, which appears also in *SGM* 1, and in the
giving of the mystery itself as opposed to the gift of knowing the mysteries in
Matt 13:11; Luke 8:10. Of course, *SGM* 1 may echo Mark 4:11–12 rather than

4:11–12's echoing a proto-Mark; and the parables are not the mystery itself in 4:11–12. They are the means by which the mystery is communicated to insiders and obscured from outsiders. To be "given" the mystery is not awkward if by definition "mystery" includes revelation, i.e., if a mystery is a secret revealed to insiders. Nor does the singular of "mystery" in 4:11 betray any awkwardness. It matches the singular of "kingdom": the kingdom (singular) is a mystery (singular). Matt 13:11 pluralizes "mystery" out of the thought that different parables exhibit different facets of the kingdom (so also *Gos. Thom.* 62, in likely dependence on Matthew). In accordance with this thought Matthew multiplies the parables of the kingdom (ch. 13). The correlation of the one mystery with the one gospel in Eph 6:19 has little if any bearing on Mark 4:11; for here exists, as we have just seen, a correlation between the one mystery and the one kingdom. And as is well known, Matthew repeatedly adds the element of knowledge, or understanding, to Mark, usually without agreement from Luke.[17] The present addition does not need to echo a proto-Mark, then; and the unusual agreement of Luke against Mark may arise by secondary influence from Matthew. Koester would have to show that in every passage where Matthew has knowledge and understanding and canonical Mark does not, canonical Mark has denuded the text of *SGM* and that most of the time Luke has independently and at corresponding locations done the same thing to an original proto-Mark. Otherwise it is easier to think that Matt 13:11 adds knowing as Matthew does elsewhere.

In 20:22–23 Matthew omits the baptism consisting in Jesus' death (Mark 10:38–39; cf. Luke 12:50) so as not to detract from his earlier portrayal of Jesus' baptism in water as a proper example for would-be disciples to follow. In Matt 3:13 Jesus comes "to the Jordan … to be baptized." Both expressions are peculiar to Matthew and highlight that Jesus had his own baptism in mind when going to the Jordan. The point is reinforced by Matthew's inserting 3:14–15, also peculiar to his Gospel. There Jesus insists on getting baptized against John the Baptist's objection and calls baptism "the fulfillment of all righteousness," i.e., the doing of what is right. As a result, *"This is* [instead of 'You are'] my beloved Son, in *whom* [instead of 'in *you*'] I am well pleased" sets forth Jesus as a proper example to be followed in baptism (cf. 28:19). That is the only baptism of Jesus which Matthew is interested in. Romans 6:1–11 presupposes that Jesus' death is a figurative baptism making believers' baptism a participation in his death.

Matthew 17:14–21 omits most of Mark 9:14b–16 because the subject matter of the argument between the scribes and the disciples lacks specificity and because the crowd's amazement at seeing Jesus lacks a readily apparent reason. Matthew 17:14–21 also omits Mark 9:21, 22b–24 and parts of Mark 9:25–27, 28 because Matthew has delayed the demonic element for later mention. Perhaps he also objects to the questioning of Jesus' ability and to the halting faith

---

[17] Gundry, *Matthew*, 650, s.v. "Understanding."

of the father (cf. Matthew's unique criticisms of "little faith" in 8:26; 14:31; 16:8; 17:20). Jesus' seeing the crowd running together in Mark drops out because of Jesus' and the disciples' coming to the crowd at the beginning of the story (Matt 17:14). In Matthew the demon exits without so much as a whimper (contrast Mark) to highlight the authority of Jesus (cf. Matt 28:18). Koester's own noting of the possible magical associations in Mark's (ἐκ)θαμβέομαι provides a possible reason for Matthew's and Luke's omission. It is gratuitous to think that deaf-muteness and epilepsy in Mark 9:25–27 exclude each other. Matthew 17:14–21 replaces "having a mute spirit" with "because he is epileptic and suffers badly" to unify the statement with the epileptic symptoms that Matthew sees in Mark's following descriptions. Such a literary unification, seen also in the frequent tightening up of parallelism, typifies Matthew's style. Since the terminology of death and resurrection recalls the terminology in which Jesus' death and resurrection are described (as Koester himself notes), the inference of a relation to *SGM* is again gratuitous.[18]

Matthew 20:17–19 omits the amazement and fear of the disciples as Jesus presses toward Jerusalem for martyrdom (Mark 10:32). Luke 18:31–34 makes the same omission. Matthew makes it because in his Gospel Jesus' disciples *do* understand his coming passion. In Matt 17:23, after the second complete passion-and-resurrection prediction, the clause "and they were exceedingly grieved" replaced "but they did not understand the saying and feared to ask him" (Mark 9:32). Their grief showed understanding – hence, the present omission. Luke's agreement in the omission shows secondary influence from Matthew; for Luke 18:34 uniquely adds a threefold statement of the disciples' ignorance, which apart from such influence should have caused Luke to retain the amazement and fear in Mark. Contrary to Koester's assertion, amazement at Jesus' going ahead makes good sense in the context of canonical Mark, where Jesuanic events are characteristically portrayed as numinous. In Mark 16:8, for example, we expect some joy and delight (as in Matt 28:8). Instead, we read of fear and trembling. Even Jesus' death by crucifixion is a numinous event, witnessed as such by a Roman centurion (Mark 15:37–39).

In its story of the youth whom Jesus raised, *SGM* seems to conflate νεανίσκος, "young man," in Matt 19:16–22, the look of love in Mark 10:17–22, and πλούσιος, "rich," in Luke 18:18–23. At least it is just as easy if not easier to think so as it is to posit a late redactor of Mark and equate him with the author of *SGM*. As often, Matthew's omitting the disciples' amazement at Jesus' teaching about wealth (cf. Matt 19:23 with Mark 10:23–24) protects the doctrine of understanding and knowledge as necessary ingredients of true discipleship. Invoking a late redactor to make an addition to canonical Mark overlooks a Mat-

---

[18] For further details and on Luke's agreements with Matthew against Mark, see Gundry, *Matthew*, 348–53.

thean trait that is much more widespread than the passages Koester makes the bases of his argument.

With regard to Mark 14:51–52, Koester considers it a remnant of the story concerning the young man whom Jesus raised in *SGM*, a story which *SGM* added to a proto-Mark but which was expurgated, except for this remnant, by the orthodox canonical Mark at an even later date. But why was the remnant of the story not expurgated along with the rest of it? Koester needs to answer this difficult question. But a convincing answer is made more difficult by the fact that the enigmatic character of Mark 14:51–52 left by itself would have provided a strong motive for deleting it at the same time that the raising of the young man was supposedly deleted (a point missed by Schenke when he weakly answers "the necessary and difficult question" by saying that the expurgator "no longer saw the connection between the two passages"[19]). It is easier to view Mark 14:51–52 as a foregleam of Jesus' resurrection,[20] to explain Matthew's and Luke's omissions of it as due to its irrelevance to their purposes, and to regard the additions in *SGM* as expansions of the sort we find everywhere in apocryphal literature.

In the passages discussed by Koester we have seen evidences of Matthew's secondary influence on Luke, detectable because the point on which Luke agrees with Matthew against Mark suits Matthew's interests and style but not Luke's. This particular phenomenon within the general phenomenon of Matthew's and Luke's agreements against Mark can be seen in a number of other passages not germane to Koester's discussion and not supportive of his thesis. Matthew's redaction of Mark and secondary influence on Luke therefore offer an explanation more comprehensive and less top-heavy than Koester's. Every other textual phenomenon to which Koester appeals can likewise be treated more adequately than by his theory.

J. D. Crossan also treats canonical Mark as a revision of *SGM*, but he goes on to argue that *SGM* 1 and 2 do not simply disappear from canonical Mark. Rather, they appear as dismembered elements scattered elsewhere in canonical Mark. The redactor of Mark, considered to be the same person as the one who redacted *SGM*, scatters these elements to offset Carpocratian corruption of his own *SGM* 1 and 2.

The general argument for this theory is that the dismembered elements do not fit the contexts to which they have been scattered and that Matthew, Luke, and modern students have consequently found it difficult to interpret these elements. More particularly, Crossan argues that since *SGM* reads "*he* comes into Jericho" in Mark 10:46a, "*they* come into Jericho" looks like a pluralization by canonical Mark. In the first place, however, the singular of Jesus' coming into Jericho in Clement's quotation of v. 46a may be influenced by the singular of

---

[19] Schenke, "Mystery," 77.
[20] Gundry, *Mark*, 861–63.

Jesus' going out of Jericho (v. 46b) or by the singular of his drawing near to Jericho in Luke 18:35[21] rather than by a hypothetical singular of Jesus' coming into Jericho in *SGM*. Moreover, a singular reading in *SGM* would say nothing about the chronological relation between *SGM* and canonical Mark. Had *SGM* come earlier, canonical Mark's deletion of *SGM* 2 would not have favored a switch to the plural; for the deletion would have given no cause for such a switch. Without *SGM* 2, on the contrary, the singular of Jesus' exit follows even more closely on the plural of his and the disciples' entrance. On the other hand, a plural reading of v. 46a in *SGM* would be no easier than the plural reading in canonical Mark. More difficult, rather; for though both have Jesus speaking to the Twelve in vv. 41–45, in *SGM* 2 the Twelve disappear and the young man (whose presence might justify the plural) is mentioned only obliquely whereas in canonical Mark v. 46a directly mentions the disciples right alongside Jesus.

Secondly and more importantly, the third person plural in v. 46a fits the third and first person plurals in vv. 32–33 ("they were going up to Jerusalem.... we are going up to Jerusalem") so nicely that even though Clement were following *SGM* in reading the singular it seems more likely that in v. 46a the third person plural, referring to Jesus and the Twelve, represents the original reading, changed to the singular by *SGM* to avoid awkwardness and confusion with *SGM*'s immediately following third person plural that refers entirely differently to the sister and mother of the young man plus Salome. Third person plurals with verbs of topographical movement in 11:1, 12a, 20, 27 further favor the originality of the same in 10:46a. The ease with which the shift to the singular in 10:46b can be explained (it prepares for Jesus' confrontation with Bartimaeus) makes that shift a nonargument for omission of *SGM* 2 by canonical Mark.[22]

Now we need to recognize that the position of *SGM* 2 presents exactly the kind of contextual problem for the greater earliness of *SGM* that Crossan tries to establish and use for his theory that dismembered elements of *SGM* are scattered throughout a later canonical Mark. Not only does *SGM*'s plural reference to the young man's sister and mother plus Salome jar against the immediately preceding and probably original plural reference to Jesus and the Twelve. But also the key statement in *SGM* 2, "and Jesus did not receive them," does not fit the immediate context. If the women had not received Jesus, *SGM* 2 would have provided the reason for his leaving Jericho in v. 46b. But the nonreception is the other way around.

We can explain the key statement only on distant contextual and extra-Markan grounds or by recourse to an abridgement of *SGM* 2. For example, a combination of Mark 15:40 and its parallel Matt 27:56 could make Salome the

---

[21] See Smith, *Clement*, 368–69, for Matthean and Lukan contaminations of Clement's quotations of Mark 10:17–31.

[22] Gundry, *Mark*, 599.

mother of James and John, who in Mark have recently asked for places of high honor and whose mother did the asking according to Matt 20:20. Her asking may prompt Jesus' nonreception; or, in reverse, his nonreception constitutes or confirms his denial of her request. Recourse to an abridgement of *SGM* 2, the missing part of which would theoretically provide the contextual point of Jesus' turning a cold shoulder to the women, is a counsel of despair, however. Clement's putative letter says that *SGM* 2 adds "only" what is then quoted. Hence Crossan is forced to consider *SGM* 2 expurgated even before canonical Mark is supposed to have expurgated it further. Not only does the necessity of adding an earlier expurgation threaten to bring down the hypothesis under its own weight, but also Jesus' nonreception of the women requires nothing more to understand the statement. We may want to know why he does not receive them, but in and of itself the statement carries a complete meaning. The supposition of an earlier expurgation of unknown additional material therefore grows out of the exigency of a theory, not out of the evidence at hand.[23]

Crossan thinks next that canonical Mark transfers "Bethany" from *SGM* 1 to 11:1, 11, 12; 14:3, and "house" from *SGM* 1 to 14:3. The awkward position of "Bethany" in 11:1 (contrast Luke 19:28–29; Matt 21:1) is supposed to support this transfer. But the awkwardness – if there is any – begins with the first position of Jerusalem! Actually, Mark will work backward quite logically and topographically from the destination, Jerusalem, through Bethphage, an intermediate point, to Bethany, the closest point.[24] It is hard to think that 11:11, 12; 14:3 originally had no name for the place where Jesus and the Twelve stayed outside Jerusalem. It is also hard to think that if these texts originally had no place name canonical Mark inserts it repeatedly rather than transferring it once. If the house in 14:3 will come from *SGM* 2, where will its owner Simon the leper come from? He does not appear in *SGM* 2. Are we to suppose that only Simon belonged to 14:3 from the start? If so, in what capacity besides owner of the house? And where besides his house did the anointing in 14:3 take place?

Canonical Mark is also supposed to transfer "'Son of David, have mercy on me.' But the disciples rebuked her" from *SGM* 1 to 10:47–48. Crossan argues this point from the awkwardness of the word order in 10:47: "Son of David, Jesus, have mercy on me." Since the request for sight will come only after a later question from Jesus in v. 51, Bartimaeus shouted only "Jesus!" in the earlier, secret version of v. 47. But this theory succeeds only in creating questions. What precedent is there for an address with the mere "Jesus"? Why would canonical Mark break up "Son of David" and "have mercy on me" and make them straddle "Jesus" rather than adding them as a unit after "Jesus" so as to produce a more

---

[23] Cf. R. Bauckham, "Salome the Sister of Jesus, Salome the Disciple of Jesus, and the Secret Gospel of Mark," *NovT* 33 (1991): 245–75.

[24] Gundry, *Mark*, 623–24.

normal word order (as in Luke 18:38)?[25] Why does "Jesus" not disappear, as in v. 48? In its specifying of the request for sight, v. 51 will go beyond the cry for mercy in vv. 47–48. Hence no redundancy will favor a later addition of that cry.

Yet again, Crossan thinks that canonical Mark transfers "rolled the stone from the door of the tomb" from *SGM* 1 to 16:3. But then we would expect canonical Mark to retain *Jesus'* rolling the stone from the door of the tomb, as in *SGM* 1. We would expect so especially because of the women's question in 16:3, "*Who* will roll the stone from the tomb for us?" Crossan takes the absence of this question in Matt 28:1; Luke 24:2 as evidence of an addition in Mark 16:3. But the absence in Matthew does not reflect the text of Mark used by Matthew. Rather, the question "drops out because [Matthew's] inserting the sealing of the stone and the guarding of the tomb [see 27:62–66, unique to Matthew] makes their [the women's] question senseless. Nobody would dare unseal the stone and roll it away for them. Because of the guard, nobody could."[26] And the question is not really absent in Luke 24:2. Rather, it is tucked into the comment that they "found the stone rolled away from the tomb," which chiastically conflates "from... the tomb" and "looking up they see that the stone is rolled away" in Mark 16:3 and 4, respectively. Within the text of Mark itself, the rolling of a stone to the door of the tomb in 15:46 prepares for and thus favors the originality of the question in 16:3. A transfer of the question from *SGM* 1 to 16:3 would probably have resulted only in a simple reference to the stone's having been rolled away as in 16:4, not in the women's questioning who will roll it away; for in *SGM* 1 rolling away the stone is not presented as a problem.

Supposedly, canonical Mark transfers Jesus' going into the tomb, where the young man was, from *SGM* 1 to 16:5 and transforms it into the women's going into the tomb of Jesus and seeing a young man. Luke 24:4 puts two men in the tomb – but for a redactional reason that Crossan himself notes in his references to Luke 9:30; Acts 1:10. So this difference from canonical Mark does not support a different text in an earlier version. Likewise unsupportive are the angel of the Lord and the happening of everything outside the tomb in Matt 28:2, for these differences from Mark are clearly redactional.[27] Crossan offers no possible reason for the putative transfer in canonical Mark. Without the women's going into the tomb of Jesus and seeing a young man, what would we suppose *SGM* had at this point that is not Lukan or Matthean redaction? What else did the women do, see, hear? These questions are pressing; for they deal in part with the very heart of the story, not with an unessential, possible add-on.

---

[25] See Gundry, *Mark*, 593–94, concerning a possible reason for the placement of "Son of David" before "Jesus."

[26] Gundry, *Matthew*, 586.

[27] Gundry, *Matthew*, 586–87.

Canonical Mark is further supposed to transfer "he raised him [by] grasping the [= his] hand" from *SGM* 1 to 1:31; 5:41; 9:27. Said to support this theory is the absence of the clause from Matt 8:15 par. Luke 4:39; Matt 17:18 par. Luke 9:42, though it is present in Matt 9:25 par. Luke 8:54. But the facts are different. There is no absence of the clause from Matt 8:15 par. Luke 4:39. Rather, Matt 8:15 changes the verb from active to passive (as in 9:25 vis-à-vis Mark 5:41) and the participle from "grasping" to "touching." Luke 4:39 changes grasping the hand to rebuking the fever, and raising to standing up. The absence in Matt 17:18 is part of a far larger omission-cum-summary of Mark 9:26b–27.[28] The same thing has happened in Luke 9:42–43, but with characteristically Lukan redaction. Even otherwise, if Matthew and Luke draw from canonical Mark rather than from *SGM*,[29] then the absence of the clause would be irrelevant to the question of the relation between canonical Mark and *SGM*. For the absence would be due to the influence of canonical Mark, not to the influence of *SGM*. On the other hand, if the absence were due to influence from *SGM*, why retention of the clause in Matt 9:25 par. Luke 8:54 (as recognized by Crossan) and in Matt 8:15 par. Luke 4:39 (as just recognized here)? Or if Matthew and Luke draw from both canonical Mark and *SGM*, then agreement with one or the other has no argumentive value. For nothing is falsifiable and therefore nothing verifiable when disagreement with the one can always be explained by dependence on the other. Further questions arise: What would motivate canonical Mark to retain and scatter the particular clause at issue but not others in *SGM*? What would motivate him not only to retain it but also to repeat it? What gesture or other means of healing is supposed instead of grasping and raising in a *SGM* earlier than canonical Mark? Is there good evidence for a more original gesture or other means?

In one respect Crossan disagrees with the foregoing criticisms by positing that when canonical Mark transfers the clause in question to 9:27 he also shifts other elements of *SGM* 1 by adding "since childhood" to 9:21 and the boy's becoming "as if dead, so that many were saying, 'He has died'" to 9:26. The absence of these elements in Matt 17:18 par. Luke 9:42 is cited in support. But we have already referred to an easier explanation, i.e., characteristically Matthean and Lukan redaction of canonical Mark. If canonical Mark has transferred the notion of youth from *SGM* 2 to 9:21, instead of ἐκ παιδιόθεν, "since childhood," in 9:21 we might expect ἐκ/ἀπὸ νεότητος, "since youth," to correspond to ὁ νεανίσκος, "the young man," in *SGM* 1. One also wonders whether the appearance of having died in 9:26 reflects very well the actuality of having died and the entombment that we read about in *SGM* 1. Furthermore, it would seem more likely that if canonical Mark were in the business of dismembering *SGM* 1

---

[28] See Gundry, *Matthew*, 351, for characteristically Matthean redaction.
[29] So Crossan, *Four Other Gospels*, 115, 119–20.

and scattering elements of it he would have put the young man's being raised from the dead in another story of healing rather than in the story of exorcism which 9:14–27 presents.

Next, canonical Mark is supposed to shift "the young man, gazing at him [Jesus], loved him… he was rich" from *SGM* 1 to 10:17–22, but with a change to "from my youth" and with a reversal that makes Jesus love the young man.[30] The transfer is also supposed to prompt addition of the young man's crestfallenness and sorrowful departure because of his having many acquisitions. But the rich man in 10:17–22 is not said to be young. He looks back on his youth. One could think that canonical Mark transforms the young man of *SGM* 1 into an adult to counter a Carpocratian pederastic interpretation of *SGM* 1, but to change the young man's loving Jesus to Jesus' loving an adult male would only expose the story to a different kind of homosexual interpretation – and a more highly charged one at that, because Jesus himself would become the initiator of homosexual love. It is hard to think that canonical Mark would blunder so badly against its own intention.

Canonical Mark is supposed to transfer "he [the young man] began to beseech him [Jesus] that he might be with him" from *SGM* 1 to 5:18. Matt 8:34 omits the statement, and Luke 8:38 rephrases it. But the plea in Mark 5:18 leads naturally into Jesus' refusal and commissioning of an ex-demoniac to go proclaim what the Lord has done for him (5:19). Without the plea the commission would be abrupt. Therefore an earlier absence of the plea seems unlikely. Other differences between *SGM* 1 and 5:1–20 increase the unlikelihood of a transfer: raising the dead versus casting out demons and Jesus' allowance of the plea to be with him versus his refusal of the plea. One could explain this last difference as stemming from canonical Mark's desire to guard against a Carpocratian homosexual interpretation, but then his blunder in making Jesus love the rich man in 10:21 stands out all the more. And what would canonical Mark do with Jesus' choosing the twelve apostles "in order that they might be with him" (3:14)? The absence of the plea to be with Jesus in Matt 8:34 belongs to a far larger redactional omission by Matthew[31] and therefore does not support an absence of the plea in an earlier version of Mark 5:18. Neither does the rephrasing of the plea in Luke 8:38 support absence; it only favors that Luke's copy of Mark had the plea.

Canonical Mark is supposed to transfer "they came into the house" from *SGM* 1 at least to 3:20 (if not also to 1:29; 2:15) to set up a rhythm of calling or visiting. Since a house appears to be forced on 3:20, as shown by the absence of 3:20–21 from Matthew and Luke, an earlier version of Mark must have lacked

---

[30] See Gundry, *Mark*, 554, for the probably physical connotation of loving as putting an arm around, patting, or such like.

[31] Gundry, *Matthew*, 161.

this addition from *SGM* 1. So runs Crossan's argument. But the coming together of a crowd is said to keep Jesus and the Twelve from being able to eat. Why then should it seem forced that Jesus goes into a house, apparently to eat? The frequency of Mark's references to Jesus' going into a house (see the concordance, s.v. οἰκία and οἶκος; cf. esp. 2:1–2) supports the originality of such an entry in 3:20. It is easily probable that Matthew and Luke omit Mark 3:20–21 because of the offensive charge that Jesus has gone berserk. Besides, Matthew immediately follows up the names of the Twelve (10:2–4 par. Mark 3:16–19) with their commission (10:5–42), which does not appear in Mark till much later (6:7–11). This clamping together of items separated in Mark makes it easy to omit what immediately follows the names of the Twelve in Mark, i.e., Mark 3:20–21. Luke finds it easy to do the same thing for the similar reason that he follows up the names of the Twelve (6:14–16) with the Sermon on the Plain, accompanied by healings (6:17–49). And in all probability, offence at the charge in Mark 3:20–21 that Jesus has gone berserk plays a part again.

Canonical Mark is supposed to transfer "after six days" from *SGM* 1 to 9:2. The unoriginality of the phrase in 9:2 is betrayed, argues Crossan, by its unclarity, which is betrayed in turn by "approximately eight days" in the parallel Luke 9:28. But "*approximately* (ὡσεί) eight days" does not clarify anything. And Matt 17:1 retains "after six days"; so Matthew seems to think Mark's phrase clear. "After six days" obviously means that six days after Jesus made the preceding statements the transfiguration occurred. The question whether the six days include or exclude the days of the statements and of the transfiguration has no bearing on the relation between canonical Mark and *SGM*, for the same sort of question attaches to the phrase in *SGM* 1: Does it include or exclude the days of coming to the young man's house and of Jesus' commanding him?

To avoid homosexuality, says Crossan, canonical Mark transfers "when evening arrived the young man comes to him wearing a linen cloth on his naked [body]" from *SGM* 1 to 14:51–52, where its awkwardness is shown by its absence from Matt 26:56 par. Luke 22:53. By contrast, the statement makes a quite natural reference in *SGM* 1 to a nude nocturnal baptism. For the sake of argument, let us grant that NT references to "taking off" and "putting on" (Gal 3:27; Eph 4:20–24; Col 3:8–14) reflect the practice of disrobing before baptism and re-robing after baptism rather than that those references generated the practice; and let us grant that for ritual reasons early Christian baptism was performed at night, though Acts 16:33 offers quite a different reason for the only NT example of nocturnal baptism and Hippolytus mentions baptism at dawn, not at night, and writes as late as the early third century (*Trad. Ap.* 21). Even granting these debatable assumptions, we have to ask why *SGM* 1 says not a syllable about baptism (Where is the water?) or about disrobing and re-robing (Where is the new garment?). We should note that against all synoptic evidence to the contrary the baptismal hypothesis requires that Jesus himself baptize the

young man (see also John 4:2, though some take it as a historically false qualification of 3:22; 4:1). We also need to know why canonical Mark would choose
the flight of the disciples as the event to which to transfer a young man's wearing a linen cloth on his naked body. To adopt Crossan's theory one has to suppose not only such a transfer but also Mark's fabrication of the young man's following with Jesus, of his being seized by Jesus' captors, and of his fleeing
naked – none of which is suggested by *SGM* 1 or, except for the fleeing, by the
context in canonical Mark. There, in canonical Mark, the young man's wearing
a linen cloth on his naked body prepares naturally for his fleeing naked out of
the grasp of his would be captors just as his fleeing and that of the disciples lead
naturally into Jesus' being taken away by himself.

The larger significance of the incident may not be immediately transparent,
but the contextual meaning of the narrative as such is crystal clear. It is in *SGM* 1,
not in 14:51–52, that contextual meaning as well as larger significance becomes
clouded. What is actually said in *SGM* 1 leaves entirely unclear even a superficial connection between wearing a linen cloth on a naked body and anything else
in the context. If, as Koester says, *SGM* had Jesus teaching the mystery of God's
kingdom in chs. 4 and 10 alike, then Jesus' teaching the young man "the mystery
of God's kingdom" can hardly count as a catechism leading to nude baptism; for
according to ch. 4 Jesus teaches this very mystery to a huge crowd that includes
outsiders. Never mind that he teaches it in such a way as to obscure it from the
outsiders. Baptismal catechism is not even addressed to outsiders. Nor does the
mystery of God's kingdom as taught in ch. 4 include moral instructions such as
characterize baptismal catechism. Matthew and Luke omit 14:51–52 probably
because they plan to replace "the young man" of Mark 16:1–8, who parallels the
one in 14:51–52, perhaps also because the incident does not suit their redactional
purposes or because its significance would escape their audiences.

Against the theory that Mark 10:13–45, including *SGM*, represents a lection
used at the nude nocturnal baptism of catechumens,[32] E. Best argues cogently
that the monotheistic confession in v. 18 is nowhere else associated with Christian baptism. Nor is the Decalogue, partly quoted in v. 19, till a post-Markan
date (cf. *Did.* 2:1–3). Christian baptism has never required prior riddance of all
one's worldly goods (v. 21; cf. vv. 28, 23–27). The rich man who goes away
downcast because he has many worldly goods (v. 22) makes a strange example
for baptizees. And the details of the passion-and-resurrection prediction
(vv. 33–34) are otiose in a baptismal confession.[33]

We may add to Best's arguments. The passion-and-resurrection prediction
defines in advance Jesus' baptism not as a rite – he has already undergone the
rite of baptism (1:9–11) – but as his suffering, to be shared by James and John

---

[32] Cf. Smith, *Clement*, 167–88.
[33] E. Best, *Disciples and Discipleship* (Edinburgh: T. & T. Clark, 1986), 83–86.

(see 10:35–40, which gives no hint that James and John have yet to undergo the rite – on the contrary, see John 1:29–42). One could argue that Jesus' prediction of suffering interprets the rite; but even in Rom 6:1–23, where Paul relates baptism to participation with Christ in his death, burial, and resurrection, the point has to do with morality, not with suffering. In *SGM*, moreover, Jesus relates his baptism of suffering to James and John, not to the young man with a linen cloth on his naked body. And σινδών, "a linen cloth," though used occasionally in noncanonical Christian literature for baptismal garb, had a wide variety of uses and so far as we can tell never turned into a technical term for baptismal garb. More seriously, since the young man comes to Jesus already wearing a σινδών, the baptismal hypothesis must treat it as the garment taken off before baptism to symbolize renunciation of the old life, not as the baptismal garment put on after baptism to symbolize new life in Christ. If in disagreement with Crossan one retains the originality of 14:51–52 as well as *SGM* 1, the baptismal hypothesis raises the question, Why is the young man still wearing the old garment in 14:51–52? Leaving the old garment in the clutches of Jesus' captors hardly represents baptism, a voluntary act, as though the baptism occurs symbolically in 14:51–52 rather than literally in *SGM* 1. For 14:27–31 has pre-interpreted the flight from Jesus' captors as scandalous. One may find a new garment of baptism in the στολή of the young man in Jesus' empty tomb (16:5).[34] One may even identify that young man with the young men of *SGM* and 14:51–52 (but not with the rich man who turns back from discipleship in 10:17–22, for he looks *back* on his youth whereas only Matt 19:20, omitting that look, turns him into a downcast *young* man for a contrast with the children who have just received Jesus' blessing – cf. also Matthew's insertion of children who praise Jesus in the temple [21:15–16]). It is certainly better not to equate the σινδών and the στολή; for στολή connotes a long formal robe such as scribes like to wear (12:38–39) whereas the earlier mentioned σινδών appears to be a mere piece of cloth, easily abandoned, or at most a scanty tunic, easily slipped out of. But στολή, like σινδών, though used occasionally in noncanonical Christian literature for baptismal garb, had a wide variety of uses and so far as we can tell never turned into a technical term for baptismal garb. And why the use for new life in Christ of a word whose only other occurrence in Mark has characterized the pompous and rapacious scribes? Why no young man's reaffirmation of the cross between scandalous flight and announcement of the resurrection (against the theory of Meyer that 16:1–8 presents a reaffirmation of baptismal loyalties after a forsaking of them in 14:51–52[35])?

---

[34] Cf. R. Scroggs and K. I. Groff, "Baptism in Mark: Dying and Rising with Christ," *JBL* 92 (1973): 531–48, though H. Fleddermann pertinently notes that the baptismal motif of dying and rising with Christ, as in Rom 6:1–11, occurs nowhere in Mark, not even in 10:38–39 ("The Flight of the Naked Young Man [Mark 14:51–52]," *CBQ* 41 [1979]: 415).

[35] Meyer, "The Youth in the Secret Gospel of Mark," 145–47; idem, *Secret Gospels*, 124.

An identification of the young men in *SGM*, Mark 14:51–52, and Mark 16:1–8 as one and the same young man in successive stages of Christian initiation might give the baptismal hypothesis some much needed help. But standing against such an identification is the lack of an anaphoric definite article after the initial mention of a young man. Instead, the second mention is accompanied by an indefinite τις (14:51) and the third mention is simply anarthrous (16:5). Yet in every comparable situation Mark starts with an indefinite expression and thereafter uses the anaphoric definite article: so with reference to the paralytic (2:3, 4, 5, 9, 10), the man with the withered hand (3:1, 3, 5), the Gergasene demoniac (5:2, 8 [cf. 15, 16, 18]), the woman with a constant flow of blood (5:25, 33), the synagogue-ruler (5:22, 35, 36), the Syrophoenician woman (7:25, 26), the blind man of Bethsaida (8:22, 23), the father of the boy with a mute spirit (9:17, 21, 24), the blind beggar (10:46, 49, 51), the inquiring scribe (12:28, 32), the widow with two mites (12:42, 43 [cf. 44]), and the servant girl (14:66, 69). The case of the synagogue-ruler has special pertinence because the second and third references to him carry the anaphoric definite article even though the story of the woman with a constant flow of blood has intervened, as in the discontinuous mentions of a young man.

Canonical Mark is supposed to transfer "the mystery of the kingdom of God" from *SGM* 1 to 4:11 to situate Jesus' teaching not in secret ritual (as in *SGM* 1, capitalized on by the Carpocratians – cf. Irenaeus, *Adv. haer.* 1.25.5) but in publicly spoken parable (4:1–2). But though Jesus teaches the mystery of God's kingdom through publicly spoken parable, even in canonical Mark – indeed, emphatically in canonical Mark – his explaining the parabolic mystery of God's kingdom takes place only in private with the disciples (see 4:10, 13–20, 33–34; cf. other Markan passages concerning the disciples' private audiences with Jesus). In 4:11, therefore, "the mystery of the kingdom of God" is not at all problematic, but right at home. It does not need to be regarded as a foreign body intruded from *SGM* 1.[36] Changes in Matthew and Luke derive from a desire to stress the culpability of outsiders and the element of understanding, an ideal trait of disciples that Matthew often emphasizes.

Finally, canonical Mark is supposed to transfer "and from there, arising, he returned to Transjordan" from *SGM* 1 to 10:1a, where the strangeness of the conjunction of "the borders of Judea and Transjordan" betrays the transfer (cf. the omission in Luke 9:51 and the revision, "the borders of Judea beyond the Jordan," in Matt 19:1). But why should canonical Mark think that he needs to preserve an unessential piece of topographical information, especially when according to Crossan's theory he lets far more essential elements of the story disappear entirely – viz., the woman who is a sister to the young man, her prostrat-

---

[36] See also J. Marcus, *The Mystery of the Kingdom of God* (SBLDS 90; Atlanta: Scholars Press, 1986), 86–87 n. 41.

ing herself before Jesus, Jesus' anger, and the loud shout from the tomb? Why does canonical Mark not omit the entire story if he finds it objectionable? If out of respect for tradition he preserves any of the story by scattering it in bits and pieces, why does his respect for tradition not lead him to preserve some more essential bits and pieces than a topographical detail that is more problematic in *SGM* 1 than it is in 10:1? For presumably *SGM* referred to Judea at 10:1a. Otherwise, a transfer of Transjordan from *SGM* 1 to 10:1a would not have produced the supposedly strange conjunction. *SGM* 1 makes Jesus leave Judea after having done a number of things there (10:1b–34) and head away from Jerusalem to Transjordan even though both editorial and Jesuanic statements have just announced that he and those with him are going up to Jerusalem (10:32–33). In canonical Mark, Jesus does nothing in Judea before he arrives in Transjordan, with the result that canonical Mark merely works backward from ultimate destination to intermediate destination, as in 11:1, to highlight the region and city where Jesus' passion-and-resurrection predictions will be fulfilled.[37]

Others have shown in detail that *SGM* is largely a confused pastiche of phrases gathered from elsewhere in Mark and the other canonical Gospels.[38] Despite Clement's supporting the Markan authenticity of *SGM*, then, and despite the efforts of some present-day scholars to date *SGM* before canonical Mark and the other Gospels, we should regard *SGM* as apocryphal non-Markan additions to canonical Mark, additions which post-date the other Gospels too and which the Carpocratians supplemented for their own purposes.[39]

To break new ground, we may note that Jesus' commanding the young man in *SGM* 1 hardly means his commanding him to come in the evening wearing a linen cloth on his naked body. For the lack of any reference to baptism makes sartorial preparation for baptism an unlikely meaning, and the lack of any references to or hint of sexual relations makes sartorial preparation for homosexual intercourse an equally unlikely meaning. Jesus is not said to be wearing a linen cloth on *his* naked body, and the text of *SGM* says nothing to suggest that the young man exposed his nakedness by taking off the linen cloth that he was wearing. On the contrary: "for Jesus was teaching him the mystery of the kingdom of God." The conjunction γάρ, "for," and the imperfect tense of ἐδίδασκε, "was teaching," define the activity of "that night" didactically rather than sexually or baptismally.

---

[37] Gundry, *Mark*, 528–29, 535, 623–24, 627.

[38] See, e.g., Bruce, "'*Secret*' *Gospel*," 11–13; D. Schmidt in *Protocol of the Center for Hermeneutical Studies in Hellenistic and Modern Culture* (Colloquy 18; Berkeley, Calif.: The Center for Hermeneutical Studies in Hellenistic and Modern Culture, 1976), 41–43.

[39] See Bruce, "'*Secret*' *Gospel*," 12–13, for other examples of Clement's credulity – against Brown ("The Longer ['Secret'] Gospel of Mark," 89–110), who favors that Mark himself added to his canonical Mark "mystical" materials (as Clement calls them) for advanced Christians as distinct from catechumens. Brown does lodge important objections of a larger sort, however, against Koester and esp. Crossan.

Only if Clement's denial is false that "naked [man] with naked [man]" and "the other things about which you [Theodore] wrote" occur in *SGM* should we allow a homosexual meaning in *SGM*. Yet Clement writes as one who knows "word for word" (κατὰ λέξιν) "the very words" of *SGM*, which was written in Alexandria, left to the church in Alexandria, and "most carefully guarded" there, being read to initiates into the great mysteries. His instruction to deny that Mark wrote *SGM* even though in his belief Mark really did write it by way of expanding the original version (in our terms, canonical Mark) – this instruction seems designed to keep Carpocratians from passing off their objectionable additions to *SGM*, such as "naked [man] with naked [man]," as having Markan authority.

To discover what Jesus commanded the young man let us step back to the preceding clause, "for he was rich." It explains why the young man has a house despite his youth. It also echoes descriptions of the adult rich man in vv. 22, 25 ("for he had many acquisitions.... a rich [man]"; cf. Luke 18:23: "for he was exceedingly rich") and recollects Jesus' commands that the adult rich man go sell all that he has, give to the poor, and come follow him (v. 21). Since then in *SGM* 1 the clause, "and after six days Jesus commanded him," immediately follows the clause, "for he was rich," and since the verb of command (ἐπέταξεν) has no direct object (contrast the infinitival and clausal direct objects in 6:27, 39; 9:25), the commands to the rich adult man are meant to fill the ellipsis in *SGM* 1 (cf. 1:27, where an ellipsis after this same verb is to be filled with an earlier command in 1:25). Like the rich adult man in 10:17–31, then, the rich young man in *SGM* is also commanded to go sell all that he has, give to the poor, and come follow Jesus. Instead of inserting the story of the rich young man right after the story of the rich adult man the author of *SGM* delays it till after the passion-and-resurrection prediction in 10:32–34 so as to put Jesus on the road to Jerusalem through Jericho, where *SGM* will set the sequel as a second insertion. *SGM* borrows the youth of the rich man from Matt 19:16–22; and his youth reminds *SGM* of the young man in Mark 14:51–52, from where *SGM* now borrows the wearing of a linen cloth on a naked body. By wearing only that much when he comes to Jesus, the young man demonstrates his obedience: during the balance of the day, i.e., between the daytime of Jesus' command and the evening, the rich young man disposed of his wealth and now has nothing left but the linen cloth, only what a corpse needs (cf. 15:46). Thus he has qualified himself to follow Jesus. As a result Jesus can teach him the mystery of God's kingdom. The linen cloth on a naked body represents dispossession, then, not baptismal or homosexual ritual; and *SGM* 1 offers a counterbalance to the rich adult man who left downcast and did not return having dispossessed himself. This contrast links up with the growing ideal of poverty in Alexandrian Christianity. The growth of this ideal causes an adverse reaction in Clement, *Q.d.s.* (*Who Is the Rich Man That Will be Saved?*) 11. Nonetheless, Clement's letter to Theodore betrays an attraction to the secrecy of *SGM*.

Anticipating the contrast between the two rich men is the young one's gazing at Jesus and loving him right after being raised. The wording ἐμβλέψας αὐτῷ ἠγάπησεν αὐτόν exactly matches v. 21a. But in *SGM* the rich young man already begins to exhibit the difference between himself and the rich adult man by doing to Jesus what Jesus unsuccessfully did to the earlier rich man. (The use of ἠγάπησεν for the young man's loving Jesus carries homosexual overtones no more than Jesus' loving the rich adult man did.) Confirming the parallel between the two rich men is the description in *SGM* 2 of the young one as him "whom Jesus loved" just as Jesus had loved the adult one. Only the verb has changed to the imperfect tense (ἠγάπα), presumably because of the linear character of the young man's following Jesus, who loves him because he is following (cf. John 11:5, 36; 13:23; 19:26; 21:2, 7, 20). His request to be with Jesus is being fulfilled. Since in *SGM* 1 Jesus seems to have given the same commands to the rich young man that he gave to the rich adult man, perhaps *SGM* 2 implies that the young man's sister and mother, accompanied by Salome, have in mind to ask for him a place of high honor such as Salome, understood as the mother of James and John, asked for them. In any case, canonical Mark looks older and better than *SGM*.

5. Jesus' Blasphemy according to Mark 14:61b–64
and *Mishnah Sanhedrin* 7:5

Mark's account of Jesus' trial before the Sanhedrin is plagued by a host of historical critical questions. Did the trial really take place, or has Mark or some Christian before him fabricated it in a parallelistic fashion out of Jesus' traditional and presumably historical trial before Pontius Pilate? If a Sanhedric trial did take place, did it proceed as Mark narrates it? How could he or a Christian before him have gotten accurate information about the trial? Has historical information suffered from Markan and pre-Markan redaction? If so, to what extent, and which elements in Mark's text represent what actually happened? What elements represent pre-Markan redaction, what elements represent Markan redaction, and what evidence favors the assignment of particular elements to this, that, or another source? Do the other canonical Gospels and perhaps other literature inside and outside the NT provide supplementary and sometimes better historical information? If Jesus stood before the Sanhedrin, did the Sanhedrin try him or only hear him, only examine him? What *was* the Sanhedrin in Jesus' time? *Who* were they? Can we even speak of the Sanhedrin in the sense of a regularly meeting, fixed body of judges? The questions go on and on.[1]

Here I do not propose to discuss them all; rather, I wish to take up one element in Mark's text to which such questions apply and with which they are implicated. That element is the charge of capital blasphemy under which Jesus is said to have been condemned by the Sanhedrin. The text of Mark 14:61b–64 reads:

Again the high priest [who according to the preceding verse had stood up] was asking him [Jesus] and says to him, "Are you the Christ, the Son of the Blessed One?" And Jesus said, "I am, and you [pl.] will see the Son of Man sitting at the right hand of the Power and coming with the clouds of heaven." And the high priest, rending his garments, says, "What need of witnesses do we still have? You have heard blasphemy [a form of ἀκούω plus the genitive, not accusative, case]. How does it appear to you?" And they all condemned him to be liable to the death penalty.

Not all blasphemy was punishable by death, but here we are presented with a case of capital blasphemy.

---

[1] See R. E. Brown, *The Death of the Messiah, From Gethsemane to the Grave* (ABRL; New York: Doubleday, 1994), 1:328–97.

The blasphemy for which Jesus is supposed to have been condemned has come in for various identifications. The notion that the Sanhedrin took the "I am" of Jesus as a claim to be the divine I AM of the OT (Exod 3:14) has not found very much favor. Following the question, "Are you the Christ, the Son of the Blessed One?" the answer "I am" is taken as elliptical much more naturally than as absolute. Filling in the ellipsis we would read, "I am *the Christ, the Son of the Blessed One*," a reading that does not conform to the I AM *of God* in the OT. Besides, even a nobody like the man born blind can say, "I am" (John 9:9), and not be charged with capital blasphemy.[2]

Agreement is likewise growing that the Sanhedrin would not have considered a self-claim to messiahship blasphemous, at least not capitally so. On the one hand, Jewish messianic expectation was too diverse to have provided a foundation firm enough for laying a capital charge against the messianic claimant. On the other hand, the purely human character of the expected Messiah or messiahs would have made it difficult to justify the charging of a messianic claimant with capital blasphemy.

The next part of Jesus' answer, "I am [the Son of the Blessed One]," has gained more votes. Of course, "the Son of the Blessed One" may mean no more than "the Christ." For in 2 Sam 7:14 Yahweh says concerning the royal offspring of David, "I will be his father, and he will be my son." An anthology from Qumran uses that passage for the Davidic messiah (4Q174). Yahweh calls a Davidic king his son in Ps 2:7, likewise used messianically in later Jewish and Christian literature.[3] And "the Son of God" may apply to a messiah in 4Q246.

But what if "the Son of the Blessed One" does not simply restate "the Christ" but qualifies "the Christ" as a superhuman, divine figure? What if the high priest drew from the false testimony concerning a prediction by Jesus that he would destroy the temple made by human hands and build another temple *not* made by human hands – what if the high priest drew from that testimony a suspicion that Jesus' claim to be the Son of the Blessed One entailed a higher kind of messiahship than that which Jewish expectation ordinarily entertained? Or what if the reference to divine sonship comes not historically from the high priest but imaginatively from Mark or an earlier Christian? What if the whole dialogue – the high priest's question plus Jesus' reply, perhaps even the whole episode or at least much of it – arises out of the Christian confession of Jesus as the Christ, God's Son in the sense of sharing deity with God, not out of the actualities of a trial? Then a fictional claim, "I am [the Son of the Blessed One]," would justify a fictional charge of capital blasphemy.

---

[2] For fuller criticism of a divine I AM in Mark 14:62 see D. R. Catchpole, *The Trial of Jesus* (StPB 18; Leiden: E. J. Brill, 1971), 132–35.

[3] Str-B 3:675–77; Acts 13:33; Heb 1:5; 5:5; and probably Mark 1:11 parr.

Whether or not we see the high priest historically suspecting a claim to superhuman messiahship or a Christian imaginatively fabricating a dialogue between the high priest and Jesus out of a Christian confession, the last part of Jesus' answer, "And you will see the Son of Man sitting at the right hand of the Power and coming with the clouds of heaven [a theophanic symbol]," draws on Ps 110:1 and Dan 7:13 and escalates Jesus' claim to messiahship and divine sonship to a superhuman level. This last part of Jesus' answer could provide blasphemy even apart from an escalation in the meaning of "the Christ, the Son of the Blessed One." For according to rabbinic tradition R. Jose asked R. Akiba how long he was going to profane the Shekinah by interpreting the thrones of Dan 7:9 as set for the Holy One, blessed be he, and one for David (*b. Sanh.* 38b). One might suppose that Jesus does not portray himself but someone else as sitting at God's right hand when he refers to "the Son of Man." But if R. Akiba could be charged with profaning the Shekinah for putting a third party (David) on a throne beside God's throne, presumably Jesus could be charged with blasphemy for putting a third party (the Son of Man) at God's right hand.

A problem remains, however. It is that *m. Sanh.* 7:5 requires capital blasphemy, such as Jesus is said to have been charged with, to include a pronunciation of the tetragrammaton, YHWH, whereas the text of Jesus' answer to the high priest contains, not "of the Lord" (τοῦ κυρίου), which we would expect for "of Yahweh," but the reverential substitute, "of the Power." The Mishnaic passage has to do with the execution of blasphemers and reads as follows:

The blasphemer is not culpable [i.e., is not liable to execution] unless he pronounces the Name itself [the tetragrammaton]. R. Joshua b. Karha says: "On every day [of the trial] they examined the witnesses with a substituted name, [such as] 'May Jose smite Jose.' When sentence was to be given they did not declare him guilty of death [on the grounds of evidence given] with the substituted name, but they sent out all the people [i.e., the audience, so that only the judges, the witnesses, and the accused were left in the courtroom] and asked the chief among the witnesses and said to him, 'Say expressly what you heard' [in other words, quote the blasphemy once again, but this time do not use a substitute for the tetragrammaton], and he says it [the blasphemy, including the tetragrammaton]; and the judges stand up on their feet and rend their garments, and they may not mend them again. And the second witness says, 'I also heard the like,' and the third says, 'I also heard the like.'"[4]

---

[4] Translation by H. Danby, *The Mishnah* (Oxford: Oxford University Press, 1933), ad loc. Cf. *m. Sanh.* 6:4: "Why was this one hanged [after being stoned to death]? Because he blessed [= a euphemism for 'cursed'] the Name, and the Name of heaven was profaned." See *m. Yoma* 3:8; 6:2; *m. Sota* 7:6 that "the Name" in *m. Sanh.* 7:5 excludes divine names other than the tetragrammaton.

Blasphemy does not consist in pronouncing the tetragrammaton; but to be judged as deserving of death, according to this text, blasphemy must include a pronunciation of the tetragrammaton. As such, blasphemy consists in cursing (the piel of the verb גדף, which the Mishnah uses as a synonym for the verb קלל or נקב in Lev 24:10–16, the OT passage providing the basis for requiring that capital blasphemy include a pronunciation of the tetragrammaton). Cursing does not carry the narrow connotation of the English word "curse," however. In Isa 37:6, for example, an Assyrian is said to have cursed God merely by saying that Yahweh the God of the Jews would not deliver Jerusalem from the Assyrians. Far from speaking against Yahweh, the Assyrian has even claimed that Yahweh sent the Assyrians and is with them (Isa 36:4–21). So if regarded as false, Jesus' description of the Son of Man as sitting at God's right hand and coming with the clouds of heaven might easily fall under blasphemy as cursing in the sense of bringing dishonor to God.[5]

But can one bring dishonor to God without pronouncing the tetragrammaton? Yes. Right in Mark, at 2:5–7, some scribes are said to have accused Jesus of blasphemy even though he had not pronounced the tetragrammaton in saying, "Child, your sins are being forgiven." Jesus' forgiving sins counted as blasphemy because by so doing he had arrogated to himself a divine prerogative. On its face, this arrogation seems just as serious as the blasphemy of his predicting that the Son of Man will sit at the right hand of the Power and come with the clouds of heaven. But no capital charge was brought against Jesus on the earlier occasion. Why then is a capital charge brought against him now? It does not satisfy to answer that in ch. 2 antagonism against Jesus had not yet heated up to such a degree as to make a capital charge politically appropriate in Mark's storyline.[6] For at the close of the section Mark 2:1–3:6 the Pharisees' going out and "immediately conspiring with the Herodians how they might destroy him" (3:6) shows that a charge of capital blasphemy would be eminently appropriate even at this early stage.[7] And we would expect that of all people the scribes, the theologians, would describe as deserving of death the blasphemy of arrogating to oneself the divine prerogative of forgiving sins. But they did not. Why?

---

[5] For a broad definition of blasphemy see D. L. Bock, *Blasphemy and Exaltation in Judaism* (Biblical Studies Library; Grand Rapids: Baker, 2000), 30–112; A. Y. Collins, "The Charge of Blasphemy in Mark 14:64," *JSNT* 26 (2004): 381–95. Collins brings into the discussion also חרף and נאץ.

[6] So D. L. Bock in open discussion at an SBL session in Atlanta, Georgia, November 2003; cf. his *Blasphemy and Exaltation*, 185.

[7] It might be argued back that the conspiracy in Mark 3:6 to destroy Jesus shows that the supposed blasphemy in 2:7 was considered deserving of death even without a pronunciation of the tetragrammaton. But several pericopes have intervened; 2:1–12 features the scribes whereas 3:1–6 features the Pharisees and Herodians; and the conspiracy to destroy Jesus in 3:6 arises out of his having violated the Sabbath, not out of blasphemy.

Sharpening the question is that in Mark 14:62 Jesus' "I am" accepts the high priest's reverential substitute, "the Blessed One"; and Jesus goes on to use another reverential substitute, "the Power." Whether or not the text of Mark accurately represents Jesus' answer to the high priest's question, how can Jesus *be said* to have spoken capital blasphemy? The answer may be seen as denigrating God so as to fall under the category of blasphemy. But *capital* blasphemy? As quoted, the answer does not contain the tetragrammaton or a Greek equivalent thereof. So again, why does this blasphemy lead to a capital charge when the former one in ch. 2 did not?

The question has received three main answers. I will offer a fourth. According to the first answer the requirement that capital blasphemy include a pronunciation of the tetragrammaton did not exist in Jesus' time. Either the Mishnaic passage represents a later idealization of Sanhedric jurisprudence, or the obliteration of the Sadducean sect in the destruction of Jerusalem and the temple in A.D. 70 led to a jurisprudence that better protected the rights of accused people by making capital convictions more difficult. So long as the Sadducees ruled the roost, says this view, capital blasphemy did not require a pronunciation of the tetragrammaton, as Jesus' case gives evidence.

According to the second answer a Christian fabrication of the dialogue between the high priest and Jesus and perhaps of the whole Sanhedric trial of Jesus makes the Mishnaic passage irrelevant. What would a Christian know or even care about a Sanhedric requirement that capital blasphemy include pronunciation of the tetragrammaton even though such a requirement was in force? The point would be to satisfy the requirement of a Christian confession, not that of Sanhedric jurisprudence.

According to the third answer Mark describes only a preliminary hearing designed "to determine if Jesus was as dangerous as the [Jewish] leadership sensed and whether he could be credibly sent to Rome [i.e., Roman authority in the personage of Pontius Pilate]" (cf. Mark 12:12–16) rather than given a formal trial governed by the rule requiring a pronunciation of the tetragrammaton in capital blasphemy.[8] But what may have started as such a hearing ended with a formal condemnation ("And they all condemned [κατέκριναν] him to be subject [ἔνοχον] to death" – Mark 14:64), which condemnation, however, the leadership could not carry out because of the Romans' overlordship.[9]

---

[8] Bock, *Blasphemy and Exaltation*, 191; see pp.190–95.

[9] At first Bock draws a fine distinction between ἔνοχος and αἴτιος, as though the former is less formal or technical than the latter (but see Mark 3:29; Matt 5:21–22). Finally, though, he admits that Mark's language could "apply to a formal judgment" in "a legal procedure" (*Blasphemy and Exaltation*, 191–92). Bock does not explain why he thinks that "the rules for examination might differ" according to the presence or absence of authority to carry out a capital condemnation. After all, the strict rules in *m. Sanh.* 7:5 exist in the absence of such authority whereas Bock's argument requires leniency in that absence.

Here again is our question: How can we explain why the Sanhedrin is said to have condemned Jesus under a charge of capital blasphemy despite the Mishnaic requirement that capital blasphemy include a pronunciation of the tetragrammaton on the one hand and despite the absence of the tetragrammaton, or a Greek equivalent of it, from the quoted version of Jesus' blasphemy on the other hand? The fourth answer to this question (my own answer) is best approached by asking another question: In view of the Mishnaic regulation that witnesses to capital blasphemy use a substitute for the tetragrammaton so long as an audience of non-jurists are present (not till all but the judges, witnesses, and accused are dismissed is the tetragrammaton itself to be pronounced in a quotation of the alleged blasphemy), how would we expect Jesus' blasphemy – if it did include or was thought to have included a pronunciation of the tetragrammaton – to be quoted by witnesses, in his case by the judges themselves, to other people? Why, of course, with a substitute for the tetragrammaton just as in Mark's text. Thus Jesus did pronounce the tetragrammaton. It is the right hand of Yahweh concerning which Ps 110:1 speaks ("Yahweh said to my lord, 'Sit at my right hand'"). So Jesus said or was thought to have said, "I am, and you will see the Son of Man sitting at the right hand of Yahweh …"; and the Sanhedrists who later reported to non-jurists what Jesus had said used "the Power" as a substitute for Jesus' "Yahweh."[10]

This view enjoys the advantage of harmonizing with indications that the Mishnaic passage may enshrine early regulations. What are those indications? First of all, the whole book of Susannah (see esp. vv. 44–59) and 11QT^a 61:9 exhibit a pre-Christian concern to protect the rights of accused people. Second, already in the LXX of Lev 24:15–16 the death penalty is prescribed for the person who not only curses God but also names the name of "Lord" in so doing (ὀνομάζων … τὸ ὄνομα κυρίου). At the beginning of v. 16 δέ, "but," seems to indicate that naming the name of "Lord" goes beyond cursing God without a pronunciation of that name. And let us remember that the pre-Christian manuscripts of the LXX probably had the tetragrammaton itself or a sign thereof rather than κυρίου, "Lord," which appears in Christian manuscripts of the LXX. Philo, a first century Jewish figure and therefore pre-Mishnaic, explicitly describes the naming of the name "Lord" as a graver offense than cursing God and one deserving of death (*Mos.* 2.37–38 §§ 203–8); and Josephus, another first century Jewish figure and therefore also pre-Mishnaic, interprets "naming the name of the Lord" and Lev 24:16 as "blaspheming God" (*Ant.* 4.8.6 § 202). Moreover, the correspondence between the standing of the high priest and of the

---

[10] C. A. Evans notes that pronunciation of the tetragrammaton in a reverential citation of Scripture would not necessarily count as blasphemous (*Jesus and his Contemporaries* [AGJU 25; Leiden: E. J. Brill, 1995], 413). But such pronunciation does make capital the blasphemy of citing Scripture in a fashion that dishonors God. See Bock, *Blasphemy and Exaltation*, 113–83, for Jesus' supposedly dishonoring God in the citation of Ps 110:1 and Dan 7:13.

judges in Mark and the Mishnah, respectively, and between the tearing of garments at the hearing of capital blasphemy in both passages favors that Mark reflects the sort of custom later enshrined in the Mishnah and therefore already practiced in the first century. D. Juel noted that of the reasons listed in Str-B 1:1007 for tearing one's garments, only the hearing of the tetragrammaton has a legal setting – a fact that makes this correspondence between the Mishnah and Mark more remarkable and therefore more supportive of an enshrinement of early jurisprudence in the Mishnaic passage.[11]

There are differences, of course. In *m. Sanh.* 7:5 all the judges are to stand and tear their garments when hearing the tetragrammaton pronounced in a report of blasphemy. Here in Mark the high priest is already standing, and only he is said to tear his garments when hearing what he tells his fellow judges is blasphemy. But these differences lend themselves to easy explanation without damage to a fundamental correspondence. In the Mishnah previous testimony has prepared all the judges to stand and tear their garments when the chief witness pronounces the tetragrammaton. In Mark the high priest has already stood up to play a role like that of the prosecutorial witnesses. Jesus' prediction comes as a surprise, and the high priest coaches the other judges into regarding it as blasphemous. Whether they tore their garments on agreement with the opinion of the high priest Mark does not say, for his interest quite naturally jumps to the condemnation of Jesus by all of them. One might even imagine that the moment for a tearing of garments had passed by the time the other judges reached agreement. In any case and contrary to usual opinion, the texts of Mark and the Mishnah do not suffer from any incompatibility; rather, they agree with each other at a fundamental level.

Against the foregoing, Bock argues that the high priest's designation of God as "the Blessed One" shows sensitivity toward the utterance of God's name, so that Jesus may have likewise used "the Power" as another substitute for God's name.[12] But this argument can cut in the opposite direction, viz., that in imitation of the high priest's substitute those who reported what Jesus said substituted "the Power" for Jesus' "Yahweh." Furthermore, in a similarly contentious situation at Mark 12:36 Jesus did not hesitate to use the divine name in quoting Ps 110:1. So in an allusive quotation of Ps 110:1 at Mark 14:62 Jesus is likely to have used the divine name again (against Bock's notation that "it was common for biblical texts to be pronounced with a substitute for the divine Name"[13]).

---

[11] D. Juel, *Messiah and Temple* (SBLDS 31; Missoula: Scholars Press, 1977), 97. See R.H. Gundry, *Mark* (Grand Rapids: Eerdmans, 1993), 914, for the high priest's tearing his *under-garment* in Mark's account.

[12] Bock, *Blasphemy and Exaltation*, 184, 200, 214–15 esp. n. 74, 220; so also Juel, *Messiah and Temple*, 97–98, though later in private conversation with me Juel pronounced himself convinced by my oral presentation of the present thesis.

[13] Bock, *Blasphemy and Exaltation*, 198.

Bock also strains to find instances of capital blasphemy that did not include a pronunciation of the tetragrammaton.[14] Since Jesus is condemned on the ground of verbal blasphemy, however, instances of capital punishment for nonverbal blasphemy carry no argumentive weight. Nor do slayings by God for blasphemy carry any argumentive weight for human jurisprudence. The opinion of Rabbi Meir (c. A.D. 140) does make an exception to the jurisprudential rule requiring a pronunciation of the tetragrammaton for capital blasphemy; but the Sages are said to have rejected his view, though allowing that a heathen as opposed to a Jew is punishable by death for blaspheming with the use of a substitute for the tetragrammaton (*m. Šebu.* 4:13; *b. Šebu.* 35a–36a; *b. Sanh.* 55b–57a, 60a). And Jesus was a Jew, not a heathen, of course.

It is puzzling how Bock deduces that *y. Sanh.* 7.25a–b (Neusner 7.8–9) "suggests that many [rabbis] made the argument that a euphemism [= a substitute for the tetragrammaton] left one liable [to the death penalty], just as blaspheming with the Name ... did." For, as he himself observes, the passage "appears to distinguish the death penalty from extirpation [exclusion from the community]," yet blaspheming with a euphemism gets only a warning or, at most, extirpation. In the end, he grants that in "the prevailing rabbinic view" capital blasphemy required a pronunciation of the tetragrammaton; that "the rabbinic position limits automatic death to the specific offense using the Name"; that with the exception of *m. Sanh.* 7:5 "there is little discussion of formal judicial examples of blasphemy"; that "warnings were certainly issued in such cases where a range of euphemisms was used for utterances, but it does not appear, at least in the rabbinic period, to have carried an automatic death sentence"; and that "the official rabbinic position is that the use of the divine Name constitutes the only clear case of capital blasphemy." Thus the best Bock can do is to say only that "detailed debate on the point [with Rabbi Meir, presumably] *might suggest* an old difference of opinion on the matter" (italics added).[15]

Optimistically thinking that he has disposed of the probability that Jesus' supposed blasphemy included a pronunciation of the tetragrammaton, Bock seeks to fill the remaining vacuum with an appeal to 11QT[a] (= 11Q19) 64:6–9:

If a man slanders his [God's] people and delivers his people up to a foreign nation and does evil to his people, you shall hang him on a tree; and he shall die. According to the mouth [i.e., testimony] of two witnesses, he shall be put to death; and they shall hang him on a tree.

---

[14] Bock, *Blasphemy and Exaltation*, 69–70, 76–77, 93–96, 99, 102–7, 110–11.

[15] Bock appeals weakly to *b. Sanh.* 81b, but as I. Epstein (editor of the Soncino edition) says, "The meaning of the passage is uncertain" and the word crucially in question may be "a disguised form of the Tetragrammaton" (p. 543 n. 1), so that utterance of the tetragrammaton *would* have to be included in a capital blasphemy. In *b. Sanh.* 60a there is debate over the requirement of tearing one's clothes upon hearing blasphemy but not on the question whether capital blasphemy has to include an utterance of the tetragrammaton.

Then Bock infers that Jesus' application to himself of Ps 110:1 and Dan 7:13 amounts not only to a high christological claim but also to an attack on the Jewish leadership, a threat that he will judge them in the end, a violation of the prohibition in Exod 22:27 of cursing or reviling a ruler, a "prospect of intense political-social unrest," an undermining of Roman authority, an exposing of the Jews to Roman recrimination, and therefore an instance of capital blasphemy – in accordance with 11QT^a 64:7–9 – apart from a pronunciation of the tetragrammaton.[16] An astonishingly long list of inferences! One might think that Bock has engaged in "illegitimate totality transfer," as though the Son of Man's sitting at the right hand of the Power and coming with clouds of heaven automatically connoted not only for Mark's audience but also for the Sanhedrin all the items listed by Bock. But in Mark 14:62 Jesus does not attack the Jewish leadership, threaten to judge them in the end, curse or revile them, speak of leading a popular uprising, or deny Roman authority. Nor in Mark 14:63–64 does the high priest or the Sanhedrin say he does. Nor in Mark 15:1–5 do they accuse him before Pilate of doing so. (It is Pilate who suggests with a question that Jesus may be "the king of the Jews"; only then do the chief priests accuse Jesus "much" [πολλά, an adverbial accusative] without any Markan specification of their accusations.) In contrast with 11QT^a 64:6–9 Jesus has not slandered God's people, delivered them up to a foreign nation, done evil to them, or been accused of any of these misdeeds or described as about to do them. Mark 14:61a–64 deals only in high Christology. Besides, the word in 11QT^a 64:7 that "slanders" translates – viz., רכיל – does not appear among the terms for blasphemy that Bock himself canvasses.[17] It means to inform or spy against with the result in 11QT^a 64:6–9 of delivering up God's people to a foreign nation. Was Jesus accused of being an informer to the Romans against his fellow Jews? No. And even if he had been, is it likely that the sectarian Temple Scroll provides a more reliable guide for Jesus' Sanhedric trial than does the tractate *Sanhedrin* in the mainline Mishnah? Hardly.

Thus far I have gingerly stepped between the possibilities of historicity and unhistoricity in Mark. But now the question presses forward: Does the fundamental correspondence between Mark and the Mishnah arise out of historical fact with regard to a Sanhedric trial of Jesus, or did Mark or someone before him more or less fabricate that trial (and do so on the point of capital blasphemy according to a known jurisprudence of the Sanhedrin)? A fundamental correspondence between Mark and the Mishnah, including a hidden "Yahweh" behind "the Power," does not depend on Markan historicity. But does that correspondence have anything to say about historicity? Perhaps so, for the subtlety of the correspondence – a subtlety seen in the difference between Jesus' not being

---

[16] Bock, *Blasphemy and Exaltation*, 28, 208, 231–32, 236.
[17] Bock, *Blasphemy and Exaltation*, 30–112.

brought to trial for capital blasphemy but uttering it on the spot and the Mishnah's dealing with cases in which the accused is brought to trial for capital blasphemy previously uttered, a subtlety seen also in the difference between avoiding the tetragrammaton in a post-trial report and avoiding the tetragrammaton in all but the final testimony during a trial – this double subtlety would require not only that a Christian fabricator have known Sanhedric jurisprudence for cases of capital blasphemy and not only that such a fabricator have taken care to keep the Sanhedrin from violating their own jurisprudence in such cases (in itself an unlikely care in view of the well-known violations of Sanhedric jurisprudence in other respects when Mark and the Mishnah are compared), but also the double subtlety would require that a Christian fabricator buried beneath the surface of the story the correspondence between the conduct of Jesus' trial as to capital blasphemy and a normal condemnation for capital blasphemy, and did so by making Jesus speak blasphemy on the spot rather than earlier and by making him speak in the words of a reporter concerned to avoid pronouncing the tetragrammaton in the presence of non-jurists rather than by quoting the very words that Jesus spoke, including the tetragrammaton.

One might argue that a Christian fabricator made Jesus avoid the tetragrammaton to portray the Sanhedrin as condemning Jesus under a false charge of capital blasphemy. But falsehood goes unmentioned in the text, and this omission contrasts sharply with the falsehood explicitly and emphatically attributed to the earlier charge involving the temple (vv. 55–59). That earlier portrayal of the Sanhedrin as seeking true testimony and rejecting inconsistent testimony as false contrasts with the redacted statement in Matt 26:59 that they were seeking false testimony[18] and militates against Christian fabrication at that earlier point in Mark just as the subtle portrayal of the Sanhedrin as following their jurisprudence on capital blasphemy as best they could, given the unforeseen special circumstances of Jesus' case, militates against Christian fabrication at this present point in Mark. Everywhere else in the NT Christians use

---

[18] Bock speaks of "planned false witnesses" (*Blasphemy and Exaltation*, 193). Similarly, Collins says that "the members of the council had sought and found persons willing to appear and bring false testimony against Jesus," and she supports this statement by saying further that "the γάρ of v. 56 links the false testimony with the activity of the members of the council reported in v. 55" ("The Charge of Blasphemy," 380). But Bock and Collins are reading Mark through Matthean lenses. According to Mark 14:55 the witnesses themselves were "sought," i.e., planned. On the other hand, the falsity of their testimony was *not* planned by those who sought the testimony, for – as noted above – they rejected the testimony on account of its falsity. The γάρ of v. 56a does not introduce an explanation to the effect that they were looking for false testimony. Rather, it introduces an explanation of the reason why the council did not find the kind of testimony they were looking for, i.e., true testimony ("they were not finding ['testimony against Jesus for putting him to death'], for many were testifying falsely and [a typically Markan paratactic καί meaning 'as shown by the fact that'] the testimonies were not consistent" [vv. 55–56]). Only at Matt 26:59 is false testimony sought – in line with Matthew's overall program of intensifying the Jewish leaders' guilt.

"God" or the rhetorical flourish "the Majesty on High," not "the Power," in quoting and interpreting Ps 110:1 (cf. Acts 2:34–35 with 2:36; Rom 8:34; Eph 1:20 with 1:17; Col 3:1; Heb 1:3, 13; 8:1; 10:12; 12:2; Mark 16:19; and see Luke 22:69 for the conflate "the power of God") whereas "the Power" does occur for God in non-Christian Jewish writings (see esp. *b. Šabb.* 87a; *b. Sota* 37a par. *'Abot R. Nat.* 35 for an absolute usage, as here; cf. a similar Samaritan usage in Acts 8:10 and a probably Jewish heretical usage in the plural at *m. Sanh.* 4:5). Nor do Christians use "the Blessed One" as a title for God elsewhere in the NT (contrast esp. "God's Son" in Mark 1:1 [probably]; 3:11; 5:7) whereas "the Blessed One" substitutes for "God" in the Jewish and probably pre-Christian *1 En.* 77:1 and sounds much like an abbreviation of the common rabbinic expression "the Holy One, blessed [is] he" (see also *m. Ber.* 7:3; *b. Ber.* 50a; *y. Ber.* 7:11c (all cited in Str-B 2:51); and *Tg. Yer. II* Gen 49:2 and possibly Mur 43 2 [DJD 2:159–60]).[19] Or should we say that the rabbinic expression represents an expansion? The alternation between the simple adjective ἀγαπητός, "beloved," and the perfect passive participle (i.e., verbal adjective) of ἀγαπάω in Mark 1:11 par.; 9:7 parr. as compared with Eph 1:6, and in Rom 1:7; Eph 5:1 as compared with Rom 9:25; Col 3:12, makes it quite possible that τοῦ εὐλογητοῦ, "of the Blessed One," goes back to the passive participle of ברך, which occurs for God in the rabbinic and targumic literature just cited. The counter appeal to H. Danby's translation, "who is to be blessed," overlooks that this translation would work well in Mark 14:61 ("the Son of the One who is to be blessed"). As for the theory that Mark is imitating Jewish style, where else can it be demonstrated that he does so rather than following Jewish Christian tradition? His frequent translations of Jewish terms and explanations of Jewish customs tend in the opposite direction. You do not imitate only to explain.[20]

So far as Mishnaic judicial regulations violated in Jesus' Sanhedric trial are concerned, *b. Sanh.* 46a allows irregularities even in capital cases for emergencies and protection of the Torah. So irregularities in that trial do not necessarily indicate its unhistoricity or rule out an origin by Jesus' lifetime of Mishnaic regulations protective of the accused. I have discussed the irregularities at some length in my commentary on Mark, as also differences between the Sanhedric and Roman trials of Jesus, between the Sanhedric trial and the trials some scholars have supposed that Mark's community had undergone, and between the Sanhedric trial and the treatment of the righteous sufferer in Wisdom 2 and 5 and certain Psalms – differences whose number and seriousness make doubtful that Mark or a Christian before him used the Roman trial, Christian experience, or Wisdom and the Psalms as a basis for fabrication.[21] As for the possibility of a

---

[19] On Mur 43 2 see Brown, *Death of the Messiah*, 469 n. 14.

[20] See further D. L. Bock, "Jewish Expressions in Mark 14:61–62 and the Authenticity of the Jewish Examination of Jesus," *Journal for the Study of the Historical Jesus* 1 (2003): 149–55.

[21] Gundry, *Mark*, 891–98.

leak concerning what happened at Jesus' Sanhedric trial, one might consider the probability that the Sanhedrin, large as it was, had its share of talkers. One might also look to Joseph of Arimathea (Mark 14:43); Nicodemus (John 3:1, 4; 7:50; 19:39); the unnamed disciple known to the high priest (John 18:15–16); Peter, who was sitting with the servants of the Sanhedrin (Mark 14:54; cf. vv. 66–72); and chief priests and Pharisees who became disciples of Jesus (John 12:42–43; Acts 6:7; 15:5). For a similar leak despite an attempt at maintaining secrecy see Josephus, *Vita* 38–41 §§ 180–204.[22]

One more argument against the historicity of Jesus' Sanhedric trial needs examination. This argument is that the Gospel of John, supported in part by Luke, has the arrested Jesus taken to Annas for private questioning and then by way of Caiaphas's house to Pilate for trial, no Sanhedric trial having taken place (John 18:12–28).[23] The subsidiary argument that an overnight meeting of the Sanhedrin would have been virtually impossible to organize on the spot[24] disregards the urgency felt by Jesus' opponents, the opportunity afforded them by Judas Iscariot, and the availability of servants to act as couriers for the chief priests.

Regarding the main argument from John's lacking a Sanhedric trial of Jesus, one can better argue that John knew Mark or Markan tradition but redacted it for compositional and theological reasons: (1) John's having Jesus say back in ch. 2, "Destroy this temple and in three days I will raise it," and then editorializing that Jesus was talking about his body (2:19, 21) evacuate the Sanhedric trial of one of its main components, viz., the false charge that Jesus said he would destroy the temple and raise it in three days (Mark 14:57–59). (2) More particularly, Jesus' saying directly to the Jews in John, "Destroy this temple," eliminates any need for the witnesses in Mark, attributes the destruction to the Jews rather than Jesus (in line with Pilate's delivering Jesus to the Jews for crucifixion according to John 19:16), replaces the witnesses' false testimony in Mark with Jesus' true testimony (a prominent theme throughout John), and – with John's editorial comment – makes Jesus raise himself from the dead just as in John 10:17–18. (3) The high priest's question in Mark 14:61, "Are you the Son of the Blessed One?" would not make sense in John because there Jesus has repeatedly and publicly proclaimed himself God's Son and otherwise divine and been so well understood to have done so that twice he was nearly stoned (John 8:59; 10:31–33). (4) Having Jesus say "I am" throughout the Fourth Gos-

---

[22] Cf. Bock, "Jewish Expressions," 148–49.

[23] See, e.g., D. M. Smith, "John and the Synoptics: Historical Tradition and the Passion Narrative," in *Light in a Spotless Mirror* (ed. J. H. Charlesworth and M. A. Daise; Faith and Scholarship Colloquies; Harrisburg, Penn.: Trinity Press International, 2003), 88–89; idem, "John a Source for Jesus?" (paper presented at the annual meeting of the SBL, Atlanta, Ga., November 2003), 7, 10–11.

[24] So P. Fredricksen, *Jesus of Nazareth, King of the Jews* (New York: Alfred A. Knopf, 1999), 223.

pel up to his trial, and especially twice in the immediately preceding arrest scene (John 18:6, 8), evacuates the Sanhedric hearing of another of its main components, viz., Jesus' saying "I am" in answer to the high priest's question (Mark 14:62). (5) Jesus' talk of the Son of Man's being seen sitting at God's right hand and coming on clouds (Mark 14:62) would tend against John's realized eschatology and omission of the so-called synoptic apocalypse (Mark 13 parr.). (6) The high priest's asking Jesus privately in John about his disciples and teaching gives Jesus an opportunity to highlight his having "spoken openly to the world" (John 18:19–20), a major theme throughout John's Gospel, which features Jesus as the Word who speaks in a cascade of words to which he repeatedly makes emphatic reference in his discourses.[25] (7) In John the Jews do not bother to condemn Jesus as the Sanhedrin does in Mark, because the Jews know and explicitly admit that they cannot execute him (John 18:31–32). (8) When Jesus is taken in John to Caiaphas the high priest nothing happens to Jesus there (John 18:24, 28); so it seems that John has eliminated the Sanhedric trial and retained only its locale. And (9) the Jews' interrogation of Jesus in John 10:22–39, his answering in terms that go beyond christhood (about which they had asked) to divine sonship and oneness with his Father, and the Jews' accusing him of capital blasphemy – all these elements in that earlier passage get rid of any need for John to tell what happened at Jesus' Sanhedric trial. We need equally good or better compositional and theological reasons for thinking that at this point Johannine historical tradition was changed into a Markan unhistorical account. Such reasons are lacking.

After delaying Jesus' Sanhedric trial till after daybreak, Luke omits the witnesses and their accusations against Jesus, the charge of blasphemy, and the condemnation of Jesus to death (Luke 22:66–71). But do these omissions indicate that Luke knew a more historical, Johannine-like tradition? No, because the omissions fit Luke's redactional program of portraying Jesus as a paragon of moral and religious virtue. In agreement with this program Luke reverses the charge that Jesus blasphemed, for Luke 22:65 makes Jesus the *object* of blasphemy. Even the possibility that he said he would destroy the temple goes out the window. And with a modest *"You* say that I am" he turns back the question whether he is God's Son. So it might seem that John knew Luke or a Lukan unhistorical tradition rather than a historical tradition known also by Luke.

All in all, then, the older account in Mark looks historically better than John's or Luke's later account.

---

[25] See below, pp. 324–62.

6. Matthew: Jewish-Christian or Christian-Jewish? At an Intersection of Sociology and Theology

Against the traditional view that locates the Gospel of Matthew in a Christian group already separated from Judaism a new view has sprung up. It advocates that Matthew's group considers itself part of the Jewish community, not a re-placement thereof, and in turn that non-Christian Jews consider Matthew's group a part of their community, though a deviant part. Influentially advocating this new view is A. J. Saldarini in his book, *Matthew's Christian-Jewish Community.*[1]

The book uses "Christian-Jewish" rather than "Jewish-Christian" (though on pp. 24–25 "Jewish-Christian" occurs several times for groups similar to Mat-thew's) and uses "community" primarily for the whole constellation of various groups, Christian and non-Christian alike, making up Judaism during the period of the Second Temple (though the prefixing of "Christian" to "Jewish" leaves the misimpression that "community" refers only to Matthew's group). Mat-thew's group is evangelistically trying to win dominance over the larger Jewish community according to this thesis and therefore does not regard Israel as re-jected by God – rather, only its leaders as so rejected because of their opposition to Matthew's group.

The Gentile mission has barely and cautiously started for this group, so that among them Gentiles are "peripheral" and "attracted" to Christian Judaism much as Gentile proselytes and God-fearers are attracted to the rest of Judaism. All members of the group, Gentiles as well as Jews, are expected to keep the OT law as interpreted by Matthew's Jesus. Hence the legalistic-sounding passages in the Gospel of Matthew reflect expectations in his group, not keepsakes of an outgrown tradition.

The Gospel presents Jesus in terms entirely at home at least somewhere in other sectors of the widely variegated Judaism which existed at the time. More easily to keep Matthew's group within the boundaries of that Judaism Saldarini supposes that the group consists of a single house church. A larger entity would open too many possibilities of "church" in the traditional sense, which implies separation from Judaism, an influx of Gentiles, and a consequent lessening of adherence to the OT law and heightening of Christology above the limits set by

---

[1] CSHJ; Chicago: The University of Chicago Press, 1994.

Jewish monotheism even after remarkably exalted forms of Jewish messianism have been granted.[2]

Saldarini succeeds in showing that Matthew's group maintained close contact with non-Christian Jews. Otherwise, too much of the Gospel of Matthew, including its distinctively and overarchingly Jewish features, becomes obsolete already at the time of writing. But Saldarini does not succeed in showing that the group considered itself, and was considered, part of the Jewish community. Much earlier than the date of Matthew by Saldarini's reckoning (A.D. 75–90), Paul maintained close contact with non-Christian Jews and even spoke of Gentile Christians as grafted into the stock of Israel, yet he also spoke of non-Christian Jews as cut off from that stock and he distinguished "the church" from "Jews" and "Greeks" (these latter two points neglected by Saldarini; see Rom 11:17–24; 1 Cor 10:32 and cf. Paul's being flogged by the Jews, though he no longer adhered to Judaism, with the suffering by Matthew's group of such flogging [10:17; 23:34; 2 Cor 11:24]). Matthew 28:15 uses "Jews" for a third party different from Matthew and his group. Saldarini proposes that for intra-Jewish polemic Matthew is taking up an opprobrious term normally used by Gentiles and is limiting it to those Jews who have accepted the falsehood that Jesus' corpse was stolen. Consequently, Matthew and his group remain Jews by religion even though not included among the "Jews" of 28:15.[3] But the text speaks generally of Jews as those among whom the falsehood has circulated, not limitedly of those who have accepted it; and elsewhere in Matthew's Gospel "Jews" is used only by non-Jews (2:2; 27:11, 29, 37).

Likewise failing is Saldarini's argument that Matthew never names his group over against the Jewish community. This argument rests on five oversights: (1) Saldarini overlooks that in 1:21 "his [Jesus'] people" cannot refer to the Jews in general because Jesus' people will consist only of those who will call him "Immanuel" (1:23) and whom he will therefore save from their sins (again 1:21), not of all those *needing* salvation as Saldarini says[4] – yet at Matthew's writing Jesus has not saved the bulk of Jewry and they have not called him "Immanuel." (2) Saldarini overlooks that Matthew does call his group "the righteous" (13:43; see also 13:49 for their counterpart, "the wicked" – both passages missed by Saldarini in his denial: "unlike the authors of many apocalyptic writings, he [Matthew] does not use the substantive 'the righteous' or 'the just' as a technical designation to set his group apart from his opponents."[5] (3) Saldarini overlooks that Paul's prominence among Christians in Syria (where Saldarini lo-

---

[2] Cf. L. W. Hurtado, *One God, One Lord* (Philadelphia: Fortress, 1988); idem, *Lord Jesus Christ* (Grand Rapids: Eerdmans, 2003); R. Bauckham, *God Crucified* (Grand Rapids: Eerdmans, 1998).

[3] Pp. 35–37, 201, 230–31.

[4] Pp. 29, 32.

[5] P. 27.

cates Matthew's group), Paul's setting "Jews," "Greeks," and "the church" over against each other (again 1 Cor 10:32), and Paul's using "churches" for Jewish Christian groups in Judea (Gal 1:22, again missed by Saldarini in his assertion, "Only the author of Acts uses the term [ἐκκλησία, 'church'] of mid first-century believers-in-Jesus in Jerusalem and Antioch"[6]) all combine to turn back the charge of anachronism in the translation "church" at Matt 16:18; 18:17, where Saldarini prefers to think less differentiatingly of an "assembly."[7] (4) Saldarini overlooks that in 16:18 Jesus' "my" differentiates the "church" from the Jewish community. And (5) Saldarini overlooks that 21:43 identifies *God's kingdom* as that which is given to the fruit-bearing nation, so that it is not Israel which is transferred from non-Christian Jewish leaders to Matthew's Christian Jews.[8]

We should not think with Saldarini of Matthew's group as trying to win dominance *over* the Jewish community, then, but of their trying to win converts *from* that community, nor of their merely attracting Gentiles or cautiously opening their boundaries to them but of their aggressively "going" (πορευθέντες) to evangelize and disciple "all the nations" (πάντα τὰ ἔθνη) "in the whole inhabited world" (ἐν ὅλῃ οἰκουμένῃ – 24:14; 28:19). The widespread success of this mission seems indicated by the uniquely Matthean statements that "the field is *the world*" (ὁ κόσμος – 13:38) and that the net "gathered together [fish] *of every kind*" and "was *filled*" (13:47–48), and by Matthew's putting the one-hundred-fold yield *first* (13:8, 23) rather than last (as in Mark 4:8, 20). Furthermore, then, we should not think with Saldarini of a small house church but of the great church afflicted with the problem of many false disciples, on whom Matthew repeatedly trains his eye (yet another factor neglected by Saldarini), and thus different from Judaism though still in contact.[9]

Correspondingly, the Matthean Jesus says to keep *his* commandments, which interpret the OT law, not to keep that law as interpreted by him. Saldarini's latter way of putting the matter strikes a more Jewish note[10] but does not conform to Matthew's wording (see 28:20 ["teaching them to observe all things whatever that I have commanded you"] with 5:21–48 ["But I (ἐγώ) say to you" (six times)] in relation to 5:17–20 ["I have come ... to fulfill ('the law' and 'the prophets')"]; cf. 11:29 ["Take my yoke upon you and learn from me"]; 23:8–10 ["for you have one teacher .... because you have one instructor, the Christ"]). And Jesus' commandments interpret the law with a penetrating emphasis on moral principles that accommodates Gentile reticence to live ritually as Jews.

---

[6] P. 118.

[7] Pp. 118–20, 130, 225–26.

[8] Against pp. 59–63, 196, 201, 243.

[9] See R. H. Gundry, "In Defense of the Church in Matthew as a *Corpus Mixtum*," *ZNW* 91 (2000): 153–65; idem, "On True and False Disciples in Matthew 8.18–22," *NTS* 40 (1994): 433–41.

[10] Pp. 7–9, 124–64.

Correspondingly again, Matthew presents Jesus in terms that rise above any brand of Jewish messianism, i.e., as "*God* with us" (not just as "God's *presence* with us" – so Saldarini[11]) and as the Son of God in a sense that entails his being sandwiched between the Father and the Holy Spirit (1:23; 28:19, the sandwiching unmentioned by Saldarini apparently because it points to an early, unphilosophical form of trinitarianism [so also Paul at an earlier date[12]] that distinguishes Matthew from Judaism at a fundamental point). Saldarini slips by saying that Matthew's Magi "honor Jesus ... even as God"[13] but seems not to appreciate that such worship goes beyond the pale of Jewish messianism.

Further distortions and neglect of Matthew's text appear on pages 32 ("The disciples are identified with the prophets and with righteous people who want to see and hear what the disciples see and hear" [13:16–17; rather, *contrasted* with those who wanted to]); 77–78 (except for two centurions Gentile authorities are treated "neutrally or negatively" [but Pilate obeys the OT law of handwashing as indicative of his innocence – see 27:24 with Deut 21:6–8 – and in 27:19 his wife declares Jesus "righteous"]); 105 (Matthew reports "the parable of the fig tree" [21:19; but Matthew reports an incident, not a parable]); 126 (24:20 does not allow the disciples to flee on the Sabbath [but the text says to pray that their flight not *occur* on the Sabbath, so that despite its undesirability they *are* allowed to flee on the Sabbath]); 146 ("nowhere are the disciples called sons" [but 5:45 calls them "sons," as recognized by Saldarini himself on p. 94]); 151 ("a [Matthean] critique of the excessive use ... [and] misuse of oaths" [but 5:34 says to swear "not at all," as Saldarini recognizes on p. 153]); and 192 (Jesus reappears in 28:9–10, 16–20 "as he said he would in chapters 24–25" [but those chapters put world-wide evangelism and end-time tribulation first and describe a coming "in clouds with much power and glory," accompanied by a gathering of the elect "from the four winds, from the extremity of earth to the extremity of heaven," *not* as in 28:9–10, 16–20]).[14]

A. F. Segal agrees with Saldarini that Matthew's group thought of itself as within the pale of Judaism and that other Jews accepted the group as within that pale despite its deviance.[15] A. C. Wire's supplementary description of Mat-

---

[11] P. 166 et passim (italics added).

[12] See 1 Cor 12:4–6; 2 Cor 13:13.

[13] P. 176.

[14] Minor errors include "happend" for "happened" (p. 78), "siezed" for "seized" (p. 116), "diety" for "deity" (p. 154, three times), "2:23" for "1:23" (p. 193), "stesses" for "stresses" (p. 261), and "Donohue" for "Donahue" (p. 294).

[15] A. F. Segal, "Matthew's Jewish Voice," in *Social History of the Matthean Community* (ed. D. L. Balch; Minneapolis: Fortress, 1991), 3–37. In the end, though, Segal nearly pulls the rug out from under his own thesis by saying, "It is difficult to ascertain whether the Matthean community, in its latest form [as] represented by the Gospel itself, was entirely sure of its Jewish identity" (p. 36). The essays cited below only by title likewise come from *Social History of the Matthean Community*. For consistency with Saldarini's foregoing use of "Matthew's group" I will use that phrase instead of "Matthean community."

thew's group as scribal, i.e., halakic, tends in the same direction.[16] So also does P. Perkin's haggadic description.[17] Both descriptions contain some truth because especially though not only under the Mark-Q hypothesis Matthew pares down narratives to make room for teaching[18] yet adds haggadah-like narratives about the nativity, Peter's walking on water, the coin in a fish's mouth, Judas's suicide, the dream of Pilate's wife, the resurrection of saints, two earthquakes, guards at Jesus' tomb, and the angel of the Lord's descent from heaven and rolling away the stone from the door of the tomb.[19]

But the imperial, cosmopolitan outlook of W. R. Schoedel's Ignatius militates against a Jewish sectarian definition of Matthew's group.[20] Ignatius does not even seem to know an alternative Jewish Christianity, much less a Christian Judaism, in Antioch or within hailing distance. So whether or not Ignatius knew and used Matthew, as J. P. Meier argues he used it,[21] but all the more if Ignatius did know and use Matthew, how did the church in Antioch or thereabouts travel so far and fast from Jewish sectarianism? The difficulty of answering this question casts doubt on the hypothesis that Matthew's group really was a Jewish sect bent on reforming Judaism or was a Jewish sect just then in the process of coming out of Judaism.[22] But if Matthew's group had already made a clean break with Judaism, regarded itself as a separate entity, and was so regarded by others, it was already on its way to becoming the Ignatian church. Matthew's great emphasis on evangelizing all the nations fits such a separation.[23] So also his urban thinking leads toward Ignatius's urban thinking.[24]

But what should we say to the arguments that Matthew's group was still only a Jewish sect? The argument that Matthew's anti-Pharisaism puts his group in an intramural debate with post-70 Judaism overlooks his special use of the Sadducees,[25] who left no heirs in post-70 Judaism and against whom the Matthean group could not carry on any kind of debate, much less an intramural one, especially not up in Syria or Galilee, far from the Sadducean base of power in Je-

---

[16] A.C. Wire, "Gender Roles in a Scribal Community," 87–121.

[17] P. Perkins, "Gender Analysis: A Response to Antoinette Clark Wire," 122–26.

[18] Cf. H.J. Held, "Matthew as Interpreter of the Miracle Stories," in G. Bornkamm, G. Barth, and H.J. Held, *Tradition and Interpretation in Matthew* (NTL; London: SCM, 1963), 168–92.

[19] Matt 1:18–2:23; 14:28–33; 17:24–27; 27:3–10, 19, 51b–53, 62–66; 28:2, 4, 11–15.

[20] W.R. Schoedel, "Ignatius and the Reception of the Gospel of Matthew in Antioch," 129–77.

[21] J.P. Meier, "Matthew and Ignatius: A Response to William R. Schoedel," 178–86.

[22] Saldarini describes as "fading" Matthew's hope that he would prevail and make his program normative for the whole Jewish community ("The Gospel of Matthew and Jewish-Christian Conflict," 41). This description gives some ground for a definition of Matthew's group as not Jewish sectarian.

[23] See esp. Matt 28:19–20.

[24] G.D. Kilpatrick, *The Origins of the Gospel according to St. Matthew* ((Oxford: Clarendon, 1946, 1959), 124–25.

[25] Matt 3:7; 6:1, 6, 11, 12; 22:23 par., 34.

rusalem and the temple, now destroyed. To say that Matthew's use of ἐθνικός, "Gentile," as a term of disapprobation[26] implies his group's membership in Judaism overlooks his use of "Jews" in 28:15 as a party different from his group. The anarthrousness of the noun (not "*the* Jews," but "Jews") stresses a qualitative difference. Alone, Matthew's multiplication of "their synagogues"[27] might be taken as an intramural epithet. But combined with the use of "Jews" as a third party the phrase seems to mean Jewish synagogues over against the church, which includes Jews without being Jewish.

Matthew's use of ἐκκλησία, "church,"[28] can hardly be taken in a Jewish, Septuagintal sense; for Paul had long since used the term in a differentiatingly Christian sense, and he himself as well as the book of Acts tells of his ministry in Antioch.[29] So his usage must have been known there and roundabout. Moreover, not only does Matt 21:43 give the kingdom to a nation (ἔθνος) producing its fruits. Matthew 1:21 identifies this nation as Jesus' people (λαός). He will save them from their sins. They are the ones who call his name Immanuel – "they," as distinguished from all known textual traditions of Isa 7:14, quoted in Matt 1:23. So we have not just a reforming sect within the people of God, Israel, or a sect barely in the process of losing its reformative spirit, but a distinctly new people whose church-assembly differs from the synagogue-gatherings of Jews. Just as this people belong to Jesus, so also does the church ("*his* people"), which the people are ("I will build *my* church," Matt 16:18).[30]

Not only are this people or church set over against the synagogues of Jews. This people or church do not enjoy "continued acceptance … within Judaism" (as Segal says they do).[31] Compared with Mark and Luke, Matthew has intensified the element of persecution,[32] including persecution in synagogues and Jewish courts;[33] and Matthew says in 23:13 not only that the scribes and Pharisees do not themselves enter the kingdom but also that they keep others from entering. So Matthew's group and non-Christian Jews reject each other. They are on the outs. Consequently, a continuing mission to the Jews aims solely at conversion, not at all toward reformation.

---

[26] Matt 5:47; 6:7; 18:17.

[27] Matt 4:23; 9:35; 10:17; 12:9; 13:54; cf. 23:34. Only 4:23 has a synoptic parallel.

[28] Matt 16:18; 18:17 (twice).

[29] Gal 2:11–14 (cf. 1:22); Acts 11:19–30; 12:25–13:3; 14:26–15:2, 30–35; 18:22–23.

[30] Against Saldarini's statement that Matthew "has no name for his group" ("The Gospel of Matthew and Jewish-Christian Conflict," 41–42).

[31] Segal, "Matthew's Jewish Voice," 31.

[32] Cf. R. H. Gundry, *Matthew* (2d ed.; Grand Rapids: Eerdmans, 1982), 682, s.v. "Flight from persecution," against Segal's dependence on D. R. A. Hare, *The Theme of Jewish Persecution of Christians in the Gospel according to St. Matthew* (SNTSMS 6; Cambridge: Cambridge University Press, 1967), who underplays the element of actual persecution.

[33] Matt 10:17, 23.

Non-Christian Jews and Matthew's group might well be on the outs. His Jesus is Immanuel, "God with us" (1:23). So Jesus says to his disciples, "I am with you always, to the end of the age" (28:20). Not only does he sandwich himself as the Son between the Father and the Holy Spirit in the Great Commission (28:19). He also replaces the "God" of "Immanuel" with his own ever-present "I" (28:20). One might think to find an analogy in the Jewish doctrine of the two powers in heaven,[34] but here in Matthew is a recent historical figure quoted as saying while he was on earth that he would stay with his disciples here, not in heaven, and do so in accordance with the divine title with which his people call him (see 18:20 too). This high Christology of Matthew and its fundamental difference from anything known to Judaism, including the two powers doctrine, is almost bound to have fixed a great gulf between Matthew's group and Judaism. Segal and Saldarini have soft-pedaled that difference (though credit goes to Saldarini for describing the rising status of Jesus as "a key change").

Segal and Saldarini have also soft-pedaled the didactic difference between Matthew's Jesus and teachers in Judaism. Matthew 28:20 enjoins obedience to all Jesus' commandments, not to the Torah. Granted, Jesus interprets the Torah in giving his own commandments (5:17–48). But the antithetical manner in which his interpretation replaces the Torah – and it is the quoted and paraphrased Torah itself, not other Jewish teachers' interpretations of it,[35] which his interpretation replaces – this antithetical manner exceeds even the first-person style in which the temple scroll of a deviant Jewish sect repromulgates the Torah.[36] Thus the antithetical manner puts distance between Matthew's group and anything recognizably Judaistic – unless one stretches "Judaistic" well beyond normal usage.

At the same time that the Matthean Torah looks more different from Judaism than Segal and Saldarini have allowed it also looks more Pauline than they have recognized. We are told that Matthew interprets the Torah according to the love commandment and fights Paulinism as well as Pharisaism. But in his most anti-Judaistic letter Paul too interprets the law as fulfilled in that commandment (Gal 5:14; cf. Rom 13:8, 10). This same Paul quotes and paraphrases other parts of the Torah as well – much of the Decalogue, for example[37] – in giving instructions to largely Gentile Christians. He does not engage in provocatively antithetical interpretation of the Torah after Matthew's manner but diplomatically describes the Torah as holy and just and good and even Spiritual (Rom 7:12, 14) and argues Matthew-like that he does not abrogate it but establishes it (Rom 3:31). Differences remain, of course. But if we take into account all the

---

[34] So Segal, "Matthew's Jewish Voice," 32.
[35] Gundry, *Matthew,* 83–84, 87, 89–90, 91–92, 94, 96–97.
[36] I allude, of course, to 11QTª (= 11Q19).
[37] Rom 7:7; 13:9.

evidence, not just Paul's slogan "not under law but under grace" (Rom 6:14), he and Matthew stand closer together than sometimes thought.

Segal's association of Matthew with Peter as opposed to Paul also runs into problems. Not only does Matthew alone mention Peter's sinking and Jesus' calling him "Little Faith" (14:30–31). Matthew is also the only one to introduce Judas's suicide and butt it up against Peter's denials (26:69–27:10), a parallel made the more unhappy for Peter both by the adverb "bitterly," which describes his weeping in 26:75 and which Mark 14:72 does not have (though Luke 22:62 does), and by Matthew's unparalleled indication that Peter "denied [Jesus] before all" (ἠρνήσατο ἔμπροσθεν πάντων [26:70]), which puts Peter in the category of those whom Jesus "will deny before [his] Father in heaven" because they have "denied [Jesus] before people" (ἀρνήσηταί με ἔμπροσθεν τῶν ἀνθρώπων [10:33]). Moreover, Matthew does not contain the command that the women tell Peter about the resurrection (as they are commanded to do in Mark 16:7) or the reference to an appearance by the risen Jesus to Peter (as it is referenced in Luke 24:34 and 1 Cor 15:5). Would a Gospel growing out of a Petrine sociological compromise allow Peter to start out so grandly and fade out so miserably?[38]

But a compromise between Judaism at large and Christian Judaism is not what Matthew aims to strike. In the first place, an evangelist who seeks such a middle course is unlikely to put such a huge emphasis as Matthew does on discipling all the nations.[39] Discipling them would only add to the sociological problem he is supposedly trying to solve. Nor does discipling all the nations look like a program for reforming Judaism. The more troublesome sociological problem of Matthew's group does not have to do with the relation of a Christian Judaism to the rest of Judaism, but with relations inside Matthew's group between tares and wheat, bad fish and good, true disciples and false. We need to recognize Matthew's group as a large and mixed body (as opposed to "a fragile minority"[40]) and focus on the desire to weed out the tares, on the counter demand for tolerance till the Last Judgment, on the prohibition of making individual judgments against the genuineness of a fellow disciple, on the occasional necessity of collective discipline, on the many's growing coldness of love, on intramural betrayal and hatred in addition to betrayal by others and hatred by all

---

[38] See also below, p. 124, in connection with Matthew's doctrine of salvation.

[39] The combination of this emphasis and Jewishness fits the description in Acts 11:19–26; 13:1–3 et passim of the church in Syrian Antioch better than it fits a Galilean church whose shape is shrouded in mystery. The emphasis on discipling all the nations also puts a roadblock in the way of Saldarini's suggestion that as a Jewish sect Matthew's group took circumcision for granted ("The Gospel of Matthew in Jewish-Christian Conflict," 49 n. 38). The greater the emphasis on bringing Gentiles into Judaism, the greater the need to emphasize circumcision – or to defend a nonrequirement of circumcision. The absence of circumcision from Matthew therefore combines with the emphasis on discipling all the nations to disfavor Jewish sectarianism.

[40] So Saldarini, "The Gospel of Matthew and Jewish-Christian Conflict," 38.

the nations, on the expansive treatment of much-needed mutual forgiveness, and on the danger of being thrown out from the wedding feast even though you are a "friend" (ἑταῖρε), like Judas, whom Matthew's Jesus ironically calls his friend.[41] Here is grist for the sociological mill. But we miss it by fixating on the relation of Matthew's group to Judaism.

And it is exactly these interior features of Matthew's group that pose some problems for sociologist R. Stark's description of the group, like other Christian groups, as a charitable organizaiton.[42] Who would want to join a group not only under persecution but also at war with itself and needing a hard kick in the seat of its pants with the moral rigorism of Matthew's Gospel? Mark 10:30 promises houses, brothers, sisters, mothers, children, and fields along with persecutions right now, in this age, as well as eternal life in the age to come. But the severity of persecution and the intramural problems brought on by it in Matthew's group forestall such a this-worldly promise in the parallel Matt 19:29, which therefore limits itself to the by-and-by. Even the traveling preachers in Matthew's group need stiffer rules than in Mark or Luke. They are not to acquire money, whereas in Mark and Luke they are not to take any along. In Matthew's group they appear to have been acquiring from their audiences gold as well as the copper and the silver mentioned by Mark and Luke, respectively.[43]

Only some in Matthew's group have risked their own safety by feeding, giving drink to, clothing, entertaining, and visiting the sick and imprisoned fugitives from persecution, those who flee from one city of Israel to another, whom Jesus calls the least of his brothers (10:23, 40–42; 25:31–46). These little ones appear not to be marginal Christians, sinning Christians, as Wire suggests,[44] but Christians suffering the results of persecution and liable to be caused to sin, i.e., to apostatize under persecution, if their fellow professing Christians do not help them as some (the goats) are failing to do though others (the sheep) are helping. Matthew's group is a sociological shambles. No wonder he wants them to go disciple all the nations. At least they will stay out of each other's hair.[45]

---

[41] Matt 5:21–26; 6:14–15; 7:1–6; 13:24–30, 36–43, 47–50; 18:15–18, 21–35; 22:11–14; 24:10, 12; 25:1–13; 26:50.

[42] R. Stark, "Antioch as the Social Situation for Matthew's Gospel," 189–210.

[43] Cf. Matt 10:9 with Mark 6:8; Luke 9:3.

[44] Wire, "Gender Roles in a Scribal Community," 116–17.

[45] See further D. A. Hagner, "Matthew: Christian Judaism or Jewish Christianity," in *The Face of New Testament Studies* (ed. S. McKnight and G. R. Osborne; Grand Rapids: Baker, 2004), 263–82; idem, "Matthew: Apostate, Reformer, Revolutionary?" *NTS* 49 (2003): 193–209; and P. Foster, *Community, Law and Mission in Matthew's Gospel* (WUNT 2/177; Tübingen: Mohr Siebeck, 2004). Hagner and Foster take up the work of A. Overman and D. Sim as well as that of Saldarini, Segal, and company.

7. Salvation in Matthew

In regard to the doctrine of salvation in Matthew a number of questions arise: What does salvation consist in? Who does the saving? Who are saved? How are they saved? When are they saved? What circumstances, real or imagined, seem to have prompted Matthew to present his version of salvation? I will conclude with some comparisons and inferences concerning Matthew's *Sitz im Leben*.

What Does Salvation Consist in?

Matthew wastes little space before introducing the topic of salvation, and his first mention of it indicates that salvation consists in deliverance from sins (1:21). The plural of "sins" seems to imply that Matthew does not conceive of sin as an external power that has enslaved its victims so as to make them sin against their will (contrast esp. Rom 6:12–23; 7:7–25). By modifying "sins," in fact, "their" (a subjective genitive in Greek) seems to fix the blame for sinning on the sinners themselves, so that deliverance from sins means deliverance from punishment for sinful acts, such as those listed in 15:19: "evil designs, murders, adulteries, fornications, thefts, false testimonies, blasphemies" (N.B. the consistent use of the plural in this list, over against the singular in the NRSV except for the first item). With this view of salvation agree Matthew's references to forgiveness of moral debts (i.e., release from having to pay them – 6:12; cf. 18:27, 32, 35), forgiveness of trespasses (6:14–15), and forgiveness of sins (9:2, 5, 6; 26:28), even every sin and blasphemy except for blasphemy against the Spirit (12:31–32). The plural of "debts," "trespasses," and "sins" is again notable, as is also the modifier "every" when "sin" and "blasphemy" occur in the singular.

On the other hand, salvation consists in rescue from τοῦ πονηροῦ (6:13). Some take the Greek expression as neuter and therefore as referring to evil in the abstract, to evil in general, or to any evil thing. Others take the expression as masculine and therefore as referring to Satan as the Evil One. The use of the masculine ὁ πονηρός in 13:19 for the one who snatches the word of the king-dom out of hearers' hearts favors a reference to Satan in both passages (cf. also 5:37, where τοῦ πονηροῦ may stand opposite God in the preceding verses, and 13:38–39, where τοῦ πονηροῦ equates with "the Devil"). With the neuter understanding, rescue from evil would presumably mean the same as salvation from sins, i.e., deliverance from punishment for the evil that one has done. With the masculine understanding, rescue from the Evil One would probably mean rescue from the Devil, Satan, as the one who tempts people to commit sins (4:1–11; 16:23).

To the woman who had the issue of blood Jesus pronounces salvation (9:22); and at his crucifixion chief priests, scribes, and elders say, "He saved others, he cannot save himself" (27:42). Since the supposed inability of Jesus to save himself has to do with physical deliverance from crucifixion, his antithetically parallel saving of others had to do with deliverance from the physical effects of their sins just as the woman's salvation had to do with stopping her issue of blood (cf. 4:23–24; 8:16–17; 11:4–5; and other stories of healings, exorcisms, and the raising of a dead person). Perhaps it is relief from these physical effects of sinning to which Jesus refers in promising rest to the weary and heavy laden who come to him (11:28–30; cf. his miracles mentioned in the earlier part of ch. 11).

For Matthew, however, salvation goes beyond deliverance from the physical effects of sinning. It extends to deliverance from condemnation (11:22–24), from being lost, from perishing (18:14), from wrath (3:7), from being thrown into a furnace of unquenchable, eternal fire and thus from weeping and gnashing of teeth (3:10–12; 7:19; 13:30, 42, 50; 18:8–9). Positively, salvation extends to justification, being pronounced righteous (12:36–37), to entrance into life (18:8–9; 19:17) with the result of having life that is eternal (19:16). This entrance into life comes by way of entrance into the kingdom of heaven (18:3) – through bodily resurrection if it is necessitated by prior death (12:41–42; 22:23–33; 27:51b–53) – and thus with the result of participation in God's heavenly rule on earth, a participation that brings with itself comfort in place of mourning, property in place of poverty, vindication in place of shame, mercy in place of judgment, a vision of God, acknowledgment as God's sons, and great reward in place of persecution (5:3–12).

Who Does the Saving?

Jesus saves, as his very name indicates (1:21; cf. Peter's outcry in 14:30, "Lord, save me," though he was asking Jesus to save him from drowning). Since salvation includes forgiveness of sins, salvation by Jesus naturally includes *his* forgiveness of sins (9:1–7). And since he acts always in consort with God, salvation naturally includes forgiveness by the Father in heaven as well (see 6:12 with 6:9). Furthermore, since Jesus' baptizing of people in the Holy Spirit and fire appears in its Matthean context to consist in his Spirit-endowed ministry, whatever the meaning of "fire" the Holy Spirit joins Jesus and God the Father in the act of saving (3:11–17). This trinitarian cast accords with Matthew's trinitarian formula for baptism (28:19).

That Jesus, God the Father, and the Holy Spirit do the saving looks like a vertical axis of salvation in Matthew. But a horizontal axis appears too. For disciples' restoration of a straying, sinning fellow disciple counts as gaining that fellow disciple so that he or she does not perish (18:12–18). Thus we can say that in Matthew disciples save each other. Not only "the Son of Man" but also "human beings" (N.B. the plural) have "authority" to forgive sins (see 9:8 with 9:1–7 and cf. 18:21–35). Since salvation includes forgiveness, as already noted, and since the authority of human beings to forgive sins parallels the Son of Man's authority to do so, we can say once again that in Matthew disciples save each other.

Matthew does not stop with trinitarian and ecclesial salvation, however. His soteriology proceeds to self-salvation. Those who lose their lives for Jesus' sake will find – i.e., save – their lives (16:24–26). Such a losing of life counts as one's own doing (τὴν πρᾶξιν αὐτοῦ – 16:27), so that you save yourself.

Who Are the Saved?

It is Jesus' people who are saved (1:21). And who are they? They are those who "call his name 'Immanuel,'" those who confess that in him "God [is] with us" (1:23), and who make this confession in public despite the threat of persecution (10:32–33). As noted in the preceding essay, the third person plural of "they will call" in Matthew's quotation of Isa 7:14 is text critically unique. No other known text of the OT passage has the third person plural. Most likely, then, Matthew himself produced this reading by altering a different one so as to define the people whom Jesus saves as those who call his name Immanuel. They are a sinful people; at least they were prior to his saving them from their sins. But he came to call sinners, not righteous people (9:9–13).

For the saved, 21:43 uses another collective term besides "people," viz., "nation." Jesus' having saved them as a people from their sins, they are now a nation that produces the fruits of God's kingdom, i.e., good deeds, righteous conduct (see, e.g., 5:16; 21:32). Comprising this nation are people of faith in Jesus and of discipleship to him from all nations (8:10–11; 28:19), plus holy ones, saints, from the past (27:51b–53) – an international nation of little people, social nobodies and mental infants as to human wisdom and prudence (10:42; 11:25; 18:6, 10, 14; 25:40, 45). But as compared with the unsaved, the saved are few, the Monaco of nations as far as population is concerned (7:13–14), so few as to be a family (5:22–24, 47; 7:3–5; 10:21; 12:46–50; 18:15, 21, 35; 25:40; 28:10). These are the saved.

How Are They Saved?

Because of their mental infantilism Jesus' people have to be saved by divine revelation (11:25–26), by God's giving them to know the mysteries of the kingdom of heaven (13:11). Because of their sins Jesus' people have to be saved by divine mercy and generosity (5:7; 19:30–20:16) and by the service of Jesus in giving his life as a ransom in substitution for them (20:28), i.e., by the shedding of his covenantal blood for the forgiveness of their sins (26:28; contrast the taunt, "Save yourself… and come down from the cross" [27:40–42], and cf. Elijah's not coming to save Jesus from death by crucifixion [27:49]). So much for what is done on behalf of Jesus' people for their salvation.

What do they need to do for themselves? They need to repent of their sins by getting baptized, confessing their sins during baptism, and producing fruit worthy of repentance, i.e., speaking and acting in a way that shows their baptism in water to have been prompted by genuine repentance (3:6–10; 7:16–20; 12:33–35; 21:43; 28:19). One produces such fruit by learning and keeping the law as explained, commanded, and exemplified by Jesus (5:20–48; 11:29; 13:1–23, 51–52; 19:16–19; 28:19); and such learning and obedience mean leaving the way of wickedness and going the way of righteousness (21:28–32), speaking good words (12:33–35), doing good deeds (5:16; 16:27; 25:14–30), converting oneself into the lowly position of a little child (18:3–4), not causing others to stumble into sin (18:6–7), and not stumbling into sin oneself (18:8–9). The list of specifics goes on and on: meekness, mercy, purity of heart, peacemaking, conciliation, avoidance of lust, maintenance of marriage, truthfulness, love of enemies, prayer for persecutors, secret charity, secret fasting, secret praying, forgiveness of debtors, forgiveness of those who have sinned against you, renunciation of earthly wealth, self-criticism, adherence to the Golden Rule (see the whole of the Sermon on the Mount, and passages such as 18:21–35; 19:21–30 among others). Matthew will not have salvation apart from these and other evidences – such as the absence of vices opposite to the foregoing virtues, for example – that repentance was genuine.

Repentance from sins and the practice of virtue do not suffice for salvation, however. One must also believe in Jesus (18:6; cf. 8:25–26; 9:2, 22; 14:31; 16:8; 28:17). Believing in him entails confessing him in public (10:32–33); calling him "Immanuel" (1:23); loving him more than you love your father, mother, son, or daughter (10:37); taking your cross and following him, which means risking persecution by open discipleship (10:38–39; 16:24–27); persevering under persecution (10:16–23; 24:9–13; cf. 13:18–23 and contrast the denials of Jesus by Peter [26:69–75] and Judas Iscariot's betrayal of Jesus [26:47–57]).

Because of a double mention by Matthew, it bears emphasis that under persecution one must persevere to be saved: "But the one persevering to the end – this one will be saved" (10:22; 24:13; contrast the one who in 13:20–21

hears the word and receives it immediately and joyfully but because of tribulation and persecution turns out to be "temporary" and stumbles into sin rather
than bearing the fruit of good deeds). Just as Judas Iscariot exemplifies disciples who show the falsity of their profession by betraying their fellows to
persecutors (cf. 24:10, unique to Matthew: "and then many will stumble into
sin and betray each other and hate each other"), Peter exemplifies disciples
who betray the falsity of their profession by denying Christ under the pressure
of persecution, as shown by Matthew's inserting the phrase "before all" concerning Peter's denial of Jesus in 26:70, so that Peter falls into the category of
those whom Jesus will deny before his Father in heaven because they have denied him before others (10:33). Naturally, then, the bitterness of Peter's weeping, paralleled in Luke 22:62 but not in Mark 14:72 (see Matt 26:75), is immediately paired with Judas Iscariot's hanging himself (Matt 27:1–10); and
Peter's name disappears from the story of Jesus' resurrection (contrast 28:7
with Mark 16:7), so that the reference in Matt 28:16 to "the eleven disciples"
shows that Peter remains as a tare among wheat, not to be separated from the
wheat until the end. (Corollaries to Peter's representation of disciples who do
not persevere to the end so as to be saved are, first, that in Matt 16:17–19 "this
bedrock," on which Jesus will build his church, is not Peter, "a stone," but "the
bedrock" of Jesus' "words," to which – not as in Luke 6:47, 49 – Matt 7:24, 26
attaches "these," corresponding to "this" with "bedrock" in Matt 16:18 and,
second, that in view of the falsity of Peter's discipleship the authority to bind
and loose, an authority represented by "the keys of the kingdom of heaven,"
has to be given in 18:18 to the disciples in general whereas it was given only
to Peter in 16:19.[1])

Belief in Jesus shows itself not only in perseverance under persecution but
also in the endangering of oneself by extending hospitality and charity to fellow
disciples who are fleeing persecution (cf. 10:40–42; 25:31–46 with 10:11–13,
23, most of this material being unique to Matthew). More generally, genuineness of repentance and belief shows itself in faithful, prudent, and kind treatment of fellow disciples. Otherwise there awaits dichotomization, a fate shared
with the hypocrites, and weeping and gnashing of teeth (24:45–51). Not exactly
salvation!

Negatively, Matthew takes pains to note that salvation does not come by baptism as such (3:7). To drive this point home he shifts the phrase "for the forgiveness of sins" from John's baptism (so Mark 1:4 par. Luke 3:3) to the Words of
Institution (Matt 26:28). Again negatively, Matthew notes twice that salvation
does not come by virtue of Abrahamic ancestry (3:9; 8:11–12).

---

[1] See further R. H. Gundry, *Matthew* (2d ed.; Grand Rapids: Eerdmans, 1994), 330–41, 664.

When Are They Saved?

Forgiveness of sins takes place in the present. "Your sins are being forgiven," Jesus says to a paralytic (9:2). Then he heals the paralytic to prove that as the Son of Man "on the earth" he has authority to be forgiving sins (9:6). Inversely, blasphemy against the Holy Spirit will not be forgiven "in this age" (12:31–32). But neither will it be forgiven "in the coming [age]." Since forgiveness of sins equates with salvation, then, salvation occurs both now and hereafter. As to the hereafter, "every careless word that human beings will speak – they will give an account concerning it in the day of judgment. For by your words you will be pronounced righteous and by your words you will be condemned" (12:36–37). By virtue of repentance and coming to hear the wisdom of Solomon, respectively, the men of Nineveh and the queen of the South will rise up "in the judgment" and condemn Jesus' generation. Correspondingly to the condemnation of Jesus' generation, then, the salvation of the men of Nineveh and the queen of the South must take place in the day of judgment, which is also the day of resurrection. Since those who do not turn and become like little children "will by no means enter the kingdom of heaven" (18:3), the entrance of those who do convert will likewise occur in the future. And the going away of the righteous into eternal life (25:46) will occur "when the Son of Man comes in his glory and all the angels with him," at which time "he will sit on his throne of glory" and judge "all the nations" (25:31–32).

What Circumstances, Real or Imagined, Seem to Have Prompted Matthew to Present His Version of Salvation?

Notably, Matthew presents a catch-all doctrine of salvation (cf. his catch-all Christology: Jesus as the Christ, Immanuel, God's Son, the Son of Man, Lord, and Wisdom). His is a soteriology of both-and rather than this-but-not-that. In 19:16–30, for example, having eternal life, inheriting eternal life, entering life, entering the kingdom, having treasure in heaven, and being saved all carry the same soteriological meaning. Fine distinctions mean little to Matthew. Though he distinguishes between repentance and belief on the one hand and evidence ("fruit," as he calls it) on the other hand, he does not distinguish cleanly between salvation as a gift and salvation as a reward or clearly deny the latter in favor of the former as Paul does. And it remains unclear what relationship, if any, exists between the covenant in which Jesus' blood is shed for the forgiveness of sins (26:28) and the various covenants that the OT talks about (again contrast Paul).

Within Matthew's soteriological potpourri, however, we can discern certain emphases. For him salvation consists primarily in forgiveness of sins (though this element is expressed in a variety of terms). But stress falls not so much on God's forgiving mercy, accepted through faith, as on human beings' saving themselves in the sense of demonstrating that they have truly repented of their sins. Thus it is the righteous who are saved, and they are saved by persevering in the superiorly righteous conduct they have learned from Jesus' teaching and example. Because they must persevere to the end their salvation occurs mainly in the future.

We are now positioned to speculate on the circumstances that may have evoked the foregoing emphases. As implied in the first paragraph of this essay, those circumstances may have existed in fact or only in the mind of Matthew, or may have consisted in a mixture of fact and fantasy. I favor the factual but will not attempt here an argument for my opinion except to say that the references of Paul to his former persecution of the church (Gal 1:13; Phil 3:6; 1 Tim 1:12; cf. Acts 8:1–3; 9:1–2, 13–14, 21; 22:4–5; 26:9–11), coupled with his references to continued persecution by non-Christian Jews (2 Cor 11:24, 26; 1 Thess 2:14– 16), favor the factual.

There, I have tipped my hand. Matthew's soteriological emphases seem to have grown out of circumstances in which he perceived Jewish Christians to be suffering persecution from fellow Jews who had not become Christians. As a result and as always happens in times of persecution – including those times when Christians have persecuted Jews – some were falling away to save their necks. Matthew saw Christians, Judas-like, betraying other Christians to their persecutors. He saw Christians, Peter-like, falsifying their profession with public denials of Christ. He saw their distinctively Christian conduct lapsing in such a way as to make them indistinguishable from their fellow Jews who made no Christian profession. He saw them failing to evangelize those fellow Jews and failing to make disciples of Gentiles as well, for such evangelistic efforts would mark them for persecution.

Warning! Your salvation depends on perseverance in the Christian life and witness. Otherwise you will be lost along with those who make no profession, many of them your very persecutors. Prove yourselves true. Do not let persecution lead you to hide your connection with Jesus. Flee if you must, but preach the gospel of the kingdom wherever you go. And do your good works as Christians in the full gaze of the public, even to the extent of endangering yourselves by openly ministering to persecuted fellow Christians. The day of judgment is coming. Show yourselves salty, not saltless; wise builders, not foolish ones; wheat, not tares; good fish, not bad; wearing a wedding garment, not lacking one; useful in service, not slothful and useless; wise virgins, not foolish ones. Do not slip into the category of goats rather than sheep. Your salvation is at stake. Make sure you are one of the few that will be saved.

Concluding Comparisons and Inferences
Concerning Matthew's *Sitz im Leben*

If Matthew's emphasis on salvation by works of righteousness arises out of a need for persecuted Christians to prove the genuineness of this profession, we might ask whether a similar emphasis in the Epistle of James arises out of the same need or out of a different one. If out of a different one, has the difference in need made a difference in the emphasis? My own impression is that in James the emphasis arises out of a need to quell contentiousness within local assemblies, so that the works of righteousness have to do with the gaining or regaining of harmony in those assemblies whereas in Matthew the emphasis arises out of a need to prove genuineness of Christian profession under persecution, so that the works of righteousness have to do with the risks of open discipleship and Christian evangelism in the larger society.

If Matthew's emphasis arises out of a need for persecuted Christians to prove the genuineness of their profession, we might also ask whether this emphasis has the purpose of combating Paul's doctrine of salvation – or, as he prefers to say, justification – by faith apart from works or of combating an antinomian aberration of Paul's doctrine. To ask the question in these terms is to cast doubt on an affirmative answer. The same is true if we ask whether Matthew's emphasis has the purpose of combating or competing with the rabbinic Judaism that was evolving in the last quarter of the first century. For it is one thing to claim superiority over that Judaism for the purpose of keeping persecuted Christians true to the faith, but it would be quite another thing to claim superiority over that Judaism for the purpose of taking command of Jewish religious life. And to suppose a synergy of both purposes founders on the unlikelihood that a persecuted minority thought of taking over the large, persecuting body. On the contrary and as already noted, Matthew underlines the comparative fewness of those who will be saved: "For the gate is small and the way is narrow that leads to life, and few are those who find it" (7:14).

So we are back to the old question whether Matthew's Gospel represents an intramural competition for power within Judaism (Christian Judaism versus protorabbinic Judaism) or an intramural crisis of discipleship within Jewish Christianity (defections from discipleship back into Judaism versus perseverance in Christian life and witness). If Matthew's soteriological emphasis on perseverance arises out of persecution, as it seems to do, score a point for an intramural crisis of discipleship within Jewish Christianity over against an intramural competition for power within Judaism. And given an intramural crisis of discipleship within a Jewish Christianity persecuted by non-Christian Judaism, then from that standpoint the possibility of an early date for Matthew looks good. For we know of such persecution prior to the destruction of Jerusalem and the temple, and one has to ask whether after that destruction non-Christian Jews had enough political clout to persecute Jewish Christians.[2]

---

[2] On the question of Matthew's date see further Gundry, *Matthew*, 599–623, 672–73.

8. The Sermon on the Mount
according to H. D. Betz[1]

Hans Dieter Betz's commentary on the Sermon on the Mount (Matt 5:3–7:27; hereafter the SM) was long-awaited. What a mighty tome it turned out to be – 640 double-columned, heavily footnoted pages of main text, plus 37 pages of preliminaries (Foreword, Preface, Reference Codes, Short Titles of Works Often Cited, and Editor's Note) and 50 pages of additional material (Bibliography and Indices) – enough to take your breath away! Earlier published work by Betz on the SM – *Essays on the Sermon on the Mount*[2] and portions of *Synoptische Studien*[3] – whetted scholarly appetites for this full treatment. Now those appetites have been sated, whatever the degree to which the commentary earns agreement.

The present review essay expresses appreciative admiration, raises higher critical questions, and offers a theological observation. The bulk belongs to higher critical questions, but first the appreciative admiration. For understanding the SM the commentary by Betz provides a treasure trove of materials both in the history of interpretation, in his own interpretation of the scriptural text, and above all in Greco-Roman background. Jewish background is not so strongly represented, but then we already have plenty of that in other treatments. The world of biblical scholarship owes Betz a very large debt of gratitude for his massive research and penetrating discussions. Nothing said from here on is meant to detract from this accolade.

Higher critically, Betz posits a primitive pool of Jesus' sayings and then argues that drawing on that pool, someone composed Q. Drawing mainly on that same pool but occasionally on Q, someone composed the SM as a free-standing entity; and in the same fashion someone composed the Sermon on the Plain (Luke 6:20–49; hereafter the SP) as another free-standing entity. Q contained a protosermon that provided a basis for the SM and the SP; but after the composi-

---

[1] H. D. Betz, *A Commentary on the Sermon on the Mount, including the Sermon on the Plain (Matthew 5:3–7:27 and Luke 6:20–49)* (ed. A. Y. Collins; Hermeneia; Minneapolis: Fortress, 1995).

[2] H. D. Betz, *Essays on the Sermon on the Mount* (Philadelphia: Fortress, 1985).

[3] H. D. Betz, *Synoptische Studien: Gesammelte Aufsätze II* (Tübingen: Mohr [Siebeck], 1992).

tions of the SM and the SP someone revised Q by substituting the SM for the protosermon and someone produced another revision of Q by substituting the SP for the protosermon. Finally, Matthew incorporated the version of Q containing the SM (Q[Matt]) into his Gospel and Luke incorporated the version of Q containing SP (Q[Luke]) into his Gospel, but these incorporations entailed no redactions of the SM and the SP by Matthew and Luke.[4]

It is unclear whether Betz thinks Matthew and Luke likewise abstained from redacting the rest of their respective versions of Q. If not, how is it that they spared only the SM and the SP, and spared them in concert though working independently and on different sermons? On the other hand, if Matthew and Luke did abstain from redacting the rest of Q too, how is it that they redacted Mark but froze up when they came to Q, and did so despite working independently on Mark and different versions of Q? And if they did not redact any of Q, on what grounds can we distinguish them from the redactors of their versions of Q? Whatever the answers to these questions, at least so far as the SM and the SP are concerned Betz has buried Matthew and Luke as authors and resurrected them as scissors-and-paste copyists, and makes no bones about having done so.

Of course, the hypothesis that both the SM and the SP drew on a protosermon that made up part of original Q explains the similarities between the SM and the SP.[5] But Betz uses the differences between the SM and the SP to argue that these sermons were composed independently from each other as well as

---

[4] Betz, *Commentary*, 7–9, 42–44, 88.

[5] For the well-known similarities see Betz, *Commentary*, 70:
"The two Sermons share component parts and overall arrangement. Both have an *exordium*, in which beatitudes constitute the major component.... Jesus' love-command plays the major role in the main body of both Sermons. Both Sermons carefully expound the meaning of this love-command .... The presuppositions and conclusions ... are on the whole the same. Both Sermons recognize the Golden Rule as a fundamental ethical principle. Both Sermons conclude with the parable of the two house builders. Beyond these major components, the two Sermons share a pool of individual sayings, images, metaphors, and theological concepts. They also have in common that they both function in the eduction [*sic*, education] of disciples."
Betz assigns the SM and the SP to a genre of *epitomai*, defined as condensations of an earlier and larger work into a systematic whole (pp. 70–80). But this assignation does not explain the similarities between the SM and the SP, nor does Betz try to explain them thus. For one thing, the similarities run too deep, wide, and detailed. For another, no other *epitomai* exhibit the special similarities that bind the SM and the SP closely to each other. Betz's admission of great variety in structure and content among *epitomai* (p. 79) further rules out this genre – if genre it is – as an explanation for the similarities between the SM and the SP. The presence of a protosermon in original Q explains not only these similarities but also the position of the SM and the SP "at about the same place in both Gospels [Matthew and Luke], and in both [Gospels] they [the sermons] are surrounded by similar narrative framework (Matt 4:24–5:2 and Luke 6:17–20a). In both Gospels they are followed by the story of the centurion's servant at Capernaum (Matt 8:5–13 and Luke 7:1–10). This sequence of textual units, independently parallel in Matthew and Luke, must have been the same in Q" (p. 43).

outside Q and prior to revisions of Q.[6] The question then arises, Are the differences so great as to require independent compositions? Betz's affirmative answer to this question prompts further questions, which he has not answered: Is Matt 10:5–42 so different from Mark 6:7–13 as to require composition independent from the Markan passage, i.e., so different as to require the hypothesizing of a protopassage on which Matthew and Mark drew independently from each other? Is Matt 13:1–52 so different from Mark 4:1–32 as to require composition independent from that Markan passage? Is Matt 18:1–35 so different from Mark 9:33–37, 42–48 as to require composition independent from Mark? And is Matthew 23–25 so different from Mark 13 as to require composition independent from Mark?

If in respect to these other discourses the differences are not so great as to require independence except for the common drawing of some material from a protodiscourse, in what ways do these differences fall short of those that are supposed to make such a requirement for the SM and the SP? The addition to 10:5b–15 of 10:16–42; to 13:1–23 of the parables concerning the wheat and tares and its explanation, the hid treasure, the pearl of great price, the good and bad fish, and the treasures new and old; to 18:1–9 of the parables concerning the lost sheep and the unforgiving servant plus intervening instructions on a sinning brother; and to the eschatological discourse in ch. 24 of chs. 23 and 25 – these extensive additions, not to detail smaller ones and other changes, create differences from Markan parallels that might appear to some people just as large as any differences that exist between the SM and the SP. Moreover, throughout the five discourses of Jesus in Matthew, differences from discourse material in the immediate Markan parallels are sometimes paralleled elsewhere in the triple tradition and sometimes apart from Mark in the double tradition, and sometimes are unique to Matthew. In these respects, then, the comparison between the SM and the SP presents nothing distinctive that would support independent composition of the SM and the SP as free-standing entities outside Q and prior to revisions of Q. Conversely, the reasoning that runs toward such composition of the SM and the SP would – if applied to Matthean discourses other than the SM – require that they too were composed independently from their Markan parallels (a conclusion unlikely to attract very many endorsements).

---

[6] For example, Betz notes that the SM contains an eschatological section absent from the SP (*Commentary*, 70). But elsewhere Matthew adds eschatological material (the wheat and tares, the good and bad fish, the wise and foolish virgins, the man without a wedding garment, the judgment of sheep and goats, etc.), so that one can justifiably suppose Matthew himself added some eschatological material to the sermon found in Q. Betz (p. 70) notes that the SM contains no threats in addition to beatitudes, as the SP does; but he himself also notes (p. 98) that in echoing the beatitude of the *Homeric Hymn to Demeter* (lines 480–83), Pindar omits the accompanying threat (frg. 121).

Betz argues further, this time not from differences between the SM and the SP but from differences between the SM and the rest of Matthew, that the evangelist did not redact the SM when he took it over from Q^Matt. Though seeing fewer and smaller differences between the SP and the rest of Luke, Betz nevertheless uses them to argue also against Lukan redaction of Q^Luke. His omitting to discuss in detail these latter differences makes it needless to consider them here. But concerning the deduction that Matthew did not redact the SM the question arises, Outside the SM are there any Matthean passages that can be compared in length even remotely to the SM and at the same time be shown to lack the evangelist's redactional interference and thus to provide support by analogy for such a lack in the SM? Betz cites no such passages, much less shows them to lack redactional interference by Matthew; and it would seem hard for anyone else to make up for this deficiency in argument.

Further questions arise concerning differences between the SM and the rest of Matthew. Are the differences so great as to justify Betz's thesis that the evangelist did not redact the SM? Are they wide or narrow? Real or imagined? Should we similarly deny to Paul the statement, "We have been *saved* by *hope*" (Rom 8:24a), because it differs from his more usual message that "we have been *justified* by *faith*"? To the alleged differences between the SM and the rest of Matthew, then.

The SM teaches meekness for Jesus' disciples (5:5), says Betz, but elsewhere in Matthew Jesus himself exhibits meekness: "Different from the SM, Jesus' meekness became an important part of Matthew's christology."[7] To be sure, the SM never presents Jesus as a model of his ethical teaching. But 5:17 does state that he came not to destroy the law or the prophets but to fulfill them, 5:19 that doing must go along with teaching, and 7:15–20 that a tree is known by its fruits, i.e., a speaker by his conduct. Therefore Jesus' exhibiting in conduct outside the SM his own teaching on meekness within that sermon can hardly set the rest of Matthew against the SM. On the contrary, the uniqueness to Matthew of Jesus' saying, "Learn from me because I am meek and lowly in heart" (11:29), unites with the borrowing of meekness from Zech 9:9 in a distinctively Matthean formula-quotation (21:5) and with Matthew's habit of conforming his sources to OT phraseology, as evident especially in the triple tradition,[8] to favor that at 5:5 Matthew has borrowed from Ps 36:11 LXX to form the beatitude on meekness.

Betz draws another contrast from 5:5: whereas that beatitude in the SM speaks of inheriting the earth, 19:28 and 25:34 point to a new earth.[9] But 5:5 too might refer to a new earth, for the SM does not specify the old earth any more

---

[7] Betz, *Commentary*, 126.

[8] R. H. Gundry, *The Use of the Old Testament in St. Matthew's Gospel with Special Reference to the Messianic Hope* (NovTSup 18; Leiden: E. J. Brill, 1967), 132–33.

[9] Betz, *Commentary*, 128.

than it specifies a new one. Though it speaks of a regeneration, 19:28 does not mention the earth. Nor does 25:34 speak of a new earth, only of inheriting a kingdom prepared since the founding of the world. And in general a regenerated and inherited earth – if 19:28 and 25:34 *had* used the term "earth" – could still be the inherited earth of 5:5.

In the SM, Betz argues, righteousness is the object of hungering and thirsting (5:6); but elsewhere in Matthew Jesus models righteousness (see, e.g., 3:15; 27:19), and righteousness already characterizes his disciples, though not perfectly.[10] But again, the SM itself demands that a teacher exhibit in conduct his teachings. And righteousness already characterizes Jesus' disciples, though not perfectly, in the SM as well as elsewhere in Matthew: "Blessed are the ones persecuted because of righteousness" (5:10); "unless your righteousness exceeds that of the scribes and Pharisees…" (5:20); "be careful not to perform your righteousness before people to be seen by them" (6:1).

Betz treats 5:13–16 as a commission by Jesus of his disciples ("let your light shine in front of people," for example) and then notes the absence there of any Christian terms such as "church," "gospel," "discipleship," and "faith," and of any reference to Christian baptism, miracle-working, Jesus' authority, and authority and power given by him to the community, all of which are found in other commissioning passages (Mark 16:15–17; Matt 16:18–19; 18:17–18; 28:18–20; John 20:23; Gal 1:16).[11] But one has to ask whether 5:13–16 really is a commissioning passage rather than an exhortation to the doing of good works in public such as we find in 1 Pet 2:11–3:17, hardly a commissioning passage. Betz does not suggest how "church" could have been worked appropriately into the figurative sayings of Matt 5:13–16. After all, they are couched in the second person plural: "*You* are the salt of the earth…. *You* are the light of the world." Outside the SM, moreover, "church" is missing from passages that Betz himself relates to the Christian witness of Matthew's church (chs. 10 and 24) as well as from all the commissioning passages listed by Betz except for 16:18–19; 18:17–18, which contain no commission and therefore do not belong on his list. Outside Mark 16:15–17, which is the spurious and only commissioning passage to carry most of the items missing from Matt 5:13–16, "gospel" appears only in Gal 1:16, "discipleship" and Christian baptism only in Matt 28:18–20, and "faith" and miracle-working in none of the commissioning passages. As usual, then, an argument from silence proves weak.

None of the hermeneutical principles apparent in 5:17–20 appear elsewhere in the synoptic tradition, including the rest of Matthew. So says Betz.[12] But in 15:3, "Why also do you ['Pharisees and scribes' – v. 1] transgress the command of

---

[10] Betz, *Commentary*, 131–32.
[11] Betz, *Commentary*, 156.
[12] Betz, *Commentary*, 172.

God on account of your tradition?" looks like a restatement in the form of an accusatory question of 5:17a ("do not think that I have come to destroy the law or the prophets") or 5:20b ("unless your righteousness exceeds that of the scribes and Pharisees ..."). Betz himself draws a parallel between 5:19 and 23:3, 23; Mark 7:8–9;[13] and since he regards 5:19 as referring to Jesus' authoritative interpretations of the Torah, by his own lights 28:20 ("teaching them to observe all things that I have commanded you") looks like 5:19. As to 5:20, it is yet again Betz himself who draws a parallel between "this rather positive stand toward the Pharisees [in that their righteousness 'is the right kind but inferior in degree']" and 23:3 4, "which states that the Pharisees have the right teaching but fall in the right practice."[14] If he appeals to pre-Matthean tradition behind chs. 15 and 23, he can hardly argue for a prefabricated SM on the ground of differences from the rest of Matthew. For it assumes what needs to be proved to say that agreements with the SM count as pre-Matthean but disagreements with the SM count as Matthean – this to preserve the thesis of a SM that Matthew did not redact.

Still on the topic of righteousness in 5:20, Betz says that the criticism of Pharisees only for inferior righteousness "has no precise parallels" elsewhere in the NT and "mentions none of the usual specifics, including the keeping of the Sabbath, tithing, purity and impurity, separation from the 'people of the land' ('*am hā-'āreṣ*), contradiction between words and deeds, and so on,"[15] and that the superior righteousness taught by Jesus has the Jewish sense of achievement by human action and therefore differs from the Matthean sense of imitating the righteousness of Christ (3:15; 10:41; 27:4, 19, 24).[16] But these observations overlook that in 5:20 Jesus is not addressing the Pharisees by way of criticism, as he does in chs. 15 and 23, so that he has no need to mention "the usual specifics." He is addressing his disciples ("Blessed are you whenever people reproach and persecute you ... because of me" – 5:11) and using the Pharisees only by way of a warning aside, a negative example. Under the rubric of "hypocrites" some specifics do come into the SM at 6:1–17 (almsgiving, prayer, and fasting). And elsewhere in Matthew imitation of Jesus' example would seem to count for "achievement by human action" as much as would obedience to his words in the SM (see 11:29 again). Furthermore, Joseph's righteousness in 1:19 cannot count as an imitation of Jesus' righteousness (Jesus was not yet born), nor can the Baptist's coming to "the chief priests and the elders ... in the way of righteousness" (21:23, 32) before ever he joined Jesus in fulfilling all righteousness and before Jesus started teaching righteousness (3:7–17). Thus breaks down the supposed difference between righteousness inside and outside the SM.

---

[13] Betz, *Commentary*, 186 nn. 135–36.
[14] Betz, *Commentary*, 192.
[15] Betz, *Commentary*, 194; cf. 191.
[16] Betz, *Commentary*, 190.

According to Betz, Matt 5:31–32 reads Deut 24:1–4 as condemning divorce by inference from the Deuteronomic declaration that a divorcee remarried to another man is unclean whereas Matt 19:8 reads Deut 24:1–4 as permitting divorce because of hardheartedness.[17] But 5:31 quotes Deut 24:1–4 as making provision for divorce while restricting it by requiring the divorcee to be given a bill of divorce; 5:32 escalates the restriction to a prohibition with but one exception; and in 19:8, where the next verse also grants a single exception, the rationale of hardheartedness casts Deuteronomic divorce in just as bad a light as does the inference from Deuteronomic uncleanness in 5:31–32. At this point, then, the SM does not stand in tension with the rest of Matthew.

Betz suggests that 5:43 omits "as yourself" from "love your neighbor" because inclusion of the comparative phrase in a framework of imitating God would have implied that he loves himself whereas the SM portrays his love as selfless and indiscriminate for evil people as well as good people, for the unrighteous as well as the righteous (v. 45). Then Betz contrasts this indiscriminateness in the SM with the Jesus-focused love of God elsewhere in Matthew (3:17; 12:18; 17:5).[18] But a God who in the SM wants you to do good works in public that others may glorify him and who wants you to pray that his name be reverenced and his rule come and his will be done on earth as it is done in heaven and to serve him rather than Mammon – this God of the SM would seem to have a rather healthy amount of self-love. And the Matthew who outside the SM sees no conflict between loving God and loving your neighbor as yourself (19:37–40) is unlikely to see a conflict between God's loving his Son and God's loving other human beings, whether righteous or unrighteous. His Son *is* one of the righteous, as noted by Pilate's wife and by Pilate himself (27:19, 24).

The use of "Gentiles" at 5:47; 6:7, 32a in the purely negative sense of "pagans" is supposed to distinguish the SM from the rest of Matthew, where Gentiles appear as objects of evangelism, many of whom have populated Matthew's church (28:19–20).[19] But 18:17 too uses "Gentile" in the negative sense ("let him be to you as a Gentile"; cf. also 10:5, 18; 20:19, 25; 24:9). On close inspection the distinction dissolves.

Throughout 6:1–6, 16–18, says Betz, "hypocrites" are neither identified explicitly with the Pharisees (cf. 5:20) – rather, with character types "displaying sham religiousness" – nor equated with Jesus' adversaries. Even the addressees of the SM can be hypocrites (7:5: "Hypocrite, first cast the beam out of your eye"). For Matthew, by contrast, all Jewish adversaries of Jesus are hypocrites (15:7; 22:18; 23:13, 14, 15, 28; 24:51).[20] But at 7:5 "hypocrite" appears

---

[17] Betz, *Commentary*, 248–49, 258.
[18] Betz, *Commentary*, 302–3.
[19] Betz, *Commentary*, 320, 524 n. 40.
[20] Betz, *Commentary*, 347, 357 n. 198.

in the singular for an individual, not in the plural for a class. More importantly, in Matthew outside the SM certain people are called "hypocrites" not because they are Jesus' adversaries but because they display sham religiousness, just as in the SM. Furthermore, in 15:7 the hypocrites – i.e., the scribes and Pharisees (cf. 5:20) – do not oppose Jesus but ask a question critical of his disciples; and at 24:51 it is a professing disciple, not an adversary of Jesus, whose fate is that of the hypocrites much as a discipular addressee of the SM is called a hypocrite at 7:5.

"The synagogues" in 6:2, 5 are not "*their* [the Jews'] synagogues," as in 4:23; 9:35, 10.17, 12.9, 13.54, and thus are "places where the members of the SM community also meet and observe what is reported."[21] But Betz himself notes that the use in 23:6 is like that in 6:2, 5, so that the latter is not distinctive of the SM.[22] Furthermore, in 6:2, 5 "the hypocrites" and "they" provide a third person plural framework for "the synagogues"; and the coordination in 23:6, 34 of "the synagogues" and "your synagogues" (the latter of which is equivalent to "their synagogues" inasmuch as Jesus is addressing "the scribes and Pharisees") should warn us against taking the absence of "their" as evidence of attendance at synagogues in contradistinction to nonattendance when "their" (or an antagonistic "your") is present. One can also question whether references to synagogal practices imply current attendance by the SM community or only recollections from past attendance. In either case, ch. 23 undermines any distinctiveness of the SM in this respect.

Matt 16:19; 18:18 (cf. John 20:23) give special authority to Peter and the church, respectively, to forgive sins or not to forgive them with regard to the guilty parties' eternal and irreversible destiny; but 6:12, 14–15 does not include such authority – rather, only an authority by which disciples are obligated to forgive those who sin against them.[23] Yet Betz himself notes a lack of the special authority not only in the SM but also in 28:18–20, so that on this point too the SM loses its distinctiveness. A further weakness in the argument lies in Betz's equation of binding and loosing with interpersonal forgiveness. The passage 6:12, 14–15 deals with such forgiveness. But the association in 16:19 with scribal keys (cf. 23:13) favors interpretive binding and loosing – i.e., prohibition and permission – of certain kinds of conduct; and the binding and loosing in 18:18 deal with ecclesiastical discipline and restoration, not with interpersonal forgiveness. Thus the passages do not stand in tension with each other so much as they deal with different issues. Moreover, since 18:15–18 is concerned for the fate of sinners whereas 6:14–15 is concerned for the fate of those sinned against

---

[21] Betz, *Commentary*, 156 n. 9 (italics original).

[22] Betz, *Commentary*, 156 n. 9 again. He adds 23:34 – wrongly, because it reads "your synagogues," not "the synagogues."

[23] Betz, *Commentary*, 156, 417.

if they do not exercise forgiveness, again no tension exists between the passages. And in the parable of the unforgiving servant at 18:23–35, which is uniquely Matthean, we find the same concern for the fate of those sinned against that we find in 6:14–15. The narrowing of interpersonal relations in society at large (so 6:12, 14–15) to interpersonal relations in the church (so ch. 18) leads to matters of discipline that could not apply in the larger society. But the concern for those sinned against is exactly the same in both passages, so that we have no reason not to see Matthew at work in 6:14–15.

According to Betz the doctrine of the kingdom in the SM is unique in the NT in that 6:25–34 defines the kingdom in terms of *creatio continua* by God the Father; hence, seeking first the kingdom and his righteousness means trusting him to provide the basic physical needs of each day.[24] But Luke 12:22–32 parallels Matt 6:25–34 and includes seeking the Father's kingdom and having "these things added to you." Again the SM proves undistinctive. Besides, the command to seek first the kingdom and God's righteousness instead of seeking first for food, drink, and clothing does not define the kingdom, as though the SM spelled out a doctrine of God's kingdom that could be contrasted with kingdom-doctrine elsewhere in the NT. The passage deals with priorities, not with the kingdom as such; i.e., the wording does not equate the kingdom with God's daily providence. This providence is something in addition to the kingdom (προστεθήσεται). As an object of seeking, therefore, the kingdom takes priority over daily needs.

In 7:15–20 the SM does not relate false prophets to the end time, but 24:11, 24 does, says Betz.[25] He himself notes, however, that the SM puts the warning against false prophets right before an account of the Last Judgment. And though 24:24 puts false prophets in the great tribulation, i.e., in the end time just preceding the Parousia, 24:11 puts false prophets also in an earlier time. There is no reason why 7:15–20 cannot correspond to 24:11 rather than contrasting with 24:24.

But according to Betz "the eschatology of the SM is conventionally Jewish, devoid of apocalyptic characteristics and quite different from the Christian apocalyptic worldview of Matthew, as expressed especially in Matthew 24–28."[26] What then of inheriting the earth, receiving mercy and being pronounced God's sons at the Last Judgment, seeing him, gaining great reward in heaven, and other promises of eschatological peripety in the Beatitudes? What of the passing away of heaven and earth (5:18)? "The gehenna of fire" (5:22)? Your whole body's being cast into that gehenna (5:29, 30)? Receiving judgment hereafter for having passed judgment here and now (7:1–2)? The broadness of the

---

[24] Betz, *Commentary*, 465; idem, "Sermon on the Mount/Sermon on the Plain," *ABD* 5:1110; idem, *Essays*, 95, 121.

[25] Betz, *Commentary*, 527–28.

[26] Betz, *Synoptische Studien*, 275.

way leading to destruction and the numerousness of those taking that way (7:13)? The narrowness of the way leading to life and the fewness of those taking that way (7:14)? The portrayal of the Last Judgment as such (7:21–23)? The comparison of that judgment to a storm (7:24–27)? Presumably Betz would describe these eschatological elements of the SM as "conventionally Jewish." Yet they find many parallels elsewhere in Matthew, the book of Revelation, and other early Christian literature as well as in Jewish literature such as *4 Ezra* and *1 Enoch*.

Above all, then, Betz tries to separate off the SM and its eschatology by building a contrast between a lack of Christology here ("the SM contains no Christology at all"[27]) and the presence of high Christology elsewhere in Matthew. In the first place, however, this argument overlooks both the dropping in Matt 10:42 of a christological reference in the parallel Mark 9:41 ("because you are Christ's") and the changing to "*You* have said [that I am 'the Christ, the Son of God']" in Matt 26:64 of Jesus' "I am ['the Christ, the Son of the Blessed One']" in Mark 14:62. Outside the SM, that is to say, Matthew shows himself capable of softening and even omitting Christology.

But what of Betz's evidence for a contrast between no Christology in the SM and high Christology elsewhere in Matthew? He begins by citing passages in the SM that portray the disciples of Jesus as God's "sons" (5:9, 45), passages in the SM that portray God as the disciples' "Father" (5:16, 45, 48; 6:1, 4, 6 [twice], 8, 9, 14, 15, 18 [twice], 26, 32; 7:11), and a passage in the SM where Jesus speaks of God as *his* "Father" too (7:21). Then Betz concludes that in the SM Jesus stands on an equal plane with the disciples, all of them sons of God their Father, whereas the rest of Matthew never calls the disciples "sons of God" but elevates Jesus to a unique kind of divine sonship: "the only son of God is Christ."[28] One can only say that this argument rests on oversights. For in 10:20, 29; 13:43; 18:14; 23:9 – all outside the SM – God is called the Father of Jesus' disciples (cf. 13:38: "the good seed are the sons of the kingdom [which is the kingdom 'of the Father' of 'the righteous' – v. 43]"); and in 17:24–27 the freedom of the disciple Peter as well as of Jesus from having to pay a tax (though they pay it anyway to avoid giving offense) rests on his as well as Jesus' being one of "the sons" of a king, i.e., of God, for the upkeep of whose temple the tax goes.

At 5:10, Betz notes, no attempt is made to connect suffering for righteousness with Jesus' death: "I regard this absence of a christology and indeed of any reference to the suffering of Jesus as evidence that the SM comes from a pre-Matthean source."[29] But such a reference would be narratively premature before the Jewish leaders start to oppose Jesus and especially before he starts to predict his

---

[27] Betz, *Synoptische Studien*, 274.
[28] Betz, *Commentary*, 142 n. 398.
[29] Betz, *Commentary*, 145.

passion. The discourses in chs. 10 and 13, which precede the passion predictions as the SM does, likewise lack any reference to the passion.[30] Are we then to infer that they too derive whole from a pre-Matthean source and underwent no redaction by Matthew? The same and similar observations apply to the absence from the SM of references to Jesus' resurrection as well as death, to the church and baptism, to the imitation of Christ – and apply as well to the absence of specifically Christian soteriology, to which absence Betz appeals.[31] These elements too would be narratively premature were they to appear in the SM.

Jesus' phrase "because of me," which in 5:11 describes the reproach and persecution of his disciples, "says no more than that the reason for the persecution is Jesus' teaching, which is dedicated to righteousness." Thus, says Betz, there is "not… a trace of high christology."[32] But if only Jesus' teaching of righteousness is in view one wonders why we do not read "because of my words," as in 7:24–27, or something like 13:21, "persecution on account of the word," instead of the intensely personal "because of me." This wonderment increases when noting both the strong ἐγώ, "I," of Jesus in the so-called Antitheses of 5:21–48 and the reference in 7:22 to using his name in successful wonder-working. That is, the context in the SM supports a high Christology for "because of me" at 5:11.

Instead of connecting with Jesus' death, notes Betz, the persecuted disciples stand in parallel with the persecuted prophets ("for thus they persecuted the prophets before you" – 5:12c).[33] But which of the prophets was persecuted because of another person, unless that person be God, who gave his word to the prophet, in which case the parallel persecution of Jesus' disciples because of him would imply a high Christology? In any case, the parallel with persecuted prophets falls short of eliminating a christological implication in the phrase "because of me."

---

[30] Even the statement in 10:38, "And the person who does not take his cross and follow after me is not worthy of me," does not connect the disciples' suffering with Jesus' death. He has not predicted that he will die by crucifixion. Nor will he make such a prediction till the eve of his entry into Jerusalem (20:19). Nor will he take his cross or carry it in the Passion Narrative; Simon of Cyrene will (27:32). Yet further, Jesus does not speak of his disciples' being *nailed* to crosses, only of their *taking* crosses, i.e., of picking up the horizontal beam and carrying it. In the Roman world condemned people might be forced to pick up that part of a cross at the beginning of their journey to the place of execution. On the way, others hurled insults at them, spat on them, and made sport of them. Though death becomes a subsequent possibility in Jesus' saying (v. 39), cross-taking only means subjecting oneself to shame, to "the howling, hostile mob," by following after Jesus wherever he goes (J. Jeremias, *New Testament Theology* [New York: Macmillan, 1971], 242). Since the text refers to a literal following at this very time, prior to the passion, taking one's cross can hardly have a literal meaning. Not only has Jesus not taken a cross or said that he would. Those who follow him from this point on will have taken crosses no more than those who earlier started following him took crosses. Nor *can* they take crosses in a literal sense, for no Roman court of law has condemned them to death by crucifixion.

[31] Betz, *Synoptische Studien*, 88–92, 246.

[32] Betz, *Commentary*, 147.

[33] Betz, *Commentary*, 152–53, esp. n. 516.

As to the recently mentioned Antitheses, Betz treats the first part of each one as a mistaken, literal interpretation of Scripture rather than as Scripture itself, so that Jesus' "but I say to you" comes across as the word of a mere interpreter of Scripture rather than as the pronouncement of one who takes a position above Scripture by ratcheting it up to new heights of intensity. And Betz sees the second part of each antithesis as based not on Jesus' authority but on reason, "as can be confirmed by [Jesus' use of] examples, proverbs, rhetorical questions, and so on."[34] But according to Scripture the Lord God himself reasons with his people by using all these devices (see, e.g., Isa 1:18 and the surrounding passage), so that Jesus' use of reason rules out a high Christology not in the least. It is hard to accept the quotations and paraphrases of Scripture – "You shall not commit murder," "You shall not commit adultery," and so on – as mistaken, literal interpretation rather than as Scripture itself.[35] And Betz admits that Jesus' declaration, "But *I* say to you," differs from the rabbinic formula, "But *you* must say." Drawing on David Daube, Betz tries to minimize this difference but has to concede that in contrast with Jesus' delaration the rabbinic formula "deemphasizes rather than emphasizes the authority of the rabbi."[36]

The address to Jesus at the Last Judgment, "Lord, Lord" (7:21, 22), does not advocate a high Christology, according to Betz. On the contrary, he says, it "ridicules the devotion of Gentile Christians" who call Jesus "Lord" but are "deluded by their christology" so as to have neglected the doing of God's will and become workers of lawlessness.[37] Betz does not discuss the damaging implications of "Marana tha" (1 Cor 16:22) in respect of his attributing to Jewish Christians antagonism toward κύριος-Christology. Those who address Jesus as Lord in the SM have certainly neglected the doing of God's will and worked lawlessness. But because of delusion by their high Christology? If so, Betz would have to say that Matthew shares with the SM this same low estimation of high Christology, because in 25:11 the foolish virgins who are shut out from the wedding feast of salvation address him in the same way: "Lord, Lord." Yet from beginning to end, from "the Christ," "the son of David," and "Immanuel... God with us" in ch. 1 to the universally authoritative and omnipresent "Son," sandwiched between "the Father" and "the Holy Spirit," in ch. 28, as Betz recognizes, Matthew puts forward a high Christology. Indeed, he writes "Lord" thirty-four times where parallel pericopes lack it and uses it another fifteen times in pericopes unique to his

---

[34] Betz, *Commentary*, 204–11.

[35] See the standard commentaries for OT references. Even the clause, "and you shall hate your enemy" (5:43c), appears to come from Ps 139:21–22, overlooked by Betz (R. H. Gundry, *Matthew* [2d ed.; Grand Rapids: Eerdmans, 1994], 96–97). Betz's statement that Matthew "usually quotes the LXX verbatim" (*Commentary*, 304) is simply untrue (see Gundry, *The Use of the Old Testament*, 147–50 et passim).

[36] Betz, *Commentary*, 208–10.

[37] Betz, *Synoptische Studien*, 236–37; cf. idem, *Commentary*, 546–49.

Gospel (as compared to thirty paralleled uses). It seems easier to see the SM and the rest of Matthew as sharing a high Christology of Jesus' lordship than to see a contrast between them at this point.

Still in 7:21, according to Betz Jesus does not say to the workers of lawlessness "our Father" or "your Father" but "my Father," not because he presents himself to them as God's Son in a unique sense but because he wants to dissociate himself from them, the Gentile Christians he is rejecting.[38] But he is not yet speaking *to* them, only *about* them. And, more importantly, are we to think that in 10:32 "my Father" dissociates Jesus from those he confesses before God because they have confessed him (Jesus) before their fellow human beings? Or in 25:34 from the Father-blessed sheep who inherit the kingdom? Or in 26:29 from the disciples with whom Jesus will drink wine anew in the kingdom? The distinction between "my Father" and "your Father"[39] – a distinction found in Matthew both inside and outside the SM – seems to give Jesus' divine sonship a different status from that of the disciples' sonship to God.

Betz speaks of prophecy, exorcism, and miracles as "performed everywhere in the ancient world in the name of all sorts of deities" and admits that in 7:22 the SM recognizes "the magical potency of the name of Jesus" in those activities.[40] Well, then, the SM must hold to a high Christology; otherwise it could hardly consider Jesus' name potent.[41] That the name has proved potent even in the mouth of rejected workers of lawlessness heightens the entailed Christology.

But Betz will have Jesus as a judge in the SM no more than he will have there Jesus as a divine Lord or unique Son of God: "In 7:21–23 Jesus does not act as the eschatological judge but as the advocate of his disciples. This role remains within the eschatological thinking of Judaism and does not require a specifically Christian christology."[42] One might ask whether Judaism of the period really does exhibit another recent historical figure who claimed for himself the role of advocate for his followers at the Last Judgment or another figure of recent history whose followers claimed such a role for him. But Betz goes on to infer that the workers of lawlessness turn to Jesus "after they have been rejected by the divine judge, presumably God himself."[43] Admittedly their plea, "Have we not …?" may imply a previous rejection. But where do we find any indi-

---

[38] Betz, *Commentary*, 548.

[39] And "our Father" too, for 6:9b instructs the disciples how to pray: "Therefore you (ὑμεῖς) pray in this way" (6:9a). The "our" does not include Jesus.

[40] Betz, *Commentary*, 550.

[41] The SM does not reject prophecy, exorcism, and miracles as such, and the rest of Matthew accepts them "not without reservations" (Betz, *Commentary*, 551), so that no basic disagreement over them divides the SM from the rest of Matthew (against Betz's near argument to the opposite effect).

[42] Betz, *Commentary*, 554.

[43] Betz, *Commentary*, 549.

cation that it was God rather than Jesus who had rejected them? At last mention God was "in the heavens" (v. 21).

Undeterred, Betz interprets Jesus' statement-cum-command, "I never knew you. Depart from me, you who work lawlessness," not as a condemnation but as a legal formula of renunciation that says, "I can't represent you as your advocate because I don't know you and don't have any responsibility for you," in accordance with Matt 25:12 and a long string of other passages.[44] But it is difficult to find in those passages evidence for a formula of refusal on grounds of unacquaintance to act as someone's advocate before a judge. Take 25:12, for example. This passage carries special significance because the foolish virgins have just addressed the bridegroom exactly as the workers of lawlessness have addressed Jesus, "Lord, Lord"; because the bridegroom's statement, "I do not know you," parallels Jesus' statement, "I never knew you"; and because the shutting out of the foolish virgins corresponds to the sending away of the workers of lawlessness. The bridegroom does not refuse to act in front of anyone else as those virgins' advocate. He alone has the authority to open and shut the door. Likewise in 7:21–23 Jesus alone determines people's fate. Whether pronounced for the first time or reaffirmed, his description of them as "workers of lawlessness" reads like a judge's verdict; and his command that they depart from him, like a judge's sentence, as in 25:46, where the goats "go away [from 'the Son of Man,' who is sitting as judge on 'the throne of his glory' – v. 31] into eternal punishment." Of course, Jesus does act as an advocate, but outside the SM (Betz lists Matt 10:32–33 par. Luke 12:8–9; Mark 8:38 par. Luke 9:26; Rev 3:5; *2 Clem.* 3:2; 4:2–5[45]). If it were true that the SM "seems determined" in its "refusal to engage in any form of 'higher' christology" by portraying Jesus only as an "authoritative teacher and advocate at the last judgment" rather than as the eschatological judge himself,[46] we might have expected in 7:23 wording of the sort found in 10:33, say, "And then I will deny them before my Father in heaven."[47]

---

[44] Betz, *Commentary,* 551. He cites Gen 29:5; 42:7–8; Job 19:14; Tob 5:2; 7:4; Matt 11:27; John 1:26, 31; 7:28–29; 8:19, 55; 10:4–5, 14–15, 27; 17:25–26; Acts 12:14; 19:15; Str-B 1:469; Wettstein 1:344–45.

[45] Betz, *Commentary,* 141.

[46] Betz, *Commentary,* 548.

[47] G. N. Stanton (*A Gospel for a New People* [Edinburgh: T. & T. Clark, 1992], 317–18) notes that to keep from weakening his thesis that the SM is un-Matthean Betz "boldly suggests" (Stanton might better have said "timidly," for Betz's suggestion – and it is only a suggestion – lies buried in a footnote) that the whole discourse in which 10:32–33 appears also represents "a pre-Matthean composition" (as Betz thinks the SM does [*Essays,* 42 n. 62]). Stanton also wonders whether Betz's thesis requires a similar treatment of the discourses in chs. 13, 19, (23) 24–25 too and notes that the vocabulary of 7:21–23 often appears to be redactional elsewhere in Matthew and thus makes it easy to think that Matthew has redactionally enlarged the saying recorded in Luke 6:46: "And why do you call me, 'Lord, Lord,' and not do the things I say?" (cf. almost every important word and phrase in the Matthean passage with the statistics in Gundry,

Finally against high Christology in the SM Betz argues that the soteriology of the SM – i.e., salvation by obedience to the Torah as interpreted by Jesus – requires belief in Jesus only as a teacher.[48] But as noted by C. E. Carlston, the binding force of Jesus' interpretation – a force so strong that it determines people's eternal fate – differs from the correctability of both Jewish teachers and Greco-Roman philosophers.[49]

Before leaving the question of differences between the SM and the rest of Matthew we need also to bring into play some differences within the SM. The beatitude in 5:11 switches from the third person plural of the preceding beatitudes to the second person plural. In 5:13–16 Jesus tells his disciples, "Thus let your light shine in front of people so that they may see your good works," but in 6:1 warns them, "be careful not to perform your righteousness in front of people to be seen by them" and in the following verses instructs them to do their good works "in secret." *"Your"* righteousness" in 6:1 differs from *"his"* [God's] righteousness" in 6:33.[50] An absolute prohibition of judging appears in 7:1; but on condition of casting a beam out of your own eye 7:5 allows you to cast a mere speck out of your brother's eye. In 7:13 "many" describes "the masses of humankind on their way to destruction" whereas in 7:22, according to Betz, "many" describes "the majority of Gentile Christians, in comparison with whom the Christians of the SM feel themselves to be in the minority (cf. 7:14: οἱ ὀλίγοι)."[51]

These pairs of sayings can be made complementary rather than contradictory, of course;[52] but it is hard to escape an impression that if the members of these pairs were found not both in the SM but one in the SM and one elsewhere in Matthew, Betz would have used the differences between them to argue for a non-Matthean character and original independence of the SM. To the extent that he sees these differences within the SM and treats them as due to drawing on different sources and to redaction that took place in the formation of the SM and earlier tradition history, both prior to Matthew's incorporating the SM by way of Q^Matt, Betz loses his argument that differences between the SM and the rest of Matthew point to a pre-Matthean sermon unredacted by Matthew when he incorporated it. For if the author and reviser of the SM drew on different sources and redacted them without making them entirely cohesive, why could

Matthew, 674–82). Deserving consideration is Stanton's opinion that Matthew and apocalyptists were not so careful as to see a contradiction between advocate and judge.

[48] Betz, *Commentary*, 189–97 et passim.

[49] C. E. Carston, "Betz on the Sermon on the Mount – A Critique," *CBQ* 50 (1988): 51.

[50] Betz does not take up the possibility that seeking God's righteousness and kingdom means seeking for the coming of God's rule, at which time he will do his persecuted people right by vindicating them (Gundry, *Matthew*, 118–19). Betz assumes that God's righteousness means the righteousness that God requires of human beings in conformity with his own character and actions.

[51] Betz, *Essays*, 127 n. 10.

[52] See, e.g., Betz, *Commentary*, 339, 346–47, 488.

not that author and reviser be Matthew himself, who did not make the SM entirely cohesive with the rest of his Gospel any more than he made the SM entirely cohesive with itself?

In other words, Betz's argument for a pre-Matthean SM unredacted by Matthew rests not just negatively on a lack of cohesion between that sermon and the rest of Matthew but also positively on cohesion within the sermon. Without such cohesion – and Betz freely acknowledges the lack of it[53] while self-contradictingly affirming it[54] – Matthew might as well be the one who put together incoherent elements within the sermon just as in Betz's view Matthew put the sermon together with elements incoherent with it elsewhere in his Gospel. For example, if he put righteousness as human achievement in the sermon together with righteousness as imitation of Christ outside the sermon, why could not he be the one who put together God's righteousness and human righteousness within the sermon? Where is the need for a pre-Matthean author of the sermon? Such questions fairly leap out of Betz's own observations:

> Within the SM a contradiction seems to exist between a theology of God's hiddenness (6:1–6, 16–18) and another theology emphasizing God's manifest activity in creation (5:45; 6:25–34; 7:11, 24–27). The contradiction is created through the combination of diverse sources. For the SM, both statements are true.[55]

And in another connection,

> Working with materials coming from different sources, the author, or rather the redactor, of the SM apparently did not care to harmonize these sources but instead shows a considerable tolerance for diversity. As the systematician that he no doubt also was, he took the diversity to be complementary rather than contradictory. The same degree of tolerance is shown later by the evangelist Matthew.[56]

Repeatedly, Betz denies that this or that in the SM could have come through Matthean redaction of material reflected more or less closely in the SP or elsewhere in Q. Though sometimes arguing for such a denial from differences between the SM and the SP, he does not seriously take up and criticize the positive efforts of other scholars to show just how the SM might have developed through Matthean redaction, differences from the SP being due to that very redaction

---

[53] See Betz, *Commentary*, 347–49:
"It is safe to assume that they [6:1–6, 16–18 and 6:7–15] cannot have come originally from the same pen because they present quite different theological perspectives.... the fact that such diverse sources could be integrated in the SM, which on the whole represents a somewhat different theology from either 6:1–6, 16–18 or 6:7–15, points to *multiple authorship* within the SM.... In other words, the author/redactor of the entire SM understood his task to be that of selecting and coordinating diverse materials from the Jesus-tradition" (italics original).

[54] As in the description of the SM as "reflecting a coherent theological thought world that is Jewish in character" (Betz, *Synoptische Studien*, 275).

[55] Betz, *Commentary*, 343.

[56] Betz, *Commentary*, 339; see also 348.

and to Lukan redaction as well.[57] Despite the prominent role recently played by word-statistics in scholars' determining the presence or absence of Matthean redaction, such statistics receive little or no attention; and Betz blithely makes assertions such as the following: "the language of vs 1 is not attributable to a specifically Matthean insertion, but it is adopted from and together with source material used by the evangelist himself."[58] No note is taken of Matthean insertions outside the SM of the same words and expressions into Markan material and, apparently, into other Q material. Betz describes the lack of "Thy will be done" in Luke's version of the Lord's Prayer as "hardly original," for example; yet though mentioning the importance for Matthew's Gospel of God's will, Betz does not bring up the statistics that would argue here for a Matthean insertion.[59]

As another example, take Betz's comment on 5:44:

There is no indication that the differences between the SM and the SP are due to the redaction of the Gospel writers Matthew and Luke, either by shortening Q/Luke or by expanding Q/Matthew. The SM and the SP agree only on one word, "pray," so that one must treat both texts as independently composed textual units. Consequently the redactional differences are due to the pre-Matthean and pre-Lukan authors of the SP and the SM, not to the authors of the final Gospels.[60]

But one might just as well say there is no indication that the differences between the SM and the SP are due to pre-Matthean and pre-Lukan redaction rather than to redaction by the evangelists themselves. Suppose that at this point the two sermons do agree on only the one word, "pray." Why should the disagreement between "for the ones persecuting you" (the SM) and "concerning the ones mistreating you" (the SP) indicate pre-gospel rather than gospel redaction? Besides, there is more agreement than on the one word, "pray." Both texts follow up with a prepositional phrase, each having an arthrous substantive participle as the object of its preposition. Though different, the prepositions are synonymous (ὑπέρ and περί, respectively). So also are the participles (τῶν διωκόντων and τῶν ἐπηρεαζόντων, respectively). Both participles have exactly the same direct object (ὑμᾶς, "you" [pl.]). And both commands to pray appear in the context of a preceding command to love your enemies, which command agrees verbatim in the two sermons – not to detail other similarities of context. Where lies the pressing need to posit redactions earlier than Matthew and Luke? And one

---

[57] Thus as the commentary progresses scholars holding different views from Betz's are cited with increasing rarity. Much less are they argued against. And U. Luz and G. Strecker appear more and more exclusively as Betz's partners in conversation, for they recognize a smaller amount of Matthean redaction than do most other Matthean scholars and to that extent seem agreeable to him.

[58] Betz, *Commentary*, 351.

[59] Betz, *Commentary*, 391–93; contrast W. Schenk, *Die Sprache des Matthäus* (Göttingen: Vandenhoeck & Ruprecht, 1987), 284–85; Gundry, *Matthew*, 106–7.

[60] Betz, *Commentary*, 312.

should question Betz's denial that evidence exists for redaction by an evangelist. For διώκω, "persecute," appears five times in Matthew where parallel pericopes lack it, and not only three times earlier in the SM (5:10, 11, 12) but also in the commissioning of the Twelve for their Galilean mission (10:23), over against only one paralleled appearance.[61]

In general, similarities between the SM and the rest of Matthew include more than diction. For example, the contrast between wise and foolish builders with which the SM closes – a contrast between true and false disciples inasmuch as the builders hear Jesus' words in the SM and the SM addresses Jesus' disciples matches the contrast elsewhere in Matthew between true and false disciples: wheat and tares, good and bad fish, wedding guests with and without a suitable garment, wise and foolish virgins (all peculiar to Matthew). Betz can say, of course, that the SM influenced Matthew's redaction elsewhere, but the dictional and other similarities attain such large proportions that it becomes gratuitous to distinguish the redactor of the SM from the redactor of the rest of Matthew. And to the degree that the SM influenced Matthew elsewhere it becomes harder for Betz to support the distinction on grounds of differences between the SM and the rest of Matthew: those differences become comparatively fewer in number, lesser in substance, and thereby weaker in argumentive value.

One more example of this sort will suffice: "the elaborate nature of the units SM/Matt 5:43–48 and SP/Luke 6:27–36 speaks clearly in favor of written texts prior to their inclusion in the Gospels."[62] But it remains mysterious why Matthew and Luke, operating on Q, should prove incapable of an elaborateness that earlier redactors proved quite capable of. The widely acknowledged though differently assessed large- and small-scale elaborateness evident throughout Matthew's Gospel outside the SM points away from Betz's thesis.[63] If the further thesis is correct that the SM "is a decisive passage for determining the theology of Matthew,"[64] then the part of Matthew's Gospel not redacted by him (the SM according to Betz) replaces Matthean redaction as the most telltale though not sole indicator of Matthew's theology. In a reversal of the usual reasoning that redactional changes provide the clearest such indicators, then, the unredacted tail (the SM) wags the redacted dog (the remainder of Matthew). But if the tail

---

[61] See Carlston, "Betz on the Sermon on the Mount," 55–56; Stanton, *A Gospel for a New People*, 314–16, for more extensive detailing of similarities in specially Matthean diction between the SM and the rest of Matthew, and for other similarities Stanton, 320–21.

[62] Betz, *Commentary*, 298.

[63] See, e.g., the discussions in D. A. Hagner, *Matthew 1–13* (WBC 33A; Dallas: Word, 1993), l–liii; U. Luz, *Matthew 1–7* (Minneapolis: Augsburg, 1989), 37–41; W. D. Davies and D. C. Allison, *Introduction and Commentary on Matthew I–VII* (vol. 1 of *A Critical and Exegetical Commentary on the Gospel according to Saint Matthew*; ICC; Edinburgh: T. & T. Clark, 1988), 58–72; C. L. Blomberg, *Matthew* (NAC 22; Nashville: Broadman, 1992), 22–25, and other literature cited by these authors.

[64] Betz, *Synoptische Studien*, 270.

wagged so decisively as Betz says it did, why did Matthew let stand those sup-posed differences from the SM that have become the basis for Betz's positing an independent origin for the sermon? Better is the older view that Matthew is him-self responsible for the shape of the SM.

As a matter of theological observation distinct from higher critical debate, both the extracting of the SM and the SP from Matthew and Luke for special commentary and the commenting on them as independent entities prior to their incorporation into Matthew and Luke, and so far as possible even prior to their incorporation into different versions of Q, make Betz's commentary *pre*canon-ical in its thrust. Accompanying this thrust is a universalizing tendency, es-pecially in discussions of what Betz considers to be the core of the SM. He makes that core represent the best in the general phenomenon of religion (cf. the unusually large number of Greco-Roman parallels – some might say forced par-allels – drawn by him). This turn comes despite the limited address to Jesus' disciples:

The petitioners of the Lord's Prayer [which according to Betz goes back to Jesus and forms the center of the SM] are defined as members of the human community, because the pronoun "our" includes all human beings living on the earth. Whatever humans have to bring before God, they can rightly bring before him only as representatives of all human beings.... This universality in regard to the concept of God, as well as to humanity, is re-markable.[65]

Similarly, Betz prefers the kinder, gentler eschatology of the Lord's Prayer, where God benevolently takes over the world, to the particularist eschatology evident elsewhere in the SM, where the world is destroyed, the wicked "end up in eternal condemnation," and only the faithful inherit the eternal kingdom.[66] Regarding the Golden Rule,

the term "doing" (ποιεῖν) includes all human interaction by deeds and words, just as "the people" (οἱ ἄνθρωποι) refers to all members of the human race, not only the outsiders to the community of Jesus' disciples. Thus the ethics of the SM is not particularistic or sep-aratist but universalist, thereby fulfilling one of the requirements of ethics [no communi-tarian postmodernism here!].... Consequently, as such the Golden Rule is neither non-Christian nor Christian; it is recognized as universal and is as such "Christianized" by its insertion in the SM. This insertion takes place first at the level of the Judaism of Jesus, then Jewish Christianity (SM), and finally by the appropriation of the SM by the Gospel of Matthew.[67]

The roughness of the narrow road leading to life consists not particularly in persecution because of Jesus but generally in "the difficulties of life itself. These difficulties consist of the myriad of pressures, dangers, and obstacles on

---

[65] Betz, *Commentary*, 382.
[66] Betz, *Commentary*, 391.
[67] Betz, *Commentary*, 517–18.

the outside, as well as of human foolishness and stubbornness on the inside."[68]
Even "at this point [7:13]," where "the SM sees itself as representing a minority
that stands in stark opposition to the majority of fellow Jews as well as fellow
humans" – "a minority status" that "is maintained throughout the SM" – Betz
tries to universalize the lack of universalism by saying, "Typical of the times
anyway, however, minority status was also claimed by other groups in the
ancient world, among them the Jews in general."[69]

And so, while agreeing with Julius Wellhausen against Adolf von Harnack
that "Jesus was not a Christian, but a Jew," Betz bows toward Harnack by making the Jesus of the SM, if not a "Christian liberal" (Harnack's position), at least
something of a Jewish liberal.[70]

---

[68] Betz, *Commentary*, 521.

[69] Betz, *Commentary*, 525; cf. the right column in the middle paragraph on 507.

[70] Cf. Betz, *Commentary*, 32–37; idem, "The Sermon on the Mount and Q: Some Aspects of
the Problem," in *Gospel Origins and Christian Beginnings* (ed. J. E. Goehring et al.; Sonoma,
Calif.: Polebridge, 1990), 26–31.

9. Spinning the Lilies and Unraveling the Ravens: An Alternative Reading of Q 12:22b–31 and P. Oxy. 655

Introduction

In a series of five elegantly argued articles James M. Robinson, three times with Christoph Heil as his coauthor, has proposed (1) that οὐ ξαίνει, "[the lilies] do not card," in P. Oxy. 655, i, 9–10 represents earlier tradition than αὐξάνει, "grow," in Q 12:27; (2) that the itacistically spelled οὐ ξένουσιν, "do not card," in Matt 6:28b ℵ* also represents that tradition; (3) that because of incoherencies and absence from P. Oxy. 655, i, 1–17a the expressions τῇ ψυχῇ ὑμῶν, "about your life," and τῷ σώματι ὑμῶν, "about your body," in Q 12:22b and the whole sayings in Q 12:23, 31 did not belong to an earlier collection of sayings adopted by Q 12:22b–31; (4) that the wording and position of the parallel to Q 12:25 in P. Oxy. 655, i, 13–17a represent tradition earlier than that of Q 12:25; and (5) that therefore P. Oxy. 655, i, 1–17a represents earlier tradition than does Q 12:22b–31 or its canonical derivatives, Luke 12:22b–31 and Matt 6:25–33.[1]

There is such massive repetition in Robinson's and Heil's articles that I will usually cite them individually only when quoting them directly. In addition I will cite as "E-mail to Robinson" a message I sent to Robinson in response to a paper he read at a meeting of the Society of Biblical Literature in Orlando, Florida, November 1998. (The paper was later published in *Harvard Theological Review*.[2]) I will cite as "E-mail to Gundry" the gracious reply of Robinson.

---

[1] J. M. Robinson and C. Heil, "Zeugnisse eines schriftlichen, griechischen vorkanonischen Textes: Mt 6,28b ℵ*, P.Oxy. 655 I,1–17 (EvTh 36) und Q 12,27," *ZNW* 89 (1998): 30–44; J. M. Robinson, "A Written Greek Sayings Cluster Older than Q: A Vestige," *HTR* 92 (1999): 61–77; idem, "The Pre-Q Text of the (Ravens and) Lilies: Q 12:22–31 and P. Oxy. 655 (*Gos. Thom.* 36)," in *Text und Geschichte* (MThSt 50; Marburg: Elwert, 1999), 143–80; J. M. Robinson and C. Heil, "The Lilies of the Field: Saying 36 of the *Gospel of Thomas* and Secondary Accretions in Q 12.22b–31," *NTS* 47 (2001): 1–25; idem, "Noch einmal: Der Schreibfehler in Q 12,27," *ZNW* 92 (2001): 113–22. See also J. M. Robinson, "Excursus on the Scribal Error in Q 12:27," in *The Critical Edition of Q* (ed. J. M. Robinson, P. Hoffmann, and J. S. Kloppenborg; Leuven: Peeters, 2000), xcix–ci.

[2] See n. 1.

Q 12:22b–31

22 διὰ τοῦτο λέγω ὑμῖν· μὴ μεριμνᾶτε τῇ ψυχῇ ὑμῶν τί φάγητε, μηδὲ τῷ σώματι ὑμῶν τί ἐνδύσησθε.

23 οὐχὶ ἡ ψυχὴ πλεῖόν ἐστιν τῆς τροφῆς καὶ τὸ σῶμα τοῦ ἐνδύματος;

24 κατανοήσατε τοὺς κόρακας ὅτι οὐ υπείρουυιν οὐδὲ θερίζουσιν οὐδὸ συνά γουσιν εἰς ἀποθήκας, καὶ ὁ θεὸς τρέφει αὐτούς· οὐχ ὑμεῖς μᾶλλον διαφέρετε τῶν πετεινῶν;

25 τίς δὲ ἐξ ὑμῶν μεριμνῶν δύναται προσθεῖναι ἐπὶ τὴν ἡλικίαν αὐτοῦ πῆχυν;

26 καὶ περὶ ἐνδύματος τί μεριμνᾶτε;

27 κατα[[μάθε]]τε τὰ κρίνα πῶς αὐξάν[[ει]]· οὐ κοπι[[ᾷ]] οὐδὲ νήθ[[ει]]· λέγω δὲ ὑμῖν, οὐδὲ Σολομὼν ἐν πάσῃ τῇ δόξῃ αὐτοῦ περιεβάλετο ὡς ἓν τούτων.

28 εἰ δὲ ἐν ἀγρῷ τὸν χόρτον ὄντα σήμερον καὶ αὔριον εἰς κλίβανον βαλ- λόμενον ὁ θεὸς οὕτως ἀμφιέ[[ννυσιν]], οὐ πολλῷ μᾶλλον ὑμᾶς, ὀλιγόπιστοι;

29 μὴ [[οὖν]] μεριμνήσητε λέγοντες· τί φάγωμεν; [[ἤ·]] τί πίωμεν; [[ἤ·]] τί περι- βαλώμεθα;

30 πάντα γὰρ ταῦτα τὰ ἔθνη ἐπιζητοῦ- σιν· οἶδεν [[γὰρ]] ὁ πατὴρ ὑμῶν ὅτι χρῄζετε τούτων [[ἁπάντων]].

31 ζητεῖτε δὲ τὴν βασιλείαν αὐτοῦ, καὶ ταῦτα [[πάντα]]προστεθήσεται ὑμῖν.

P. Oxy. 655, i, 1–23

a (1) [λέγει Ἰ(ησοῦ)ς· μὴ μεριμνᾶ-
1 τε ἀ]πὸ πρωΐ ἕ[ως ὀψέ,
2 μήτ]ε ἀφ᾽ ἑσπ[έρας
3 ἕως π]ρωΐ, μήτε [τῇ
4 τροφῇ ὑ]μῶν τί φά-
5 [γητε, μήτε] τῇ στ[ο-
6 λῇ ὑμῶν] τί ἐνδύ-
7 [ση]σθε. (2) [πολ]λῷ κρεί[σ-
8 σον]ές ἐ[στε] τῶν [κρί-]
9 νων, ἅτι[να ο]ὐ ξα[ί-]
10 νει οὐδὲ ν[ήθ]ει. (3) χ[αὶ]
11 ἓν ἔχοντ[ες ἔ]νδ[υ-]
12 μα, τί ἐν[.....]..αι
13 ὑμεῖς; (4) τίς ἂν προσθ<εί>η
14 ἐπὶ τὴν εἱλικίαν
15 ὑμῶν; αὐτὸ[ς δ]ώσει
16 ὑμεῖν τὸ ἔνδυμα ὑ-
17 μῶν. λέγουσιν αὐ-
18 τῷ οἱ μαθηταὶ αὐτοῦ·
19 πότε ἡμεῖν ἐμφα-
20 νὴς ἔσει καὶ πότε
21 σε ὀψόμεθα; λέγει·
22 ὅταν ἐκδύσησθε καὶ
23 μὴ αἰσχυνθῆτε.

Since I will contest neither the decipherment of P. Oxy. 655 on which he and Heil depend[3] nor, with one exception, the reconstruction of Q 12:22b–31 in *The Critical Edition of Q*, sigla indicating emendations, doubtful readings, unreadable texts, and restored lettering in lacunae appear, again with one exception, only in the full texts on page 150 above.[4]

Robinson has written that the "divergences [of P. Oxy. 655] from Q are clearly not secondary to the Q text, since they cannot be explained as a reduction due to the 'gnostic' influence of Saying 37 [in the *Gospel of Thomas*]."[5] I will not try to prove gnostic influence from *Gos. Thom.* 37, but I will try to show that the divergences of P. Oxy. 655 from Q are better explained as redactions of Q 12:22b–31 or its canonical derivatives.

Q 12:22b–23 and P. Oxy. 655

Robinson and Heil regard Q 12:23 as secondary: "Isn't life more than food, and the body than clothing?" Robinson observes first that this verse distinguishes between life and food and between the body and clothing but asserts that v. 22b does not. Rather, v. 22b "makes them equivalent," as follows: "Do not worry about your life, (namely) what you shall eat, nor about your body, (namely) what you shall put on."[6] Robinson has twice inserted "namely" into his translation as though your life *is* what you eat and as though your body *is* what you put on. These equations are self-evidently false; so Robinson shifts, perhaps unconsciously, from equivalence to representation: "The original point has been

---

[3] Robinson and Heil, "Lilies," 4–9. But for caution see S. E. Porter, "P. Oxy. 655 and James Robinson's Proposals for Q: Brief Points of Clarification," *JTS* ns 52 (2000): 84–92. J. Schröter suggests restoring lines 10b–13a of P. Oxy. 655 as follows: π[όθ]εν ἔχοντ[ες ἔ]νδ[υ]μα τι ἐν[δύ-σεσθε κ]αὶ ὑμεῖς; "Woher (irgend)ein Kleid habend, werden aber ihr euch anziehen?" ("Rezeptionsprozesse in der Jesusüberlieferung: Überlegungen zum historischen Charakter der neutestamentlichen Wissenschaft am Beispiel der Sorgensprüche," *NTS* 47 [2001]: 452–68, and "Verschrieben? Klärende Bemerkungen zu einem vermeintlichen Schreibfehler in Q und tatsächlichen Irrtümern," *ZNW* 92 [2001]: 283–89). But in this restoration καί, "too, also, even," is meaningless because P. Oxy. 655 does not mention a clothing of lilies to which a clothing of the disciples could be added. And an enclitic τι weakens ἔνδυμα with indefiniteness whereas Schröter's understanding of a future heavenly garment hardly tolerates such a weakening or indefiniteness. This understanding also requires an unheralded jump from present, earthly food and clothing to future, heavenly clothing. Alternatively, Schröter restores lines 10b–13a to read κ[αὶ] ἐν ἔχοντ[α ἔ]νδ[υ]μα, τί ἐν[δύσεσθε κ]αὶ ὑμεῖς; "und (dennoch) ein Kleid haben. Was aber zieht ihr an?" But for a parallel with ξα[ί]νει and ν[ή]θ]ει this translation requires not the neuter plural participle ἔχοντα but the finite verb ἔχει, which the clearly lettered εχοντ in line 11 resists. Furthermore, the emphatic position of ἕν ill accords with an indefinite sense.

[4] For the sigla and the reconstructed text of Q 12:22b–31 see *The Critical Edition of Q*, lxxxvii and 334–53, respectively.

[5] Robinson, "Pre-Q Text," 179.

[6] Robinson, "Sayings Cluster," 68–69.

that one should not worry about life and the body, as represented by one's physical necessities such as food and clothing."[7] This shift shows a belated recognition that v. 22b does in fact distinguish between life and food, between the body and clothing, as v. 23 does. But even representation does not interpret accurately the distinction in v. 22b. Food does not represent life; it is necessary to life (for sustenance). Clothing does not represent the body; it is necessary to the body (for warmth). Robinson himself calls food and clothing "basic necessities for survival."[8]

Next, Robinson and Heil take the qualitative distinction in v. 23 between life and food, between the body and clothing, as a putdown of food and clothing. Then they contrast the putdown with the contextual portrayal of food and clothing as necessities for life and the body and infer the secondariness of the putdown.[9] Robinson writes, "It is as if suddenly one should not be anxiety laden about food, so as to be able to give priority to life, or about clothing, so as to be able to give priority to the body," and then hypothesizes that "the community's economic level must have risen enough that anxiety over food and clothing would only reveal an unworthy worldly concern" inasmuch as "food and clothing … are not worth it [anxiety], in contrast to higher values such as life and the body."[10] We should certainly accept a qualitative distinction between life and food, between the body and clothing. For you do not live to eat, you eat to live. You do not have a body to accommodate your clothes, you wear clothes to accommodate your body. So food and clothing are indeed subsidiary to life and the body even though the subsidiaries are necessary.

But there is no need to see in the qualitative distinction an elevation of life and the body into a realm of "higher, spiritual values that are far above such worldly concerns as food or clothing."[11] The body is obviously of worldly concern, and in this context τῇ ψυχῇ connotes physical life. The qualitative distinction is that food *serves* life and that clothing *serves* the body, so that "God will take care of life and the body [items of superior value] by providing such necessities as food and clothing [items of inferior value]" (to gloss Robinson's own statement).[12] Thus v. 23 fits quite well what Robinson calls "the point of the original collection" and does not interrupt the flow of thought from the prohibition of anxiety to the illustrations of God's caring for ravens and lilies. On the contrary, v. 23 provides a rationale for nonanxiety: if life and the body are of superior value, then God will provide them with their necessities of inferior value, as shown by his doing the same even for ravens and lilies (cf. Matt 10:29–

---

[7] Ibid.
[8] Ibid.
[9] Robinson and Heil, "Lilies," 10–11.
[10] Robinson, "Sayings Cluster," 69.
[11] Ibid.
[12] Ibid.

31/Luke 12:6–7). N.B.: whether or not it represents Q in this respect the most likely text of Luke 12:23 begins with a rationalizing γάρ, "for."

Robinson and Heil refine their argument by defining ἡ ... ψυχή quasi-philo-sophically as "the soul" in contrast to "the body" and therefore as of higher value than "food" whereas in v. 22b τῇ ψυχῇ carries the nonphilosophical meaning "life." This difference is supposed to expose further the secondariness of v. 23. But the purported difference is unlikely, for in v. 23 food relates to ψυχή as clothing relates to the body. Since clothing relates to the body by way of serving a physical need, food must likewise relate to ψυχή by way of serving a physical need. The soul does not need food; so ψυχή must mean "life," the kind of physical life which does need food, just as in v. 22b the ψυχή as physical life needs something to eat.

Yet further against the originality of Q 12:23 Robinson and Heil note that vv. 29 and 30b ("Therefore do not be anxious, saying, 'What are we to eat?' or 'What are we to drink?' or 'What are we to wear?' ... For your Father knows that you need all these things") make an *inclusio* with v. 22b but not with v. 23; for vv. 29, 30b do not remention the superiority of life and the body over food and clothing, about which superiority v. 23 speaks. Verse 23 is the second saying in the passage, however; so vv. 29, 30b omit to remention that superiority not because v. 23 was lacking in a pre-Q collection but because vv. 29, 30b hark back to the first saying in the passage, v. 22b, just as expected in an *inclusio*.

For Robinson and Heil the absence of a parallel in P. Oxy. 655 to Q 12:23 also counts against the latter's originality. But "food" in P. Oxy. 655 seems to echo "food" in Q 12:23. The word appears nowhere else in the canonical texts out of which Q is reconstructed. And in P. Oxy. 655 πολλῷ, "much," in the statement, "You are much better than ...," seems to echo πλεῖον, "more," a comparative of the very same adjective in the question of Q 12:23, "Is not the soul more than ... and the body [more] than ...?" These probable echoes support the originality of Q 12:23 and the view that P. Oxy. 655 echoes Q 12:22b–31 or its canonical de-rivatives at the same time it subtracts therefrom.

After excluding Q 12:23 from a pre-Q collection and noting the absence of "life" and "the body" both from the second member of the *inclusio* in vv. 29, 30b and from P. Oxy. 655, Robinson and Heil proceed to infer behind Q 12:22b a saying without any reference to life and the body: "Do not be anxious about what you are to eat nor about what you are to wear." But a retention of Q 12:23 in a pre-Q collection (for which retention see above) would erase the first el-ement in Robinson's and Heil's argument and make "life" and "the body" in v. 22b a natural lead into the affirmation of their superiority to food and clothing in v. 23. The second member of an *inclusio* need not repeat everything men-tioned in the first member anyway, nor would a repetition of τῇ ψυχῇ ὑμῶν and τῷ σώματι ὑμῶν (v. 22b) fit easily into the construction μὴ ζητεῖτε τί φάγητε καὶ τί πίητε (v. 29). One might think that if τῇ ψυχῇ ὑμῶν and τῷ σώματι ὑμῶν are original to the saying in v. 22b they would appear also in v. 29 as datives of advantage, but elsewhere in the NT a dative of advantage never appears in a ζητέω-clause though there are nearly a hundred such clauses. Therefore the absence of "your life" and "your body" from v. 29 does not imply their absence from a saying that underlies Q 12:22b.

As to the absence of "your life" and "your body" from P. Oxy. 655, there datives of respect precede the "what"-clauses: "Do not be anxious ... neither about your food (τῇ τροφῇ ὑμῶν), what you are to eat, nor about your robe (τῇ στολῇ ὑμῶν), what you are to wear." This construction matches Q 12:22b. Only the nouns are different, "food" instead of "life" and "robe" instead of "body." So P. Oxy. 655 does not support "what"-clauses *un*introduced by dative nouns, as in Robinson's and Heil's reconstruction; and the question arises, Which is more likely, that "food" was changed to "life" before "what you are to eat" and that "robe" was changed to "body" before "what you are to wear" or that "life" was changed to "food" to conform to the immediately following "what you are to eat" and that "body" was changed to "robe" to conform to the immediately following "what you are to wear"? Surely this latter. Well, then, P. Oxy. 655 looks secondary to Q 12:22b.

Furthermore, P. Oxy. 655 seems reductionistic; for it begins with a twofold reference to food for eating and a robe for wearing but afterwards mentions only clothing. The reference to food looks like the vestige of an earlier tradition, a vestige discarded in succeeding lines.[13] If P. Oxy. 655 is in the business of reduction, then, down goes its value for arguing that behind Q 12:22b lies a saying without reference to life and the body unless – since eating is present in both P. Oxy. 655 and Q 12:22b – one were to argue further that the putative saying lacked also a reference to eating. And it would seem odd that at its start P. Oxy. 655 added a reference to food as well as to eating but at its end – *not* as in Q 12:29, which also adds drinking as a natural complement to eating – omitted a reference even to eating. (Since eating implies food, Q 12:29 does not need to rementuon food along with eating; and since human beings do not work to produce water as they do work to produce food, water did not accompany food in the earlier prohibition of anxiety over food.)

Finally against the presence of "life" and "the body" in a saying underlying Q 12:22b Robinson and Heil argue that the need of clothing for the body does not match the need of food for bodily life and that the body needs food as well as clothing. This twofold argument lacks literary sensitivity. Just as bodily life needs food for sustenance, so the body needs clothing for protection. One could almost as easily say that bodily life requires clothing for warmth and that the body needs food for sustenance. But the ingestion of food makes more

---

[13] Cf. J. Schröter, "Vorsynoptische Überlieferung auf P.Oxy. 655? Kritische Bemerkungen zu einer erneuerten These," *ZNW* 90 (1999): 270; idem, "Rezeptionsprozesse," 461–62.

appropriate the association of food with the life that animates the body, and the exteriority of clothing makes more appropriate the association of clothing with the body. In either case, it is wrong to inject comparison into complementarity. But if one were to insist on judging food as more needed than clothing and therefore neither as original, consistency would require us to dismiss even the putatively earlier version, "Do not be anxious about what you are to eat nor about what you are to wear," as an imbalanced and therefore late pairing. For the same logic that counts food as more needed than clothing should count eating as more needed than being clothed. And P. Oxy. 655 gives no support to the jettisoning of food and clothing from an earlier version of Q 12:22b–23. On the contrary, P. Oxy. 655 supports their originality by mentioning "food" and a "robe."

Q 12:25 and P. Oxy. 655

For three reasons Robinson and Heil regard as secondary the traditionally accepted wording and middle position of Q 12:25 ("But who of you by being anxious can add a bit to his lifespan [or 'a cubit to his stature']?"): (1) the saying has nothing to do with ravens or lilies; (2) against the contextual optimism of trust in God the notation of inability to add a bit to one's lifespan or a cubit to one's stature amounts to a cynical reflection on human impotence whereas P. Oxy. 655, representing a more authentic wording and last position, carries to a climax the contextual optimism with this question and answer: "Who might add to your stature [or 'lifespan']? He himself [God] will give you your clothing"; and (3) Q 12:25 interrupts parallelism by coming between the illustrations of ravens and lilies, so that "it even became necessary in the next verse, Q 12:26, to restore the original train of thought by repeating the exhortation not to be anxious about clothing."[14]

The first reason demands a preliminary discussion of ἐπὶ τὴν ἡλικίαν αὐτοῦ πῆχυν. Several observations favor that here it means "a bit to his lifespan" rather than "a cubit to his stature": (1) Jesus is discussing food for survival, not for growth; (2) unlike adding a bit – say, an hour – to one's lifespan, adding a whole cubit (18–22 inches) to one's stature would count as a very big thing rather than the "very little thing" that Luke 12:26 calls it; and (3) the reference to the short life of grass (Q 12:28) favors the temporal meanings of ἡλικίαν and πῆχυν and disfavors that the lilies' growing supports a dimensional meaning.[15]

---

[14] Robinson, "Sayings Cluster," 70.

[15] See R. H. Gundry, *Matthew* (2d ed.; Grand Rapids: Eerdmans, 1994), 658, against the attempt to limit ἡλικία to a certain age, such as "old age," rather than the totality of one's age, i.e.,

Now adding a bit to one's lifespan has to do with bodily life inasmuch as the eating of food is necessary to such life. The just-mentioned ravens have such life and therefore need to eat food (so Q 12:24: "and God feeds them"). Lilies appear in the passage not till later (Q 12:27), so that the saying in v. 25 need not relate to them. It would be out of place, in fact, for that saying to do so. The saying on lifespan does relate to the one on ravens, however, in that human beings need food to live out their lives just as ravens, but not lilies, need it. Yet anxiety over food does not increase your lifespan even a bit; so trust God to feed you as he feeds the ravens.

As to disagreement with contextual optimism, reflection on human impotence exposes the futility of anxiety and thereby discourages anxiety (so Luke 12:26: "If therefore you cannot do even a very little thing [adding a bit to your lifespan by being anxious about it], why are you anxious about the remaining things [food and clothing]?"). This exposure and discouragement pave the way for trust in God's provision. Even P. Oxy. 655 observes that lilies do not card or spin. Of course they do not; they are impotent to do so. But this observation does not betray a cynicism disharmonious with trust in God's provision any more than Q 12:25 does.

Robinson and Heil take the coming of Q 12:25 between the illustrations of ravens and lilies not as a sign of secondary content, for P. Oxy. 655 has something similar, so much as a sign of secondary location, for P. Oxy. 655 has its similar saying in last position. But the illustration of divinely fed ravens, which has nothing to do with the exhortation against anxiety over clothing, comes between the two occurrences of that exhortation in Q 12:22b and Q 12:26 and suffices to explain its repetition in the latter verse. And we have to ask whether it is more likely that the saying about inability to add to one's ἡλικίαν was advanced from an originally last, climactic position (so P. Oxy. 655) to a position where it disjoins the illustrations of ravens and lilies or that it was shifted out of a disjunctive position into a climactic last position. More likely the latter.

I am inclined to regard Matt 6:28a ("And why are you anxious about clothing?"), which *The Critical Edition of Q* adopts, as more distant from Q than is Luke 12:26 ("If therefore you are able to do not even a very little thing, why are you anxious about the other things?"). Thus the addition of "one" to "bit [of time]" in Matt 6:27 compensates for the omission of Q 12:26 (= Luke 12:26) and corresponds to the omitted "not even a very little thing."[16] More especially, without a reference to "not even a very little thing" the further reference to "the

---

lifespan, and against the attempt to attach the ἡλικίαν-saying to the following one on clothing rather than to the preceding one on food.

[16] See ibid., 682 ("Compensation" in "Topical Index"), for discussions of habitual compensations in Matthew's Gospel.

other things" does not make easy sense. So Matthew replaces "the other things" with ἐνδύματος, "clothing," a favorite of his. It appears in his Gospel six times without parallel in paralleled pericopes[17] and only once with a parallel.[18] If then Luke 12:26 represents Q better than Matt 6:28a does, Q 12:25 looks even less like a fly of secular cynicism dropped into the ointment of theistic optimism. Rather, it looks well integrated in that the inability of human beings to do even a very small thing like adding a bit to their lifespan by worrying about it supports the contextual exhortation not to worry about other things even though they are necessary, but to trust God for them.

For another reason Q 12:25 may not be so disjunctive as claimed. The noting of inability to add a bit to your lifespan by worrying about it may follow up the exhortation not to worry about your life, what you are to eat, as illustrated by the ravens just as the noting of the fate of grass thrown into an oven (Q 12:28) follows up the exhortation not to worry about your body, what you are to wear, as illustrated by the lilies.

More generally, Robinson and Heil argue that "it is the high degree of parallelism in the Q text itself that suggests that the interruptions to that parallelism may be interpolations." Suddenly, however, Robinson and Heil reverse field by saying that "on any reading, the well-organized text Q 12:22b–31 [which has 'strikingly parallel structure'] would seem to be secondary in comparison with P. Oxy. 655, which is nearer a simpler oral tradition...."[19] When comparing Q 12:22b–31 with P. Oxy. 655 they regard the better parallelistic organization in Q 12:22b–31 as a sign of secondariness. When hypothetically reconstructing a text earlier than Q 12:22b–31 (which is itself reconstructed from Luke and Matthew) they regard better parallelistic organization as a sign of priority. Robinson and Heil are trying to have it both ways.

What then of the position of the saying on εἰλικίαν in P. Oxy. 655? First, the illustration of divinely fed ravens makes no appearance even though P. Oxy. 655 began with an exhortation against anxiety over food. As a result, all attention shifts to the exhortation against anxiety over a robe, the illustration of lilies does make an appearance, and the saying on εἰλικίαν enters as a followup. But since the illustration of lilies has to do with clothing, here εἰλικίαν more naturally takes its other meaning, "stature."

Why does P. Oxy. 655 introduce the saying on stature at all, though, and especially why in a climactic later position? Let us note first that instead of an ordinary garment (ἔνδυμα), as in Q 12:23, we read initially about something fancier: στολῇ, "robe,... esp. a long, flowing robe."[20] Economically speaking,

---

[17] Matt 3:4; 6:28; 7:15; 22:11, 12; 28:3.
[18] Matt 6:25.
[19] Robinson and Heil, "Lilies," 21–23.
[20] BDAG, s.v. στολή.

it looks as though the community behind P. Oxy. 655 rather than one behind Q had enjoyed upward mobility. But in lines 10–12 of P. Oxy. 655 we read about having an ordinary garment, not a robe, and about having only one ordinary garment at that, with emphasis on its oneness (ἓν ἔχοντες ἔνδυμα – N.B. the shoving of ἓν ahead of ἔχοντες even though ἓν modifies the following ἔνδυ-μα). So do not worry about having a fancy robe to wear. Trust God for a single ordinary garment. Downward mobility replaces upward mobility. Asceticism replaces worrying about material prosperity. And as an encouragement to trust in God's provision of the only garment an ascetic needs P. Oxy. 655 introduces God's ability to add to a person's stature. A God who can do that will surely give you a garment sufficient to the stature you have in fact attained. To gain this encouragement P. Oxy. 655 shifts the referent of τίς ("Who?") from inca-pable human beings to the omnicapable God and adds a forthright answer ("He himself will give you your garment") instead of leaving the question purely rhetorical (as in Q 12:25). Is it more likely that an answered question was changed to an unanswered one or that an unanswered question was sec-ondarily provided with an answer? The latter.

It appears that P. Oxy. 655 has shifted "one" from "one of these [lilies]" (Luke 12:27/Matt 6:29) or from "one bit" (Matt 6:27) to produce "one gar-ment." P. Oxy. 655 also omits the comparison of the lilies with the inferior glory of Solomon's clothing. This omission joins the switch from a robe to an ordinary garment and the addition of that garment's oneness to further an as-cetic trajectory.

The position of Robinson and Heil that a change by P. Oxy. 655 in the place-ment of Q 12:25 is unlikely stumbles over the equal unlikelihood that Q, ac-cording to their view, inserted v. 25 inappropriately not only in terms of posi-tion (by breaking up the ravens and lilies) but also in terms of content (by put-ting "a grumbling, helpless reflection on human impotence …. right in the middle of a group of otherwise so amazingly optimistic, trusting state-ments").[21] Nowhere do Robinson and Heil try to explain how and why such a purportedly horrendous maiming of a beautifully integrated original took place. Nor do they make anything of the emphatic limitation in P. Oxy. 655 to "*one* garment." This limitation suggests that for P. Oxy. 655 trust in God's provision is related to an asceticism that rejects the owning and wearing of more than one garment. We might associate such a rejection with ascetic ten-dencies that appear throughout the *Gospel of Thomas* (cf. the limitation to one tunic in Mark 6:9; Matt 10:9; Luke 9:3, which may have influenced P. Oxy. 655 at this point).[22]

---

[21] Robinson and Heil, "Lilies," 12–13, 15.

[22] Cf. S. J. Patterson and J. M. Robinson, *The Fifth Gospel* (Harrisburg, Pa.: Trinity Press In-ternational, 1998), 46–48, 59–65.

Robinson writes that "the cluster [in P. Oxy. 655] concludes with the reassurance that God, to whom one readily gives credit for one's stature, can hence be trusted to provide for one's human needs."[23] On the subordinate point, however, the optative of προσθείη bespeaks the *ability* of God to add to one's stature, not an *actuality* of his having done so. On the main point, the plural of "needs" (so Robinson) disagrees with the singularity of the garment God will provide. Again, then, P. Oxy. 655 has the tenor of asceticism, not of ordinary living.

Robinson and Heil wish to interpret Coptic *Gos. Thom.* 36 ("Jesus says: 'Do not worry from morning to evening and from evening to morning about what you will wear,'" a shortened version of P. Oxy. 655) separately from 37 ("His disciples said: 'When will you appear to us and when will we see you?' Jesus said: 'When you undress without being ashamed [thus far also lines 17b–23 of P. Oxy. 655, almost exactly] and take your clothes (and) put them under your feet like little children (and) trample on them, then [you] will see the son of the Living One and not be afraid'"). Thus Coptic *Gos. Thom.* 36 supposedly preserves the theme of P. Oxy. 655, i.e., trust in God's provision, while *Gos. Thom.* 37 goes in the gnostic direction of liberation from bodily existence. But Coptic *Gos. Thom.* 36 completely omits the theme of God's provision found in the source text, P. Oxy. 655. This omission combines with the shared theme of clothing in the very next saying to give the prohibition of anxiety over clothing a basis not in God's provision of one garment, as in P. Oxy. 655, but in the coming gnostic-like riddance of clothing altogether. Though Coptic *Gos. Thom.* 36 has nothing corresponding to the undressing in *Gos. Thom.* 37, then, we can still detect a trajectory from the theme of God's provision of food and clothing in Q 12:22b–31, its canonical derivatives, and P. Oxy. 655, through an ascetic limitation of God's provision of clothing to one ordinary garment in lines 10–17a of P. Oxy. 655, to an ultimate riddance of all clothing as detestable in lines 17b–23 of P. Oxy. 655 and Coptic *Gos. Thom.* 36–37. Supporting the last part of this trajectory is a possibility that the undressing in both the Greek and the Coptic of Saying 37 led the Coptic of Saying 36 to drop from the earlier Greek version of that saying in P. Oxy. 655 its vestige of food, its illustration of lilies, and its emphasis on having one garment.

To avoid understanding Coptic *Gos. Thom.* 36 in the light of *Gos. Thom.* 37 Robinson and Heil assert that "the individual sayings of the *Gospel of Thomas* elsewhere stand on their own feet" and therefore are not to be interpreted in terms "of adjoining sayings."[24] This assertion not only neglects the significance

---

[23] Robinson, "Pre-Q Text," 179.
[24] Robinson and Heil, "Lilies," 14 n. 41. In "Pre-Q Text," 152, Robinson words himself more cautiously: "[In *Gos. Thom.*] each saying is *normally* independent of the immediate context of adjoining sayings" (italics added).

of Saying 36's omission of trust in divine provision. It also overreaches in its denial that a collocation of sayings may sometimes affect their meaning, especially when they share a theme, as here.[25] For example, the juxtaposition of *Gos. Thom.* 25 and 26 makes for an interpretation of protecting your brother "like the apple of your eye" (25) in terms of "see[ing] clearly (enough) [after removing the beam from your own eye] to remove the splinter from your brother's eye" (26). And the juxtaposition of *Gos. Thom.* 18 and 19 bases the promise of not tasting death (a theme shared by both sayings) on the disciples' paying heed to Jesus' sayings and interprets standing at the beginning (18) as existence before coming into existence (19).[26]

Q 12:27, Matt 6:28 ℵ*, and P. Oxy. 655

Q 12:27 tells how lilies grow without performing tasks; it does not include growing among the tasks that lilies do not perform. Here Robinson perceives a problem:

In the place where one would expect to find the first chore involved in making clothes by hand, as some form of work one need not perform if freed from anxiety, one finds instead the distracting reference to lilies "growing." The fact that lilies grow adds nothing to the point of trusting in God's care and hence not working, that is to say, it has nothing to do with the main thrust of the two illustrations of ravens and lilies.[27]

But the text does not speak about "the *fact* that lilies grow" (italics added). It speaks about the *manner* of their growth. Robinson has taken no account of πῶς, "how," in the exhortation, "Consider the lilies – *how* they grow." The next two clauses, "They do not toil, neither do they spin," define the manner of growth negatively; and the final clause, "not even Solomon in all his glory was clothed as one of these," defines that manner positively. Where is the claimed distraction?

Since lilies are not said to be glorious it might be objected that their manner of growth does not point to the development of a glory surpassing that of Solomon's clothing and thus betrays itself as foreign to the thought of the saying. But growing takes no effort, so that in this respect it fits not toiling and not spinning; and the resultant glory of lilies' effortless growth *is* contained in an ellipsis: "not even Solomon in all his glory was clothed as one of these [lilies is clothed in glory]."

Now Robinson cites T. C. Skeat:

We expect to be asked, not to reflect on the growth of the lilies, but on the appearance of the lilies themselves. That this is a valid criticism can be seen by comparing the parallel

---

[25] Cf. Schröter, "Vorsynoptische Überlieferung auf P.Oxy. 655?" 271–72.
[26] See further idem, "Rezeptionsprozesse," 451–54.
[27] Robinson, "Sayings Cluster," 72.

"logion" of the "fowls of the air". Here we find ἐμβλέψατε εἰς τὰ πετεινὰ τοῦ οὐρανοῦ (Mt 6:26), or κατανοήσατε τοὺς κόρακας (Lc 12 24), but not, for example, κατ-ανοήσατε τοὺς κόρακας πῶς πέτονται. The unsuitability of αὐξάνει was clearly felt by the scribe of *e*, who added *et florescunt* ["and flower"], after *crescunt* ["grow"], in an ef-fort to bring the subject back to the appearance of the lilies.[28]

On the contrary, we do not expect the lilies' appearance to come into view im-mediately; for the feeding of ravens came into view only after their not sowing, not reaping, and not gathering into barns. In P. Oxy. 655 the lilies' appearance does not come into view at all! We are not told to consider how the ravens fly, because their flying does not lead to God's feeding them, whereas we *are* told to observe how lilies grow, because their growing does lead to God's clothing them with a glory that surpasses that of Solomon's clothing. And it is question-able whether the scribe of *e* thought αὐξάνει unsuitable. Just as likely he added flowering to growing to bring out the glorious result of growing. A dissatisfac-tion over the original text's leaving the lilies' glory in an ellipsis may have con-tributed to his addition.

Robinson and Heil refer to "the parallel of three activities that ravens and lilies do not carry out."[29] But since lilies do grow, the verb of growing does not count as one of those negated activities. Therefore no parallel exists in Q between three-somes of activity that ravens and lilies do not carry out. To make an argument that the positive of growing spoils an earlier threesome of negatives involving lilies and paralleling the threesome of negatives involving ravens Robinson and Heil replace growing in Q with the not carding of P. Oxy. 655, supported by Matt 6:28 ℵ*. But then not toiling breaks up the complementary pair of not carding and not spinning, and to save that pair with an omission of not toiling would be to lose the desired threefold parallel with what ravens do not do.

For Robinson earlier-than-Q does not imply originality, for he denies knowl-edge whether the ravens originally accompanied the lilies (in which case P. Oxy. 655 represents a later omission) or whether the ravens came alongside the lilies later (in which case P. Oxy. 655 represents an earlier version).[30] If the latter, the lilies would not have needed three verbs for parallelism with the three verbs associated with ravens. But then the argument from such a parallelism against the priority of growing would evaporate.

I have noted that a replacement of growing with not carding would leave not toiling to break up the complementary pair of not carding and not spinning. So Robinson argues that "they do not toil" is "more probably secondary" on the ground of the generality of toiling as opposed to the specificity of sowing, reap-ing, and gathering in the case of ravens and of carding and spinning in the case

---

[28] T. C. Skeat, "The Lilies of the Field," *ZNW* 37 (1938): 213.
[29] Robinson and Heil, "Lilies," 16.
[30] Robinson, "E-mail to Gundry."

of lilies; and "it was the need to have a third verb, since one had three verbs with the ravens, that led to [οὐ] κοπιᾷ being introduced, once the parallel of the two illustrations was present."[31] Here Robinson loses his ignorance and seems to know that the ravens came alongside the lilies later, so that – as just noted – the argument against the priority of growing from parallelism with three negated verbs involving ravens really does evaporate. Furthermore, a late addition of not toiling would not have produced a parallel with the three verbs negated in connection with ravens; for growing is not negated and an addition of not toiling earlier than a change of not carding to growing would likely have put not toiling first or last, just as in Matt 6:28 ℵ* (on which *v.l.* see the next footnote), so as to avoid a breakup of not carding and not spinning.

Let us note that in replacing a verb that is not negated, "grow," Robinson and Heil draw a negated one, "not card," from a source, P. Oxy. 655, which has only one pair of verbs, "not card nor spin," attached to only one illustration, that of lilies. So the question is whether an earlier full parallelism that appears in no known text outside Matt 6:28 ℵ*, which Robinson agrees does not contain what Matthew wrote,[32] was broken down in the Q used by Matthew and Luke (and in P. Oxy. 655 too unless it represents a stage of the tradition prior to a building up of the putatively full parallelism that Matthew's and Luke's Q broke down by replacing "not card" with "grow") or whether an earlier partial parallelism was retained in the known texts of Matthew and Luke (and obliterated by omission in P. Oxy. 655).

If the lilies were originally independent from the ravens and possibly earlier as well, the lilies would have had no parallelistic need of three negated verbs. I do not argue for this possibility; but Robinson, who thinks of Q 12:22b–31 as a collection gradually built up with originally independent sayings,[33] should recognize that this way of thinking weakens the argument from parallelism against the earliness of "grow." It should also be noted that since people do not usually speak or write in perfect parallelism, imperfect parallelism may signal a greater originality than would perfect parallelism, which might signal some polishing by a redactor.

In my e-mail to Robinson I observed, "Ordinarily, and other things being equal, we prefer a rough reading as more likely original than a smooth reading," and asked, "So isn't it easier to imagine a scribe's changing the anacoluthon in

---

[31] Ibid.

[32] Robinson, "Pre-Q Text," 157. Matt 6:28 ℵ* says to observe the manner, not the fact, of the lilies' not carding, not spinning, and not toiling. But it is the manner of their growing, not that of these negated activities, that leads to the lilies' glory greater than that of Solomon's clothing. So P. Oxy. 655 reads ἅτινα, "which," rather than πῶς, "how," and thus avoids the incoherence in Matt 6:28 ℵ*. Robinson and Heil say that neither they nor Skeat has argued for or against the priority of ἅτινα in P. Oxy. 655 ("Noch einmal," 117).

[33] Robinson, "E-mail to Gundry": "One has all along assumed that this collection grew, i.e. by definition a collection has to be collected from smaller units."

τὰ κρίνα πῶς ('the lilies – how') to the grammatically smooth τῶν κρίνων, ἅτινα ('the lilies, which') and thus also the dropping of κοπιᾷ ('toil') for ξαίνει ('card'), a sound-alike of αὐξάνει, to complement νήθει ('spin') than it is to imagine a scribe's introducing anacoluthon and destroying the complementarity of carding and spinning?" In his reply Robinson reasoned that "once the negative [represented in P. Oxy. 655] had been eliminated [as in Q 12:27], the ἅτινα construction needed somehow to be recast, and apparently πῶς αὐξάνει οὐ κοπιᾷ served the purpose of producing the negative prior to οὐδὲ νήθει. That a corrector is somewhat clumsy is not unusual, indeed the roughness of the resultant text can draw attention to the tampering."

This last observation is fair enough, though it enjoys no advantage over the usual preferring of a rough reading to a smooth one. But we still have to ask why a scribe would eliminate οὐ before ξαίνει, change carding to growing with a substitution of αὐξάνει, and add not toiling – all at the expense of destroying the complementarity of carding and spinning. Robinson said he is unsure that the scribe who he thinks substituted growing for not carding destroyed the complementarity of carding and spinning "intentionally." "I assume," Robinson continued, "it was on his part an honest mistake, due to a lacunae in his Vorlage or an unclear lettering that led him to mistake the relatively rare verb 'card' for the more common verb 'grow.'" That Robinson has to resort to such an assumption exposes a weakness in his and Heil's view. Of course, it requires some guesswork to explain the reading in P. Oxy. 655 if that of Q 12:27 is considered earlier. But at least this guesswork requires no assumption of a damaged or unclear text. Nor does the complexity of Robinson's hypothesis stand it in good stead. For unless the earlier text said to consider *how* the lilies do not card (against which see n. 32), the hypothesis has it that a scribe's honestly mistaking οὐ ξαίνει for αὐξάνει led him to back up, eliminate ἅτινα, substitute πῶς, and then – following πῶς αὐξάνει – insert οὐ κοπιᾷ in order that οὐδὲ νήθει might have a negative preceding it. In addition to making a smooth text rough this supposed procedure is overly complex.

Robinson also cites Skeat as dismissing "the 'sound-alike' explanation" of a change from οὐ ξαίνει to αὐξάνει: "for the phonetic similarity is by no means strong."[34] But the rhythmic and visual as well as phonetic similarities do seem fairly strong. For the two expressions share their only consonants, ξ and ν. Both start with an unaccented diphthong ending in υ and finish with exactly the same diphthong ει. Both accent the middle syllable of three. And in both, that middle syllable contains an α, the only difference consisting in P. Oxy. 655's adding an ι for the diphthong αι. Furthermore, "in the Greek of the first century A.D. as indicated by orthographic variations in papyri, ostraca, and inscriptions from Egypt and elsewhere in the Mediterranean world…. an -ι is often added erron-

---

[34] Skeat, "Lilies," 213.

eously to a simple α, η, or ω," and "the long diphthongs αι, ηι, and ωι show evidence of having been reduced to their corresponding simple vowels ...."[35] This slipperiness might have helped a shift from the -α- of αὐξάνει to the -αι- of οὐ ξαίνει or vice versa. Again by the first century A.D. there is "a very frequent interchange of vowels in unaccented syllables."[36]

Despite having cited Skeat to the contrary Robinson writes:

The letters for "not carding" (οὐ ξαίνει) are practically the same as for "growing" (αὐξάνει), especially when one takes into consideration that there was no word division to make clear whether it was a case of two words (οὐ ξαίνει) or one word (αὐξάνει). What is worse, vowels that were pronounced much the same were often carelessly inter changed.[37]

I therefore suggest that the rhythmic, visual, and phonetic similarities may have contributed to a change in the opposite direction from that envisioned by Robinson, i.e., from αὐξάνει to οὐ ξαίνει, a change aided by the following negatives with toiling and spinning. Not necessarily that those similarities led to a confusion of αὐξάνει with οὐ ξαίνει. For the fact that ἅτινα in P. Oxy. 655 reads more smoothly than does the anacoluthonic πῶς in Q 12:27 suggests that a scribe both deliberately replaced πῶς with ἅτινα to improve style and deliberately replaced αὐξάνει with οὐ ξαίνει to improve substance with the complementary pair of carding and spinning. In this case the rhythmic, visual, and phonetic similarities simply oiled the latter replacement.

To the contrary Robinson and Heil quote Skeat as arguing in a letter to them (15 July 1998) that since all the statements about ravens and lilies are negative except for the one about growing, a presumption exists "that αὐξάνει is likely to be a corruption of a negative statement."[38] But a copyist's "improvement" by conforming a positive statement to surrounding negatives is just as likely, as confirmed by the entirely negative variant readings, generally acknowledged as corruptions, not only of ℵ* at Matt 6:28 but also of D it[(a),d] sy[c,s] eth (Diatessaron[syr]) (Marcion[acc. to Tertullian]) Clement at Luke 12:27 (οὔτε νήθει οὔτε ὑφαίνει, "they neither spin nor weave").

What then of the argument that the generality of not toiling does not fit the specificity of all the other negated verbs? To build on a previous point, the specificity of carding as a complement to spinning is the very characteristic that may have induced someone to substitute carding for toiling. And the generality of toiling suits the variety of shepherding and sheep-shearing for wool, of plant-

---

[35] F. Gignac, "Phonological Phenomena in the Greek Papyri Significant for the Text and Language of the New Testament," in *To Touch the Text* (ed. M. P. Horgan and P. J. Kobelski; New York: Crossroad, 1989), 35–37.

[36] Ibid.

[37] Robinson, "Sayings Cluster," 63; see also idem, "Pre-Q Text," 154.

[38] Robinson and Heil, "Lilies," 4.

ing and harvesting flax for linen. In that case, toiling refers to men's contribution to the production of clothing, spinning to women's contribution. Of course, women's contribution includes carding, weaving, and sewing as well as spinning (hence the variant readings in Matt 6:28 and Luke 12:27), so that spinning is only exemplary. But unlike spinning, neither shepherding nor shearing, neither planting nor harvesting, has an association with the production of clothing distinctive enough to provide a readily understood example thereof. At the same time the connotation of κοπιᾷ as exhausting work suits the toiling of men out in the hot sun as a complement to women's spinning thread at home.[39]

The foregoing interpretation has a venerable history, but it has recently been proposed that since the ravens' not sowing, reaping, or gathering has to do with men's work, the lilies' not toiling or spinning must have to do with women's work. Those who like Robinson regard the ravens and lilies as originally independent from each other cannot use this argument legitimately for a pre-Q text, however. So the further argument fails that the parallel with men's work that ravens do not do favors an earlier pair of not carding and not spinning instead of Q 12:27's pair of not toiling and not spinning.

Since κοπιᾷ does not suit the work of women at home very well, the interpretation of Q 12:27 in terms of such work tends to depend on accepting the aforementioned "Western" text of Luke 12:27: "they neither spin nor weave." This text points solely to women's work at home but also looks like a refinement. For why would a scribe spoil so fitting a pair of verbs? Yet the following reference to Solomon's glorious clothing and the assumption that its glory was the effect of artistic weaving might easily induce a scribe to introduce weaving alongside spinning and at the expense of toiling. Besides, the external evidence favoring "they do not toil nor spin" is massive.[40]

Sowing seed, harvesting, and gathering into barns runs the gamut of activities in food production. So it might be argued that carding should be added to spinning for the running of a gamut in the production of clothing. But the addition of carding would not result in such a gamut, for the final processes of weaving and sewing would be left outstanding. And though the tidiness of a parallel between men's work in connection with ravens and women's work in connection with lilies possesses a certain attractiveness, we have noted that in other respects the parallel between vv. 24 and 27 is not entirely tidy (as, e.g., in the difference between "Consider… *that*" and "Observe… *how*"). All in all, then, the interpretation of toiling and spinning as references to men's and women's work in the production of clothing passes muster.[41]

---

[39] See F. Hauck, "κόπος, κοπιάω," *TDNT* 3:827–30.

[40] P[45,75] *rell.* See also Robinson and Heil, "Zeugnisse," 33–35.

[41] The suggestion of an underlying Aramaic wordplay between עמל, "toil," and עזל, "spin" (so T. W. Manson, *The Sayings of Jesus* [London: SCM, 1949], 112) may support the originality of "they do not toil nor spin."

Q 12:31 and P. Oxy. 655

For the secondariness of Q 12.31 Robinson and Heil argue:

a final high-point had already been reached in the two preceding verses, and there within the terminology of the sayings collection itself, namely in the summarizing exhortation not to be anxiety-laden.... the text closes fittingly with the reassurance: "for your Father knows that you need them all ['food, (drink) and clothing']" This leaves the following verse referring to βασιλεία indeed as a kind of unexpected appendix or an anticlimax, whose positioning as well as its new language make it questionable whether the verse actually did form the original conclusion of this sayings collection.[42]

But we should not assume that a reference to God's kingdom weakens rather than strengthens the climax. Nor should the "obvious absence" of God's kingdom from "the body of this sayings collection" forestall the possibility of a kingdom-reference added *originally* for the sake of climax.[43] Moreover, seeking God's kingdom forms so fitting a contrast with the Gentiles' seeking after "all these things" (Q 12:30) that it looks doubtful we should regard Q 12:31 as secondary. The echoing of "all these things" in "these things" at Q 12:31 points in the same direction. And if we were to assign to Q the wording of Luke 12:29 ("And you – do not seek ...") rather than that of Matt 6:31 ("Therefore you should not be anxious, saying ...") – though the assignment would be questioned – then Q 12:31, "But seek his kingdom," would form another fitting contrast, this time with the just-cited Q 12:29: "And you – do not seek ...."

The possibility of taking God's kingdom eschatologically nettles Robinson and Heil, who want a noneschatological collection of sayings earlier than Q 12:22b–31:

the mentioning of the kingdom of God, which often is automatically taken to be a future reference by Jesus, is in any case to be classified as a foreign element in this sayings collection. Originally the sayings collection drew attention to God's ... care of humans, without suggesting that God's care is conditioned by the nearness or the inbreaking of his kingdom.[44]

It is often observed, however, that from the OT onward the eschatological and the sapiential occur in original combinations. In the present passage, seeking God's kingdom means looking with desire (so the frequent meaning of ζητέω) for the arrival of God's rule in the coming age as an alternative to seeking what to eat, drink, and wear in the present age (N.B. the adversatives δέ in Matt 6:33 and πλήν in Luke 12:31). That God will provide now these necessities to those who look and long for his coming kingdom makes anxiety over present physical

---

[42] Robinson and Heil, "Lilies," 18.

[43] Ibid., 20. See also Schröter, "Rezeptionsprozesse," 465–68.

[44] Robinson and Heil, "Lilies," 17; see further Robinson, "Pre-Q Text," 165–73.

needs unnecessary. So no intrinsic reason exists to pit futuristic eschatology against sapiential presentism. The argument that because the imminent arrival of God's kingdom does not appear in preceding verses the verse where it does appear must be secondary – this argument assumes what needs to be proved, viz., that the line of thought does not progress from one point to another. And the argument that God's kingdom is not necessarily eschatological, and certainly not here because of no pointer thereto, neglects the meaning of seeking as looking and longing for something not presently at hand.

Yet again for the secondariness of Q 12:31 Robinson and Heil argue that "the closing *inclusio* in Q 12.29–30 ... refers back to Q 12.22b and thus rounds out the small sayings collection."[45] In reality, however, only Q 12:29 ("Therefore do not be anxious, saying, 'What are we to eat?' or 'What are we to drink?' or 'What are we to wear?'") forms an *inclusio* with Q 12:22b ("On account of this I say to you, do not be anxious about your life, what you are to eat, neither about your body, what you are to wear"). On Robinson's and Heil's reasoning, then, we should regard as secondary Q 12:30 as well ("For the Gentiles seek after all these things, for your Father knows that you need them all"). Yet Robinson and Heil describe this saying as "the reassurance" with which the sayings collection "closes fittingly."[46]

Finally, Robinson and Heil appeal to the absence of Q 12:31 from P. Oxy. 655: "Apparently it is not necessary to refer to the βασιλεία as an explanation for God's constant care."[47] Unnecessary – yes. But unnecessariness does not equate with secondariness. P. Oxy. 655 lacks the ravens. Are they therefore secondary? Not necessarily. The lilies are unnecessary to the point of God's provision; they merely illustrate that point. But Robinson and Heil do not regard them as therefore secondary.

Since "the last several verses of the Q sayings collection [vv. 28–30 as well as v. 31] are missing from *P. Oxy.* 655," Robinson moderates his argument: "*to this extent* it [the absence of Q 12:31 from P. Oxy. 655] conforms to the conjecture of those who thought that the collection originally had no climax referring to the kingdom."[48] Are we then to think that the sayings about grass, about not seeking what to eat or drink or wear, and about the Father's knowing our need for all these things that the Gentiles seek – as well as the saying about seeking God's kingdom – were all added to a pre-Q collection which like P. Oxy. 655 lacked them rather than that P. Oxy. 655 deleted them? If not, the argument from P. Oxy. 655 for the secondariness of Q 12:31 falls flat. But the sayings in Q 12:28–31 are so seamlessly integrated with Q 12:22b–27 – they all have to do

---

[45] Robinson and Heil, "Lilies," 19. "Those" refers to scholars whom he has cited.
[46] Ibid., 18.
[47] Ibid.
[48] Robinson, "Sayings Cluster," 73 (italics added). "Those" refers to scholars whom he has cited.

with God's provision of daily necessities – that it is easier to think of them as original and of their lack in P. Oxy. 655 as secondary.

Can we think of good reasons why P. Oxy. 655 might have deleted the sayings in Q 12:28–31? Yes. Q 12:28 talks about God's clothing the grass "in this way" (οὕτως), i.e., with a glory surpassing that of Solomon's clothing. But P. Oxy. 655 delays till last the saying about adding to your stature, does so to bring the passage to an ascetic climax in God's giving you one ordinary garment instead of the robe about which you should not be anxious, and therefore discards the saying that alludes to clothing more glorious than Solomon's. Q 12:29 prohibits anxiety over what to eat, drink, and wear. But though mentioning first "your food, what you are to eat," P. Oxy. 655 has long since turned its attention exclusively to clothing, so that Q 12:29 too suffers deletion just as did the saying about ravens for the same reason. Both Q 12:30 and Q 12:31 speak of "all these things" that the Gentiles seek and that God will add to his own. And what are these things? They are what you are to eat, drink, and wear in the preceding saying. Out go these sayings, then, and again for the same reason as before, viz., the turning of attention in P. Oxy. 655 exclusively to a single garment. It is not that Q adds. It is that P. Oxy. 655 tendentiously subtracts.

Conclusion

Q 12:22b–31 reads well as an original unity. A prohibition against anxiety over what to eat for maintaining life and over what to wear for protecting the body is buttressed by an evaluation of the body and its life as higher in value than food and clothing. God's feeding the ravens, which do not work for their food, illustrates the value he puts on life and contrasts with the ineffectiveness of anxiety to prolong lifespan even a bit. The illustrative and contrastive elaboration of the prohibition against anxiety over food has created the need for a renewed prohibition against anxiety over clothing. Enter such a prohibition, plus an illustration concerning the lilies' growing without working in such a way as to surpass in glory Solomon's clothing. The short life and fiery fate of the thus-clothed grass contrast with the life and fate of Jesus' addressees to show how much more they may trust God for clothing. The illustrative and contrastive elaboration of the prohibition against anxiety over clothing has created the need for a summarizing prohibition against anxiety. Enter such a prohibition, plus supportive references to Gentiles' misspent efforts and to God's knowing the needs of Jesus' addressees, in view of which references they are commanded to look and long for the coming kingdom of God and trust him to supply their present needs.[49]

---

[49] For reasons to think that Matt 6:34 is a redactional alternative to Luke 12:32, which there-

P. Oxy. 655 reads well as a redacted version of Q 12:22b–31 or its canonical derivatives. The prohibition against anxiety is strengthened with temporal specifications. Nonanxiety over food comes over only to be dropped as the attention reduces to nonanxiety over clothing, in particular over an unnecessary robe (cf. the dropping of nonanxiety over food altogether in Coptic *Gos. Thom.* 36). Because of the reduction to nonanxiety over a robe the sayings about the greater value of life and the body and about God's feeding the ravens drop out. As a result of their omission and a delay of the saying on adding to one's lifespan there is no need for a renewed prohibition of anxiety over clothing. So it drops out too. But the statement, "You are much better than the lilies," echoes the omitted question about ravens, "You are worth more than the birds, aren't you?" and "much" may also echo "more" in the omitted statement about the greater value of life and the body. The combination of "You are better than" with "the lilies" forces an omission of the command, "Observe." "The lilies, which…" gets rid of the anacoluthon in "the lilies – how…." With the aid of rhythmic, visual, and phonetic similarities αὐξάνει, "they grow," is exchanged for οὐ ξαίνει, "they do not card," for a closer complement of "nor spin." "They do not toil" drops out to bring the complementary pair right next to each other. "Having one garment" recommends satisfaction with an ascetic lifestyle – a single ordinary garment is enough – over anxiety-causing aspiration to a high standard of living, represented by a robe, and contrasts with having many things in Luke 12:19. The sayings about a glory greater than that of Solomon's clothing and about God's clothing the grass with such greater glory disagree with the emphasis on a single ordinary garment as opposed to a robe. Therefore they drop out. And since attention has shifted to clothing alone, the prohibition against anxiety over food and drink as well as clothing and the two further sayings about "all these things" also drop out. At this point damage to P. Oxy. 655 prevents decipherment. Finally there enters the saying about adding to one's lifespan. But because of the shift from food to clothing εἰλικίαν now means "stature" rather than "lifespan." And to encourage trust in God's provision of the ascetic's single ordinary garment this last saying turns into a question-and-answer with regard to God's ability.

Robinson and Heil deny that they assume textual development to proceed always from the shorter and simpler to the longer and more complex.[50] But they argue for the priority of P. Oxy. 655 over Q 12:22b–31 because the former "is nearer a *simpler* oral tradition."[51] So despite their arguing also from what they consider to be incoherencies in Q 12:22b–31 one can hardly escape the impres-

---

fore concluded this passage in Q, see Gundry, *Matthew*, 119, 658. Robinson and Heil do not include Luke 12:32 in their discussion, but its command not to fear and its assurance that the Father will give the kingdom to Jesus' addressees follow up nicely the command to seek God's kingdom and the assurance that he knows their needs.
[50] Robinson and Heil, "Noch einmal," 116.
[51] Robinson and Heil, "Lilies," 23 (italics added).

sion that favoritism toward brevity and simplicity has forestalled a reasonably strong effort to make good sense of the passage as it stands and inclines them to see incoherence where none exists. I hope to have shown that a reading of Q 12:22b–31 alternative to their reading makes good sense, perhaps better sense. And even if Robinson and Heil were correct in their tracing the pre-history of Q 12:22b–31, the traditional reading of P. Oxy. 655 as a redaction of Q 12:22b–31 or its canonical derivatives would still make good sense, perhaps better sense than their reading.[52]

---

[52] Because of freedom from translation Greek, Robinson and Heil (ibid., 23–24) discount underlying Aramaic wordplays that have been proposed and describe Q 12:22b–31 as "a Greek composition … a secondary literary composition" and go on to suggest that behind it lies "a more archaic unit … with the same kind of indications of an Aramaic background as is typical of the rest of Q, and with which Saying 36 of the [Greek] Gospel of Thomas [as represented by P. Oxy. 655] may have had a close affinity." But Robinson and Heil offer no evidence that P. Oxy. 655 contains any translation Greek, so why do they associate P. Oxy. 655 rather than Q 12:22b–31 with a possible but nonextant, more archaic unit containing Aramaic character-istics?

10. The Essential Physicality of Jesus' Resurrection according to the New Testament

The present essay deals with the nature of Jesus' resurrection as the NT presents it. Many believers in the resurrection understand it as a more or less spiritual phenomenon. Some of them say the story of the empty tomb is unhistorical, the corpse of Jesus having suffered the normal fate of corpses, but that he himself enjoyed resurrection in the form of disembodied exaltation to heavenly existence.[1] Putting more trust in the story of the empty tomb, others say the tomb was empty because the corpse of Jesus evaporated, in a manner of speaking, so that the risen Jesus is nonphysical.[2] Or Jesus' corpse metamorphosed into a living but essentially nonphysical body that took on physical characteristics only as the occasion of earthly appearances demanded.[3]

Some but not all who hold these views do so to insulate Jesus' resurrection from the rigors, vagaries, and fluctuations of historical inquiry,[4] perhaps also to

---

[1] Though she does not deny the emptiness of Jesus' tomb P. Perkins argues, "Nor ... can one insist that if a tomb containing the body of Jesus were to be found by archaeologists, the Christian proclamation of Jesus as the one who has been raised and exalted by God would be destroyed and with it the Christian claims about Jesus' place in salvation" (*Resurrection: New Testament Witness and Contemporary Reflection* [Garden City, N.Y.: Doubleday, 1984], 84; cf. the very influential book by H. Grass, *Ostergeschehen und Osterberichte* [3d ed.; Göttingen: Vandenhoeck & Ruprecht, 1970]).

[2] Cf. L. D. Weatherhead, *The Resurrection of Christ in the Light of Modern Science and Psychical Research* (London: Hodder, 1959), 43–57; S. H. Hooke, *The Resurrection of Christ* (London: Darton, Longman & Todd, 1967), 128–33; W. Pannenberg, *Jesus – God and Man* (London: SCM, 1968), 88–106 with 74–88; C. F. D. Moule, "Introduction," in *The Significance of the Message of the Resurrection for Faith in Jesus Christ* (ed. C. F. D. Moule; SBT 2/8; London: SCM, 1968), 9–10. Moule thinks of Jesus' material remains as being "taken up into and superseded by" a new and different mode of existence "rather as fuel is used up into energy." This view of the resurrection then allows him to suggest elsewhere that in his *pre*existence Jesus had, or was, a "spiritual body" (*The Origin of Christology* [New York: Cambridge University Press, 1977], 139–40).

[3] M. J. Harris, *Raised Immortal* (Grand Rapids: Eerdmans, 1983), passim; idem, *From Grave to Glory* (Grand Rapids: Zondervan, 1990), passim.

[4] Cf. the biblical theological description of Jesus' resurrection as eschatological and therefore as not subject, or only restrictedly subject, to the canons of historical research (so, e.g., Perkins, who infers from the eschatological character of Jesus' resurrection that "the 'bodily' reality involved is discontinuous with the material reality we experience" and thus *not* "a miraculous intervention in the natural order, such as the revival of a corpse" [*Resurrection*, 29–30], and F. Mussner, who goes on to weaken the connection with historical inquiry [*Die Auferste-*

soften the supernatural element and thereby avoid sacrificing their intellects, though under the latter motive it is puzzling why the sudden evaporation or metamorphosis of a corpse should be thought very much easier to believe in than the raising of one. But motivation of belief is beside the points of truth or falsity and of significance. If Jesus' corpse suffered the normal fate of corpses, a spiritual resurrection of him is minimally open to historical investigation; for only the claim that the risen Jesus made a number of appearances needs explanation. The evaporation or metamorphosis of a corpse so as to leave an empty tomb leaves the door somewhat more open to historical inquiry; for the emptiness of the tomb, or at least the claim that it was empty, needs to be explained along with the claim that the risen Jesus made a number of appearances. But whatever the fate of his corpse, a Jesus risen only or at least essentially in spiritual form tends to give more explanatory room to psychology and sociology than to history.[5]

I will try to show that the NT presents the resurrection of Jesus in a way that leaves it more open to historical inquiry. My attempt does not imply that brute facts carry their own interpretation, or that we have direct access to the brute facts concerning the historical Jesus, or even that there are such items as brute facts. Those questions remain open in this essay, as do also philosophical questions of material and personal identity and such like. Nor will I discuss the historicity of Jesus' resurrection. That would require a further effort, one undertaken massively with a positive result by N. T. Wright.[6] I want to find out what the NT means when it talks about Jesus' resurrection. Only then will we discover the degree to which historical inquiry may apply to it, and only then will we be able to decide the degree to which dematerializing views represent the NT itself or represent efforts at a cultural translation of it.

---

hung Jesu (Biblische Handbibliothek 7; Munich: Kösel, 1969), 123–27]; also R. H. Fuller, *The Formation of the Resurrection Narratives* [Philadelphia: Fortress, 1980], ix-x, 22–23). But why should an eschatological event be considered beyond the pale or at the fringe of historical inquiry if the event is purported to have taken place in time and space and to have provided observable evidence of its occurrence? And it takes more than an *obiter dictum* to establish that eschatology implies discontinuity with present materiality. See H. Harris, *The Tübingen School* (Grand Rapids: Baker, 1990), 179–80.

[5] M. J. Harris allows historical inquiry to the extent that he sees the tomb of Jesus as empty and his appearances as physical, but he disallows historical inquiry to the extent that "there were no witnesses of the Resurrection itself, and in his resurrected state Jesus was normally not visible to the human eye" (*From Grave to Glory*, 103–4). But the denial that Jesus' resurrection was "even an incident that *could* have been observed by mortal gaze" (italics added) arises out of Harris's definition of resurrection as essentially nonphysical and thereby destabilizes the basis on which he himself argues for openness to historical inquiry.

[6] N. T. Wright, *The Resurrection of the Son of God* (vol. 3 of *Christian Origins and the Question of God*; Minneapolis: Fortress, 2003). For my own contribution to the debate over historicity see "Trimming the Debate" in *Jesus' Resurrection: Fact or Figment?* (ed. P. Copan and R. K. Tacelli; Downers Grove, Ill.: InterVarsity, 2000), 104–23.

My position is threefold: (1) the NT presents a unified view of the nature of Jesus' resurrection; (2) according to that view he rose from the dead in a physical body; and (3) the physicality of that body forms an essential element of his risen being. The first part of my position disagrees with the view that the NT presents conflicting versions of Jesus' resurrection, such as one version that he rose spiritually to appear luminously and another version that he rose bodily to appear physically.[7] The second part of my position disagrees with the view that the NT presents the risen Jesus as nonphysical. The third part of my position disagrees with the view that though the NT portrays him as occasionally appearing in a physical form it does not portray that form as essential to his risen being.

A Presentation of Arguments for the Essential Physicality of Jesus' Resurrection according to the New Testament

We find the earliest literary references to Jesus' resurrection in the Epistles of Paul. By his own account Paul had been a Pharisee (Phil 3:5). According to Josephus, *J.W.* 2.8.14 § 163, the Pharisees held that the incorruptible (i.e., immortal) soul of a good person passes into another body whereas the incorruptible souls of wicked people suffer eternal punishment. Granted, Josephus used phraseology that reflects Hellenistic dualistic language concerning body and soul rather than the language which Pharisees might have used among themselves. But the really significant point is that he should have mentioned the Pharisees' belief in corporeal immortality at all, and this despite two competing considerations: (1) that his Greco-Roman audience were liable to find the belief reprehensible or foolish (witness the Athenian reaction to Paul's preaching of the resurrection in Acts 17:32 – this point stands whether or not we regard Luke's account as historical) and (2) that throughout his book Josephus was trying to make the Pharisees look good in the eyes of his Greco-Roman audience. The Pharisees – among whom Josephus counted himself; so he should have known about their belief – must have held to physical resurrection for him to have attributed to them a Hellenistically phrased position that ran counter to his purpose in writing.

---

[7] J. M. Robinson, "Jesus: From Easter to Valentinus (or to the Apostles' Creed)," *JBL* 101 (1982): 7–17; idem, *Trajectories through Early Christianity* (Philadelphia: Fortress, 1971), 48–49 n. 43; Fuller, *The Formation*, 45–49; cf. 32–34. J. D. G. Dunn canvasses other views that see disparity (*Jesus and the Spirit* [Philadelphia: Westminster, 1975], 115–22). In Dunn's own view the first Jewish Christians believed in a physical resurrection of Jesus; Paul substituted a nonphysical resurrection; and Luke and perhaps John reacted against Paul with a return to physical resurrection. In general against Robinson, see G. O'Collins, "Luminous Appearances of the Risen Christ," *CBQ* 46 (1984): 247–54; and W. L. Craig, "From Easter to Valentinus and the Apostles' Creed Once More: A Critical Examination of James Robinson's Proposed Resurrection Appearance Trajectories," *JSNT* 52 (1993): 19–39.

At Acts 23:6–8 the Pharisees' belief in resurrection is distinguished from be-lief in angels and spirits.[8] The distinction implies belief in the physicality of res-urrection. This belief corresponds to the very meaning of the noun for resurrec-tion, ἀνάστασις, as the "standing up" of corpses buried like sleepers in a supine position (likewise the cognate verb ἀνίστημι, "stand up") and shows up in later rabbinic literature too.[9] Some rabbis even debated whether dead bodies will rise wearing the same clothes in which they were buried.[10] Paul's having been "a Pharisee of the Pharisees" therefore creates the presumption that unless strong evidence to the contrary comes forward, we may assume that his vocabulary of resurrection carries the Pharisaical connotation of physicality. And the theory that physical portrayals of Jesus' resurrection arose later out of antidocetic ten-dencies in the early church will be preempted.[11] Whether Paul thought of the reanimation of the whole person, including the body, or of the reunion of the old but reanimated body with the preserved soul, or of the union with the preserved soul of a new body raised out of the old one (and there may be other possibil-ities)[12] does not matter a great deal so far as the point of physicality as such is concerned.

In 1 Cor 15:3–4; Acts 13:29–30 Paul's juxtaposing not only Jesus' death but also his burial with his resurrection, the last of which means "rising" or "raising," entails that the resurrection means the rising or raising of Jesus' bu-ried body.[13] Further description of the resurrected bodies of believers will add

---

[8] On the interpretation of angels and spirits see G. Juhász, "Translating Resurrection: The Importance of the Sadducees' Belief in the Tyndale-Joye Controversy," in *Resurrection in the New Testament* (ed. R. Bieringer, V. Koperski, and B. Lataire; BETL 165; Leuven: Leuven University Press, 2002), 115–16, and earlier literature cited there.

[9] Str-B 3:473–74, 481; 4/2:815–16.

[10] Str-B 2:551; 3:475.

[11] See further Gundry, "Trimming the Debate," 19–21.

[12] P. Volz, *Die Eschatologie der jüdischen Gemeinde* (Tübingen: J. C. B. Mohr [Paul Sie-beck], 1934), 249–55.

[13] On the question of "rising" versus "raising" see O. Hofius, "'Am dritten Tage aufer-standen von den Toten': Erwägungen zum Passiv ἐγείρεσθαι in christologischen Aussagen des Neutestaments," in *Resurrection in the New Testament* (ed. R. Bieringer, V. Koperski, and B. Lataire; BETL 165; Leuven: Leuven University Press, 2002), 93–106, and earlier literature cited there. Some have thought that the mention of Jesus' burial does not prepare for the rising or raising of his physical body but insures the reality of his physical death (see, e.g., Grass, *Os-tergeschehen und Osterberichte*, 146–47). It is true, of course, that burial is often associated with death – but not for the insurance of death; rather, as a usual consequence thereof (see the list of references provided by Grass himself). If death leads to burial, resurrection leads to a re-versal of burial (cf. Ezek 37:13: "when I open your graves and bring you up from them"; see M. Hengel, "Das Begräbnis Jesu bei Paulus und die leibliche Auferstehung aus dem Grabe," in *Auferstehung – Resurrection* [ed. F. Avemarie and H. Lichtenberger; WUNT 135; Tübingen: Mohr Siebeck, 2001], 119–83, with massive documentation). And where in pre-Pauline Chris-tianity do we find evidence of a need to insure the death of Jesus? Later, in Mark 15:44, the question is not whether Jesus has *died*, but whether he has died *already*. The later Gospels ig-nore this question. In 1 John 5:6–7 the coming of Jesus Christ in blood as well as water prob-ably denies the Cerinthian or pre-Cerinthian separation of a non-dying spiritual Christ from a

glorification, immortalization, and other enhancements (1 Cor 15:42–44); but the raising of Jesus' buried body provides the physical starting point and *sine qua non* of resurrection. Since Paul is citing tradition, this entailment represents a common, pre-Pauline Christian view, i.e., a very early traditional view. Since he is citing tradition agreeably it represents his own view as well as that of Christians before him. And since he is citing tradition that provides common ground on which both he and his Corinthian readers stand it represents a view of Jesus' resurrection that even those at Corinth who denied the future resurrection of believers, and supposedly inclined toward docetism, adhered to.

In the further part of 1 Corinthians 15 Paul writes about the future resurrection of believers after the pattern and on the ground of Jesus' resurrection. His use of the Greek word σῶμα in this discussion therefore says something about the nature of Jesus' resurrection. If the future resurrection of believers will be somatic, so also was Jesus' resurrection, as is only natural to deduce from the aforementioned juxtaposition of burial and raising. Now σῶμα means the physical body. Even as a metaphor it means the physical body, but the physical body as an analogy for something else. Here in 1 Corinthians, for example, Paul's famous metaphor of the body for the church goes down to the physical details of different bodily parts – head, eyes, ears, nose, hands, feet, and genitals (12:12–27).

The evidence is massive that σῶμα means a physical body, not a person without reference to the physical body (though by synecdoche it may represent the rest of the person as well).[14] But particularly pertinent to our present topic is Paul's interchanging of σῶμα, "body," and σάρξ, "flesh," in his argument for the resurrection (1 Cor 15:35–40). He does not speak of the resurrection of the flesh, probably because in other associations the word "flesh" connotes weak-

---

dying physical Jesus, so that the resurrection of the indivisible Jesus Christ – if it were in view – would include the physical body. In 1 Cor 15:4 the second ὅτι disengages Jesus' resurrection from his burial no more than the first ὅτι disengages his burial from his death and no more than the ὅτι in v. 5 disengages his appearances from his resurrection. In Acts 13:30 δέ, "but," forges an adversative link between the entombment of Jesus and his being raised.

[14] See R. H. Gundry, *Sōma in Biblical Theology with Emphasis on Pauline Anthropology* (SNTSMS 29; Cambridge: Cambridge University Press, 1976; reprinted, Grand Rapids: Zondervan, 1987]). The criticism of this book by J. D. G. Dunn (in *SJT* 31 [1978]: 290–91) that it proceeds on "an intention to push a line" has no argumentive value. Intentions do not determine the validity or invalidity of arguments. The second, "more serious" criticism that the book wrongly poses the issue "as a sharp either-or between *sōma* = 'the whole person' and *sōma* = 'the physical body alone'" stumbles over the scriptural passages cited by Dunn as undermining this either-or. One might have thought that the first one, for example, favors the either-or in that it takes a mention of the mind as well as of the body to encompass the whole person (Rom 12:1–2). Similarly, one might have thought that the future making alive of believers' mortal bodies in Rom 8:11 favors an understanding of Rom 8:10, "The body [is] dead," in terms of physical mortality, i.e., proleptic death (cf. 2 Cor 4:10–12), over Dunn's vague understanding in terms of death "in one dimension of his [the believer's] relationships." This dimension would have to exclude all physicality if Dunn were to maintain his argument that "Paul can hardly mean that the physical body is dead here and now."

ness and sinfulness; but he does use body and flesh without any fundamental distinction in his drawing of analogies to the resurrection.[15] And he even uses the phrase "flesh of human beings" (v. 39), which comes as close as possible to equating resurrection of the body with resurrection of the flesh without falling prey to the negative connotations that the word "flesh" carries elsewhere.[16]

Paul speaks of earthly bodies as well as of heavenly bodies. He speaks about the flesh of birds as well as about the flesh of earthbound creatures. The order of the overall analogy does not seem to ascend from flesh to body; for though he moves from "flesh" (v. 39) to "bodies" (v. 40), he started with "body" (vv. 37–38). Nor does the order of the particular analogies seem to ascend from earth to heaven or from low grade to high grade; for though he moves from seeds up to human beings, he then meanders through beasts, birds, fish, heavenly bodies, earthly bodies, sun, moon, and stars. He stresses differences by saying that we do not sow the seed-like body that will be, by listing widely varying kinds of flesh, and by calling attention to varying degrees of glory. But none of these differences have to do with materiality versus immateriality just as later the heavenly human being is a human being originating "from heaven" (Paul's own phrase), not a human being made out of heaven as though heaven were an ethereal substance (so we should interpret the "earthy" human being as originating "from earth" [again Paul's own phrase], not as made of earth – vv. 47–48). Also pertinent is Paul's use of οἰκοδομήν, "building," and οἰκοτήριον, "house," terms that connote greater solidity than does ἡ … οἰκία τοῦ σκήνους, which means a house that is comparatively unsubstantial, like a tent (2 Cor 5:1–2). C. S. Lewis was following a biblical instinct when in *The Great Divorce* he portrayed heaven and its inhabitants as possessing greater physical density, not less physical density, let alone ethereality.

---

[15] J. Plevnik says that Paul "uses σάρξ for the living things on earth, and σῶμα … for the heavenly things" (*Paul and the Parousia* [Peabody, Mass.: Hendrickson, 1997], 162–63). Wrong! First Corinthians 15:37–38 uses σῶμα for earthly plant life. First Corinthians 15:40 speaks of "earthly σώματα." And 1 Corinthians 15:44–49 describes the σῶμα ψυχικόν as "from earth" and "earthy."

[16] Cf. T. Peters, "Resurrection: The Conceptual Challenge," in *Resurrection: Theological and Scientific Assessments* (ed. T. Peters, R. J. Russell, and M. Welker; Grand Rapids: Eerdmans, 2002), 302–3, against J. D. G. Dunn, who states, "Paul's theology of the resurrection does not require or depend on Jesus' tomb being empty. But Paul's conceptualization of the resurrection body is a very sophisticated one, involving a subtle distinction between 'flesh' and 'body'" ("Beyond the Historical Impasse? In Dialogue with A. J. M. Wedderburn," in *Paul, Luke and the Graeco-Roman World* [ed. A. Christophersen et al.; JSNTSup 217; Sheffield: Sheffield Academic Press, 2002], 253; cf. idem, "The Ascension of Jesus: A Test Case for Hermeneutics," in *Auferstehung – Resurrection* [ed. F. Avemarie and H. Lichtenberger; WUNT 135; Tübingen: Mohr Siebeck, 2001], 309). Also against M. J. Harris, *From Grave to Glory*, 388, where "bodily" is set against "fleshly" as though in Col 2:9 Paul means to imply that though the fullness of deity dwelt in the fleshly body of Jesus during his earthly ministry this fullness no longer does so because Jesus now has an unfleshly body.

Moving to the Gospels and Acts let us note the conjunction of Jesus' empty tomb, the statement "He is risen," and the reported bodily manifestations of the risen Jesus. This conjunction indicates that the Gospels present Jesus' resurrection as physical, even essentially so. Matthew 28:9 reports that women grasped the risen Jesus' feet, John 20:17 that he told Mary Magdalene to stop touching his feet, Luke 24:39–40 that he showed the disciples his hands and feet and invited the disciples to handle him and see, John 20:20 that he showed the disciples his hands and side, and John 20:24–29 that he invited Thomas to feel the scars of crucifixion that remained on his risen body.[17] Luke 24:42–43 reports that the risen Jesus ate food in front of the disciples as part of a demonstration that he was not a spirit.[18] Acts 1:4;[19] 10:41 add that the disciples ate and drank with the risen Jesus.[20] And in Acts 2:26b the citation of Ps 16:9b with reference to Jesus' resurrection, "Moreover, my flesh will dwell in hope," puts a fleshly stamp on it.

It has been said that Jesus reportedly presented himself in a material fashion not to prove that he was physical but to prove that he was real. But a real what? A real person? That would require only an overpowering vision. Old Testament theophanies, which are sometimes put forward as models of the culturally appropriate way that early Christians used for expressing their experience of the risen Jesus[21] – these theophanies may have portrayed God in human guise, but they fell far short of having him invite his human subjects to handle a body that he had put on just for the human needs of an occasion. And in the NT the association of Jesus' appearances with his death, burial, and resurrection disfa-

---

[17] Robinson sees the following beatitude on those who have not seen yet believe as correcting the materialism of the risen Jesus' appearances earlier in John 20 ("Jesus: From Easter to Valentinus," 12). On the contrary, by compensating for the lack of material evidence once the risen Jesus stopped appearing the beatitude protects the materiality of his appearances.

[18] See Grass, *Ostergeschehen und Osterberichte*, 40–41, on the escalation of evidences for physicality in Luke 24:36–43.

[19] Reading συναλιζόμενος instead of the very weakly supported συναυλιζόμενος.

[20] According to G. O'Collins, Luke mitigates an excessive realism in Luke 24:42–43 by saying in Acts 1:4 that the apostles ate with the risen Jesus and in Acts 10:41 that they both ate and drank in his company (*Interpreting the Resurrection* [New York/Mahwah, N. J.: Paulist], 47–48). But Acts 1:4 says that he ate with them, not they with him, so that far from mitigating an excessive realism in Jesus' eating with the apostles Luke has doubled his emphasis on realism; and after two statements that the risen Jesus ate, the further statement in Acts 10:41 naturally means that the apostles joined him in eating and, as to be expected, that drinking accompanied the eating. O'Collins also considers it a problem that if the risen Jesus ate food, "We must face the questions: What happened to the food taken by the risen Jesus? Can a risen body digest food and grow?" (ibid., 40–43). Taking a biblical rather than systematic theological or philosophical standpoint (as throughout the present essay) we may ask for evidence that Luke and John would not have answered affirmatively these questions of digestion and elimination. It is another matter whether Paul would have so answered (see the comments below on 1 Cor 6:13, however).

[21] J. E. Alsup, *The Post-Resurrection Appearance Stories of the Gospel-Tradition* (Calwer theologische Monographien A 5; Stuttgart: Calwer, 1975), 239–74.

vors OT theophanies as the generative force behind the tradition of his appearances; for OT theophanies had no similar associations with death, burial, and resurrection. The only suitable matrix for the tradition of the appearances is the companion tradition of death, burial, and reversal of death and burial by resurrection. Similarly, the only suitable matrix for the tradition of the risen Jesus' invitation to feel his scars is the desire to prove his physical continuity with the Jesus who had died on a cross. We may say the same with regard to his eating of food. Whether Jesus' body is portrayed as requiring food is beside the point that at least part of his essential being is portrayed as a resurrected physical body.

The physical implication is not so strong in Mark because we do not have there a text-critically accepted account of an appearance by the risen Jesus. But the conjunction of the women's coming to anoint his corpse, the young man's reference to him as "the crucified one," his announcement that Jesus "has been raised, he is not here. Look! The place where they laid him," and his reminder that the disciples will see Jesus in Galilee because Jesus is preceding them there all point in the same direction of a physical resurrection (Mark 16:1–8). Further factors in Matthew also point in this direction: the conjunction of Jesus' resurrection with the resurrection of saints' bodies (σώματα) that came out of tombs after Jesus' resurrection, entered Jerusalem, and appeared to many (Matt 27:51b–53); also the connection between Jesus' resurrection and the rumor that his disciples had stolen his body – plus an actual appearance in Galilee. These can hardly be understood in any way but physical.

A Refutation of Arguments against the Essential Physicality of Jesus' Resurrection according to the New Testament

But what of arguments that at least in part the NT portrays Jesus' resurrection as nonphysical? This time I begin with the Gospels and Acts and work backward to Paul. It is often argued that the mysterious abilities of the risen Jesus to appear and disappear suddenly, even to pass through closed doors (Luke 24:31, 36, 44; Acts 1:3; 10:40–41; John 20:19, 26), portray him as essentially nonphysical even though able to project himself occasionally in a physical form for the purpose of accommodating himself to the disciples' need of physical verification.[22] If so, however, the evangelists portray a risen Jesus who deliberately misled his disciples not only by projecting himself physically for the sake of visual verification but also by leaving the impression of essential physicality through eating food, drinking liquid, subjecting himself to physical contact, and inviting such contact with the scars that he had suffered before his resurrection. The statement attributed to him in Luke 24:39, "A spirit does not have flesh and

---

[22] See, e.g., M.J. Harris, *Raised Immortal*, 53–57.

bones as you see that I have," sounds like a description of essential nature, not like a description of passing accommodation.[23]

Admittedly there is eating of a meal in the theophany at Gen 18:1–8, but nothing like the risen Jesus' eating and drinking for the express purpose of proving his physicality. It is true that according to Matt 28:17 some of the eleven disciples doubted. But the text does not tell what they doubted or why; so it is reading a lot into the text to say they doubted that the risen Jesus was physical or because there was so much visual ambiguity they could not be sure of his physicality. The text localizes the event on an appointed mountain in Galilee. The text says the disciples saw Jesus. The text says they prostrated themselves before him. Earlier, Matthew stressed their little faith (6:30; 8:26; 14:31; 16:8; 17:20). It was an emphasis peculiar to his Gospel (with the sole exception of 6:30 par. Luke 12:28) and of course had nothing to do with visual ambiguity since Jesus had not yet died and risen. So it does not seem likely that the doubt in 28:17 had anything to do with the composition of Jesus' risen body. It probably had to do quite simply with doubt that Jesus *could* have risen despite the physical evidence standing before them.[24] Likewise the variety which we see in the evan-

---

[23] According to M.J. Harris the resurrected body of Jesus "was 'customarily immaterial' in the sense that in *his customary mode of existence* during the forty days [of post-resurrection appearances], he did not have a material body of 'flesh and bones'.... But when, on occasion, he chose to appear to various persons in a material form, this was just as really the 'spiritual body' of Jesus as when he was not visible or tangible" (*From Grave to Glory*, 404–5). So then Jesus' statement in Luke 24:39 must mean that he has flesh and bones *only at the moment* and that when not appearing to people, as he usually does not, he is a spirit who though having a body does not have flesh and bones. Apart from his misleading the disciples if such was the meaning, we need to ask whether under this view he got a fresh set of flesh and bones every time he appeared to people and, if not (cf. ibid., 388: "But these resurrection appearances were certainly not successive reincarnations of Christ"), where the single set was stored and how it managed to stay alive, if it did, during the longer periods of his customary immateriality, and what has happened to those flesh and bones now that he has altogether ceased appearing. Surely these questions are more telling than the question concerning the whereabouts of the risen Jesus' physical body when he was not appearing to the disciples – to which question the answer is easy: if not in heaven, incommunicado on earth. The defense that though turning into flesh and bones under earthly conditions but not under other conditions the present body of Jesus is the same body under all conditions (ibid., 392–94 [with appeals to B.F. Westcott and W.J. Sparrow-Simpson], 404–5) – this defense entails the difficulty of having flesh and bones which under unearthly conditions *exist* but do not exist *as flesh and bones*. Otherwise, we are back to the earlier questions of freshness, storage, preservation, and continuance. I regard the observation that neither the disciples nor the women who out of their means ministered to them and to Jesus are said to have offered provisions for his ordinary human need of shelter and food once he had risen (ibid., 391) as a particularly weak argument from silence for the risen Jesus' essential immateriality, especially in view of his asking for food and in view of the rarity with which this sort of service to him is mentioned prior to the resurrection.

[24] Against Dunn, who makes Matt 28:17 his parade example of ambiguity on the basis of which he casts doubt on the physicality of Jesus' resurrection (*Jesus and the Spirit*, 123–28, 131, 133). M.J. Harris suggests that some of the eleven failed to recognize Jesus because they remained at some distance from him (cf. προσελθών in v. 18a; *Raised Immortal*, 20–21). But he appeared to all the eleven; so they all seem to have been at the same distance from him.

gelic accounts of Jesus' appearances is due to different theological concerns and to a multiplicity of sources, not to any ambiguity in what the women and the disciples saw.

The evangelists who describe the mysterious abilities of the risen Jesus – viz., Luke and John – are none other than the evangelists who most emphasize his physicality.[25] By twice narrating a visible ascension of Jesus "into heaven" (Luke 24:50–51; Acts 1:9–11; cf. the catching up of Elijah to heaven without death and resurrection or any other transformation according to 2 Kgs 2:1–12) Luke implies that this physicality was not unessential and occasional but was essential and permanent   and Luke is the only NT writer to provide a narrative of the ascension, a fact that strengthens the physical implication over against a false deduction of nonphysicality from Jesus' ability to appear and disappear in Luke's Gospel. John does not provide a narrative of Jesus' ascension, but he does refer to the ascension by quoting Jesus as saying to Mary Magdalene, "for I have not yet ascended to the Father" (John 20:17). The immediately preceding words, on which the just-quoted "for"-clause depends, read, "Stop touching me." It is hard not to understand John as saying that the risen Jesus not only appeared physically to Mary but also ascended to appear physically before God his Father. Sometimes Jesus' command to stop touching him is taken as an indication of his essential nonphysicality, as though he meant to say that Mary should learn to think of him from then on in different terms. But he gave the reason why Mary should stop touching him. It was not that he did not want to be thought of as physical. It was that he now needed to ascend to the Father. And when he came back that evening to breathe the Holy Spirit on the disciples he showed them his scars and a week later invited Thomas to feel them. Apparently, ascending to the Father changed nothing with regard to his physicality. Thomas did not feel the scars, not because he could not have done so or because Jesus did not want him to but because the physical reality was so visually unambiguous, after the ascension as before, that he did not need to (see John 7:37–39 for the necessity that Jesus ascend to the Father between appearances so as to give the Spirit in the second appearance).

So also Revelation 5 portrays Jesus as a lamb in the presence of God. As "standing," Jesus the lamb is risen rather than lying on an altar dead. "As slain" he bears the scars of crucifixion on his physical body *in heaven* just as he bore them on earth when he showed them to his disciples and invited Thomas to feel them.[26] These two items of description – as standing and as slain – show that the

---

[25] Additionally M. McClymond points out in private communication that "sudden translation of a corporeal body is no more mysterious than a sudden transformation of an incorporeal Jesus from an invisible into a visible state."

[26] We are not meant to think that John saw the physical form of a lamb, but that he saw Jesus in the physical form of a human being and described him in terms of a sacrificed lamb brought back to life with visible scars remaining.

risen Jesus is physical in heaven as well as on earth (cf. Paul's contemplation in 2 Cor 12:2–4 of the possibility that he may have been caught up into the third heaven "in the body," i.e., in his present body of flesh and blood – a possibility that demonstrates the compatibility of physicality and heavenliness).[27] The physicality of Jesus' resurrection appearances on earth does not seem to have been a passing accommodation to the needs of his earthbound disciples. Common authorship of the Fourth Gospel and Revelation would make this argument stronger, but the mere origin of the two books in the same Johannine school (the least that can be said in view of the many interrelationships between John and Revelation) makes the argument strong enough. We can hardly think that in Revelation the risen Jesus is portrayed as physical in heaven simply to accommodate John's need to see and recognize him for who he is, for John portrays himself in 6:9 as quite capable of seeing and recognizing the souls of martyrs for who they are prior to their resurrection. And it is not advisable to think that the Fourth Gospel and Revelation offer competing traditions of nonphysical and physical versions of Jesus' resurrection, perhaps offering the nonphysical for the purpose of negating it with the physical; for the textual evidence favoring a nonphysical version lacks the strength to convince us that there ever was such a version.

An essentially nonphysical resurrection does not necessarily follow from sudden appearance, from sudden disappearance, or from luminosity of appearance. If the shining of Moses' face when he came down from Mt. Sinai and of Jesus' face and clothing at the transfiguration did not imply essential nonphysicality, neither does it follow that the shining of the face of the risen Jesus in Rev 1:16 implies *his* essential nonphysicality. The risen Jesus looks luminous only after his earthly appearances to the disciples have ceased and therefore falls due to his heavenly exaltation. No inference concerning nonphysicality can legitimately be drawn. If the sudden transportation of Philip from the desert road near Gaza to Azotus, so that he disappeared suddenly from one locality and appeared suddenly in another, does not imply his essential nonphysicality (Acts 8:39–40), neither do the sudden appearances and disappearances of the risen Jesus carry such an implication. In other words, sudden appearance on a

---

[27] Against M. J. Harris, who equates earthliness with physical decay, and heavenliness with immortality (*Raised Immortal*, 121). Besides, we should avoid the assumption that resurrected saints will dwell with God and Christ forever in heaven. Establishing an earthly locale for eternal life are the doctrines of the second coming (a descent from heaven to earth – see esp. 1 Thess 4:16–17 and pp. 292–309 in the present volume against the notion that the catching up of saints to meet the Lord in the air entails a taking to heaven) and of the new creation, in which the new Jerusalem, indwelt by God and Christ, comes down out of heaven to earth (see esp. Revelation 21–22; cf. the description of the "eternal not-handmade house in the heavens," i.e., the new body, as "our building from heaven" – 2 Cor 5:1–2; against M. J. Harris, *Raised Immortal*, 124–25; idem, *From Grave to Glory*, 425). To the physicality of a renewed earth is matched the physicality of resurrected saints and their resurrected Lord (cf. pp. 399–408 in the present volume).

scene does not imply nonphysicality away from the scene, much less nonphysicality at the scene.

The text does not say that the risen Jesus passed *through* a closed door. So under the assumption of a physical resurrection we need not imagine that John wanted us to suppose that one physical body, that of Jesus, passed through another physical body, that of a closed door. All John says is that "Jesus came and stood in the midst" (20:19, 26; similarly, Luke 24:36). We do not know whether John wanted his audience to understand that Jesus' risen body passed through a closed door, or that he gained entry by virtue of the disciples' opening it for him when he came, or that the door did not need to be opened because he came by translation from heaven or elsewhere on earth *directly* into their midst. Since John relates the closed door to the disciples' fear of the Jews and mentions neither a passing through the closed door nor an opening of it, the last possibility seems most likely. It also seems to fit best John's phraseology of "coming" and "standing in the midst," as though Jesus appeared out of the blue rather than passing through anything. In any case, we do know that John stresses Jesus' physicality once the risen Jesus stood in the midst of his disciples.

So also does Luke stress the physicality of the risen Jesus, only without reference to a closed door. Thus we can hardly say that in Luke's book of Acts Paul heard Jesus speaking but saw only a blinding light because Jesus' postresurrection physicality lasted only until the ascension and was therefore unessential. The function of the blinding light was not to dematerialize the exalted Jesus; it was rather to strike Paul down and bring him to conversion. Besides, Acts 9:3; 22:6–11 do not say that Paul saw only a blinding light. They say that a blinding light flashed around him, and Acts 26:16 should make us wary of thinking that on the Damascus road Paul did not see the risen Jesus: "For to this end I [Jesus] have appeared [ὤφθην] to you [Paul]."

The beginning of the risen Jesus' appearances are invariably mentioned, but rarely his disappearances (only in Luke 24:31, apart from the ascension). This textual phenomenon suggests, it has been argued, that after his resurrection Jesus' essential state was one of invisible nonphysicality.[28] Not only does this argument leave the exceptions unaccounted for. It also rests on a *non sequitur*: emphasizing the appearances does not necessarily imply an essential state of invisible nonphysicality. Take the more obvious implication: emphasis falls on the appearances to stress evidence of resurrection. Equal emphasis on the disappearances would have been counterproductive in this respect. Moreover, given the strong emphasis on indications of physicality, the appearances imply more naturally that the risen Jesus was not usually with his disciples than that he was essentially nonphysical.

---

[28] M. J. Harris, *Raised Immortal*, 53.

To say that the risen Jesus is portrayed as having the ability to "materialize" and thereby "localize" himself assumes his essential nonphysicality rather than arguing for it. The physicality of his body when he appears may equally well imply *coming* rather than materialization – more naturally, in fact, because the Gospels actually use verbs of coming, going ahead into Galilee, and ascending into heaven for the actions of the risen Jesus. These common verbs favor shifts in location rather than shifts in modes of being.

Unless all unmarried people are ghosts, the abolition of the institution of marriage in the resurrection does not imply nonphysicality (Mark 12:25; Matt 22:30; Luke 20:35). Nor does the angel-likeness of resurrected people imply it, for there is more than one possible likeness between them and angels. Luke 20:36 makes it out to be immortality. We might also think of non-marrying as such.[29]

Paul's claim that he has "seen" the Lord (1 Cor 9:1) forestalls interpreting his reference to God's revealing his Son "in" him (Gal 1:16) as an inward experience that excludes an objective vision of physical reality.[30] Paul writes that God will destroy the belly and the foods that we eat to fill it (1 Cor 6:13b). But Paul also and immediately writes that the body – i.e., the present physical body – is for the Lord and the Lord for it (6:13c), that it is a "member" of Christ and the "temple" of the Holy Spirit (6:15, 19), and later that it will be raised (ch. 15). So we dare not conclude that a coming destruction of the belly and its foods implies an essential nonphysicality in the resurrection. By dealing only with the present belly and its foods this destruction in no way reflects on the makeup of the resurrected body.[31]

The argument that Paul nowhere uses the phrase "the resurrection of the body" stumbles over his writing that the body is raised (1 Cor 15:44). The retort that it is a spiritual rather than physical body which is raised mistakes the meaning of

---

[29] Against Perkins, who thinks that the Sadducees "mock a literalist version of resurrection" and that Jesus' answer "has already accepted a hellenized spiritualizing of resurrection" (*Resurrection*, 21). On the contrary, the Sadducees mock resurrection as such because resurrection was understood only in literalistic terms; and nonmarriage does not equate with Hellenistic spiritualization. Also against J. R. Donahue, "A Neglected Factor in the Theology of Mark," *JBL* 101 (1982): 574–78, from whom Perkins draws; and M. J. Harris, *Raised Immortal*, 123–24, though on p. 210 Harris interprets Jesus as referring to "the angelic property of deathlessness."

[30] In Gal 1:16 ἐν ἐμοί means "in my case," not "inside me." Paul is presenting the revelation as an argument that the Galatians can see personified in his experience. Dunn's explanation of ἐν ἐμοί in terms of subjectivity slights the element of physical objectivity (*Jesus and the Spirit*, 105–6, 115). See C. M. Pate, *The Reverse of the Curse* (WUNT 2/114; Tübingen: Mohr Siebeck, 2000), 183–85 n. 31, and cf. D. A. Carson, "The Vindication of Imputation: On Fields of Discourse and Semantic Fields," in *Justification: What's at Stake in the Current Debates* (ed. M. Husbands and D. J. Treier; Downers Grove, Ill.: InterVarsity/Leicester, UK: Apollos, 2004), 74–75 n. 54.

[31] Against M. J. Harris, who writes, "Paul hints that the resurrection body will not have the anatomy or physiology of the earthly body" (*Raised Immortal*, 124).

"spiritual." Earlier, in 1 Cor 2:13, 15; 3:1, Paul used the word to describe a certain class of Christians as different from fleshly ones. He certainly was not contrasting ghostly Christians with physical Christians, and nobody understands him thus. As he himself said, spiritual Christians are those who are informed by the Holy Spirit (see the whole of 1 Cor 2:10–16). In Col 1:9 "spiritual" similarly describes understanding as given by the Holy Spirit and in Gal 6:1; 1 Cor 14:37 describes persons as filled with the Holy Spirit. Elsewhere in Paul "spiritual" describes gifts as given by the Holy Spirit (1 Cor 12:1; 14:1; Rom 1:11); a blessing as given by the Holy Spirit (Eph 1:3; cf. vv. 13–14); songs as inspired by the Holy Spirit (Eph 5:19; Col 3.16), the manna, the water-supplying rock, and the law as given by the Holy Spirit (1 Cor 10:3, 4; Rom 7:14, respectively); and the gospel ("spiritual things" in contrast with the "fleshly things" of financial and other support) as given by the Holy Spirit (1 Cor 9:11; Rom 15:27). Only Eph 6:12 forms an exception by putting "the spiritual things of evil" (τὰ πνευματικὰ τῆς πονηρίας) side by side with "rulerships," "authorities," and "the cosmic rulers of this darkness," all of which stand in contrast with "blood and flesh." But the contrast does not thus lie between immateriality and materiality; rather, between the weakness of human beings and the strength of superhuman beings.[32]

Since throughout his letters Paul uses the word "spiritual" not for immateriality but in reference to various functions of the Holy Spirit, we should understand that the spiritual body of resurrection is brought into being by the supernatural operation of the Holy Spirit rather than by natural generation. Paul himself goes on to say as much: "the last Adam became a life-producing Spirit" (1 Cor 15:45) – this with specific reference to resurrection of the body, not just to eternal life in general.[33] The statement that the last Adam became a

---

[32] Even R.E. Brown, who speaks of the resurrected body as only *"less* physical," succumbs somewhat to a false understanding of "spiritual" and "flesh and blood" (*The Virginal Conception and Bodily Resurrection of Jesus* [New York: Paulist, 1973], 85–92 [italics added]; cf. the statement of D.J. Harrington that "Paul's response is noteworthy for ... its vagueness about the nature of the 'spiritual body'" ["Afterlife Expectations in Pseudo-Philo, 4 Ezra, and 2 Baruch, and Their Implications for the New Testament," in *Resurrection in the New Testament* (ed. R. Bieringer, V. Koperski, and B. Lataire; BETL 165; Leuven: Leuven University Press, 2002), 32]). D.B. Martin makes the old mistake of understanding a spiritual body as "a body composed only of pneuma [a kind of heavenly stuff] with sarx and psyche having been sloughed off along the way" (*The Corinthian Body* [New Haven, Conn.: Yale University Press, 1995], 126). M.J. Harris inclines to a definition of the spiritual body as a body animated by the human spirit which has been transformed by the Holy Spirit. In support of this definition he cites the parallel with σῶμα ψυχικόν, a body animated by the human soul (*From Grave to Glory*, 195, 401–2; idem, *Raised Immortal*, 120–21). But this definition is unnecessarily complicated. The parallel carries a contrast favoring the divine Spirit instead of rather than in addition to the human spirit. Any reference to the human spirit would make Paul uncharacteristically contrast the human spirit with the human soul. And we have just seen that with only a single exception, and that one having to do with superhuman rather than human spirits, his other uses of πνευματικός have to do solely with the Holy Spirit.

[33] M.J. Harris sees a "potential difficulty" in saying that "the spiritual body is simply a body

life-producing Spirit links up with "the Lord is the Spirit.... the Spirit of the Lord.... from [the] Lord [the] Spirit" (2 Cor 3:17–18) to confirm a reference to the divine Spirit in a "spiritual body." "But the one joining himself to the Lord is one spirit" (1 Cor 6:17) shows that in 1 Cor 15:45 the risen Jesus' having become a spirit does not entail an essential nonphysicality, for in 1 Cor 6:17 Paul is speaking of a human being who exists in an essentially physical body.[34] So we must not infer an essential nonphysicality for the risen Jesus from the spirituality of the bodies of raised believers.[35] Nor must we infer the nonphysicality of the risen Jesus from his having become a life-producing Spirit any more than in the same verse we infer the nonphysicality of the first human being Adam from his having become a living soul.

True, "flesh and blood will not inherit the kingdom of God" (1 Cor 15:50). But "flesh and blood" connotes the frailty of the present mortal body, as Paul's next, synonymously parallel clause indicates: "neither does corruption inherit incorruption." He simply means that the present mortal, corruptible body will not inherit God's kingdom; and he goes on to say that this present mortal, corruptible body will put on incorruption and immortality (1 Cor 15:51–55; N.B. the neuter gender as referring to the body in v. 53 and cf. Rom 8:23). This statement sounds not at all like an exchange of physicality for nonphysicality, but like an exchange of inferior physicality for superior physicality – a physicality so superior, in fact, that in 2 Cor 5:1–4 Paul will come to speak not merely of an exchange of bodily characteristics but of putting on a new, more substantial body over the old, less substantial one. (He mixes the metaphors of dwellings and garments.) So once again we must not infer an essential nonphysicality for the risen Jesus from the incorruptibility and immortality of the bodies of raised believers. Quite the reverse![36]

By the same token, the glory of Christ's risen body does not exclude physicality, but adorns it.[37] It is argued to the contrary that the contrast between "the body of his glory" (Phil 3:21) and "the body of his flesh" (Col 1:22) shows the resurrected Jesus to be essentially unfleshly even though he might appear on occasion to have flesh and bones.[38] But this argument overlooks that in

---

of flesh totally under the control of the Spirit," for then "Jesus had a spiritual body before his resurrection" (*From Grave to Glory*, 198). But here "spiritual" means "made alive by the Spirit," not "controlled by the Spirit." So also in Rom 8:11: "And if the Spirit of the one who raised Jesus from [the] dead dwells in you, the one who raised Christ from [the] dead will make alive also your mortal bodies through his Spirit that indwells you."

[34] Against M. J. Harris, *From Grace to Glory*, 404.

[35] Also against Hooke, *Resurrection*, 55; Perkins, *Resurrection*, 21. Correctly, P. Lampe, "Paul's Concept of a Spiritual Body," in *Resurrection: Theological and Scientific Assessments* (ed. T. Peters, R. J. Russell, and M. Welker; Grand Rapids: Eerdmans, 2002), 103–14, esp. 108–10.

[36] See also Gundry, "Trimming the Debate," 121–23.

[37] Against Hooke, *Resurrection*, 55–56.

[38] M. J. Harris, *From Grave to Glory*, 387–88.

Phil 3:21 "glory" contrasts with "humiliation" and therefore does not in the least denote an unfleshly material out of which the resurrected body is made. In Col 1:22, conversely, "flesh" does identify the material out of which the crucified body of Jesus was made. Perhaps this identification militates against an incipiently gnostic denial of the incarnation (cf. 2:9). Almost certainly it distinguishes the crucified body of Jesus from his metaphorical body, the church, mentioned both before and after in the passage (1:18, 24; 2:17, 19; 3:15). There is no contextual reason to think that Paul means to distinguish between the crucified and resurrected bodies of Jesus as essentially material and essentially immaterial, respectively.

Paul's description of the resurrected body as ἀχειροποίητον, "not handmade" (2 Cor 5:1), does not deny physicality.[39] It denies human origin. God's Spirit brings the resurrected body into being; the present mortal body is procreated humanly. Similarly the temple not handmade (Mark 14:58) is a work of divine rather than human artisanship (cf. Acts 7:48; 17:24). The circumcision not handmade (Col 2:11) is divinely performed rather than humanly performed. The tabernacle not handmade (Heb 9:11) is divinely constructed rather than humanly constructed (cf. Heb 9:24). The stone cut out of a mountain without hands (Dan 2:34, 45) represents the kingdom of God as opposed to a human kingdom. Since this stone smites an image and breaks in pieces its iron, brass, clay, silver, and gold, the description of the stone as cut without hands cannot point to immateriality. If circumcision not handmade is nonphysical, it is so because of the description "in the divestment of the body of the flesh" (cf. Eph 2:11), not because of the description "not handmade." This latter description does not touch the question of materiality or physicality.[40]

The argument that the earliest layers of the NT portray Jesus as personally exalted but not as bodily resurrected and that only later layers portray him as also bodily resurrected because people could not conceive of disembodied existence – this argument rests on a failure of observation and a mistaken presupposition. It

---

[39] As thought by M. J. Harris, *Raised Immortal*, 114; idem, *From Grave to Glory*, 195.

[40] M. J. Harris tries to steer a middle course between materiality and incorporeality, as though the resurrected body is immaterial yet corporeal: "Paul was implicitly rejecting not only a materialistic view of immortality (since it was a *spiritual* body) but also a spiritualistic view of immortality (since it was a spiritual *body*)" (*Raised Immortal*, 234, italics original). But what makes up the resurrected body if it is constituted neither of flesh and bones nor of spirit, both of which constitutions Harris rejects? His definition of "spiritual" as "animated or controlled by the spirit" does not answer this question. In the absence of an answer one wonders whether the denial of essential materiality, i.e., essential physicality, may not derive from an assumption that an essential materiality or physicality would entail corruptibility. Harris seems to assume so, for he characterizes a physical body as corruptible and a spiritual body as incorruptible without considering the possibility of a difference between the present physical body as corruptible and a future physical body as incorruptible (ibid., 121). We need to think temporally and ethically as well as constitutionally. In the Pauline and generally biblical view corruptibility stems from evil, not from materiality or physicality.

fails to observe that the earliest datable tradition of what happened to Jesus after his death and burial speaks of his resurrection, not of his exaltation; and it is pre-Pauline, which makes it as early as anything we have in the NT (1 Cor 15:3–7). The argument falsely presupposes that first-century Jews – in particular, those who resisted Hellenism – found it difficult or impossible to conceive of disembodied existence. But Paul had grown up "a Hebrew of the Hebrews" (Phil 3:5) yet spoke of being away from the body and out of the body in a conscious state (2 Cor 5:6–10; 12:2–4; Phil 1:20–24). According to Matthew, the most Jewish of the Gospels, Jesus spoke of those who can "kill the body but cannot kill the soul" (10:28). According to *1 En.* 9:3, 10 the souls of righteous martyrs make suit to God, and in 22:3 we read that certain "hollow places have been created… that the spirits of the souls of the dead should assemble therein." According to 2 Esd 7:75–101, at death the soul of the wicked wanders in torture and grief. *Apocalypse of Moses* 32:4 tells Eve that her husband Adam "has gone out of his body" and that she should "rise up and behold his spirit borne aloft to his Maker." And so on and on in non-Hellenistic as well as Hellenistic Jewish literature.[41] And we are supposed to believe that the first Jewish Christians could not conceive of a personally exalted Jesus without inventing the story of his resurrection and an empty tomb? It seems then that the NT presents us with a view of Jesus' resurrection that some people would describe, *have* described, as "crass" and "crude."[42] The NT may be swimming against a strong Platonic current in the stream of Western culture, but we may well hesitate to describe as crass and crude a portrayal concrete enough to examine from a historical standpoint. For historiography too has now become deeply embedded in Western culture – and increasingly elsewhere as well. And as ancient as that Platonic current is in its origins, the old Roman creed that affirms "the resurrection of the flesh" better captures the NT meaning of resurrection as it pertains to Jesus as well as others.

Addendum: A Biblical and Philosophical-Scientific Conversation with Christian Nonreductive Physicalists

Traditionally the physicality of resurrection in the NT has gone along with anthropological dualism, a view of human beings as made up of physical and nonphysical parts that are separable, as in death, yet normally in union with each

---

[41] See Gundry, Sōma *in Biblical Theology*, 87–109; cf. M. E. Thrall, "Paul's Understanding of Continuity between the Present Life and the Life of the Resurrection," in *Resurrection in the New Testament* (ed. R. Bieringer, V. Koperski, and B. Lataire; BETL 165; Leuven: Leuven University Press, 2002), 283–300.

[42] See, e.g., Perkins, *Resurrection*, 74 ("crudely materialistic images of resurrection"); D. E. Nineham, *The Gospel of St. Mark* (PNTC; Baltimore: Penguin, 1963), 321 ("crudely materialistic traits").

other. But unconvinced that the Bible teaches or represents such an anthropology and influenced by the successes of cognitive science and various neurosciences, a number of Christian thinkers are now wedding a monistic interpretation of biblical anthropology with nonreductive physicalism. This brand of physicalism denies that human beings consist partly of a soul/spirit/mind and affirms nonphysical properties that emerge bottomup from physical states, particularly brain states. As supervenient, these nonphysical properties then effect physical states topdown. In this view, naturally, there can be no supervenient state apart from a physical one.[43]

The following comments and questions engage in conversation those Christian thinkers who advocate nonreductive physicalism. First I will defend anthropological dualism as the view taken in the Bible. Then I will call in question the philosophical-scientific advantages of nonreductive physicalism.

There is much more to biblical anthropology than the question of monism versus dualism. But let us center our conversation on that question. Though using the term "dualism" because of its popularity, however, I register here my preference for the terms "duality" and "dichotomy," because "dualism" tends to connote wrongly an uneasy or even antagonistic relation between the physical and the nonphysical.

On some points we can agree: (1) The Bible uses a multiplicity of terms for both the inner and the outer parts, aspects, or functions (take your pick) of human beings, terms such as "spirit," "soul," "heart," "mind" for the inward, and "body," "flesh," "flesh and bones," "members" for the outward. (2) Whether or not the Bible ever uses such terms in a partitive sense, sometimes it does use them by synecdoche for the whole human being (as in the nonbiblical expression, "All hands on deck!" where "hands" is used as a part for the whole). (3) Whether or not the Bible ever puts these terms together analytically, it does sometimes put them together nonanalytically – i.e., synthetically – to stress wholeness of human being, so that the combination of "spirit," "soul," and "body" in 1 Thess 5:23 may not support trichotomy any more than the combination of "heart," "soul," "mind," and "strength" in Mark 12:30 supports quadratomy. (4) A term such as "soul" may carry different meanings in accordance

---

[43] See *Whatever Happened to the Soul? Scientific and Theological Portraits of Human Nature* (ed. W. S. Brown, N. Murphy, and H. N. Malony; Theology and the Sciences; Minneapolis: Fortress, 1998). The Templeton Foundation Press has included this book among its "Books of Distinction." The authors of essays in it are R. S. Anderson, V. E. Anderson, F. J. Ayala, W. S. Brown Jr., J. B. Green, M. Jeeves, H. N. Malony, N. Murphy, and S. G. Post. Only occasionally will I cite particular passages in the book. For the argument from advances in cognitive science and various neurosciences see esp. Murphy, "Human Nature: Historical, Scientific, and Religious Issues," 13–19, and Jeeves, "Brain, Mind, and Behavior," 73–98; idem, "The Resurrection Body and Personal Identity: Possibilities and Limits of Eschatological Knowledge," in *Resurrection: Theological and Scientific Assessments* (ed. T. Peters, R. J. Russell, and M. Welker; Grand Rapids: Eerdmans, 2002), 202–18.

with different contexts. (5) The Bible does not teach a natural immortality (much less a preexistence) of the soul; for whether or not the soul survives the death of the body, the soul's existence depends on God's will and power. (6) A variety of anthropological beliefs existed side by side in the biblical writers' environments, pagan and Jewish environments alike – beliefs ranging from monism to dualism, from material souls to immaterial souls, from no afterlife to immortality of the soul to resurrection of the bodies only of the righteous to a general resurrection, and so on.[44] (7) The biblical emphasis falls on anthropological wholeness, but it remains a question whether that wholeness is monadic or unitive.

Despite terminological and environmental variety and synecdochic and synthetic usages, however, I wish to argue that the Bible presents an anthropological dualism of the nontensive sort. And I will limit myself largely to the NT. Many passages in it range anthropological terms on two sides opposite each other: "outer person" on the one side and "inner person" on the other side in 2 Cor 4:16; "inner person/mind" on the one side and "members/flesh/body" on the other side in Rom 7:22–23, 25; "bodies" and "mind" in Rom 12:1–2; "body" and "spirit" in 1 Cor 7:34; "flesh/body" and "spirit" in 1 Cor 5:3–5; 2 Cor 7:1; Col 2:5; "heart/soul/mind" and "face/eye/ear/flesh" in Rom 2:8–9; 1 Cor 2:9; 2 Cor 5:12; Eph 6:5–7; Col 3:22–23; "hearts" (in an agreed-upon nonphysical sense) and "bodies" in Heb 10:22; "heart" and "eye/hand/members/body" in Matt 5:29–30; "heart" and "stomach" in Mark 7:19; Matt 15:17; "heart" and "mouth" in Mark 7:20–23; Matt 12:34; 15:18–19; Luke 6:45; Rom 10:9–10; 2 Cor 6:11; "heart" and "lips" in Isa 29:13; Mark 7:6; Matt 15:8; "hearts/mind" and "hands" in Jas 4:8; and "conscience" and "flesh" in 1 Pet 3:21.

But you monists regularly regard these pairs as representing inner and outer aspects of an indivisible whole and as representing functions rather than constituent parts. Because terms like "body," "flesh," "flesh and bones," and "members" point more naturally to objects rather than functions (though some scholars would demur) the functional interpretation is usually restricted to terms concerning the inner life: "mind" for the function of thinking, "heart" for that of thinking and feeling, "soul" for that of living, "spirit" for that of relating to other beings, and so on. But do these terms refer *only* to aspects and functions of human being? That they refer also to inner and outer *parts* of human being is evident, I think, from their separability.

Though their flesh returns to dust, in the OT the deceased are regularly gathered to their ancestors *before* they are buried in the family sepulchre and even when they are buried far from it and alone (Gen 15:15; 25:8–9; 35:29; 49:28–50:14; Num 20:24, 26; 27:13; 31:2; Deut 31:16; 32:50; 1 Kgs 2:19; 2 Kgs 21:18). In Isa 14:9, 18–20 the "shades" (or however we should translate רפאים in Sheol are distinguished from their corpses in the tombs and stirred up

---

[44] On this variety of ancient anthropological beliefs see Martin, *The Corinthian Body*, 3–37.

to meet and address the king of Babylon, whose death brings him to their underworld. And the witch of Endor calls up Samuel from the dead for a conversation with King Saul (1 Sam 28:8–19).

After Jesus committed his "spirit" to God and expired, according to Luke 23:39–55, Jesus' "body" was "put in a rock-hewn tomb" while he – obviously his disembodied spirit that he had committed to God – joined the repentant thief in "Paradise" that very day. Similarly, Stephen prayed just before he was stoned to death and buried, "Lord Jesus, receive my spirit" (Acts 7:59). And after rising from the dead Jesus declared that a "spirit" does not have "flesh and bones" as he had (Luke 24:37, 39).

First Corinthians 5:3–5 talks about the destruction of the "flesh" while the "spirit" is saved. James 2:26 says that the "body" apart from the "spirit" is dead. And Jesus warned, "Do not fear those who kill the body but cannot kill the soul. Fear, rather, the one who can destroy both body and soul in gehenna" (Matt 10:28). The inability of human beings to kill the soul though they can kill the body shows that body and soul are distinct and separable and that the soul cannot here mean the life or vitality of the body. The parallel in Luke 12:4–5 does not mention the soul and therefore does not give a clear expression of dualism: "do not fear those who kill the body and afterwards have no more that they can do.… fear the one who after he has killed [the body] has authority to cast into gehenna." But Luke's version does not rule out Matthew's explicitly dualistic version; and since God must have something to cast into gehenna after he has killed the body, Luke's version implies the casting there of either a bodiless soul or, in accordance with Matthew's version, both body and soul.[45]

Second Corinthians 12:1–4 contemplates the possibility that Paul was outside his body when he was caught up to "the third heaven," i.e., "Paradise," already in this life. Philippians 1:20–24 opposes "dying/departing and being with Christ" to "living/staying in the flesh." Similarly, 2 Cor 5:6–9 opposes being "away from the body/at home with the Lord" to being "away from the Lord/at home in the body."

In 2 Cor 4:7–5:5 Paul writes, "We [he and his fellow workers] are always carrying in our bodies the death of Jesus" and "always being given over to death on account of Jesus" – obvious references to the constant threat of martyrdom (as also in Rom 8:36; 1 Cor 15:31; 2 Cor 11:23), against the mistaken assertion that Paul is unconcerned with thanatology in this passage. Then he writes that they long to have their more substantial "heavenly dwelling," a figure of speech for the resurrected body, put on right over their less substantial "earthly tent," a figure of speech for the present mortal body, so as not to be found naked after taking off the present mortal body without having yet put on the resurrected body. That is to say,

---

[45] Against Green, "'Bodies – That Is, Human, Lives': A Re-Examination of Human Nature in the Bible," 102.

the best possibility consists in living up to the resurrection at Jesus' return and thus avoiding an interim of disembodied existence – against the notion that nakedness has to do with shame or not being clothed with Christ at the Last Judgment, which does not come into view till 2 Cor 5:10 (cf. 1 Cor 15:37, where the nakedness of a sown seed describes a postmortem, preresurrection state rather than indicating shame or Christlessness at the Last Judgment); also against what can only be called the wildly wrong claim that a concern of Paul with thanatology here would be "uncharacteristically subjective and individualistic"[46] (for not to make too much of Paul's using the plural of the first person pronoun, everybody recognizes an almost unrelenting subjectivity and individualism of Paul throughout 2 Corinthians, starting immediately in the very first chapter and continuing without letup into the present passage and most of the time beyond – see especially chs. 10–13, not to detail similarly subjective and individualistic passages: Rom 1:8–17; 9:1–5; 10:1; 1 Cor 1:10–17; 2:1–5; 3:5–15; 4:1–21; 7:25–26; 9:1–27; 10:33–11:1; 14:18–19; Eph 3:1–13; Phil 1:12–26; 3:4b–17; Col 1:24–2:5; and, of course, passages in the highly personal letters to Timothy, Titus, and Philemon). Paul's concern with thanatology in 2 Cor 5: 1–5 is proved, finally, by the clause in v. 4, "in order that the mortal [literally, 'what has to do with death'] may be swallowed up by life."

In Rev 6:9–11 the disembodied "souls" of martyrs eager for the first resurrection are told to wait in heaven till the number of martyrs reaches completion. So even there, in heaven, an interim separates death and resurrection. Apparently Jesus and biblical authors would not subscribe to physicalism, even a physicalism that regards spiritual or mental properties as supervenient states that cease to exist with the death of the body. But more on that kind of physicalism later.

How would the biblical language surveyed above have been understood in the biblical era? Without any comment by me the answer should be clear from the following extrabiblical, typical samples: (1) The dead are those "in hades whose spirit has been taken from their bodies" (Bar 2:17). (2) Tobit prays for the release of his "spirit" in death for the enjoyment of "the everlasting place" (Tob 3:6). (3) The souls and bodies of the righteous will be united at the resurrection but the souls of the wicked will continue in a grief-laden disembodied existence (*2 Bar.* 30:25). (4) At death the mortals "who were made of earth" return "to the earth" while their "souls" return to God who lent them (Wis 15:8).

This biblical and extrabiblical evidence belies the confidently repeated statements, larded with supportive quotations from supposedly authoritative scholars and often substituting for careful attention to the biblical and extrabiblical texts themselves, that Jesus and biblical writers thought of human being only holistically, never partitively and never in terms of a disembodied part. Furthermore, the frequency of the dualistically partitive language and the ab-

---

[46] So Green, "Bodies," 171.

sence of contradictory language are the more striking and significant in view of the diversity of anthropological opinion in the ancient environment – and yet even more striking and significant in that the most Jewish of the Gospels, Matthew, presents a version of Jesus' saying on human ability to kill the body and inability to kill the soul that is more explicitly dualistic than the parallel version in that most Hellenistic of the Gospels, Luke. And that most Jewish of the Epistles, James, addressed as it is to Jewish Christians, is no less dualistic in its anthropology than are those Epistles of the apostle to the Gentiles, Paul. So although the NT authors used various anthropological terms available to them in the surrounding culture, their anthropology does not evince the kind of tailoring to different audiences that we might have expected if those authors were simply accommodating their language and anthropology to various prevailing norms among their different intended audiences. Apart from the dualistic anthropology on which they rest, moreover, a number of biblical statements would lose their meaning entirely. In other words, it is not so much that the Bible teaches dualistic anthropology as it is that what it teaches on other matters often depends on the dualistic anthropology it presupposes.

But to the biblical evidence that resists nonreductive physicalism I add a batch of questions that undermine its philosophical and scientific viability:

1) Does the increasingly successful answering of questions concerning human being with the use of empirical methods point toward physicalism? Natural scientists might be tempted to think so. But with each new answer a new question seems to appear. So far as a *final* answer to the riddle of human being is concerned, then, is there any progress even in the empirical sphere? Does not the rainbow of an ultimate solution to the riddle recede with every forward stride of discovery? At the least, is it not as much a leap of faith to assume that empirical discoveries regarding the human constitution are bringing us closer to a fixed goal as it is to assume that progress will continue to be matched by the opening of newly recognized fields of the unknown? Therefore does the physicalistic deduction rest on a firm base even in the terms of empirical method?

2) If we have to take account of causal influence of the whole on the part as well as of the part on the whole, from the standpoint of *reductive* materialism why cannot the whole consist of brain functions as a whole, as distinct from functions localized in different parts of the brain, without recourse to nonphysical emergent properties as well? Thus, bottomup from different parts of the brain, topdown from the brain as a whole – period. Therefore does taking account of causal influence from the whole on the part really give nonreductive physicalism an advantage over reductive materialism?

3) As to the reductive materialistic reasoning that if the mind were nonphysical it could not be the source of the energy required for the body (or, more specifically, the brain) to act – cannot the same reasoning be brought against top-

down causation of bodily acts by supervenient states? For though those states are caused bottomup by physical states, they themselves – or at least some of them – are hypothesized to be nonphysical, are they not? Do not you nonreductive physicalists, then, have to join dualists in questioning the assumption that a physical event requires physical energy in the form of a physical stimulus? If so, as nonreductive physicalists do you not have to give up your argument against dualists that a nonphysical entity could not act effectively on a physical entity? And for a Christian, does not the effective acting of God, who is Spirit, on and in physical entities require a giving up of that argument?[47]

4) If for the sake of topdownism you say that emergent mental functions are not *wholly* accounted for by brain functions at the lower level, what *does* account for those mental functions that brain functions do not account for? What kind of nonphysical stimulus is it, and what is its source? If you answer that the stimulus consists in the shaping influence of a pattern in the totality of information being processed in the interactive network of brain-processing modules, is it not true that a pattern does not shape anything but that it is the *result* of shaping, so that a process produces a pattern rather than vice versa? If so, does it not require some nonbiologically bound interference in the ongoing neurobiological processes of the brain to recognize a pattern?

5) You may say that variability in circumstances, i.e., environments, may make for a difference between supervenient states emerging from the same brain state. But in and of themselves circumstances are hermeneutically mute, are they not? Do they not require interpretation to determine whether they, or variations within them, make for a difference between supervenient states? If so, where does the interpretation of circumstances come from? If you answer that it comes from a mental set, i.e., an expectation, the question arises, Where does the mental set or expectation come from? Presumably from circumstances experienced in the past. But they too had to be interpreted. So the question, Where do interpretations of circumstances come from? keeps being pushed back in an infinite series of regressions. Thus your nonreductive physicalism does not provide an answer to the question of how variability in circumstances can make for a difference between supervenient states emerging from the same brain state, does it?

6) If you build on I. Lakatos's thinking about scientific progress, take nonreductive physicalism as a thetic hardcore, and project that the positive heuristic of this hardcore will be to explain physicalistically all the operations once attributed to the mind or soul – but then feel forced to appeal to circumstances exterior both to the brain and to its emergent properties – how can hardcore nonreductive physicalism explain by itself all the operations once attributed to the mind or soul? Do not circumstances now substitute for the mind or soul as the

---

[47] Against Murphy, "Human Nature," 7–8, with a citation of O. Flanagan.

"ghost in the machine" – and a not very convincing ghost at that if it is correct that in and of themselves circumstances are hermeneutically mute?[48]

7) For example, if you say that circumstances justify the interpretation of certain experiences as acts of, or encounters with, the divine, do you not have to ask what makes circumstances any more interpretive than an experience that takes place within them? Where does the determination that some circumstances point to the divine and others do not – where does that determination come from? Say you interpret an illness as punishment from God because of the twin circumstances of your having committed a sin and of your believing that God punishes sin. How did you arrive at the conviction that such and such was a sin and at the belief that God punishes sin? Where is the explanatory power of a nonreductive physicalism that has to seek help from circumstances which themselves require interpretation from an outside source?

8) Or again, how can you say that nonreductive physicalism explains neurobiolgoically why an approach to moral analysis and moral education based on narrative accounts of virtuous lives – say, those of St. Francis and Mother Theresa – should be more effective than rule-based ethics when it is questionable how neurobiological processes, even with the addition of supervenient states, can arrive at a judgment that life A is virtuous whereas life B is evil?[49]

For Christian thinkers the combination of these questions with biblical anthropology, rightly understood, rules out nonreductive physicalism. Better is the old dualism.

[48] Against Murphy, "Nonreductive Physicalism: Philosophical Issues," 139–40, with a citation of Lakatos.

[49] Against Post, "A Moral Case for Nonreductive Physicalism," 210–12; Brown, "Conclusion: Reconciling Scientific and Biblical Portraits of Human Nature," 226–27.

11. The Inferiority of the New Perspective on Paul

The publication of E. P. Sanders' *Paul and Palestinian Judaism* stirred up the study of Paul's theology.[1] Reviewers regularly noted the importance of the book (from here on, *PPJ*). Despite his suffering the barb of Sanders' criticism one reviewer went so far as to endorse the claim on the dust cover of *PPJ* that here we have the most important work on its subject to appear in a generation.[2] In *PPJ*, however, Sanders gave far more space to Palestinian Judaism than to Paul. Then Sanders wrote another book, *Paul, the Law and the Jewish People* (from here on *PLJP*), which redressed that imbalance and made possible a fuller and fairer account of his thoughts.[3] Its first and third chapters "expand and clarify, and sometimes correct, the account of Paul's view of the law which was sketched in *Paul and Palestinian Judaism*."[4] Special lectures in Europe, Great Britain, and North America gave Sanders further opportunity to broadcast his thoughts. Their influence on Pauline studies led to what is now called "The New Perspective on Paul."

Particularly impressive to NT scholars have been the breadth and depth of Sanders' discussions in *PPJ* concerning both primary Jewish materials and secondary literature (especially that stemming from modern Jewish scholarship) devoted to those materials. We should heed his call to relate the materials to each other in ways that take account of hortatory purpose as well as of theological dogma and not to seize on certain statements that appeal to Christian prejudice and neglect others which from the Christian standpoint put Palestinian Judaism in a better light. His striving to compare whole patterns of religion, not merely particular themes, and to do so initially with scholarly objectivity rather than with theological evaluation, merit applause. Sanders may not live up to his own ideals – his comparison turns out to be not so holistic as announced and his apology for Palestinian Judaism (not just description of it) as well-balanced between God's grace and the good works of human beings shows some intrusion of Sanders' own theological preferences[5] – but those ideals have enlarged and

---

[1] Philadelphia: Fortress Press, 1977.
[2] M. McNamara, *JSNT* 5 (1979): 71; cf. *PPJ*, 24–29. Here and below, reviews are cited only by the journal in which they appeared.
[3] Philadelphia: Fortress, 1983.
[4] *PLJP*, ix.
[5] Sanders, *PPJ*, 426–27.

purified the descriptive task he set for himself to a larger degree than is evident in some other treatments of the same topic.

Since the bulk of *PPJ* dealt with Palestinian Judaism and a comparatively small portion with Paul's theology, most reviewers of that book followed suit. By contrast the present evaluation deals briefly with Palestinian Judaism and at some length with Paul's theology. It also takes account of various articles written by Sanders and most especially of his *PLJP*.

Sanders excludes from the consideration of Paul's pattern of religion 2 Thessalonians, Colossians, Ephesians, the Pastorals, and passages about Paul in Acts. Inclusion might strengthen certain criticisms of Sanders' thesis (see esp. Eph 2:8–9; 1 Tim 1:7; Titus 3:4–7; and possibly Acts 13:39), though the thesis might also gain some points (e.g., from Acts 16:3; 18:18; 21:17–26; Eph 2:10; Titus 3:8). The overall picture would not alter, however; nor would it with the inclusion on the Jewish side of the Targumim and Pseudo-Philo's *Biblical Antiquities*, for the neglect of which Sanders has been criticized.[6]

Reviewers have regularly noted that Sanders does not, in fact, compare whole patterns of religion; rather, he compares soteriologies dealing with "getting in and staying in" (his phrase).[7] He nearly admits as much ("one might call this pattern the soteriological pattern") but prefers the more general term "pattern of religion."[8] This limitation to soteriologies has seemed to reduce the argumentative weight of the supposed holism of his comparisons. Furthermore, it is charged, not only has Sanders succumbed to the temptation of building too much on too little; he has also fallen prey to the danger of leaving a generally false impression of Palestinian Judaism by concentrating on its soteriology (with which the literature of Palestinian Judaism shows little concern), by disregarding the atomistic nature of rabbinic literature when it comes to soteriology, by overlooking the questions that generated rabbinic literature, by pa-

---

[6] N. King, *Bib* 61 (1980): 141–44; McNamara, *JSNT* 5 (1979): 73; G. Brooke, *JJS* 30 (1979): 248. The question of Christian influence in the *Testaments of the Twelve Patriarchs*, which Sanders also excludes, leaves the *Testaments* in limbo. On the other hand, J. Neusner thinks Sanders should have shown the same reticence to use rabbinic materials because of great uncertainties concerning their dates, historical reliability, original meanings, theological redactions, etc. ("The Use of the Later Rabbinic Evidence for the Study of Paul," in *Approaches to Ancient Judaism* [ed. W. S. Green; BJS 9; Chico, Calif.: Scholars Press, 1980], 2:56–59; cf. an earlier form of this article in *HR* 18 [1978–79]: 177–91, there titled "Comparing Judaisms").

[7] See N. A. Dahl, *RelSRev* 4 (1978): 155–57; A. J. Saldarini, *JBL* 98 (1979): 300; McNamara, *JSNT* 5 (1979): 72; Brooke, *JJS* 30 (1979): 248; W. A. Meeks, "Toward a Social Description of Pauline Christianity," in *Approaches to Ancient Judaism* (ed. W. S. Green; BJS 9; Chico, Calif.: Scholars Press, 1980), 2:27; B. R. Gaventa, "Comparing Paul and Judaism," *BTB* 10 (1980): 39–41. Gaventa adds the objection that there are no wholes to compare since we have only a few, occasional letters of Paul and since our knowledge of rabbinic Judaism in Paul's day is sketchy. But this objection only expresses the limits of historical research. Surely Sanders means "whole" so far as data are available.

[8] Sanders, "Patterns of Religion in Paul and Rabbinic Judaism: A Holistic Method of Comparison," *HTR* 66 (1973): 457.

pering over differences among various sectors of Palestinian Judaism, by failing to take account of its historical developments, by playing down certain elements (in particular, apocalyptic), and by ignoring the distinction between abstract theology and lived religion.[9]

In Sanders' defense, however, he has not conceived of soteriology narrowly. It covers all the essential points of religion, i.e., all the requirements for getting in and staying in. Whatever their number, these essentials include both beliefs and practices. Formally, then, Sanders' inability to discuss in the confines of *PPJ* the mass of halakic minutiae developed in Palestinian Judaism (however systematic or atomistic that development may have been) does not invalidate his description of them as soteriologically designed to help people stay in. Quite simply, those minutiae helped form the nomistic side of "covenantal nomism" (Sanders' phrase describing the pattern of religion in Palestinian Judaism).

A careful reading of *PPJ* will falsify the charges that Sanders is inattentive to the atomistic nature of rabbinic literature when it comes to soteriology, to the differences among various sectors of Palestinian Judaism, and to its historical developments. In fact, he gives a reasonable amount of attention to these matters; and in a responsive article he turns back the charge of overlooking the questions which generated rabbinic literature by noting that there must have been a pattern of religion behind those questions – otherwise Judaism would have disintegrated in the flux of time – and by arguing that the Mishnah discusses disputed points because points of agreement (i.e., those that made up the pattern of Palestinian Judaism) needed no discussion.[10]

---

[9] J.C. Beker, *ThTo* 35 (1978): 108, 110–11; Dahl, *RelSRev* 4 (1978): 155; J. Murphy-O'Connor, *RB* 85 (1978): 123; D.A. Hagner, *The Reformed Journal* 29 (1979): 26; Saldarini, *JBL* 98 (1979): 300, 302; McNamara, *JSNT* 5 (1979): 72; Brooke, *JJS* 30 (1979): 247–49; Neusner, "The Use of the Later Rabbinic Evidence," 43–63; W.D. Davies, *Paul and Rabbinic Judaism* (Philadelphia: Fortress, 1980), xxxi–xxxvi; cf. H. Räisänen, "Legalism and Salvation by the Law," in *Die paulinische Literatur und Theologie* (ed. S. Pedersen; Teologiske Studier 7; Aarhus/Göttingen: Vandenhoeck & Ruprecht, 1980), 67 n. 27.

[10] E.P. Sanders, "Puzzling Out Rabbinic Judaism," in *Approaches to Ancient Judaism* (ed. W.S. Green; BJS 9; Chico, Calif.: Scholars Press, 1980), 2:66–67, 70–73; cf. already idem, *PPJ*, 234–37, 420–21. Saldarini's complaint that to see the same pattern of religion in *1 Enoch*, an apocalyptic book, as in Tannaitic literature is to overlook obvious differences hits the mark to the extent that a truly holistic comparison is insisted on, but not to the extent that soteriology is in view and can be shown to be similar in *1 Enoch* and Tannaitic literature (*JBL* 98 [1979]: 302). In the Dead Sea Scrolls trust in elective grace and emphasis on strict observance of the law stand side by side despite the presence of interest in apocalyptic. So we have no reason to think the apocalyptic character of *1 Enoch* (itself represented at Qumran) subverts the similarities between *1 Enoch* and Tannaitic literature with respect to covenantal nomism. On the other hand, Sanders' argument that Weber's theory of Israel's falling from grace through worship of the golden calf is necessary to the affirmation of legalism in Judaism needs to be faulted (*PPJ*, 38; cf. F.W. Weber, *Jüdische Theologie* [2d ed.; Leipzig: Dörffling & Franke, 1897], 274–77). Jewish theologians of the NT era might still teach legalism without holding to such a theory.

Sanders affirms the importance of apocalyptic in Paul's theology even though he does not discuss it at length,[11] and his lack of emphasis on Jewish apocalyptic poses no problem unless someone can show that such apocalyptic negated covenantal nomism. He admits a partial negation of this sort in *4 Ezra* but can explain it as due to disappointment resulting from the destruction of Jerusalem and the temple in A.D. 70.[12] Here, indeed, a crack opens in the pattern of Palestinian Judaism. J. C. Beker tries to drive a wedge into the crack by asking why we should accept such an explanation when most of Tannaitic literature post-dates A.D. 70 yet loses nothing of covenantal nomism.[13] The question is not telling, however, since a historical event can evoke quite different responses among people belonging to the same religion. There is no reason why *4 Ezra* may not be the exception that proves the rule. As historians of religion we want to know what *was* (as a matter of fact), not what *should* have been (as a matter of consistency).

So far as the distinction between abstract theology and lived religion is concerned, Sanders' emphasis on exhortation as the primary framework of nomistic language and on prayer as the primary framework of covenantal language (i.e., the language of elective grace) pays due to the importance of lived religion. D. A. Hagner is almost certainly correct in saying that "adherents of a religious faith seldom reflect the balance of its theology holistically conceived."[14] But the suggestion that despite theoretical balance one-sided legalism sometimes characterized the practice of Palestinian Judaism not only misses the hortatory and prayerful nature of the theologoumena cited by Sanders. It also needs literary evidence, else we cannot know whether a disparity between theology and practice did in fact develop.

Is there very much literary evidence of such a disparity? Probably not if we exclude the NT and analyze the Jewish literature only *formally* with the question of contradiction in our minds and the handy explanation of logically loose hortatory and prayerful language in our pockets. This kind of analysis allows Sanders to state a thesis part of which the rest of the present essay is written to refute: "on the point at which many have found the decisive contrast between Paul and Judaism – grace and works – Paul is in agreement with Palestinian Judaism .... *salvation is by grace but judgment is according to works; works are the condition of remaining 'in', but they do not earn salvation.*"[15] But if we treat the literatures

---

[11] Sanders, *PLJP*, 12 n. 13, with references to *PPJ*, 441–42, 549, 552.

[12] Sanders, *PPJ*, 427–28.

[13] Beker, *ThTo* 35 (1978): 110; cf. B. Byrne (*"Sons of God" – "Seed of Abraham"* [AnBib 83; Rome: Pontifical Biblical Institute, 1979], 229–30), who adds a consideration of *2 Baruch*.

[14] Hagner, *The Reformed Journal* 29 (1979): 26.

[15] *PPJ*, 543 (italics original). Because for Paul Christian faith entails an active decision (whereas Jews have only to be born into the covenant) and because for Paul soteriology grows out of union with Christ (whereas in Palestinian Judaism it grows out of a person's relation to the law), Sanders describes the two patterns of religion as "totally different" ("Patterns of Religion,"

(the Pauline and the Palestinian Jewish) *materially* – i.e., if we weigh their emphases – quite a different impression is gained, an impression of Palestinian Judaism as centered on works-righteousness and of Paul's theology as centered on grace. Such an impression need not include theological judgments, only historical descriptions; for it is another question (though an important one) whether we ourselves should prefer legalism, grace, or a combination of the two.

Weighing the materials of Palestinian Judaism shows a preponderance of emphasis on obedience to the law as the way of staying in. The covenant, based on God's elective grace, may be presupposed; but it has no prominence (as Sanders admits).[16] Rather, the law is searched, pulled, stretched, and applied. The rabbis start building a fence around it in order that people may not even come close to breaking it. A body of interpretive or applicatory traditions starts piling up, also a body of oral legal traditions (written down finally in the Mishnah) which parallel the written law of the OT. These traditions draw the criticism in the NT *outside Pauline literature* that they smother the original intent of the law (see Mark 7:6–13 par. Matt 15:3–9 for the classic passage). Whether it was Jesus or the early church that was originally responsible for the criticism and whether or not the criticism was just, the very raising of the issue establishes a Palestinian Jewish preoccupation with the law and with its careful observance and indicates a basic disagreement between Palestinian Judaism and Christianity at this point (even in sectors of Christianity where the law was valued – see, e.g., the Gospel of Matthew).

Josephus's descriptions of the Jewish sects confirm this preoccupation (*Life* 38 § 191; *J.W.* 1.5.2. § 110; 2.8.6, 9, 12, 14 §§ 136, 147, 159, 162; *Ant.* 17.2.4 § 41; 18.1.3–4 §§ 12–18), as do the contents of the Mishnah and other early rabbinic literature. J. Neusner is even able to portray the Pharisees before A.D. 70 and after Hillel as trying to extend the laws of purity concerning the temple to everyday life.[17] Much more do the rabbis after A.D. 70 set their sights on exact delineation of legal responsibilities. The punctiliousness of the sect at Qumran proves that we cannot legitimately use end-time fervor to dilute preoccupation with careful observance of the law. And whatever enjoyment Palestinian Jews derived from such observance is immaterial to the fact of this preoccupation. Sanders has succeeded in undermining the notion that in Palesti-

---

474–76) and "essentially different" (*PPJ*, 543). These descriptions do not fully agree, however, with his strong insistence that Paul and Palestinian Judaism agree on grace and works. Such a fundamental agreement, if proved, would weaken the adverbs "totally" and "essentially" and tend toward a view Sanders denies, viz., that the patterns are alike, only the materials different.

[16] See, e.g., *PPJ*, 236.

[17] J. Neusner, *From Politics to Piety* (Englewood Cliffs, N.J.: Prentice-Hall, 1973), 14, 67, 73, 80, 83–90, 119–20, 146, 152; idem, *The Rabbinic Traditions about the Pharisees before 70* (Leiden: E. J. Brill, 1971), Part I, 62–65, 70, 304–7; Part II, 295; Part III, 244, 286–300. Cf. W. Horbury's criticism of Sanders for neglecting tendencies in Palestinian Judaism to "moral absolutism and asceticism" ("Paul and Judaism," *ExpTim* 90 [1979]: 116–18).

nian Judaism the retention of salvation always depended on producing at least a bare majority of good deeds; but he has not succeeded in relating the law to elective grace in a way that materially scales down preoccupation with legal interpretation, extension, application, and observance.

Though obedience is integral and important to Paul's theology, alongside Palestinian Jewish absorption in legal questions his comments on obedience look proportionately slight. Furthermore, they usually take the form of exhortations, not of legal interpretation, extension, and application.[18] Where amoral questions arise (as concerning meat offered to idols in 1 Corinthians 8–10; cf. Romans 14), Paul tends to freedom of conscience rather than to legal definition. The moral demands of the law he takes, not as distinctive of Judaism, but as matters of universal obligation (see esp. Rom 1:18–32). Therefore it would not cross his mind that commanding Gentile as well as Jewish Christians to meet these demands might disagree with his insistence on freedom from the law. In the Judaizing debate he is concerned with specially Jewish features of the law (circumcision, "days and months and seasons and years" [Gal 4:10], and dietary restrictions),[19] the kind that capture most attention in Palestinian Judaism. The fact he does not defend himself against inconsistency suggests that even his opponents took the moral and ethical demands of the law as matters of universal obligation rather than as specially Jewish requirements.[20]

As noted, Sanders sees an agreement in principle between Paul and Palestinian Judaism: a person gets in by God's elective grace and stays in by works of the law. But for Paul, of course, God's elective grace works through Christ. Sanders' view therefore requires us to think that after defining in an un-Jewish christological way the grace that gets a person in, Paul lapses back to his inherited Jewish, unchristological way of thinking with regard to staying in: "Christians are judged according to how well they fulfill the law" and will be excluded if they do not fulfill it well enough.[21] "When he had to deal in detail with transgression within the Christian community, reward and punishment, and the possibility of postconversion atonement, he did so in a thoroughly Jewish way."[22] This view of Paul's thought implies that the question of staying in was not a theological point of debate between him and the Judaizers; for other-

---

[18] Cf. Sanders, *PLJP*, 95–96, 106–7; P. Steensgaard, "Erwägungen zum Problem Evangelium und Paränese bei Paulus," *ASTI* 10 (1975/76): 110–28.

[19] Sanders, *PLJP*, 104.

[20] Cf. C. Haufe, "Die Stellung des Paulus zum Gesetz," *TLZ* 91 (1966): 171–78; P. Bläser, *Das Gesetz bei Paulus* (NTAbh 19/1–2; Münster: Aschendorff, 1941), 38–44; P. Stuhlmacher, "Das Gesetz als Thema biblischer Theologie," *ZTK* 75 (1978): 271–76.

[21] Sanders, *PLJP*, 112; see again *PPJ*, 543, and almost identical statements on pp. 517, 518; also *PLJP*, 10. Sanders' statement that Paul opposes obeying the law as the condition of remaining among the elect seems to contradict these other, repeated statements ("Paul's Attitude toward the Jewish People," *USQR* 33 [1978]: 184).

[22] Sanders, *PLJP*, 107.

wise we would have expected him to carry over his un-Jewish thinking from getting in to staying in so as to avoid a charge of inconsistency and keep the focus of his soteriology on faith in Christ.

In fact, however, the question of staying in *is* the issue, at least the primary one, in Galatians. There, contrary to Sanders' statement that "the subject of Galatians is ... the condition on which Gentiles enter the people of God,"[23] Paul does not deal with a question whether believing Gentiles had *gotten* in. Rather, he deals with the question whether believing Gentiles could *stay* in without submitting to circumcision and keeping other parts of the law. "Having begun by the Spirit, are you now being perfected by the flesh?" (3:3). It is a question of "abiding," not of starting, according to Paul's quotation of Deut 27:26 (3:10). "You have been severed from Christ, you who are seeking to be justified by the law; you have fallen from grace .... You were running well; who hindered you from obeying the truth?" (5:4, 7).

Someone might say that the Judaizers were concerned with the question of getting in – thus they did not regard Gentile believers as "in" – and that Paul, regarding Gentile believers as already in, transposed the question to one of staying in. Apart from the unlikelihood that he was badly misinformed or knowingly and foolishly misrepresented his opponents' position, his view of the question determines his response, which we want to understand. So it does not matter to *his* theology whether his understanding of the Judaizers' soteriology was accurate or not. Since for him staying in was the question, it is hard to think he lapsed back – perhaps carelessly, perhaps inconsistently – into Jewish thinking with respect to continuing in the Christian life. Even in the less polemical Romans, staying in by faith in Christ seems to be as much on Paul's mind as getting in; for he devotes chs. 6–8 to the ongoing life of believers as being not under law but under grace. And whatever else the phrase "from faith to faith" in 1:17a may mean, it surely means that from beginning to end, faith alone (which Paul expressly contrasts with works – see esp. 4:4–5) forms the overarching principle of soteriology, staying in as well as getting in. Similarly we read in Rom 11:20, "You *stand* by faith," and in 15:18, "For I will not presume to say anything [except] those things that *Christ* has accomplished through me."

Outside Galatians and Romans, too, Paul repeatedly identifies faith and rejects works as the principle of continuance in salvation. He repeatedly affirms the activity of God and denies human effort as the fundament of perseverance.

---

[23] Sanders, *PLJP*, 17–20. Sanders describes the point as "absolutely vital." Taking the issue as one of getting in rather than as one of staying in enables him to say that in Galatians Paul is not arguing against Judaism in general; rather, against a position concerning a particular point advocated in Christian circles (*PLJP*, 19–20). But if Paul's opponents took their cue from Judaism and if the issue had to do with staying in, Paul's remarks hit against Judaism *via* his opponents' Judaistic false gospel (as Sanders admits in *PLJP*, 46, though as usual he limits Paul's criticism to privileged status – a limitation we will later find reasons to reject).

Human effort is an effect, not a cause. "For you stand by faith" (2 Cor 1:24). "Not that we are adequate in ourselves so as to consider anything as [coming] from ourselves, but our adequacy is from God" (2 Cor 3:5). "Being confident of this very thing, that he who has begun a good work in you will perfect it until the day of Jesus Christ" (Phil 1:6). "Work out your salvation with fear and trembling, for it is God who effects in you both the willing and the doing for his good pleasure" (Phil 2:12b–13). "We ... put no confidence in the flesh .... I count [N.B. the present tense after the preceding perfect tense 'I counted'] all things to be loss ... and I count [them] rubbish in order that I be found in him, not having my righteousness from the law but [having] the [righteousness] through faith in Christ, the righteousness from God, [based] on faith" (Phil 3:3, 8–9). Likewise in disputed epistles: "Striving according to his working which works in me with power" (Col 1:29); "being established by the [probably = 'your'] faith" (Col 2:7); "that Christ may dwell in your hearts through faith" (Eph 3:17). Cf. 2 Cor 4:7, 10; 12:9; 13:4; Eph 2:10; 6:10.[24]

Paul did not dispute with the Judaizers because he thought they taught that believing Gentiles had to be circumcised and start keeping the rest of the law as a means of getting in, then. In *PPJ* Sanders himself showed that strictly speaking not even non-Christian Palestinian Judaism represented such a view (and if it did – i.e., if circumcision was considered a good work by which Gentiles earned entry – his view that the circumcision of Jews was not so considered would look questionable). Instead, entering the covenant preceded taking the yoke of the commandments. Thus Gentile proselytes entered the covenant by

---

[24] Cf. K. T. Cooper, "Paul and Rabbinic Soteriology," *WTJ* 44 (1982): 137, and the comments on a different but related topic by E. Synofzik, *Die Gerichts- und Vergeltungsaussagen bei Paulus* (GTA 8; Göttingen: Vandenhoeck & Ruprecht, 1977), 59–61. Sanders does not believe, of course, that "faith stopped functioning after entry" (*PLJP*, 114). In a letter to me dated 3 December 1981 he wrote, "I need to sharpen the formulation and clarify the point .... I did not intend to imply that 'entry' is only momentary. There is nevertheless a distinction between an entry requirement (what is necessary in order to be considered a member *at all*) and behavioural requirements within the group. Circumcision, I think, is the former in the Galatians debate. When considered in the latter category, it is a matter of indifference (*Gal. 6.15*; I Cor. 7.19), as are 'days' and food (Rom. 14.1–6)" (italics original). These words and longer statements in *PLJP*, 20, 52 n. 20, 159, represent a basic shift rather than the sharpening and clarification of an original point. For it used to be in Sanders' view that getting in was solely by God's elective grace in both Paul and Palestinian Judaism. Now Sanders is saying that getting in requires circumcision in Palestinian Judaism and among Christian Judaizers; otherwise a person cannot be considered a member at all. It used to be in Sanders' view that for both Paul and Palestinian Judaism, keeping the law was only the means of staying in. Now Sanders is saying that at least one aspect of keeping the law – viz., submitting to circumcision – is a means of getting in for Palestinian Judaism and Christian Judaizers whereas Paul goes in the opposite direction by making circumcision a matter of indifference. It seems that the fundamental and original thesis that Paul and Palestinian Judaism were at one on getting in by grace and staying in by obeying the law has broken down. In effect, Sanders now admits that Jews and Judaizers were synergists on the topic of getting in and that at least on the question of circumcision Paul was not a synergist even with respect to staying in, much less with respect to getting in.

indicating their acceptance of it and their intention to obey the commandments in it, and circumcision and similar acts that followed constituted evidence rather than means of entry.[25] We can hardly suppose, then – and Paul gives us no reason to suppose – that Judaizers in the church taught that believing Gentiles had to be circumcised and start keeping the rest of the law to get in. On the contrary, Paul battles against circumcision and keeping the rest of the law as necessary to stay in, i.e., against *falling* from grace, not against failure to enter it (Gal 5:4).

At the same time Paul demands good works, and Sanders appeals to this demand. But Paul's un-Jewish extension of faith and grace to staying in makes good works evidential of having received grace through faith, not instrumental in keeping grace through works.[26] This extension also means we cannot accept Sanders' view that Paul's attacks on the Judaizers' teaching are to be explained simply as a dogmatic denial: Judaism (and therefore the Judaizing element in the church) is wrong because it is not Christianity.[27] On the contrary, Paul attacks the Judaizers' teaching as a *corruption* of grace and faith (again see Gal 3:3, 10; 5:4, 7). For him, then, getting in and staying in are covered by the seamless robe of faith as opposed to works with the result that works come in as evidential rather than instrumental. Sanders' bisection of getting in and staying in cuts a line through Paul's religion where the pattern shows a whole piece of cloth.

Paul's insistence on faith rather than on law for staying in as well as for getting in raises the question, Why did he regard law and faith as excluding each other? In what respect did he consider them incompatible? Sanders offers an answer limited to salvation history: "God's will to save by Christ is changeless .... the law was *never* intended by God to be a means of righteousness. It is not only *lately* that it has come to an end as such."[28] But a historical intention of God that salvation should *always* be by faith in Christ for all people, Gentiles as well as Jews, does not explain why Paul can speak of faith as "coming" late in history (Gal 3:23–29), why he can speak of the salvation of Gentiles as an only recent historical development (see esp. Rom 11:11–32), why he can assume that faith and the law were compatible in the OT (not only was Abraham justified by

---

[25] Sanders, *PPJ*, 206–12; cf. 85–101.

[26] Cf. E. Jüngel, *Paulus and Jesus* (3d ed.; Tübingen: Mohr [Siebeck], 1967), 66–70. We may partly agree with Sanders that in Paul "good deeds are the *condition* of remaining 'in', but they do not *earn* salvation" (*PPJ*, 517; idem, *PLJP*, 114). On the other hand, the condition must be evidential rather than instrumental if it is to stand beside Paul's much stronger emphasis on staying in by faith, not by works. Therefore the view that those professing Christians whose sin is so serious, prolonged, and unforsaken that they apparently lose their salvation never really had it in the first place looks like a fair extrapolation from Paul's thinking (see esp. 2 Cor 13:5–6; cf. Matt 7:23; 1 John 2:18–19). This issue will occupy our attention later.

[27] So Sanders' understanding of Paul (*PPJ*, 550–52 et passim; idem, *PLJP*, 27, 47). He stresses Paul's "exclusivist soteriology" so one-sidedly that he thinks Paul's own emphatic, extended formulation "by faith and not by works ... actually misstates the fundamental point of disagreement [with Judaism and Judaizing]" (*PPJ*, 551).

[28] Sanders, *PLJP*, 85–86 (italics original); so also 47.

faith prior to the law but also David was justified by faith *during the period of law* [Rom 4:1–8]), or why Paul can say that "the righteous requirement of the law should be fulfilled in us, who walk not according to the flesh but according to the Spirit" (Rom 8:4).[29] Apparently there is something about the law in human experience as illustrated in Palestinian Judaism that is incompatible with faith whereas the law as originally given by God and as now immersed in the Spirit and revised in accordance with Christ's coming, the hardening of Israel, and the grafting in of Gentiles is not incompatible with faith.[30] Statements that speak of fulfilling the law imply the new work of the Spirit. Statements such as "faith came" (Gal 3:23) and "you are not under the law but under grace" (Rom 6:14–15) reflect a failure of the law in past human experience.

Where in past human experience does the incompatibility of the law with faith lie? We are forced back to an old answer that Sanders rejects: for Paul the incompatibility lies in the self-righteousness to which unbelievers who try to keep the law succumb. Sanders counters that we find Paul's main objection to Jewish self-righteousness not in self-dependent pride of accomplishment but in the Jews' dependence on their status as God's covenant people who possess the law and in their consequently missing the better righteousness based solely on believing participation in Christ, not on having the law: "What is wrong with Judaism is not that Jews seek to save themselves and become self-righteous about it, but that their seeking is not directed toward the right goal.... They do not know that, as far as salvation goes, Christ has put an end to the law and provides a different righteousness from that provided by Torah obedience (Rom. 10.2–4)."[31] Thus the difference between Jewish righteousness and God's righteousness in Christ "is not the distinction between merit and grace, but between two dispensations. There is a righteousness which comes by law, but it is now worth nothing because of a different dispensation.... It is this concrete fact of *Heilsgeschichte* which makes the other righteousness wrong."[32]

To be sure, Paul sees a shift in dispensations. But he sees more than that. The key passage Phil 3:2–11 starts with his boasting in the givens of Jewish status ("as to circumcision, an eight-dayer; from the stock of Israel; of the tribe of Benjamin"), but it builds up to confidence in personal accomplishments ("a Hebrew of the Hebrews; as to the law, a Pharisee; as to zeal, persecuting the church; as to the righteousness in the law, having become blameless"). So salvation history does not account for all that Paul says, much less for the passion

---

[29] On Paul's expecting Christians to fulfill the law, see Sanders, *PLJP*, 93–122.

[30] Paul does not, however, carefully and consciously distinguish the revisions. See the well-balanced comments by Sanders, *PLJP*, 97–105.

[31] Sanders, *PPJ*, 550.

[32] Sanders, *PLJP*, 140. Pages 137–41 deal with the shift in dispensations. To avoid a developmental view of *Heilsgeschichte*, "salvation history," Sanders also refers to God's "plan of salvation" (*PLJP*, 26–27, 55 n. 50).

with which he says it. We are dealing with an autobiographical as well as dispensational shift. Sanders admits that in Phil 3:2–11 Paul makes personal accomplishments as well as the givens of Jewish status the objects of his former confidence in the flesh, but he argues that Paul does not charge himself with "the attitudinal sin of self-righteousness." Rather, "he [had] put confidence in something other than faith in Jesus Christ."[33] "The only thing that is wrong with the old righteousness seems to be that it is not the new one; it has no fault which is described in other terms."[34] But a long list of items in Phil 3:2–11 points to the attitudinal sin of self-righteousness alongside the mistake of missing God's righteousness in Christ: (1) "boast"; (2) "have confidence"; (3) "*think* (δοκεῖ) to have confidence"; (4) "to me" (μοι) in connection with "gain"; (5) "I regard"; (6) Paul's setting out his past achievements as superior to the achievements of his opponents, who boast in the flesh, as though there is a contest over who can boast the most; (7) his following denial that he now "considers" himself to have arrived (vv. 12–16); and (8) his exhortation to be similarly "minded" (φρο-νῶμεν – v. 15). These attitudinal elements show that "self-righteousness" accurately expresses an important feature of Paul's thought. Zeal for the law was good, but not the self-righteousness which followed. That self-righteousness was wrong both in itself and in its posing a hindrance to accepting God's righteousness through faith in Jesus Christ.

That a dispensational shift does not by itself account for all Paul says is evident also in his parade example, Abraham; for he, according to Paul, was justified by faith long before Christ ushered in the new dispensation (Galatians 3; Romans 4). David is just as troublesome to Sanders' purely salvation-historical explanation; for Paul has David too justified by faith (Rom 4:6–8). Yet David lived not only long before the new dispensation but also right within the old dispensation of law. With regard to Abraham and David, Sanders suddenly drops salvation history:

It seems to me to be a mistake to read Romans 4 as implying the continuous, or at least sporadic, existence of people of faith between Abraham and Christ. David (4:6) is not cited as a second historical person who also had faith, but rather a psalm (traditionally attributed to David) is quoted which pronounces a blessing on those who have faith. Abraham is immediately returned to (4:9), and he continues to be employed in a typological way.[35]

The modern critical view that Davidic authorship of Psalm 32 is only traditional, not actual, has no relevance. On Paul's lips "David says" means that the historical David pronounced the following beatitude. Only by having Paul exclude David and David's contemporaries from the beatitude – an unlikely and certainly unstated qualification which goes against the autobiographical char-

---

[33] Sanders, *PLJP*, 44.
[34] Sanders, *PLJP*, 139–41.
[35] Sanders, *PLJP*, 62 n. 125.

acter of Psalm 32 – could Sanders escape the implication that people of faith existed between Abraham and Christ. Furthermore, Paul thinks chronologically, not just typologically, concerning Abraham, the law, and justification by faith (Gal 3:15–18).

Since Paul's own righteousness had included works accomplished as well as status granted, we must say that his opposing the works of the law to faith in Christ includes on attack on self-dependence as well as an indication of the dispensational shift. What Paul says about Abraham in Rom 4:2, 4 supports this point: "For if Abraham was justified by works he has a ground for boasting .... But to the one who works the reward is not reckoned according to grace but according to debt" (contrast *Pr. Man.* 8; *Jub.* 23:10; *m. Qidd.* 4:14).[36] Sanders tries to avoid the force of these statements by noting that in fact the reward was given to Abraham on the basis of faith and that Paul neither mentions nor criticizes an attempt by Abraham to be justified by works.[37] Nevertheless, Paul's statements imply that Abraham *could* have boasted if his justification *had* come by works. Paul's ruling out even the possibility of Abraham's having been justified by works which he could have boasted about shows that self-dependence as well as salvation history has come into view.

Sanders recognizes that according to Paul "it was never … God's intention that one should accept the law in order to become one of the elect."[38] "It has always been by faith."[39] Well, then, so far as God's intention is concerned, salvation history did not shift from righteousness that comes by the law to God's righteousness in Christ (as Sanders self-contradictorily says in his attempt to load everything on Paul's notion of salvation history),[40] but from promise to ful-

---

[36] The intervening words, "but not before God," do not imply that justification by works would have enabled Abraham to boast before his fellow human beings (against Räisänen, "Legalism and Salvation by the Law," 70). Rather, "but not before God" prepares for the scriptural citation of Gen 15:6 in v. 3 (which opens with the connective γάϱ, "For") and interprets the passive verb in the statement, "And it [Abraham's believing God] was reckoned to him for righteousness," as the action of God himself (which amounts to his denying that Abraham was justified by works and had any ground for boasting). If Abraham's fellow human beings come into view at all, Paul is implying that they would set up a system of justification by works contrary to God's way of justification. The suggestion that "but not before God" calls attention to the impropriety of human boasting before God no matter how good one's works might be (so H. Hübner, *Das Gesetz bei Paulus* (FRLANT 119; Göttingen: Vandenhoeck & Ruprecht, 1978], 99–100) does not establish a good base for the following γάϱ-clause. See further C.E.B. Cranfield, *A Critical and Exegetical Commentary on the Epistle to the Romans* (ICC; Edinburgh: T. & T. Clark, 1975), 1:228.

[37] Sanders, *PLJP*, 33–34. Sanders notes the expressions "law of works" (3:27) and "the one who works" (4:4) but by-passes them in favor of expressions concerning status: "Jews" (3:29); "the circumcision" (3:30; 4:9, 12); "those of the law" (4:14, 16). Yet the textual data require a both-and rather than an either-or.

[38] Sanders, *PLJP*, 46.

[39] Sanders, *PLJP*, 33–34.

[40] Sanders, *PLJP*, 550–51 ("He [Paul] simply saw the old dispensation as worthless in comparison with the new"); idem, *PLJP*, 140–41.

fillment (cf. Galatians 3–4). The use of the law to establish one's own right-eousness is what Paul finds wrong in Palestinian Judaism, including his own past life.

Romans 9:30–10:13 comes into play here. Sanders admits that "at first blush" and taken alone 9:30–32 means that Israel failed to fulfill the law because they rested on works rather than on faith. But the rest of the passage, Sanders argues, identifies the reason for this failure not with a wrong manner of trying to fulfill the law (works instead of faith) but with lack of faith in Christ, so that "their own righteousness" (10:3) means "the righteousness which the Jews alone are privileged to obtain" rather than "self-righteousness which consists in individuals' presenting their merits as a claim upon God."[41] We may agree that Paul blames Israel for their lack of faith in Christ. But to make that lack displace rather than complement wrong dependence on one's own works fails to carry conviction. Sanders is reduced to saying that in 9:31 Paul uses νόμος a second time even though he means "the righteousness of God which comes by faith in Christ," that this use is "certainly curious," and that "Paul did not say precisely what he meant" but "the desire for a balanced antithesis [νόμος having just occurred for the Mosaic law] led Paul to an almost incomprehensible combination of words." Sanders then draws a parallel with 8:10.[42] But in 8:10 Paul achieves balance with pairs of antonyms – "body" vs. "Spirit," "dead" vs. "life" (the problem here lies in the inconcinnity of adjective vs. noun, which has no bearing on 9:31), and "sin" vs. "righteousness" – whereas Sanders asks us to believe that in 9:31 the *same* word "law" refers in one breath to the Mosaic law, in the next breath to the righteousness of God which comes by faith in Christ.

Another view is preferable. Paul's speaking of faith in 9:32 looks like a contrast with νόμον in the sense of law. Indeed, the strongly adversative ἀλλ᾽ ὡς ἐξ ἔργων, "but as [if it were] by works," confirms this contrast and interprets νόμον in v. 31 as the law used for works-righteousness. Otherwise the question, "Why [did they not attain it]?" and its answer, "Because [they did] not [pursue it] by faith but as [if it were] by works," makes doubtful sense. For if the second occurrence of νόμον in v. 31 means the righteousness of God by faith, Paul has *already* (in the first phrase of v. 31) told why Israel did not attain it: they were pursuing the law. As it is, the contrast in pursuing but not attaining requires that the object be the same. Thus νόμον has one referent, the law, and the second occurrence of νόμον has no qualifier attached because the qualifier attached to the first occurrence – viz., "of righteousness" – carries over. The verb ἔφθασεν means "attained," not "fulfilled," says Sanders.[43] But "attained" in the sense "achieved" comes out to much the same as "fulfilled." The verb κατέλαβεν means "took hold

---

[41] Sanders, *PLJP*, 36–38; cf. N. T. Wright, "The Paul of History and the Apostle of Faith," *TynBul* 29 (1978): 82–83.

[42] Sanders, *PLJP*, 42; cf. the less exegetical discussion on pp. 155–58.

[43] Sanders, *PLJP*, 42.

of" and by virtue of synonymous parallelism determines a similar meaning for ἔφθασεν. Therefore we do best to understand Paul as saying that Israel pursued the law as a way of establishing self-righteousness but because of sin (cf. esp. 2:1–3, 23) failed to attain it.[44] In view of the statement that it is Gentiles who have taken hold of righteousness (v. 30) Paul probably chooses ἔφθασεν to indicate not only that Israel did not arrive at all but also that Israel did not arrive *first* (the basic meaning of φθάνω), i.e., ahead of the Gentiles.

At 10:3 the infinitive "to establish" in the phrase "seeking to establish their own [righteousness]" and the contrast with subjection to God's righteousness show that it is not pride of privilege so much as self reliance Paul is objecting to. Yet again, in 10:5 it is performance rather than privilege which contrasts with faith: "for Moses writes that the one who *does* [ποιήσας] the righteousness which is from the law will live by it." And in 10:8 Paul's *dropping* "that you may do it" from his quotation of Deut 30:14 concerning "the word of faith" favors the view that here faith contrasts with the Jewish attempt to perform the law, not with Jewish privilege in having the law.

Sanders tries to blunt the argument from Rom 10:5 by saying that the immediately following verses show Paul to be in disagreement with Moses: life (eternal life in Paul's view) comes only by faith and confession, not by doing the law.[45] But a possible disagreement with Moses is immaterial. The point remains that in this verse and throughout the surrounding passage Paul sets faith against an attempted performance of the law for righteousness, not only against unbelief. Moreover, in view of his high view of scriptural authority and in view of his earlier defenses of the law (Rom 3:31; 7:7–14; 9:30–33) a disagreement with

---

[44] Sanders' strongest argument against this understanding – viz., the argument that Phil 3:6–9 shows righteousness by the law to be attainable (*PLJP*, 43–45) – rests on a failure to recognize that Paul there speaks from the standpoint of a false human estimate: "If anyone else *thinks* … I more" (v. 4b). He is not implying that except for God's righteousness God would have been satisfied with Paul's righteousness. Paul's rhetorical contest with the Judaizer determines his taking the standpoint of a false human estimate. Against Sanders, understanding "my righteousness" as "my individual righteousness" does not depend on a conflation with Rom 3:27; 4:2; for right within Philippians 3 the phrases "according to [the] law, a Pharisee; according to zeal, persecuting the church; according to the righteousness in [the] law, having become blameless" point to individual performance alongside Jewish status. Sanders admits as much in his statement, "Paul says that his former confidence in the flesh was partly in status … and partly in accomplishment" (*PLJP*, 44). Understanding "law of righteousness" in Rom 9:31 as "the law which promises a righteousness to be attained by faith" (so C. T. Rhyne, *Faith Establishes the Law* [SBLDS 55; Chico, Calif.: Scholars Press, 1981], 98–102, with an appeal to Rom 3:21–4:25) would not substantially alter the argument against Sanders' denying a criticism of the Jews' manner of pursuit. Nevertheless, "seeking to establish their own righteousness" in 10:3 favors understanding 9:31 as "pursuing the law for self-righteousness."

[45] E. P. Sanders, "On the Question of Fulfilling the Law in Paul and Rabbinic Judaism," in *Donum Gentilicium* (ed. E. Bammel, C. K. Barrett, and W. D. Davies: Oxford: Clarendon, 1978), 106–7; *PLJP*, 41 ("Moses [according to Paul] was incorrect when he wrote that everyone who fulfills the law will 'live'").

Moses seems unlikely. Paul probably thought Moses' statement was theoretically true but – because of human depravity – practically impossible (cf. the exposé of Jewish failure to keep the law and the lumping of Jews with Gentiles as sinners in Rom 2:1–3:23).[46]

We conclude, then, that Paul is not criticizing the Jews' unbelief in Christ *instead of* their attempt to perform the law, but that he is criticizing their unbelief *as caused by* an attempt to perform the law. That attempt leads to self-righteousness, but not because of any fault in the law itself or in obedience as such. Rather, boasting corrupts Spirit-less obedience to the law. Such obedience ends in man-made religion (if it does not already arise out of man-made religion). The law itself, however, is Spiritual (Rom 7:14 – πνευματικός, related to the Holy Spirit in Paul's usage and therefore capitalized here in English translation), so that Spiritual believers naturally fulfill the righteous ordinance of the law (Rom 8:4). The same Spirit that determines their conduct determined the precepts of the law. And no true believer is un-Spiritual (Rom 8:9). Hence prolonged carnality calls in question a profession of faith (see esp. Gal 5:19–24). In view of Sanders' discussion it may be too much to say that in Palestinian Judaism good works were always thought to earn God's favor according to a bookish weighing of merits. But in view of the many passages in Palestinian Jewish literature that Sanders cites concerning atonement by good works,[47] it is not too much to say that in Paul's presentation of Palestinian Judaism good works constitute a righteousness necessary at least to activate God's grace for the forgiveness of sins.[48] Paul will have none of this synergism. For him salvation is *wholly* by grace through faith. Good works do not activate God's grace when they are enough (however little or much might be enough – Sanders rightly points to a lack of systematization in Palestinian Jewish passages dealing with this question[49]). Instead, good works are an outgrowth of the new creation in Christ.

Paul is not content to argue that trying to keep the law is incompatible with faith. He takes unbelieving Jews and Christian Judaizers on their own terms and argues also that trying to keep the law never turns out to be successful. This failure of the Jews is the point of Rom 2:1–3:23, which leads into the detailed explanation of justification by faith in 3:24–5:21.[50]

---

[46] Cf. J. Murray, *The Epistle to the Romans* (NICNT; Grand Rapids: Eerdmans, 1965), 2:249–51. There is no need to deny Sanders' point that Paul was concerned to give Jews and Gentiles equal access by faith to God's righteousness.

[47] See the pages cited under "Atonement" in the subject-index of *PPJ.*

[48] See W. L. Lane, "Paul's Legacy from Pharisaism: Light from the Psalms of Solomon," *Concordia Journal* 8 (1982): 130–38.

[49] Sanders, *PPJ*, 125–47.

[50] See U. Wilckens, *Rechtfertigung als Freiheit: Paulusstudien* (Neukirchen-Vluyn: Neukirchener Verlag, 1974): 79–84.

In support of Sanders, N. T. Wright argues that "Paul's accusations are not against legalism, but against sin, the breaking of the law."[51] They are against breaking the law, yes. But Paul levels his accusations (whether he borrows them or constructs them himself) to puncture Jewish boasting in the law. Such boasting arises from legalism. Sanders, seconded by Wright, argues back that this boasting does not have to do with merits, what we would call self-righteousness based on keeping the law, but with a special relation to God, as in Rom 2:17–20, 23a.[52] But Paul's contextual exposé of the Jews' disobedience to the law keeps him from saying they boast in their obedience. To avoid appearing to contradict himself he says only that they boast in the law, in God, etc. It is simply assumed they boast in the law because they think they keep it well enough. As we have already noted, Rom 4:2 clearly shows that the objects of boasting include works of obedience as well as pride of possession: "for if Abraham was justified by works he has a ground of boasting" (cf. Phil 3:4, 6). Sanders is correct to deny that for Paul obedience to the law is bad, but wrong in denying Paul's criticism that such obedience has led to the sin of pride.

According to Sanders, however, the inconsistency and unconvincingness of Paul's statements concerning universal sinfulness show that he posited justification by faith before thinking of universal sinfulness rather than that he reached justification by faith as a conclusion based on universal sinfulness.[53] We might quibble with Sanders over his opinion that Paul is inconsistent and unconvincing. But if Sanders' hypothesis that in 1:18–2:29 Paul draws on a Jewish synagogue sermon which serves his purpose to show the equality of Jews and Gentiles under God's judgment and that he does so even though the sermon presupposes that some people do keep the law satisfactorily, not only does the inconsistency with Paul's own view that nobody keeps the law satisfactorily turn into a mere side effect of his drawing on the sermon, but also the hyperbole in his statements in ch. 3 concerning universal sinfulness is more easily recognized as showing the strength of his appeal to the need for justification by faith. In the end, however, it does not matter whether in Paul's mind universal sinfulness came before justification by faith or vice versa, or whether the two occurred to him simultaneously. The fact remains that he includes Jews with Gentiles as law-breakers to undermine dependence on the law and thereby support justification by faith.

Sanders also argues that in the early chapters of Romans Paul is not attacking legalism but is trying to put Jews and Gentiles on an equal footing so as to establish faith as a universal way of salvation instead of the law as a peculiarly Jewish way.[54] But could there not have been equality *under the law* for Jews and Gen-

---

[51] Wright, "The Paul of History and the Apostle of Faith," 82.
[52] Sanders, *PLJP*, 32–35; Wright, "The Paul of History and the Apostle of Faith," 82.
[53] Sanders, *PLJP*, 35–36; cf. 123–35.
[54] Sanders, *PPJ*, 490–91; cf. idem, *PLJP*, 29–30 et passim.

tiles? Why should not Paul have seen equal footing for Gentiles if they, like proselytes to Judaism, submitted to circumcision and tried to keep the rest of the law on coming into the church? Sanders answers by pointing to Gal 2:14 as indicating that Paul did not think Gentiles were able to live by the law.[55] But Gal 2:14 says nothing of the sort. The question of ability does not come up. Paul makes only a factual statement that Cephas, a Jew, is living like the Gentiles rather than like the Jews; and he asks why Cephas is trying to force Gentiles to live like Jews.

Elsewhere the question of ability does arise, but with particular reference to *Jews*. Whether Paul or someone else, the "I" in Rom 7:7–25 is under the law and therefore must be Jewish. At least the "I" must *include* the Jew. This "I" despairs over inability to keep the law. Whether the despair is *ex post facto* (as Sanders thinks[56]) or reflects a feeling at the time of the experience, the fact itself of Jewish inability to keep the law remains.[57] So Paul strengthens his attack on works-righteousness by calling attention to Jewish inability not to sin as well as to the actuality of Jewish sinning. Sanders attributes the passion of Rom 7:7–25 "partly" to Paul's desire to exonerate God from intending the law to bring sin and from having given a law that brought death.[58] But where did the rest of the passion come from? And the passion in the passage relates directly to human inability, not to God's honor: "Wretched man that I am! Who will rescue me from the body of this death?" (v. 24). At the end of his discussion Sanders betrays the weakness of his position by saying, "We must back away from strict exegesis of Romans 7 to understand Paul's thought."

The Jews and Judaizers would presumably take as much encouragement as possible in their successes (as Paul expressly does from his past Judaistic standpoint in Phil 3:5–6) and take care of their failures with repentance and forgiveness.[59] But according to Paul obedience would have to be total to be successful in establishing one's own righteousness before God. For Paul, apparently, the fact that repentance and forgiveness have to take up the slack caused by disobedience shows the inadequacy of works-righteousness. Thus he will not allow the law to be divided, as though a person could work up sufficient righteousness by keeping part of the law but not the rest: "for as many as are of the works of the law are under a curse; for it is written, 'Cursed is everyone who does not abide by all things written in the book of the law so as to do them'" (Gal 3:10, with a quotation of Deut 27:26).[60] Sanders thinks Paul chose to quote

---

[55] Sanders, *PPJ*, 496.

[56] Sanders, *PPJ*, 442–43.

[57] For a full discussion see the next chapter in the present volume. This discussion includes a consideration of Acts 22:3; Gal 1:13–14; and esp. Phil 3:4–6, which are often used incorrectly to deny Jewish inability to keep the law.

[58] Sanders, *PLJP*, 76–81, 124.

[59] Sanders, *PPJ*, passim.

[60] Discovery of Paul's phrase "works of the law" in 4QMMT has caused a flurry of scholarly excitement. Though 4QMMT shows that at least some Jews considered such works as justifi-

Deut 27:26 because only here does the LXX connect "law" with "curse"; that therefore Paul's emphasis falls on those words, not on the word "all," which only happens to appear; and finally that the weight of Paul's argument rests in the quotations of Gen 15:16 and Hab 2:4 (Gal 3:8, 11), since the further quotation of Lev 18:5 in v. 12 shows the law to be wrong because it does not rest on faith, not because it is impossible to fulfill the law completely. The quotation in Gal 3:10 is designed, then, as a sidelight "to discourage Gentiles from accepting circumcision,"[61] for "failure to fulfil the law perfectly leads to damnation by the law; while true life *cannot in any case* come by obedience to the law, even if the obedience is faultless."[62]

But should we shunt aside Gal 3:10 as an "even if," a mere spur alongside the main track of Paul's argument? A whole train of considerations favors that we should not. Sanders lays down the principle that it is not the OT quotations that tell us what Paul means, but Paul's own words that tell us what he took the OT quotations to mean. Then Sanders notes that in his own words Paul mentions only the curse which comes on those who accept the law.[63] For the sake of argument let us accept Sanders' principle and ask whether Paul's own words are in fact limited to the curse. The answer is no. Paul starts introducing the quotation with the words, "For as many as are of the *works* of the law." If he has in mind merely acceptance of the law we would have expected a reference only to the law, not to the works of the law. "Works" shows that he has in mind performance, which relates to the bulk of the quotation, "everyone who does not continue in all things written in the book of the law so as to do them."[64] The large amount of space he devotes in Rom 2:1–3:23 to Jewish failure to abide by everything in the law confirms this observation.

---

catory the excitement is slightly overheated because the meaning of the phrase is determined largely by its usage in context – Paul's in the one case, that of 4QMMT in the other – so that the meaning in 4QMMT does not necessarily determine the meaning in Paul. The Pauline contextual reference to "*all things*" written in the book of the law" rules out a limitation of "the works of the law" to Jewish identity markers, such as Mosaically prescribed circumcision, observance of the Sabbath, and food laws. As it happens, though, the references to "fornications," "deceit," "betrayal," and "evil" in 4QMMT rule out a limitation to Jewish identity markers there too. At the same time, such markers do attain prominence because of their visibility and influence on social relations. The highlighting of ecclesiastical social problems arising out of the Judaizing controversy, with which J. D. G. Dunn above all is to be credited, offers the main and perhaps only positive contribution of the New Perspective on Paul. But highlighting such problems falls short of a limitation to them. Similarly, what might be called the New Perspective on Judaism corrects a view of Judaistic soteriology as based solely on human merit, but the correction does not erase the synergistic blend of human merit and divine grace in that soteriology. Of course, the proportions of emphasis on human merit and divine grace differ from one author or Jewish teacher and circumstance to another.

[61] Sanders, *PPJ*, 483; cf. idem, *PLJP*, 17–27.
[62] Sanders, "On the Question of Fulfilling the Law," 105–6 (italics original); cf. idem, *PLJP*, 152.
[63] Sanders, *PLJP*, 20–22.
[64] Cf. D. J. Moo, "'Law,' 'Works of the Law,' and Legalism in Paul," *WTJ* 45 (1983): 90–99.

Furthermore and as Sanders himself notes elsewhere,[65] within the quotation of Deut 27:26 Paul takes from the LXX the verb ἐμμένει, "abides by," which requires legal perfection, rather than giving a more accurate translation of the Hebrew יקים, "confirms," which requires only a basic intention to keep the law. This point gains in strength from the fact that in several other respects he does *not* follow the LXX of Deut 27:26.

Yet again Paul returns to the question of performance in v. 12: "but the law is not of faith; rather, 'the one who does them [the things written in the law] will live [ζήσεται, which for Paul means to have eternal life] by them'" (Lev 18:5). Is Paul pitting Hab 2:4, which he quotes in the preceding verse for righteousness or eternal life by faith, against Lev 18:5 and disagreeing with the Mosaic statement?[66] Though he might have changed opinion between epistles,[67] his defense of the law in Romans casts doubt on an affirmative answer (cf. the foregoing comments on Rom 10:5). The interest in the question of performance evident in Gal 3:10 ("works of the law" and "abides by") substantiates the doubt. More probably Paul quotes Hab 2:4 to show that in fact faith underlies righteousness or eternal life and quotes Lev 18:5 to show that eternal life might have come through complete obedience to the law.[68] Then in v. 13 he returns to the theme of the curse that comes because of a breakdown in obedience. Since according to v. 10 the curse falls on the one who fails to abide by everything in the law Paul's statement, "Christ redeemed us from the curse of the law," clearly implies that it is failure to abide by everything in the law which necessitates faith in Christ's redemptive work. Otherwise Paul has no reason to bring up the curse again. Thus nonperformance lies on the main track, not on a spur, of his argument; and his argument is not that eternal life *could* not come *even though* a person perfectly obeyed the law, but that eternal life *does* not come *because* a person obeys the law only imperfectly.[69]

---

[65] Sanders, *PPJ*, 137.

[66] It does not matter to the present argument whether in Gal 3:11b we attach "by faith" to "the one who is righteous" or to "will live." Either way, faith contrasts with doing the law.

[67] Hübner has stressed the differences between Galatians and Romans (*Das Gesetz bei Paulus*). But see U. Luz's review of Hübner's book that the differences have been overestimated and that too much theological significance has been read into those that do exist (*TZ* 35 [1979]: 122–23).

[68] See Hübner, *Das Gesetz bei Paulus*, 39–42, though his explanation that "quantitative Erfüllung ist nicht möglich, weil die Torah Bestimmungen besitzt, die 'qualitativ erfüllt' werden müssen" does not carry conviction.

[69] See U. Wilckens, "Zur Entwicklung des paulinischen Gesetzesverständnisses," *NTS* 28 (1982): 166–69 et passim; idem, *Rechtfertigung als Freiheit*, 84–94; idem, *Der Brief an die Römer* (EKK 6/1; Cologne/Neukirchen-Vluyn: Neukirchener Verlag, 1978), 93, 178–80, 201, 233–43. Despite the criticisms of G. Klein ("Sündenverständnis und theologia crucis bei Paulus," in *Theologia Crucis – Signum Crucis* [ed. C. Andersen and G. Klein; Tübingen: Mohr, 1979], 249–82), Wilckens is right to see the importance of concrete transgressions in Paul's thought.

Final confirmation comes from Gal 5:3, which Sanders admits "shows that, although Paul quoted Deut 27:26 for the connection of 'curse' and *nomos*, he did not forget that it said 'all'":[70] "But I testify again to every man who is circumcised [or 'gets himself circumcised'] that he is a debtor to do the whole law." We may note first that these are Paul's own words, which therefore show what he got from the quotation of Deut 27:26 in Gal 3:10. Secondly, the adverb "again" (πάλιν, which is not to be omitted with D* G 1739 *pc* it goth arm) shows that he is indeed reflecting on the earlier passage. And the accusation in Gal 6:13, "For not even those who are getting circumcised keep the law themselves," shows that he is contrasting incomplete performance, such as mere submission to circumcision, with complete performance.

According to Sanders, however, Paul infers that accepting circumcision entails accepting the whole law, "not to argue that the law should not be accepted *because* all of it *cannot* be kept, but as a kind of threat: if you start it *must* all be kept." Sanders goes on:

To make this support the view that Paul argues against the law because it is impossible to keep all of it quantitatively, one must make a long list of assumptions about Paul's and the Galatians' presuppositions about the law: one must keep it all; one cannot do so; there is no forgiveness of transgression; therefore accepting the law necessarily leads to being cursed. The middle terms of this thought-sequence are never stated by Paul, and this sequence of views cannot be found in contemporary Jewish literature.[71]

Actually, these presuppositions need be only Paul's, not the Galatians' as well. The first, that one must keep all the law, is not an assumption on our part but Paul's outright statement in Gal 5:3 (cf. 3:10 too and the foregoing discussion of it). The second, that one cannot keep all the law (in fact, *does* not keep all the law suffices for the argument in Galatians[72]), is hardly missing. We have seen that Gal 3:13a compared with v. 10 clearly implies such failure, that Gal 6:13 states it outright, that Rom 2:1–3:23 details it, and that Rom 7:7–25 adds pathos to it.[73] Moreover Gal 5:17–21, which comes not very far after the verse presently in question, indicates that without the Spirit a person does not avoid the works of the flesh, which will prevent the inheriting of God's kingdom. The third presupposition, that there is no forgiveness of transgression, is put wrongly; rather, Paul adopts the earlier Christian view that Jesus' vicarious death (therefore not our obedience to the law) takes care of transgression; and he does not leave this presupposition unstated (see Gal 3:13; cf. Rom 3:23–25; 4:25; 5:6–10; 1 Cor 15:3; 2 Cor 5:21; Gal 1:4). Thus the "middle terms" *are*

---

[70] Sanders, *PLJP*, 27.

[71] Sanders, *PLJP*, 27 (italics original).

[72] See the foregoing discussion, p. 213.

[73] These passages in Romans cast doubt on the view that Paul writes in a quantitative vein in Galatians but switches to a qualitative vein in Romans (as Hübner says in *Das Gesetz bei Paulus*, 76–80).

stated by Paul; and for *his* theology it makes no difference whether or not they can be found in contemporary Jewish literature. As Sanders does not deny, the fourth presupposition, that accepting the law necessarily leads to being cursed, appears in the text (Gal 3:10). G. Howard has argued from the word order in the Greek text that "debtor" rather than "the whole law" receives the emphasis.[74] "Debtor" does indeed receive emphasis; but so also does "the whole law" because of its position before the infinitive "to do" whereas in 3:10, to which Paul is harking back, "to do" has its object following. It stands fast, then, that Gal 5:3 confirms the necessity and failure to keep the whole law as a main feature of Paul's argument for justification by faith alone.

But the argument does not stop with the law's failure to help people produce sufficient righteousness of their own. Paul twists the screw tighter by saying that the law actually increases sin (Gal 3:19, 22; Rom 5:20; 6:15–16; 7:5–6, 7–25, esp. 13; 11:32). Since Sanders does not dispute the point but affirms it,[75] we have only to ask how he can deny that the unfulfillability of the law poses a major problem to Paul. Why does Paul attempt this tour de force of saying the law *increases* sin if not even inability to keep it perfectly troubles him? It appears that the twin pillars of human weakness and salvation history, not just salvation history, uphold justification by faith alone. To counter that Paul's thinking runs from the solution in Christ to the human plight, so that Paul's anthropology is only a reflex effect of his Christian soteriology,[76] makes the strength of his emphasis on the lordship of sin using the law and the pathos in his description of life under that lordship hard to explain adequately. Sanders does not appreciate these problems sufficiently but emphasizes corresponding problems in seeing a development from plight to solution.[77] We should call in question that there was any devel-

---

[74] G. Howard, *Paul: Crisis in Galatia* (SNTSMS 35; Cambridge: Cambridge University Press, 1979), 14–17.

[75] Sanders, *PLJP*, 70–71. Hübner does dispute the point so far as Romans is concerned (*Das Gesetz bei Paulus*, 71–76; cf. Wilckens, "Zur Entwicklung," 182–83). His strongest argument – viz., that the singular of τὸ παράπτωμα, "the transgression," in Rom 5:20 points away from increased sinning on the part of individual human beings and toward an increase in the transsubjective rule of sin – comes to grief in ch. 6, where the transsubjective rule of sin works out in individual sinning (see, e.g., the exhortation in v. 12: "Therefore do not let sin reign in your mortal body with the result of obeying its lusts [pl.!].")

[76] Sanders, *PPL*, 442–47, 474–511; idem, *PLJP*, 68, 125. Räisänen singles out Gal 2:21 as the strongest support for the view that Paul rejected the law for a christological rather than anthropological reason ("Legalism and Salvation," 69); but P. Garnet points to a slightly earlier statement in Gal 2:15 as indicating that the human problem precedes the christological solution ("Qumran Light on Pauline Soteriology," in *Pauline Studies* [ed. D. A. Hagner and M. J. Harris; Grand Rapids: Eerdmans, 1980], 29–31). For a modern example of psychological turmoil over failure to keep the law perfectly, see the autobiographical statement of the Jewish scholar E. Rivkin in his book *A Hidden Revolution* (Nashville: Abingdon, 1978), 22.

[77] Sanders, *PLJP*, 68–70, 81, 138, 149–54. It is hard to understand why Sanders thinks the universality of sin implies that Paul thought backwards from solution to plight. Why could not Paul have thought that since all need salvation Christ came to save all? According to

opment in either direction. The problems suggest that Paul thought simultaneously rather than consecutively of plight and solution.

But as Paul's soteriology needs balancing by the lordship of sin in his thinking, so the lordship of sin needs balancing by the forensic meaning of justification and the concept of sin as guilt which that meaning implies.[78] As is popular to do nowadays, Sanders stresses the power of sin more than the guilt of sin as the quintessence of Paul's hamartiology.[79] Thus justification denotes transferal from sin's lordship to Christ's lordship more than an exchange of guilt for God's righteousness.[80] But in Galatians Paul introduces justification as the solution to the problem of transgressions, which cause the law to bring a curse. Only then does bondage come into his discussion – and even so, primarily bondage to false religion (4:1–10, 21–5:1), only secondarily to sinning (3:22; 5:17–21).[81] This pattern repeats itself in Romans: emphasis on guilt comes first, reaching a climax in 3:19–23; forensic justification follows in 3:24–5:19; and only later comes the emphasis on sin's lordship (5:20–8:17). See also 1 Cor 6:9–11; 2 Cor 5:21.

It is not satisfactory to pass off the earlier passages as merely traditional and undistinctive of Paul's thought. He uses too much papyrus on guilt and on its removal by God's righteousness. Sanders correctly calls attention to the possibility of substituting "life" and "Spirit" for "righteousness" in Rom 6:16; Gal 3:3, 6, 21.[82] But this possibility in no way negates or scales down the forensic element. Since union with Christ makes possible the exchange of guilt for God's righteousness (see esp. Phil 3:7–11) Paul naturally mixes the forensic benefit of

---

Gal 2:15–16, Sanders argues, Paul "knows full well that observant Jews are not in fact sinners by the biblical standard" (*PLJP*, 68, in reference to Paul's mentioning "Jews" who are "not sinners from [the] Gentiles"). But because of the contrast with "Jews," the term "Gentiles" rather than the phrase "not sinners" receives the emphasis, as is confirmed by the emphatic position of ἐξ ἐθνῶν before ἁμαρτωλοί, against normal word order. Paul's formal use of the Jewish epithet "sinners" for Gentiles does not imply that he did not regard Jews too as sinful (cf. Rom 2:1–3:24; 7:7–25). We may appreciate, even endorse, Sanders' argument for rhetorical exaggeration in Rom 1:18–3:23; 7:7–25 (see *PLJP*, 123–35). But his deduction that such exaggeration is due to Paul's moving from solution to plight does not follow. We might equally well say that Paul uses rhetorical exaggeration because of his preoccupation with the human plight. In fact, such a view would make it easier to understand the rhetorical flights, which gain rather than lose pathos in the hyperbole Paul uses.

[78] See, e.g., pp. 242 n. 43, 247–48 in the present volume.

[79] Much modern psychology views guilt as an incapacitating complex. Though this view may have alerted us to sin as an incapacitating power in the theology of Paul it may also have dulled many of us to sin as objective guilt in his theology. Adding moral relativism to such a psychological view of sin insures a theological devaluation of objective guilt. This devaluation carries with itself, of course, a corresponding devaluation of the propitiatory and expiatory value of Jesus' death. To the extent that psychology is a natural science it is merely descriptive and lacks the capacity to address moral questions.

[80] Sanders, "Patterns of Religion," 470–74; idem, *PPJ*, 502–8.

[81] Against Sanders, "Patterns of Religion," 478.

[82] Sanders, "Patterns of Religion," 470–74.

that union, "righteousness," with other benefits (cf. the mixture of forensic language, "one died for all," with participatory language, "therefore all died," in 2 Cor 5:14).[83] The benefits of union with Christ are not equivalent to each other; they accompany each other and are distinguished from each other (cf. Rom 5:17–21; 8:1–11).

Sanders objects that even in Rom 1:18–3:23 Paul does not reach the conclusion "guilty"; rather, "under sin" (3:9).[84] But how can we read about the inexcusability of heathen in the latter half of ch. 1, about the inexcusability of Jews in ch. 2, about the accountability – i.e., subjection to trial (ὑπόδικος) – of Jews and heathen alike in 3:19, and about propitiation and expiation in Christ's blood and the passing over of sins committed beforetime (3:25) without taking "under sin" as referring to sin that brings guilt as well as to sin that brings bondage?[85] The time is surely past when we could think, as Sanders wants us to, that the lack of the *term* "guilty" (ἔνοχος, which Paul uses only once and nonsoteriologically in 1 Cor 11:27) means that Paul was not exercised by the *idea* of guilt. James Barr has not done his work for nothing.[86]

Certainly, illegitimate sexual unions contradict union with Christ (1 Cor 6:12–20; 10:1–22). But Paul warns against other sins that by their nature have nothing to do with union (e.g., thievery, covetousness, drunkenness, reviling, and rapaciousness in 1 Cor 6:10 – the list could grow longer with additions from Gal 5:20–21 and other passages). And why should he be so concerned about the lordship of sin if not for the reason that sinning brings guilt? Otherwise not even certain sexual unions would contradict union with Christ. It is simply untrue to say that Paul never presses his participatory language into the service of his juristic language as he sometimes presses his juristic language into the service of his participatory language (for the latter see Gal 3:21, where "righteousness" appears instead of the expected "life," and Rom 6:7, where "justified from sin" has the contextual meaning "set free from the dominion of sin"). In Gal 5:16–24 participation in Christ and the Spirit serves the warning against the works of the flesh. The fact that Paul describes the contrasting fruit of the Spirit as that "against which there is no law" reveals a juristic frame of reference to which the language of walking by the Spirit and belonging to Christ

---

[83] G. Caird calls attention to 2 Cor 5:14 and criticizes Sanders for failing to analyze what "participation" means and for failing to take seriously the metaphorical nature of Paul's juristic language (*JTS* ns 29 [1978]: 541–42). We may wonder, however, whether Caird's interest in figurative language (see his book *The Language and Imagery of the Bible* [Philadelphia: Westminster, 1980]) leads him to underestimate the degree to which Paul intended his juristic language to express the state of affairs itself, not an analogy to it.

[84] Sanders, *PPJ*, 503.

[85] C. Bryan shows good sense in combining the notions of propitiation and expiation in ἱλαστήριον (*A Preface to Romans* [Oxford: Oxford University Press, 2000], 111).

[86] J. Barr, *The Semantics of Biblical Language* (London: Oxford University Press, 1961), 35–45 et passim.

is bent. Similarly, where union with Christ in Rom 6:1–11 would lead us to expect a recapitulation of that idea in v. 14, which supports the intervening exhortation (vv. 12–13), Paul is not content to stop with the statement, "For sin shall not lord it over you" (v. 14a), but locates the ultimate ground of his exhortation in a juristic theologoumenon: "for you are not under law but under grace" (v. 14b). And instead of reading that in Christ there is liberation from the lordship of sin, as we would expect from Rom 7:7–25, we read in 8:1 the juristic statement that there is "no condemnation" to those who are in him.[87] Not till v. 2 does Paul write about liberation, but he immediately goes back to juristic language in the phrases "as a sin-offering," "condemned sin," and "righteous requirement of the law" (vv. 3–4). In short, the dynamics of union with Christ are pressed into the service of forensic justification as well as vice versa.[88]

---

[87] Rom 8:1 harks back to Rom 5:16, 18, where κατάκριμα does not refer to the lordship of sin over conduct but to the sentence of death and its execution *because of* sin's lordship. In 8:1, then, Paul is reminding his audience of the reversal of condemnation for those who are in Christ Jesus. It is argued that "condemned sin" in 8:3–4 means "broke the power of sin in human conduct" because the condemnation was something the law could not do whereas the law certainly could, and did, condemn sin in the sense of pronouncing judicial sentence against it. But this argument overlooks the possibility that the inability of the law has its counterpart not in God's condemning sin in the flesh but in the ἵνα-clause concerning the fulfillment of the righteous requirement of the law. God's condemning sin in the flesh would then lay the juristic foundation for the superstructure of freedom from sin's lordship.

The argument that the inferential ἄρα, "then," in v. 1 relates "condemnation" to the preceding discussion of sin's lordship rather than to guilt is overrated. We can see a tight connection drawn with the preceding context by ἄρα οὖν, "therefore then," in 7:25. But here in 8:1 Paul drops οὖν. As a result ἄρα draws only a loose connection, probably with earlier discussions of forensic justification, especially the one in ch. 5, the only preceding passage in Romans where κατάκριμα has occurred. The γάρ-clause in v. 2 does indeed talk of deliverance from sin's lordship (described in 7:7–25). In so doing it does not define "condemnation" in v. 1; rather, it makes deliverance from sin's lordship a sign or evidence of the judicial pronouncement "no condemnation." The γάρ-clause in v. 3 starts with the same purpose but returns in its second half to the judicial aspect, grounded in Jesus' sacrifice for sin.

God's sending his Son in the likeness of sinful flesh and as a sin-offering defines God's condemning sin in the flesh much more easily (these expressions all occur in the same clause in relation to each other) than does the subsequent ἵνα-clause concerning the fulfillment of the righteous requirement of the law. That fulfillment gives the purpose, not the definition, of God's condemning sin in the flesh and makes up for the inability of the law. Though admitting the well-known use of περὶ ἁμαρτίας for "sin-offering" in the LXX, some commentators shy away from it here with a generalizing interpretation that they fail to support with counter evidence. The phrase is so frequent in the LXX for sin-offerings, however, that we need powerful reasons not to accept this meaning in Rom 8:3. The bond between "condemned sin in the flesh" and περὶ ἁμαρτίας gives us a positive reason to accept it (cf. 2 Cor 5:21). A general meaning, such as "for sin" or "to deal with sin," would be superfluous in the context. Therefore eliminating v. 1 (usually along with 7:25a) as an alien juristic gloss does not leave the way clear to see only a discussion of liberation from sin's power and to deny a reminder of liberation from the guilt of sin (against R. Bultmann, *Exegetica* [Tübingen: Mohr (Paul Siebeck), 1967], 279, and others in his wake; cf. H. Hübner's complaint that Sanders separates the juristic and the participatory too much ["Pauli Theologiae Proprium," *NTS* 26 (1980): 468–69]).

[88] Therefore it is hard to accept Sanders' waving aside 1 Cor 6:9–11, which he recognizes to

But if juristic thinking marks Paul's theology deeply, why does he not write more about atonement, repentance, and forgiveness?[89] He may not write very much about them (see below), and at least some of what he does write comes from early Christian tradition. But in addressing the already converted he can in the main assume that tradition. Atonement, repentance, and forgiveness need not be any the less foundational to his theology or important to his thinking for being traditional. (Sanders should be the first to grant the principle behind this statement since in Palestinian Judaism the covenantal side of nomism admittedly gets little attention in the literature but, according to his interpretation, has fundamental importance.[90]) In fact, when citing the tradition concerning Christ's death "for our sins" Paul describes the tradition "as of first importance" (1 Cor 15:3). Whether traditional or not, the statement concerning propitiation and expiation in Rom 3:25 comes at a crucial juncture in his argument, viz., at the point of transition from sin to justification. Paul hardly needs to cite a juristic tradition here if he is mainly concerned about the power, not the guilt, of sin. Furthermore, this juristic tradition, if tradition it is and not Paul's own words, agrees with his emphasis on the inexcusability of sin in 1:18–3:23,[91] with further statements in 4:7–8:25; 5:6–11; 8:3, 32; 14:15 (most of which are obviously juristic and the rest of which are most naturally taken so), and with his delaying a discussion of the lordship of sin till 5:21 and the following chapters. Even Sanders admits that the juristic statements in 2 Cor 5:11–21 belong to Paul.[92] When we add to these 1 Cor 5:7; 11:24–25; Gal 1:4; 2:20; 3:13; 1 Thess 5:10 (cf. Eph 2:13; Col 1:20), the supposition that Paul lacked interest in the juristic value of Christ's death looks false. Two studies by H. N. Ridderbos and J. D. G. Dunn strengthen this verdict.[93]

---

be nonparticipatory, as hortatory (*PPJ*, 498, 500). It would be truer to say that the levitical and juristic language of the passage provides the firm foundation of Paul's exhortation. See Byrne, "*Sons of God*," 231–33, and Cooper, "Paul and Rabbinic Soteriology," 135, on the interdependence of juristic and participatory categories and their eschatological framework.

[89] Sanders, *PPJ*, 497–508.

[90] See esp. the response to Neusner in Sanders, "Puzzling Out Rabbinic Judaism," 72–73; also idem, *PPJ*, 234–37, 420–21.

[91] The point stands whether or not we accept Sanders' thesis that much of Rom 1:18–3:23 stems from Jewish homiletical tradition, for Paul would at least be using such tradition to stress the inexcusability of sin.

[92] Sanders, *PPJ*, 502–3.

[93] H. N. Ridderbos, "The Earliest Confession of the Atonement in Paul," and J. D. G. Dunn, "Paul's Understanding of the Death of Jesus," both in *Reconciliation and Hope* (ed. R. Banks; Grand Rapids: Eerdmans, 1974), 76–89, 125–41. See also R. H. Gundry, *Sōma in Biblical Theology* (SNTSMS 29; Cambridge: Cambridge University Press, 1976), 204–16; P. Stuhlmacher, "Achtzehn Thesen zur paulinischen Kreuzestheologie," in *Rechtfertigung* (ed. J. Friedrich, W. Pöhlmann, and P. Stuhlmacher; Tübingen: Mohr/Göttingen: Vandenhoeck & Ruprecht, 1976), 512–14; idem, "Zur paulinische Christologie," *ZTK* 74 (1977): 455–60. S. Kim criticizes Dunn for playing down the penal, substitutionary character of Jesus' death in Paul's theology after having presented good evidence for it (*The Origin of Paul's Gospel* [WUNT 2/4; Tübingen: J. C. B. Mohr, 1981], 276–77 n. 3).

On the other hand repentance and forgiveness, which are prominent in Palestinian Judaism, do not appear so often in Paul as atonement does (but see Rom 2:4–5; 4:6–8; 2 Cor 3:16; 7:9–10; 1 Thess 1:9–10). Why not? Sanders answers: Paul was too interested in the problem of sin's lordship, for which repentance and forgiveness provide no solution but for which union with Christ and receiving his Spirit do provide a solution.[94] Here Sanders is partly right. Repentance does not sound a christological note as faith, which has Christ as its object, does. Nor does forgiveness in comparison with justification, which entails a removal of guilt because of Christ's atonement. But Sanders misses the boat in thinking Paul favored the christologically oriented terms and avoided the Judaistic terms purely for the dogmatic reason that Christianity is not Judaism. Rather, as we have seen, Paul so deeply felt the falling short of God's glory through sin that he did not think trying to keep the law, *much less repenting to receive forgiveness for failures to keep it*, adequate. The more the law abets sin's lordship because of human weakness, the less adequate is repentance to take care of guilt. *For repentance implies a change of behavior.*

For this same reason Paul cannot ascribe atoning value to good works. Juristically Christ's self-sacrifice makes them unnecessary and by comparison inferior. Dynamically sin's lordship, exercised through the law, frustrates efforts to keep the law well enough to make atonement. Despite his very full discussions of atonement by good works in Palestinian Judaism Sanders neglects to emphasize how differently Paul thinks of atonement.[95] This neglect grows out of a mistaken belief that Paul has little concern over the question of guilt. A greater appreciation of just such a concern enables us to understand his rejection of Judaism better.

Even Paul, however, says that in the end people will be judged according to their works. Citing Rom 2:12–16; 11:22; 14:10; 1 Cor 3:10–13; 4:2–5; 6:9–10; 10:21; 11:29–32; 2 Cor 5:8–10; Gal 5:21, Sanders uses such statements to argue that on the question of staying in, Paul holds fast the Jewish mode of thinking, according to which avoiding evil works and doing good works are the condition of staying in but do not earn salvation.[96] "The point is that God *saves* by grace, but that *within* the framework established by grace he rewards good deeds and punishes transgression."[97]

---

[94] Sanders, "Patterns of Religion," 468–69; idem, *PPJ* 499–501, 507, 549–51.

[95] See "Atonement" in the subject-index of *PPJ*. With regard to Paul's view of staying in, Sanders thinks 1 Cor 3:5–4:6; 5:1–5; 11:27–34; and 2 Cor 12:21 indicate a belief in atonement through repentance and the suffering of punishment by the Christian who has sinned (*PLJP*, 107–9). But Paul does not use the language of atonement in these passages, only that of discipline. The language of atonement he reserves for Christ's death alone.

[96] Sanders, *PPJ*, 515–18; idem, *PLJP*, 113–14. See also *PLJP*, 123–35, esp. 125–26, for a retraction of Rom 2:12–16 from this point.

[97] Sanders, *PPJ*, 543 (italics original); cf. K.P. Donfried, "Justification and Last Judgment in Paul," *ZNW* 67 (1976): 92–103.

But we cannot afford to let this apparent similarity between Paul and Palestinian Judaism go unscrutinized. Again it is necessary to recall that whatever else Paul's phrase "from faith to faith" may mean in Rom 1:17, it surely means that salvation continues as well as starts on the principle of faith alone, which, as Paul makes clear, excludes works (see Rom 4:4–5 for the most explicit statement; cf. 11:17–22). And we have already noted that his letter to the Galatians, which emphasizes faith instead of works, deals more with staying in than with getting in. So we have to ask whether in Paul's doctrine of judgment according to works synergism has watered down the doctrine of grace or whether the danger consists in false profession (so that loss of salvation is only the loss of what falsely appeared to be salvation) rather than in the negating of a salvation genuinely received. The evidence Sanders cites from Palestinian Jewish literature shows overwhelmingly that good works are a *condition* as well as a sign of staying in. It appears, however, that for Paul good works are only (but not unimportantly!) a *sign* of staying in as well as of getting in. Not only do we have the phrase "from faith to faith" and the whole Epistle to the Galatians. Paul expresses his thought unambiguously in 2 Cor 13:5: "Test yourselves whether you are in the faith. Prove yourselves. Or do you not recognize concerning yourselves that Jesus Christ is in you unless indeed you are disapproved (ἀδόκιμοι)?" In particular, the admonition "Test yourselves" points to evidence rather than means. Paul goes on to talk of doing good and not evil (v. 7). Thus good works are a way of proving the genuineness of salvation. There is no need to make Paul contradict himself by deducing that he regards good works as a *means* of retaining salvation.[98]

Contrastingly the rabbis make varying and sometimes contradictory statements about merit and the weighing of fulfillments and transgressions at the Last Judgment.[99] (Some rabbis even rested God's election of Israel on the merit of the patriarchs, of Israel at the exodus, or of Israel in the future.[100]) Sanders takes these statements as unsystematically hortatory rather than as contrary to grace. Even so, the rabbis' mixing of merit-language and grace-language makes synergism an applicable designation and stands in sharp opposition to Paul's avoiding all talk of merit – indeed, denying merit outright.

---

[98] Cf. H. N. Ridderbos, *Paul: An Outline of His Theology* (Grand Rapids: Eerdmans, 1975), 178–81. Failure to observe the distinction between good works as the evidence of salvation retained as well as received solely by faith and good works as the means of retaining salvation received by faith underlies H. Räisänen's seeing an incoherence at this point in Paul's thought ("Paul's Theological Difficulties with the Law," in *Studia Biblica 1978, III: Papers on Paul and Other New Testament Authors* [ed. E. A. Livingstone; JSNTSup 3; Sheffield: University of Sheffield, 1980], 307).

[99] Sanders, *PPJ*, 125–47; cf. Byrne's remark that "in *practice* … works *are* a means of gaining salvation" in Judaism ("*Sons of God*," 230–31 [italics original]).

[100] Sanders, *PPJ*, 87–101.

Everyone recognizes that judgment according to works provides Paul a basis of exhortation and that his affirmations of justification by faith, not by works, are theological, even polemically so. But his waxing polemical on the doctrine casts a shadow on Sanders' insistence that works-righteousness in Palestinian Judaism was only a hortatory device, not a soteriological principle as well (which, combined with elective grace, produces synergism). Are we to prefer Paul's interpretation or Sanders'? Paul was closer. He had been a zealous proponent of Palestinian Judaism. His statements not only comment on others in Palestinian Judaism but also reflect on the nature of his own participation in it (Gal 1:13 14). To be sure, he converted to Christianity. But conversion does not necessarily blind a person to past realities. So we are not at liberty to say Paul misconstrued his own experience of Judaism.[101]

Despite his call to obey the commandments that he thinks Christians are obligated to obey, it is hard to imagine Paul as engaging in the careful attempts to define the commandments exactly and, further, to "build a fence" around them by adding regulations to keep people from even coming close to breaking them.[102] Sanders interprets such attempts on the part of the rabbis as growing out of a sincere desire to please God. Well and good. But Paul's failure to follow the rabbinic pattern reveals a world of difference between him and the rabbis: they show much more confidence in human nature than he does.[103] He is far less sanguine. His dependence on the Holy Spirit relates to this malism and forestalls the need for scholastic definition and protection of the commandments.

Sanders tries to counteract a relatively sanguine estimate of human nature in Palestinian Judaism by stressing the language of unworthiness and dependence on God's grace that we find especially in Jewish prayers *to* God as opposed to descriptions *of* God, where the language of justice, reward, and punishment prevails.[104] But Paul characteristically stresses God's grace in speaking *of* him (the references are too numerous to list). Furthermore, in the literature of Palestinian Judaism the people of God are typically called "the pious" and "the righteous" – terms that point to good conduct – but in Paul's epistles "the believers," "the called," and "the saints" – terms that reflect God's grace.[105] Despite some for-

---

[101] For merit theology in Palestinian Judaism, see D. A. Carson, *Divine Sovereignty and Human Responsibility* (Atlanta: John Knox, 1980), 49–53, 68–74, 78 (in part), 89–92, 104–21.

[102] Cf. Sanders, *PLJP*, 95–96, 106–7. Saldarini notes that "halaka is not derived from covenant in any concrete way in Tannaitic literature; it is itself central and primary" (*JBL* 98 [1979]: 300). As a result of the rabbis' preoccupation with legal minutiae Caird wonders whether their religion "was not *in toto* at the third remove from principles which are central to Christian theology" (*JTS* ns 29 [1978]: 539).

[103] See Carson, *Divine Sovereignty*, 92–93.

[104] See, e.g., Sanders, *PPJ*, 395.

[105] "The saints" emphasizes divine consecration rather than holy living, though of course holy living stems from such consecration. Presumably Paul might have used the Jewish terms too had they not in his view become overlaid with legalistic connotations. The Dead Sea Scrolls

mal similarities, then, Paul and Palestinian Judaism look materially different at the point of grace and works.[106] We may conclude that he rejected Judaism and Judaistic Christianity not only because of a conviction that God had revealed his Son Jesus in him (Gal 1:15–16) – after all, he could have preached Christ as the messianic establisher of law-observance – but also because of a conviction that works-righteousness lay at the heart of Judaism and Judaistic Christianity and that it would corrupt what he had come to believe concerning God's grace in Jesus Christ.[107]

In summary, then, for a true estimate of Pauline soteriology in comparison with Judaistic soteriology:

– The question is not whether Judaism *taught* salvation by works but whether Paul *presented* it as teaching salvation by works. If Paul presented Judaism as teaching salvation by works the debate whether Judaism taught salvation by grace or by works is basically irrelevant (though in spelling out Judaistic soteriology, one would need to take into account Paul's presentation of it).

– The question is not whether salvation by works means salvation is earned wholly by good works as opposed to faith in God's grace but whether salvation by such works means earning salvation *in part* by them, with faith in God's grace to make up for sins of omission and commission. If salvation by works means the latter, then passages in nonchristian Jewish literature that

---

form a partial exception to typical Jewish usage (see G. L. Carr, "The Provenance of the Term 'Saints': A *religionsgeschichtliche* Study," *JETS* 24 [1981]: 107–16).

[106] This judgment runs opposite that of M. D. Hooker, "Paul and 'Covenantal Nomism,'" in *Paul and Paulinism* (ed. M. D. Hooker and S. G. Wilson; London: SPCK, 1982), 47–56. She agrees with Sanders that Paul and Palestinian Judaism look similar at the point of grace and works and uses that agreement to argue against Sanders that the patterns of religion therefore look similar despite the intrusion of Paul's "participation theology."

[107] Of course Paul did not think that by becoming a Christian he had departed from his ancestral religion as represented in the OT and in the remnant of grace (see esp. Romans 11). Nor did he think it wrong to practice Judaism apart from an attempt to establish one's standing before God (see esp. 1 Cor 9:20; Romans 14; also the portrait of Paul in Acts 13–28, which some would discount, however, as due to a catholicizing tendency). But the great autobiographical reversal that Paul details in Gal 1:13–14; Phil 3:4–9 and his battle against the Judaizers show it is appropriate to speak of his getting out of Judaism. The possibility that he reacted against Hellenistic or Diaspora Judaism rather than against Palestinian Judaism has not entered the present discussion because Sanders dismisses it, probably rightly (*PPL*, 1–12; see further idem, "The Covenant as a Soteriological Category and the Nature of Salvation in Palestinian and Hellenistic Judaism," in *Jews, Greeks and Christians* [ed. R. Hamerton-Kelly and S. Scroggs; SJLA 21; Leiden: E. J. Brill, 1976], 11–44, that covenantal nomism characterized Hellenistic as well as Palestinian Judaism anyway). Nor have Jesus' quarrels with his opponents on legal questions – though his opinions could only support Paul's estimate – come under consideration. Form and redaction critical issues would attenuate any argument so derived. Finally, for present purposes it has not seemed necessary to discuss the question whether or not justification by faith is the center of Paul's theology (see R. Y. K. Fung, "The Status of Justification by Faith in Paul's Thought: A Brief Survey of a Modern Debate," *Themelios* 6 [3, 1981]: 4–11).

extol God's grace do not disprove a Pauline presentation of Judaism as teaching salvation by works.

– The question is not whether Paul taught the necessity of good works but whether such necessary works are evidential of salvation or contributory to salvation. If Paul taught them as necessary evidence of salvation but not as a necessary contribution to it, then his teaching on works does not create an inconsistency with his teaching on justification by faith apart from meritorious works.

– The question is not whether Paul taught "getting in" by faith and "staying in" by works (as in Judaism, according to Sanders, yet with Paul's addition of Christ's redemptive work) but whether Paul taught staying in by works or by faith. If he taught staying in by faith as well as getting in by faith he does not agree with a Judaistic soteriology that taught getting in by faith but staying in by works.

– The question is not whether "the works of the law" consist in Jewish identity markers but whether "the works of the law" are limited to them. If "the works of the law" include more than Jewish identity markers Paul's soteriology goes deeper than social relations between Jews and Gentiles in the church, though it certainly encompasses those relations.

All in all, then, hurrah for the Old Perspective on Paul! Its superiority over the New Perspective consists in a denial of synergism in favor of staying in as well as getting in by faith alone, and in a stress on the justified sinner's relation to God as foundational for social relations in the church. Whether or not written by Paul, Eph 2:8–10 summarizes this soteriology admirably well:

For *by grace* you have been saved through faith – and this [being saved by grace through faith] not from (ἐκ) you! *God's* gift! Not from (ἐκ)) works, lest anyone boast! For we are *his* workmanship by having been created in Christ Jesus for good works, which God prepared in advance that *in them* we should walk [italics for emphases in the Greek word order; N. B. also the exclamatory effect of three omissions of "is"].[108]

---

[108] For an up-to-date bibliography as well as extensive discussion see esp. S. Westerholm, *Perspectives New and Old on Paul* (Grand Rapids: Eerdmans, 2004). My thanks to Sanders for graciously and voluntarily sending me a manuscript of *PLJP* long before its publication.

12. The Nonimputation of Christ's Righteousness[1]

The leading Protestant Reformers came to think not only that our sins were imputed to Christ but also that his righteousness is imputed to us who believe in him.[2] The symmetry of such an exchange has proved attractive in systematics; but in biblical theological quarters its second half, the imputation of Christ's righteousness to believers, is losing support – with good scriptural reasons and possibly with a good theological benefit, I will try to show, though I dissociate myself from tendencies sometimes evident in those quarters, such as the tendencies to blur a distinction between declarative righteousness and behavioral righteousness, to interpret justification solely in terms of Jewish-Gentile relations in the church, and to enlarge the doctrine of justification into a doctrine of universal salvation. Naturally my discussion will center on the Epistles of Paul, where an imputation of Christ's righteousness has been thought present.

The imputation – i.e., charging – of our sins to Christ is not in dispute. About that imputation Paul writes explicitly, "In Christ, God was reconciling the world to himself by not counting their trespasses against them .... He made the one who did not know sin [to be] sin on our behalf" (2 Cor 5:19–21), and quotes Ps 32:2 to the same effect: "Blessed is the man whose sin the Lord will not count" (Rom 4:8; cf. 1 Cor 15:3: "Christ died for our sins").[3] But what about the imputation – i.e., crediting – of righteousness? Here are all the NT texts that refer explicitly to imputation in relation to righteousness:

---

[1] This essay grows out of some comments I made on the doctrine of imputation in *Books & Culture* 7/1 (January–February 2001): 6–9 and 7/2 (March–April 2001): 14–15, 39 and to a considerable degree responds to the book-length critique of those comments by J. Piper, *Counted Righteous in Christ* (Wheaton, Ill.: Crossway Books, 2002). References below to "public dialogue" have to do with such dialogue at the Wheaton College Theology Conference held there in April 2003.

[2] See J. Buchanan, *The Doctrine of Justification* (Edinburgh: T&T Clark, 1867), 131–32, for a brief statement of this classic Protestant doctrine but also *Diogn.* 9:1–5 for a much earlier version of the doctrine.

[3] As D. A. Carson correctly points out, "Strictly speaking, there is no passage in the New Testament that says that our sins are imputed to Christ" ("The Vindication of Imputation: On Fields of Discourses and Semantic Fields," in *Justification: What's at Stake in the Current Debates* [ed. M. Husbands and D. J. Treier; Downers Grove, Ill.: InterVarsity/Leicester, UK.: Apollos, 2004], 78). But the parallelism between the negative of not counting trespasses and the positive of making Christ sin makes clear an imputation of sins to Christ. We will see whether any similar parallelism supports an imputation of Christ's righteousness.

- Gal 3:6; Rom 4:3, 22: "it [Abraham's believing God] was counted for him as righteousness."
- Rom 4:5: "his [the believer's] faith is counted as righteousness."
- Rom 4:6: "the person for whom God counts righteousness apart from works."
- Rom 4:9: "faith was counted for Abraham as righteousness."
- Rom 4:11: "in order that he [Abraham] might be the father of all who believe without being circumcised, in order that righteousness might be counted also for them."
- Rom 4:22–24: "therefore also it [faith] was counted for him [Abraham] as righteousness; but not on account of him alone was it written, 'It was counted for him,' but also on account of us, for whom it is going to be counted, [i.e., us] who believe on the one who raised Jesus our Lord from the dead."

But none of these texts says that Christ's righteousness was counted. With the exception of Rom 4:6, 11, which will come up later, they say that Abraham's faith was counted and that our faith is counted, so that righteousness comes into view not as what is counted but as what God counts faith to be. Nor does Paul ascribe this righteousness to Christ; rather, he portrays Christ as the object of faith, for example in Gal 2:16b, "even we believed in (εἰς) Jesus Christ in order that we might be declared righteous."[4]

Those who understand these texts to teach an imputation of Christ's righteousness, alien to sinners, argue on the contrary that Paul's phraseology is shorthand for faith as the *instrument* by which that righteousness is received. An expansive paraphrase might read, "Faith was counted with the result that Christ's alien righteousness was imputed."[5] To test this understanding we need to examine the way Paul and others elsewhere use the phraseology of "counting

---

[4] See also Phil 1:29, "to believe in (εἰς) him ['Christ']"; Phlm 5, "the faith that you have toward (πρός) the Lord Jesus" (cf. Rom 10:9–14; Gal 3:26[?]; Eph 1:15; Col 1:4; 2:5; 1 Tim 3:13; 2 Tim 1:13; 3:15). I leave aside the question whether the phrase "by the faith of Christ" (so a literal translation of the Greek), which occurs in Rom 3:22, 26; Gal 2:16a,c, 20, 22; Eph 3:12; Phil 3:9, refers to Christ's faith or faithfulness rather than to faith in him. Among others, see M. Silva, "Faith Versus Works of Law in Galatians," in *The Paradoxes of Paul* (vol. 2 of *Justification and Variegated Nomism*; ed. D. A. Carson, P. T. O'Brien, and M. A. Seifrid; WUNT 2/181; Tübingen: Mohr Siebeck, 2004), 217–20, 227–34, for what seems to me a devastating refutation of this view (see also S. E. Porter, "The Rhetorical Scribe: Textual Variants in Romans and Their Possible Rhetorical Purpose," in *Rhetorical Criticism and the Bible* [ed. S. E. Porter and D. L. Stamps; JSNTSup 195; Sheffield: Sheffield Academic Press, 2002], 416–17, that the *v.l.* πίστεως ἐν Χριστῷ 'Ιησοῦ in Codex Alexandrinus at Rom 3:22 "is much more compatible with the traditional objective interpretation of the genitive phrase"). But even with the understanding of Christ's faith or faithfulness it remains that only the faith of Abraham and others like him is said to be counted as righteousness.

[5] See, e.g., J. Murray, *Redemption – Accomplished and Applied* (Grand Rapids: Eerdmans, 1955), 155–61; Piper, *Counted Righteous in Christ*, 57; Carson, "The Vindication of Imputation," 63–68.

as" and "being counted as" (λογίζομαι εἰς, Greek texts without εἰς, "as," being less relevant to our purpose):

(All the Pauline texts)

– Rom 2:26: "his [a Gentile law-keeper's] uncircumcision will be counted as circumcision, won't it?"
– Rom 9:8: "the children of the promise are counted as seed."
– 2 Cor 12:6: "lest anyone count as me more than what he sees me [to be] or [more than] anything he hears from me" (a somewhat literal translation).

(All the non-Pauline texts in the NT)

– Acts 19:27: "that the temple of the great goddess Artemis be counted as nothing."
– Jas 2:23: "it [Abraham's believing God] was counted for him as righteousness."

(Some Greek texts outside the New Testament)

– Gen 15:6 LXX: "he [the Lord] counted it [Abraham's believing in the Lord] for him as righteousness."
– Job 41:24 LXX: "the fathomless deep was counted as a place for walking around."
– Ps 105:31 LXX (106:31 HB): "it [Phinehas's zeal] was counted for him as righteousness."
– 1 Macc 2:52: "and was not it [Abraham's being found faithful when tested; cf. Genesis 22] counted for him as righteousness?"
– Philo, *Her.* 94: "and it is well said, 'His faith was counted as righteousness for him,' for nothing is so righteous as to put in God alone a pure and unmixed faith."

(Some non-Greek texts with similar phraseology)

– Gen 31:15: "are we [Rachel and Leah] not counted by him [Laban] as foreigners?"
– Lev 25:31: "the houses of the villages that have no surrounding wall will be counted as open fields."
– Num 18:27: "your offering will be counted for you as the grain from the threshing floor or the full produce from the wine vat."
– Num 18:30: "when you have offered from it the best of it, then the rest of it [i.e., the rest of the offering] will be counted for the Levites as the product of the threshing floor and as the product of the wine vat."
– 2 Sam 19:19 (19:20 HB): "let not my lord count to me iniquity nor remember what your servant did wrong" (Shimei to David).
– Job 13:24: "why ... do you count me as your enemy?" (so also Job 19:11; 33:10).

– Job 19:15: "those who live in my house and my maids count me as a stranger."
– Job 41:27: "he counts iron as straw."
– Prov 27:14: "it will be counted to him as a curse."
– 4QpsJbᵃ (= 4Q225) 2 I: "And Abraham believed God, and righteousness was counted for him."
– *Jub.* 14:6: "and he [Abraham] believed the LORD and it was counted for him as righteousness" (cf. 31:23).
– *Jub.* 30:17: "and it [the killing of the Shechemites by two of Jacob's sons] was a righteousness for them, and it was written down for them for righteousness."
– *Jub.* 35:2: "This thing [the obedience of Jacob to his mother] is… a righteousness for me before the LORD."
– 4QMMT 117 (= 4Q398 1 II, 4, and 2 II, 7): "it will be counted for you as righteousness when you do what is upright and good before him."

Now it is hard if not impossible to think that Rom 2:26 presents a Gentile law-keeper's uncircumcision as the instrument by which an alien circumcision is received. Or that Rom 9:8 presents the children of the promise as the instrument by which an alien seed is received. Or that 2 Cor 12:6 presents more than what others see in Paul or hear from him as the instrument by which an alien Paul might be received. Or that Acts 19:27 presents Artemis's temple as the instrument by which an alien nothingness might be received. Or that Jas 2:23 presents Abraham's faith as the instrument by which an alien righteousness was received (for James emphasizes faith as needing the evidence of the believer's own behavioral righteousness[6]). Or that in its context Gen 15:6 presents Abraham's faith as the instrument by which an alien righteousness was received.[7] Or that Ps 105(106):31 presents Phinehas's zeal as the instrument by which an alien righteousness was received. Or that 1 Macc 2:52 presents Abraham's faithfulness in offering Isaac as the instrument by which an alien righteousness was received. Or that 4QMMT 117 presents upright, good behavior as the instrument by which an alien righteousness is received.

In none of these cases does an instrumental interpretation make good contextual sense. In most of them it makes absolute nonsense, as the foregoing gobble-dygook shows. And in all of them the counting results in an *identification* of what is counted with what it is counted as, not in the introduction of something to be distinguished from what is counted – hence the propriety of translating the Greek preposition εἰς with "as" when used in conjunction with λογίζομαι,

---

[6] "This faith-completed-by-works *is* righteousness and naturally is reckoned as such" (J. A. Ziesler, *The Meaning of Righteousness in Paul* [SNTSMS 20; Cambridge: Cambridge University Press, 1972], 132 [italics original]).
[7] Here and below, those who distinguish between context as the situation in which something is spoken or written and cotext as the language that surrounds a particular expression or passage and helps determine its meaning may substitute "cotext(ual)" for "context(ual)."

"count."[8] Paul's parallel use of ὡς, regularly translated "as," with λογίζομαι confirms this usage (Rom 8:36; 1 Cor 4:1; 2 Cor 10:2; so also Num 18:27, 30 and Job 41:24[27] in the LXX). As intimated before, "counted *to be*" would also convey the intended meaning,[9] *and this counting to be occurs whether or not what is counted is intrinsically what it is counted to be.*

In *Jub.* 30:17 the killing of the Shechemites is counted to be righteousness because by the author's lights (though in disagreement with Gen 34:30; 49:5–7) it was intrinsically righteous. So also Phinehas's zeal in Ps 105(106):31 (in agreement with Num 25:6–13). But in Rom 2:26 a Gentile law-keeper's uncircumcision will be counted as circumcision even though it is not. In Acts 19:27 the temple of Artemis is in danger of being counted as nothing even though in the opinion of the speaker it is a wonder of the world.[10] In Job 41:24 LXX the watery depths are counted as terra firma even though they are not. In Gen 31:15 Laban counts his daughters as foreigners even though they are not foreign to him. In Lev 25:31 the law counts houses in unwalled villages as open fields even though they are not. In Num 18:27, 30 the law counts offerings as the whole of a harvest or vintage even though they are only a small part of it. And in 2 Sam 19:19 Shimei asks David not to count him guilty even though he is in fact guilty. The lack of any reference in Galatians 3 and Romans 4 to Christ's righteousness confirms this linguistic conclusion that the counting of faith as righteousness is *not* shorthand for faith as the instrument by which an alien righteousness – Christ's – is received.[11] (N.B. that the counting of faith as righteousness is no less forensic than a counting of Christ's righteousness would be.)

To get around the plain and simple meaning of Paul's language advocates of the instrumental view may argue that faith includes its object, in this instance

---

[8] As any Greek lexicon indicates, εἰς has a variety of meanings determined in part by context.

[9] Often λογίζομαι occurs without an εἰς-phrase and means "consider to be," as in Rom 3:28, for example: "for we consider a person to be justified by faith apart from works of the law" (see the Greek lexicons).

[10] Cf. Antipater the epigrammist, *Greek Anthology* 9.58: "I have set eyes on the wall of lofty Babylon, on which is a road for chariots; and the statue of Zeus by the Alpheus; and the hanging gardens; and the colossus of the Sun; and the huge labor of the high pyramids; and the vast tomb of Mausolus. But when I saw the house of Artemis that mounted to the clouds, those other marvels lost their brilliance; and I said, 'Lo, apart from Olympus, the Sun never looked on anything so grand.'"

[11] On the linguistic evidence see also Ziesler, *The Meaning of Righteousness in Paul*, 180–85, though he does not concern himself with the question of instrumentality. J. Hervey draws an analogy between hyssop as the instrument of purgation in David's prayer, "Purge me with hyssop" (Ps 51:7), and faith as the instrument of the imputation of Christ's righteousness; but he overlooks that David does not say hyssop is counted as purgation as Paul says faith is counted as righteousness (*Aspasio Vindicated and the Scripture Doctrine of Imputed Righteousness Defended, in eleven letters from Mr. Hervey to Mr. John Wesley, in answer to that gentleman's remarks on Theron and Aspasio* [earlier volumes written by Hervey]. *With Mr. Wesley's letter prefixed. To which is annexed, A Defence of Theron and Aspasio, against the objections contained in Mr. Sandeman's letters on Theron and Aspasio. With Mr. Hervey's letters to the Author prefixed* [London: R. Aiken & Son, 1794], 123).

Christ and therefore his righteousness. Faith is only as good as its object – true, so that the faith which God counts as righteousness requires Christ as its object. But the object of God's counting is faith in Christ, not Christ as the object of faith. To include Christ in the faith that God counts as righteousness would be to confuse the object of faith with faith as the object of imputation or, more simply, to confuse faith with its object.

It might be asked whether an instrumental view of faith is necessary to the doctrine of an imputed righteousness of Christ. Yes, it is, because all Paul's language of imputation involves faith (even the two statements in Rom 4:6, 11 that speak of righteousness as counted occur in a passage heavily oriented to faith); and if – given an imputation of Christ's righteousness – faith too were correctly taken to be counted as righteousness rather than as instrumental toward it, the imputed righteousness that consists in faith would imply an insufficiency in the imputed righteousness of Christ. Not an attractive implication!

Since Paul writes that a wage is counted and since a wage is external to a person whereas faith is internal to a person, it is argued – again on the contrary – that faith must not be counted but must rather be instrumental toward the counting of something external like a wage though in other respects different from a wage, viz., the righteousness of Christ. But this argument neglects the switch away from the counting of a wage "not *according to* grace but *according to* debt" – a wage being paid to eliminate a debt and therefore not equivalent to a debt (Rom 4:4) – over to faith's being counted "*as* righteousness," i.e., as equivalent to righteousness. Besides, the contrast between external and internal is being imposed on the text. Paul does not draw such a contrast.

But it is asked, "Would he not rather say something like, 'Now to him who works, his works are credited as (= treated as) his righteousness according to debt ...,'" if Paul means that faith as the counterpart of a wage is counted as righteousness?[12] The answer is no, because in the matter of justification he does not want even to suggest that God credits works as righteousness. So Paul avoids the crediting of works, writes instead about the counting of a wage, and thus gains a contrast with the already mentioned and now echoed "grace" by which believers are "justified as a gift" (3:24; see also 4:16; 5:2, 15–17, 20–6:1 for ongoing references to this grace). The contrast backs up Paul's immediately foregoing assertion that before God Abraham has nothing to boast about (4:2).

Theologically it is objected that a straightforward counting of faith as righteousness not only gives righteousness an internal human origin rather than an external divine one but also makes faith a work of righteousness and thereby puts justification on a synergistic rather than solely gracious basis.[13] But insofar

---

[12] Piper, *Counted Righteous in Christ*, 56.
[13] Murray, *Redemption – Accomplished and Applied*, 159–60.

as Reformed soteriology takes faith to be a gift of God, the objection sounds hollow.[14] And this view of faith as a gift has Pauline support: "for Christ's sake it was graciously given you ... to believe in him" (Phil 1:29); "faith [comes] from hearing [or 'what is heard'] and hearing [or 'what is heard'] through the word of Christ" (Rom 10:17); "God has allotted to each [of you] an allotment of faith" (Rom 12:3).[15]

If we were to assign to faith a human origin, or to the extent that to preserve the element of human responsibility we were to assign to faith a human origin,[16] it would remain that Paul emphatically puts faith and works in opposing categories: "But to the one who works the wage is not counted according to grace but according to debt; and to the one who does not work but believes on the one who justifies the ungodly his faith is counted as righteousness, just as David mentions the blessedness of the person for whom God counts righteousness apart from works" (Rom 4:4–6a; see also 3:27–28). In other words, Paul rejects the Jewish tradition that God counted Abraham's faith as righteousness because it was a good work.[17] Paul rejects this tradition not by making faith the instrument by which Christ's righteousness is received but by saying that God counted Abraham's faith as righteousness even though it was *not* a good work. For "in believing [which by its nature is trusting], Abraham did not work, but let God work."[18] Therefore the charge of synergism does not stick. Moreover, the antithetical parallel between faith and works militates against an instrumental view of faith, for works are not instrumental in the reception of one's own righteousness (cf. Rom 10:3, "their own righteousness," and Phil 3:9, "my own righteousness"). That kind of righteousness *consists* in works. Likewise, what God counts as righteousness *consists* in faith.

Does God's counting of righteousness in Rom 4:6, 11 differ from the counting of faith in the surrounding passage so as to make righteousness *rather than* faith the direct object of counting and faith the instrument toward the counting of righteousness? Again no, for grammatically Paul makes faith a direct object of counting just as he makes righteousness its direct object. The conclusion to

---

[14] Piper writes that Christ "sovereignly works faith ... in us," yet makes the objection (*Counted Righteous in Christ*, 125; so also Buchanan, *The Doctrine of Justification*, 387).

[15] Cf. 1 Cor 15:10; Eph 2:8; Phil 2:12–13; 3:12; 1 Thess 2:13. God does not believe for us, of course, so that believing is a human activity even in Reformed soteriology. On the question of synergism, therefore, an imputation of Christ's righteousness on the basis of faith offers no advantage over the counting of faith as righteousness.

[16] Cf. H. Lee, "Biblical, Theological Reflections on the Tension between Divine Sovereignty and Human Responsibility in Paul's Letters," *Chongshin Theological Journal* 6 (2001): 50–72.

[17] For references to ancient Jewish literature in this regard see Ziesler, *The Meaning of Righteousness in Paul*, 43, 103–4, 109, 123, 125–26, 175, 182–83; C. E. B. Cranfield, *The Epistle to the Romans* (ICC; Edinburgh: T&T Clark, 1975, 1979), 1:229.

[18] M. A. Seifrid, *Christ, Our Righteousness* (Downers Grove, Ill.: InterVarsity, 2000), 68; see also the comments on Gen 15:6 by G. von Rad, "Faith Reckoned as Righteousness," in *The Problem of the Hexateuch and Other Essays* (New York: McGraw-Hill, 1966), 129.

draw is that God counts both faith and righteousness because he counts them as identical to each other.

D. A. Carson lodges several objections against identifying the righteousness that is counted with the faith that is counted as righteousness.[19] First, he calls the locutional difference a "problem" for such an identification and then reasons that "if God has counted or imputed our faith to us as righteousness, then, once he has so counted or imputed it, does he *then* count or impute the righteousness to us, a kind of *second* imputation?" (italics added). But there is no problem if we allow – as we should and Carson himself does throughout the rest of his essay – for different ways of saying the same thing. And if the counting of righteousness equates with the counting of faith as righteousness we have synonymity, not a sequence of two imputations.

Second, Carson objects that the preceding context in Romans "of human ungodliness and wickedness" implies God's "imputing an (alien) righteousness" rather than his "imputing faith to us as righteousness." But the preceding context does not keep Paul from saying in Rom 4:3, 9 that God counts faith as righteousness, so that Carson has to undermine his own argument by describing the counting of faith as righteousness as "a slightly adjacent thought." Slightly adjacent? It is what Paul brings up first and develops most emphatically. And proof that a context of human ungodliness and wickedness does not imply the imputation of an alien righteousness comes from passages where God's righteousness saves from sin with no thought (as everyone would agree) that God imputes an alien righteousness (see Ps 51:14; *4 Ezra* 8:36, 39–40; 1QS 11:11–15, quoted below, and also Isa 46:3–13). That is to say, Carson's objection rests on a neglect of the OT and other Jewish background of God's righteousness as salvific activity rather than as imputed moral character that replaces human sin. More to follow on this activity.

Third, Carson objects that in Rom 4:23–24 God's crediting righteousness to "us ... who believe on him who raised Jesus our Lord from the dead" portrays faith "as *the means or the condition or the instrument* of the imputation of righteousness, not as that which is imputed as righteousness" (italics original). But in those verses (to which should be added vv. 18–22) it is faith, not righteousness, that is counted; and it is counted "as righteousness," so that the reference to "us ... who believe" is designed to bring both Jewish and Gentile believers under the umbrella of an Abrahamic faith that God counts as righteousness, not to make it an instrument of gaining an alien righteousness of Christ (cf. v. 11: "that he [Abraham] might be the father of all who believe").

Fourth, however, Carson appeals to Rom 3:21–26 and especially 27–31, plus 5:1 and Phil 3:8–9, as indicating "the instrumental nature of faith" as a "commonplace in the New Testament." Fair enough, but only in the sense noted

---

[19] Carson, "The Vindication of Imputation," 63–67.

above, viz., that faith lays hold of God's righteousness, his salvific action of counting the faith as righteousness, not of Christ's righteousness.

Fifth, Carson objects that since λογίζομαι has "an astonishingly wide range of meaning" and in Rom 3:28 "certainly [does] not [mean] imputation in any technical sense.... it seems a bit doctrinaire to read the Genesis 15:6 citation in Romans 4 in the controlling way that Gundry advocates." But it seems a bit doctrinaire *not* to read Romans 4, with its use of λογίζομαι, in the light of Gen 15:6, which Romans 4 cites heavily. After all, "we," not God, do the reckoning in Rom 3:28 whereas God does it in Gen 15:6 and Romans 4.

For us, then, justification is both negative and positive. Negatively, God does not count our sins against us. Jesus took them away. Positively, God counts our faith as righteousness. These complementary elements suffice to eliminate any exegetical need to import into Romans 4 an unmentioned righteousness of Christ – and also any pastoral need to do so for the healing of Christians' hurting consciences.

It is further objected, however, that since the first three chapters of Romans feature *God's* righteousness (1:17; 3:5, 21, 22, 25, 26), the righteousness in ch. 4 can hardly consist in anything so human as faith. But whatever the meaning of God's righteousness (on which see below), this chapter substitutes "the righteousness of faith" for "the righteousness of God" (4:11, 13; cf. 9:30; 10:6); and in view of the linguistically demonstrated fact that according to ch. 4 God counts faith as righteousness, "the righteousness of faith" in this same chapter must mean yet again the righteousness which by God's counting consists in faith. Similarly, the righteousness that comes "from" (ἐκ) faith (Rom 9:30; 10:6) and from God "through" (διά) faith and "on the basis of" (ἐπί) faith (Phil 3:9) is the faith that God counts as righteousness. Paul's language is supple: faith is the origin, the means, and the basis of righteousness in that God counts it as righteousness.[20]

Similarly once more, believing has "the result of righteousness" according to Rom 10:10 in the sense that God counts faith as righteousness. The notion that the use of εἰς to indicate a result demands an alien righteousness, that of Christ, does not pass muster. Since for Paul faith is not a work – i.e., not intrinsically righteous – God's counting faith as righteousness agrees perfectly well with righteousness as the result of faith. And the argument that in the parallel clause of Rom 10:10 confession does not *consist* in salvation but only *results* in salvation fails to consider Paul's earlier use of the verb of counting with righteousness but not with salvation.[21]

---

[20] Cf. Heb 11:7: "[Noah] became heir of the righteousness according to faith." Murray argues that faith is not counted as righteousness, because Paul never says justification is "on account of" or "because of" faith; rather, "by," "through," and "upon" faith (*Redemption – Accomplished and Applied*, 155). But at least ἐπί, "on the basis of," amounts to what Murray calls for.

[21] Against Piper, *Counted Righteous in Christ*, 62.

So far the discussion has revolved around the technical term for counting, λογίζομαι. But another term used in connection with justification may be synonymous. That is the verb καθίστημι, "establish," in Rom 5:19: "For just as through the disobedience of the one man [Adam] the many were established [as] sinful, in this way also through the obedience of the one [man Jesus Christ] the many will be established [as] righteous." The verb means to establish physically by way of bringing, conducting, or taking, or to establish nonphysically by way of appointment, ordination, or making. It is particularly the frequent use of this verb for appointing that may be synonymous with counting because to be appointed as this or that means to be counted as such. Therefore Rom 5:19 could mean that through Adam's disobedience human beings were counted as sinful, and through Christ's obedience (i.e., righteousness) human beings will be counted as righteous.

This meaning is favored by Paul's using "justify" in the sense of "declaring righteous." So let us ask, How will Christ's obedience enable sinners to be declared, counted, or established as righteous? By the imputation of that obedience or by some other means? Paul did not bring Christ's obedience into the discussion of imputation in Romans 4 (or in Galatians 3). But he did indicate in Rom 3:21–31 that it is the expiatory and propitiatory death of Christ, represented by his blood, which enables God to be righteous even in declaring righteous those sinners who exercise faith, *which declaration Paul proceeds to explain in ch. 4 as God's counting their faith as righteousness.* So in 5:19 the obedience of Christ refers again to his submission to that expiatory and propitiatory death (as also in Phil 2:8: "by becoming obedient to the extent of death, even the death of a cross"), which death enables God to be righteous when he declares sinners to be righteous by counting their faith as righteousness.[22]

To the contrary and in support of counting Christ's righteousness as ours, appeal is made to the parallel Paul draws between Christ's obedience and Adam's disobedience. So the further question has to be asked, How did Adam's disobedience establish people as sinful? By the imputation of that disobedience or by some other means? This question moves us backward to Rom 5:12–18. The passage starts with statements that "sin entered the world" through Adam, that death entered the world "through sin," and that death spread to all human beings

---

[22] Declaring sinners righteous by counting their faith as righteousness is not to be merged with making them behaviorally righteous by the infusion of righteousness. Some think that according to Rom 3:26 God is righteous *in that* he justifies sinners who believe rather than that justifying them does not contradict his righteousness (so S.K. Williams, "The 'Righteousness of God' in Romans," *JBL* 99 [1980]: 277–78; cf. C. Blackman, "Romans 3 26b: A Question of Translation," *JBL* 87 [1968]: 203–4; D. A. Campbell, *The Rhetoric of Righteousness in Romans 3.21–26* [JSNTSup 65; Sheffield: Sheffield Academic Press, 1992], 166–70). But this view overlooks the background of God's wrath against the unrighteousness of human beings, of Christ's propitiation, of God's passing over the sins committed earlier, and – in the OT – of God's not justifying the wicked (Exod 23:7; cf. Prov 17:15; Isa 5:23).

"in this way" (not "so" in the inferential sense of "therefore," which the underlying Greek word does not bear). "In this way" means that death spread to all
human beings "through sin."

Paul then identifies more expansively the ground on which death spread to all
human beings.[23] It is that "all have sinned." Does this statement mean Adam's
sin counted as everybody's sin, so that we should infer God's imputing the original sin of Adam to all Adam's descendants? One might think so from
1 Cor 15:22a, "For just as in Adam all are dying ...," by reasoning that since
death is the consequence of sin, dying in Adam entails having sinned in Adam.
But dying in Adam does not mean that Adam's death counted as everybody's
death, for Paul does not use the past tense, "In Adam all died." He uses the present tense, "In Adam all are dying." So dying in Adam means dying one's own
death as a consequence of one's own sinning, which resulted in turn from sin's
having entered the world through Adam.

"All have sinned" in Rom 5:12 echoes "all have sinned" in Rom 3:23, where
the statement summarizes Paul's preceding delineation of the manifold sins
committed by human beings throughout history, with nary a word about
Adam's original sin (Rom 1:18–3:20); and Paul refers to "our transgression*s*"
(pl.) in 4:25 and to "*many* transgressions" right here in 5:16. All Paul's other
uses of the verb "sin" also refer to human beings' sinning for themselves.[24] But
J. Murray argues that 5:12 cannot refer to such sinning because infants die without having sinned for themselves.[25] Alongside infants other theologians add
mentally deficient youth and adults. To sustain this argument it is necessary to
think that "all have sinned" in 3:23 at least includes a reference to the sinning of
infants and the mentally deficient together with that of everybody else in
Adam's original sin. Yet this inclusion so overshoots the context of 3:23 – the
context of manifold sins – that one may detect some embarrassment in Murray's
comment on that verse: "it would not be defensible *to restrict* the reference to
the sin of Adam and the involvement of posterity therein."[26] Paul's emphasis on
the lack of distinction between Jews and Greeks in the matter of sin, however
(see esp. 2:9; 3:9, 22b–23 but also the whole of 1:18–3:23), shows that "all"
means Jews and Gentiles alike, the question of mental capacity not in view.

Further showing that "all have sinned" in Rom 5:12 does not mean God imputed Adam's original sin to the rest of the human race is an immediately following explanation, introduced with the conjunction "for," concerning the sin-

---

[23] See T. L. Carter, *Paul and the Power of Sin* (SNTSMS 115; Cambridge: Cambridge University Press, 2002), 170–73, for translating ἐφ' ᾧ in 5:12 with "inasmuch as."

[24] See Rom 2:12; 5:14, 16; 6:15; 1 Cor 6:18; 7:28, 36; 8:12; 15:34; Eph 4:26; 1 Tim 5:20;
Titus 3:11.

[25] J. Murray, *The Imputation of Adam's Sin* (Phillipsburg, N.J.: Presbyterian and Reformed,
1959), 10; idem, *The Epistle to the Romans* (NICNT; Grand Rapids: Eerdmans, 1959), 1:183.

[26] Murray, *Romans*, 1:112, italics added.

ning of people before the law was given, i.e., during the period between Adam and Moses (vv. 13–14). These people's sinning "not after the likeness of Adam's transgression" shows that Paul distinguishes their sins from Adam's original sin and attributes their sins to the presence of sin in the world due to its *entrance* through Adam. So "all have sinned" means that under the influence of sin all have sinned for themselves, not that they sinned in the original sin of Adam.

The reference to people's sinning between Adam and Moses temporarily interrupts the comparison begun in v. 12 ("On account of this, just as…"; see v. 15 for its resumption: "But not as…, in this way also…"). Does this interruption arise from a fear that "all have sinned" in v. 12 would be *mis*understood in terms of all individuals' sinning for themselves, so that it would follow naturally but erroneously that "through Jesus Christ, righteousness and life entered the world, and life spread to all *because all individually did acts of righteousness*"?[27] Certainly Paul wants to avoid self-righteousness, but because it would contradict 1:18–3:20 ("There is no righteous person, not even one" in 3:10, for example), not because he wants 5:12 to be understood differently from 3:23, i.e., in terms of an imputation of Adam's sin.

Sin got its start, then, in the original sin, which consisted in a transgression of God's stated command not to eat from the tree of the knowledge of good and evil. Since the law, consisting in stated commands as distinct from the compunctions of conscience (cf. 2:14–15 with 1:32), was not given till much later, sins committed during the intervening period were unlike Adam's sin in that they did not consist in transgressions which would have been entered as debits on an account (cf. 4:15) but consisted in slavish service to sin as a dominating force.[28] Likewise death, having entered the world through Adam's transgression, ruled illegally, so to speak; death usurped power outside the law or, rather, before the law. "The many died by the transgression of one" in that through Adam's transgression death, like sin, entered the world as a force to which people fell subject in their own sinning. Then it turns out in v. 18 that Adam's "transgression" in Eden contrasts not only with the sins committed between him and Moses but also with Christ's "act of righteousness." The contrast between Adam's sin and the sins committed between him and Moses has to do with a freely chosen transgression versus servitude. The contrast between Adam's sin and Christ's act of righteousness has to do with disobedience versus obedience.[29]

---

[27] So Piper, *Counted Righteous in Christ*, 92–93 (italics original).

[28] So also Seifrid, *Christ, Our Righteousness*, 70 n. 91, though Seifrid follows T. Zahn's understanding of ἐφ᾽ ᾧ in 5:12: "under which circumstance."

[29] Because Paul excoriates Gentiles for violating what they know to be God's righteous requirement (1:32) and for doing so apparently from earliest times, not just after the law was given through Moses (see the entirety of 1:18–3:20), some interpreters identify those who sinned and died between Adam and Moses as a subset of the general population, viz. (as in the similar interpretation of 3:23; 5:12 discussed above), infants who died too young to have known God's

Verses 16–21 also speak of righteousness as a gift that originated in abundant grace and came by way of Christ's act of righteousness, and of grace as reigning. Since 3:24; 4:4–5, 16 associated righteousness with grace and since the whole of ch. 4 defined righteousness as the faith that God graciously counts as righteousness, the gracious gift of righteousness in 5:16–21 must consist in God's counting faith as righteousness rather than in Christ's act of righteousness which made possible such a counting.[30] The language of giving and receiving a gift, though it would be compatible with imputation, neither demands nor favors it. In Acts 5:31; 10:43, for example, forgiveness of sins is given and received through Christ but not imputed; for he did not sin, was not forgiven, and therefore had no forgiveness that could be imputed to others. Paul puts in parallel Adam's transgression and Christ's act of righteousness, then, not in that both have been imputed but in that both have occasioned the entry into the world of reigning forces: sin and death on the one hand, life-giving grace on the other hand.

---

righteous requirement and therefore died because God imputed to them Adam's transgression – likewise in regard to mentally deficient youth and adults. Because it takes a Sherlock Holmes to detect here any reference to infants and the mentally deficient this interpretation smacks of desperation to save the passage for an imputation of Adam's sin. The interpretation also underestimates Paul's seeing the promulgation of the Mosaic law as inaugurating a new though now outmoded dispensation of legal demands (Rom 4:13–15; 5:20; Gal 3:17–19, 23–25). Piper argues that "even" in the phrase "even over the ones who did not sin after the likeness of Adam's transgression" (5:14) "implies … a special and particular class of sinners, not all sinners before Moses" (*Counted Righteous in Christ*, 100–101 n. 44). But Paul's "even" more naturally emphasizes the whole of those who sinned apart from the law between Adam and Moses, as distinguished from Adam and from those who transgressed the law after it was given. I say "more naturally" because it is very uncertain – as Piper's self-confessed wrestling shows – what subset Paul might be referring to if he is indeed referring to a subset (cf. Murray's finding it "difficult to determine" whom Rom 5:13–14 has in view [*The Imputation of Adam's Sin*, 10]).

[30] Piper argues that since the free gift results in a sentence of justification (εἰς δικαίωμα – v. 16) the two cannot be equated, so that the free gift consists in Christ's righteousness as the basis of that sentence (*Counted Righteous in Christ*, 105–6). But since the free gift is admittedly "the gift of righteousness" (v. 17) and, as explained above, harks back to God's counting faith as righteousness, it is this counting that constitutes the free gift and results in a sentence of justification. Besides, only a whisper of difference distinguishes "judgment" (κρίμα) from its result, "condemnation" (κατάκριμα, literally, "judgment against"), so that it is wrong to press the parallel difference between "the free gift" and its result, "a sentence of justification" (see v. 18 as well as v. 16). I reject a distinction between "righteousness" in Rom 5:17 as a gracious gift and "the righteousness of God" in Rom 3:3–8; 4:9–25 (cf. Romans 9–11) as his faithfulness to the Jews and to "all the families of the earth" in accord with the Abrahamic covenant (Gen 12:1–3). For in Rom 3:21–26 Paul explains "the righteousness of God" in terms of our "being justified as a *gift* by his *grace*" (against Williams, "The 'Righteousness of God' in Romans," 259). Agreed, Paul puts God's righteousness in parallel with God's faithfulness and truthfulness; but Paul defines the means by which God keeps his promise to Abraham as the counting of Abraham-like faith to be righteousness. When Paul wants to emphasize the grace of God in such counting, he portrays God's righteousness as a gift. But this emphasis does not characterize all passages dealing with the righteousness of God, so that it does not cut ice to ask, How can one submit to a gift of righteousness any more than to a gift of some other kind? (ibid.; see Rom 10:3 for such submission).

Paul will later say that the wages of sin is death in contrast with eternal life as God's gift in Christ Jesus (6:23). But neither there do we find the language of imputation. For sin is portrayed throughout 6:12–23 as a slavemaster, so that death is not the wages you get paid *for* sinning; rather, death is the wages you get paid *by* sin. Just as God is the giver of eternal life, not its cause, so in this passage sin is the paymaster of death, not its cause. Which fact brings us back to 5:12–14, where sin entered the world and death entered the world "*through* sin," not "*because of* sin." Whatever the rest of Scripture says about death as the penalty for sinning, here the entry of sin and death to take dominion exhibits the apocalyptic language of personified forces, not of penalty or of imputation, so that the sinning and dying of people between Adam and Moses were the effects of sin and death as forces (cf. Gal 2:17, where sin functions as someone to whom service is rendered; 3:22, where sin functions as a prison warden; and Rom 1:17, where Paul launches his discussion of justification with the language of apocalyptic: "for in it ['the gospel'] the righteousness of God is being revealed [ἀποκαλύπτεται]"). This language, plus that of grace as reigning, shows that Paul does *not* delay such personifications till ch. 6, where they are generally recognized. In fact, sin appeared as a personified force in Romans as early as 3:9, where the statement that "all are under sin" means in context that sin dominates all people in that God has given them over to it.[31] With the giving of the law, of course, the legal framework of transgression and penalty comes in alongside the framework of personified forces, so that Paul's question in 6:1 whether we should sin in order that grace may abound implies a false legalistic argument just as by common consent the further part of ch. 6, particularly vv. 12–23, and ch. 7, particularly vv. 7–25, reprise the language of personified forces.[32]

Those who advocate an imputation of Christ's righteousness usually regard the crucifixion as "the *climax* of his atoning sufferings" and "the *climax* of a perfect life of righteousness."[33] Thus the righteousness of Christ includes his

---

[31] See esp. Rom 1:24, 26, 28; against Piper, *Counted Righteous in Christ*, 100–101 n. 44. D. J. Moo details the active role of sin as a dominating force in Romans 5–7: sin not only enters the world (5:12) but also reigns (5:21; cf. 6:13–14), gains obedience (6:16–17), pays wages (6:23), seizes opportunity (7:8, 11), and deceives and kills (7:11, 13; *The Epistle to the Romans* [NICNT; Grand Rapids: Eerdmans, 1996], 319). See also C. Forbes, "Paul's Principalities and Powers: Demythologizing Apocalyptic?" *JSNT* 82 (2001): 61–88, esp. 72–74, with further bibliography; J. L. Martyn, *Galatians* (AB 33A; New York: Doubleday, 1997), 272–73, 308–9, 317, 388–89, 536–37, for similar personifications in Galatians; and Rev 20:14 for an example of personifications in apocalyptic ("Death and Hades were cast into the lake of fire").

[32] On the tension in one and the same document between sin as a personified force and sin as a responsible act of the human will, see J. K. Riches, "Conflicting Mythologies: Mythical Narration in the Gospel of Mark," *JSNT* 84 (2001): 29–50.

[33] Piper, *Counted Righteous in Christ*, 41–42 (italics added). Much fuller is A. Ritschl, *A Critical History of the Christian Doctrine of Justification and Reconciliation* (Edinburgh: Edmonston and Douglas, 1872), 213–14, 248–67 et passim, though he surveys the doctrine from a systematic theological rather than biblical exegetical standpoint.

law-abiding obedience prior to and in addition to his obedient submission to crucifixion.[34] But a number of data show not only that Christ's "act of righteousness" (v. 18) equates with his "obedience" (v. 19) but also that the act of righteousness consisted in obeying God the Father to the extent of dying on a cross and did not include the totality of Christ's earthly life:

– The parallel with Phil 2:8, where the obedience of Christ is tied specifically to his death on a cross, not to his preceding life on earth or even to his incarnation[35]

– The references earlier in Romans 5 to Christ's dying for the ungodly, dying for us while we were still sinners, shedding his blood for our justification, and reconciling us to God through his death (vv. 6–11)

– The absence of any contextual indication that Christ's obedience included a previous life of obedience to the law

– The failure of Paul, despite his extensive discussions of the law and writing that Christ was born "under the law" (Gal 4:4), ever to make a point of Christ's keeping the law perfectly or on our behalf (not even his sinlessness in 2 Cor 5:21 being put in relation to law-keeping)

– The extremely scant attention that Paul pays elsewhere to Christ's previous life in any respect

– The extremely heavy emphasis that Paul does lay elsewhere on the death of Christ

---

[34] The technical terms are "active obedience" and "passive obedience" respectively. But these are not meant to be distinguished chronologically, for the active obedience is thought to run through the crucifixion and the passive obedience to start at the incarnation. A systematic theological objection is lodged that to exclude an imputation of Christ's active obedience leaves the door open for the introduction of believers' own obedience as the only ground for hope after obtaining the remission of past sins (Buchanan, *The Doctrine of Justification*, 189, in reference to the teaching of Piscator). But whether or not the active obedience of Christ is imputed, why should his death suffice only for past sins, those committed prior to conversion?

[35] In Phil 2:5b–11 Christ's emptying himself by taking the form of a slave implies obedience but refers solely to his death in that "he emptied himself" is a Greek way of echoing what Isa 53:12 says about the suffering Servant – i.e., Slave – of the LORD: "he poured out his soul unto death." "He emptied" echoes "he poured out." "Himself" echoes "his soul," which is the Semitic equivalent of a reflexive pronoun (cf. 1 Tim 2:6 with Isa 53:10; Mark 10:45 par. Matt 20:28). Paul delays Isaiah's "unto death" for incorporation in the statement, "he humbled himself by becoming obedient unto death, even the death of a cross," crucifixion being called in the Roman world "a slave's death." So the incarnation is expressed not in the self-emptying phrase but in the phrases "having come to be in the likeness of human beings" and "having been found in fashion as a human being"; and these phrases simply represent the precondition of obedience unto death (cf. Heb 2:10, 14–18, esp. v. 14: "Therefore since the children have shared in blood and flesh, in the same way he himself also partook of the same that through death he might render impotent him who had the power of death, i.e., the devil"; see pp. 279–91 in the present volume and Wesley's letter to Hervey, dated 15 October 1756, as quoted in Hervey, *Aspasio Vindicated*, xiv–xv).

– The present antithetical parallel with Adam's transgression, which hardly refers to a whole life of sinning but refers instead to the original sin in Eden, the only sin of Adam mentioned in Scripture
– The probable singularizing of both Adam's transgression and Christ's act of righteousness by the modifier "one"

This last datum requires elaboration because a number of commentators translate the relevant phrases in v. 18 "through one's [Adam's] transgression" and "through one's [Christ's] act of righteousness" rather than "through one transgression" and "through one act of righteousness." In favor of "one's" it is argued that the whole passage deals with a comparison between the two individuals Adam and Christ, that "one" refers to Adam and Christ a number of times in vv. 12, 15–17, 19, and that in v. 18 "one's" would strengthen the contrast with "all people" (twice) in the same verse and in v. 12, and with "the many" in vv. 15 (twice), 19 (twice). In v. 18, on the other hand, "one" lacks the definite article that it has when referring to Adam and Christ in vv. 15, 17, 19 and does not modify "man" as it does in vv. 12, 15, 19. Moreover, when in vv. 15, 17, 19 "one" refers to Adam in connection with his "transgression" or "disobedience" and to Christ in connection with his "grace" or "obedience," "one" always has the definite article.[36] The absence of definite articles with "one" in v. 18 therefore favors that "one" modifies "transgression" and "act of righteousness," and this construal makes for an expansion of "one transgression" to the "many transgressions" in v. 16 and to the multiplication of sin in v. 20, and for a contrastive expansion of "one act of righteousness" to "abundance" of grace in v. 15 and to the "superabundance" of grace in v. 20. All in all, then, this datum and the other data belie the notion that God imputes to believers a righteousness of Christ that he built up over a lifetime of obedience to God and the law; and it would be odd for the righteousness that believers do gain to be described as "*of*" God if it consists of Christ's obedience *to* God.

According to a counter argument Paul makes no distinction between Christ's prior life of obedience and his propitiatory death. But Paul's putting Christ's act of righteousness in parallel with Adam's single act of disobedience and probably limiting the act of obedience to "one" make precisely that distinction. It is then argued that there were "many acts of obedience in Jesus' final days and hours," such as "the obedience of Gethsemane, or the obedience when the mob took him away, or the obedience when he was interrogated, [and so forth]."[37] But we are dealing with Paul, not with the Gospels; and he writes about an or one act of obedience, not about many acts of obedience during the passion,

---

[36] "One" lacks the definite article in v. 12 because there is no previous reference to the man Adam. Verse 16 is only a partial exception, if an exception at all, because as a participle "having sinned" modifies "one" directly rather than governing a genitive, as in "the transgression *of* the one," "the grace *of* the one man," and so on.

[37] Piper, *Counted Righteous in Christ*, 112.

much less about prior acts of obedience. Moreover, "a unified act involving many acts of obedience"[38] would make a poor parallel with Adam's initial, solitary act of disobedience.[39]

To be sure, δικαίωμα, translated "act of righteousness" in 5:18 and "righteous requirement" in 8:4 (also in 1:32), may be collective in 8:4 for all the requirements of the law. But that collective meaning is unsure, even unlikely, for Paul writes in Gal 5:14 that "the whole law is fulfilled in *one* command, 'You shall love your neighbor as yourself.'"[40] Even if δικαίωμα be collective in Rom 8:4, there it is not modified by "one" as it probably is in 5:18; and in 5:18 the word lacks the qualifying phrase "of the law" that it has in 8:4, and refers in 5:18 to an act, not to a set of requirements.

To be sure again, whereas Adam's act of disobedience brought the entrance of sin and death, an act of disobedience by Jesus would have disqualified him from dying for our sins. But this fact does not imply that his whole life of obedience is imputed to believers. It implies only that his obedience prior to crucifixion – what Matt 3:15 calls the "fulfilling of all righteousness" – qualified him to die for our sins.[41] It is Christ's act of righteousness, then, the obedient dying

---

[38] Piper, *Counted Righteous in Christ*, 112.

[39] One and the same person may commit many acts, including acts of different and even diametrically opposed sorts; so the singularity of the person, whether Adam or Christ, does not explain the singularity of each one's act (against Murray, *Romans*, 1:201–2). The statement in 2 Cor 8:9 that though Christ was rich he became poor is sometimes used to encompass the whole of his life in one act of obedience. But his becoming poor is put in terms of "grace," not of obedience; and it is an open question whether the becoming poor has to do with his incarnation, with his itinerant ministry, or alone with his crucifixion.

[40] See the full discussion by H. W. M. van de Sandt, "Research into Rom. 8,4a: The Legal Claim of the Law," *Bijdr* 37 (1976): 252–69, and cf. Rom 13:8–10. The love-commandment does not include all the commandments in the law, as though it were collective for them. Rather, it provides their point of convergence (ἀνακεφαλαιοῦται), so that fulfilling it results in fulfilling them too (cf. Christ as the point of convergence for "all things in heaven and on earth" in Eph 1:10, where he is hardly collective for everything in the universe – Paul was no christopantheist).

[41] In public dialogue D. A. Carson argued that inasmuch as John's baptism had to do with repentance, the submission of Jesus to that baptism despite his sinlessness marked his fulfillment of all righteousness on our behalf (Matt 3:15). But "on our behalf" does not tally with Matthew's emphasis on Jesus' exemplary righteousness. Matthew is the only evangelist to say that Jesus went to John "for the purpose of being baptized by him" (3:13), so that Jesus sets the example to be followed in the Great Commission (28:19–20, unique to Matthew in respect to baptism). Only Matthew's Jesus says, "Take my yoke upon you and learn from me because I am meek and lowly in heart" (11:29). To make Jesus an example of obeying his own prohibition of oaths (5:33–37, again unique to Matthew among the Gospels, though see Jas 5:12) Matthew alone has Caiaphas put Jesus under oath ("I adjure you") and Jesus answer, "*You* said [it]" instead of "I am," to the high priest's question whether he (Jesus) is "the Christ, the Son of God" (26:63–64; contrast Mark 14:61–62; Luke 22:62–63). And so on. Therefore Jesus' fulfilling all righteousness in baptism at Matt 3:15 looks exemplary rather than vicarious. Matthew's transferring "for the remission of sins" from "the baptism of repentance" (Mark 1:4; Luke 3:3) to the Word of Institution over the cup (Matt 26:28) adds to this impression.

of a propitiatory death, that assuaged the wrath of God so as to make God's declaration of believing sinners to be righteous both right in the upholding of his
moral character and right in the exercise of his saving grace.[42] The resurrection
of Christ demonstrates God's acceptance of that death as the basis of this declaration (Rom 4:25). Thus the talk of a legal fiction, or of "justifiction" according to an unfortunate typographical error in *Right with God: Justification in the
Bible and the World*, 49, is off the mark.[43]

Earlier I noted that in Romans 4 Paul shifts to "the righteousness of faith" from
"the righteousness of God" in Romans 1–3. Do these two expressions refer to different kinds of righteousness? Yes, but they are intertwined because in 3:21–26
"the righteousness of God" comes "to all who exercise faith." His righteousness,
which is never said to be counted or imputed (passive voice), consists in his
counting (active voice) of our faith as righteousness while at the same time maintaining his moral character. The righteousness of faith is the moral accomplishment that God counts faith to be even though it is not intrinsically such an accomplishment.[44] The active element in God's righteousness should not surprise
us, for overwhelming evidence exists that in Paul and his Jewish heritage the
righteousness of God is not a merely static moral attribute. Rather, his righteousness takes the form of justificatory action. Sometimes this action consists in meting out justice by way of punishment. Usually it consists in meting out justice by

---

[42] "There can be no justification of the sinner which is not simultaneously a justification of
God in his wrath against the sinner" (Seifrid, *Christ, Our Righteousness*, 171.)

[43] Ed. D. A. Carson; Grand Rapids: Baker, 1992. The death of Christ as an expiation and propitiation in Rom 3:25 implies that sin requires the penalty of death. But this implication does not
negate Paul's switching in Rom 5:12–21; 6:12–23 to sin and death as dominating forces. It is
popular nowadays to interpret biblical righteousness not as behavior according to a moral norm
but as behavior according to the terms of a covenant. This view is correct in what it affirms but
wrong in what it denies; for at least where God is concerned the terms of a covenant are rooted in
his moral character (N.B.: not in a moral norm external to him). Take, e.g., Lev 11:45; 19:2;
20:26: "You shall be holy, for I am holy" (G. Schrenk, "δίκη, δίκαιος, κτλ," *TDNT* 2:195; Moo,
Romans, 83–84). If righteousness were covenantal apart from God's moral character no need
would arise for Christ to be made sin for us, to become a curse for us, to shed his blood as an expiation of our sin and a propitiation of God's wrath against our unrighteousness – a wrath that
derives from the righteousness of God as a moral attribute. What saves justification from the
realm of fiction is Christ's propitiation, not an amorally covenantal character of righteousness.
Nor does a covenantal setting dispossess justification of its legal, juridical connotation; for in the
biblical world covenants were legally binding treaties. See further M. A. Seifrid, "Righteousness
Language in the Hebrew Scriptures and Early Judaism," in *The Complexities of Second Temple
Judaism* (vol. 1 of *Justification and Variegated Nomism*; ed. D. A. Carson, P. T. O'Brien, and
M. A. Seifrid; Grand Rapids: Baker, 2001), 416–42; Moo, *Romans*, 241–42.

[44] According to Seifrid God's word of promise effected Abraham's faith (Rom 4:16–22), so
that faith was counted as righteousness because it really was righteousness, a work of God
(*Christ, Our Righteousness*, 136–37). But the passage seems to emphasize Abraham's not succumbing to doubt rather than the faith-producing effectiveness of God's promissory word. Even
on Seifrid's reading, why does Paul take care at the beginning of Romans 4 to oppose faith and
works instead of saying from the start that faith is God's work and omitting the opposition between faith and works, especially since the law was not yet given in Abraham's time?

way of salvation, though the salvation of some may entail the punishment of others – and does entail Christ's suffering punishment for our sins that we might be saved. Often God's righteousness and salvation appear in juxtaposition:

- Ps 24:6: "He will receive ... **righteousness** from the God of his **salvation**."
- Ps 51:14: "Deliver me from bloodguiltiness, O God, the God of my **salvation**; [then] my tongue will joyfully sing of your **righteousness**."
- Ps 71:15–16: "My mouth will tell of your **righteousness**, of your **salvation** all day long. I will come with the mighty deeds of the Lord GOD; I will make mention of your **righteousness**, yours alone."
- Ps 98:1–3: "His right hand and his holy arm have accomplished **salvation** for him. The LORD has made known his **salvation**; he has revealed his **righteousness** in the sight of the nations.... All the ends of the earth have seen the **salvation** of our God."
- Isa 45:8: "Let the clouds pour down **righteousness**; let the earth open up and **salvation** bear fruit, and **righteousness** spring up with it."
- Isa 45:21–25: "And there is no other God besides me, a **righteous** God and a **Savior**.... Turn to me and be **saved**.... The word has gone forth from my mouth in **righteousness**.... Only in the LORD are **righteousness** and strength.... In the LORD all the offspring of Israel will be **declared righteous**."
- Isa 46:13: "I bring near my **righteousness**, it is not far off. And my **salvation** will not delay, and I will grant **salvation** in Zion."
- Isa 51:5–6, 8: "My **righteousness** is near; my **salvation** has gone forth.... But my **salvation** will be forever, and my **righteousness** will not be broken.... But my **righteousness** will be forever, and my **salvation** to all generations."
- Isa 56:1: "For my **salvation** is about to come, and my **righteousness** to be revealed."
- Isa 59:17: "He [the LORD] put on **righteousness** like a breastplate and a helmet of **salvation** on his head."
- Isa 61:10: "He has clothed me with garments of **salvation**; he has wrapped me with a robe of **righteousness**."
- Isa 62:1: "For Jerusalem's sake I will not keep quiet, until her **righteousness** goes forth like brightness, and her **salvation** like a torch that is burning."
- Isa 63:1: "Who is this ... marching in the greatness of his strength? It is I who speak in **righteousness**, mighty to **save**."
- Jer 23:5–6: "'Behold, the days are coming,' declares the LORD, 'when I will raise up for David a **righteous** branch; and he will ... do justice and **righteousness** in the land. In his days Judah will be **saved**.... And this is his name by which he will be called: "The LORD [is] our **righteousness**."'"
- *4 Ezra* 8:36, 39–40: "'For in this, O Lord, your **righteousness** and goodness will be declared, when you are merciful to those who have no store of good works.' ... He answered me and said, '... I will rejoice over the creation of the righteous ... and their **salvation**.'"

- CD 20:20: "**Salvation** and **righteousness** will be revealed to those who fear God."
- 1QS 11:11–15: "As for me, if I stumble, God's mercies will always be my **salvation**; and if I fall in the sin of the flesh, in the **righteousness** of God, which endures eternally, will my judgment be.... he judges me in the **righteousness** of his truth, and in his great goodness he always atones for all my sins; in his **righteousness** he will cleanse me from the uncleanness of human being and from the sin of the sons of Adam, in order [that I might] praise God for his **righteousness**."
- 1QM 18:7 8: "Many times you have opened for us the gates of salvations [pl.].... You, O God of **righteousness**, have acted for the sake of your name."
- *1 En.* 99:10: "They will walk in the path of his [the Most High's] **righteousness** ... and they will be **saved**.

See also Pss 31:1; 35:23–24; 71:2; 89:17; 96:13; 98:9; 111:3; 143:11; Isa 1:27; 51:6, 8; 53:11; 1QS 11:2–3(?); 1QH^a 12:37.[45]

So oriented is this usage to action that "righteousness" occurs in the plural for righteous acts:

- Judg 5:11: "There they will recount the **righteousnesses** [i.e., righteous acts] of the LORD, the **righteousnesses** for his warriors in Israel."
- 1 Sam 12:7: "concerning all the **righteousnesses** of the LORD that he did for you and your fathers."
- Ps 103:6: "The LORD performs **righteousnesses** and judgments for all who are oppressed."
- Dan 9:16, 18: "O Lord, in accordance with all your **righteousnesses**, let now your anger and your wrath turn away.... For we are not presenting our supplications before you on account of our **righteousnesses**, but on account of your great compassion."
- Mic 6:5: "to know the **righteousnesses** of the LORD [referring to his saving Israel from King Balak of Moab]."[46]

Clearly Paul too uses "righteousness" in this salvifically active way, as to be expected from his writing that God's righteousness is "being witnessed by the Law and the Prophets" (Rom 3:21) and as shown almost immediately in Romans by his juxtaposing "salvation" with "the righteousness of God": "For I am not ashamed of the gospel, for it is God's power resulting in **salvation** to everyone who believes.... For in it the **righteousness** of God is being revealed from

---

[45] Seifrid figures that in the OT divine righteousness appears as salvific four times more often than it appears as punitive, and he mounts an impressive argument against a reference to divine righteousness in 1QS 11:2–3 ("Righteousness Language," 415–16, 429–30, 435–38).

[46] For a general survey of righteousness as an action, human as well as divine, behavioral as well as declarative, see Ziesler, *The Meaning of Righteousness in Paul*, 22–34. Paul portrays righteousness as so active that it wields weapons and speaks in Rom 6:13; 10:6–10; 2 Cor 6:7.

faith to faith, as it is written, 'But the righteous person by faith will live'"
(Rom 1:16–17; note the echo of Ps 98:1–3, quoted above, in the universal revelation of God's righteousness).[47] And Rom 3:26 defines the righteousness of
God ("his righteousness") in terms of an action as well as an attribute: "for the
demonstration of his righteousness at the present time in order that he might be
righteous [an attribute; cf. 3:5] and declaring righteous [an action] the person of
faith in Jesus." The righteousness is God's, not Christ's, because God, not
Christ, is the one who according to the next chapter counts faith as righteousness. As already noted, Christ enters the picture as the object of faith, whose
obediently righteous act of expiation and propitiation made it right for God to
count faith as righteousness. In that God set forth Christ as an expiatory, propitiatory sacrifice the righteousness of God is a punitive action. But in that as a
result he counts faith as righteousness his righteousness is a salvific action. If
we correlate Jewish usage starting in the OT with its distinctively Pauline, christologically based elaboration in Romans 1–4 we have excellent reason to inter-
twine the righteousness of faith and the righteousness of God.[48]

Similarly in Rom 9:30–10:4 Paul says that "righteousness" derives "from
faith" and again calls it "the righteousness of God" in that according to his earlier explanation God is the one who counts faith as righteousness. Furthermore,
"Christ is the end of the law for righteousness to everyone who believes" in that
he is the object of their believing. Piper gives what he calls "the most literal,
straightforward translation of Romans 10:4" – i.e., "The goal (or end) of the law
is *Christ for righteousness* for everyone who believes" (italics original) – and
interprets the italicized phrase as meaning that Christ *is* their righteousness.[49]
But Paul's earlier explanation requires Christ to be the object of the faith that

---

[47] The fact that the gospel rather than the righteousness of God is his power resulting in salvation does not undermine the meaning of righteousness as salvific action. Nor is it absurd for
Paul to say that in the gospel God's salvifically active righteousness is being revealed (along
with his righteous character). For the gospel is powerful *as proclaimed* (1 Cor 1:18, 23–25),
and the proclamation of it is revealing God's salvifically active righteousness just as in the parallelistically constructed statement of Rom 1:18 the wrath of God is being revealed through his
action of giving sinners over to their own depravity (Rom 1:24, 26, 28; cf. the revelation of each
person's "work" [an action] in 1 Cor 3:13 and of "faith" [an action] in Gal 3:23; against Williams, "The 'Righteousness of God' in Romans," 259–62, though Williams admits that "God's
righteousness" at Rom 1:17 "would likely bring to mind ideas of deliverance or salvation" and
also recognizes that the gospel is powerful as proclaimed [255–57]).
[48] Carson's calling the righteousness of God "alien to Paul" because it is God's assumes, apparently, that θεοῦ is a genitive of possession or description, so that the righteousness is understood as moral character that replaces human sinfulness ("The Vindication of Imputation," 69).
But inasmuch as the righteousness of God regularly refers to his activity, most often his salvific
activity, the genitive is better understood as subjective. Then sinners who believe become the
forensic objects of God's salvific activity rather than forensic recipients of his moral character,
and the description "alien" becomes inappropriate in the sense intended.
[49] Piper, *Counted Righteous in Christ*, 87–89. For the present purpose it is unnecessary to decide whether "end" indicates a goal, a termination, or both.

God counts as righteousness rather than that Christ be the righteousness of believers. Besides, the word order in Piper's literal translation misleadingly makes "end" the subject of the sentence, makes "Christ" the predicate nominative, and ties "Christ" closely with "for righteousness." Apparently Paul's advancing the predicate nominative, "the end of the law," to the head of the sentence for emphasis has deceived Piper into thinking the phrase is the subject, whereas "Christ" is the subject, so that "for righteousness" relates to "the end of the law" (see the standard translations).[50] And even Piper's misleading translation leaves open the question, Christ for *whose* righteousness or for *what* righteousness? In view of Paul's earlier writing in Romans we should answer that he is referencing not the righteousness of Christ but either God's righteousness or the righteousness that faith is counted to be – probably the latter since Paul immediately goes on to mention "the righteousness of (ἐκ) faith" as opposed to "the righteousness of (ἐκ) the law" (Rom 10:5–6).

Since the righteousness of God stands opposite righteousness that derives "from the law" it is also "righteousness *from* God," i.e., from the God who counts faith rather than works of the law (see Phil 3:6–9 with Rom 4:1–6).[51] Similarly according to 1 Cor 1:30 Christ became "wisdom for us" who by faith are in him. Since this wisdom is made up of "both righteousness and sanctification and redemption," Christ became those too. But unlike the wisdom of the world this wisdom comes "from God," so that the righteousness which helps make it up also comes from God just as in Phil 3:9. Earlier in 1 Corinthians 1 Paul referenced "the word of the cross" and told his addressees, "God was pleased through the foolishness of the proclamation to save those who exercise faith.... But we proclaim Christ crucified .... Christ the power of God and the wisdom of God.... For look at your calling, brothers and sisters .... God has elected the foolish things of the world ... in order that no flesh should boast in God's presence" (vv. 18–29, excerpts).

So the crucified Christ became for us wisdom from God in that believing in Christ makes us the objects of God's electively, salvifically active wisdom. He became for us sanctification from God in that believing in Christ makes us the objects of God's electively, salvifically active sanctification. He became for us redemption from God in that believing in Christ makes us the objects of God's

---

[50] Cf. John 1:1c, where the Greek text puts the predicate nominative "God" first for emphasis in the statement that "the Word was God." See Williams, "The 'Righteousness of God' in Romans," 284. The two foregoing paragraphs oppose also Cranfield, *Romans*, 1:97–98; 2:515.

[51] For "righteousness from God" see also Ps 24:6; Isa 54:17; Bar 5:2, 9. The Greek genitive that underlies "the righteousness *of* God" may convey the meaning "from." In fact, the looseness of the relation between a Greek noun in the genitive (most often introduced by "of" in English translation) and the noun on which it depends allows a wide variety of meanings to be determined by context: possession, separation, origin, description, apposition, comparison, content, agency, etc.

electively, salvifically active redemption. Parallelistically, then, he became for us righteousness from God in that believing in Christ makes us the objects of God's electively, salvifically active righteousness.

And Paul's linking the cross with our exercise of faith meshes with the explanation in Romans 3–4 that the expiatory, propitiatory death of Christ enables God to count our faith as righteousness and to be righteous in doing so. The death is Christ's; but the righteousness is God's, comes from God, not from Christ, and does not consist in an imputed righteousness of Christ any more than God imputes to believers a wisdom of Christ, a sanctification of Christ, or a redemption of Christ. Nowhere, for example, does Paul say that Christ was redeemed, so that Christ's redemption could be counted as ours. Hence the righteousness from God that Christ became for us is God's elective, salvific action of counting our faith in Christ to be righteousness.

With a view toward making the righteousness Christ's in 1 Cor 1:30 Carson stressed in public dialogue the word "Christ."[52] But is Christ righteousness from God in respect to having his own righteous conduct counted as ours or in respect to him as the object of the faith that God in *his* righteousness counts as equivalent to righteousness? Stressing "Christ" does not answer this question, but the latter answer – Christ as the object of faith-counted-as-righteousness – has the advantage of Paul's other statements.

In 2 Cor 5:21 the making of him who did not know sin to be sin on our behalf refers again to the expiatory, propitiatory death of Christ, for which his sinlessness qualified him (cf. 1 Pet 3:18); and our becoming the righteousness of God in him refers to the attained purpose of that death, viz., God's counting as righteousness the faith that united us to the Christ who died for us.[53] We do not become the sinlessness of Christ, much less his righteousness, by having it imputed to us as a moral accomplishment on his part and our behalf. We become *God's* righteousness, but not God's righteousness as a moral quality. Just as in Gal 3:13 Christ "became" a curse in the sense that he became the object of God's curse (see Deut 21:23 for God as the curser in the passage Paul quotes), so also in 2 Cor 5:21 we "become" the righteousness of God in the sense that we become the objects of his salvifically active righteousness, of his declaring us righteous because we have believed in his Son, whose death as the sinless-one-made-sin expiated our sins and propitiated God's wrath against them (cf. Rom 10:3, which speaks of subjection to the righteousness of God and therefore implies being an object of its action; also Isa 53:11, which says that the Servant of the LORD "will justify the many, as he will bear their in-

---

[52] Cf. Carson, "The Vindication of Imputation," 76.

[53] Since elsewhere Paul uses the phrase "in Christ" predominantly for the location of believers 2 Cor 5:21 is best taken as indicating the location of believers where they become God's righteousness, not the location of that righteousness.

iquities," but says nothing about imputing to them his righteousness as a moral quality).[54]

If Paul had meant that the righteousness of Christ replaces our sins we would expect him to have said so. How easy it would have been for him to write in 2 Cor 5:21, "in order that we might become the righteousness *of Christ.*" But he did not. Or to write in Phil 3:8–9, "in order that I might gain Christ and be found in him, not having my righteousness [derived] from the law but [having] *his* righteousness [based] on faith." But Paul did not. Instead, he writes about the righteousness of or from God (eleven times), almost always in passages where God and Christ are distinguished from each other (nine times).[55] It is perfectly astounding that time after time after time those who advocate an imputation of Christ's righteousness – my former self included and, for that matter, those who advocate its infusion and others who advocate participation in it through union with Christ – quote Pauline passages that speak of God's righteousness only to substitute the righteousness of Christ in their expositions of those passages. This shift in gears seems to occur by automatic transmission.

The only NT passage, non-Pauline, that mentions the righteousness of Christ does not deal in imputation, infusion, or union with him but attributes our faith to his righteousness: "to those who have received a faith of equal value to ours through the righteousness of our God and Savior Jesus Christ" (2 Pet 1:1).[56] One could note Peter's linking the righteousness and deity of Christ and, moving over to Paul, argue that he presents the righteousness of God as worked out in the obedient life and death of his divine Son. To make this argument, in fact, appeal is regularly made to the unity of Father and Son in the Trinity, as though that unity demands that God's righteousness be Christ's too.[57]

I wonder why on this basis a righteousness of the Holy Spirit is not added to the mix and whether God the Father along with the Holy Spirit lived and died obediently in union with God the Son. Not everything said about one person of the Trinity applies to the other persons. The Father does not obey the Son, for

---

[54] In his interpretation of 2 Cor 5:21 Carson again neglects God's righteousness as salvific activity ("The Vindication of Imputation," 69–71).

[55] Rom 1:17; 3:5, 21, 22, 25, 26; 10:3 (twice); 1 Cor 1:30; 2 Cor 5:21; Phil 3:9. Only Rom 1:17 and 3:5 lack a nearby distinction between God and Christ, but neither do they associate God and Christ. To paper over the inconvenient fact that Paul never speaks of Christ's righteousness but does speak of the righteousness of God as distinct from Christ, Piper repeatedly refers to "divine righteousness," as though "divine" would include Christ as well as God the Father (*Counted Righteous in Christ*).

[56] This translation interprets the Greek preposition ἐν as instrumental: "through." Alternatively, the phrase locates our faith "in" Christ's righteousness. Tied as it is to the designation of him as "our God and Savior," his righteousness carries the usual meaning of divine salvific action (see above).

[57] Cf. Piper, *Counted Righteous in Christ*, 181 n. 26: "the absence of doctrinal explicitness and systematization in Paul may be no more problematic for the doctrine of the imputation of Christ's righteousness than it is for the doctrine of the Trinity."

example, as the Son is said to obey the Father.[58] Moreover, there are explicit scriptural affirmations of the deity, differentiation, and unity of God the Father, Son, and Holy Spirit on which the development of trinitarian doctrine rests but no similar affirmations on which the doctrine of an imputation of Christ's righteousness can validly be developed. And the trinitarian appeal fails to account for this absence despite repeated mentions of God's righteousness in passages that distinguish God and Christ from each other. So it would be specious to say that the denial of an imputed righteousness of Christ robs him of glory that belongs to him.[59] We are not dealing with a question of Christ's glory, but with the questions of what the Bible does and does not teach and of whether the doctrine of an imputation of Christ's righteousness represents a valid development of biblical teaching. *Of course* theologians are not limited to repeating what the Bible says, but what they develop in and for their own circumstances should at least arise out of what the Bible says. So long as the Bible does not provide such statements, and in the present case says much that points in a contrary direction, an appeal to the difference between an exegetical field of discourse and a systematic theological field of discourse does no good for the putative doctrine.[60]

In summary, where can sinners find righteousness? In Christ. Whose righteousness can they find there? God's. What does it consist in? God's counting faith as righteousness. How does he do so without contravening his wrath against our unrighteousness? By setting forth Christ as an expiatory, propitiatory sacrifice.[61]

Finally, what practical difference does it make whether we affirm or deny an imputation of Christ's righteousness? Well, M. A. Seifrid observes that "in reducing 'justification' to a present possession of 'Christ's imputed righteousness', Protestant divines inadvertently bruised the nerve which runs between justification and obedience."[62] I therefore suggest that *Paul does not match the*

---

[58] Matt 26:39, 42, 44; Mark 14:36, 39; Luke 22:42; John 5:30; 6:38; 10:18; 12:49–50; 17:4; Heb 5:8.

[59] Contrast Piper, *Counted Righteous in Christ*, 51.

[60] Against Carson, "The Vindication of Imputation," 46–78. Upon systematizing Pauline statements about imputation by God with the Son's doing everything the Father does according to John 5:16–30, Carson goes so far as to deduce that Christ too imputes righteousness – presumably his own (Christ's) – to believers (ibid., 69–71). Such systematization seems to me a violation of scriptural contexts, a violation that if practiced consistently would produce intractable problems in that apart from contextual differences many scriptural theologoumena would flatly contradict each other.

[61] Cf. the extrabiblical use of προτίθημι, "set forth," used in Rom 3:25, and its nominal cognate πρόθεσις for the laying out of a dead body. The exclusion of "propitiatory" and "propitiation" in favor of "expiatory" and "expiation" alone would affect the basic arguments of this essay very little.

[62] Seifrid, *Christ, Our Righteousness*, 175; cf. J. Wesley's early (but later abandoned) rejection of an imputation of Christ's active obedience: "It is not scriptural; it is not necessary.... But it has done immediate hurt. I have abundant proof, that the frequent use of this phrase ['the

imputation of our sins to Christ with an imputation of Christ's righteousness to us believers because he (Paul) wants to emphasize the obedient life of righteousness that we are supposed to live – and indeed will live if we are true believers – apart from the OT law, under which Christ was born, and to emphasize the judgment of our works at the end. This suggestion does not imply that an imputed righteousness of Christ would contradict the need of believers to live a life of righteousness apart from the OT law and in view of the Last Judgment. But it is to say that the absence from Paul of an imputed righteousness of Christ, especially one that includes a lifetime of obedience to the law, leaves more theological and rhetorical space for emphasizing that need and therefore helps Paul resist antinomianism with the doctrines of union with Christ in death to sin and coming alive to righteousness (i.e., behavorial righteousness) and of the gift of the Holy Spirit as a sanctifying influence (see, e.g., Rom 6:1–7:6; 1 Cor 6:9–11, 17–20; Gal 5:13–26). This emphasis may go a long way toward evacuating the longstanding complaint that despite protestations to the contrary the classic Protestant doctrine of double imputation tends to shortchange sanctification[63] and thus may also go a long way toward satisfying legitimate concerns not only of Roman Catholics but also of pietists in the Lutheran tradition, in the Anabaptist and Baptist traditions, in the Keswick movement, in the Holiness movement, and in Pentecostalism. That most of these pietists hold to double imputation means only that they should consider dropping the doctrine of an imputation of Christ's righteousness, a doctrine which at least at the subconscious level may prompt them – wrongly, in my view – to portray sanctification, perfect love, life on the highest plain,[64] or baptism in the Holy Spirit as a second

---

imputed righteousness of Christ'], instead of 'furthering men's progress in vital holiness,' has made them satisfied without any holiness at all; yea, and encouraged them to work all uncleanness with greediness" (letter to Hervey as quoted in Hervey, *Aspasio Vindicated*, vii; cf. p. ix, "But the *nice, metaphysical* doctrine of *imputed righteousness*, leads not to repentance, but to licentiousness" [italics original], and p. xxiv, "We swarm with Antinomians on every side. Why are you at such pains to increase their number?"). Hervey's response that God's goodness prompts thankful obedience (pp. 70, 79, 245–46, and "Assertion IX" on p. 407) contains an important point but neglects the equally important point that Paul threatens professing Christians with damnation if they do "the works of the flesh" (Gal 5:19–21; for Wesley's change of mind, see "The Lord Our Righteousness" [a sermon preached 24 November 1765], in *The Works of John Wesley*, vol. 1: *Sermons*, I, 1–33 [ed. A. C. Outler; Nashville: Abingdon, 1984], 447–65). Seifrid believes in an imputation of Christ's righteousness but wants to balance its present imputation with final justification at the Last Judgment.

[63] I use "sanctification" here in the popular sense of godly living. The biblical usage is richer, of course. See Ziesler, *The Meaning of Righteousness in Paul*, 5–7, for a survey of different ways in which Protestants have dealt with the criticism that "there is no road from it [forensic justification] to ethics" and A. Schweitzer, *The Mysticism of Paul the Apostle* (New York: Seabury, 1968), 225, for the most famous statement of this criticism.

[64] An allusion to R. Paxson's once popular book, *Life on the Highest Plain* (Chicago: Moody Press, 1928); cf. Dr. and Mrs. Howard Taylor, *Hudson Taylor's Spiritual Secret* (London: China Inland Mission, 1935). For details on the theology of a second blessing see J. D. G. Dunn, *Pneu-*

blessing normally delayed till after conversion inasmuch as Christ's righteousness is supposedly imputed at conversion (cf. the concerns of those who emphasize the lordship of Christ as part of salvation from its very start[65]). Besides, though an imputation of Christ's righteousness made entry into the Protestant doctrine of justification at an early date, the earlier – and therefore most traditional – version of that Protestant doctrine did not include such an imputation.[66]

---

matology (vol. 2 of *The Christ and the Spirit*; Grand Rapids: Eerdmans, 1998), 81–85, 222–42, with criticism and bibliography.

[65] See, e.g., J. F. MacArthur Jr., *The Gospel according to Jesus* (Grand Rapids: Zondervan, 1988). In public dialogue B. McCormack claimed that to reject an imputation of Christ's righteousness leaves no basis for distinguishing sanctification from justification and therefore leads to an understanding of justification as transformative rather than forensic, as infusive rather than declarative. But in the absence of an imputation of Christ's righteousness why should not sanctification be ascribed to a distinct though not delayed work of the Holy Spirit instead of being drawn under the umbrella of justification in terms of infusion?

[66] See M. A. Seifrid, "Luther, Melanchthon and Paul on the Question of Imputation," in *Justification: What's at Stake in the Current Debates* (ed. M. Husbands and D. J. Treier; Downers Grove, Ill.: InterVarsity/Leicester, UK: Apollos, 2004), 143–45, 149, with documentation.

13. The Moral Frustration of Paul before His Conversion: Sexual Lusts in Romans 7:7–25

Despite announcements that W. G. Kümmel cut down once and for all the interpretation of Rom 7:7–25, or at least 7:14–25, as both paradigmatically autobiographical of Paul and psychologically descriptive of his Christian experience,[1] that interpretation has enjoyed something of a comeback.[2] I will urge with Kümmel's critics that Paul describes an experience he himself had, but against them that he had this experience before converting to Christianity.

Arguments for understanding Paul as describing his *Christian* experience of moral frustration often begin with an appeal to the present tense in 7:14–25. This appeal depends on recognizing the *pre*-Christian orientation of 7:7–13. Otherwise the past tenses in 7:7–13 become just as problematic for a Christian orientation as the present tense in 7:14–25 purportedly is for a pre-Christian orientation.

It is argued that the present tense throughout 7:14–25 "is here sustained too consistently and for too long and contrasts too strongly with the past tenses characteristic of vv. 7–13 to be at all plausibly explained as an example of the present used for the sake of vividness in describing past events which are vividly re-

---

[1] W. G. Kümmel, *Römer 7 und die Bekehrung des Paulus* (Leipzig: J. G. Hinrichs, 1929), reprinted in *Römer 7 und das Bild des Menschen im Neuen Testament* (TB 53; Munich: Chr. Kaiser, 1974). Typical of the announcements that Kümmel settled the matter are those of R. Schnackenburg ("Römer 7 im Zusammenhang des Römerbriefes," in *Jesus und Paulus* [2d ed.; ed. E. E. Ellis and E. Grässer; Göttingen: Vandenhoeck & Ruprecht, 1978], 293) and G. Schunack (*Das hermeneutische Problem des Todes* [HUT 7; Tübingen: Mohr, 1967], 108–9).

[2] Especially noteworthy is the support given to one or both sides of the interpretation by A. Nygren, *Commentary on Romans* (Philadelphia: Muhlenberg, 1949), 277–303; K. Stalder, *Das Werk des Geistes in der Heiligung bei Paulus* (Zurich: EVZ-Verlag, 1962), 295–307; C. E. B. Cranfield, *A Critical and Exegetical Commentary on the Epistle to the Romans* (ICC; Edinburgh: T. & T. Clark, 1975), 1:340–70; J. D. G. Dunn, "Rom. 7,14–25 in the Theology of Paul," *TZ* 5 (1975): 257–73; idem, *Jesus and the Spirit* (Philadelphia: Westminster, 1975), 313–16; idem, *Romans 1–8* (WBC 38A; Dallas: Word, 1988), 374–412; A. F. Segal, *Paul the Convert* (New Haven, Conn.: Yale University Press, 1990), 224ff.; D. B. Garlington, "Romans 7:14–25 and the Creation Theology of Paul," *TJ* ns 11 (1990): 197–235; L. Thurén, *Derhetorizing Paul* (WUNT 124; Tübingen: Mohr Siebeck, 2000), 122–30; idem, "Romans 7 Derhetorized," in *Rhetorical Criticism and the Bible* (ed. S. E. Porter and D. L. Stamps; JSNTSup 195; Sheffield: Sheffield Academic Press, 2002), 420–40.

membered."[3] But the argument does not hold up. Not only does recent research on Greek tenses as more aspectual than temporal undercut it,[4] but also Paul uses the present tense in Phil 3:3–6 to describe his Judaistic past. This use has been overlooked because it occurs in ellipses. It is there, nonetheless: "For we are the circumcision, who worship by God's Spirit and boast in Christ Jesus and do not put confidence in flesh, even though I myself [am] having confidence even in flesh. If anyone else thinks it good to put confidence in flesh, I more [think it good to put confidence in the flesh]: with respect to circumcision, [I am] an eight-dayer; [I am] from the stock of Israel; [I am] of the tribe of Benjamin; [I am] a Hebrew of Hebrews; as to the law, [I am] a Pharisee; as to zeal, [I am] one who is persecuting the church; as to the righteousness in the law, [I am] one who has become blameless." The expressed present in vv. 3–4 establishes the tense that needs supplying in the list of vv. 4–6. That we instinctively resist supplying the present in the last three items only shows how vivid was Paul's recollection of his Judaistic past and therefore how easily the present tense in Rom 7:14–25 may be taken as a similarly vivid recollection. In both passages Paul sustains the present tense at some length. In both he juxtaposes it with past tenses referring to his pre-Christian days (in Romans 7 past tenses precede in vv. 7–13; in Philippians 3 the imperfect follows in v. 7).[5] In both the present tense concerning Paul is triggered by a preceding present tense concerning another subject ("the law is Spiritual" [Rom 7:14a]; "If anyone else thinks it good" [Phil. 3:4b]). And in both, Paul uses the present tense in conjunction with ἐγώ, "I."

The autobiographical character of the "I" in Phil 3:4–6 brooks no questioning. The parallels between that passage and Rom 7:14–25 therefore create a presumption that the "I" in Rom 7:14–25 (and by association in 7:7–13) is also autobiographical. That Paul *might* have used a merely fictive "I" Kümmel established. But considerable doubt greets the claim that Paul *did* use such an "I." Perhaps the best and most extensive critique is that of G. Theissen, who notes the failure of Kümmel's analogies to the "I"-statements of Romans 7 to occur, as they should for a Pauline fictive "I," in unconditional declarative sentences as opposed to questions and conditional sentences or statements. The details of

---

[3] Cranfield, *Romans*, 1:344–45. Dunn's arguing that ᾔδειν in v. 7 probably implies an experience of lust that has continued into the present ("Rom. 7,14–25," 261) flounders in its failure to maintain the difference between vv. 7–13 and 14–25 that would be indispensable to an argument from the present tense and in its requiring the imperfect force of the pluperfect ᾔδειν to carry the action into the present.

[4] See, e.g., S. E. Porter, *Verbal Aspect in the Greek of the New Testament with Reference to Tense and Mood* (New York: P. Lang, 1989). Because definitions of the verbal aspects contain a measure of inherently temporal elements, however, one hesitates to take the tenses as purely aspectual.

[5] Garlington seems to think that the recapitulative imperfect in Phil 3:7 cancels out Paul's preceding use of the present tense for his Judaistic past ("Romans 7:14–15," 212–13 n. 69). On the contrary, the recapitulative imperfect confirms the use of the present tense for the past.

Theissen's critique need no rehearsal here.[6] Representative is N. A. Dahl's earlier statement that "the element of personal confession in vv. 24–25a (cf. 14b–15, 18b–19) makes it difficult [to] acquiesce with the interpretation of the 'I'-style as being simply a rhetorical device."[7] The poignant anguish and pathetic frustration voiced by the "I" demand that Paul wrote out of his own experience.[8] To reverse a famous comment by T. W. Manson, we may call it the biography of Everyman if we like, but here Everyman's biography is the autobiography of Paul.[9] Surely Paul puts forward his experience as typical – otherwise it would fail to carry the argument (cf. "we" and "our" in vv. 5–7a) – but it remains *his*. What could be plainer than the αὐτὸς ἐγώ of doubly emphatic self reference in v. 25? Nobody doubts the self-references of αὐτὸς ἐγώ later in this epistle at 9:3–4a, "For I could pray that *I myself* were accursed [so as to be separated] from Christ for the sake of my brothers and sisters, my relatives according to flesh, who are Israelites," and 15:14, "And I am persuaded, my brothers and sisters – even *I myself* [am persuaded] concerning you" – nor in 2 Cor 10:1, "But *I myself*, Paul, urge you," or 2 Cor 12:13, "except that *I myself* did not burden you." That is, every other Pauline instance of αὐτὸς ἐγώ is indubitably autobiographical, as are also the instances of αὐτός with only a first person singular verb in 1 Cor 9:20, 27; Phil 2:24, so that we must reject S. K. Stower's claim that Romans carries no hint of autobiography.[10] Combined with the pathos of the preceding outcry in 7:24, "Wretched man [that] I [am]! Who will deliver me from the body of this death?" a fictive "I myself" in 7:25 would be incredibly theatrical.[11] Even a vicarious ex-

---

[6] See G. Theissen, *Psychological Aspects of Pauline Theology* (Philadelphia: Fortress, 1987), 191–201; also D. J. Moo, *The Epistle to the Romans* (NICNT; Grand Rapids: Eerdmans, 1996), 427–28 n. 12; idem, "Israel and Paul in Romans 7.7–12," *NTS* 32 (1986): 128–29.

[7] N. A. Dahl, "The Pauline Letters: Proposal for a Study Project of an SBL Seminar on Paul" (unpublished paper), 17. Similar opinions may be found in C. L. Mitton, "Romans vii Reconsidered," *ExpTim* 65 (1953–54): 78; M. Goguel, *The Birth of Christianity* (New York: Macmillan, 1954), 213–14; S. Sandmel, *The Genius of Paul* (New York: Farrar, Straus, and Cudahy, 1958), 28, 56; J. I. Packer, "The 'Wretched Man' in Romans 7," *SE* 2/1 (1964): 621–27; K. Kertelge, "Exegetische Überlegungen zum Verständnis der paulinischen Anthropologie nach Römer 7," *ZNW* 62 (1971): 106–7; J. Lambrecht, "Man Before and Without Christ: Rom 7 and Pauline Anthropology," *LS* 5 (1974): 29, 31–32; G. W. Burnett, *Paul and the Salvation of the Individual* (Biblical Interpretation Series 57; Leiden: E. J. Brill, 2001), 173–214.

[8] Inexplicably N. T. Wright describes our passage as "not emotional" (*The Climax of the Covenant* [Minneapolis: Fortress, 1992], 198).

[9] 6. Cf. T. W. Manson, "Romans," in *Peake's Commentary on the Bible* (eds. M. Black and H. H. Rowley; London: Nelson, 1962), 945.

[10] S. K. Stowers, *A Rereading of Romans* (New Haven, Conn.: Yale University Press, 1994), 270; idem, "Romans 7.7–25 as a Speech-in-Character (προσωποποιία)," in *Paul in His Hellenistic Context* (ed. T. Engberg-Pedersen; Studies of the New Testament and Its World: Edinburgh: T&T Clark, 1994), 192.

[11] To advance his thesis of Paul's using the rhetorical device of speech-in-character, Stowers cites pathetic outcries in the Medea-tradition regarding lack of self-mastery (*A Rereading of Romans*, 260–72; cf. idem, "Romans 7.7–25," 180–202; T. Engberg-Pedersen, "The Reception

perience in Adam at the fall or in the apostasy of Israel would leave the intensity of emotion curious, to say the least.[12] And what would a rhetorical "I" gain for solving exegetical problems? Nothing, unless it excluded Paul. But elsewhere it does *not* (see Rom 3:7; 1 Cor 6:12, 15; 10:29–30; 13:1–3, 11–12; 14:11, 14–15; Gal 2:18–21).

Nevertheless, a number of scholars have recently appealed to the Greco-Roman rhetorical technique of impersonation to argue for Paul's "I" as a reference to Adam and/or Israel and to himself and others in solidarity with Adam and/or Israel.[13] But besides the foregoing there are other reasons to doubt that Paul means to portray the fall of Adam under "I," a view that first gained its recent popularity largely through the writings of S. Lyonnet.[14] To be sure, the fall

---

of Graeco-Roman Culture in the New Testament: The Case of Romans 7.7–25," in *The New Testament as Reception* [ed. M. Müller and H. Tronier; JSNTSup 230; Sheffield: Sheffield Academic Press, 2002], 32–57). But Medea speaks about herself; she does not impersonate anyone else (see Thurén, "Romans 7 Derhetorized," 429, in favor of "impersonation" rather than "speech-in-character" and for impersonation as "usually refer[ring] to the personification of inanimate objects or abstract concepts" and as "sometimes used of people who have died or had never lived, but were represented as living"). αὐτὸς ἐγώ hardly means "I by myself" (i.e., without the help of the Holy Spirit) despite Mitton's lengthy attempt to establish that understanding ("Romans vii Reconsidered," 78–80, 99–103, 132–35). Under it the preceding bulk of the passage would be unintelligible so far as this sense of "I" is concerned; and elsewhere in Paul the expression is simply intensive, not technical in the sense suggested (see U. Luz, *Das Geschichtsverständnis des Paulus* [BEvT 49; Munich: Chr. Kaiser, 1968], 160; R. Y.-K. Fung, "The Impotence of the Law: Toward a Fresh Understanding of Romans 7:14–25," in *Scripture, Tradition, and Interpretation* [eds. W. W. Gasque and W. S. LaSor; Grand Rapids: Eerdmans, 1978], 39–40).

[12] Dunn makes this point very well ("Rom. 7,14–25," 260–61; *Jesus and the Spirit*, 314).

[13] For Adam see, e.g., B. Witherington III with D. Hyatt, *Paul's Letter to the Romans* (Grand Rapids: Eerdmans, 2004), 184–96; M. A. Seifrid, *Justification by Faith* (NovTSup 68; Leiden: E. J. Brill, 1992), 150; Theissen, *Psychological Aspects*, 206–8, 250–60; J.-N. Aletti, "Rm 7.7–25 encore une fois: enjeux et propositions," *NTS* 48 (2002): 363–64; C. Grappe, "Quime délivrera de ce corps de mort? L'Esprit de le vie! *Romains* 7,24 et 8,2 comme éléments de typologie adamique," *Bib* 83 (2002): 472–92. For Israel see Moo, "Israel and Paul," 122–35; idem, *Romans*, 423–67; C. Bryan, *A Preface to Romans* (Oxford: Oxford University Press, 2000), 139–45; P. F. Esler, *Conflict and Identity in Romans* (Minneapolis: Fortress, 2003), 237–38. For both Adam and Israel see Wright, *Climax of the Covenant*, 196–200, 217–19, 227. B. Dodd understands "I" as "a composite of various elements .... elements of Adam's story, elements of Paul's experience, ... Jewish, and perhaps Christian, believers" (*Paul's Paradigmatic "I"* [JSNTSup 177; Sheffield: Sheffield Academic Press, 1999], 223). Strangely, Israel does not make it into Dodd's composite "I." Because of the virtual absence of the future tense in Rom 7:7–25 (that tense occurs only in a question at v. 24b) R. F. Hock casts some doubt on Paul's use of impersonation, which according to Hermogenes requires the temporal sequence of past (as in Rom 7:7–11), present (as in 7:14–24a, 25), and future ("Paul and Greco-Roman Education," in *Paul in the Greco-Roman World: A Handbook* [ed. J. P. Sampley; Harrisburg, Penn.: Trinity Press International, 2003], 211–12).

[14] S. Lyonnet, "Quaestiones ad Rom 7, 7–13," *VD* 40 (1962): 163–83; idem, "L'histoire du salut selon le chapitre vii de l'Epître aux Romains," *Bib* 43 (1962): 117–51; idem, "Tu ne convoiteras pas," *Neotestamentica et Patristica* (NovTSup 6; Leiden: E. J. Brill, 1962), 157–65; idem, "History of Salvation in Romans 7," *TD* 13 (1965): 35–38 (a summary of the article in

has already received special notice in Rom 5:12–21. Adam's prominence in that earlier passage may therefore suggest that he is the referent in a rhetorical "I" incorporating the whole human race (cf. 2 Esd 7:118; also 3:7; 2 Bar. 48:42–43; Str-B 3:227–29). And a number of parallels may be drawn between Rom 7:7–25 and Genesis 1–3: (1) Paul's relating "I" to the law may correspond to Adam's being put in Eden according to Tg. Neofiti Genesis 1–3 to keep the law rather than to cultivate the garden, the tree of life even being identified with the law. (2) Living apart from the law once upon a time (Rom 7:9a) may parallel Adam's life in Eden prior to the command not to eat from the tree of the knowledge of good and evil (Gen 2:16–17). (3) The command Paul cites in Rom 7.7b, "You shall not lust [literally, 'desire strongly' – ἐπιθυμήσεις]," is similar to the command not to eat from the tree of knowledge, a command sometimes said to contain the germ of the whole law[15] and begun to be broken when desire, the quintessential sin, arose. (4) In both passages a prohibiting command becomes an instrument of sin. (5) Personified sin in Rom 7:7–25 may correspond to the serpent in Genesis 3. (6) Deception takes place in both passages (Gen 3:13; Rom 7:11). (7) In both, death results from sin.

Nevertheless Eve, not Adam, was deceived in Genesis 3 and Eve, not Adam, desired the forbidden fruit. Consequently not only do the parallels between Romans 7 and Genesis 3 suffer but also the supportive backdrop of Rom 5:12–21 drops away, for that earlier Pauline passage says nothing about Eve. And elsewhere Paul makes a clear distinction between Adam and Eve in this matter: "the serpent deceived Eve" (2 Cor 11:3); "and Adam was not deceived; but the woman, having been deceived, fell into transgression" (1 Tim 2:14).[16] The omission of Adam's name in Rom 7:7–25 (contrast 5:12–21; 1 Cor 15:22) agrees with saying that Eve rather than Adam was deceived. So how can Paul's audience be expected "to recognize themselves … as children of Adam who have also had desire, sinned, and died"?[17] Furthermore, though desire led to sin in Genesis 3 the broken command consisted in a prohibition of eating, not in a prohibition of desiring. Paul quotes the prohibition of desiring straight out of the decalogue (Exod 20:17 LXX; Deut 5:21

Biblica); idem, Les étapes de l'histoire du salut selon l'Epître aux Romains (Bibliothèque oecuménique 8; Paris: Cerf, 1969), 113–37.

[15] Gen 3:6; cf. 1 John 2:15–17; Tg. Neof. Exod 20:17 and Deut 5:18[21]; Apoc. Mos. 19:3; Philo, De decal. 142, 150, 173; 4 Macc. 2:6; b. Šabb. 145b–146a.

[16] Against Garlington, who thinks it wrong to distinguish "so sharply between Adam and Eve," for "Eve, after all, was the instigator of her husband's sin" ("Romans 7:14–25," 210). Garlington's argument is with Paul, who in Rom 7:7–25 personifies not Eve but sin, using the commandment, as the instigator of lust.

[17] As thought by Witherington, 190. Thurén also asks how Paul's audience would know he was impersonating Adam (Derhetorizing Paul, 119; see also idem, "Romans 7 Derhetorized," 426–30).

LXX; cf. Rom 13:9), not out of the fall-narrative, where (as just noted) it does not appear.

Nor does cutting short the period without law at the fall work.[18] That period would require a cutting short *before* the fall, in particular at the giving of the command not to eat from the tree of knowledge of good and evil. But where is the evidence for positing such a period? The command came right after the creation of Adam and his being set in Eden. Birds and beasts had yet to be formed, and Eve had yet to come into existence after them (see Gen 2:15–25). There is no hint of an interval during which Adam lived between his creation and the giving of the command, both of which events preceded the completion of creation in the birds, beasts, and Eve.[19] If by some trick of the imagination it could be thought there was such an interval, its extreme brevity militates against Paul's making it a discrete period of salvation history and describing life during it with an imperfect tense, which implies some duration of action (ἔζων, "I was living").

Feeling these difficulties, Lyonnet suggests that Adam was without law in Eden not in the sense that God had yet to give the command but in the sense that Adam looked on the command not as such but as the natural state of things. Thus the period without law lasted up to the fall, when Adam first began to regard the command as externally imposed rather than internally created. It takes considerable ingenuity to read into Paul's statements a distinction between internalized law and externalized law. That the distinction arises out of the necessities of the interpretation rather than out of the data of the text suggests that the interpretation itself is being imposed from without. Elsewhere in Paul the internalization of the law depends on the work of the Spirit in believers (Rom 8:12–14; Gal 5:16–26). But such a work of the Spirit is notably absent in Romans 7. We may also wonder how much is gained by extending the period without law up to the fall, for the narrative in Genesis seems to indicate that the fall occurred immediately after God put Adam and Eve in the garden. If there was an intervening period at all, it was so short as to call into question the interpretation that makes Paul divide salvation history in such a way.

By no means have we reached the end of difficulties in this salvation historical view of Rom 7:7–25. When the commandment came, sin sprang to life. It was already dwelling within the "I" (vv. 8, 18, 20–21, 23). But the serpent was external to Adam and did not even confront him – rather, Eve. Paul recognizes that sin was not dwelling within Adam before the fall, for he explicitly says

---

[18] Against Lyonnet, *Les étapes*, 113–37.

[19] Against F. Watson, who thinks "it is enough for Paul that Genesis does not exclude such an interval" (*Paul, Judaism and the Gentiles* [SNTSMS 56; Cambridge: Cambridge University Press, 1986], 225 n. 36). Witherington states that "the only person said in the Bible to be living before or without any law was Adam" (*Romans*, 189). Where does the Bible say so? As noted, it puts the creation of Adam and his placement in Eden with God's command in an uninterrupted succession.

that "sin *entered* the world" at the fall (Rom 5:12). ἀνέζησεν (Rom 7:9) is inappropriate to the entrance of sin even though the term means "sprang to life" rather than "revived."[20] Because Paul writes that Eve rather than Adam was deceived it does not seem to be his view that Adam was powerless to resist sin. Yet the "I" in Rom 7:7–25 *is* thus powerless. In Rom 5:12–14 Paul's discussion depends on the giving of the law not until Moses. In Gal 3:17–19 Paul stresses that the law was a latecomer, 430 years after Abraham. How then can we think that in Rom 7:7–25 he sees a period of law as beginning and immediately ending in Eden? For *Targum Neofiti* to support his relating Adam to the law, the tree of knowledge rather than the tree of life should have been identified with the law; for lawbreaking could only be represented by eating from the tree of knowledge.[21]

If the commandment, "You shall not lust," did not come when God put Adam and Eve in Eden, when did it come? It came when God gave the Mosaic law, including that commandment, at Sinai.[22] Perhaps then Paul uses "I" to impersonate Israel, of which he has been a member, with reference to Israel's failure to keep the law. But the extreme pathos and highly individualistic "I myself" of the passage are hard to square with such a view.[23] Moreover, this view requires that the statement of Paul, "For apart from the law sin [is] dead" (Rom 7:8b), describe the state of affairs prior to the giving of the Mosaic law. But then he would be contradicting his earlier statements not only that "sin was in the world until the law" but also that sin's accomplice, death, "reigned from Adam till Moses even over those who had not sinned after the likeness of Adam's transgression" (5:13–14). And the state of affairs subsequent to the giving of the Mosaic law, i.e., the state of Is-

---

[20] F. Godet, *Commentary on the Epistle to the Romans* (Grand Rapids: Zondervan, 1969 repr.), 280.

[21] According to H. Schlier "the command *came*" (Rom 7:9b) makes sense only in terms of Genesis 1–3 (*Der Römerbrief* [HTKNT; Freiburg: Herder, 1977], 224). But the argument requires a discrete period from creation to the prohibiting of the tree of knowledge, *not* a period lasting till the fall. For at the fall the command could not have come in the sense of being given but only in that of impinging on Adam's consciousness as a broken command. Yet the latter sense would agree with a Pauline autobiography. On the other hand, we have just noted the lack of evidence for a discrete period from creation to the prohibiting of the tree of knowledge. At the opposite extreme E. Brandenburger illegitimately modernizes Paul by making him dehistoricize Adam's fall and treat it as typical of what happens to post-Mosaic human beings when the law comes (*Adam und Christus* [WMANT 7; Neukirchen: Neukirchener Verlag, 1962], 215–16). Engberg-Pedersen argues against the Adamic interpretation ("The Reception," 42–43).

[22] See esp. Moo, *Romans*, 423–67; idem, "Israel and Paul," 122–35; P. F. Esler, *Conflict and Identity in Romans*, 230–38.

[23] The book of Lamentations also displays an "I"-style full of emotion, but the alternation between "I," "we," and third person references to Zion, Jerusalem, and Judah indicates clearly that its "I" carries a communal reference as well as referring individually to the author (similarly in Jer 10:19–22; Mic 7:7–10, *Pss. Sol.* 1:1–2:6). Romans 7:7–25 contains no such indication of a communal reference. As for the "I"-style in the Psalms and 1QH, it represents the experiences and sentiments of their individual authors. A communal use of them does not affect their original individualistic meaning (cf. Segal, *Paul the Convert*, 225).

rael's boasting in the law (2:23), does not square easily with the despair suffered by the "I" after the commandment came. Moreover again, Paul has earlier associated lusts with the world of pagans, to whom the Mosaic prohibition against lusting had not come, as he himself recognizes (1:24; 3:3). And he later lists that prohibition as only one among equals (13:9), so that despite extrabiblical indications to the contrary it is hard to think that in ch. 7 he presents the prohibition as the quintessence of the law. Why then a singling out of this prohibition for a summary of Israel's sinning? Those who think Paul impersonates both Adam and Israel, as in the statement that "Israel recapitulated the sin of Adam,"[24] face the difficulties attached to both putative impersonations.

To take Paul as referring to his attaining the status of bar mitzvah remains the best interpretation. *Indeed, we may say that Paul slips into the ἐγώ-style precisely because becoming bar mitzvah applied to him but not to the Gentiles who made up the majority of his audience* (1:5–6). His Jewish experience illustrates a universal principle and establishes the inability of the law to sanctify anybody, of course; but only a minority of his audience shared the specifics of that experience.

Paul's reference to becoming bar mitzvah needs qualification, however. He singles out a particular commandment to establish his autobiographical point and only then refers to an early period of freedom from the law. When sin finally springs to life it does so in response to the particular commandment just cited. The succeeding discussion plays on Paul's confrontation with *that* commandment even though he implies the inability of the whole law to sanctify a person. *Failure to pay attention to this restriction underlies the otherwise valid criticism that Jewish lads had some considerable relation to the law from circumcision onward.*

The commandment Paul singles out prohibits lust, the very sin which, in its sexual sense, is dead (i.e., inactive – see Jas 2:17, 26) prior to puberty but springs to life (i.e., becomes active) in a lad about the time he becomes bar mitzvah and therefore legally and morally responsible. And lust in Paul's vocabulary often carries a sexual connotation (most clearly in Rom 1:24; 13:14; 1 Thess 4:5; cf. Rom 7:5). It is usually thought that Paul lops off the objects of lust in the tenth commandment – "your neighbor's house … wife … male servant [et al.]" – to make the commandment a general prohibition of all sins which grow from the seed of lust. On the contrary, the omissions probably represent a simple abbreviation, as in Rom 13:9 where as already noted the tenth commandment is one among equals, all of which are subsumed under "You shall love your neighbor as yourself." And the abbreviation serves Paul's lim-

---

[24] Wright, *Climax of the Covenant*, 197; see also P. W. Meyer, "The Worm at the Core of the Apple: Exegetical Reflections on Romans 7," in *The Conversation Continues* (ed. R. T. Fortna and B. R. Gaventa; Nashville: Abingdon, 1990), 73; J. A. Ziesler, "The Role of the Tenth Commandment in Romans 7," *JSNT* 33 (1988): 47.

ited purview of the awakening of sexual desire at the very time his obligation to the law matured.[25]

Moo argues to the contrary that "Paul's own usage [of the tenth commandment] and the context [of its quotation in Rom 7:7] give no support to this restriction [to sexual desire]."[26] Ziesler expands this point to include the use of ἐπιθυμέω and ἐπιθυμία in the rest of the NT, the LXX, and other ancient Jewish literature.[27] But Paul's usage is decisive, and everyone recognizes the sexual meaning of "lusts" earlier in Rom 1:24, where it is associated with "bodies." The attachment of "lusts" to the "body" in Rom 6:12 favors a similar meaning there. "The passions of sins" at work in bodily "members" tend in the same direction just preceding our passage in Rom 7:5. So also do the "lusts" of "the flesh" in Rom 1:14. Though farther distant, "passion of lust" is associated with "sexual immorality" (πορνείας) in 1 Thess 4:3–5; "passions" and "lusts" are correlated in Gal 5:24; and "lusting" is linked with "fornicating" in 1 Cor 10:6–8.[28] Paul's predominant use of the plural ("lusts" and "passions") shows that in Rom 7:8 his modifying "lust" with "every [sort of]" (πᾶσαν) does not necessarily expand the meaning of ἐπιθυμίαν to coveting of nonsexual sorts (cf. the detailing in 1:24–27 of different kinds of sexual lust in distinction from other sins, such as failure to glorify God, unthankfulness, vain reasonings, idolatry, covetousness [πλεονεξία], envy, murder, deceit, boastfulness et al. in the surrounding context, just as the prohibition of lusting stands in distinction from other prohibitions in Rom 13:9).

---

[25] G. Bornkamm says that Paul omits particular objects from the tenth commandment to leave room for "the possibility that 'desire' can express itself nomistically just as much as antinomistically, i.e. in the zeal for one's own righteousness (Rom 10.3)" (*Early Christian Experience* [New York: Harper & Row, 1969], 90). This opinion ties in with his adopting Bultmann's trans-subjective interpretation and the attempt to see the doctrine of justification at every possible turn in Paul. Whether or not Paul's theology centers on justification, he can talk about other topics; and here he is discussing sanctification. See R. Bultmann, *Theology of the New Testament* (New York: Scribner's, 1951), 1:247–48; idem, *The Old and New Man in the Letters of Paul* (Richmond: John Knox, 1967 repr.), 16, 33 ff.; and, for sufficient criticisms, H. Ridderbos, *Paul: An Outline of His Theology* (Grand Rapids: Eerdmans, 1975), 146; Kertelge, "Exegetische Überlegungen," 107; A. van Dülmen, *Die Theologie des Gesetzes bei Paulus* (SBM 5; Stuttgart: Katholisches Bibelwerk, 1968), 114 n. 134; O. Kuss, *Der Römerbrief* (RNT 6; Regensburg: Pustet, 1959), 2:469–70; H. Räisänen, "Zum Gebrauch von ΕΠΙΘΥΜΙΑ und ΕΠΙΘΥΜΕΙΝ bei Paulus," *ST* 33 (1979): 85–99; M. A. Seifrid, "The Subject of Rom 7:14–25," *NovT* 34 (1992): 315–17. It seems that Meyer agrees essentially with Bultmann: "the religious self is put in the wretched position of serving sin in the very service of God.... there is no distinction between the 'godly' and the 'ungodly'" ("Worm," 80). Similarly see Luz, *Geschichtsverständnis*, 162, against interpretations in terms of a person who is developing into a Christian, a Christian who has not yet received the Spirit, or a Christian who has fallen away or lapsed into dependence on the law.

[26] Moo, "Israel and the Law," 131 n. 9.

[27] Ziesler, "Role of the Tenth Commandment," 44–46, 54 nn. 15–17.

[28] Cf. Watson, *Paul, Judaism and the Gentiles*, 151–57.

The medieval origin of the bar mitzvah *ceremony* does not stand against this view, for the legal shift occurring at age thirteen originated much earlier (cf. the apparently preparatory taking of Jesus to the temple at the age of twelve).[29] Nor does instruction in the law during boyhood present an obstacle, for Paul correlates knowing sin with sin's springing to life. Not instruction alone is in view, then, but instruction accompanied by the activity of sin; and not till puberty does sin use the prohibition of lust.[30] According to the rabbis the evil impulse, which is to be tamed by the law, is largely sexual in nature. Any sensitive bar mitzvah would be worried by the tenth commandment,[31] especially because he is catapulted into adult responsibility to keep the law at the very time his sexual urges become so active that he is unable to avoid defiling seminal emissions (cf. Leviticus 15).[32] Even Lyonnet recognizes the special relation of becoming bar mitzvah and certain sexual prohibitions.[33]

"Apart from the law" does not mean the absence of the law in Jewish or universal history, then, but the absence of the tenth commandment as an instrument of sin and death in Paul's prepuberal boyhood. Sin's springing to life and using that commandment define the coming of the commandment as a coming in Paul's life rather than in Jewish or world history. His consequent death cannot be physical or eternal, for it has already taken place ("I died, and for me this commandment... was found to result in death"). Rather, the contrast with the ability of sin to carry out its design – an activity that defines sin's life – determines that Paul's death consisted in his inability to carry out a contrary design.[34] A description of this kind of death occupies the rest of the chapter.[35] By the same token Paul's earlier living, when sin was dead, means that lust did not tyrannize over him during his boyhood. His remaining a bachelor, if so he did, would make a

---

[29] Luke 2:41–52. See Z. Kaplan, "Bar Mitzvah, Bat Mitzvah," *EncJud* 4:243–44.

[30] Burnett argues at first that an inner sense of duty to obey the law must have preceded puberty but in the end admits that "the full meaning of the 10th commandment, in particular, would not have had much bearing on his life as a child" (*Paul and the Salvation of the Individual*, 193–95). M. P. Middendorf cites Gal 5:3 and Phil 3:5 for the argument that according to Paul circumcision put one under obligation to keep the law (*The "I" in the Storm* [Saint Louis: Concordia Academic Press, 1997], 159–60). But Gal 5:3 has to do with adult Gentiles getting circumcised, and Phil 3:5 says nothing about an obligation to keep the law. Was an infant expected to start keeping the law at the age of eight days?

[31] W. D. Davies, *Paul and Rabbinic Judaism* (2d ed.; London: SPCK, 1962), 20–26, 30–31.

[32] G. W. Buchanan, *The Consequences of the Covenant* (NovTSup 20; Leiden: E. J. Brill, 1970), 182–84.

[33] S. Lyonnet, "L'histoire du salut," 122 n. 2.

[34] According to Middendorf, Paul means that "the notion that 'I' am able to utilize the Law's command as a means to life has 'died'" (*The "I" in the Storm*, 169). But Paul writes, "*I* died." He does not write that some "notion" died (cf. Gal 2:19: "For through the law I died to the law").

[35] Concerning extrabiblical parallels see F. F. Bruce, "Paul and the Law of Moses," *BJRL* 57 (1974–75): 271. The objection that Paul does not elsewhere engage in introspection is ill-founded (see Rom 9:1–3; 1 Cor 4:4a; 2 Cor 1:8–9, 12, 17; 4:16; 10:1; 12:1–10; Phil 1:23–26; 3:7–14; 4:11–13; Col 2:1; 1 Thess 2:3–12; 3:1, 5; 2 Tim 1:3).

later unsuccessful struggle with lust (lasting till the Spirit of Christ liberated him – v. 25a and ch. 8) quite understandable.[36] Even under a wider view of "every [sort of] lust," sexual lusts would be included and would connect both with the onset of sexual urges at puberty and with a concurrent coming into adult responsibility to keep the whole law (*m. 'Abot* 5:21: "At five years old [one is] fit for the Scripture, at ten years for the Mishnah, at thirteen for [the fulfilling of] the commandments"). The foregoing is the only view that adequately entertains Paul's statement in Rom 7:9a that he was once living apart from the law and the related surrounding statements that apart from the law sin is dead, that when the commandment came sin sprang to life, and that he died.[37]

I must now face the objection that other passages – in particular, Acts 22:3; 23:6; 26:4–5; Gal 1:13–14; Phil 3:4–6 – show Paul to have been self-righteously content rather than upset with frustration before his conversion. First, it must be said that Paul's zeal for Judaism and advancement in it do not contradict an internal struggle with sexual and perhaps other desires. More than one sincerely zealous and eminently successful religionist has entered that contest and lost. Second, such a struggle need not have been the decisive element in Paul's conversion, which he consistently attributes to an appearance of the risen Lord. His defeat at the one point of the tenth commandment may have prepared him for conversion, but it could hardly have turned him into a Christian. Third, confidence in the flesh need not imply a claim to perfection, but only to right ancestry and a preponderance of right conduct, so that the minority of sins are forgiven.[38] These three considerations take care of Gal 1:13–14; Acts 22:3; and most of Phil 3:4–6.

Only the phrase, "as to the righteousness in the law, being blameless" (Phil 3:6), remains. But Paul writes it from the standpoint of externals, whereas Rom 7:7–25 describes an internal struggle.[39] The preceding items on the list in Philippians 3 are all observable – circumcision, national and tribal origins, cultural identification as a Hebraist, sectarian identification as a Pharisee, persecution of the church – and provide the details behind the summarizing "blameless." Furthermore, Paul is describing himself as a whole; but in Rom 7:7–25 he describes a narrow aspect – his confrontation with the tenth commandment. Only by making "blameless" mean sinlessly perfect could we pit the term

---

[36] Verse 25a shows that deliverance did not come till conversion.

[37] Stowers interprets Paul to be impersonating Gentiles who once lived apart from the law but then took on its yoke only to find themselves haunted and overpowered by their pre-Judaic lusts (*A Rereading of Romans*, 273–84). This interpretation makes sense of having once lived apart from the law; but Paul's addressing "those who know the law" (7:1) must at least include Jews, whom the interpretation does not fit. And in view of his repeatedly identifying himself as a Jew in this very epistle (see 3:9; 4:1; 9:3–5; 11:1, 13–14) he could hardly expect his audience to understand him as impersonating without further ado a Gentile trying to keep the OT law.

[38] Cf. E. P. Sanders, *Paul and Palestinian Judaism* (Philadelphia: Fortress, 1977), passim.

[39] Cf. A. C. Purdy, "Paul the Apostle," *IDB* 3:685; Dodd, *Paul's Paradigmatic "I,"* 223.

against a pre-Christian autobiographical view of Rom 7:7–25. The people at Qumran out-Phariseed the Pharisees, yet among them a deep sense of personal sin co-existed with the conviction that they were the righteous (see esp. 1QH).[40]

If "blameless" poses a problem at all it does so for an impersonating "I" too. The impersonated Adamic Everyman would include Paul. So also would an impersonated Israel. Therefore the supposed contradiction of Phil 3:6 would still stand. Only by excluding Paul from the "I" (a usage few admit and fewer on other sides of this debate take into account at this point) could the problem be solved in a way different from one that relieves the pre-Christian autobiographical interpretation. To make Paul blameless in himself (Phil 3:4–6) and blameworthy only in Adam and/or Israel runs up against the affirmation that all, Jews and Gentiles alike, have sinned for themselves. Indeed, the necessary qualification of "blameless" by Rom 1:18–3:23 – especially by 2:17–29; 3:9–23, dealing with Jews, like Paul – makes a knock-down argument from Phil 3:4–6 impossible. (N.B.: in Phil 3:6 Paul does not say he *felt* blameless, i.e., had no awareness of sin; it is Rom 7:7–25 that deals in introspection.[41]) The very Jews Paul describes as zealously active in establishing their own righteousness (Rom 10:2–3) are the same as those he accuses of law-breaking (Rom 2:17 ff.). Galatians 3:10 provides an even clearer qualification: "For as many as are of the works of the law are under a curse; for it is written, 'Cursed is everyone who does not abide in all the things that are written in the book of the law by doing them.'" Since the expression "as many as are of the works of the law" must include Paul before his conversion, he must have been under the curse for having failed to keep the law wholly.[42]

If Paul's blamelessness and defeat do not contradict each other, then, does his wretchedness in Rom 7:14–25 necessarily contradict his pre-Christian Pharisaism? No. Frustration with regard to a single commandment does not tell the whole tale concerning his experience of the law; nor does the general pleasure that Pharisees took in keeping the law rule out particular frustrations over besetting sins. We get more than a hint of such frustrations in *b. Ber.* 17a, a passage that includes the element of pleasure. Like the Pharisee in Luke 18:9–13 the rich

---

[40] Cf. Esler, who correctly describes "blameless" as "a relative (or comparative)" term "expressing moral excellence, inasmuch as it differentiated someone in a particular context from others" (see Gal 1:14 with Phil 2:14–15; 1 Thess 2:10; 3:13; 5:23; *Conflict and Identity*, 232–33).

[41] K. Stendahl to the contrary notwithstanding. Among others, see A. A. Das, *Paul and the Jews* (Library of Pauline Studies; Peabody, Mass.: Hendrickson, 2003), 142–48, esp. 146–47, and J. M. Espy, "Paul's 'Robust Conscience' Re-examined," *NTS* 31 (1985): 162–67, against an overinterpretation of Phil 3:6.

[42] Sanders neglects Gal 3:10 in appealing to Gal 3:11–12 for the position that Paul repudiates the law on grounds of Christology and soteriology but not on the ground of the unfulfillability of the law (*Paul and Palestinian Judaism*, 443 n. 4). Verse 10 affirms what Sanders denies and subverts his primary thesis that Paul did not start with human beings' need of salvation, but with God's deed of salvation. Do we need to put either one ahead of the other in Paul's thought?

young ruler was generally self-satisfied, but one commandment – the very tenth which Paul stumbled at and Jesus led up to but left unquoted – proved his undoing (Mark 10:17–22; Matt 19:15–22; Luke 18:18–23). Agreement with and delight in God's law (Rom 7:16, 22) do not adequately reflect Christian experience, which would have to include performance as well (8:4). Instead, they correspond to the zeal for the law that Paul attributes to his pre-Christian self and to unbelieving Jews (Acts 22:3; Rom 10:2–3; Gal 1:13–14; Phil 3:4–6). Since this zeal does not preclude lawbreaking, the parallel with Rom 7:7–25 holds up. Those who delight in sin are the heathen (Rom 1:18–32). The zealous but unbelieving Jews Paul writes about do not delight in breaking the law. Though they break it, they learn it, rely on it, approve the excellent things it teaches, teach it to others, and boast in God – a description that matches agreeing with and delighting in the law (Rom 2:17–20).

The delight of OT saints in God's law included performance and therefore does not correspond to the frustrated delight in Rom 7:14–25. Similarly the willing of God's good pleasure in Phil 2:13 is a willing accompanied by performance. That God is its source, therefore, does not contradict the unregenerate willing that fails to issue in performance in Rom 7:14–25, where not the whole person but only the inner person, or mind, delights in the law.[43] The inner person is not the person in Christ, which has to do with sanctification (Eph 2:15; 4:24; Col 3:10), but the nonphysical part of a person's constitution, which has to do with psychical feelings.[44] Likewise the mind is not a Christian's renewed mind, for such a mind transforms conduct into a demonstration of God's will (Rom 12:1–2). Furthermore, since even the mind of a Christian has to be exhorted to renewal (Rom 12:2), the mind as such does not imply regeneration. Even the heathen recognize God's righteous edict that sinners deserve to die (Rom 1:32); so it should not surprise us that the unrenewed mind of a nomistic Jew agrees with and delights in God's law.

Serving sin in Rom 6:16–20 has to do with actions performed through the body (see esp. the term "members" in v. 19; cf. vv. 12–14). Serving God's law in 7:25b has to do only with the mind, expressly mentioned. Hence there is no disharmony in taking both passages as descriptive of unregenerate life. In fact 7:25b also speaks of serving the law of sin with the flesh, which because of the interchangeability of "flesh" and "members" matches serving sin with one's members in 6:16–20.

---

[43] For this reason Paul can say on the one hand, "It is no longer I that do it [the bad]," and on the other hand, "What I hate [the bad], this I do." It is not regeneration that splits the "I" from its actions, as Nygren argues (*Romans*, 286), but a constitutional distinction true of all human beings – a distinction between physical and nonphysical parts, so that the "I" may identify itself with the inner person, or mind, and distance itself from the flesh, members, or body, whose actions sin determines much to the distress of the inner person, or mind.

[44] See a much fuller discussion in Gundry, Sōma *in Biblical Theology with Emphasis on Pauline Anthropology* (SNTSMS 29; Cambridge: Cambridge University Press, 1976), 135–40.

Those who oppose the pre-Christian view cite the hostility of the unregenerate mind toward God in Rom 8:5–7 and deduce that the mind which agrees with and delights in God's law in 7:16, 22 is regenerate. But the mind of 7:14–25 is a moral monitor such as even pagans have, though it may be corrupted (again see 1:32; also 1:18–20 and perhaps 2:14–15).[45] According to 10:2–3 the Jews, motivated by such a monitor and seeking to establish their own righteousness, "did not subject themselves to God's righteousness." The phraseology echoes 8:7: "the mind of the flesh does not subject itself to God's law." In its agreement with and delight in God's law, then, the mind stands over against sin in the flesh, members, and body. In its attempt to establish a person's own righteousness (so among the Jews) as well as in its succumbing to corruption (so among the heathen) the mind stands over against God and his righteousness. The switch from νοῦς in 7:16, 22 to φρόνημα in 8:5–7 and the qualification "of the flesh" in 8:5–7 signal the shift in connotations.

"Mind" and "inner person" resist the notion that Paul is delineating pre-Christian experience from a later, Christian point of view and that at the time a non-Christian would be unaware of the nature of the struggle going on within him- or herself. This way of harmonizing the self-satisfaction in Phil 3:4–6 with the turmoil in Rom 7:7–25 also runs up against the emotional intensity of the latter passage, an intensity that seizes on the vivid historical present, interjects the emphatic ἐγώ, adds the intensive αὐτός, lurches back and forth between confession and self-exoneration, suffers the tension of willing the good and doing the bad, takes enjoyment in God's law, and pitches into despair over inability to carry out that law. No alien analysis from a distant standpoint here! To speak the way he does the subject must have been self-conscious at the time the warfare raged within him.[46]

His defeat at the hands of sin brings us to well-known connections and contrasts between 7:7–25 and 6:1–7:6; 8:1–39, connections and contrasts widely considered to offer the strongest evidence for taking the whole of 7:7–25 as pre-Christian. "When the commandment came, sin sprang to life and I died"

---

[45] I incline toward the view, however, that 2:14–15 anticipates 8:11ff. and therefore refers proleptically to Gentile Christians. To avoid treating the mind as an unregenerate moral monitor, Garlington appeals to the covenantal context of OT passages such as Psalms 19, 119; Jer 31:33; Ezek 36:26 ("Romans 7:14–25," 218). But the cited noncovenantal passages earlier in Romans take interpretive precedence.

[46] Against J.-N. Aletti, "Romans 7,7–25: Rhetorical Criticism and Its Usefulness," *SEÅ* 61 (1996): 90–91, as well as many others. In favor of later Christian analysis Luz argues that a *dead* "I" could have neither spoken of its death nor distinguished between life and death (*Geschichtsverständnis*, 162). The argument misconstrues "I died" (v. 10). Paul does not mean that he lost consciousness. He means that he lost control. Later Christian analysis would allow a temporal meaning of "now" and "no longer" in vv. 17 and 20; but since the logical meaning would remain possible, no point of argument arises. The appeal to "depth psychology" by Theissen (*Psychological Aspects*, 229–43, esp. 235) does not alleviate the problem of Paul's emotional intensity for a later Christian analysis.

(7:9b–10a) surely describes what happened before conversion. Yet Paul links this description, the whole of which occupies vv. 7–13, to vv. 14–25 with γάρ, "For" (v. 14a). At this point we would have expected disjunction rather than linkage if Paul had meant to shift from pre-Christian to Christian experience. As it is, he immediately announces that he is "fleshly" (v. 14). This announcement recalls v. 5, "For when we were in the flesh," which because of the past tense and the context of vv. 1–6 clearly refers to an unregenerate state.[47] To be sure, Paul is capable of calling Christians "fleshly" (1 Cor 3:1–3) and saying that they are "in the flesh" (2 Cor 10:3; Gal 2:20; Phil 1:22, 24; Phlm 16). But in context the latter expression has no moral connotations; it refers simply to earthly life. And the behavior of a "fleshly" Christian calls in question the genuineness of his or her faith (Gal 5:19–21). The immediate context of chs. 7–8 determines that the fleshly "I" of 7:14 is unregenerate.[48] For "those who are in Christ Jesus .... do not walk according to the flesh .... For the mind of the flesh is death .... because the mind of the flesh is hostile toward God .... And those who are in the flesh cannot please God. But you are not in the flesh; rather, in the Spirit, if indeed the Spirit of God dwells in you. And if anyone does not have the Spirit of Christ, this person does not belong to him" (8:1–9, excerpts). So Paul is discussing a difference in conduct between Christians and non-Christians, not between victorious Christians and defeated Christians.[49]

The difference cannot be evaded by limiting 7:7–25 (or 14–25) to sensitivity to sin.[50] No, sinful conduct ("What I hate, this I *do* .... the bad which I do not want [to do], this I *practice*" [vv. 15, 19]) versus right conduct ("resulting in sanctification" [6:22]; "walk" [a common metaphor for conduct; 8:4]) spells the difference (cf. 1 Cor 6:9–11; 2 Cor 5:21; Eph 2:1–3; 1 John 3:4–12). On the non-Christian side there is extended domination by sin. Otherwise the expressed frustration over inability to do the good and avoid the bad becomes nonsensical and the outcry in 7:24 affected. On the Christian side possession of the Spirit makes the difference. Paul's statement that anyone who does not have the Spirit of Christ does not belong to Christ looks like a comment on the absence

---

[47] With all due respect to Stalder, who denies that justification takes place once for all (but see Rom 5:1, 9) and therefore assigns even Rom 7:4–5 to present Christian experience (*Das Werk des Geistes*, 292–93).

[48] Strictly speaking, the fleshly "I" in 7:14 is not a sinful "I," but an "I" whose physical weakness and needs make it easy prey for sin (see Gundry, Sōma *in Biblical Theology*, 137–38).

[49] Seifrid makes Paul speak of "the inherent *capacities* of the individual [to sin] despite awareness of a broader context [of redemption in Christ]" ("The Subject of Rom 7:14–25," 326, italics added). But Paul speaks of actualities.

[50] For example, C. E. B. Cranfield, "The Freedom of the Christian according to Romans 8.2," in *New Testament Christianity for Africa and the World* (eds. M. E. Glasswell and E. W. Fasholé-Luke; London: SPCK, 1974), 94–96. Cf. further minimization of the difference by saying that 7:7–25 shows the "tainting" with sin of even the Christian's best actions (Cranfield, *Romans*, 1:361; cf. Packer, "The 'Wretched Man' in Romans 7," 626; Stalder, *Das Werk des Geistes*, 293–94).

of the Spirit in 7:7–25.[51] The comment implies that the "I" in 7:7–25 does not belong to Christ. To this agrees the contrast between the moral defeat of the "I," which is "sold under sin" and "captive to the law of sin," and the moral victory of "those who are in Christ Jesus," who are "set free from the law of sin and of death," who fulfill "the righteous requirement of the law," and who "walk... according to the Spirit" (see also 6:17–18, 22). The law of sin and of death recalls "the passions of sins which were aroused by the law [and] worked in our members so as to bear fruit" (7:5). Since the earlier passage undoubtedly relates to those outside Christ, so also does the latter.[52]

The serving of righteousness "in newness of the Spirit" rests on believers' being "released from the law" (7:6). Yet 7:7–25 presumes being under the law:

when the commandment came... I died .... For sin, taking opportunity through the commandment, deceived me and through it killed me... effecting my death through that which is good .... For we know that the law is Spiritual .... I agree with the law, that it is good .... I delight in the law of God in the inner person, but I see a different law in my members... making me captive to the law of sin which is in my members.

Paul wants not only to exonerate the law but also to show its worse-than-inability to sanctify those who are under it – and they do *not* include Christians, as he has made plain with respect to sanctification as well as justification (6:14–7:6; cf. 8:1–4, where justification shades into sanctification[53]). The emphatic "Now then" and the back reference to release from condemnation for those who are in Christ Jesus at the start of ch. 8 (cf. 3:19–5:21) seal the exclusion: Paul is no longer talking about his pre-Christian self, captured by sin and condemned under the law, but about all those who are free from the law and justified in

---

[51] Dunn thinks the battle with sin in 7:14–25 contrasts with a lack of resistance to sin in 7:7–13 and implies that the Spirit is joining Paul in battle with the flesh (cf. Gal 5:16–17; "Rom. 7, 14–25," 261–62). But the admission that Paul "is still defeated" casts doubt on the Spirit's combat. And, as already noted, Paul joins rather than breaks apart 7:7–13 and 14–25. Hence his discussion simply progresses with the addition of a new element. The victory of sin (vv. 14–25) does not disagree with the deceit of sin (vv. 7–13). More than one battle has been won by deceit. Cranfield's attempt to read the Spirit between the lines of 7:14–25 is equally weak: he reasons that the qualification "in my flesh" (v. 18) implies that the Holy Spirit dwells elsewhere in the "I" (*Romans*, 1:360–361). But in this passage "flesh" parallels "members" and "body," and according to 1 Cor 6:19 the Christian's "body is a temple of the Holy Spirit."

[52] J. Murray tries to make an argument for the Christian view out of being sold under sin and captive to it: in 1 Kgs 21:20, 25; 2 Kgs 17:17 the wicked are active agents in selling themselves to sin whereas in Rom 7:14 the self is victimized and the "I" in 7:14–23 is captive to sin rather than wicked per se; therefore the true character of the "I" must be regenerate (*The Epistle to the Romans* [NICNT; Grand Rapids: Eerdmans, 1959], 1:260–61). One wonders what would happen to "redemption" under such reasoning.

[53] C. Hodge tries to eliminate the contrast between chs. 7 and 8 by settling on the "no condemnation" of 8:1 (*Commentary on the Epistle to the Romans* [Grand Rapids: Eerdmans, 1968 repr.], 244–45). But though 8:1 refers to justification (so that the referent of the inferential "then" becomes a question), 8:2 ff. immediately returns to sanctification and sustains the contrasts already evident in a comparison of 6:1–7:6 and 7:7–25.

Christ. Thus the "I" of 7:7–25 is never said to be "in Christ." Its wretchedness
(v. 24a) contrasts sharply with the assured "Abba! Father!" of those who in
Christ have the Spirit (8:15).[54]

It has become somewhat popular to use the overlapping of the present age and
the age to come as a means of making the contrasts between 7:14–25 and
6:1–7:6; 8:1–39 compatible with a Christian referent in 7:14–25.[55] Living in
both ages at the same time, Christians are simultaneously sinners and saints. It
is not that they are sometimes good, sometimes bad. Rather, everything they do
is conditioned by both the Spirit and sin. Thus Christians and their conduct may
be described in seemingly contradictory ways. So it is said.

Undeniably Christians live in the ambiguity of an eschatological overlap. That
they are not sinless and do die yet are called "saints" and have eternal life proves
as much.[56] But this situation does not adequately explain the contrasts between
7:14–25 and 6:1–7:6; 8:1–39. The "I" in 7:14–25 is not merely unable to avoid a
mixture of the good and the bad. With respect to the commandment at issue he
cannot do the good at all, only the bad. Sin has taken over so completely that the
"I" is imprisoned.[57] Contrariwise those who are in Christ "do not walk according
to the flesh but according to the Spirit" (8:4). The wording is exclusive.[58]

Nevertheless those who are in Christ need exhortations not to walk according
to the flesh but to walk according to the Spirit. There is an ambiguity, then; but it
is not so much an eschatological one as an ambiguity arising out of the possibility of false profession and the consequent possibility of apostasy. Ultimately,
of course, the overlapping of the ages gives rise to these possibilities. But it is
the ambiguity of profession vis-à-vis inner reality that provides the immediate
reason for exhortations not to forfeit salvation by failing to live holily. These exhortations crop up throughout the NT. Representative are Matt 5:19–20;

---

[54] The wretchedness of a captive to the law of sin and of death differs from the sighing of
Christians, liberated from that law but suffering with the rest of creation the pains of the old age
while awaiting the new (contrast 7:23–24 with 8:18–25).

[55] See, e.g., Dunn, *Romans 1–8*, 377; Garlington, "Romans 7:14–25," 197–235; Seifrid,
"The Subject of Romans 7:14–25," 320–33.

[56] Dunn's discussion suffers at this point, however, because he confuses Christians' sharing
in the death of Jesus through their persecutions and their suffering of death as the lingering effect of their own and Adam's sin ("Rom 7, 14–25," 269–71).

[57] The contextual restriction to the particular commandment used by sin qualifies this inability. But those who appeal to eschatological tension usually cut 7:14–25 loose from 7:7–13 since
7:7–13 most naturally antedates conversion. The consequent generalizing of 7:14–25 exacer-
bates the problem of inability. Without the restriction totally sinful conduct is required in
7:14–25 and sinless perfection in 8:1 ff., for Paul's language brooks no softening.

[58] To maintain that Rom 7:7–25 describes Christian experience Thurén describes as "hyperbole" the exclusivity of wording between chs. 7 and 8 and compares the seeming exclusivity of
Paul's saying Christians are not under the law yet also implying in 1 Cor 15:56 that because of
their mortality they are still under the law ("Romans 7 Derhetorized," 433–38). But
1 Cor 15:56 has to do with the eschatological overlap, and the appeal to hyperbole leaves unexplained Paul's saying he was once living apart from the law.

13:24–30, 36–43; 22:11–14; 25:1–13; John 15:1–6; Rom 6:12–13; 13:14; 1 Cor 9:27; 15:2; 2 Cor 13:5; Gal 5:16–6:10; Heb 4:11–13; 6:1–12; 10:26–31; 2 Pet 1:4–11; and Revelation 2–3.

One of the exhortations merits special discussion because some have used it to argue for the Christian view of Rom 7:14–25. It is Gal 5:16–17, which according to the argument describes the same tension we find in Rom 7:14–25 yet incontestably deals with Christian experience. But wide differences separate the two passages. The desire of the Spirit figures prominently in Gal 5:16–17; but delight in God's law is related to the inner person or mind, not the Spirit, in Rom 7:14–25.[59] In Gal 5:16–17 the Spirit opposes the flesh; in Rom 7:14–25 the mind, or inner person, opposes sin. In Gal 5:16–17 the flesh is virtually equivalent to sin (cf. vv. 19–21); in Rom 7:14–25 flesh is equivalent to the members and the body, differs from sin as its dwelling place and means of action, and is sin's victim rather than the Spirit's opponent. The "I" suffers utter defeat in Rom 7:14–25; the Spirit gives victory in Gal 5:16, 22–24. Rom 7:14–25 is a dismal description, Gal. 5:16–17 a confident exhortation. In Rom 7:14–25 Paul speaks of actualities; in Gal 5:16–17, about purposes – the desire of the flesh, the desire of the Spirit [ἵνα μή + the subjunctive].[60] When actualities finally come into view in Galatians 5 Paul makes clear that the person whose life is characterized by the deeds of the flesh is not regenerate: "Now the deeds of the flesh are evident... those who practice such things will not inherit the kingdom of God" (vv. 19–21). Since "those who belong to Christ Jesus have crucified the flesh with its passions and desires" (Gal 5:24), the power of sin in Rom 7:14–25 makes Gal 5:16–24 damaging rather than helpful to the case for regenerate experience in Rom 7:14–25.

The power of sin leads to the outcry, "Wretched man that I am! Who will rescue me from the body of this death?" (v. 24). Some have seen a parallel with "the body is dead because of sin" in 8:10 and reasoned that since this statement, introduced with the clause "but if Christ is in you," has to do with Christians, "the body of this death" in 7:24 must also belong to a Christian. His cry for deliverance and the thanksgiving in v. 25a look forward, then, to translation and resurrection (cf. 8:23; 1 Cor 15:50–58). But in 8:10 the body is dead in the sense that

---

[59] We have already seen that "mind" and "inner person" do not imply regeneration.

[60] "In order that you may not do the things that you want" apparently means that the flesh aims to thwart the Spirit when you want to do good and that the Spirit aims to thwart the flesh when you want to do evil. Some interpret ἵνα μή as ecbatic here; but in the thirty-eight other passages where Paul uses this construction it is telic. The sole exception comes in 1 Cor 1:10. There it is epexegetical, however, and does not make a real exception; for the epexegetical is a brand of the telic in that purpose is wrapped up in the content of what ἵνα μή introduces. In a few other Pauline passages the ecbatic meaning is possible but the normal telic meaning more natural. Even Fung, who takes the ecbatic meaning and interprets Rom 7:14–25 as the experience of a Christian who tries to keep God's law by his or her own efforts, admits that Gal 5:16–17 envisions a different situation ("The Impotence of the Law," 36–37).

it is mortal, under the sentence of death (see v. 11 and 6:12[61]). Physical death is in view. But "*this* death" in 7:24 looks back to a different kind of death, the one mentioned in vv. 10, 11, and 13 (cf. 8:2) – i.e., Paul's inability to carry out his designs when sin sprang to life. (The word order in 7:24 and the antecedents in vv. 10, 11, and 13 favor "the body of this death" over "this body of death.") Therefore the pre-Christian "I," shackled by a body that sin dominates, cries out for a deliverance that would consist in a body which, though mortal, is freed and filled by the Spirit, its members "instruments of righteousness to God" (see 6:12–23 for the best commentary; also 1 Cor 6:19–20). Such a deliverance takes place at conversion, not at the last day. And it is God who effects that deliverance through Jesus Christ our Lord – therefore the thanksgiving in v. 25a (cf. a similar thanksgiving in 6:17, which unquestionably deals with conversion).

The thanksgiving in v. 25a follows naturally upon the outcry and question in v. 24. But the stepping back in v. 25b to summarize vv. 7–23 or 14–23 has seemed so awkward that it has been considered a gloss.[62] No text critical evidence supports the theory of a gloss, however; and if v. 25b were a gloss, some such evidence would probably bear witness to the pure text.[63] Furthermore, Witherington calls attention to the Greco-Roman rhetorical technique of overlapping;[64] and Dahl points out that vv. 6b and 25b bracket vv. 7–25a:

> Drawing the conclusion of the section, v. 25b corrects a possible misunderstanding of what was said in v. 6b. To be enslaved *palaiotēti grammatos* is not really to be subservient to the law of God, which is served by the *nous* only; in the sphere of the flesh (in which actions are done), "I serve the law of sin." A delayed conclusion, inserted after the beginning of a new trend of thought, would not be without analogy (cf. e.g. Rom 10:17).[65]

Therefore the argument that under the pre-Christian view v. 25b is anticlimactic proves weak. Those who put it forward fail to recognize that under *any* view Paul steps back in v. 25b to draw a conclusion concerning vv. 7–24 or 14–24. We would have to say so even though a Christian were speaking in ch. 7 as well as in ch. 8. Either the backward step is radical from the chronological standpoint (a Christian

---

[61] See also Gundry, *Sōma in Biblical Theology*, 37–47, though the interpretation of 7:24 needs modification by the following comments here.

[62] See, e.g., R. Bultmann, *Exegetica* (ed. E. Dinkler; Tübingen: Mohr [Paul Siebeck], 1967), 278–79. His drawing a line between serving God's law with the mind (v. 25b) and agreeing with and delighting in God's law according to the inner person (vv. 16, 22) is forced. Also arguing for a gloss is H. Lichtenberger, "Der Beginn der Auslegungsgeschichte von Römer 7: Röm 7,25b," *ZNW* 88 (1997): 284–95.

[63] K. Aland, "Glosse, Interpolation, Redaktion und Komposition in der Sicht der neutestamentlichen Textkritik," *Apophoreta* (BZNW 30; Berlin: Töpelmann, 1964), 27–31.

[64] Witherington, *Romans*, 196, with reference to Quintilian, *Instit. Or.* 9.4.129–30.

[65] Dahl, "The Pauline Letters," 25. Cf. also the doxology in 1:25b, after which Paul goes back to finish his former line of thought. Dahl's explanation is better than W. Keuk's attempt to make 7:25b a question beginning a new section ("Dienst des Geistes und des Fleisches: Zur Auslegungsgeschichte und Auslegung von Rm 7,25 b," *TQ* 141 [1961]: 257–80).

"I" looks forward to his resurrection at the last day in v. 25a and reverts to his present struggle in v. 25b), or it is radical in the shifting role of the speaker (the "I" speaks as a victorious Christian in v. 25a but as a wretchedly defeated Christian or non-Christian in v. 25b). In fact, there is a backward step in 8:1 too – all the way back to justification – before Paul takes up sanctification again (cf. the parallel between "Therefore then" in 7:25b and "Now then" in 8:1). Since not even a Christian view of 7:14–25 can avoid the backward step in 8:1, little room is left for denying what is inherently likely, viz., that at an emotional pitch Paul felt his lament and question in v. 24 needed an immediate response before the drawing of a conclusion and the building of a counter theme.[66]

The threefold outcome: (1) Rom 7:14–25 does not describe, much less excuse, moral defeat as a necessary experience of true Christians. Rather, the whole of Rom 7:7–25 leads up to the availability of moral victory in Rom 8:1–17, a victory that is characteristic of them as well as possible for them. Hence, an extended suffering of moral defeat should cause either a questioning of Christian profession or a questioning of the picayunish standards by which Christians sometimes evaluate their lives. (2) Though Paul's pre-Christian moral defeat may have contributed little or nothing to his Christian conversion, a correct reading of Rom 7:7–25 makes him more like the early, conscience-stricken Luther than the New Perspective on Paul allows.[67] (3) Augustine of Hippo made a mistake in changing his mind on the meaning of Rom 7:7–25. His older view was better. And of all people he should have understood Paul's allusion to sexual lusts in sin's springing to life.[68]

---

[66] Cranfield thinks the emotional pitch "highly melodramatic" if a Christian "I" is not crying for deliverance from present distress (*Romans*, 1:345). But is the cry any less melodramatic on the lips of a Christian "I" for whom deliverance from the power of sin is readily available and whose bodily resurrection is assured and expected as a matter of creed? The further argument that if 7:14–25 were pre-Christian it would have appeared in Paul's discussion of humanity without Christ (1:18–3:20) deserves treatment only in a footnote. The argument either leaves 7:7–13 pre-Christian and by doing so forfeits itself, or it demands a Christian referent for 7:7–13, which goes against the wording of the passage. In 1:18–3:20 Paul shows the powerlessness of the law to justify, in 7:7–25 its powerlessness to sanctify: there is no duplication (Godet, *Romans*, 271). Chapter 7 helps ch. 6 draw out 5:20–21; ch. 6 seeks to counteract the domination of sin; ch. 7 describes the role of the law in that domination (Schnackenburg, "Römer 7," 297). And 7:5 sets the theme for 7:7–25; similarly, 7:6 sets the theme for 8:1 ff. (Luz, *Geschichtsverständnis*, 161; idem, "Zum Aufbau von Rom 1–8," *TZ* 25 [1969], 161–81).

[67] See above, pp. 195–224, on the New Perspective.

[68] On Augustine's change of mind see Kümmel, *Römer 7*, 90–94.

14. Style and Substance
in Philippians 2:6–11

It may seem foolhardy to suppose one can add anything profitable to all that has already been written on Phil 2:6–11. Indeed, what is written here will build on what others have written elsewhere. But for all the attention devoted to the style of this passage and to the ways its style affects our understanding of its substance – i.e., its meaning – we may find more of style-cum-substance than has thus far been identified.

When we divide up Phil 2:6–11 according to its participial and finite verbal phrases, there comes to light an overall concentric structure of meaning.[1] This meaning receives additional emphasis from a number of chiasms, some of them unnoted before, as well as from other parallels often noted in earlier studies. The division according to participial and finite verbal phases yields the following:

---

[1] Cf. R. P. Martin, *Carmen Christi* (2d ed.; Grand Rapids: Eerdmans, 1983), 36–38; W. Schenk, *Die Philipperbriefe des Paulus* (Stuttgart: Kohlhammer, 1984), 172–73, 186. In the third edition of his book (*A Hymn of Christ* [Downers Grove, Ill.: InterVarsity, 1997], lvii–lx) Martin follows W. Stenger (*Introduction to New Testament Exegesis* [Grand Rapids: Eerdmans, 1993], 118–32) in dropping from v. 7 μορφὴν δούλου λαβών, "taking a slave's form," as Paul's interpolation into a quoted hymn. But to get a series of synthetically parallel couplets Martin has to combine *two* verbal phrases in one line of a couplet at v. 8: ἐταπείνωσεν ἑαυτὸν γενόμενος ὑπήκοος μέχρι θανάτου, "he humbled himself, becoming obedient unto death." Apart from the "Preface to the 1997 Edition," page numbers in *A Hymn of Christ* match those in *Carmen Christi*. On the Semitic use of participles as finite verbs see E. Lohmeyer, *Kyrios Jesus* (2d ed.; Heidelberg: Winter, 1961), 9–11; Martin, *Carmen Christi/A Hymn of Christ*, 39. Unlike attributive, substantival, and periphrastic participles those in Phil 2:6–11, being circumstantial and therefore adverbial, can stand more or less alone, as illustrated by the ability of such participles to be used as commands (cf. D. Daube, "Appended Note: Participle and Imperative in I Peter," in E. G. Selwyn's *The First Epistle of St. Peter* [New York: St. Martin's, 1958], 467–88; cf. also the independence of participles in absolute constructions). It is another question, of course, whether the more or less independent use of participles reflects an Aramaic original, betrays Aramaic influence on a Greek original, or bears no relation to Aramaic.

$$
\begin{array}{ll}
& \quad\quad\quad\quad a \quad\quad\quad\quad b \\
\text{I.} & \text{ὃς ἐν μορφῇ θεοῦ ὑπάρχων} \\
& \quad\quad\quad\quad\quad\quad b' \quad\quad\quad\quad a' \\
\text{II.} & \text{οὐχ ἁρπαγμὸν ἡγήσατο τὸ εἶναι ἴσα θεῷ}
\end{array}
$$

A

$$
\begin{array}{ll}
& \quad\quad\quad c \quad\quad\quad d \\
\text{III.} & \text{ἀλλὰ ἑαυτὸν ἐκένωσεν} \\
& \quad\quad a'' \quad\quad\quad b'' \\
\text{IV.} & \text{μορφὴν δούλου λαβών}
\end{array}
$$

B

$$
\begin{array}{ll}
& \quad\quad e \quad\quad\quad\quad f \quad\quad\quad\quad g \\
\text{V.} & \text{ἐν ὁμοιώματι ἀνθρώπων γενόμενος} \\
& \quad\quad e' \quad\quad g' \quad\quad f' \\
\text{VI.} & \text{καὶ σχήματι εὑρεθεὶς ὡς ἄνθρωπος}
\end{array}
$$

C

$$
\begin{array}{ll}
& \quad\quad d' \quad\quad\quad c' \\
\text{VII.} & \text{ἐταπείνωσεν ἑαυτὸν} \\
& \quad\quad b''' \quad\quad\quad\quad a''' \quad\quad\quad\quad\quad h \\
\text{VIII.} & \text{γενόμενος ὑπήκοος μέχρι θανάτου, θανάτου δὲ σταυροῦ}
\end{array}
$$

B′

$$
\begin{array}{ll}
& \quad\quad\quad\quad\quad i \quad\quad\quad\quad j \\
\text{IX.} & \text{διὸ καὶ ὁ θεὸς αὐτὸν ὑπερύψωσεν} \\
& \quad\quad\quad\quad j' \quad\quad\quad i' \quad\quad\quad\quad h' \\
\text{X.} & \text{καὶ ἐχαρίσατο αὐτῷ τὸ ὄνομα τὸ ὑπὲρ πᾶν ὄνομα} \\
& \quad\quad\quad\quad k \quad\quad\quad\quad\quad l \\
\text{XI.} & \text{ἵνα ἐν τῷ ὀνόματι Ἰησοῦ πᾶν γόνυ κάμψῃ} \\
& \quad\quad\quad\quad\quad\quad\quad\quad\quad m \\
& \text{ἐπουρανίων καὶ ἐπιγείων καὶ καταχθονίων} \\
& \quad\quad\quad\quad\quad\quad l' \\
\text{XII.} & \text{καὶ πᾶσα γλῶσσα ἐξομολογήσηται} \\
& \quad\quad\quad\quad k' \quad\quad\quad\quad\quad\quad m' \\
& \text{ὅτι}^2 \text{ κύριος Ἰησοῦς Χριστὸς εἰς δόξαν θεοῦ πατρός}
\end{array}
$$

A′

We are now positioned to take up in detail the concentric, chiastic, and other parallel arrangements and to spell out their interpretive implications. The following discussion will require readers to keep looking back at the text as divided and tagged above.

---

[2] I take this ὅτι to be recitative, equivalent to quotation marks setting apart the confession, "Jesus Christ [is] Lord."

Concentricity and Related Other Parallels

Indubitably the pair *VII–VIII* deals with death on a cross, and the quartet *IX–XII* almost certainly with postexistent acknowledgment as divine.[3] Most probably the pair *V–VI* deals with incarnation as a human being.[4] The fact that a concentric arrangement of *A–B–C–B'–A'* would emerge if the pair *I–II* deals with preexistent divine being and the pair *III–IV* deals with slave-like death on a cross favors that the pair *I–II* does indeed deal with preexistent divine being and that the pair *III–IV* does indeed deal with slave-like death on a cross.

A. Preexistent divine being (*I–II*)
  B. Slave-like death (*III–IV*)
    C. Incarnation as a human being (*V–VI*)
  B'. Death on a cross (*VII–VIII*)
A'. Postexistent acknowledgment as divine (*IX–XII*)

Thus existence in the form of God does not refer to Adam-like human existence in God's image, as argued by some[5] though controverted on other grounds by most.[6] Nor does self-emptying refer to the incarnation, as usually thought, but to death on a cross. Also favoring a reference in self-emptying to death on a cross, as argued linguistically above all by J. Jeremias,[7] is the parallel between self-emptying and taking the form of a slave; for in the Roman world crucifixion was associated especially with the execution of slaves.[8] Thus further, *C* (incarnation as a human being in *V–VI*) meets a condition that makes possible the preceding *B* and the following *B'* (slave-like death on a cross in both *III–IV* and *VII–VIII*); and *B* (slave-like death in *III–IV*) contrasts with the preceding *A* (preexistent divine

---

[3] The great height (ὑπερ-) of God's exaltation of Jesus strongly disfavors the view of G. Howard that *IX–XII* has to do only with earthly glory following the resurrection ("Phil 2:6–11 and the Human Christ," *CBQ* 40 [1978]: 378–87).

[4] To take advantage of equality with God implies that Christ Jesus had such equality and that therefore his coming to be in the likeness of human beings and being found in fashion as a human being represent a new phenomenon, i.e., incarnation. On οὐχ ἁρπαγμὸν ἡγάσατο as not taking advantage see R. W. Hoover, "The Harpagmos Enigma: A Philological Solution," *HTR* 64 (1971): 95–119.

[5] See most prominently J. D. G. Dunn, *Christology in the Making* (2d ed.; London: SCM, 1989), xlvii–xix, 114–21. For further bibliography, see C. M. Pate, *The Reverse of the Curse* (WUNT 2/114; Tübingen: Mohr Siebeck, 2000), 308.

[6] See most prominently O. Hofius, *Christushymnus Philipper 2,6–11* (2d ed.; WUNT 17; Tübingen: Mohr [Siebeck], 1991), 115–22, but also Martin, *Carmen Christi/A Hymn of Christ*, xxi; P. T. O'Brien, *The Epistle to the Philippians* (NIGTC; Grand Rapids: Eerdmans, 1991), 263–68, and other literature cited there.

[7] J. Jeremias, *Abba* (Göttingen: Vandenhoeck & Ruprecht, 1966), 208, 275 n. 22, 312–13; idem, "παῖς, παιδίον, κτλ," *TDNT* 5:711–12, esp. n. 445. See the second addendum to this present essay for a treatment of objections to this view.

[8] M. Hengel, *Crucifixion* (Philadelphia: Fortress, 1977), 51–63 (= ch. 8, "The 'Slaves' Punishment'").

being in *I–II*) just as *B'* (death on a cross in *VII–VIII*) contrasts with the following *A'* (postexistent acknowledgment as divine in *IX–XII*).

Though appearing at the center, *C* (incarnation as a human being in *V–VI*) gets the least attention (only two participial phrases are devoted to it) because the incarnation merely meets a condition making possible *B* and *B'* (slave-like death on a cross in *III–IV* and *VII–VIII*) and thus lets emphasis fall on the contrast between the high of pre- and postexistent divine honor and the low of the most shameful of human deaths, the incarnation lying between these extremes.[9] *A'* subdivides into the pair *IX–X*, dealing with postexistent past acknowledgment as divine by God, and *XI–XII*, dealing with postexistent future acknowledgment as divine by every creature.[10] The doubled length of *A'* (it takes up four verbal phrases instead of the usual two each in *A*, *B*, *C*, and *B'*) makes for an outweighing, not just a counterbalancing, of death on a cross (shame) by acknowledgment as divine (honor).[11] Moreover, the independence of the διό-clause ("therefore…") in *IX–X*, the follow-up with a ἵνα-clause ("in order that…"), and the compounding of each clause by the placement of two finite verbs in each one help give even greater weight to postexistent acknowledgment as divine in the outweighing of death on a cross. Moreover again, the unnecessary καί, "also," immediately following διό calls special attention to the complexly and compoundly stated acknowledgments of Jesus as divine. And moreover yet again, the compound subordinate clause that caps the whole passage with references to postexistent future acknowledgment as divine (ἵνα… πᾶν γόνυ κάμψῃ… καὶ πᾶσα γλῶσσα ἐξομολογήσηται…, "in order that… every knee should bow… and every tongue should confess…") forms some-

---

[9] Concentric arrangement does not necessarily put emphasis on the centerpiece. It is just as possible that repetition and first and last mention put emphasis on the flanks (cf. the observation of J. W. Welch that though an emphatic focus on the center may elevate the importance of a central concept or dramatize a radical shift of events, flanking elements may equally effectively emphasize a comparison, a contrast, a complement, or a completion ["Introduction," in *Chiasmus in Antiquity* (ed. J. W. Welch; Hildesheim: Gerstenberg, 1981), 10]). The doubling in length of the final element in Phil 2:6–11 (*IX–XII*; see the following discussion) shows that here the emphasis does not fall on the central element of incarnation.

[10] Schenk includes present Christian worship and confession of Jesus Christ as Lord along with future such worship and confession (*Philipperbriefe*, 193–95). Though this inclusion would leave the worship and confession still future to Jesus' exaltation and name-giving, it seems more natural to see the emphasis on universality ("every knee… every tongue") as pointing to the climactic acclamation of Jesus at the end rather than to an acclamation that evolves throughout the present age.

[11] Martin objects that *A'* "is so gigantic that it throws the preceding chiasms out of balance and makes the total picture look decidedly odd," but he undercuts his own objection by describing himself as "supportive" of my "seeing verses 9–11 [i.e., *A'*] as the 'center of gravity' [quoting my phrase]" (*A Hymn of Christ*, lvi n. 24). Martin's objection is driven by a desire to discover an underlying hymn that can be described as "a *symmetrical whole*" once supposedly Pauline interpolations have been deleted (p. lix [italics original]). But even granted a deletion of such interpolations, by combining two verbal phrases in one line of a couplet at v. 8 (see n. 1 above) he has spoiled the symmetry.

thing of a grammatical *inclusio* with the compound subordinate clause that begins the whole passage with references to divine being, servile self-emptying, and human self-humbling (ὅς… οὐχ… ἡγήσατο… ἀλλὰ ἑαυτὸν ἐκένωσεν… καί… ἐταπείνωσεν ἑαυτόν…, "who… did not consider… but emptied himself… and… humbled himself…"), all in the past.

God's granting Jesus the name κύριος, which means "Master" as well as "Lord," or "Lord" in the sense of "Master" (*X*), compensates for Jesus' taking the form "of a slave" (δούλου – *IV*). Emphasizing the honor of this name are (1) the use of ὄνομα no fewer than three times, plus an implied fourth occurrence after the second τό in *X*; (2) the identification of the name as κύριος, "Lord," in *XII*; (3) the anterior position of κύριος despite its function as a predicate nominative, usually posterior to the subject and to a linking verb; (4) the omission of such a verb, so that emphasis falls undividedly on Lordship; and (5) the aforementioned contrast between κύριος and δοῦλος. The arthrousness of ὄνομα already in its first occurrence (*X*)[12] anticipates the identification of Jesus Christ's name as κύριος (*XII*).

Contributing to the parallel between *A* and *A'* in this concentric structure are the double occurrence in each of different cases of θεός, "God," and by way of contrast the double occurrence in *C*, at the center, of different cases of ἄνθρωπος, "human being." Not only does the double occurrence of θεός both in *A* and in *A'* help form an *inclusio* for the passage as a whole. So also does the double occurrence of θεός in *I* and *II* form an *inclusio* for *A*, and the double occurrence of θεός in *IX* and *XII* an *inclusio* for *A'*. But the parallel between *A* and *A'* does not stop with the double occurrence in each of different cases of θεός. In *A* Christ Jesus acts in respect to God; in *A'* God acts correspondingly in respect to Jesus Christ. Not only does the ὑπερ- of ὑπερύψωσεν (*IX*) anticipate the ὑπέρ of τὸ ὑπὲρ πᾶν ὄνομα (*X*) to stress the supreme height to which God exalts Jesus by granting him the name "Lord." ὑπερ- also recalls ὑπάρχων (*I*), so that existence in the divine form is matched by reception of the divine name.

"For [the] glory of God [the] Father" (*XII*) contributes further to the parallel between *A* and *A'* and recommends itself as an original part of our passage, not a later addition to it by Paul or someone earlier in quotation of a pre-Pauline hymn,[13] by keeping the universal confession of Jesus Christ as Lord from running counter to his not considering equality with God something to be taken advantage of (*II*).[14] And if original to our passage, "for [the] glory of God [the] Father" favors Pauline authorship of the whole inasmuch as the phrase

---

[12] See J. B. Lightfoot, *Saint Paul's Epistle to the Philippians* (London: Macmillan, 1894), 114; O'Brien, *Philippians*, 203 n. d, on the text critical question.

[13] Against Jeremias, *Abba*, 275. For originality see M. Hengel, "Das Christuslied im frühesten Gottesdienst," in *Weisheit Gottes – Weisheit der Welt* (ed. W. Baier et al.; St. Ottilien: EOS Verlag, 1987), 1:402.

[14] For other arguments see Hofius, *Christushymnus*, 7–8, 54–55, 65–66.

echoes "grace (χάρις) to you … from God our Father and [from the] Lord, Jesus Christ" (1:2; cf. the "gracing [ἐχαρίσατο]" of Jesus Christ with the name "Lord" in 2:9–11) and anticipates "glory to God, even our Father" right after a mention of "Christ Jesus" (4:19–20; cf. the following of "Jesus Christ" by the "glory of God [the] Father" in 2:11). Likewise the anticipation of "every knee" (*XI*) and of "every tongue" (*XII*) by "every name" (*X*) insures the originality to our passage of τὸ ὑπὲρ πᾶν ὄνομα, and the triple use of "every" lends weight to the element of universality. Again likewise, the progressive descent from high (ὑπερ-) exaltation (*IX*) and the name above (ὑπέρ) every name (*X*) to heavenly beings (ἐπουρανίων) and then to earthly beings (ἐπιγείων; N.B. the repetition of ἐπ[ί], merely "on" rather than "over" [ὑπέρ]) and finally to subterranean beings (καταχθονίων: κατα-, "down," striking an even stronger contrast with ὑπέρ) favors the originality of the reference to heavenly, earthly, and subterranean beings.[15]

Stepping back, we might take ἀλλά, "but," as starting a new and independent clause in *III*. But no change of subject occurs in the second finite verb vis-à-vis the first finite verb: he who in *II* did not consider equality of being with God something to be taken advantage of is one and the same with him who in *III* emptied himself. Therefore we have no need to think of a new and independent clause in ἀλλὰ ἑαυτὸν ἐκένωσεν, "But he emptied himself"; rather, "but emptied himself," the ὅς, "who," of *I* carrying over to *III* (and also to *VII*, as we will discover; see 1 Tim 3:16 for ὅς as the subject of a multiplicity of verbs and

---

[15] Against Jeremias, *Abba*, 275. Among others, O'Brien (*Philippians*, 239–40) notes that bowing in the name of Jesus has no corresponding value in secular Greek (BDAG, s.v. ὄνομα 1dγℷ, where Phil 2:10a is paraphrased as follows: "that when the name of Jesus is mentioned every knee should bow"), though parallels using other verbs are to be found in the LXX of 3 Kgdms 8:44; Pss 43:9; 62:5; 104:3. In Phil 2:10 we do not have a formula of verbal invocation, exorcism, or prayer; rather, a description of physical worship. O'Brien goes on to say (p. 243) that ἐν τῷ ὀνόματι Ἰησοῦ, "in the name of Jesus," replaces ἐμοί, "to me," of Isa 45:23 LXX "to make plain the astonishing idea that homage is to be paid to Jesus as Lord." I suggest that since "every knee should bow" is paralleled by "every tongue should confess (ἐξομολογήσηται)," the Aramaizing use of ὁμολογέω, "confess," with ἐν (= ℶ; cf. Matt 10:32 par. Luke 12:8; Ps 43:9b LXX; BDAG, s.v. ὁμολογέω 4b) has led here to the unusual but emphatically parallel use of κάμψῃ, "bow," with ἐν (cf. Schenk, *Philipperbriefe*, 189). Alternatively or additionally one might suggest that κάμψῃ here takes ἐν rather than the usual πρός through assimilation to ἐν ὁμοιώματι (*V*), to which ἐν τῷ ὀνόματι comes close in assonance and rhythm of pronunciation. (N.B. the identical number of syllables and the identical number of accents when secondary accents are included in the first and last syllables of ὁμοιώματι and in the last syllable of ὀνόματι as well as in grammatical construction.) If adopted, these suggestions would still not settle the issue whether every knee will bow to worship God in Jesus' name, as favored by the final phrase, "for [the] glory of God [the] Father," or to worship Jesus, as favored by every tongue's confessing, "Jesus Christ [is] Lord." I take the latter view because of the emphasis on Jesus' high exaltation and on God's granting him the name above every name (for discussion, see G. F. Hawthorne, *Philippians* [WBC 43; Waco, Tex.: Word, 1983], 92–93).

Rom 1:21, 32; 2:29; 4:2, 4, 10, 12, 13 and many other passages for continuations of the same subject after ἀλλά).

Or we might take ἐταπείνωσεν ἑαυτόν as the centerpiece of an independent clause, " ... he [not 'who'] emptied himself..." (*VII*), signalled either by asyndeton at the start of *V* if the participial phrase therein (ἐν ὁμοιώματι ἀνθρώπων γενόμενος, "in [the] likeness of human beings having become") goes with the subject in *VII* (the "he" who humbled himself) or – if that participial phrase goes with the subject in *III* (the "he" who emptied himself) – signalled by the conjunction in *VI* (καί, "and"). Putting a full stop after self-emptying would create asyndeton both between the dependent clause concerning self-emptying and the independent clause concerning self-humbling and between the participial phrase concerning the taking of a slave's form and the participial phrases concerning the coming to be in the likeness of human beings and being found as to fashion like a human being. It would also load the "he" who humbled himself with three preceding participial phrases in succession, plus a fourth one following. Putting a full stop after being found as to fashion like a human being would again create asyndeton between the participial phrase concerning the taking of a slave's form and the following two participial phrases, would load the "he" who emptied himself with three following participial phrases in succession, and would leave the "he" who humbled himself with only the participial phrase following it (γενόμενος ὑπήκοος ..., "becoming obedient ..."). A full stop after taking a slave's form would give the "he" who emptied himself only one, subsequent participial phrase, would load the "he" who humbled himself with two preceding participial phrases plus a third one following, and would create asyndeton between clauses though avoiding it between participial phrases in the same clause. A full stop after becoming in human beings' likeness would give two participial phrases each to the "he" who emptied himself and to the "he" who humbled himself (though the former two both follow their "he," whereas the latter two straddle their "he") and would avoid asyndeton between clauses though creating it between the former two participial phrases. Taking the participial phrases as conceptually though not grammatically independent, i.e., as conceptually though not grammatically equivalent to finite verbs, would subtract problems of unequal loading by bringing over, in effect, the subjects of finite verbs to the participles but would multiply problems of asyndeton by creating asyndeta, again in effect, at the openings of *IV, V, VII,* and *VIII*.

It seems best to equalize the participial loads of the "he" who emptied himself and the "he" who humbled himself. Though the equalization creates asyndeton between the participial phrases concerning the taking of a slave's form and the coming to be in human beings' fashion, this asyndeton poses less awkwardness than an asyndeton between clauses would pose; and the greater awkwardness of asyndeton between clauses would entail the added disadvantage of inequality in

participial loads. Galatians 4:4 demonstrates the acceptability in Pauline literature of asyndeton between participial phrases;[16] and a natural differentiation between μορφὴν δούλου λαβών as expressing an action contemporaneous with
that of ἑαυτὸν ἐκένωσεν, "[who] emptied himself *by* taking [the] form of a
slave," and ἐν ὁμοιώματι ἀνθρώπων γενόμενος as expressing an action prior
to that of ἑαυτὸν ἐκένωσεν, "[who] emptied himself *after* coming to be in [the]
likeness of human beings" (more on this difference below), relieves most if not
all of the asyndetic awkwardness between these two participial phrases. But if
we take them as both modifying the "he" who emptied himself we need not put
a full stop after γενόμενος at the end of *V*; for then the καί, "and," following immediately at the start of *VI* simply introduces the third main-verbal phrase in a
compound dependent clause for which ὅς, "who," provides the common subject.[17] Inasmuch as "having come to be in [the] likeness of human beings" (*V*)
and "as to fashion having been found as a human being" (*VI*) both refer to the
incarnation, they make a couplet (*C*). But inasmuch as the second of these participial phrases starts with "and," the first relates back to the subject of "emptied
himself" and the second forward to the subject of "humbled himself" so as to
equalize the number of participial phrases modifying each subject (though from
another standpoint, as just argued, "each subject" is really the same subject
"who," carried over from the very start).

Between the compound subordinate clauses beginning with ὅς, "who," and
with ἵνα, "in order that," lies the compound independent clause signalled by διὸ
καί, "therefore also," and featuring the new subject ὁ θεός, "God," and its verbs
ὑπερύψωσεν, "highly exalted," and ἐχαρίσατο, "granted." It bears repeating
that as the only independent clause in the whole passage and therefore as its
grammatical center of gravity, this indication of God's high exaltation of Christ
Jesus and of God's granting him the name above every name carries more
weight than any other clause or participial unit in the passage.[18]

Chiasm and Related Other Parallels

Supplemented by related other parallels, chiastic arrangements abound in
Phil 2:6–11. Taking the form of a slave, which signifies a slave-like death (*IV*),
makes an antithetic parallel with existing in the form of God (*I*). Similarly self-

---

[16] Gal 4:4: "When the fullness of time had come God sent forth his Son, born (γενόμενον) of
a woman, [asyndeton] born (γενόμενον) under [the] law."

[17] Cf. G. D. Fee, "Philippians 2:5–11: Hymn or Exalted Pauline Prose?" *BBR* 2 (1992):
40–41 n. 42, except that Fee sees the start of a new sentence rather than the start of a new main-
verbal phrase in a compound dependent clause.

[18] See O'Brien, *Philippians*, 249–50, that *XII* would not make an independent clause even
though the future indicative *v.l.* ἐξομολογήσεται were accepted.

emptying, which again signifies death (*III*), makes an antithetic parallel with refusal to consider equality of being with God something to be taken advantage of (*II*). In *I–IV*, then, we have a contentually chiastic arrangement of a–b–b'–a'.[19] The order of participial phrase (*I*: "existing ...")–finite verbal phrase (*II*: "did not consider ...")–finite verbal phrase (*III*: "but emptied himself")–participial phrase (*IV*: "having taken ...") adds grammatical chiasm to contentual chiasm.[20]

a ("in [the] form of God")–*b* ("existing")–*b'* ("considered")–*a'* ("being equal with God") presents a chiastic arrangement in reference to preexistent divine being. *c* ("himself")–*d* ("emptied")–*d'* ("humbled")–*c'* ("himself") presents a chiastic arrangement in reference to death on a cross.[21] Though *a–b–a"–b"* presents a nonchiastic arrangement in reference to the antithesis between existing in the form of God and taking the form of a slave (N.B. the use of μορφή, "form," in both expressions, as often noted), *a"* ("[the] form of a slave")–*b"* ("taking")–*b'''* ("becoming")–*a'''* ("obedient unto death") presents a chiastic arrangement, again in reference to death on a cross.[22]

Though *V* and *VI* start alike with *e* ("in [the] likeness") and *e'* ("as to fashion"), respectively, *f* ("of human beings")–*g* ("having become")–*g'* ("having been found")–*f'* ("as a human being") presents a chiastic arrangement in reference to the incarnation.[23] *h* ("rather, death of a cross") and *h'* ("the [name] above every name") present a pair of tailpieces, both of them appositives at the close of references to death on a cross and to acknowledgment as divine, respectively, and both of them adding a fillip to the contrast between shame and honor in those respective events. The antithetic parallel between *h* and *h'* favors that h belongs to this composition as an original element.[24]

---

[19] So H.-W. Bartsch, *Die konkrete Wahrheit und die Lüge der Spekulation* (Theologie und Wirklichkeit 1; Frankfurt/Main: P. Lang, 1974), 17–18. But Bartsch errs in seeing chiasm in the next four verbal units; for coming to be in the likeness of human beings (*V*) does not have a counterpart in becoming obedient unto death (*VIII*), nor does being found in fashion as a human being (*VI*) have a counterpart in self-humbling (*VII*).

[20] Cf. Jeremias, *Abba*, 279, with F. Manns, "Philippians 2:6–11: A Judeo-Christian Hymn," *TD* 26 (1978): 5–6. Manns errs, however, in separating out τὸ εἶναι ἴσα θεῷ, "the being equal with God," for treatment as c in a concentric arrangement a–b–c–b'–a'. That phrase must stay in b for a parallel with "existing in the form of God" in a. Likewise forced several other attempts of Manns to find concentric structure by dividing single verbal units.

[21] As recognized by Jeremias, *Abba*, 312, and others. Hofius (*Christushymnus*, 7) considers ἑαυτὸν ἐκένωσεν, "himself emptied" (*III*), to be in chiastic antithetical parallelism with ἡγήσατο τὸ εἶναι ἴσα θεῷ, "considered being equal with God" (*II*). But the reflexive pronoun does not make a very good counterpart to the articular infinitival phrase. Equality of being with God relates much better to existence in God's form (*I*), and self-emptying relates much better to self-humbling (*VII*).

[22] So also Schenk, *Philipperbriefe*, 187.

[23] So also Manns, "Philippians 2:6–11," 5–6.

[24] See esp. Hofius, *Christushymnus*, 3–17, 61–64.

i ("him")–*j* ("highly exalted")–*j'* ("granted")–*i'* ("him the name") presents a chiastic arrangement in reference to postexistent *past* acknowledgment as divine by God. *k* ("in the name of Jesus")–*l* ("every knee should bow")–*l'* ("every tongue should confess")–*k'* ("Jesus Christ [is] Lord") presents a chiastic arrangement in reference to *future* postexistent acknowledgment as divine by every creature (N.B. esp. the parallel between "every knee" and "every tongue").[25] *m* ("of heavenly and earthly and subterranean [beings]") and *m'* ("for [the] glory of God [the] Father") present another pair of tailpieces, neither of them necessary to the overall thought but both of them adding a fillip each to the final clauses referring to future postexistent acknowledgment as divine. The successiveness of the verbal phrases in which these tailpieces occur (contrast the separation of the tailpieces *h* and *h'*) again increases the outweighing of death on a cross by acknowledgment as divine. Respectively, these tailpieces specify the range of knee-bowing and the purpose-cum-result of tongue-confessing.

The chiasms emphasize the element mentioned first and again last. Thus emphasis falls on Jesus' preexistent divine being (*a* and *a'*), on him as the object of his self-emptying/humbling (*c* and *c'*), on his slave-like death by crucifixion (*a''* and *a'''*), on his humanity (*f* and *f*), on him as the object of God's acknowledgment (*i* and *i'*), and on Jesus' divine name (*k* and *k'*). Alone, the forward positions of *a, c, a'', f, i,* and *k* would have carried an emphasis on the elements just noted. But the combination of forward positions with chiasm increases the emphasis immensely. Except for conjunctions and subjects, plus a negative and four tailpieces, the only elements lying outside these chiastic arrangements are the logically second accusative ἁρπαγμόν, "something to be taken advantage of" (*II*), the referential prepositional phrase ἐν ὁμοιώματι, "in [the] likeness" (*V*), and the referential dative σχήματι, "as to fashion" (VI). Like the conjunctions, subjects, and negative the referential expressions are introductory. The logically second accusative has taken a textually first position after the negative, where emphasis falls on equality of being with God as *not* being considered something to be taken advantage of.[26]

Further Interpretive Implications

The chiasm of *k–l–l'–k'* favors that despite the arguments of C. F. D. Moule and M. Silva to the contrary "the name above every name" does not refer to "Jesus."[27] For "the name of Jesus" corresponds to "Jesus Christ [is] Lord," with

[25] So also O'Brien, *Philippians*, 247.

[26] Cf. Schenk, *Philipperbriefe*, 189.

[27] Against C. F. D. Moule, "Further Reflexions on Philippians 2:5–11," in *Apostolic History and the Gospel* (ed. W. W. Gasque and R. P. Martin; Grand Rapids: Eerdmans, 1970), 270; M. Silva, *Philippians* (Wycliffe Exegetical Commentary; Chicago: Moody, 1988), 128–29.

κύριος, "Lord," put first for emphasis on this name as the honorific one in view. And to carry over "in the name of Jesus" to the last line, producing "and [in order that] every tongue should confess *in the name of Jesus*, 'Jesus Christ [is] Lord,' …,"[28] would both spoil the chiasm of *k–l–l'–k'* and threaten to make *k'* ("Jesus Christ [is] Lord") superfluous; for "in his name" would probably say all that needs saying about the confession.[29]

The correspondence between Jesus Christ's equality of being with God (*A*) and God's high exaltation of him (*A'*) undermines the growingly popular view that we should take ἐν μορφῇ θεοῦ ὑπάρχων as causative ("*because* he existed in [the] form of God") rather than concessive ("*although* he existed in [the] form of God"). For to the extent that becoming human and dying a shameful death lay in the very nature of divine preexistence the διό, "therefore," which introduces the high exaltation looks misplaced: it should have introduced incarnation and death on a cross. By introducing the exaltation instead, and a doubly emphasized exaltation at that, διό makes the incarnation and especially death on a cross the reason for an exaltation matching the preexistent equality with God which made that incarnation and death so lovingly irregular (cf. vv. 1–5) as to deserve such a compensation.[30]

Pairing and chiasm favor the synonymity of the form of God with equality to God and thus disfavor taking the ἐν before μορφῇ θεοῦ to diminish the meaning of "[the] form of God," as though existence *in* God's form meant less than *being* God's form.[31] This argument increases in strength if the τό before εἶναι is anaphoric, referring the being equal with God back to existence in his form,[32] and if the ἐν before ὁμοιώματι ἀνθρώπων does not diminish the meaning of "[the] likeness of human beings" as though being *in* human likeness meant less than *being* human. In and of itself, we should note, incarnation need not connote humiliation – quite oppositely, it may connote glory (John 1:14; cf. the sacrifi-

---

Though supported by the fact that elsewhere a genitive following ὄνομα indicates the name itself, not the possessor of another name, Moule's and Silva's view would notably require that the name which is Jesus differ from Jesus' name that is above every name. For God granted the name above every name in consequence (διο) of Jesus' humbling himself to the point of death on a cross, yet God did not grant the name "Jesus" in consequence of that self-humbling. Jesus had borne this name since his circumcision (Luke 2:2; cf. Matt 1:22; so, correctly, Martin, *Carmen Christi/A Hymn of Christ*, 235; see also O'Brien, *Philippians*, 237–38).

[28] Suggested by O'Brien, *Philippians*, 248.

[29] One may detect a chiasm in "Christ Jesus" (v. 5) and "Jesus Christ" (v. 11). But the components of this chiasm are quite far apart from each other, a lone "Jesus" intervenes in v. 10, and "Christ" follows "Jesus" in v. 11 probably to avoid the placement of two titles, "Lord" and "Christ," in side-by-side competition (κύριος, "Lord," coming first in the Greek text).

[30] Against, O'Brien, *Philippians*, 214, and those listed by him in n. 55.

[31] Against E. Käsemann, "A Critical Analysis of Philippians 2:5–11," *JTC* 5 (1968): 61–62.

[32] So Hawthorne, *Philippians*, 84, with supportive references to L. Cerfaux and M. Dibelius. See Silva, *Philippians*, 124, that equality of *being* with God (an adverbial ἴσα) does not fall below equality of *personhood* with God (for which we would expect ἴσος).

cial worship proferred Barnabas and Paul, thought to be Zeus and Hermes come down in human likeness [Acts 14:11–13]) – much less the extreme of humiliation entailed by crucifixion, as here. So chronological order gives way to rhetorical contrast.

In its structure – ἐν plus a singular noun followed by a dependent genitive and a participle – ἐν ὁμοιώματι ἀνθρώπων γενόμενος, "in [the] likeness of human beings having become" (*V*), parallels ἐν μορφῇ θεοῦ ὑπάρχων, "in [the] form of God existing" (*I*). Though "likeness" is more or less synonymous with "form," "of human beings" contrasts with "of God"; and "having become," which rests on a Greek aorist participle, contrasts with "existing," which rests on a Greek present participle. "As to fashion like a human being" (*VI*) similarly contrasts with "being equal to God" (*II*), though not considering the equality something to take advantage of led to being found in fashion as a human being.[33] More immediate and stronger than the contrast between deity and humanity, however, is the contrast between deity and death (see esp. the forceful ἀλλά, "but," and διό, "therefore").

The striking and oft-noted parallel between the reflexive constructions ἑαυτὸν ἐκένωσεν (*III*, the first member of *B*) and ἐταπείνωσεν ἑαυτόν (*VII*, the first member of *B'*), a parallel buttressed by the assonance of the verbs (and we should remind ourselves that Philippians was more heard than read[34]), is not quite matched by the parallel between γενόμενος in *V* and γενόμενος in *VIII*. Though one cannot deny a certain echo, in its second occurrence this participle takes a predicate adjective (ὑπήκοος, "obedient") but not in its first occurrence; nor does the participle appear in corresponding sections (rather, in *C* and *B'*). Thus it deals with unlike topics, viz., incarnation on the one hand and death on the other. Hence the two occurrences can hardly bear the weight of bounding a strophe on Jesus' earthly life.[35]

Both *IV* and *VIII* are best taken as participial phrases of means: "[who] emptied himself *by* taking [the] form of a slave" and "[who] humbled himself *by* becoming obedient unto death." For becoming obedient unto death did not precede self-humbling. Much less did self-humbling precede becoming obedient unto death, because the aorist tense of γενόμενος, "becoming," indicates action prior to or concurrent with and even equivalent to that of the main verb but hardly action subsequent to that of the main verb as required by a self-humbling that preceded becoming obedient unto death. Therefore self-humbling does not refer to the incarnation, which preceded death. By the same token, i.e., because of the parallel between *B* and *B'*, taking the form of a slave does not refer to the

---

[33] Cf. Jeremias, *Abba*, 312.

[34] P. J. Achtemeier, "*Omne verbum sonat*: The New Testament and the Oral Environment of Late Western Antiquity," *JBL* 109 (1990): 3–27.

[35] Against Jeremias, *Abba*, 274–76, 312–13. For further criticisms see Hofius, *Christushymnus*, 6 n. 15.

incarnation but to death, the death of a convicted slave, death on a cross. And just as becoming obedient unto death defines self-humbling, so taking the form of a slave defines self-emptying. Christ Jesus did not take a slave's form before emptying himself, much less take a slave's form after emptying himself (this latter being disallowed by the aorist tense of λαβών, "taking"), but emptied himself by taking the cruciform of a slave. Once again, then, self-emptying does not refer to the incarnation; and ἑαυτὸν ἐκένωσεν should be understood as an idiomatic Greek allusion to נפשו ... הערה in Isa 53:12. Not till the following participial phrases, "having come to be in the likeness of human beings" and "as to fashion, having been found as a human being," does the antecedent action of incarnation come into view. The parallel between *III* and *IV* in *B* also favors an allusion to Isa 53:12 in that the one who according to that passage poured out his soul is a slave to whose "form" (תאר) the prophet makes reference (Isa 52:14; 53:2) just as the Jesus who emptied himself is a slave to whose "form" (μορφήν) Paul makes reference (cf. the use of μορφή for תאר in Judg 8:18 LXX^A; Isa 52:14 Aq).

The parallel between *V* and *VI* in *C* disfavors a taking of *V* ("in [the] likeness of human beings having become") as equivalent to and therefore incarnationally interpretive of *IV* ("[the] form of a slave taking"); rather, as equivalent to and expressive of the incarnation along with *VI* ("as to fashion having been found as a human being"). In turn, these expressions of the incarnation favor that *I* and *II* in *A* describe a preincarnate state of being and a preincarnate action, which correspond to what later follows the incarnational actions, i.e., to *IX–XII* in *A'*, rather than describing already in *I* and *II* of *A* a human state of being and a human action, both comparable to Adam's. Moreover, the already noted chiasm in *I* and *II* favors that equality of being with God (*a'*) defines God's form (*a*) in terms of deity as opposed to Adam-like creaturehood in God's image. It would seem a bit much to have in succession a finite verbal expression ("emptied himself") and three participial phrases ("taking [the] form of a slave," "coming to be in the likeness of human beings," and "as to fashion being found as a human being") all referring to the incarnation.[36] And the form of a slave need not equate with the likeness of human beings or with human fashion; for by no means are *all* human beings slaves, unless without other indication the passage is implying the slavery of human beings in general, Jesus Christ included, to the elemental spirits of the universe[37] or to corruption.[38]

---

[36] Against O'Brien, who takes both λαβών and the first γενόμενος as coincident with ἐκένωσεν and expressive of manner (*Philippians*, 217).

[37] So Käsemann, "Critical Analysis," 66–67. G. Bornkamm supports Käsemann on the ground that this view explains why incarnation and slavery go together (*Studien zu Antike und Christentum* [BEvT 28; Munich: Chr. Kaiser, 1970], 181). But if self-emptying by taking the form of a slave refers to death, incarnation does not go together with slavery. A certain kind of death does, viz., death on a cross.

The parallel between *V* and *VI* also undermines the interpretation of ὁμοιώματι, "likeness" (*V*), as something less than "identity or equivalence" with
human beings, the statement of "a real incarnation" not coming till *VI* ("and as
to fashion having been found as a human being").[39] The fashion of a human
being does not differ from the likeness of human beings. It is only *being found*
in fashion as a human being that marks an advance by way of consequence on
coming to be in the likeness of human beings. That is to say, synthetic parallelism characterizes *V* and *VI*: being found in fashion as a human being ensued
from coming to be in the likeness of human beings.[40] But both statements relate
to the incarnation.[41]

Calling all possible attention to crucifixion as such, its utter shamefulness,
are the repetition of θανάτου, "death," the addition of σταυροῦ, "of a cross,"
the use of an adversative δέ, "rather," instead of the expected ascensive καί,
"even," thus making death on a cross contrast with every other kind of death,[42]
and the anarthrousness of both θανάτου and σταυροῦ. The correspondence
between death on a cross, which carried the connotation of a slave's execution
(*B'*), and a slave's emptying himself in death (*B*) again speaks for the originality of θανάτου δὲ σταυροῦ (*VIII*), often regarded as an addition by Paul or
someone earlier to a pre-Pauline hymn.[43] Much more does the concentric structure disfavor treating the whole of v. 8 (*VII–VIII*) as a Pauline gloss on an earlier hymn.[44]

Just as God's high exaltation of Jesus (*IX*) compensates for Jesus' lowering
himself (*VII*), so also does God's granting Jesus the name above every name
(*X*) compensate for Jesus' becoming obedient to death on a cross (*VIII*). Thus
we have in *VII–X* an a–b–a'–b' arrangement that further magnifies the outweighing of Jesus' shameful death with highest honor. Synthetic parallelism
characterizes *IX* and *X*: God's high exaltation of Jesus leads to God's granting

---

[38] So Dunn, *Christology in the Making*, 115–16, with reference to Rom 8:18–21.

[39] Against R. P. Martin, *Philippians* (NCB; London: Oliphants, 1976), 98, in dependence on
O. Michel.

[40] J. Weiss, "Beiträge zur paulinischen Rhetorik," in *Theologische Studien* (Göttingen: Vandenhoeck & Ruprecht, 1897), 190–91.

[41] The view of Schenk that σχήματι depends on ἐν would strengthen the correspondence
with ὁμοιώματι, which most certainly depends on ἐν, to produce "in likeness … and in
fashion" (*Philipperbriefe*, 187). But the intervention of γενόμενος, "having come to be," the
construal of σχήματι with a new participle, εὑρεθείς, "having been found," and perhaps the
difference between a genitive in ἀνθρώπων, "of human beings," and a conjunction plus a
nominative in ὡς ἄνθρωπος, "as a human being," disfavor a carry-over of ἐν and favor the
dative of respect in σχήματι, "as to fashion."

[42] Cf. Rom 3:22 and 9:30, in both of which passages δέ contrasts the righteousness of God
with all other righteousness to which people might lay claim.

[43] For the originality of θανάτου δὲ σταυροῦ see also Hengel, "Das Christuslied," 402.

[44] Against G. Strecker, "Redaktion und Tradition im Christushymnus Phil 2 6–11," *ZNW* 55
(1964): 63–78.

him the name above every name. Synthetic parallelism characterizes *XI* and *XII* too: every knee's bowing in honor of Jesus' name leads to every tongue's confessing, "Jesus Christ [is] Lord."[45] Furthermore, every knee's bowing in honor of his name (*IX*; N.B. the downward direction of the action) not only corresponds to Jesus' lowering himself (*VII*) but also, along with that self-lowering, forms a counterpart to God's lifting Jesus up on high (*IX*; N.B. the contrastive upward direction of the action): the bowing acknowledges the exaltation.[46] And every tongue's confessing that Jesus Christ is Lord (*XII*) is the counterpart to God's granting Jesus the name above every name (*X*): the confessing acknowledges the name giving. Thus we have in *IX–XII* another a–b–a'–b' arrangement that yet further magnifies the outweighing of Jesus' shameful death with highest honor.[47]

Finally, the concentricity, chiasms, and related other parallels in Phil 2:6–11 rather favor the view that this passage represents Paul's own exalted prose (a view gradually regaining favor[48]) rather than an early Christian hymn whose lines of fairly equal length Paul has disequalized with additions. For as noted above, the supposed additions form integral parts of the overall style and substance. It does not matter how many of the concentric, chiastic, and related other parallels stemmed from deliberate art well aware of itself, how many from spontaneous art quite unaware of itself, and how many from art of intermediate gradations of self-awareness. (Could Paul himself or any other author always make such distinctions?) All that we have is the text, and we can only analyze it whatever the degree of deliberation or spontaneity that fed into its production. But what a text![49] A correct interpretation of it lays more emphasis on the old,

---

[45] E. Lohmeyer (*Kyrios Jesus*, 6) thinks that every knee's bowing in the name of Jesus (*XI*) parallels God's granting Jesus the name above every name (*X*). Certainly the giving of the name makes possible the knee-bowing in that name; but it seems misguided to speak of parallelism. The shift from an independent clause to a subordinate one combines with grammatical and conceptual parallels between *IX* and *X* and between *XI* and *XII*, and with chiasms in both pairs (see the preceding discussion), to favor parallelism instead between exaltation and name-giving and between knee-bowing and confession (so, correctly, Jeremias, *Abba*, 311).

[46] On bowing the knee as a mark of extreme abasement and submission inasmuch as people usually stood to pray see Martin, *Carmen Christi/A Hymn of Christ*, 265; O'Brien, *Philippians*, 240–41.

[47] Cf. J. Weiss, "Beiträge zur paulinischen Rhetorik," 190–91.

[48] See Fee, "Philippians 2:5–11," 29–46, and except for his denial of Pauline authorship J. Reumann, "Resurrection in Philippi and Paul's Letter(s) to the Philippians," in *Resurrection in the New Testament* (ed. R. Bieringer, V. Koperski, and B. Lataire; BETL 165; Leuven: Leuven University Press, 2000), 411 n.11. Hengel argues for a hymn, but one possibly composed by Paul ("Das Christuslied," 401–2); and Martin maintains the pre-Pauline hymnic hypothesis (*A Hymn of Christ*, lv–lxv).

[49] With this exclamation I acknowledge that the present essay leaves many matters undiscussed, so fascinatingly rich is the text.

primitive contrast between Christ's crucifixion and exaltation than on the younger contrast between his incarnation and preexistent glory.

Addendum I: Assonance and Euphony in Philippians 2:6–11

The following certain and possible instances of assonance and euphony may be noted in Phil 2:6–11:

1) αϱ in ὑπάϱχων and ἁϱπαγμόν (*I–II*);
2) ων/ον in ὑπάϱχων and ἁϱπαγμόν (*I–II*);[50]
3) σα in ἡγήσατο and ἴσα (*II*);
4) το in ἡγήσατο and τό (*II*);
5) ει/ι in εἶναι and ἴσα (*II*);[51]
6) the whole of ἑαυτόν (twice in *III* and *VII*);
7) ἐ–νωσεν in ἐκένωσεν and ἐταπείνωσεν (*III* and *VII*);
8) ματι in ὁμοιώματι and σχήματι (*V* and *VI*);
9) ἀνθϱωπω/ο in ἀνθϱώπων and ἄνθϱωπος (*V* and *VI*);
10) ος in γενόμενος and ἄνθϱωπος (*V* and *VI*);
11) the whole of γενόμενος (twice in *V* and *VIII*);
12) η and ι in σχήματι (*VI*);[52]
13) ως in ὡς and ἐταπείνωσεν (*VI* and *VII*);
14) νω, ον, and νο in ἐταπείνωσεν, ἑαυτόν, and γενόμενος (*VII* and *VIII*);
15) ος in γενόμενος and ὑπήκοος (*VIII*);
16) the whole of θανάτου (twice in *VIII*);
17) ου in θανάτου (twice) and σταυϱοῦ (*VIII*);
18) the whole of καί (twice in *IX* and *X*);
19) αὐτο/-ῳ in αὐτόν and αὐτῷ (*IX* and *X*);
20) ὑπεϱ in ὑπεϱύψωσεν and ὑπέϱ (*IX* and *X*);
21) το/τῳ in ἐχαϱίσατο, αὐτῷ, and τό (twice – *X*);
22) ο/ω in ἐχαϱίσατο, αὐτῷ (twice), and ὄνομα (twice – *X*);
23) το/τῳ ονομα in τὸ ὄνομα (twice) and τῷ ὀνόματι (*X* and *XI*);
24) ον/αν in ὄνομα (three times), πᾶν (twice), γόνυ, and δόξαν (*X*, *XI*, and *XII*);
25) ου/υ in Ἰησοῦ, γόνυ, and ἐπουϱανίων (*XI*);[53]

---

[50] For the loss of a quantitative distinction between long and short vowels see F. T. Gignac, "Phonological Phenomena in the Greek Papyri Significant for the Text and Language of the New Testament," in *To Touch the Text* (ed. M. P. Horgan and P. J. Kobelski; New York: Crossroad, 1989), 37.

[51] For the identical pronunciations of ει and ι see Gignac, "Phonological Phenomena," 34–35.

[52] See Gignac, "Phonological Phenomena," 39.

[53] See Gignac, "Phonological Phenomena," 36–37.

26) ἐπ in ἐπουρανίων and ἐπιγείων (XI);
27) ανιων/ονιων in ἐπουρανίων and καταχθονίων (XI);
28) ιων/ειων in ἐπουρανίων, ἐπιγείων, and καταχθονίων (XI);
29) the whole of καί (three times in XI and XII);
30) α/ο in πᾶσα, γλώσσα, ἐξομολογήσηται, ὅτι, κύριος, Χριστός, δόξαν, and πατρός (XII);
31) σα in πᾶσα and γλώσσα (XII);
32) ος in κύριος, Χριστός, and πατρός (cf. ους in Ἰησοῦς – XII); and
33) ισ/εις in Χριστός and εἰς (XII).

Addendum II: Self-Emptying as Death, Not Incarnation

The high number of likely allusions to Isa 52:13–53:12 in Phil 2:6–11 and the indubitable allusion to Isa 45:23 in v. 11 – all in the context of servanthood – strengthen the case for an allusion to "poured out his soul unto death" (Isa 53:12) in "emptied himself ... unto death" (vv. 7–8).[54] The placement of "taking the form of a slave/servant" right after the reference to self-emptying looks like a signal to the allusion. O'Brien puts much weight on the linguistic objection that the use of נפשׁ as a reflexive "is extremely rare, both in biblical Hebrew and in the Qumran texts, while μεχρὶ θανάτου appears to be too far from μορφὴν δούλου λαβών to justify its being a direct translation of the Hebrew expression [למות] and only supports the argument that the phrase 'taking the form of a servant' is a reference to Jesus' incarnation, not his death."[55] But "becoming obedient unto death" occurs right after self-humbling, which corresponds very well to abasement in Isa 52:13–53:12, just as obedience corresponds to servanthood in that same passage. And elsewhere too individual elements in a borrowed text are sep-

---

[54] L. Cerfaux, "L'hymne au Christ-Serviteur de Dieu (*Phil.* II, 6–11 = *Is.* LII, 13–LIII, 12)," *Recueil Lucien Cerfaux II* (Gembloux: Duculot, 1954), 425–37; idem, *Christ in the Theology of St. Paul* (New York: Herder & Herder, 1959), 377–82, 385–86, 390–96; L. Krinetzki, "Der Einfluss von Is 52,13–53,12 par auf Phil 2,6–11, *TQ* 139 (1959): 157–93, 291–336; A. Feuillet, "L'hymne christologique de l'épître aux Philippiens," *RB* 72 (1965): 359–65. Both Cerfaux ("L'hymne au Christ," 428; *Christ*, 390–91) and M. Rissi ("Der Christushymnus in Phil 2,6–11," *ANRW* II 25.4:3320–21) argue that ὡς ἄνθρωπος (*VI*) alludes to ἄνθρωπος ἐν πληγῇ ὤν, "being a man in misfortune," in Isa 53:3 LXX rather than to ὡς υἱὸς ἀνθρώπου, "as a son of man," in Dan 7:13 LXX Theod, as thought by E. Lohmeyer on the ground that ὡς, "as," would not follow εὑρεθείς, "having been found," in normal Greek (*Die Brief an die Philipper, an die Kolosser und an Philemon* [19th ed.; MeyerK; Göttingen: Vandenhoeck & Ruprecht, 1953], 95; *Kyrios Jesus*, 38–41). Even if Lohmeyer is correct, however, the many other allusions to Isa 52:13–53:12 are not thereby negated; for the NT often dovetails allusions to different OT passages. A possible advantage of Lohmeyer's view lies in the presence of ὡς in Dan 7:13 LXX Theod but not in Isa 53:3 LXX. On the other hand, the supposition of an ellipsis after Paul's ὡς ἄνθρωπος, to be filled with εὑρίσκεται, producing "as a human being is found," weakens the advantage of Lohmeyer's view.

[55] O'Brien, *Philippians*, 269, with references to R. Deichgräber and T. Nagata.

arated in the borrowing just as emptying one's soul, i.e., self, and "unto death," which appear together in Isa 53:12, are separated in Phil 2:7–8. For examples of such separation see Mark 11:9–10 parr. with Ps 118:25–26; Rom 10:6–8 with Deut 30:12–14; and compare the distribution of Mark 11:25 in the separated passages Matt 5:23–24; 6:5, 14.[56] The rarity of נפש as a reflexive is overstated[57] and counterbalanced by the much greater rarity of נפש with ערה, as in Isa 53:12 (elsewhere in the Hebrew Bible only at Ps 141:8, there too referring most probably to death; cf. the reference to Sheol's mouth in the immediately preceding verse), and by the uniqueness in ancient Greek literature of ἑαυτόν with κενόω at Phil 2:7. This rarity and uniqueness make the correspondence between the Hebrew and Greek expressions most striking, and weight should also be assigned to the idiomatic use of ἑαυτόν for τὴν ψυχὴν αὐτοῦ (= נפשו) in the two Pauline or deutero-Pauline texts 1 Tim 2:6; Titus 2:14 as compared with Mark 10:45 par. Matt 20:28.[58] As to differences from the LXX of Isa 52:13– 53:12, many acknowledged quotations of and allusions to the OT in the NT differ from the LXX. One thinks not only of the formula-quotations in Matthew[59] but also of differences from the LXX in Pauline quotations of the OT.[60] A non-Septuagintal text does not rule out use of the OT.[61]

Martin notes that the linguistic arguments lodged against taking ἑαυτὸν ἐκένωσεν as an idiomatic Greek translation of נפשו ... הערה in Isa 53:12 do not hold up; but he considers a chronological objection decisive, viz., that the leap from preexistence to the crucifixion is too long in that it by-passes the incarnation.[62] But H. W. Robinson notes that in Rom 2:12–16 Paul inserts a chronologically backward reference between chronologically forward references

---

[56] R. H. Gundry, *Matthew* (2d ed.; Grand Rapids: Eerdmans, 1994), 85–86, 103, 109–10.

[57] See J. A. Fitzmyer, *According to Paul* (New York: Paulist, 1993), 96, for good attestation of נפש as a reflexive pronoun in Palestinian Aramaic.

[58] Cf. Jeremias, *Abba*, 208.

[59] K. Stendahl, *The School of St. Matthew and Its Use of the Old Testament, with a New Introduction by the Author* (Philadelphia: Fortress, 1968); R. H. Gundry, *The Use of the Old Testament in St. Matthew's Gospel with Special Reference to the Messianic Hope* (NovTSup 18; Leiden: Brill, 1967); W. Rothfuchs, *Die Erfüllungszitate des Matthäus-Evangelium* (BWANT 88; Stuttgart: Kohlhammer, 1969); G. M. Soares Prabhu, *The Formula Quotations in the Infancy Narrative of Matthew* (AnBib 63; Rome: Biblical Institute, 1976).

[60] E. E. Ellis, *Paul's Use of the Old Testament* (Grand Rapids: Eerdmans, 1957), 11–20, esp. 12.

[61] Against D. Seeley, *The Noble Death* (JSNTSup 28; Sheffield: JSOT, 1990), 50–57. See O'Brien, *Philippians*, 270–71, for admissions along the above line and for further literature, esp. with regard to the difference between παῖς in Isa 52:13–53:12 LXX and δοῦλος in Phil 2:6–11 (but the cognate verb δουλεύω does appear in Isa 53:11 LXX). See L. G. Bloomquist, *The Function of Suffering in Philippians* (JSNTSup 78; Sheffield: JSOT, 1993), 164–68, on the present portrayal of Jesus as a servant over against Paul's portrayal of himself as a servant elsewhere: Paul appeals to the example of Jesus in Phil 2:6–11 to clarify the appeals to his own, i.e., Paul's, example as a fulfillment of the Christ-type in 1:27–30 and 2:12–18.

[62] Martin, *Carmen Christi/A Hymn of Christ*, 182–90.

290 Style and Substance in Philippians 2:6-11

just as required here under an interpretation of self-emptying in terms of death rather than incarnation.[63] More importantly, the chronological objection that the leap from preexistence to the crucifixion is too long in that it by-passes the incarnation rests on a failure to appreciate the dramatic extreme of the contrast between divine preexistence and slave-like death – a contrast best served by juxtaposition, as agreed by all interpreters when it comes to *B′* and *A′*. So if the juxtaposition of self-humbling to the extent of death on a cross and high exaltation by God serves the contrast best there, why not a similar juxtaposition in *A* and *B*? An insertion of the incarnation between preexistence and crucifixion would have cushioned and thereby weakened the contrast. As it is, references to the incarnation in *V* and *VI* (= *C*) come between the two statements of contrast (*A–B* and *B′–A′*) without interrupting either one. In this connection we should remind ourselves of the usualness with which aorist participles – such as the first, γενόμενος, "having become," referring to incarnation (*V*) – describe action antecedent to that of the main verb (here, ἐκένωσεν, "emptied" – *III*). Even those who deny that self-emptying means death interpret the aorist participle εὑρεθείς, "having been found" (*VI*), as referring to incarnation antecedent to the self-humbling expressed in another main verb, a self-humbling that takes the course of obedience unto death (*VII–VIII*).

The decision of Martin "to proceed in chronological fashion to cover the *curriculum vitae* of Christ"[64] turns out to be more a presupposition which casts a blind eye on evidence of allusion to Isa 52:13–53:12 than an argument which subverts that evidence.[65] Disfavoring this procedure is its outcome of no fewer than four uninterrupted references to the incarnation (*III–VI*) – surely over-repetitiousness – whereas concentricity, though carrying four references to death (*III–IV* and *VII–VIII*), interrupts them with two references to incarnation (*V–VI*). And a fourfold reference to Jesus' death, shameful as it was, suits the fourfold reference to his exaltation (*IX–XII*) better than a fourfold reference to the incarnation would do. As noted before, the incarnation was not shameful.

The further objection that an allusion to Isa 52:13–53:12 would require "slave" to be an honorific title, as in Isaiah, whereas in Philippians the term carries a connotation of abasement – this objection curiously overlooks the very strong motif of abasement also in the Isaianic passage. And both passages speak of high exaltation as outweighing abasement (cf. esp. Phil 2:9 with Isa 52:13). The possibility of allusion is thus enhanced right at the point where the objection is lodged.[66]

---

[63] H. W. Robinson, *The Cross in the Old Testament* (Philadelphia: Westminster, 1955), 104–5 n. 23.

[64] Martin, *Carmen Christi/A Hymn of Christ*, 186.

[65] So also against O'Brien (*Philippians*, 270), who speaks of an expectation.

[66] Also against Seeley, *The Noble Death*, 52–53.

It is true that high exaltation stands as "the frontispiece" of the Isaianic passage "whereas in the Philippians text at ii. 9 it comes as the climax of the hymn and as the result of His [Jesus'] obedience unto death."[67] But we cannot expect the NT to follow the order of the OT (see, e.g., the use of Deuteronomic texts in reverse order at Matt 4:4, 7, 10). The Philippians text starts with preexistence in the form of God, which does not sound very different from the high exaltation with which the Isaianic text starts.[68] And the Isaianic text ends with reward, apparently the same as the earlier-mentioned exaltation, as a result of abasement.

The lack of soteriology in Phil 2:6–11 hardly argues against an allusion to Isa 52:13–53:12; for the two passages do share the prominent themes of abasement and exaltation and we cannot expect NT use of the OT to incorporate all elements of the OT text. Nor does that use do so elsewhere (if the OT text is used *at all* in a way corresponding to its originally intended meaning).[69] Conversely, the presence in Phil 2:6–11 of obedience, a theme missing from Isa 52:13–53:12, causes no problem; for the OT is constantly brought into NT passages that contain themes absent from the OT passage.

---

[67] Martin, *Carmen Christi/A Hymn of Christ*, 186.

[68] Cf. Martin, *Carmen Christi/A Hymn of Christ*, 186–87.

[69] Against Martin, *Philippians*, 98. Cf. 1 Cor 9:9 with Deut 25:4 for a well-known instance of noncorrespondence; and see Pate, *Reverse of the Curse*, 306–7.

15. The Hellenization of Dominical Tradition and Christianization of Jewish Tradition in the Eschatology of 1–2 Thessalonians

The eschatological teachings in 1–2 Thessalonians have a common purpose: correction. In 1 Thessalonians Paul wants to correct a disbelief that caused sorrow over the fate of deceased Christians. The author of 2 Thessalonians wants to correct a belief in the immediacy of Christ's return, a belief that may have had its origin in (or at least have been abetted by) exhortations to readiness in 1 Thessalonians. In both letters earlier traditions come into play for the purposes of correcting the disbelief that caused sorrow, of exhorting the recipients to readiness, and of correcting the belief in immediacy. Both dominical and Jewish materials make up these traditions. Though we will take a side-glance at the question of authorship in 2 Thessalonians, an examination of the ways in which the traditions are molded to make the correction in that epistle depends very little on an answer to the question. We will find that Paul (whose name will cover the authorship of both letters without prejudice) hellenizes dominical tradition and christianizes Jewish tradition to make his corrections and reinforce his exhortations.

Hellenization of Dominical Tradition

E. Best effectively criticized J. Dupont's theory that in 1 Thess 4:16–17 Paul borrows from the theophany at Mount Sinai.[1] Dupont had denied very much Hellenistic influence on Paul and had attributed the clouds, the trumpet, the descent, and the meeting in Paul's description of Jesus' παρουσία, "coming," to the influence of Exod 19:10–18, where the Lord comes down on Mount Sinai in a cloud and with the blast of a trumpet and the Israelites go out to meet him. Best pointed out that (1) at Sinai the cloud conceals the Lord (emphasis falls on its thickness) whereas in Paul it is a vehicle (and for believers, we might add, not for the Lord); (2) the word for "meet" in Exod 19:17 LXX

---

[1] E. Best, *The First and Second Epistles to the Thessalonians* (HNTC; New York: Harper & Row, 1972), 199; cf. J. Dupont, ΣΥΝ ΧΡΙΣΤΩΙ: *L'Union avec le Christ suivant Saint Paul* (Paris: Desclée de Brouwer, 1952), 64–73.

is συνάντησιν, not Paul's ἀπάντησιν (though the synonymity of these terms weakens Best's point); (3) the Israelites are not caught up into the air, as Christians are in Paul; (4) Paul writes "nothing comparable to the giving of the Ten Commandments to which Exod 19. 16–25 serves as an introduction"; and (5) "clouds and trumpets are common apocalyptic images." To these criticisms of Dupont's theory J. Plevnik adds that it "does not explain ... the raising of the dead" in 1 Thessalonians or Paul's "insistence that the dead are raised first" or "life with the Lord forever" according to Paul or "the voice of command ... and the voice of the archangel" as opposed to "voices, lightning, and thunder" at Sinai.[2]

The doctrine of Jesus' return rests, of course, on dominical tradition (no matter what one's opinion of its reliability might be). We meet the possibility of Paul's hellenizing that tradition first of all in the term παρουσία itself, which does not occur in Jewish literature of the period for a messianic coming. Most scholars probably take it for granted that this term had come into Christian parlance before Paul wrote 1 Thessalonians and that in using the term he merely borrowed from common Christian vocabulary (1 Thess 2:19; 3:13; 4:15; 5:23; 2 Thess 2:1, 8 and later epistles).[3]

We may discount the occurrences of παρουσία in Matt 24:3, 27, 37, 39 as due to Matthew's later redaction, not to Jesus' own words.[4] Matthew wrote his

---

[2] J. Plevnik, *Paul and the Parousia* (Peabody, Mass.: Hendrickson, 1999), 10. Plevnik does allow for the possibility of some indirect influence from the Sinaitic theophany, however.

[3] For example B. Rigaux, who is inclined to reject Dupont's exclusive attention to OT and Jewish backgrounds, follows him in supposing that the use of παρουσία for the second coming antedates Paul (see Rigaux's commentary, *Saint Paul: Les Épîtres aux Thessaloniciens* [EBib; Paris: Gabalda, 1956], 232–33). Dupont himself, finding no suitable occurrence of παρουσία in the LXX, derives Christian use of the term from its cognate verb πάρειμι, which occurs twice in Dan 7:13 LXX, an important text for the NT doctrine of the Son of Man (*L'Union avec le Christ*, 49–64). But not only does the absence of the noun from that passage weaken Dupont's suggestion. So also does the use of this verb for the coming of angelic hosts as well as of the man-like figure. Even though we were to follow Dupont's suggestion that πάρειμι in Dan 7:13 LXX led to παρουσία in the NT, the possibility remains open that the latter carried Hellenistic connotations. It is wrong of Dupont to dismiss the possibility of Paul's influence, direct or indirect, on later NT writers (cf. 2 Pet 3:12 with 15–16). This criticism applies also to P. Siber, *Mit Christus leben* (ATANT 61; Zurich: Theologischer Verlag, 1971), 36. A. Oepke makes Paul responsible for the special Christian use of παρουσία but provides no argumentation apart from the early date of Paul's writings ("παρουσία, πάρειμι," *TDNT* 5:865).

[4] Contrast the parallel passages Mark 13:4; Luke 17:24, 26, 30; 21:7, which do not have παρουσία, and see R. H. Gundry, *Matthew* (2d ed.; Grand Rapids: Eerdmans, 1994), 476, 486, 492, 493. T. Holtz argues for pre-Pauline tradition not only from Matthew's use but also from the un-Pauline character of surrounding elements in 1 Thess 4:15–17: φθάνω in the sense "precede," οὐ μή, and sleep as a euphemism for death ("Traditionen im 1. Thessalonicherbrief," in *Die Mitte des Neuen Testaments* [ed. U. Luz and H. Weder; Göttingen: Vandenhoeck & Ruprecht, 1983], 63). But in Rom 9:30–31 φθάνω does appear to denote precedence: since the Gentiles have attained righteousness, Israel, though pursuing it, did not beat

Gospel later than Paul wrote 1 Thessalonians (and there are a number of other hints of Pauline influence, direct or indirect, on Matthew;[5] cf. the usually favored view that that Gospel emanated from Syria, perhaps from Antioch in Syria,[6] and Paul's ministry in and goings to and from Syrian Antioch according to the book of Acts; also the striking fact that the first Christian use of παρουσία outside the NT turns up at Antioch in a letter written by Ignatius, bishop of the church there [*Phld* 9:2], though in reference to Jesus' first coming). The first hard evidence of a Christian use of παρουσία for the second coming appears, then, in 1 Thessalonians. This datum creates a presumption that Paul was responsible for introducing the term into Christian eschatological vocabulary. Can this presumption count any other points in its favor?

Negatively, we may apply Occam's razor by saying it is gratuitous to suppose that Paul must have borrowed from earlier Christian usage. Positively, if the special connotation that παρουσία often carried in the Hellenistic world made the term peculiarly useful for solving a problem in the Thessalonian church, the presumption that Paul introduced the term into Christian eschatological vocabulary gains a point. In his writings and the Hellenistic world at large, παρουσία did not always carry a special connotation but referred to an ordinary coming, arrival, or presence. Often, however, παρουσία did carry a special connotation: the coming of an emperor, king, or other dignitary to visit a city. The fanfare that accompanied these arrivals – including acclamation, shouting, applause, the wearing of bright clothing, the wearing and presentation of crowns, and other expressions of joy – has often been documented. The documentation needs no rehearsal here.[7] The associations of παρουσία in 1 Thessalonians show that Paul must have had in mind the special παρουσία of a sovereign.[8]

---

them to it. Holtz himself notes that outside quotations from the LXX Paul uses οὐ μή in 1 Cor 8:13; Gal 5:16; 1 Thess 5:3. Holtz also admits that Paul has used the euphemism of sleep outside traditional material (1 Thess 4:13–14), but he suggests that Paul borrowed it from the Thessalonians' question. If so, however, the euphemism does not favor his borrowing from earlier Christian tradition in 1 Thess 4:15–17 (and the same possibility applies to φθάνω). Moreover, Paul uses the euphemism a number of times elsewhere in his own composition (1 Cor 7:39; 11:30; 15:6, 18, 20, 51).

[5] See Part II of M. D. Goulder's *Midrash and Lection in Matthew* (London: SPCK, 1974), passim.

[6] See esp. B. H. Streeter, *The Four Gospels* (2d ed.; London: MacMillan, 1930), 500–23; also Gundry, *Matthew*, 609. Not all Streeter's arguments are acceptable.

[7] See esp. E. Peterson, "Die Einholung des Kyrios," *ZST* 7 (1930): 682–702; also idem, "ἀπάντησις," *TDNT* 1:380–81; A. Deissmann, *Light from the Ancient East* (2d Engl. ed.; New York: Doran, 1927), 368–73; A. Oepke, "παρουσία, πάρειμι," *TDNT* 5:860; and Rigaux, *Thessaloniciens*, 196–201; and further literature, both primary and secondary, cited in BDAG, s.v. παρουσία 2b.

[8] To avoid the connotation of a hellenistically conceived imperial coming of the Lord, Plevnik argues that Paul uses παρουσία for his and his associates' comings slightly more often (six times: 1 Cor 16:17; 2 Cor 7:6, 7; 10:10; Phil 1:26; 2:12) than for the second coming of Christ (five times: 1 Cor 15:23; 1 Thess 2:19; 3:13; 4:15; 5:23; *Paul and the Parousia*, 4–5, 8).

In the first occurrence at 1 Thess 2:19–20 "hope," "joy," "crown of exultation [boasting]," and "glory" surround the παρουσία. Furthermore, it is the παρουσία of Jesus "our Lord." The word for "Lord," κύριος, also means "emperor." In fact, it was increasingly used for the emperor in the first and second centuries.[9] Hellenistic readers such as the Thessalonians could hardly have read such a collocation of terms without comparing Jesus' coming to that of an emperor.[10] Some have argued that Paul assumes the Thessalonians already knew παρουσία as a stereotyped reference to Jesus' coming, for he provides no explanation. But the term is self-explanatory. Its meaning "coming, arrival" needs no exposition. And when it occurs among other terms indicating imperial celebration its connotation is clear.[11] In 3:13 the παρουσία is again that of Jesus "our Lord [or 'Emperor']." The accompaniment of "all his holy ones" – probably an angelic army, as in Zech 14:5 (which Paul allusively quotes; cf. 2 Thess 1:7)[12] – adds dignity to the imperial visit. Naturally, Hellenistic emperors came accompanied by soldiers. The loudest fanfare to indicate an imperial παρουσία is heard, however, in 4:15–17, where Paul mentions the shout of command, the sounding of God's trumpet, and the voice of the archangel. All this noise is calculated to wake the dead in Christ (after all, Paul has just referred to them as asleep – vv. 13–14 [twice]), but it does so by announcing Jesus' imperial παρουσία.

The fanfare that Paul attaches to the Lord's παρουσία evacuates this argument of its force, however; and Plevnik himself has to acknowledge that "παρουσία comes from Hellenistic Greek" and that "the Hebrew Bible does not have a comparable noun" (p. 5). Then he backtracks with the observation that "παρουσία occurs only in the earliest Pauline epistles" and with the argument that the word occurs "only in apocalyptic sections, where Hellenistic influence is least likely" (p. 7). But the doctrine of a rapture, or "assumption" as Plevnik prefers to call it, on which he places great emphasis, occurs only in this one early epistle of 1 Thessalonians; and the history of Christian theology displays much hellenization of apocalyptic.

[9] W. Foerster, "κύριος," *TDNT* 3:1054–58.

[10] W. Radl overlooks this near certainty in suggesting that παρουσία may here mean the epiphany of a god (*Ankunft des Herrn* [Beiträge zur biblische Exegese und Theologie 15; Frankfurt: Peter D. Lang, 1981], 173–81). The suggestion is part of Radl's scaling down Paul's interest in apocalyptic. Dupont suggests that the exultation and crown at the παρουσία may reflect OT themes, but he does not account for the clustering of terms that would carry a Hellenistic connotation (*L'Union avec le Christ*, 71–72). The eschatological cry "Maranatha" (1 Cor 16:22) doubtless aided the eschatological use of κύριος.

[11] Against U. Luz, *Das Geschichtsverständnis des Paulus* (BEvT 49; Munich: Chr. Kaiser, 1968), 310 n. 47; H. H. Schade, *Apokalyptische Christologie bei Paulus* (GTA 18; Göttingen: Vandenhoeck & Ruprecht, 1981), 27.

[12] For powerful arguments in favor of angels and against saints see esp. Best, *Thessalonians*, 152–53; also J. E. Frame, *A Critical and Exegetical Commentary on the Epistles of St. Paul to the Thessalonians* (ICC; Edinburgh: T&T Clark, 1912), 139; D. E. H. Whiteley, *Thessalonians* (New Clarendon Bible, NT; London: Oxford University Press, 1969), 57–58; C. Masson, *Les deux épîtres de Saint Paul aux Thessaloniciens* (Neuchatel: Delachaux & Niestlé, 1957), 43–44. Of course, an army of saints would support the connotation of an imperial visit just as an angelic army supports it.

To be sure, trumpets were stock items in theophanies and apocalypses;[13] and Paul may have borrowed his archangel from Dan 12:1–2, where Michael is mentioned alongside the resurrection. But in Dan 12:1–2 Michael utters not even a peep; in fact, that passage gives him no function whatever in the raising of the dead. Rather, he stands as protector of Israel during the preceding period of tribulation. Paul's omitting the name "Michael" and giving the archangel a voice to help wake the dead therefore seem to represent an advance beyond Dan 12:1–2 and to tie in with the announcement of an imperial visit for which those who are sleeping supinely in death should "stand up" in resurrection (ἀναστήσονται – v. 16). In the same manner and for the same purpose the shout of command appears to come from Paul himself, not from any known tradition; and its use for military commands (see, e.g., Hdt. 4.141 al.) harmonizes with his making "the holy ones" the imperial guard (3:13). "Will descend from heaven" substitutes for "coming in clouds" in the dominical tradition (Mark 13:26; Matt 24:30; Luke 21:27; cf. Dan 7:13) because Paul's saving the clouds for a later, different use leaves a need to indicate direction. The substitution also sets up for a complementary upward movement of believers.[14]

Three objections might be lodged: (1) Paul's reference to a "word of the Lord" rules out his inventing the shout, voice, and trumpet as announcements of an imperial visit; (2) unless that word was a prophetic revelation to Paul himself[15] the reference favors a non-Pauline origin possibly having nothing to

---

[13] Exod 19:13, 16, 19; 20:18; Isa 27:13; Joel 2:1; Zeph 1:14–16; Zech 9:14; Matt 24:31; Rev 1:10; 4:1; 8:2, 6, 7, 8, 10, 12, 13; 9:1, 13, 14; 10:7; 11:15; G. Friedrich, "σάλπιγξ," TDNT 7:80, 84, 86–88. At least three possibilities exist concerning the interrelation of the trumpets in Matt 24:31 and 1 Thess 4:16: (1) Matthew represents dominical tradition at this point and Paul draws on that same tradition; (2) Paul draws on Jewish tradition and Matthew shows direct or indirect influence from Paul; and (3) Matthew and Paul independently draw on Jewish tradition.

[14] Plevnik (Paul and the Parousia, 40–60, 63–64, 84–88, 323–24) strays from the immediate Thessalonian context to the OT and Jewish pseudepigraphal literature to interpret the shout of command, the archangel's voice, and God's trumpet in terms of "the power of God ... to establish his rule over hostile forces and sinners in the world" (p. 64). Plevnik even interprets the shout of command (κέλευσμα) as equivalent to גער, "rebuke," and its cognate noun, normally translated ἐπιτιμάω and ἐπιτίμησις in the LXX, though κέλευσμα occurs in the LXX only at Prov 30:27. Sinful forces hostile to God do not appear in 1 Thessalonians 4, however, so that it is easier to think of the shout of command, the archangel's voice, and God's trumpet as waking the sleeping dead, who do appear in the passage.

[15] Cf. B. Henneken, Verkündigung und Prophetie im Ersten Thessalonicherbrief (SBS 29; Stuttgart: KBW, 1969), 92. For several reasons the objection of P. Hoffmann (Die Toten in Christus [NTAbh nf 2; Münster: Aschendorff, 1966], 219) that Paul uses κατὰ ἀποκάλυψιν for divine revelation to himself (Gal 2:2) has little force: (1) Paul does not quote the revelation in Galatians as he does quote the word of the Lord in 1 Thessalonians; (2) the revelation appears to have been for private direction whereas the word of the Lord is directed to the community; (3) "according to revelation" does not really tell us that the revelation came to Paul directly rather than through someone else (as in Acts 21:4, 11); and (4) single instances of each expression are not enough to establish a distinction of meaning in Paul's usage.

do with a hellenistically conceived παρουσία; and (3) the un-Pauline character of expressions such as "command," "voice of the archangel," and "trumpet of God" (but see "the last trumpet" in 1 Cor 15:52) disfavors both a prophetic word from Paul himself and his inventing the shout, voice, and trumpet.[16] But the easy contextual rationale for these and other expressions negates the third objection and favors Paul's own hand in tailoring and embellishing material to suit the needs of the Thessalonians. To suppose that the word of the Lord is an otherwise unknown saying of Jesus[17] or the saying of a Christian prophet other than Paul[18] offers an untestable hypothesis and therefore a last resort.[19]

"By the word of the Lord" (ἐν λόγῳ κυρίου) became technical in the OT for God's message delivered through a prophet.[20] Paul's *"We say* by the word of the Lord" favors that he is neither quoting another Christian prophet's word from the Lord nor quoting a saying of the earthly Jesus[21] but in conjunction with the

---

[16] Cf. Luz, *Geschichtsverständnis*, 326–29.

[17] J. Jeremias, *Unknown Sayings of Jesus* (2d Engl. ed.; London: SPCK, 1964), 80–83; Holtz, "Traditionen," 55–78.

[18] So, e.g., Luz, *Geschichtsverständnis*, 327–29; W. Harnisch, *Eschatologische Existenz* (FRLANT 110; Göttingen: Vandenhoeck & Ruprecht, 1973), 42–43; J. Baumgarten, *Paulus und die Apokalyptik* (WMANT 44; Neukirchen-Vluyn: Neukirchener Verlag, 1975), 94 n. 186; Best, *Thessalonians*, 193–94. If Paul is responsible for introducing some of the apocalyptic furniture, as I am urging, it will be hard for Harnisch and Baumgarten to maintain that he reduces the apocalyptic element in favor of existential considerations.

[19] Cf. A. J. Malherbe, *The Letters to the Thessalonians* (AB 32B; New York: Doubleday, 2000), 267–69.

[20] See the LXX in 3 Kgdms 13:2, 5, 32; 21:35; 1 Chron 15:15; Sir 48:3 (with slight variations in 3 Kgdms 13:9, 17, 18, 20, 27; Sir 48:5).

[21] With the exception of John 11:25–26 (on which see the next footnote) none of the earthly Jesus' sayings offered as candidates for Paul's "word of the Lord" provide a solid basis for Paul's inference concerning the relative fates of deceased saints and living saints on the last day (see Mark 8:35; 9:1; 12:26–27; 13:27, 30; Matt 10:39; 16:25; 19:28; 20:1–16; 22:32; 23:36; 24:31, 34; 25:6; Luke 9:24, 27; 11:50–51; 17:33; 20:37–38; John 5:25; 6:39–40). The synoptic sayings do not even mention a resurrection, which is essential to Paul's argument. J. R. Michaels hypothesizes that Paul plays on the dominical saying in Matt 20:16: "Thus the last will be first and the first, last" ("Everything That Rises Must Converge: Paul's Word from the Lord," in *To Tell the Mystery* [ed. T. E. Schmidt and M. Silva; JSNTSup 100; Sheffield: JSOT, 1994], 182–95). But questions have to be asked: Why would Paul's mind have gravitated to a dominical saying about the reversal of first and last if the Thessalonians did not expect their deceased fellow Christians to rise at all (see below)? Does the deceased Christians' having died first yet also rising first square with the reversal of first and last in Jesus' saying? Do Paul's use of the adverb πρῶτον to describe the action of resurrection instead of the adjective πρῶτοι to describe the resurrected (apart from the *v.l.*) and his nonuse of ἔσχατοι weaken a correlation with the dominical saying? According to A. Lindemann 1 Thess 4:16 does not mean that the dead in Christ will rise; rather, all the dead will be raised in Christ, though unbelievers have no hope of a resurrection to eternal life ("Paulus und die Korinthische Eschatologie: Zur These von einer 'Entwicklung' im paulinischen Denken," *NTS* 37 [1991]: 377–80). Against this view see H. Merklein, "Der Theologe als Prophet: Zur Funktion prophetischen Redens im theologischen Diskurs des Paulus," *NTS* 38 (1992): 403–4.

Holy Spirit is delivering his own prophetic word of the Lord, presumably Jesus as the exalted Lord (cf. 1 Cor 14:37, "If anyone thinks himself to be a prophet or Spiritual [i.e., filled with God's Spirit], let him acknowledge the things I write to you, that they are the Lord's commandment," and 7:40, "I think that I too have the Spirit of God").[22] Paul's main point – in fact, the *only* point that he identifies as coming from a word of the Lord – is that "we who are alive, who remain till the coming of the Lord, will not precede the ones who have fallen asleep" (v. 15). The rest (vv. 16–17) consists in an elaboration of dominical tradition about Jesus' return. The elaboration combines Paul's "word of the Lord" concerning the fates of deceased and living saints with a portrayal of that return as an imperial visit in the Hellenistic style.

But we have not reached the end of Paul's additions to the tradition. He writes of meeting the Lord (εἰς ἀπάντησιν). In and of itself ἀπάντησις need not carry a special connotation; it occurs often for ordinary meetings.[23] In conjunction with the fanfare just described, however, and in relation to the παρουσία of Jesus as Lord or Emperor (here is the place to note that Paul does not use "the Son of Man," which occurs in comparable synoptic sayings, but switches from Ἰησοῦς [v. 14 (twice)] to κύριος [vv. 15–16 (three times)] and intensifies κύριος with αὐτός [v. 16] to stress the grandeur of the imperial visit), ἀπάντησις is bound to conjure up the Hellenistic practice of going out to meet the approaching dignitary in order that he might enjoy an honorary escort into the city (cf. the meeting-cum-escorting of Jesus at the triumphal entry [John 12:13], of the bridegroom in the parable of the Ten Virgins [Matt 25:1, 6], and of the

---

[22] N.B.: Paul is not transferring a saying of Jesus as the exalted Lord to the earthly Jesus. The foregoing represents a retraction of my earlier position that Paul quotes the dominical saying found in John 11:25–26 (R. H. Gundry, "The Hellenization of Dominical Tradition and Christianization of Jewish Tradition in the Eschatology of 1–2 Thessalonian," *NTS* 33 [1987]: 164–66). I now think that John 11:25–26 echoes 1 Thess 4:15–17 (cf. the Johannine emphases on believing and on abiding in Jesus with Paul's emphases on faith and on being "in Christ"). The Thessalonian text distinguishes between the dead in Christ who will rise first (ἀναστήσονται) and those who are alive (οἱ ζῶντες) at the second coming, so that they will never die. Similarly the Johannine text distinguishes between the believer in Jesus who dies but will live because Jesus is the resurrection (ἀνάστασις) and the believer who is alive (ὁ ζῶν) and never dies. See A. Guilding, *The Fourth Gospel and Jewish Worship* (Oxford: Clarendon, 1960), 148–49; P. Nepper-Christensen, "Das verborgene Herrnwort: Eine Untersuchung über 1. Thess. 4,13–18," *ST* 19 (1965): 152–53; Holtz, "Traditionen," 61, 64; and for "the word of the Lord" as Paul's prophetic speech see Merklein, "Der Theologe als Prophet," 412–19; Plevnik, *Paul and the Parousia*, 71–81.

[23] See, e.g., Matt 25:1, 6; Acts 28:15; 1 Kgdms 9:14 LXX et al. The attempt to derive εἰς ἀπάντησιν in 1 Thess 4:17 from the same or a similar phrase in tradition behind Matt 25:1, 6 (so, e.g., W. Schenk, "Auferweckung der Toten oder Gericht nach den Wirken: Tradition und Redaktion in Matthäus xxv 1–13," *NovT* 20 [1978]: 294–98) must turn aside the possibilities of Pauline influence on Matthew and of Matthean redaction in the phrase (cf. Gundry, *Matthew*, 498). Even though Paul were to have drawn the phrase from dominical tradition he would be hellenizing it with the element of imperial pageantry.

Apostle Paul [Acts 28:15]). The evidence of this practice has been set out else-where and, as in the case of royal παρουσίαι, needs no rehearsal here.[24]

On the other hand, M. R. Cosby draws several contrasts between Hellenistic formal receptions and Paul's use of ἀπάντησις in 1 Thess 4:17.[25] First-men-tioned is the unexpectedness of the παρουσία: "Christians anticipate Christ's arrival but are unaware of when it will happen (1 Thess 5:1–4)" over against the expectedness of Hellenistic παρουσίαι "at a particular time."[26] In 1 Thess 5:4, however, Paul says to his Christain audience, "But *you*, brothers and sisters, are *not* in darkness that the Day [of the Lord] should overtake *you* as a thief" (italics added). It is only the sleepers, who are "of the night" and "of darkness" and say, "Peace and safety," but "will by no means escape," on whom that day "comes as a thief in the night" (vv. 2–5). Christian brothers and sisters have no need to be informed "concerning the times and seasons" (v. 1). They have already been informed and will therefore be well aware of the near-ness of the παρουσία (2 Thess 2:3–12, esp. v. 5; cf. Mark 13:28–29 par. Matt 24:32–33 and Luke 21:29–30; also Luke 21:28).[27]

"Secondly, participants [in the παρουσία] do not put on special garments or wear laurel wreaths [as do participants in Hellenistic formal receptions].... This transformation [of being given resurrection bodies at the παρουσία] greatly overshadows the wearing of festal clothing at normal [formal?] receptions."[28] Yet for Paul the resurrection of Christians at the second coming does entail the putting on of festal clothing: "For this perishable [body] must put on (ἐνδύ-σασθαι) imperishability; and when this perishable [body] puts on (ἐνδύσηται) imperishability and this mortal [body] puts on (ἐνδύσηται) immortality ..." (1 Cor 15:53–54a); "longing to put on in addition (ἐπενδύσασθαι) our building

---

[24] A convenient collection may be found in Rigaux, *Thessaloniciens*, 230–34. Dupont also sets out the primary materials but rejects Hellenistic influence on Paul (*L'Union avec le Christ*, 64–73). H.-A. Wilcke argues against a technical Hellenistic usage by Paul (*Das Problem eines messianischen Zwischenreich bei Paulus* [ATANT 51; Zurich: Zwingli, 1967], 143–47). True, there is no set phrase. But the suggestion that εἰς ἀπάντησιν amounts to little or no more than a preposition meaning "to, toward" overlooks that Paul's "in the air" puts some weight of mean-ing on ἀπάντησιν as a distinct meeting. Peterson is able to cite evidence that the idea of meet-ing kept its liveliness through and beyond NT times ("Einholung," 701–2).

[25] M. R. Cosby, "Hellenistic Formal Receptions and Paul's use of ΑΠΑΝΤΗΣΙΣ in 1 Thes-salonians 4:17," *BBR* 4 (1994): 15–34.

[26] Ibid., 29.

[27] Against G. Holland ("Let No One Deceive You in Any Way: 2 Thessalonians as a Refor-mulation of the Apocalyptic Tradition," in *SBL Seminar Papers, 1985* [SBLSP 24; Atlanta: Scholars Press, 1985], 332: "The elect ... know that they don't know when the Day of the Lord will come and so are prepared at all times for its coming"). Holland's appeal to other thief-in-the-night passages (Luke 12:39–40; Rev 3:3; 16:15) overlooks that they occur in conjunction with presaging signs that watchful Christians will recognize as such. So too against Plevnik, who avers that Paul simply "sidesteps the quest for the date of the Lord's coming" (*Paul and the Parousia*, 120).

[28] Cosby, loc cit.

from heaven, if indeed also being clothed (ἐνδυσάμενοι) we will not be found naked.... we do not want to be unclothed (ἐκδύσασθαι) but to be additionally clothed (ἐπενδύσασθαι)" (2 Cor 5:2–4). As for wearing a laurel wreath (στέφ-ανος), Paul does speak of wearing one at the second coming, and so speaks right here in 1 Thessalonians: "For what [is] our hope or joy or laurel wreath of exultation or – it's you, isn't it? – before our Lord Jesus at his παρουσία?" (2:19; see also 1 Cor 9:24–27; Phil 4:1 with 3:20–21; 2 Tim 4:8, always in es-chatological contexts[29]).

Cosby is correct to note the difference between the summoning shout and trumpet blast at the παρουσία (1 Thess 4:16) and the shouts of acclamation at Hellenistic formal receptions.[30] But this difference is understandable in view of the need for supernatural action in the raising of deceased Christians and in the catching of them and living Christians up to meet the Lord in the air (see below). At least the παρουσία and Hellenistic formal receptions share the el-ement of happy noise.

Cosby argues further that for the παρουσία "no donations are encouraged nor taxes levied to purchase presents to honor the heavenly king [as at Hellen-istic formal receptions]. Instead, he brings rewards for his faithful servants."[31] But no such rewards are mentioned in the passage at hand (1 Thess 4:15–17), and going elsewhere in Pauline literature we find not only rewards for faithful servants of the king at his παρουσία but also a reception-like presentation to him: "to present you holy and blameless and irreproachable before him... that we may present every person mature (τέλειον) in Christ" (Col 1:22, 28b; cf. 2 Cor 11:2: "to present you as a pure virgin to the Christ").

The execution of "wrathful judgment of the wicked" at the παρουσία does not lack a counterpart in Hellenistic formal receptions,[32] for Cosby himself ref-erences the execution of prisoners at those events.[33] The comment that "divine judgment occurring as part of the event [of the παρουσία] ... is far different from Peterson's assertion that arriving dignitaries sometimes pronounced judg-ment as part of the ceremonies" looks itself like an assertion having little or no probative value.[34]

Again, Cosby himself supplies a reason why "Paul makes no mention of the Hellenistic custom of a dignitary offering sacrifices on local altars after the re-ception," i.e., "in Paul's thinking... Jesus already offered himself as the defini-

---

[29] Against Plevnik, who misses the eschatological context of Phil 4:1 in the immediately preceding verses (Phil 3:20–21; *Paul and the Parousia*, 8). Paul even introduces Phil 4:1 with ὥστε, "and so"!

[30] Ibid., 29–30.

[31] Ibid., 30.

[32] Against ibid., 30–31.

[33] Ibid., 18, 21, 22.

[34] Ibid., 30–31.

tive sacrifice, so this aspect of the formal reception would be abhorrent, a grim reminder of the paganism from which he sought to deliver people."[35]

Plevnik adds the objection that imperial visits ended with the emperor's departure whereas Paul says the saints will be with the Lord always.[36] Weakening this objection is the fact that Paul does not say the Lord will always be with the saints. In view is their presence with him, not his staying with them. And Paul is dealing with eschatology, the doctrine of the *end*, so that the analogy of emperors' comings and goings breaks off with Jesus' coming.

On the whole, then, Paul's description of the παρουσία in 1 Thess 4:15–17 comes closer to what we know of Hellenistic formal receptions than Cosby and Plevnik allow. The Thessalonian context, the αὐτός which calls special attention to Jesus' dignity as Lord or Emperor ("the Lord himself" – 1 Thess 4:15), the remarkable fact that only here in the NT are Christians said "to meet the Lord" (1 Thess 4:17, though cf. Matt 25:1, 6), and the appearance of elements of Hellenistic formal receptions also in other Pauline mentions of the παρουσία all combine to favor such a connotation for ἀπάντησις.

Paul adds a catching up of believers for the purpose of meeting the Lord. Where did this idea of a rapture come from? Not from the dominical tradition later recorded in the Olivet Discourse (Mark 13:27; Matt 24:31). There the Son of Man sends out his angels to "gather" the elect from the extremities of the earth. The language echoes OT descriptions of the gathering of exiles (Deut 30:4; Isa 52:12 LXX; Zech 2:10 LXX; cf. 2 Macc 1:27; 2:7–8; *T. Naph.* 8:3; *T. Asher* 7:7; *Did.* 9:4; 10:5). One would assume that there is nothing more than horizontal movement across the face of the earth.[37] To be sure, Paul uses the term "gathering" for the rapture in 2 Thess 2:1,[38] but it is a gathering to Jesus (ἐπ᾿ αὐτόν),

---

[35] Ibid., 20–21.

[36] Plevnik, *Paul and the Parousia*, 8.

[37] Against D. Wenham, who argues that the agency of angels in gathering the elect implies that "the elect are lifted up from the earth to the Lord" ("Paul and the Synoptic Apocalypse," in *Gospel Perspectives* [ed. R. T. France and D. Wenham; Sheffield: JSOT, 1981], 2:348). The hidden, false presupposition of this argument is that angelic activity cannot be limited to the earth. Contrast, e.g., Rev 9:13–21.

[38] See E. Best in *Bib* 55 (1974): 446–49 for telling criticisms of W. Trilling's attempt to establish the inauthenticity of 2 Thessalonians (*Untersuchungen zum zweiten Thessalonicherbrief* [ETS 27; Leipzig: St. Benno, 1972]). For further criticisms see G. F. Snyder in *JBL* 92 (1973): 614; Best, *Thessalonians*, 50–58; A. E. Harvey, "'The Workman is Worthy of His Hire': Fortunes of a Proverb in the Early Church," *NovT* 24 (1982): 215–16 (against an argument of J. A. Bailey, "Who Wrote II Thessalonians?" *NTS* 25 [1979]: 131–45); J. C. Hurd, "Concerning the Authenticity of 2 Thessalonians" (paper presented at the annual meeting of the SBL, Dallas, 19–22 December 1983); G. D. Fee, "Pneuma and Eschatology in 2 Thessalonians 2:1–2: A Proposal About 'Testing the Prophets' and the Purpose of 2 Thessalonians," in *To Tell the Mystery* (ed. T. E. Schmidt and M. Silva; JSNTSup 100; Sheffield: Sheffield Academic Press, 1994), 196–215; Malherbe, *The Letters to the Thessalonians*, 364–74. In addition, the nonexplanation of the restraint and restrainer in 2 Thess 2:6–7 does not look like the work of a pious forger, who would probably have appealed to something in Paul's genuine writing or

which the catching up in 1 Thess 4:17 requires to be an upward, vertical move-ment. Likewise, the absence of upward, vertical movement in the taking of one and leaving of another disqualifies the saying recorded in Matt 24:37–41 (par. Luke 17:26–30) from being Paul's source.[39]

As a result of the catching up and meeting, God will bring believers with Jesus – not just believers who in a disembodied state start out from heaven, the point of departure for Jesus' descent, but also these same believers reembodied by virtue of resurrection, plus believers who have never died, from the point where they meet the Lord in the air (v. 14b thus covering both the disembodied and the reembodied stages of the descent of the deceased whom God will bring with Jesus[40]). After the pattern of Hellenistic practice, in other words, believers will escort Jesus into the world during the last leg of his descent.[41] Again, we read nothing of believers' coming with Jesus in the Olivet Discourse. There the elect are not yet with the Son of Man when he sends out his angels to gather them; and, as noted before, nothing in the Synoptics indicates an upward gathering that would result in a coming with Jesus.

---

said nothing at all here rather than grasping at thin air with a reference wholly mysterious to his audience. According to Trilling the forger had nothing particular in mind (*Der zweite Brief an die Thessalonicher* [EKKNT 14; Zurich: Benziger Verlag/Neukirchen-Vluyn: Neukirchener Verlag, 1980], 71–72, 85–86, 89–90, 102). This supposition makes the shift from neuter to mas-culine harder than ever to understand. Why would a forger who had nothing particular in mind have bothered to make so tantalizing a shift? Though Paul's reminder in v. 5 has to do with the preceding verses, it probably triggered his references to the restraint and restrainer on the basis of past oral teaching, which made the shift in genders intelligible. Against E. E. Popkes ("Die Bedeutung des zweiten Thessalonicherbriefs für das Verständnis paulinischer und deuteropau-linischer Eschatologie," *BZ* 48 [2004]: 52), 2 Thess 2:1–12 denies only an *immediate* return of Christ and therefore does not contradict the possibility of a *near* return of Christ as implied by the exhortations to watchfulness in 1 Thess 5:1–11. That such watchfulness can take into its purview presaging signs is proved by the juxtaposition of exhortations to watch and predictions of such signs in the Olivet Discourse and the book of Revelation (cf. the indeterminate short-ening of the tribulation in Mark 13:20; Matt 24:22 and the cancellation of the seven thunders in Rev 10:1–7, where sealing up must mean *not* bringing to pass because opening the seven seals *has* brought to pass a series of calamities; also, since writing the prophetic word effects its coming to pass the command *not* to write down the seven thunders means they cannot come to pass). The argument of Whiteley (*Thessalonians*, 13–14) that the "peace and safety" preceding the Day of the Lord in 1 Thess 5:2–3 disagrees with the disturbing events preceding the Day of the Lord in 2 Thess 2:1–12, and therefore speaks against common authorship, stumbles over the failure of the latter passage to describe the preceding events as those that would or will be un-peaceful and unsafe *from the standpoint of unbelievers.*

[39] This difference is the more remarkable if to be taken means to be judged and to be left means to be saved (cf. R. F. Collins, "Tradition, Redaction, and Exhortation in 1 Th 4,13–5,11," in *L'Apocalypse johannique et l'Apocalyptique dans le Nouveau Testament* [ed. J. Lambrecht; BETL 53; Leuven: Leuven University Press, 1980], 333; but see also Gundry, *Matthew*, 494).

[40] See Holtz, "Traditionen," 59–61, on v. 14b as Paul's interpretation of a Christian confes-sion in v. 14a.

[41] A descent to earth implies nothing one way or the other about a chiliastic view on Paul's part, though some have tried to pair a positive implication with an absence of chiliasm else-where in his Epistles to argue against a descent to earth (so Siber, *Mit Christus leben*, 30–32).

Paul writes from an earthly standpoint: "the Lord himself will descend from heaven… we who are alive and remain… will be caught up." Interpreting him to mean that God will bring believers with Jesus *to heaven* misses this standpoint and neglects the paraphernalian indications of an imperial παρουσία. Masson argues correctly against a heavenly destination that then the Lord would be meeting the saints.[42] For a heavenly destination we might have expected Paul to write something like the following: "because the dead in Christ will rise first. Then we who are alive and remain will be caught up together with them in clouds, and the Lord himself will descend from heaven with a shout, with the archangel's voice, and with God's trumpet to meet us in the air; and thus we will always be with the Lord." In fact, R. L. Thomas is so intent on seeing a heavenly destination that he reverses Paul's phraseology: "the saints continue on to heaven with the Lord *who has come to meet them*."[43] Similarly Harnisch says the saints are caught up into the sphere of heaven,[44] whereas Paul refers to the air, not to heaven. Plevnik sees an exodus-motif and appeals to believers' heavenly citizenship and heavenly bodies to argue that in Paul's view God will bring believers to heaven with Jesus.[45] But though our citizenship is *in* heaven according to Phil 3:20–21, Paul says there that we wait for Jesus to come *from* heaven; and he gives no indication that Jesus will go back to heaven with us in tow.[46] Likewise, according to 2 Cor 5:1–4 our new body is *from* heaven. So also 1 Cor 15:47–49 has to do with origin, not with ultimate location. Similarly, Plevnik's arguments that Paul "does not mention a return [of the saints] to earth" and that Mark 9:7 (par. Matt 17:5; Luke 9:34); Acts 1:9–11; and Rev 11:12 point to the clouds' taking believers up to heaven in 1 Thess 4:15–17[47] overlooks that Paul writes of "a meeting in the air," not of a going "to heaven." The argument also overlooks that the cited synoptic passages speak only of disappearance, not of being taken up to heaven.[48]

In 1 Thess 4:14 Paul states that "God will bring the ones who have fallen asleep through Jesus with him [Jesus]." In 2 Cor 4:14 Paul states that "the one who raised the Lord Jesus will raise us too with Jesus and present [us] with you

---

[42] Masson, *Thessaloniciens*, 59–60.

[43] R. L. Thomas, "1 Thessalonians, 2 Thessalonians," in *The Expositor's Bible Commentary* (Grand Rapids: Zondervan, 1978), 11:279 (italics added).

[44] Harnisch, *Eschatologische Existenz*, 43–44 n. 23.

[45] J. Plevnik, "The Parousia as Implication of Christ's Resurrection: An Exegesis of 1 Thes 4:13–18," in *Word and Spirit* (ed. J. Plevnik; Willowdale, Ontario, Canada: Regis College Press, 1975), 212–24, 226, 229, 265–67.

[46] Against Plevnik, who vacillates between saying "the text suggests that heaven is the ultimate goal" and admitting "the text does not depict … a translation from the earth to heaven" (*Paul and the Parousia*, 192–93).

[47] Plevnik, *Paul and the Parousia*, 63; idem, "The Parousia as Implication," 267–72.

[48] Also against M. Stowasser, who thinks that Mark 13:26–27 as well as 1 Thess 4:15–17 indicates a heavenly destination ("Mk 13, 26f und die urchristliche Rezeption des Menschensohns: Eine Anfrage an Anton Vögtle," *BZ* 39 [1995]: 251–52).

[Corinthian believers]." Plevnik understands 2 Cor 4:14 to mean that God will present Paul and the Corinthian believers to himself and argues that since God resides in heaven he will bring deceased Christians (along with living ones) to heaven at the second coming in accordance with 1 Thess 4:14–17.[49] Astonishingly, indeed, Plevnik translates the last clause of 2 Cor 4:14, "and will bring us with you *into his presence*," and comments, "Here the ultimate goal *is clearly stated to be the presence of God.... into heaven.*"[50] As a matter of fact, however, the Greek text does not mention God's presence or heaven, nor does it say that God will present believers to himself. And almost exclusively, someone makes a presentation to someone else.[51] Therefore we might better think of God's presenting the saints to Jesus, as Paul aimed to present the Corinthian Christians as a pure virgin to Christ (2 Cor 11:2; cf. 1 Thess 4:17b: "and thus we will always be with the Lord"), or perhaps of God's presenting the glorified saints to the eschatologically liberated creation (Rom 8:18–23, esp. v. 19: "for the eager expectation of the creation earnestly awaits the revelation of the sons of God"). We might also ask why the presently groaning creation "will be liberated from the slavery of corruption into the liberty of the glory of God's children" (Rom 8:21) if not to be the habitat of a redeemed humanity.[52] An uninhabited new earth? Hardly. And why a bodily resurrection if not for dwelling on the new earth? In any case, 2 Cor 4:14 does not say that God will present the saints to himself in heaven and therefore does not support that in 1 Thess 4:14 he will bring them to heaven or that in 1 Thess 4:16–17 the Lord Christ ascends back to heaven after descending only part way to earth.[53] Rather, as J. Becker says, "In vs. 16–17 [of 1 Thessalonians 4] the church, to whom the resurrected ones are added, takes in the Lord like an honored guest, in order to be together with him on earth 'always.'"[54]

---

[49] J. Plevnik, "The Destination of the Apostle and the Faithful: Second Corinthians 4:13b–14 and First Thessalonians 4:14," *CBQ* 62 (2000): 83–95; idem *Paul and the Parousia*, 71–75, 89, 204.

[50] Ibid. 74 (italics added).

[51] For Pauline usage elsewhere see Rom 6:13 (twice), 16, 19 (twice); 12:1; 14:10 (if παραστησόμεθα is understood as a reflexive middle voice, "we will present ourselves to the judgment seat of God"); 16:2; 1 Cor 8:8; 2 Cor 11:2; Col 1:22 (?), 28 (?); 2 Tim 2:15; and elsewhere in the NT at Matt 26:53; Mark 4:29 (implicitly); Luke 2:22; Acts 1:3; 9:41; 23:24, 33; 24:13. An exception appears in Eph 5:27, but – not as in 2 Cor 4:14 – "to himself" is stated explicitly.

[52] Cf. C. Hoegen-Rohls, "Κτίσις and καινὴ κτίσις in Paul's Letters," in *Paul, Luke and the Graeco-Roman World* (ed. A. Christophersen et al.; JSNTSup 217; Sheffield: Sheffield Academic Press, 2002), 112–15.

[53] Also against J. Plevnik, "1 Thessalonians 4,17: The Bringing in of the Lord or the Bringing in of the Faithful?" *Bib* 80 (1999): 537–46.

[54] J. Becker, *Paul: Apostle to the Gentiles* (Louisville, Ky.: Westminster/John Knox, 1993), 144.

Citizens of a Hellenistic city took the initiative in going out to meet a visiting emperor.[55] But in the very nature of the case God has to take the initiative in bringing believers with Jesus. They cannot raise themselves from the dead, nor can they levitate by pulling up on their own bootstraps. God will have to raise them and bring them "with Jesus," whom he has already raised and exalted (v. 14). But though accomplished by God's power, their joining the Lord in his descent corresponds so closely to Hellenistic practice that a Hellenistic audience could hardly have missed the correspondence; and a Hellenistic author could hardly have failed to intend it.

Being caught up to Jesus and being brought with him both appear to be Paul's contributions to the doctrine of the second coming, then.[56] The latter is consequent on the former. Some have suggested that Paul plays on the Jewish apocalyptic theme of being caught up to see heavenly visions.[57] If so, he radically de-Judaizes the theme – the catching up goes no farther than midair, deals with a group of people rather than with an individual, has a bodily character without exception or doubt, and includes no revelation of heavenly secrets[58] – so as to fit a hellenistically conceived παρουσία-cum-ἀπάντησις. Because of its festive connotations this concept enhances the consolation he seeks to bring the grief-stricken Thessalonians.

But why does Paul deem such an enhancement necessary? He does not argue vehemently for a future resurrection as he does in 1 Corinthians 15. So it does not seem likely that the Thessalonians were denying it despite his having taught it to them. Though it may at first seem unlikely that he had not informed them of a future resurrection, a number of pointers direct us to the view either that he had not informed them of it or that he had emphasized so strongly the possibility of Jesus' returning in the near future that the expectation of being alive at the time had swallowed up what little that Paul had taught them about a future resurrection. These pointers include (1) the predominantly Gentile background of the

---

[55] Cf. the objection of Plevnik that in contrast with citizens of a Hellenistic city "the faithful are acted upon – they will be taken up [passive voice]" (*Paul and the Parousia*, 8–9).

[56] See I. H. Marshall, "Martyrdom and the Parousia in the Revelation of John," in *SE* 4/1 (= TU 102): 337–38, that the harvest in Rev 14:14–16 represents the gathering of the saints, which is then omitted in 19:11–16; 20: 4 as already taken care of. By the time Revelation was written Paul's doctrine of the rapture, if not 1 Thessalonians itself, might have circulated. Even in Rev 14:14–16, however, it is not explicitly stated that the saints are gathered *up*, though we might infer an upward gathering from the location of the reaper on a cloud and from the contrastive judgment just outside the earthly city in 14:17–20.

[57] See the mass of references to primary and secondary literature in Baumgarten, *Paulus und die Apokalyptik*, 131.

[58] See G. Lohfink, *Die Himmelfahrt Jesu* (SANT 26; Munich: Kösel, 1971): 32–74. Lohfink also notes that in both Judaism and Hellenism bodily rapture replaced death. In 1 Thess 4:15–17 it includes the deceased who will rise as well as the still living. Cf. J. Plevnik, "The Taking Up of the Faithful and the Resurrection of the Dead," *CBQ* 46 (1984): 275–76.

Thessalonian Christians (1 Thess 1:9; 2:14; Acts 17:4; cf. Acts 17:32), which opens the door to Greek skepticism regarding bodily resurrection and a consequent recession of the prospect in their thinking; (2) the shortness of the time Paul had spent in Thessalonica (Acts 17:2, 5–10; 1 Thess 2:17–18; 3:1–5, 10); (3) the shortness of the time they had been Christians (Acts 17:1–18:17; 1 Thess 3:1–2); (4) the severity of their persecution (1 Thess 1:6–7; 2:14–16; 3:1–10; 2 Thess 1:4, 7), which must have heightened the wish that in turn fathered the thought of Jesus' soon return; (5) the implication of the matter-of-fact way in which Paul includes himself and his readers among those who will be alive at Jesus' return (1 Thess 4.15) that his preaching left people expecting to survive till then; (6) his not wanting the Thessalonians to sorrow as "those who do not have hope" (1 Thess 4:13); (7) his implying their ignorance with respect to Christian hope regarding the dead (1 Thess 4:13); and (8) the strength of his consolation (1 Thess 4:18 and esp. 5:10–11, where the consolation emphasizes "*living* together with him" even for those who are presently "sleeping").[59]

The rising of the dead "first" (v. 16) need not imply a mistaken view that the resurrection of believers will take place some time later than Christ's coming. A mere delay would hardly have provided a sufficient basis for the Thessalonians' sorrow.[60] Rather, the rising of the dead "first" strengthens the promise of resurrection by giving it priority on the agenda over the catching up of the living. If "the living ... will not precede the sleeping," if not even those who survive till Christ's coming will enjoy its benefits till the deceased arise, how sure their resurrection! How little reason the Thessalonians have to sorrow for their deceased! The stress on the uniting of those who are alive with those who are de-

---

[59] See Becker, *Paul*, 141. Cf. the view of Plevnik that the Thessalonians thought of rapture as confined to the living – hence the Thessalonians' sorrow in mistakenly thinking their deceased fellow Christians would miss the rapture and Paul's consequent need to establish an on-time resurrection of deceased saints (*Paul and the Parousia*, 68–76, 83, 94–96; idem, "Taking Up," 281). But Plevnik's argument that rapture indicates "the termination of present earthly existence" so as to dwell "in heaven" (ibid., 280, 282) overlooks Paul's use of παρουσία and ἀπάντησις to rule out a rapture to heaven and imply instead a meeting in the air to escort Jesus to earth. Moreover, Luke 24:50–51; Acts 1:9–11; Rev 11:3–13 show that rapture can follow resurrection of the dead.

[60] According to S. Turner, Paul's denying the precedence of living believers implies the Thessalonians were sorrowing out of a wrong belief that their deceased fellow Christians would not be resurrected till after Christ's earthly kingdom, which Paul had taught would follow the Parousia ("The Interim, Earthly Messianic Kingdom in Paul," *JSNT* 25 [2003]: 323–42). Turner's argument merits serious consideration, but one still suspects that to assuage sorrow over a merely delayed resurrection Paul would have stopped short of adding "as also the rest [unbelievers], who do not have hope [surely the hope of resurrection to eternal life]." "That you not sorrow" would have sufficed without the addition. Merklein makes a good point that the Thessalonians were not necessarily sorrowing *hopelessly* as non-Christians do ("Der Theologe als Prophet," 408–9). Nevertheless, a mistaken belief that the resurrection of deceased Christians will follow after rather than coincide with the παρουσία still seems insufficient to have prompted Paul's *exhortation* not to sorrow as non-Christians do.

ceased ("together with them" – v. 17) serves this argument. We can conclude that Paul does not aim at correcting an erroneous view of the order in which events are going to occur. The degree of Paul's consolation outruns such a view. Nor does he aim at correcting the denial of a taught doctrine. The degree of Paul's consolation lags behind such a denial, and he shows no argumentative vehemence.[61] He aims at informing them about a future resurrection of which they were ignorant or neglectful (cf. v. 13).[62]

A. J. Malherbe adds a suggestion that the Hellenistic use of ἁρπάζω (plus its compound forms and its Latin counterpart *eripio*) for snatching away by death led Paul to turn the word upside down in order to console the Thessalonians: though some fellow believers have been snatched away from them by death, together with them they are going to be snatched up to meet the Lord. Thus the snatching up of togetherness will replace the snatching away of separation.[63] Just as Paul's calling the trumpet "God's" links up with his statement that "God will bring the ones who have fallen asleep" (v. 14) – i. e., the trumpet is a means by which God will bring them – so also the "divine passive" in the verb "will be caught up" implies God's action.[64]

---

[61] Against Malherbe, who infers from the vehemently negative οὐ μή with φθάσωμεν, "shall by no means have precedence," that "some people in Thessalonica" propounded the precedence of living believers over deceased ones (*The Letters to the Thessalonians*, 272–73). But this vehemence need be only consolatory, not argumentative as well.

[62] Particularly in view of Paul's writing that "the dead in Christ will rise first" and his doing so to keep the Thessalonians from sorrowing as those "who do not have hope," it is hard to understand A. F. J. Klijn's argument that "Paul omits every opportunity to speak of the resurrection of the dead" ("1 Thessalonians 4:13–18 and its Background in Apocalyptic Literature," in *Paul and Paulinism* [ed. M. D. Hooker and S. G. Wilson; London: SPCK, 1982], 68). As Klijn points out, *4 Ezra* 13:16–24 puts the living at an advantage over the dead because the living will witness firsthand the Lord's salvation at the end (cf. Isa 52:10; Dan 12:12–13; *4 Ezra* 6:25; *Pss. Sol.* 17:50; 18:7; *2 Bar.* 29:2; 40:2; 71:1; Luke 2:30; 10:23–24). But such an advantage fails to explain Paul's comparison to those who "have no hope," for in *4 Ezra* 13:16–24 the disadvantage of the dead consists only in not being able "to see what will happen in the last time." Similarly, Klijn's citations of *4 Ezra* 5:41–45; 6:20; *2 Bar.* 30:2b; 51:13; *L.A.B.* 19:20 as background for the catching up "together" of the living and the resurrected fall somewhat short; for Paul writes earlier, and those passages have to do with the simultaneity of resurrection, or of presence at the Last Judgment, or of enjoyment of eternal blessedness, not with the simultaneity of anything similar to the rapture in Paul's teaching.

[63] A. J. Malherbe, "Exhortation in First Thessalonians," *NovT* 25 (1983): 255–56; idem, *The Letters to the Thessalonians*, 275–76.

[64] Cf. Wis 4:11; Acts 8:39; 2 Cor 12: 2; Rev 12:5; and on the use of the passive voice for God's actions see J. Jeremias, *New Testament Theology* (New York: Scribners, 1971), 9–14, and a caveat by E. M. Sidebottom, "The So-Called Divine Passive in the Gospel Tradition," *Exp-Tim* 87 (1976): 200–204. See also Lohfink, *Himmelfahrt*, 40, on the divine passive of ἁρπάζω in Hellenistic stories of bodily rapture. By no means does the catching up imply a nonphysical body at the resurrection (against Rigaux, *Thessaloniciens*, 243). B. Spörlein points out that in 2 Cor 12:2, 4 Paul entertains the possibility of having been caught up to the third heaven in his present physical body (*Die Leugnung der Auferstehung* [Biblische Untersuchungen 7; Regensburg: Pustet, 1971]: 128).

Strikingly, Paul shifts the clouds from the Son of Man, who comes riding down in them according to the dominical tradition (Mark 13:26; 14:62; Matt 24:30; 26:64; Luke 21:27; cf. Rev 1:7; 14:14–16), to believers, who he says will be snatched up in those clouds (cf. Acts 1:9, 11; Rev 11:12; Str-B 3:635–36). By this shift Paul tailors the tradition to suit a Hellenistic ἀπάντησις on the occasion of an imperial παρουσία.[65] The unique phrase "in the air" serves the same purpose, for Paul needs some location outside the world-city where believers may meet Jesus. Heaven will not do, for the Lord will have already left there. Besides, it is too far away from the world-city. The citizens and magistrates of a city met an approaching emperor only a short distance outside their city to escort him into it. The clouds therefore suggest the air.[66] The statement that "we will always be with the Lord" (cf. 5:10 too) may represent Paul's pirating the Hellenistic notion of being "with the gods" and his laundering it for Christian use.[67] "With the Lord" also picks up and plays on the other meaning of παρουσία besides "coming," viz., "presence." Finally, Paul's adding ἐπιφάνεια to παρουσία in 2 Thess 2:8, where we read the phrase "the appearance of his coming," fits Hellenistic influence in the use of παρουσία, for little doubt exists concerning the Hellenistic connotation of ἐπιφάνεια.[68]

Paul, then, has hellenized the tradition in conjunction with his use of παρουσία. The hellenizations aim at strengthening his consolation of the Thessalonian believers. The term παρουσία was itself one of the hellenizations. Paul gets credit for introducing this word into Christian vocabulary for the second coming (though "second" was, of course, a later addition which overlooked the difference that the first coming was neither sudden nor imperial). The meeting in the air and the joining in descent provide another Hellenistic touch by virtue

---

[65] Clouds appear also in Hellenistic stories of rapture (Lohfink, *Himmelfahrt*, 44, 73).

[66] Some commentators have suggested that Paul refers to the air because in Hellenistic thought it was the abode of the spiritual principalities and powers which dominate the world and because Paul wants to imply that Jesus is Lord over that realm and that the saints share, or will share, in that lordship (Eph 2:2; 6:12). If so, we have further evidence of Paul's hellenization of the tradition. But perhaps the air is simply the natural meeting place between heaven, from which the Lord descends, and earth, from which believers are caught up.

[67] See Book I, Chapter 9, of Epictetus's *Discourses* for an example contemporaneous with Paul; for a brief survey, W. Grundmann, "σύν-μετά," *TDNT* 7:781; for more details from primary sources, Dupont, *L'Union avec le Christ*, 166–69, 181–82; cf. Malherbe, "Exhortation," 255–56. One might also think of the dominical saying in Luke 23:43.

[68] R. Bultmann/D. Lührmann, "ἐπιφαίνω κτλ," *TDNT* 9:7–10; Rigaux, *Thessaloniciens*, 201–4. Rigaux (p. 203 n. 4) rejects Dupont's effort (*L'Union avec le Christ*, 73–77) to avoid the implication of a Hellenistic connotation in ἐπιφάνεια. Plevnik joins Dupont in denying the Hellenistic character of ἐπιφάνεια (*Paul and the Parousia*, 43). But should not his cross-references to 2 Macc 2:21; 3:24; 5:4; 12:22; 14:15; 15:27; *3 Macc.* 2:9; 5:8, 51 count as Hellenistic? And although Jesus' ἐπιφάνεια in 2 Thess 2:8 proves destructive to the man of lawlessness, it proves very beneficial – like Hellenistic ἐπιφάνειαι – to the saints (see 2 Thess 1:3–10 [against Plevnik's n. 116 on p. 43]).

of which Paul also gets credit for introducing an upward rapture of all believers right after the resurrection of deceased ones.

Christianization of Jewish Tradition

If Paul has hellenized dominical eschatological and apocalyptic tradition in 1 Thess 2:19–20; 3:13; 4:15–17, he christianizes Jewish eschatological and apocalyptic tradition in the rest of 1–2 Thessalonians. By including substantive metamorphosis, christianization goes beyond the mere borrowing of phraseology from the OT and other Jewish sources. Again we do not take up every tradition that Paul uses, only those accurately described by our title.

The Day of the Lord had become an important theme in the OT prophets. So far as our documentary evidence goes, however, Paul was the first to equate the Day of the Lord with "the παρουσία of the Lord" (1 Thess 5:1–11). That he did so is evident (1) from the phraseological parallel between "the παρουσία of the Lord" (4:15) and "the Day of the Lord" (5:2); (2) from the way "the times and the seasons" in 1 Thess 5:1 relate back to the coming of Christ in ch. 4 and make a bridge to the coming of the Day of the Lord in ch. 5; (3) from Paul's making the Day of the Lord the object of Christian watchfulness (as the coming of Christ is) and the source of Christian consolation (again as the coming of Christ is; cf. παρακαλεῖτε ἀλλήλους in 5:11 with the same phrase in 4:18); (4) from his applying the notions of suddenness and surprise, which in the dominical tradition describe the coming of the Son of Man (Mark 13:35–36; Matt 24:37–51; 25:13; Luke 12:39–46; 17:26–27, 34–35; 21:34–35), to the coming of the Day of the Lord; and (5) from the interchangeability of "the Day of the Lord" with "the παρουσία of our Lord Jesus Christ and our gathering together to him" in 2 Thess 2:1–2. Thus the day of the one true God, Yahweh, turns into the day of the one true Emperor, Jesus. As a result, Paul will later change the stereotyped phrase by adding other christological terms: "the Day of the Lord" will become "the Day of our Lord Jesus [Christ]" (1 Cor 1:8), "the Day of our Lord Jesus" (2 Cor 1:14; cf. 1 Cor 5:5 *v.l.*), "the Day of Christ Jesus" (Phil 1:6), and "the Day of Christ" (Phil 1:10; 2:16).

Paul christianizes the Day of the Lord also by saying it comes as a thief (1 Thess 5:2). The metaphor does not apply to the Day of the Lord in the OT or other Jewish tradition.[69] It comes, rather, from dominical tradition. But there it applies to the coming of the Son of Man, represented as a householder (Matt 24:42–43; Luke 12:39–40; cf. Rev 3:3; 16:15; *Gos. Thom.* 21). By switching the metaphor to the coming of the Day of the Lord – which is equivalent to the παρουσία of the Lord Jesus Christ, who is the Son of Man – Paul

---

[69] See Harnisch, *Eschatologische Existenz*, 60–62.

further christianizes the Day of the Lord (cf. 2 Pet 3:10).[70] The additional phrase "in the night" (so also 2 Pet 3:10 *v.l.*) reflects the dominical tradition leading up to the parable of the householder and the thief – viz., the parable of the master and his slaves, which has its setting in the night (Luke 12:35–38; see esp. the reference in v. 38 to the second and third watches of the night – and confirms Paul's christianizing the Day of the Lord.[71]

Yet further christianizing of the Day of the Lord occurs in Paul's making it the basis of an exhortation to watch for Jesus' coming: he hybridizes "the Day of the Lord" with "the sons of light" (which is also traditional – see Luke 16:8 and Qumran literature, passim) to produce "sons of day" for believers who, belonging to daytime, ought to stay awake and keep sober (1 Thess 5:5–10).[72] They ought also to put on the armor which belongs to Yahweh in Isa 59:17 but which Paul christianizes by transferring it to believers, changing "righteousness" (so Isaiah) to "faith and love," and making "salvation" (so Isaiah) qualify "hope," which Paul adds to produce the triad of Christian virtues faith, love, and hope already mentioned in ch. 1 (cf. 5:8 with 1:3).[73]

In the Jewish tradition that was taken over into dominical tradition the figure of birthpangs stood for the horrors to take place during the tribulation (Str-B 1:950; Mark 13:8; Matt 24:8). Since Paul equates the Day of the Lord with the παρουσία of the Lord Jesus Christ, he also switches the figure of birthpangs to the παρουσία-Day of the Lord (1 Thess 5:3). The figure therefore

---

[70] Harnisch is hypercritical in denying that Paul draws on dominical tradition and in supporting the denial with the argument that in 1 Thess 5:2 the thief represents the manner of the coming of the Day of the Lord whereas Matt 24:43 par. Luke 12:39 speaks of a householder who would have watched had he known what hour the thief was going to come and steal his effects (*Eschatologische Existenz*, 94–95). Paul merely seizes on the point of unexpected disaster, as was easy to do because the next dominical saying interprets the unexpected coming of a thief in terms of the Son of Man's unexpected coming, and we have no good reason to break up these sayings. It is gratuitous of Harnisch to suppose that both NT passages derive from earlier Jewish apocalyptic. Why multiply sources unnecessarily? See J. Plevnik, "1 Thess 5,1–11: Its Authenticity, Intention and Message," *Bib* 60 (1979): 80–87.

[71] Cf. C.-P. März, "Das Gleichnis vom Dieb: Überlegungen zur Verbindung von Lk 12,39 par Mt 24,43 und 1 Thess 5,24," in *The Four Gospels 1992* (ed. F. Van Segbroeck et al.; BETL 100; Leuven: Leuven University Press, 1992), 1:633–48.

[72] Collins, "Tradition, Redaction, and Exhortation," 338; F. Laub, *Eschatologische Verkündigung und Lebensgestaltung nach Paulus* (Biblische Untersuchungen 10; Regensburg: Pustet, 1973), 159.

[73] Collins, "Tradition, Redaction, and Exhortation," 339. Against Paul's direct use of Isa 59:17 Holtz asks why Paul did not take up Yahweh's garment or mantle for the third Christian virtue rather than packing two Christian virtues into one piece of armor ("Traditionen," 68–69). The answer probably lies in Isaiah's associating the garment and mantle with vengeance and retribution, which hardly offer possibilities of linkage with Christian virtue as "righteousness" and "salvation" do. Besides, garments and mantles are not pieces of armor such as Paul wants to portray as Christians' defense against worldliness. His other uses of Isa 59:17 (see Rom 6:13; 13:12; 2 Cor 6:7; 10:3–6; Eph 6:11–17) do not demand his borrowing from an intermediate Christian tradition.

loses its original meaning, intensity of pain, and takes on a new one that is less natural, viz., suddenness. Just as birthpangs suddenly stab the body of a pregnant woman who has come to term, so also destruction will suddenly strike the wicked when the Day of the Lord arrives. Furthermore, the unstoppability of giving birth once the pangs start leads Paul to add "and they will not escape." All in all, he christianizes the birthpangs by making them part of Jesus' παρουσία rather than preliminaries to it. Perhaps the change from the dominical plural, "birthpangs," to the singular, "birthpang," is due to this concentration on the single event of Christ's coming, though rabbinic usage favors the singular. It may also be that the dominical tradition behind Luke 21:34–36, which mentions suddenness in connection with "that day," the avoidance of drunkenness, the practice of watching (cf. 1 Thess 5:6–7), and "a snare" (παγίς, perhaps going back to חֶבֶל and capable of being pointed חֵבֶל, "birth pang," as in 1 Thess 5:3), helped Paul make this shift.[74].

As we can infer from 2 Thess 2:1–2, the Thessalonian Christians did not follow Paul's shifting the birthpangs from the tribulation to the παρουσία. Nor failing that shift did they limit the Day of the Lord to the παρουσία. Rather, in their minds that day included preliminary birthpangs, which they thought had already started (and thus the Day of the Lord too) in the persecutions they were suffering (cf. Paul's starting with the topic of persecution and relating it to the second coming in 2 Thess 1:3–12; see also 1 Thess 1: 6–7; 2:14–16; 3:1–10 and the intense hostility of Jewish unbelievers in Thessalonica according to Acts 17:1–15).

As a number of commentators have noted, the Thessalonian Christians could hardly have thought that Jesus had already come back (a view that would have entailed their and Paul's having missed the event and that Paul would surely have countered by emphasizing its publicity as Matt 24:23–28 does). Therefore the Thessalonians must have included the preceding tribulation in their view of the Day of the Lord and, thinking the tribulation had started, concluded that Jesus was about to come.[75] The second epistle, then, solidifies the christianiza-

---

[74] Cf. L. Hartman, *Prophecy Interpreted* (ConBNT 1; Lund: Gleerup, 1966), 192–93; but see D. Wenham, "Paul and the Synoptic Apocalypse," 353–56. On birth-pangs as indicating inescapability see Harnisch, *Eschatologische Existenz*, 69–77, with citations of Isa 66:9; *4 Ezra* 4:40–42; *6 Ezra* 2:36–40.

[75] See, e.g., R. D. Aus, "The Relevance of Isaiah 66. 7 to Revelation 12 and 2 Thessalonians 1," *ZNW* 67 (1976): 263–64. The gnostic hypothesis of W. Schmithals (*Paul and the Gnostics* [Nashville: Abingdon, 1971]: 166–67, 202–8) and others that the Thessalonians thought the Day of the Lord had already come in a spiritualized form, Gnosticism being a kind of over-realized eschatology, has rightly been rejected by most NT scholars. For one thing, the arrival and presence of such a Day of the Lord would bring joy and confidence, not the consternation characterizing the Thessalonians in 2 Thess 2:1–2 (cf. 1 Thess 4:13 and see Trilling, *Untersuchungen*, 125–26 – also against Popkes ["Bedeutung," 45–48], who with an appeal esp. to 2 Tim 2:17–18 supposes an over-realized eschatology that falls short of Gnosticism). Furthermore, over-realized eschatology does not normally arise out of intense persecution such as

tion of the Day of the Lord by making it unmistakably clear that that day, identical only with "the παρουσία of our Lord Jesus Christ and our gathering together to him," will not arrive till after the tribulation. To do so, Paul points out two events of the tribulation that obviously have not yet taken place: the ἀποστασία, "rebellion," and the revelation of the man of lawlessness.

The expectation of a rebellion against God was common in Jewish circles[76] and came into Christianity as well.[77] But Paul christianizes the expectation by bringing it into association with the man of lawlessness, who was to lead (if not initiate) the rebellion.[78] Jews did not look for such an eschatological figure.[79] The dominical tradition speaks only of false christs and false prophets – in the

---

the Thessalonian believers were suffering. Out of intense persecution, on the contrary, arises futuristic eschatology: things will get better in the sweet-by-and-by. And a gnostic sort of spiritual enthusiasm makes Paul's exhortation not to quench the Spirit (1 Thess 5:19) hit the wrong note. Against the gnostic hypothesis as it relates to 1 Thessalonians see N. Hyldahl, "Auferstehung Christi – Auferstehung der Toten," in *Die Paulinische Literatur und Theologie* (ed. S. Pedersen; Teologiske Studier 7; Göttingen: Vandenhoeck & Ruprecht, 1980), 124–26.

[76] 1QpHab 2:1–10; *1 En.* 90:22–27; 91:7; 93:9; *Jub.* 23:14–16; *4 Ezra* 5:1–2; and further references in Str-B 3:637; 4/2:977–1015.

[77] Mark 13:5–6, 21–23; Matt 24:10–12, 23–24; 1 Tim 4:1–5; 2 Tim 3:1–13; Jude 17–19.

[78] K. Staab thinks the man of lawlessness does not instigate the rebellion but only appears at its high point (*Die Thessalonicherbriefe* [RNT 7/1; 5th ed.; Regensburg: Pustet, 1969], 51). But πρῶτον, "first," may modify the whole protasis rather than indicate that the rebellion will take place before the man of lawlessness is revealed. See Best (*Thessalonians*, 281–83), Rigaux (*Thessaloniciens*, 253–58), and Frame (*Thessalonians*, 251) that Paul does not mean an apostasy of Christians. Cf. Rom 1:18–32 for the kind of general rebellion against God in the world at large that Paul has in mind. Best thinks more narrowly of Jewish rejection of the gospel. Thomas argues that the rebellion comes first *within* the Day of the Lord, not before it, and cites the use of πρῶτον in Mark 3:27; Matt 12:29; John 7:51; Rom 15:24 ("1 Thessalonians, 2 Thessalonians," 320–21, 323). But none of these cross-references have in view a period of time (such as the Day of the Lord) within which different events occur. As Staab does, Thomas takes πρῶτον in 2 Thess 2:3 as indicating the priority of the rebellion to the revelation of the lawless one and then avers that the rebellion is not absolutely first in the Day of the Lord (or in the tribulational part of it) but only first in relation to the revelation of the lawless one. To say so, however, breaks the connection with vv. 1–2, which requires Paul to tell why the Day of the Lord is not present, not irrelevantly to sort out the order of events within the Day of the Lord after the rapture has occurred. The exhortations in 1 Thess 5:1–11 to be watchful and ready for the Day of the Lord imply that however long or short it may be, it starts with the παρουσία. Thomas's further argument that "if Paul had given oral or written instruction to this effect [viz., that the παρουσία as a single event initiates the Day of the Lord after the tribulation], the false claim that the day of the Lord was already present could hardly have alarmed these Christians" (p. 318) does not take account of the reproachful tone of Paul's question in v. 5: "Don't you remember that I told you these things when I was still with you?" They should have known better than to be persuaded by the false teaching that the Day of the Lord was already present. Later, Thomas himself recognizes Paul's reproachful tone (p. 324). On p. 319 Thomas strangely says the false teachers were denying the deliverance from the tribulation he thinks Paul promised them in 1 Thess 5:9. Thomas's argument on p. 318 that the Thessalonians would not have believed a contradiction of Paul's genuine teaching therefore disagrees with Thomas's own view on p. 319. But he rightly avoids equating ἡ ἀποστασία with the rapture.

[79] Str-B 3:637–40.

plural (Mark 13:22; Matt 24:11, 24) – and of the abomination of desolation (Mark 13:14; Matt 24:15). Mark refers to the latter with the masculine participle ἑστηκότα, "standing." But "standing" contrasts with "sitting" in 2 Thess 2:4. Furthermore, standing suits an image of some person, human or divine (cf. Rev 13:14–15); sitting suits the person himself. (An image stands even though it portrays its subject in a seated position; but a person receiving worship sits.[80]) Hence, it looks as though the man of lawlessness himself sits in God's temple. That is to say, Paul completely personalizes the abomination of desolation. Matthew goes the opposite direction by changing Mark's masculine participle to a more grammatical neuter (ἑστός). On the other hand, his phrase "in the holy place," which replaces Mark's "where it [or 'he'] ought not," is closer to Paul's "in the temple of God."

Paul is borrowing ideas and phraseology from Dan 11:32 (οἱ ἀνομοῦντες Theod), 36–37, which deals with Antiochus Epiphanes. But Ezek 28:2, which deals with the ruler of Tyre and is immediately followed by a reference to Daniel,[81] has given Paul the posture of sitting in connection with a claim to deity (cf. Isa 14:13–15).[82] It appears, then, that he models the man of lawlessness after Antiochus Epiphanes, amalgamates him with the ruler of Tyre, and christianizes this already hybrid figure by giving him the characteristics of the false christs and false prophets predicted in the dominical tradition underlying the Olivet Discourse (Mark 13:22; Matt 24:11, 24). For not only does the man of lawlessness exalt himself against God and every sacred object. Paul also gives him a παρουσία counter to that of Christ (v. 9), an ἀποκάλυψις counter to that of Christ (cf. 2:3, 8 with 1:7[83]), and signs and wonders like those of false christs and false prophets (Mark 13:22; Matt 24:24).[84] Paul even associates a mystery

---

[80] Cf. G. Vos, *The Pauline Eschatology* (Grand Rapids: Eerdmans, 1952 repr.), 95–96 n. 2.

[81] It makes no difference to Paul's linking the passages in Daniel and Ezekiel who the Daniel referred to in Ezekiel might have been. Hartman thinks Paul drew on Deut 13:2–3, 11, 14 too (*Prophecy Interpreted*, 199).

[82] Antiochus Epiphanes did not himself sit in the temple at Jerusalem but only had a pagan altar set up there (1 Macc 1:36–40, 54, 59). Nor did Caligula sit in the temple; he only ordered a statue of himself to be erected there (Philo, *Leg. Gaius* 188; Josephus, *J.W.* 2.10.1 § 185; *Ant.* 18.8.2 § 26l). Despite their actual and attempted desecrations of the temple, then, these emperors do not provide fully adequate models for Paul's man of lawlessness. R. D. Aus suggests that 2 Thess 2:1–12 rests in part on christianizing Isa 66:7 as a reference to the Messiah, whom God will not "hold back" (cf. Isa 66:9 MT; "God's Plan and God's Power: Isaiah 66 and the Restraining Factors of 2 Thess 2:6–7," *JBL* 96 [1977]: 537–53). Speculativeness makes the suggestion hard to verify or falsify.

[83] Paul's use of ἀποκάλυψις for Jesus' παρουσία appears to be another christianization of a Jewish theme, that of God's revealing himself (cf. A. Oepke, "ἀποκαλύπτω," *TDNT* 3:571–92). Passages in the Similitudes of Enoch (*1 En.* 48:6; 62:7) and *4 Ezra* 13:32; *2 Bar.* 29:3; 39:7 are probably too late to have affected Paul's usage.

[84] Cf. the somewhat similar remarks of Hartman, *Prophecy Interpreted*, 202. But he thinks Paul used a gospel tradition related to and lying behind Matthew. We might rather suppose that Paul influenced Matthew directly or indirectly (see notes 3 and 5 above and the discussion in

with the man of lawlessness (2:7; cf. 1QS 4:1; 1Q27 1:2, 3–4; 1QM 3:8–9; 14:9; 1QH 5:36) just as he often associates mysteries with God, Christ, and the gospel. Thus the man of lawlessness starts out as anti-God, but because of Paul's christianizing the Jewish tradition he goes well on his way toward becoming the Antichrist of 1 John 2:18 (cf. 1 John 2:22; 4:3; 2 John 7; Revelation 13).

In summary, then, Paul hellenizes dominical tradition by portraying Christ's return as a festive imperial visit in which deceased as well as living Christians will participate. This hellenization has the purpose of correcting a wrong belief that the return will not involve the deceased. Paul then christianizes Jewish tradition to heighten readiness for Christ's return, a readiness that he feared might be suffering from disappointment caused by the falsely supposed nonparticipation of the deceased. Finally, he christianizes Jewish tradition to cool down an overheated belief in the immediacy of Christ's return, the wish for quick release from persecution having fathered the thought of such a release.[85] And recent attempts to make Paul teach a taking of the saints to heaven after a midair U-turn by Jesus at the παρουσία suffer by comparison with the old understanding that in Paul's view Christ will descend with them all the way to earth.

---

the body of the text to which they refer). H. N. Ridderbos pays too much attention to the man of lawlessness as a false prophet, deceiving people with signs and wonders, and so neglects the man of lawlessness as anti-God, demanding to be worshipped, and (implicitly) as anti-Christ, having a revelation and a παρουσία (*Paul: An Outline of His Theology* [Grand Rapids: Eerdmans, 1975], 513; cf. Best's criticism [*Thessalonians*, 283–84] of Giblin). Vos makes the same kind of mistake by centering on the man of lawlessness as anti-God to argue against the similarly incorrect view that he is a false Messiah of the Jews (*The Pauline Eschatology*, 114–16). So also Trilling, who puts undue emphasis on ἄνθρωπος (in the phrase "the man of lawlessness") over against θεός (*Der zweite Brief an die Thessalonicher*, 86–87). The primary emphasis falls on the lawlessness of the man rather than on the humanity of the lawless one. Ridderbos thinks Paul contrasts the *man* of lawlessness with Christ the man just as in later epistles he will contrast the first man Adam and the last man Christ (*Paul*, 514). But again too much emphasis is falling on ἄνθρωπος. Adam is a given in the OT – and his very name means "man" – whereas the man of lawlessness is Paul's construction. See Rigaux, *Thessaloniciens*, 270–72, 656–57, against deriving the man of lawlessness from Beliar or Belial.

[85] As to G. Luedemann's *Paul, Apostle to the Gentiles* (Philadelphia: Fortress, 1984), there is large scale agreement with his view that in Thessalonica Paul had not preached the resurrection of deceased Christians (pp. 219–20). The present article refutes Luedemann's appeal to word statistics (which, however, he is not the first to have put forward) in favor of denying apocalyptic elements to Paul (pp. 222–25). More importantly, Luedemann attributes "the word of the Lord" to Jewish apocalyptic tradition in which the resurrection of the dead chronologically followed the withdrawal of the living. Accordingly, Paul inverted the order (pp. 225–36). But Luedemann can find no Jewish apocalyptic precedent for an aerial meeting. The most glaring weakness of all: on the order of resurrection and withdrawal he makes Paul appeal to an apocalyptic tradition that said exactly the contrary of what Paul wanted to say, and did say.

16. Is John's Gospel Sectarian?

To discuss properly whether the Gospel of John is sectarian we must not play a semantic game with various definitions of the word *sectarian*. Instead, we must settle on a definition and then determine whether John's Gospel fits it. N.B.: John's *Gospel*, not John himself or the community, communities, or church at large in and for which he wrote. The degree to which the text may or may not mirror his or their past, current, and anticipated conditions and characteristics is another question.

For the present discussion let us settle on the definition adopted by most modern sociologists as classically expressed by Benton Johnson: a sect is "a religious group that rejects the social environment in which it exists."[1] Whatever else a sect does, it regards itself as at odds with the rest of the world, in our case the non-Christian world. The opposition a sect feels to and from the outside world (from here on, simply "the world") naturally encourages cohesion within the sect as a defense mechanism. But this cohesion does not necessarily inhibit attempts to win converts. The opposite often happens – hence the subcategory of "conversionist sects" that do not isolate themselves spatially (in contrast with the community at Qumran), not to delineate other subcategories. Nor does the cohesion necessarily imply a breakaway from other bodies sharing broadly similar beliefs and practices – in the case of John, the rest of what became mainstream Christianity. No, according to the definition we have adopted the issue has to do with opposition to and from the non-Christian environment; and elements in John tend against a breakaway from what became mainstream Christianity. For example, the Johannine Jesus has "other sheep that are not of this fold" (10:16) and prays for the oneness of all believers in him, both present and future (17:20–23).

The degree to which opposition to and from the world is felt and the internal cohesion thereby encouraged varies from sect to sect, so that one may legitimately speak in the plural of degrees of sectarianism. To some degree all NT Christianity can be described as sectarian under our definition. Luke-Acts represents a low degree, however, inasmuch as there a friendly hand is extended to the world and a concerted effort is made to present Christianity as healthful to the world despite the antagonism felt to be perpetrated on it by the world. To-

---

[1] B. Johnson, "On Church and Sect," *American Sociological Review* 28 (1963): 542.

ward the other end of the spectrum the Gospel of John is often described as representing a significantly high degree of feeling opposed by the world and opposed to it. In line with this probably prevalent view among Johannine experts I devoted a whole chapter and several extended endnotes, complete with more documentation from sociological literature than ever before assembled, to just such a description in my book *Jesus the Word according to John the Sectarian.*[2]

What evidence supports a description of John as heavily sectarian in accordance with our adopted definition? Well, John paints the world in very dark colors. It is full of darkness. Those human beings who make up the world are children of darkness. They do not belong to the light. They do not comprehend the light. Their deeds are evil. They do not acknowledge God, God's Son Jesus, or God's children, who believe in him and in Jesus. Moreover, they hate God, God's Son, and God's children. They murdered God's Son, rejoiced over his death, and excommunicate and kill God's children as well.

Satan dominates worldlings. He is their father. God loved the world; but because of their unbelief his wrath rests on them already, so that they are headed for a resurrection of judgment. And *only* God is said to love the world. Though John often portrays Jesus as loving those who believe in him, he never says that Jesus loved the world. So in stark contrast with the synoptic Jesus, who regularly eats with tax collectors and sinners, the Jesus of John is never said to eat with people of the world. He eats only with believers. He reveals himself to believers but not to the world. He makes a point of saying that he does not pray for the world, but only for those that God his Father has given him out of the world. He says that to gain eternal life a person must hate his or her life in this world and be born all over again, from above, of the Spirit, so that believers thus born constitute a new species. Loving their own kind is therefore never said to entail loving those born only once, from below, of the flesh. It follows that the synoptic Jesus's command to love your neighbor, whomever in need that you meet on the Jericho road (so to speak), shrinks to the command to love one another in the Christian community (a shrinkage quite objectionable to many ethicists but typical of sectarian resocialization, so that close fellowship within the sect replaces a wide range of friendships outside the sect).[3] Thus John also presents a strong doctrine of election distinguishing those whom God draws into the sectarian circle from those whom he does not draw. Those whom he draws speak and understand what sociologists call an antilanguage, one that outsiders do not understand, at least not salvifically, but that insiders do understand, at least with

---

[2] R. H. Gundry, *Jesus the Word according to John the Sectarian* (Grand Rapids: Eerdmans, 2002), 51–70, 103–5, 106–8, 110–13.

[3] Cf. the command in 1 John 2:15–17 that goes even further by way of telling believers not to love "the world" (= unbelievers as distinct from "the *things* in the world," i.e., the lusts and pride that characterize the world of unbelievers; see Gundry, *Jesus the Word*, 105–6, against attempts to mitigate the passage).

instruction. And this antilanguage bespeaks the absolute of a totalizing narrative that encompasses all time and eternity, all space (the things above and those below), and all that exists in time and space. Because they arise out of the world, all other narratives offer falsehood.[4]

But John's canonical status throughout the church has understandably led some pluralists, universalists, inclusivists, accommodationists, and systematicians to try softening if not eliminating the hard sectarianism that has come to be traditionally associated with the Fourth Gospel.[5] What are the arguments for such a softening, and do they succeed? I will argue that they do not.

We may start with the argument that God's creation of all things through the Word (1:3) implies an acceptance of social plurality as a good – an acceptance which deeply qualifies a sectarian description of John, for sectarians consider the outside world to be bad. This argument takes no account, however, of the distinction between all things as God created them through the Word and the world's presently degraded state because of the world's having believed Satan's lie (8:44). The effect of that lie corresponds perfectly to a sectarian view of the world that far from accepting social plurality as a divinely created good considers the world en masse as evil.

A related argument is that the only kind of exclusion characterizing John has to do with soteriology, with whether a person believes or disbelieves in Jesus. John knows nothing of other sorts of exclusion, such as ethnic and economic exclusions. The gospel as John presents it is for the whole world without regard to social differences. Quite so! But sectarianism has to do with a *religious* difference, not with other sorts of differences, so that the universality of the gospel as John presents it does not produce a soft sectarianism, much less a nonsectarian gospel. The Johanninely described disastrous result of disbelief in the universally offered gospel runs in a sectarian direction.

According to John, the Word shone among all human beings (1:4–5, 9–10) and true worship of God occurs "in spirit and truth" (4:24) – unsectarian statements, it is said. But it is an exegetical question whether the Word shone among all human beings prior to the incarnation as well as afterwards, or only afterwards. Even in the case of a preincarnational shining, a sectarian emphasis falls

---

[4] See Gundry, *Jesus the Word*, 51–70, for extensive documentation in John's Gospel as well as in the sociological literature.

[5] Apart from scattered reviews of my *Jesus the Word* see esp. R. A. Culpepper, "Inclusivism and Exclusivism in the Fourth Gospel," in *Word, Theology, and Community in John* (ed. J. Painter, R. A. Culpepper, and F. F. Segovia; St. Louis: Chalice, 2002), 85–108; in the same volume, D. M. Smith, "Ethics and the Interpretation of the Fourth Gospel," 109–22; and, most comprehensively, M. Volf, "Johannine Dualism and Contemporary Pluralism" (paper presented at a conference on "St. John and Theology" held at St. Andrew's University, Scotland, July 2003, and soon to be published). By softening John's sectarianism Volf aims to salvage the Fourth Gospel for public theology, specifically for the resolution of political conflicts (N.B. the reference to contemporary pluralism in his title).

on the failure of human beings, portrayed as "the darkness" and as "the world," to recognize or apprehend the light that is the Word. And the spirit and truth in which true worship of God must occur are to be identified with the Holy Spirit as given by the crucified, resurrected, and glorified Christ (7:37–39; 20:22) and with Jesus himself as having incarnated the truth (14:6). The events that produced the truth in Jesus and the gift of the Spirit made possible what is now the only acceptable kind of worship, as shown by the statement, "But the hour is coming and now is when the true worshipers will worship the Father in Spirit and Truth" (4:23). There is no acceptance of a merely inward, sincere worship practiced outside the bounds of the gospel as presented by John.

But does not John exhibit a soft sectarianism by showing less interest in negating other religions as ways of salvation than in presenting Jesus as the universal Savior who affirms the pillars of Judaism, such as the OT and the Jewish temple, while simultaneously competing with Judaism? One might quibble over the question whether hard sectarians necessarily spend a lot of their energy negating other religions in addition to propagating their own religion. More importantly, though, the statement of John's Jesus, "No one comes to the Father except through me" (14:6c), clearly negates other religions; and it will not do to reduce that statement to a consequence of Jesus' preceding claim to be "the way and the truth and the life" (14:6b). Consequence or not, the statement carries a strong, indeed absolute negation; and consequences do not have to be rhetorically weaker than their bases. The opposite could equally well be true.

Yes, in cleansing the temple Jesus exhibited "zeal" for it as his Father's house (2:14–17). Yes again, he appealed to Moses and the OT (5:39, 45–46; 10:35 et passim). But John presents Jesus' body as the new temple that has outmoded the Jewish temple (2:18–22; 4:21), and he presents Moses and the OT as witnesses to this new reality of grace and truth that has replaced the law (1:17), to the wine of the gospel that has retired the Jewish water of purification (2:1–11), and to the true bread from heaven to which the manna given to Israel only pointed (6:26–58). Salvation may be "from (ἐκ) the Jews" (4:22c), but it is no longer to be found in their Jesus-less religion. Nor will it do to always limit John's negative portrayals of "the Jews" to the Jewish authorities in Jerusalem and say that those portrayals only follow upon the authorities' calling him demon-possessed and trying to kill him. For 2:18–22 already portrays "the Jews" negatively in that they challenge Jesus' authority, in that he tells them, "[You] destroy this temple ['of his body']," and in that they question his ability to raise it in three days. And though John often identifies "the Jews" with authorities in Jerusalem, one need not read into this and some other passages a limitation of "the Jews" to those authorities. Jews other than the authorities frequented the temple, and the Jews whom John portrays negatively as grumbling about Jesus and arguing against his claims (6:41, 52) cannot count as Jewish authorities in or from Jerusalem. For they consist of the five thousand Galileans whom he fed on "the other side of the Sea of Galilee" (6:1). Though it must not be translated into anti-Semitism (yet sadly has been so translated), John's sectarianism brooks no softening here.

Over against John's shrinking the broad command to love your neighbor into the narrow command to love your fellow believer, opponents of sectarianism in John put Jesus' and the disciples' attending a wedding of unbelievers and Jesus' helping to make it a more jovial occasion by turning water into wine (2:1–11). It is further argued that given his initial unwillingness to change the water to wine, he participated in the wedding not qua Savior of the world but qua friend or relative of the unbelievers, so that John does not prohibit association with unbelievers. Well, of course, Jesus and the disciples constantly associate with unbelievers in John. They repeatedly attend Jewish festivals with them, for instance. But we should avoid equivocating on the word *association*, as though mingling with unbelievers amounted to loving them or even to befriending them. The Johannine Jesus and his disciples are never said to befriend unbelievers, much less to love them. Only on unbelievers' turning into believers are friendship and love realized.[6]

Jesus' question and statement, "What do I and you have in common, woman? My hour has not yet come," are not to be taken as an initial unwillingness to change the water to wine, but as a declaration of independence from his mother. If he is to perform the sign, he will do so at his Father's bidding even though his hour has not yet come. And to say that Jesus turned the water into wine to make the wedding a more jovial occasion (in view of the remark by the master of ceremonies, a more *drunken* occasion would capture the implication better) is to read into the text a mundane understanding made otiose by John's calling the miracle a "sign," i.e., a symbol of the outmoding of Judaism, represented in the water (otherwise why describe the water as purificatory?), by the gospel, represented in the wine (hence John's omission of the institution of the Eucharist at the Last Supper – in a sense it is already instituted right here at Cana and then at the feeding of the five thousand and bread-of-life, eat-my-flesh, drink-my-blood discourse in ch. 6). Incidentally, John says nothing about Jesus' eating and drinking with the other wedding guests (contrast Jesus' reclining at dinner with Lazarus, Martha, and Mary in 12:1–2 and with the disciples in ch. 13).

But John and Jesus do not hurl threats of divine wrath against the world such as you would expect a hard, antiworldly sectarian to hurl. Instead, Jesus says that he has not come into the world to judge it; rather, to save it (3:17; 12:47). Though 3:36 says that God's wrath rests on the unbelieving, judgment comes only as the effect of unbelief, not as the direct result of Jesus' activity, at least

---

[6] It is irrelevant to argue, as some do, that John contains no command to hate enemies such as we read in 1QS 1:4, 9–10, as if a high degree of antiworldliness requires the hating of one's enemies. It does not, though such a command would admittedly indicate an even higher degree of antiworldiness.

not until the last day (5:24–29). Meanwhile, the words and deeds of Jesus do the judging, not he himself. Or so it is argued. But Jesus also says, "I have come into this world for judgment, that those who do not see may see and [that] those who do not see may become blind," and then and there he himself pronounces the judgment, "Your sin remains" (9:39, 41). He even declares the laying down of his life at his own initiative to be "the judgment of this world" (12:31 with 10:17–18). And we cannot legitimately separate his judgmental words from his purportedly nonjudgmental activity, because John portrays Jesus the Word as one with his words, and his activity as his words made visible.[7] However we resolve the tension between Jesus' not coming into the world to judge it but to save it and his coming for the execution of judgment, it remains that Jesus' judging the world is not limited to the last day.

According to 3:16, though, God loved the world, so that his love for it must translate into believers' positive valuation of it, must it not? No, because the command not to love the world in 1 John 2:15 appears close to a passage in the same epistle on divine and Christian love that says God sent his Son to be the Savior of the world (1 John 4:4–21). Therefore it does not follow that in the Fourth Gospel God's love for the world dictates for believers an unsectarianly positive valuation of it *as such*. It does follow, however, that God's love for the world dictates for believers a positive valuation of it as a reservoir out of which he will draw the elect through the believers' witness ("As the Father sent me I also send you," Jesus says in 20:21; cf. 17:18 and see 15:19; 17:6, 14, 16 for the elect as not of [ἐκ] the world any more than Jesus is). There is nothing unsectarian about such a valuation, for saving *from* the world those who are not *of* the world typifies conversionist sects. And once again, John presents Jesus' charitable deeds, such as feeding the hungry and healing the sick, as "signs" and "works" designed to symbolize salvation rather than to portray an altruistic doing of good – and also to elicit belief (20:30–31). This utilitarian purpose of the charitable deeds also fits sectarianism, in which they are done as tools for the extraction of the elect from the world, not for philanthropy per se.

But since God loved the world, does not the oneness of Jesus the Son with his Father and their dwelling in each other require that Jesus too loved the world, as evidenced by the giving of his life for it? And since believers indwell Jesus and he and the Father indwell believers, are not believers bound to love the world? Again no, for as just noted the command not to love the world in 1 John 2:15 is not negated by God's loving the world so as to send his Son to save it in 1 John 4:4–21. The point is not that 1 John determines the interpretation of the Gospel of John. It is rather that 1 John shows this antisectarian argument concerning John's Gospel to be a non sequitur. Similarly, the Son's working out the Father's love for the world does not require the Son to have loved the world.

---

[7] See pp. 324–62 below.

What is striking about John's saying that God loved the world but not saying that Jesus did the same is that John contrariwise *does* say that God draws the elect and Jesus does too, that God works on the Sabbath and Jesus does too, that God loves believers and Jesus does too, and that God indwells believers and Jesus does too.[8]

Though the mutual indwelling of Father, Son, and believers may indicate a nonoppositional and inclusive account of personal identity, that account has to do with close communion among *them*, not with the world, and thus links up with the cohesion of sectarians *with each other in opposition to the world*. And though Jesus' not praying for the world could mean only that he was not praying for them on the particular occasion of ch. 17, his drawing a sharp distinction between the world and those the Father had given him out of the world, his drawing attention to not praying for the world, and his not praying for the world elsewhere in John all point in an antiworldly direction.

But to maintain the sharp distinction, it is argued, sects have to emphasize law and church discipline, i.e., behavioral rules and authoritative ways of enforcing them. Yet these are missing from John. In their place we find emphases on faith and self-giving love. Therefore John is not sectarian, or his sectarianism is surprisingly soft. So goes the argument. But John wants people to believe or, better, to keep believing that the Christ, the Son of God, is Jesus rather than to apostatize into a Gnostic denial of such belief (20:30–31).[9] Emphases on such belief and on the self-giving love that guards against apostasy by building cohesiveness within the community fit John's purpose and sit comfortably in a sectarian view of John.

More particularly, 6:60–71 speaks of leaving the fold *voluntarily* (cf. 1 John 2:19). Hence an emphasis on disciplining people *out* of the fold would have been irrelevant and even counterproductive to his wanting to keep people *in* the fold both doctrinally and socially. We simply do not know whether given a different purpose the Fourth Gospel would have emphasized law and church discipline. Yet the warning in 3:19–20 of judgment on those who practice evil things and Jesus' statement to the disciples in 20:23, "Whosoever's sins you forgive are forgiven them, and whosoever's sins you retain are retained," may well imply behavioral rules and authoritative ways of enforcing them even though the christological focus has pushed them into the background. As often, the argument from silence (perhaps only partial in this case) proves weak.

Finally it is argued against hard sectarianism in John that this Gospel puts too many people in a gray zone where their salvific status remains unclear or the degree of their darkness or lightness seems less than optimal. There are the disciples of John the Baptist (3:25–36). They seem not to belong to the light but

---

[8] John 5:17; 6:44; 11:3, 5, 36; 12:32; 13:1, 23, 34; 14:21, 23; 15:4, 5, 9, 10, 12; 16:27; 17:23; 19: 26; 20:2; 21:7, 20.

[9] See, e.g., U. Schnelle, *Antidocetic Christology in the Gospel of John* (Minneapolis: Fortress, 1992).

neither does John assign them to the darkness. Some in a crowd say that Jesus is truly a prophet, others that he is the Christ, others that he is not the Christ; and some want to seize him (7:27, 40–44). Where do those that believe Jesus to be a prophet belong? Are those who believe him to be the Christ to be considered children of light? Their belief is not said to go so far as Jesus' divine sonship. He also has disciples who do *not* believe and therefore go away and no longer accompany him (6:60–66). How should they be classified? Does Nicodemus belong entirely on either side of a great divide? He comes to Jesus by night and addresses him as a teacher who has come from God, but Nicodemus is not said to believe in Jesus as the Christ and Son of God (3:1–21). Before the chief priests and his fellow Pharisees, on the other hand, he objects to their judging Jesus apart from giving him a hearing (7:45–52). Then he helps Joseph of Arimathea give Jesus a lavish burial. As for Joseph, John describes him as a disciple of Jesus but a secret one because of his fearing the Jews (19:38–42). John even attributes a true prophecy to the high priest Caiaphas (11: 47–53).[10]

The disciples who do not believe and who leave Jesus because of his incarnational language count as apostates and therefore must belong to the realm of darkness. So also must Caiaphas; for he advised the killing of Jesus and though prophesying truly, did so unconsciously and against his intended meaning. The Baptists regarded Jesus as a rival of their John; so they hardly belonged to the light. After all, the Fourth Evangelist calls them "disciples *of John*," not of Jesus (4:25). But the emphasis on John's testimony in Jesus' behalf may indicate that the Fourth Evangelist regards any Baptists of his own time as good prospects for conversion just as Paul did in Ephesus (Acts 18:24–19:7; cf. the early tradition that the Fourth Gospel was written in Ephesus). There would be nothing unsectarian about that. Nor is there anything substandard about the confession of some in a crowd that Jesus is "the prophet who was coming into the world" or "the Christ." After all, Jesus portrays himself both as a prophet (4:44; cf. 4:19; 6:14; 9:17) and as the Christ (4:25–26; 10:24–25; 17:3; so also the Fourth Evangelist in 1:17; 9:22; 20:31 as well as others in 1:41; 4:29; 11:27). The only question – a typically sectarian one – is whether all those in the crowd who confess him as a prophet and the Christ will persevere or (to use John's own term) "abide." Some do not, so that though formerly "in" they are now "out." They do not occupy a gray zone at any given time. John's calling Joseph of Arimathea a disciple of Jesus rules him in, as does also the lavishness of the burial he provides Jesus (a lavishness so extreme that it is hard to explain apart from a high christological belief on his part). The secrecy of Joseph's discipleship does not falsify his discipleship, for the very same "fear of the Jews" that motivated the

---

[10] I leave aside as argumentatively null the so-called "apostolic Christians" like Peter and the rest of the Twelve as distinct from the beloved disciple. Jesus' bestowing them peace, commissioning them, breathing the Holy Spirit on them, and giving them the authority to remit and retain others' sins put them obviously in the realm of light (20:21–23).

secrecy is attributed also to the apostles, to whom Jesus proceeded to give the Great Commission and on whom he proceeded to breathe the Holy Spirit and bestow the authority to forgive and retain people's sins (20:19–22). Nicodemus's joining Joseph in the provision of Jesus' lavish burial as well as publicly objecting to Jesus' being treated unjustly rules him in alongside Joseph. But we should rule him in even from his very first appearance in John's text (3:1–21). For though a crowd once addresses Jesus with "Rabbi" (6:25) Nicodemus addresses him with the same honorific designation just as Jesus' disciples do throughout the Gospel, beginning with Andrew and Nathaniel (1:38, 49; 4:31; 9:2; 11:8; 20:16), and as the disciples of John the Baptist address John as their rabbi. Moreover, Nicodemus designates Jesus as a teacher just as Jesus' disciples do (1:38; 11:28; 20:16) and Jesus himself does (13:13–14): "You call me 'the Teacher' and 'the Lord' and you speak well, for I am [the Teacher and the Lord]. Therefore if I the Teacher and the Lord washed your feet..."; cf. the frequent use of διδάσκω and διδαχή for his teaching in 6:59; 7:14, 16, 17, 28, 35; 8:20, 28; 18:19, 20). Most significant, however, is Nicodemus's saying to Jesus, "You have come from God," just as Jesus repeatedly says the same thing about himself – and his disciples and the Fourth Evangelist likewise (1:9; 3:19, 31; 5:43; 7:28–29; 8:14, 42; 13:3; 16:27–28, 30; 17:8). Nicodemus adds that "no one is able to do these signs that you [Jesus] are doing unless God is with him" just as Jesus says, "He who sent me is with me" (8:29) and "The Father is with me" (16:32; cf. 20:30–31 for the signs as written to foster believing in Jesus). And Jesus' saying that "the one who is doing the truth comes to the light" (3:21) looks like a theological commentary on the statement, "This one [Nicodemus] came to him [Jesus the light of the world] at night" (3:2). Nicodemus's ignorance of birth from above and Jesus' question, "Are you the teacher of Israel and do not know these things?" falsify Nicodemus's belief in Jesus no more than Jesus'saying, "Am I so long a time with you [pl.] and you [sg.] have not known me, Philip?" (in response to Philip's request, "Lord, show us the Father and it suffices us") falsifies Philip's belief in Jesus (14:8–9).

Is John sectarian, then, and strongly so? Yes. This traditional answer holds fast. And the irony that this strongly sectarian Gospel has attained great popularity even in the large and relatively unsectarian sectors of Christendom is just that – an irony – but one bought at the cost, I dare say, of filing smooth the rough edges of John's sectariansm.[11]

---

[11] Cf. G. van den Heever, "'From the Pragmatics of Textures to a Christian Utopia': The Case of the Gospel of John," in *Rhetorical Criticism and the Bible* (ed. S. E. Porter and D. L. Stamps; JSNTSup 195; Sheffield: Sheffield Academic Press, 2002), 297–334, esp. 328–31.

17. How the Word in John's Prologue Pervades the Rest of the Fourth Gospel

In the late nineteenth century A. Harnack argued for John's Prologue as a secondary addition to the rest of the Gospel, for the Prologue as designed to prepare a Hellenistic audience for the rest, and for the rest as containing nothing of the Prologue's Word-Christology.[1] Inversely M.-J. Lagrange argued that the rest of John was not written in view of the Prologue.[2] Perhaps J. A. T. Robinson represented this position most prominently in more recent times: "It has been said by no less a Johannine scholar than E. F. Scott that 'in the Fourth Gospel the Messianic idea is replaced by that of the Logos'. But this is precisely what does not happen. The word λόγος never recurs as a title, and the dominant christology of the Gospel is expressed rather in terms of 'the Christ, the Son of God' (20.21)." Thus the Prologue consists of a late addition, though Robinson detects within it, specifically in vv. 6–9, 15, the original beginning of the Gospel.[3]

Robinson acknowledged thematic interrelations between the Prologue and the rest of John. The themes include the preexistence of Christ, the contrast between light and darkness, the seeing of Jesus' glory, the seeing of God by no one except Jesus, etc. But in the Prologue such themes reflect the rest of the Gospel, written earlier; and since in Robinson's view the rest contains no Word-Christology this Christology injects into the Prologue, written later, something new and unrelated.

On the ground of those themes that the Prologue and the rest of John do share, plus similarities of vocabulary and style, other scholars deny a late addition of the Prologue but with Harnack, Lagrange, and Robinson see no Word-Christology in the rest of the Gospel.[4] Still other scholars think not only that whatever its back-

---

[1] A. Harnack, "Ueber das Verhältnis des Prologs des vierten Evangeliums zum ganzen Werk," *ZTK* 2 (1892): 189–231, esp. 230–31.

[2] M.-J. Lagrange, *Évangile selon Saint Jean* (5th ed.; EBib; Paris: Gabalda, 1936), CLXX.

[3] J. A. T. Robinson, *Twelve More New Testament Studies* (London: SCM, 1984), 65–76, esp. 69 for the quotation; cf. C. H. Dodd, *The Interpretation of the Fourth Gospel* (Cambridge: Cambridge University Press, 1960), 292–96; B. Lindars, *Behind the Fourth Gospel* (Studies in Creative Criticism 3; London: SPCK, 1971), 74; J. Ashton, *Understanding the Fourth Gospel* (Oxford: Clarendon, 1991), 345 n. 27.

[4] See, e.g., J. D. G. Dunn, "Let John Be John: A Gospel for Its Time," in *The Gospel and the Gospels* (ed. P. Stuhlmacher; Grand Rapids: Eerdmans, 1991), 313 n. 78: "I find it impossible to regard the prologue of John's Gospel as redactional (i.e., added after the evangelist put the Gos-

ground the Prologue belonged to the original version of John but also that the Word in the Prologue "gives expression to the idea of revelation which dominates the whole Gospel."[5] Thus the portrayal of Jesus as the Word in John's Prologue works itself out in an emphasis on Jesus' word, or words, in the rest of the Gospel. R. Bultmann developed this view theologically, and E. L. Miller has developed it historicocritically by exposing the weaknesses of standard views concerning the origin of Word-Christology and by substituting the informal emphasis on Jesus' words in the rest of the Gospel as grist for the mill that ground out the formal concept of Jesus as the Word.[6] I will try to show that a Christology of the Word pervades the whole of John's Gospel much more than has been recognized before.

To discover the pervasiveness of Word-Christology and simultaneously pay due to the authority of Scripture in its final form let us adopt the synchronic approach, take John's text as it presently stands, and use the Prologue to illuminate the rest in respect to Jesus' words. For whether or not John wrote his Prologue last and prefixed it to the rest, the Prologue comes first in the text and therefore casts the later words of Jesus in the light of Word-Christology.[7] As a result his words appear not as the soil out of which grew Word-Christology but as the fruit, the outworking in Jesus' earthly ministry, of Word-Christology. At least for the audience of the Fourth Gospel, if not for its author, Word-Christology is

---

pel into its present form); the themes of the prologue are too closely integrated into the Gospel as a whole and are so clearly intended to introduce these themes that such a conclusion is rendered implausible." But except in dependence on Wisdom-Christology, Word-Christology makes no appearance in Dunn's list and discussion of these common themes (pp. 314–17). Cf. J. Painter, "Inclined to God: The Quest for Eternal Life – Bultmannian Hermeneutics and the Theology of the Fourth Gospel," in *Exploring the Gospel of John* (ed. R. A. Culpepper and C. C. Black; Louisville, Ky.: Westminster John Knox, 1996), 348: "this use of the Logos [as giving 'expression to the theme of revelation'] is restricted to the prologue."

[5] R. Bultmann, *The Gospel of John* (Oxford: Blackwell, 1971), 13 n. 1.

[6] E. L. Miller, "The Johannine Origins of the Johannine Logos," *JBL* 112 (1993): 445–57. Yet Miller countenances the possibility, it should be added, that the association of λόγος with σοφία exercised some influence on the choice of λόγος over ῥῆμα, another Greek word that John often uses in the plural for Jesus' words. Against an origin in hypostatized Wisdom we might ask why John never uses the feminine noun σοφία, "wisdom," for Jesus alongside the masculine λόγος despite John's famous fondness for synonyms and despite his frequent use of other feminine nouns for Jesus: θύρα, "door," ὁδός, "way," ἀλήθεια, "truth," ἀνάστασις, "resurrection," ζωή, "life," and ἄμπελος, "vine" (John 10:7, 9; 11:25; 14:6; 15:1, 5). Cf. W. H. Kelber, "The Authority of the Word in St. John's Gospel: Charismatic Speech, Narrative Text, Logocentric Metaphysics," *Oral Tradition* 2 (1987): 109; and contrast with John's disuse of σοφία the use of σοφία for Jesus in Matt 11:19 with 11:2 (par. Luke 7:35); 1 Cor 1:24, 30.

[7] Cf. J. Zumstein ("Le prologue, seuil du Quatrième Évangile," *RSR* 83 [1995]: 225–34), who assigns John's Prologue to "le genre littéraire du prédiscours": "Le prologue est donc un prédiscours dont la fonction consiste à diriger la lecture, à contrôler le décodage du récit, à prévenir les interprétations erronées" (p. 228). Zumstein misses the extension of Word-Christology past the Prologue into the rest of John's Gospel, however. My adoption of the synchronic approach denies neither the validity of a diachronic approach, such as is used in source criticism and redaction criticism, nor the possibility that a diachronic approach proves useful when applied to John. That it does prove useful is debatable, however.

cause rather than effect, not vice versa. Perhaps so for the author as well, for what else would have prompted him to put so much emphasis on Jesus' words (an emphasis about to be delineated)? Yet we can think of a number of possibilities other than that emphasis for the prompting of Word-Christology, hypostatized Wisdom being the current favorite, though whether we should regard Word-Christology as pro-Wisdom or anti-Wisdom poses yet another question.[8]

To the business of delineating John's emphasis on the words of Jesus – first, their volume. Following the Prologue we have what someone has called a "sheer avalanche" of them, so that F. Kermode has described the Johannine Jesus as "by far the most communicative of the four [Jesuses portrayed in the canonical Gospels]."[9] Jesus' speech occupies vast stretches of John's text. After discounting ch. 21 as a redactional addition W. H. Kelber calculates that about four-fifths of chs. 1–17 and about three-fourths of chs. 1–20 consist in Jesus' sayings, dialogues, and monologues.[10] The addition of ch. 21 would not reduce that figure appreciably. We can see the emphasis on Jesus' words most clearly in comparisons with synoptic parallels. John adds to the feeding of the five thousand Jesus' long discourse on the bread of life (6:26–66). The Synoptics have nothing of the sort, though they all narrate the feeding. Similarly John adds to the triumphal entry, also narrated in the Synoptics, Jesus' discourse on his death like that of a grain of wheat (12:20–36, 44–50). Even more extensively, in John the few words of Jesus at the Last Supper according to the Synoptics balloon into almost four whole chapters (13–16). A chapter-long prayer (17) replaces his short prayers in Gethsemane according to the Synoptics. And though John inserts no discourse into the passion narrative, his Jesus certainly speaks a lot more than the synoptic

---

[8] For just two of many possible examples of a positive attitude toward Wisdom see B. Witherington III, *John's Wisdom* (Louisville, Ky.: Westminster John Knox, 1995), and M. Scott, *Sophia and the Johannine Jesus* (JSNTSup 71; Sheffield: Sheffield Academic Press, 1992). Scott argues that Wisdom, i.e., Sophia, was so thoroughly female in the way she was presented throughout the ancient Near East (he even introduces as background various goddesses) that in view of Jesus' maleness John shifted to the masculine noun λόγος. On the other hand, Scott continues, "because it [the Logos] is merely a vehicle accomodating [*sic*] the introduction of Jesus Sophia, whose progress is then mapped throughout the Gospel, it is immediately dispensable" (p. 173). We are in the process of discovering that by no means does John dispense with the Logos after the Prologue. For an example of negativity toward Wisdom see N. R. Petersen, *The Gospel of John and the Sociology of Light* (Valley Forge, Pa.: Trinity Press International, 1993), 110–32. Along the same line K. H. Jobes calls attention to distinctions in Jewish wisdom tradition which undercut the supposition that John was drawing on a unified such tradition ("Sophia Christology: The Way of Wisdom?" in *The Way of Wisdom* [ed. J. I. Packer and S. K. Soderlund; Grand Rapids: Zondervan, 2000], 226–50).

[9] F. Kermode, "John," in *The Literary Guide to the Bible* (eds. R. Alter and F. Kermode; Cambridge, Mass.: Harvard University Press, 1987), 453.

[10] W. H. Kelber, "The Authority of the Word in St. John's Gospel," 110–11; idem, "Die Fleischwerdung des Wortes in der Körperlichkeit des Textes," in *Materialität der Kommunikation* (ed. H. U. Gumbrecht and K. L. Pfeiffer; Suhrkamp Taschenbuch Wissenschaft 70; Frankfurt am Main: Suhrkamp, 1988), 33–34; idem, "In the Beginning Were the Words: The Apotheosis and Narrative Displacement of the Logos," *JAAR* 58 (1990): 82.

Jesus does, particularly during Jesus' trial. John's Jesus is a lamb (1:29, 36), but no lamb dumb before his shearers, as mostly in the Synoptics.

To make room for Jesus' added speech John has greatly reduced both the volume and the number of narratives concerning Jesus' deeds. This reduction comes despite an emphasis on Jesus' "works," which John also calls "signs." Of 666 verses in Mark, according to G. M. Burge, 209 (= 31%) deal with Jesus' miracles. If the passion narrative is left out of account, 200 verses out of 425 (= 47%) do. Matthew and Luke tend to add to the number of miracles in Mark. But John, though he knows of more and says so (20:30–31; 21:25), narrates only seven and treats them (I might add) not as "miracles" (i.e., "acts of power") to be admired but as the aforementioned "works" and "signs" to be explained by Jesus' words, so that the works and signs turn into *verba visibilia*.[11]

But we have in John not just a huge proportion of Jesus' words. John continually takes pains to highlight Jesus' words qua words. Here we must bring in John's use of ῥήματα, "words," alongside λόγος. Always in the plural, ῥήματα occurs nine times for Jesus' words[12] and three times for the words of God that Jesus speaks,[13] so that the references to Jesus' ῥήματα are to be understood as also the ῥήματα of God. Outside the Prologue John uses λόγος three times in the plural for Jesus' words,[14] but eighteen times in the singular for Jesus' word,[15] six times in the singular for God's word,[16] and twice in the singular for the word of God that Jesus speaks,[17] so that as in the case of ῥήματα, the λόγος and λόγοι of Jesus are to be understood as also those of God. Naturally the predominant singular of λόγος recalls the initial portrayal of Jesus as the Word (sg.).[18]

The Synoptics barely call attention to Jesus' λόγοι, only once in Mark, four times in Matthew, and three times in Luke, and only in the plural, never in the singular.[19] ῥῆμα fares slightly better in the Synoptics, where it occurs for Jesus'

---

[11] For the statistics see G. M. Burge, *The Anointed Community* (Grand Rapids: Eerdmans, 1987), 74–78; and for the works and signs as "visible words" see R. Bultmann, *Theology of the New Testament* (New York: Scribner's, 1955), 2:60; cf. idem, *John*, 163: "If in Jesus the λόγος became flesh, then God's action is carried out in Jesus' words." Bultmann errs, however, in collapsing works into words. One is reminded that Goethe's Faust translated John 1:1, "In the beginning was the Deed [*Tat*, a possible translation for ἔργον, which John uses for Jesus' works]." More pertinent is that the Hebrew דָּבָר means deed as well as word.

[12] John 5:47; 6:63, 68; 8:20; 10:21; 12:47, 48; 14:10; 15:7.

[13] John 3:34; 8:47; 17:8.

[14] John 7:40; 10:19; 14:24.

[15] John 2:22; 4:41, 50; 5:24; 6:60; 7:36; 8:31, 37, 43, 51, 52; 12:48; 14:23; 15:3, 20 (twice); 18:9, 32. These occurrences are divided almost evenly between Jesus' message in general and particular sayings of Jesus. Even in the case of his particular sayings the point remains that John calls attention to Jesus' word to a degree far from matched in the Synoptics.

[16] John 5:38; 8:55; 10:35; 17:6, 14, 17.

[17] John 14:24; 17:14.

[18] John 1:1 (three times), 14.

[19] Mark 8:38 (par. Luke 9:26); 13:31 (par. Matt 24:35 and Luke 21:33); Matt 7:24 (par. Luke 6:47), 26, 28.

words in Luke twice in the plural[20] and in the singular twice in Mark, once in Matthew, and eight times in Luke as never in John.[21] It appears that John has gone far out of his way to multiply references to Jesus' words qua words – there are almost twice as many occurrences of these terms in John as in all three Synoptics put together, almost three times as many if we count paralleled occurrences in the Synoptics once each – and to concentrate them primarily into the singular of λόγος and thus line them up with Jesus the λόγος. The words that Jesus speaks he speaks as the Word; and since he speaks as the Word the plurality of his words constitutes the singularity of his word, a reminder of who he is. And since as the Word he was with God in the beginning and was God his word is at one and the same time God's word. Thus the rest of the Fourth Gospel dovetails with the Prologue.

The synonymity of the singular and plural of λόγος is evident in John 14:24: "The one not loving me does not keep my *words*, and the *word* which you hear is not mine, but [is the word] of the Father who sent me." The synonymity of the singular of λόγος with the plural of ῥῆμα is evident in John 8:47, 51–52: "The one who is of God hears the *words* of God.... if anyone keeps my *word* .... if anyone keeps my *word*" (cf. 3:34: "for he whom God sent speaks the *words* of God"); 12:48: "The one ... not receiving my *words* has the one judging him; the *word* that I spoke – that will judge him at the last day"; 15:3, 7: "Already you are clean on account of the *word* that I have spoken to you.... If you abide in me and my *words* abide in you..."; and 17:6, 8, 14, 17: "they have kept your *word*.... the *words* that you gave me I have given them .... I have given them your *word* .... Your *word* is truth."[22] F.-M. Braun devotes a whole article to the synonymity of singular and plural expressions in John,[23] and John's penchant for using synonyms is too well known to need very much detailing.[24]

---

[20] Luke 7:1; 24:8.

[21] Mark 9:32 (par. Luke 9:45); 14:72 (par. Matt 26:75 and Luke 22:61); Luke 2:50; 5:5; 9:45 (twice); 18:34; 20:26.

[22] Cf. A. Corell, *Consummatum Est* (London: SPCK, 1958), 119–22; I. de la Potterie, *La vérité dans Saint Jean* (AnBib 73–74; Rome: Biblical Institute Press, 1977), 1:43–44; G. Kittel, "λέγω, λόγος, κτλ," *TDNT* 4:105–6.

[23] F.-M. Braun, "La Réduction du Pluriel au Singulier dans l'Évangile et la Première Lettre de Jean," *NTS* 24 (1977–78): 40–67; cf. idem, *Les Grandes Traditions d'Israël l'accord des Écritures d'après le Quatrième Évangile* (vol. 2 of *Jean le Théologien*; EBib; Paris: Gabalda, 1964), 140–41. Other examples of the synonymity of singular and plural include "commandment" and "commandments" (John 15:10–12; cf. 15:17: "These things I command you"), "work" and "works" (6:28–29), and "sin" and "sins" (8:21, 24; 15:22, 24).

[24] Since we are dealing with synonymous nouns I example κόλπος and στῆθος for "bosom" (1:18; 13:23, 25; 21:20), παιδίον, παῖς, and υἱός for "child, son" (4:46–54), ἄρτος and βρῶσις for "bread, food" (6:26–59), ὀψάριον and προσφάγιον for "fish relish" (21:1–13), and Ἰουδαῖοι and Φαρισαῖοι for Jesus' opponents (9:13–41), not to identify synonymous verbs for eating, washing, drawing, carrying, rising, sending, going, loving, and emoting as well as other sorts of expressions, such as prepositional phrases.

The synonymous use of λόγος, λόγοι, and ῥήματα has enjoyed wide recognition. Comparatively unrecognized is John's frequent and synonymous use of ἐντολή(-αί), "commandment(s)," as in 14:15, 21; 15:10, 12, all of which speak of keeping Jesus' commandments, or commandment, and 8:51, 52; 14:23, 24; 15:20; 17:6, all of which speak of keeping his word (λόγον).[25] Though the verb of commanding (ἐντέλλομαι) has Jesus as its subject in Matt 17:9; 28:20, as in John 15:17, the cognate noun never occurs in the Synoptics for Jesus' words. It occurs only for OT commandments except for Luke 15:29, where it occurs as a collective singular for the commands of the prodigal son's father. By contrast neither the noun nor the verb ever occurs in John for OT commandments, only for Jesus' commandments and for the Father's commanding Jesus (with the sole exception of the chief priests' and Pharisees' commands in 11:57 concerning Jesus' arrest).[26]

But to appreciate adequately the wordfulness of Jesus the Word in John and the attention that John calls to it we must expand our semantic field beyond λόγος, ῥῆμα, and ἐντολή.[27] In John's Gospel μαρτυρέω and μαρτυρία occur sixteen times for Jesus' testimony but never for it in the Synoptic Gospels.[28] Though the Synoptics have Jesus as the subject of φωνέω, "produce a sound, call, speak loudly," a number of times,[29] they use φωνή for Jesus' voice only in the cry of dereliction and death-cry[30] whereas John calls attention to the voice of Jesus nine times.[31] The Word has a voice (cf. *Acts of Peter* 38 [9], where

---

[25] The OT uses "words" for commandments in many passages (for references see BDB, s.v. דבר II 2).

[26] John 10:18; 12:49, 50; 13:34; 14:15, 21, 31; 15:10, 12, 14, 17.

[27] T. Müller expands the semantic field but does not go into sufficient detail (*Das Heilsgeschehen im Johannesevangelium* [Frankfurt am Main: Gotthelf-Verlag, 1961], 21–22).

[28] See John 3:11, 32, 33; 4:44; 5:31; 7:7; 8:13, 14, 18; 13:21; 18:37. Cf. the association of testimony with "the word of God" in the book of Revelation. There, 19:13 says that Jesus' name is "the Word of God." Therefore testifying "to the word of God" and John's exile on Patmos "because of the word of God" in 1:2, 9 probably mean testifying to Jesus himself and exile because of him. And since in 1:2, 9; 20:4 "the testimony of Jesus (Christ)" is paired with "the Word of God," we should probably consider "the Testimony of Jesus" another christological title (cf. the pairing of "the testimony of Jesus" with "the commandments of God" in 12:17). Favoring this view are (1) the designation of Jesus as "the faithful (and true) testifier" in 1:5; 3:14 (in the latter passage with the apposition, "the beginning of God's creation" – cf. John 1:1–3); (2) the description of Jesus himself and "the words of God" as "(faithful and) true" in 3:7; 6:10; 19:9, 11 (cf. 17:17; 21:5; 22:6); (3) the pairing of his word with his name in 3:8; (4) the pairing of "the word of God" with "the testimony that they had" in 6:9; (5) the combination of "word" and "testimony" in the phrase "the word of their testimony"; (6) the pairing of that phrase with "the blood of the Lamb" in 12:11; (7) the combining of "word" and "endurance" in the phrase "my word of endurance" after "endurance" has been located "in Jesus" (1:9); and (8) the equation of "the testimony of Jesus" with "the Spirit of prophecy" in 19:10. Throughout these passages "word" goes back to λόγος.

[29] Mark 9:35; 10:49; 15:35 (par. Matt 27:47); Matt 20:32; Luke 8:8, 54; 24:46.

[30] Mark 15:34, 37 (par. Matt 27:46, 50 and Luke 23:46).

[31] John 3:29; 5:25, 28; 10:3, 4, 16, 27; 11:43; 18:37. For more detailed contrasts between the

Christ is identified as "the Word stretched out [on the cross], the one and only, concerning whom the Spirit says, 'For what is Christ but the Word, the sound [ἦχος] of God?'")! To emphasize the words spoken with that voice John doubles the "Amen" in front of Jesus' "I say to you" no fewer than twenty-five times. The Synoptics never double the "Amen."[32] Very often φωνή, "voice," is used for "the sound of a cry or shout."[33] So it comes as no surprise that Jesus "shouts" (κράζω, κραυγάζω) several times in John[34] as he does only in the cry of dereliction in a single one of the Synoptics.[35] He shouts in John even when he teaches as he never does when teaching in the Synoptics.[36] We are far from the Jesus who in Matt 12:19 does not shout and whose voice no one hears in the streets.

Though the Synoptics portray Jesus as teaching more often than John portrays him as teaching, John portrays Jesus as a rabbi (ῥαββί and ῥαββουνί) significantly more often (eight times) than the Synoptics do (Mark – five times; Matthew – two times, or three if 23:8 implies as much; Luke – none) and twice takes care to translate the term with "Teacher."[37] Only in John, moreover, does Jesus repeatedly describe his teaching as God's, which description reminds one of the Prologue's Word who was with God and was God.[38] Thus the Word will publicly make announcement (ἀπαγγελῶ) concerning the Father[39] and has exegeted (ἐξηγήσατο) him.[40]

In John Jesus appears as a prophet, the scriptural connotation of which is a conveyor of God's word, almost as many times (six) as he does in Luke (seven, as against three times each in Mark and Matthew). Though the portrayal of Jesus as a prophet falls below a high Christology we should not discount it; for Jesus portrays himself as such – and if anyone in the Gospels counts as a re-

---

use of φωνή in the Synoptics and in John see F.-M. Braun, *Sa théologie: Le mystère de Jésus-Christ* (vol. 3, part 1, of *Jean le Théologien*; Paris: Gabalda, 1966), 102.

[32] Cf. B. Hinrichs, *"Ich Bin"* (Stuttgarter Bibelstudien 133; Stuttgart: Katholisches Bibelwerk, 1988), 31. A. J. B. Higgins suggests that the double preliminary "Amen" in John "corresponds to a variation from the single 'amen' in Jesus' own speech," but Higgins offers no evidence or argument that Jesus himself doubled the preliminary "Amen" ("The Words of Jesus according to St. John," *BJRL* 49 [1966–67]: 371–72).

[33] L&N 1:398 § 33.80; cf. E. Harris, *Prologue and Gospel* (JSNTSup 107; Sheffield: Sheffield Academic Press, 1994), 35, on the use of κράζω as an emphatic verb that introduces "solemn, oracular utterances" and A. E. Harvey, *Jesus on Trial* (Atlanta: John Knox, 1977), 23–24, on its forensic use, with which we might compare the testifying of Jesus in John.

[34] John 7:28, 37; 11:43; 12:44.

[35] Matt 27:50.

[36] John 7:28.

[37] Cf. A. J. Köstenberger, "Jesus as Rabbi in the Fourth Gospel," *BBR* 8 (1998): 97–128, esp. 112–15. Whereas I am arguing for a theological point – viz., the pervasiveness of the Word as a wordsmith throughout John – Köstenberger argues for the historicity of Johannine tradition.

[38] John 6:44–46; 7:14–17; 8:28.

[39] John 16:25: ἀλλὰ παρρησίᾳ περὶ τοῦ πατρὸς ἀπαγγελῶ ὑμῖν.

[40] John 1:18: ἐκεῖνος ἐξηγήσατο.

liable character, he does.[41] Though the comparative statistics on λέγω, "say," are unenlightening,[42] as also those on φημί, "say,"[43] the statistics on λαλέω, "speak," and λαλιά, "speech," speak volumes. Of their sixty-one occurrences in John, fifty have to do with Jesus' speaking, as compared with only nine such occurrences in Mark, twelve in Matthew, and ten in Luke. And as in the case of Jesus' teaching, John repeatedly describes Jesus' speaking (λαλέω) as God's ("I do not speak [λαλῶ] from myself" – John 14:10),[44] and in 8:43 he couples Jesus' speech (λαλιάν) with Jesus' word (λόγον).

Again it does not surprise us to learn that John refers eleven times to hearing Jesus' word, words, and voice[45] over against four such references in Mark,[46] eight in Matthew,[47] and four, possibly only two, in Luke.[48] More impressively, John refers to believing Jesus' word, or words,[49] and to abiding in Jesus' word and its abiding in the disciples, as the Synoptics never do.[50] Matthew refers once to keeping whatever Jesus has commanded but John refers eight times to keeping Jesus' commands, word, and words (not so at all in Mark and Luke).[51]

But enough of semantic fields, synonyms, and statistics. Let us go to individual texts. According to what is generally considered the last verse of John's Prologue (1:18), "A unique one, [who was] God, the one existing in the bosom of the Father – that one has exegeted (ἐξηγήσατο) [him]."[52] Exegeting the Father at the end of the Prologue forms a nice *inclusio* with the Word at the start of the Prologue in that "a unique one, [who was] God," corresponds to "the Word was God" and in that the unique one's having exegeted God indicates why the unique one is called "the Word" in relation to God. Jesus Christ was the exegetical Word of God.[53] Thus 1:18 leads into the word, words, speech, testimony, commandment, commandments, voice, and shouting of the Word.[54]

---

[41] John 4:44; Mark 6:4; Matt 13:57; Luke 4:24; 13:33. Cf. A. Reinhartz, "Jesus as Prophet: Predictive Prolepses in the Fourth Gospel," *JSNT* 36 (1989): 3–16. She traces through John the theme of Jesus as a prophet whose predictions have come to pass and thus support the divine origin of his words and his deity.

[42] Matthew – 475x; Mark – 289x; Luke – 515x; John – 474x.

[43] Matthew – 16x; Mark – 6x; Luke – 8x; John – 25x.

[44] See also 3:10–13, 34; 7:16–18; 8:25–30, 38, 40, 42–44; 12:48–50; 16:25 (?); 17:13–14; cf. 16:13.

[45] John 5:24, 25, 28; 7:40; 8:43; 10:3, 16, 27; 12:47; 14:24; 18:37.

[46] Mark 4:15, 16, 18, 20.

[47] Matt 7:24, 26; 13:19, 20, 22, 23; 15:12; 19:22.

[48] Luke 6:47; 8:8, 15; 10:39, though in view of "the word *of God*" in 8:21 we may need to subtract 8:8, 15.

[49] John 2:22; 4:50; 5:47; cf. 3:12; 10:25; 12:38.

[50] John 5:38; 15:7.

[51] Matt 28:20; John 8:51, 52; 14:15, 21, 23, 24; 15:10, 20.

[52] For this reading and translation of 1:18 see H.-C. Kammler, *Christologie und Eschatologie* (WUNT 126; Tübingen: Mohr Siebeck, 2000), 113–15.

[53] See further the second addendum below, "In Defense of 'Exegesis' in John 1:18."

[54] Inasmuch as ἐξηγέομαι means to tell at length, to relate in full, F.J. Moloney notes the tran-

In 1:51 this exegete turns into Jacob's ladder: "you [pl.: Nathaniel and others] will see the heaven opened and the angels of God ascending and descending on the Son of Man" (cf. Jesus' calling Nathaniel "truly an Israelite" – "Israel" being Jacob's new name, of course – in 1:47). Ascending precedes descending, surprisingly in view of the reverse order in 3:13; 6:62, under the influence of Gen 28:12, the passage having to do with Jacob's ladder.[55] Since by definition angels are messengers, Jesus the ladder is a vertical information highway between an open heaven and the earth. Elsewhere in John ascent and descent take place between heaven and earth, not within heaven, so that we should not think of the Son of Man as a ladder located up there and of the angels' ascending and descending on him as restricted to the heavenly sphere, or of the angels as ascending to him from lower in heaven and descending to him from higher in heaven. Unless he were in heaven and on earth at the same time (against which notion see, e.g., John 6:62, "If therefore you should see the Son of Man ascending to where he was before," and 17:11, "I am no longer in the world"), the angels' ascending from earth to him in heaven would leave their descent without him as its destination just as their descending from heaven to him on earth would leave their ascent without him as its destination.[56] The Son of Man is not located at the bottom or the top of the ladder as the destination *to* which the angels ascend and descend. He is the ladder *on* which they ascend and descend.[57]

Whereas the Synoptics have the Son of Man seated at God's right hand and coming with the clouds of heaven and with angels as gatherers of the elect,[58] John has the Son of Man positioned as a ladder linking the open heaven to believers below, with angels acting as messengers.[59] The angels' use of this ladder resonates with the underestimated angelomorphic Christology found in John's Gospel as well as in the Apocalypse of John,[60] where Jesus is also por-

---

sitional function of 1:18 as a lead into the following narrative (*Belief in the Word: Reading the Fourth Gospel: John 1–4* [Minneapolis: Fortress, 1993], 50; cf. Zumstein, "Le prologue," 221).

[55] Cf. A. T. Hanson, *The Prophetic Gospel* (Edinburgh: T&T Clark, 1991), 37.

[56] Against Witherington, who has the angels ascending "from" the Son of Man (*John's Wisdom*, 72; so also E. Käsemann, *The Testament of Jesus* [Philadelphia: Fortress, 1968], 70; R. Schnackenburg, *The Gospel according to St John, Volume One: Introduction and Commentary on Chapters 1–4* [Herder's Theological Commentary on the New Testament; New York: Herder, 1968], 321). But ἐπί means "on" or "to," not "from."

[57] For some especially pertinent Johannine examples of ἐπί plus an accusative as indicating location rather than destination see 1:32, 33; 3:36; 12:14, 15; 13:25; 21:20 – against Gen 28:12 LXX, which has the genitive following ἐπί, and against C. Rowland, "John 1. 51, Jewish Apocalyptic and Targumic Tradition," *NTS* 30 (1984): 498–507.

[58] Mark 13:26–27 par. Matt 24:30–31 and Luke 21:27; Mark 14:62 par. Matt 26:64 and Luke 22:67–70.

[59] S. Schulz, *Untersuchungen zur Menschensohn-Christologie im Johannesevangelium* (Göttingen: Vandenhoeck & Ruprecht, 1957), 102–3.

[60] For angelomorphic Christology in John's Gospel and a bibliography of recent work along the same line by J.-A. Bühner, C. H. Talbert, J. Ashton, and R. Paschal see C. A. Gieschen, *Angelomorphic Christology* (AGJU 42; Leiden: E. J. Brill, 1998), 18–19, 270–93. For angelo-

trayed as "the Word of God" (Rev 19:13; cf. Philo's calling "the Word" [ὁ λόγος] God's "chief messenger" [ἀρχάγγελος] in *Her.* 42 § 205). Message and messenger merge.[61]

The view of J. Painter that Jesus is not Jacob's ladder but the Son of Man enthroned in heaven by way of a ladder-like cross (in correction of Nathaniel's notion of an earthly kingship) disagrees with the angels' descending on the Son of Man. Painter's argument that no angelic mediators appear in John fails to consider the coalescence of Son of Man-Christology with angelomorphic Christology, a coalescence mediated by Word-Christology, so that the ladder and the angels ascending and descending on it are to be seen as an indivisible figure of speech referring to Jesus the Word. Apart from them as messengers the allusion to Jacob's ladder does not convey any thought of communication, for the absence of "ladder" would keep the allusion obscure and therefore God's speaking to Jacob out of the picture. The angels are just as christological as is the ladder, then. Nathaniel and his fellow disciples will see Jesus in these communicative terms throughout Jesus' earthly ministry.[62]

The story of Jesus' first sign, the turning of water to wine, resonates with Word-Christology in the Prologue. Mary his mother tells the servants, "Do whatever he *says* (λέγει) to you" (2:5). Apparently she believes in Jesus' word, or in Jesus as the Word, even before he performs his first sign. She has read the Prologue, so to speak. Then Jesus proceeds to perform the sign by speaking. John doubles the introduction to Jesus' speaking, both times with a vivid historical present tense: (1) "And Jesus says (λέγει) to them, 'Fill the jars with water'" (2:7); "And he says (λέγει) to them, 'Draw now and carry [it] to the toastmaster'" (2:8).[63] As a result Jesus "manifested his glory" (2:11a), previously defined as the glory of "the Word" who "became flesh and tabernacled among us" (1:14); and "his disciples believed in him" (2:11b) in accordance with the Prologue's equating those who received the Word with those who believed in his name, i.e., in him as "the Word" who has now begun to manifest his glory.[64]

---

morphic Christology in the Apocalypse of John see below, pp. 377–98; Gieschen, *Angelomorphic Christology*, 245–69, again with bibliography.

[61] Cf. S. S. Smalley, "Johannes 1,51 und die Einleitung zum vierten Evangelium," in *Jesus und der Menschensohn* (ed. R. Pesch and R. Schnackenburg with O. Kaiser; Freiburg: Herder, 1975), 312–13: "Himmel und Erde sind in der Person Jesu, des Menschensohnes, einzigartig zusammengebracht worden, aufgrund seiner engen Beziehung zum Vater.... Joh 1,51 blickt auf Jesus als des Wort (Joh 1,1.14) zurück." See also J. J. Kanagaraj, "Jesus the King, Merkabah Mysticism and the Gospel of John," *TynBul* 47 (1996): 352: "their [the angels'] movements highlight the communication that is possible between heaven and earth in Jesus."

[62] Against J. Painter, *Reading John's Gospel Today* (Atlanta: John Knox, 1975), 56.

[63] On John's use of the vivid historical present tense see J. Frey, *Das johanneische Zeitverständnis* (vol. 2 of *Die johanneische Eschatologie*; WUNT 110; Tübingen: Mohr Siebeck, 1998), 148–49.

[64] See C. E. B. Cranfield, "John 1 14: 'became,'" *ExpTim* 93 (1981–82): 215, that in John 1:14

In 2:22 John writes, "When therefore he [Jesus] had risen from the dead his disciples remembered that he had been saying (ἔλεγεν) this, and they believed ... the word (τῷ λόγῳ) that Jesus had spoken (εἶπεν)." "This" refers to Jesus' word to the Jews, "Tear down this temple and in three days I will raise it" (2:19). John has interpreted this word as a statement "concerning the temple of his [Jesus'] body" (2:21), which again recalls the Word's becoming flesh and ta-bernacling among us (1:14). The disciples' believing Jesus' word plays again on their believing in Jesus as the Word, his name in the Prologue (1:12). And the believing of many "in his name" at 2:23 echoes yet again the Prologue's tagging Jesus with the name "Word."[65]

John 3:8 refers to the φωνήν, "sound, voice," of the πνεῦμα, "wind, Spirit." Since the wind that "blows where it wishes" is the Spirit (cf. 3:5), the wind's "sound" – i.e., the Spirit's "voice" – is Jesus. For just as Nicodemus "is hearing" (ἀκούεις) the wind, representing the Spirit, but "does not know where it is coming from and going to," so Jesus says in 8:14 that his listeners do not know where *he* has come from and where *he* is going to.[66] In other words, Jesus sets up a parallel between himself and the Spirit, whose voice he is. Thus in 3:11 the "we" who speak (λαλοῦμεν) and the "our" whose testimony "you [pl.] do not receive" (cf. the Prologue on the Word, particularly 1:11–13, in connection with not receiving versus believing and [re]birth, as here in ch. 3) – the "we" and the "our" are Jesus and the Spirit, who testify in conjunction with each other (see 8:14, 18a with 15:26 and cf. the conjunction of voice and testimony in 5:37).[67] The parallel between the Spirit in 3:8 and Jesus in 8:14 eliminates any need to identify the "we" and the "our" in 3:11 with the Johannine community.

John 3:18 mentions "the name of the unique Son of God," in which name people are to believe. The Son of God's uniqueness recalls the Prologue (1:14, 18, both times in connection with the Father). Since in the Prologue the unique one's name, in which people are to believe (1:12), is "the Word" (1:1 [three times], 14), identified there with "the light" that came into the world just as here in 3:19–21, presumably the name of the unique Son of God in which people are to believe at 3:18 is again "the Word." This is the name which God's unique Son

---

ἐγένετο means "became" or "was made" without implication that the Word ceased to be the Word, so that the translation, "The Word came on the scene as flesh," is unnecessary. Though ἐγένετο means "came on the scene" for John the Baptist in 1:6, there it lacks a predicate nomi-native such as σάρξ, "flesh," in 1:14 (against C. K. Barrett, *The Gospel according to St. John* [2d ed.; Philadelphia: Westminster, 1978], 165).

[65] On the Word as Jesus' name cf. 1 John 5:13; 3 John 7 with 1 John 1:1 and see J. E. Fos-sum, *The Image of the Invisible God* (NTOA 30; Göttingen: Vandenhoeck & Ruprecht, 1995), 109–33, esp. 125–26, and, more briefly, H. Van den Bussche, *Le discours d'adieu de Jésus* (Tournai: Casterman, 1959), 143.

[66] 7:27–28b seems to indicate otherwise, but 7:28c–29 corrects the earlier statements by re-ducing them to Jesus' earthly origin.

[67] Braun notes the parallel between the testimony and the Word (*Sa théologie*, 120).

has (genitive of possession) as opposed to the name which *is* "the unique Son of God" (genitive of apposition).[68]

That "the unique Son of God" is a descriptive phrase, not a name, is supported by several further considerations: (1) the insertion in attributive position of an adjective, "unique," into "the ... Son of God"; (2) the absence of the phrase "of God" with "the unique Son" a couple of verses earlier in 3:16; (3) the absence of both "unique" and "of God" from "the Son" just one verse earlier in 3:17 and often elsewhere in John (see the concordance); and (4) the pairing and parallel-ing of "the Son of God" with other descriptive phrases as opposed to names: with "the one baptizing in the Holy Spirit" in 1:33–34, with "the King of Israel" in 1:49, and with "the Christ" in 11:27; 20:31. Because "the unique Son of God" in 3:18 appears to be a descriptive phrase for the owner of a name, then, and be-cause the Prologue has established "the Word" as that owner's name, further ref-erences to Jesus' name should be taken likewise (14:13, 14, 26; 15:16, 21; 16:23, 24, 26; 20:31). The large number and wide distribution of these references dis-play the pervasiveness of Word-Christology throughout John.

In contrast with Mark 2:19–20 par. Matt 9:15 and Luke 5:34–35, which por-tray Jesus as a bridegroom only by inference, John 3:29–34 portrays Jesus out-right as a bridegroom, describes him as "the one coming from heaven," and gives him a "voice" with which he "testifies" to "what he has seen and heard" there and with which he "speaks the words of God" (τὰ ῥήματα τοῦ θεοῦ λαλεῖ). "Nobody receives his testimony," except that "the one receiving his tes-timony has certified that God is true." The passage reverberates with echoes of the Prologue and its portrayal of the Word, full of truth, who was in the begin-ning with God, came into the world, exegeted God, and was not received by his own though he was received by some.[69] The statement that "he whom God has sent speaks the words (ῥήματα) of God" (3:34a) parallels the statement that "he

---

[68] Cf. Phil 2:9–11, where "the name of Jesus" is not the name "Jesus" but is the name "Lord" which Jesus has and which every tongue will confess Jesus Christ to be. Against the notion that in John's Prologue "the light" has as much claim as "the Word" has to be considered the unique one's name, the unique one is never said to be the Word – he is simply called the Word, and this from the very start – whereas the Word is said to be the light, which has earlier been identified with the life that was "in" the Word. It is true that the fourth evangelist does not write concern-ing Jesus, "His name was the Word," as he writes concerning the Baptist, "His name was John" (1:6). But the evangelist does not have to because he used "the Word" from the very start and then referred back to that expression as "the name of him" (τὸ ὄνομα αὐτοῦ – N.B. the an-aphoric definite article as opposed to the anarthrous ὄνομα that introduces the name John) whereas the evangelist first called the Baptist "a man," so that it became natural, almost neces-sary, to write that his name was John.

[69] Cf. Braun, *Sa théologie*, 103; Harris, *Prologue and Gospel*, 161. J. Jeremias understands the voice of the bridegroom culturally: it is his joyous voice heard emanating from the nuptial chamber on discovering evidence of his bride's virginity ("νύμφη, νυμφίος," *TDNT* 4:1101). To the contrary see M. and R. Zimmermann, "Der Freud des Bräutigams (Joh 3,29): Deflorations-oder Christuszeuge?" *ZNW* 90 (1999): 123–30. John understands the voice christologically.

[again Jesus, whom God has sent] gives the Spirit without measure" (3:34b, each statement being introduced with γάϱ, "for").[70] That the "words" (ϱήματα) that Jesus speaks "are Spirit" (6:63) suits both the parallel in 3:34 between his speaking God's words and giving the Spirit without measure and his identification with the voice of the Spirit (see the foregoing discussion of 3:18).

To the woman of Samaria in 4:10 Jesus mentions "the gift of God" and pairs it in apparently synonymous parallelism with "the one speaking to you" (ὁ λέγων σοι) – this in connection with "living water" that "springs up into eternal life" (4:14). John 3:16 has already said, "God ... gave his unique Son that everyone believing in him   might have eternal life." So Jesus himself is God's gift, and God's gift is a speaker. Since Jesus immediately quotes what he has spoken earlier ("Give me to drink") we might think his self-identification as a speaker to be christologically insignificant: he identifies himself thus only to introduce the quotation. But later in his conversation with the Samaritan woman, 4:26 arouses second thoughts. There in response to her statements, "I know that Messiah, the one called Christ, is coming. When that one comes, he will announce (ἀναγγελεῖ) to us all things," Jesus says, "I am, the one speaking to you (ὁ λαλῶν σοι)." In view of the woman's reference to Messiah, i.e., Christ, it seems judicious to treat Jesus' response initially as elliptical and to fill it out: "I am Messiah, the one called Christ" (cf. 9:8–9). But the prominence of Jesus' divine "I am" elsewhere in John, most strikingly at 8:58 ("Before Abraham came into existence, I am"[71]), suggests a secondary such allusion here in 4:26.[72] F. J. Moloney goes so far as to translate 4:26, "I AM [is] the one speaking to you."[73] "The one speaking to you" might also make some characteristically Johannine sense if taken as a predicate nominative without an ellipsis of

---

[70] For Jesus' giving the Spirit without measure to believers rather than God's doing so to Jesus see 7:37–39; 20:22; 1 John 3:24; and H.-C. Kammler, "Jesus Christus und der Geistparaklet: Eine Studie zur johanneische Verhältnisbestimmung von Pneumatologie und Christologie," in O. Hofius and H.-C. Kammler, *Johannesstudien* (WUNT 88; Tübingen: Mohr-Siebeck, 1996), 170 ff. Supporting Kammler is Hofius, "'Er gibt den Geist ohne Mass' Joh 3,34b," *ZNW* 90 (1999): 131–34; see also F. Porsch, *Anwalt der Glaubenden* (Geist und Leben; Stuttgart: Katholisches Bibelwerk, 1978), 24–26.

[71] M. Davies tries to evade the obvious by supposing an ellipsis in 8:58: "I am ['the light of the world,' as in 8:12]," so that "before Abraham" has to do with rank (*Rhetoric and Reference in the Fourth Gospel* [JSNTSup 69; Sheffield: JSOT Press, 1992], 84–86). But an ellipsis should not hark back so far as 8:12 is from 8:58; and πρίν means "before" in a temporal sense, not in the sense of rank.

[72] For conflicting views see G. R. O'Day, *Revelation in the Fourth Gospel* (Philadelphia: Fortress, 1986), 72, and J. Painter, *The Quest for the Messiah* (2d ed.; Nashville: Abingdon, 1993), 205; A. Link, *"Was redest du mit ihr?"* (Biblische Untersuchungen 24; Regensburg: Pustet, 1992), 286–91; D. M. Ball, *"I Am" in John's Gospel* (JSNTSup 124; Sheffield: Sheffield Academic Press, 1996), 60–67, 178–81.

[73] Moloney, *Belief in the Word*, 154–56; idem, *The Gospel of John* (SP 4; Collegeville, Minn.: Liturgical Press, 1998), 130, 134.

"is" and in line with other Jesuanic statements strewn throughout John: "I am the one speaking to you" (cf. "I am the bread of life," "I am the light of the world," and so forth[74]).

Be those possibilities as they may, Jesus' response might well have stopped with "I am." But it does not. The added phrase, "the one speaking to you," harks back to 4:10 but is otiose here in 4:26 unless emphasis falls on Jesus as the speaker of a word or as the Word who speaks. The probable allusion to Yahweh's statement in Isa 52:6 LXX, ἐγώ εἰμι αὐτὸς ὁ λαλῶν ("I myself am the one speaking") – a statement made in the immediate context of knowing Yahweh's "name" – supports an understanding of John 4:10, 26 in terms of Jesus' name "the Word."[75] In 9:37 Jesus will likewise say to the man born blind but then healed, "You have both seen him ['the Son of Man' – 9:35] and the one speaking with you (ὁ λαλῶν μετὰ σοῦ) is that one." Since 1:51 introduced the Son of Man as the angelic ladder of communication from an opened heaven to human beings on earth, it seems likely that Jesus' self-identification as the Son of Man and speaker in 9:37 also carries overtones of Word-Christology.

Back in 4:27 "his disciples came and were marveling that he was speaking (ἐλάλει) with a woman, yet no one said, 'What are you seeking?' or 'Why are you speaking (λαλεῖς) with her?'" She herself had asked, "How is it that you, being a Jew, ask to drink from me, being a woman, a Samaritan?" (4:9). But the Prologue has taught us that because Jesus is the Word it is in his very nature to speak – even to a Samaritan woman, it turns out. She proceeds to report to her fellow townspeople, "Here! See a man who told me all that I ever did. Is this perhaps the Christ?" (4:29). As in 4:25–26, speech and Christhood appear in conjunction. And though "the word" (ὁ λόγος) in 4:37 refers to Jesus' saying, "One sows and another reaps," may there be a christological hint in the statement that "the word is true," especially in view of the description of the incarnate Word as "full ... of truth" (1:14; cf. 4:42: "This is truly the Savior of the world"; 14:6: "I am ... the truth"; and the many generally recognized instances of double entendre scattered throughout John)?

John 4:39 says that many Samaritans believed in Jesus "because of the word (τὸν λόγον) of the woman." What was the word that she "testified"? John quotes it again: "He told me all that I ever did." Her word reports his word. Then when he had stayed two days many more believed because of their direct hearing of his word (διὰ τὸν λόγον αὐτοῦ – 4:41). "And they were saying to the woman, 'No longer do we believe because of your speech (διὰ τὴν σὴν λα-

---

[74] John 6:35, 41, 48, 51; 8:12; 10:7, 9, 11, 14; 11:25; 14:6; 15:1, 5.

[75] "Den unerhörten Anspruch, den Jesus zuvor durch sein Wort vertreten hat, begründet er durch sich selbst als den zu der Frau Redenden, durch – wie im Prolog angekündigt – seine Gegenwart im Logos" (Hinrichs, "*Ich Bin*," 25). See also B. Olsson, *Structure and Meaning in the Fourth Gospel* (ConBNT 6; Lund: Gleerup, 1974), 178–79.

λιάν), for we ourselves have heard and come to know that this one is truly the Savior of the world'" (4:42). Salvation by the word of Jesus the Word![76]

John 4:46–54 tells of Jesus' healing the son of a royal official. In Matt 8:5–13 and Luke 7:1–10 emphasis falls on the faith of a Gentile centurion as expressed in his plea, "But [Matthew: + 'only'] speak with a word...," and as asterisked by Jesus' saying he had not found such great faith in Israel. In the comparable Matt 15:21–28 emphasis falls similarly on a Gentile woman's faith ("O woman, great is your faith"). The parallel Mark 7:24–30 emphasizes that same woman's "word" (τοῦτον τὸν λόγον). John 4:50, 53 puts the stress on *Jesus'* word: "The man believed the word (τῷ λόγῳ) which Jesus had spoken (εἶπεν) to him [cf. 2:22] .... Therefore the father knew that in the hour in which Jesus had said to him, 'Your sons lives,' ['the fever left him']; and he himself and his whole household believed." The royal official believed but did not ask Jesus to heal at a distance with a mere word, as in the Synoptics. John has Jesus the Word take the initiative to do so against the request of the royal official that Jesus come down to Capernaum and perform a cure. And in contrast with Mark on the Syrophoenician woman, John does not underline any word of the royal official. The official had asked that Jesus "should heal his son (ἰάσηται αὐτοῦ τὸν υἱόν), for he was about to die" (4:47). But instead of hearing a word of healing we hear a word of life: "Your son lives." What has the Prologue said about the Word? "In him was life" (1:4).[77]

Another of Jesus' signs follows immediately in 5:1–9. As in the first two signs, Jesus performs this one by speaking a word instead of putting the cripple in a pool when its water was troubled.[78] The subsequent discourse plays emphatically on Jesus' verbal method: "Amen, amen I say to you that the one hearing my word (τὸν λόγον μου) and believing the one who sent me has eternal life .... Amen, amen I say to you that an hour is coming and now is when the dead will hear the voice (τῆς φωνῆς) of the Son of God; and the ones who have heard will live" (5:24–25). If we think ahead to 14:1, where believing in Jesus parallels believing in God, the parallel in 5:24 between hearing Jesus' word and believing the one who sent him, viz., God, suggests that believing Jesus' word equates with believing in him himself. If the saying in Mark 9:37 par. Luke 9:48 ("and whoever accepts me accepts ... the one who sent me") underlies

---

[76] Bultmann draws a contrast between the woman's λαλιάν as "mere words which in themselves do not contain that to which witness is borne" and Jesus' λόγον, "which refers to a statement of definite content" (*John*, 201). Has Bultmann forgotten that only two verses earlier John used λόγον for the woman's word? See further Schnackenburg, *John*, 1:456; Hinrichs, *"Ich Bin,"* 27–28.

[77] The comparison between John and the Synoptics does not depend on John's use of them, but for such use see I. Dunderberg, "Johannine Anomalies and the Synoptics," in *New Readings in John* (ed. J. Nissen and S. Pedersen; JSNTSup 182; Sheffield: Sheffield Academic Press, 1999), 116–17.

[78] Cf. Painter, *Quest*, 223.

John 5:24 it is notable that the Johannine version adds the element of Jesus' word for eternal life. And as R. Schnackenburg has commented, Jesus' word is *verbum Verbi*, "the word of the Word."[79] The voice that makes this word audible and lifegiving sounds again in 5:28–29: "the hour is coming in which all who are in the tombs will hear his voice and come out." The voiced W/word is performative, as the case of Lazarus will demonstrate.

In 5:38 Jesus says to unbelievers in reference to God the Father, "And you do not have his word (λόγον) abiding in you, because he whom that one has sent – you do not believe this one." First to notice is the close association, almost a synonymous parallelism, between the Father's word and the one whom the Father has sent. Second, we know from the Prologue that Jesus is the Word who came into the world; from 6:56; 14:23; 15:4, 5 that Jesus abides in believers; and from 15:7 that Jesus' words (ῥήματα), which he got from the Father, abide in believers. And in 5:46–47 believing Jesus' words (ῥήμασιν) is the same as believing Jesus himself just as believing Moses is the same as believing the Mosaic text. Therefore it appears that in 5:38 to have the Father's word abiding in you equates with having Jesus the Word, whom the Father sent, abiding in you. Supporting this interpretation is Jesus' statement in 5:31, "I am testifying concerning myself." The followup, "my testimony is true," recalls again John's description of the incarnate Word as "full ... truth" (1:14).[80] And the references in 5:32–35 to the testimony of John the Baptist and to his being a lamplight recall his testifying in the Prologue concerning the Word as the true light.[81]

Jesus is "the bread of life" (6:35, 48, 51) in that he has "the words (ῥήματα) of eternal life" (6:68); and just as he is himself the bread of life that he gives, so also he is himself the words of life that he speaks. Since he is the bread, the bread that he gives is he himself, more particularly his "flesh" (6:51, 53–55), i.e., the flesh that the Word became (1:14) so as to voice those words of eternal life. And since the Word was God (1:1, 18) the quotation of Isa 54:13 in John 6:45, "And they

---

[79] R. Schnackenburg, *The Gospel according to St John, Volume Two: Commentary on Chapters 5–12* (A Crossroad Book; New York: Seabury, 1980), 109. Cf. Painter, *Quest*, 233, and Bultmann, *John*, 252 ("the word of Jesus cannot be separated from his person"). Potterie agrees with Bultmann but rightly warns against him that Jesus' word is not he himself in the purely functional sense of revealing that he is the Revealer; rather, as himself the Word he reveals God (*La vérité*, 1:55 n. 40).

[80] Cf. D. Tovey, *Narrative Art and Act in the Fourth Gospel* (JSNTSup 151; Sheffield: Sheffield Academic Press, 1997), 102, esp. n. 69, and Bultmann, *John*, 163: "the word of witness and that to which the word bears witness are identical."

[81] First John 1:10 implies that God's word (λόγος) is in true believers: "If we say that we have not sinned we make him [God] a liar and his word is not in us." The only word mentioned thus far in 1 John is "the Word of life," i.e., Jesus (1:1; cf. John 1:4); and according to 1 John 3:15, "eternal life," which acts as a christological title in 1:2; 5:20, abides in believers. So also 2:14: "the word (λόγος) of God abides in you." According to 1 John 2:4 and 2 John 2 the truth, which Jesus is according to John 14:6, abides in believers (cf. the abiding of God's seed and of the Father in believers according to 1 John 3:9, 24; 4:12–13, 15–16 with the statement in 2 John 9 that to have the Father is to have the Son too).

will all be taught by God" (διδακτοὶ θεοῦ – taking the genitive as subjective), implies being taught by Jesus as the Word who was God. Of course, the rest of 6:45 speaks of hearing and learning from alongside the Father.[82] But the next verse makes Jesus the one existing alongside God and the only one who has seen the Father, and this section closes with a reference to Jesus' teaching (6:59), so that to be taught by God means to be taught by Jesus the Word. Thus coming to Jesus is the means as well as the result of hearing and learning from alongside the Father (6:45).

John 6:56 says it is the person that eats Jesus' flesh and drinks his blood who abides in him and he in that person. But drinking Jesus' blood drops out in the immediately following vv. 57–59, so that Jesus' flesh captures the spotlight; for flesh is what the Word became (1:14). The reaction of many disciples follows naturally: "This word (λόγος) is hard. Who can hear it?" (6:60). As a saying of Jesus this word is hard to hear, so that "his disciples grumble about *it*" (6:61). As Jesus himself this Word is hard to hear, so that "many of his disciples backslid and were no longer walking around with *him*" (6:66). So hard this word/ Word, in fact, that whether it is Jesus' saying or Jesus himself, no one can come to him unless it be given that person to do so (6:65; see also 6:44).[83]

But according to 6:63 "the flesh is profitable in no way." Why not, if the bread that Jesus gives for the life of the world is his flesh (6:51)? If being profitable in no way contrasts with making alive, as it does in 6:63, surely Jesus' flesh *is* profitable. He does not say, "*My* flesh is profitable in no way," however; rather, "*The* flesh is profitable in no way" just as in 3:6 "that which is born of the flesh" contrasts with "that which is born of the Spirit" and just as in 8:15 Jesus says that the Pharisees judge "according to the flesh." By contrast his flesh is profitable, makes alive, because it is not ordinary flesh. It is the Word-made-flesh on whom the Spirit descended and abode (1:32). So he says, "The words (τὰ ῥήματα, synonymous with ὁ λόγος οὗτος in 6:60) that I have spoken (λελάληκα) to you are Spirit and are life," for "the Spirit is what makes alive" (6:63). The life-giving words that Jesus speaks are the Word-made-flesh that he is; for he not only *has* life in himself (1:4), he *is* the life (11:25; 14:6; cf. 1 John 1:1–2, where "the word [λόγου] of life," "the life" that "was manifested," and "the eternal life that was with the Father and was manifested to us" function virtually as christological titles).[84]

---

[82] Here and below I have awkwardly and literalistically translated παρά with "alongside," preceded by "from" when followed by the Greek genitive, to emphasize the allusion to the Word's preexistent presence with God the Father (cf. R. Robert, "La double intention du mot final du prologue johannique," *Revue Thomiste* 87 [1987]: 439).

[83] On the ambiguity, or double meaning, of the word as Jesus' saying and as Jesus himself, see B.J. Malina and R.L. Rohrbaugh, *Social-Science Commentary on the Gospel of John* (Minneapolis: Fortress, 1998), 137.

[84] On the equation of Jesus' words with Spirit see F. Porsch, *Pneuma und Wort* (Frankfurter

Flesh as such profits in no way, then, so that apart from the Spirit the flesh of the Word would have done no good but imbued with the Spirit did immense good.[85] For at the cross water as well as blood flowed out of Jesus' riven flesh. Water represents the Spirit as the agent of rebirth from above and the source of life (3:5; 7:37–39).[86] Put the equation of Jesus' words with *Spirit* and life (6:63) together with the statement that *Jesus* has the words of eternal life (6:68) and you get Jesus' identification with the Spirit alongside a distinction from the Spirit similar to the Word's identification with God alongside a distinction from God in the Prologue.[87]

The world's hating Jesus because of his testimony concerning it (7:7) recalls the statement in 1:11 that his own did not receive him as the Word. That is, the rejection of Jesus' testimony evinces his status and function as the rejected Word. In 7:11–17 his teaching replaces his testimony and contrasts with nobody's daring to speak about him openly for fear of the Jews. But despite the world's hatred and in contrast with the crowd's speaking about him only sub rosa Jesus is loquacious – openly so, daringly so, as recognized by some Jerusalemites, "Look! He's speaking openly" (7:26), and as later emphasized by the Word himself, "I have spoken openly to the world. I always taught in the synagogue and in the temple, where all the Jews come together; and in secret I spoke nothing" (18:20; see also 8:20: "he spoke these words in the treasury while teaching in the temple"). The Word is loud and clear: "Therefore Jesus shouted as he was teaching in the temple and saying, 'You both know me and you know where I am from'" (7:28). Notably he himself is the subject matter of his didactic shout (see also 7:37–39; 12:44–50). And his teaching is marvelous: "therefore the Jews were marveling, saying, 'How does this [man] know letters though he has never learned [them]?'" (7:15). He knows them because his teaching and speech come from God, who sent him. Hence he is true just as the Word in the Prologue is true and full of truth because he was with the Father in the beginning and came into the world to exegete the Father.

Theologische Studien 16; Frankfurt: Knecht, 1974), 71–72, 195–204, 210–12; idem, *Anwalt der Glaubenden* 120–31.

[85] On the differences in John between flesh without the Spirit and flesh with the Spirit see M. M. Thompson, *The Incarnate Word* (Peabody, Mass.: Hendrickson, 1988), 39–49. This book was originally titled *The Humanity of Jesus in the Fourth Gospel* (Philadelphia: Fortress, 1988).

[86] Porsch, *Pneuma und Wort*, 53–81.

[87] "The Spirit is christified; Christ is spiritualized" (C. F. D. Moule, *The Origin of Christology* [Cambridge: Cambridge University Press, 1977], 105). Cf. Jesus' "I am ... the truth" (John 14:6) with "the Spirit is the truth" (1 John 5:8), and see G. R. Beasley-Murray, *Gospel of Life* (Peabody, Mass.: Hendrickson, 1991), 98, and esp. Burge, *Anointed Community*, 83–84, 102: "the Spirit itself is identified with the Word. That is, the Spirit Jesus possesses and the Spirit he can offer are the words he speaks. Jesus as the Logos (the Word) becomes one with his message and presents himself in the words he offers."

The Jews ask, "What is this word (ὁ λόγος οὗτος) that he spoke (εἶπεν)?" It features Jesus himself: "You will seek me and not find me, and where I am you cannot come" (7:36), so that one could translate the preceding question, "*Who* (τίς) is this Word that he spoke?" Such a translation would not fit the Jews' point of view, of course; but it would fit John's point of view in that for him Jesus is himself the Word that he speaks. The word, "where I am you cannot come," reminds us that in the beginning and before coming into the world the Word was with God (1:1–2 with 9–11, 14). That the Jews do not comprehend this word ("What is this word?" they ask) reminds us that according to the Prologue the darkness did not comprehend the light that was the life of the Word (1:4–5). And the failure of the chief priests and the Pharisees to seize Jesus when he speaks about himself (7:32 with 44–46; see also 8:20 for Jesus' speaking "words" [ῥήματα] about himself as he was teaching in the temple) reminds us that according to the Prologue the darkness did not *ap*prehend the light which was the life of the Word any more than the darkness *com*prehended it (N.B. the double meaning of κατέλαβεν and Jesus' later volunteering himself to the band that came to seize him [cf. 11:57], so that instead of seizing him – i.e., apprehending him – they merely "took Jesus with [them]," συνέλαβον τὸν Ἰησοῦν [18:12; contrast the seizing of Jesus in Mark 14:44, 46 par. Matt 26:48, 50]).

After he cites himself as the source of living water (7:37–39) Jesus' listeners refer to "these words" (this time the plural of λόγος rather than of the synonymous ῥῆμα – 7:40) and split up into factions that confess him as "truly the prophet" and as "the Christ" and that deny his Christhood (7:40–43) just as in the Prologue some receive the λόγος and others do not. The current attempt to seize Jesus ends with the exclamation of chief priests' and Pharisees' officers, "A human being has never spoken like this!" (7:46). Of course not, because the Word who in Jesus became flesh was God![88] One is reminded that because of his rhetorical skill with words (λόγους) Protagoras was nicknamed "Word" (λόγος).[89]

Despite an earlier statement that if Jesus testifies concerning himself his testimony is not true, not admissible in a Jewish trial, he testifies extensively concerning himself in 8:12–20 and describes his testimony as true. It would be false of the Godman, who is full of truth and whose very name is "Word," not to testify concerning himself. So he makes himself the subject matter of his testimony just as he makes himself the subject matter of his words (cf. the use of ῥήματα, "words," in 8:20 to summarize Jesus' preceding self-testimony that he is "the light of the world" just as in the Prologue the Word is the light that comes

---

[88] Cf. D. A. Carson, *The Gospel according to John* (Leicester, UK: Inter-Varsity Press, 1991), 331.

[89] διὸ καὶ ἐπεκλήθη λόγος. So Hesychius in a scholium on Plato's *Republic* 600C as quoted by Suidas. For the text, see *Platonis Dialogi secundum Thrasylli Tetralogias* (ed. C. F. Hermann; Leipzig: Teubner, 1892), 6:361; and for notices of this text, see F. Passow, *Handwörterbuch der griechischen Sprache* (Leipzig: Fr. Chr. Wilh. Vogel, 1852), 2:78; LSJ, s.v. λόγος IX 1. Cf. the use of λόγος in the plural for eloquence (Isocrates 3.1, 3; 9.11).

into the world; also the parallel between ῥήματα and μαρτυρίαν, "testimony," in 3:32–34). It follows naturally that during his trial before Pilate Jesus says, "I have been born for this purpose and I have come into the world for this purpose, that I might testify to the truth [which is Jesus himself – 14:6]. Everyone who is of the truth hears my voice" (18:37). Jesus' voice testifies concerning himself as the truth embodied in the Word-made-flesh.

Back in 8:25 the Jews ask Jesus, "Who are you?" His answer, τὴν ἀρχὴν ὅ τι καὶ λαλῶ ὑμῖν, has caused commentators endless problems. Even so skillful a commentator as Bultmann gives up trying to solve them.[90] Are Jesus' words a counter question or an exclamation rather than an answer? Should we treat ὅ τι as a conjunction (ὅτι, "that") rather than as a relative pronoun ("whatever")? Why the present tense of the verb when ἀρχήν, "beginning," belongs to the past? Are we dealing with an ellipsis, or with ellipses, and if so what should we supply? Most nettlesome of all, what use of the accusative does τὴν ἀρχήν represent? Standard commentaries survey the conflicting answers to these questions and provide pros and cons. I take the words of Jesus to be an answer, indeed a self-testimony in line with his immediately preceding self-testimony, not as a counter question. After all, the Jews have just asked about his identity. I take ὅ τι as a relative pronoun that introduces the meat of Jesus' answer to the question of his identity. And I take "I am," which has appeared three times in the verses leading up to the answer (8:23 [twice], 24), as implied in the answer. What then of τὴν ἀρχήν?

At this point we need to think in terms of John's text rather than in terms of what the historical Jesus said. For an analogy, take the Baptist's testimony to Jesus' preexistence (1:15, 30). Though D. A. Carson defends the historicity of the Baptist's testimony that Jesus is God's lamb who takes away the sin of the world (1:29) – but defends it at the cost of saying that the Baptist did not understand the expiatory meaning of his own words – not even Carson mounts a defense of the historicity of the Baptist's testimony that Jesus preexisted.[91] Surely the testimony refers intratextually to the Word's preexistence according to the Prologue rather than to anything that the historical Baptist said. This sort of phenomenon is widely accepted as typical of John's Gospel.

Now the evangelist John uses the accusative of reference rather often,[92] and just two verses after the one in question there appears such an accusative: "They did not know that he was speaking to them in reference to the Father (τὸν πατέ-

---

[90] Bultmann, *John*, 351–53.

[91] Carson, *John*, 149–51; similarly C. L. Blomberg, *The Historical Reliability of John's Gospel* (Downers Grove, Ill.: InterVarsity, 2001), 79, though Blomberg appears to reduce the Baptist's statement, "He [Jesus] was before me" (πρῶτός μου ἦν), to superiority within Jesus' and the Baptist's lifetimes.

[92] Besides the two discussed in this paragraph, see 4:38 (ὅ), 52 (τὴν ὥραν); 6:10 (τὸν ἀριθμόν), 71 (τὸν Ἰούδαν); 8:54 (ὅν); 11:44 (τοὺς πόδας καὶ τὰς χεῖρας); 14:26 (πάντα); 21:21 (τί).

ϱα)" (8:27). The word order in Greek puts this accusative at the head of its clause just as τὴν ἀϱχήν enjoys a forward position. If we take the accusative of reference in 8:27 as a cue for interpreting 8:25 and capitalize on the possibility of an intratextual reference in τὴν ἀϱχήν, what emerges is an allusion to the Prologue: "In reference to the beginning [mentioned twice in 1:1–2]." Only at 8:25 does John put the definite article with ἀϱχή. It is anaphoric; it harks back to the beginning in which the Word was. To be sure, ἀϱχή has appeared in other connections between the Prologue and 8:25[93] and will reappear in other connections,[94] but only in the Prologue and 8:25 does ἀϱχή appear in connection with Jesus' identity. The Prologue identifies Jesus as the Word, of course; and in 8:25 Jesus correspondingly identifies himself in terms of his speaking: "⌊I am⌋ whatever I even speak to you." He is the Word being spoken by himself much as he testifies concerning himself.

Summarily, Jesus' statement, "In reference to the beginning [I am] whatever I even speak to you" (8:25), harks back to 8:24, "if you do not believe that I am." It connects the "I am" in 8:24 with the preexistence of the Word in the beginning according to 1:1. It prepares for Jesus' claim to preexistence in 8:58, "Before Abraham came into existence, I am." And it brings out Jesus' identity as the Word by calling attention to his speaking about himself. The following verses put further emphasis on his speech, which he got from the Father who sent him: "the things that I heard from alongside him ['the one who sent me'] – these things I speak (λαλῶ) in the world…. just as the Father taught me, I speak (λαλῶ) these things" (8:26–30, excerpts).[95]

In 8:31–38 Jesus addresses "the Jews who had believed him": "If you abide in my word (ἐν τῷ λόγῳ τῷ ἐμῷ) you are truly my disciples; and you will know the truth and the truth will set you free" (vv. 31–32). The parallel between abiding in Jesus' word and abiding in Jesus (15:4–7) suggests that he himself is his word in which believers should abide to demonstrate the truth of their discipleship. John 15:2, 6, 8 too deal with abiding in Jesus to demonstrate the truth of disci-

---

[93] See 2:11, "this beginning of the signs," and 6:64, "For Jesus knew from [the] beginning who they were that did not believe and who it was that was going to betray him."

[94] See 8:44; 15:27; 16:4.

[95] On the whole question of 8:25, including textual criticism and arguments for and against the main views, see esp. B. M. Metzger, *A Textual Commentary on the Greek New Testament* (3d ed.; London: United Bible Societies, 1971), 223–24; R. W. Funk, "Papyrus Bodmer II (P66) and John 8, 25," *HTR* 51 (1958): 95–100; E. R. Smothers, "Two Readings in Papyrus Bodmer II," *HTR* 51 (1958): 111–22; M. A. Pertini, "La genialidad grammatical de Jn 8, 25," *EstBib* 56 (1998): 371–408; E. L. Miller, "The Christology of John 8:25," *TZ* 36 (1980): 257–65. Coming close to the interpretation offered above but not treating τὴν ἀϱχήν as an accusative of reference are Miller, loc. cit., T. L. Brodie (*The Gospel according to John* [New York: Oxford University Press, 1993], 327), R. H. Lightfoot (*Saint John's Gospel* [Oxford: Clarendon, 1956], 191), I. de la Potterie ("La notion de 'commencement' dans les écrits johanniques," in *Die Kirche des Anfangs* [ed. R. Schnackenburg, J. Ernst, and J. Wanke; ETS 38; Leipzig: St. Benno-Verlag, 1977], 386–89), and H. Alford (*The Greek Testament*; 6th ed.; London: Rivingtons, 1868], 1:793).

pleship, so that the parallel between these two passages grows stronger.[96] Moreover, knowing the truth as a result of abiding in Jesus' word links with the incarnate Word, who is full of truth (1:14, 17) and is the truth (14:6). Right within 8:31–38, "the truth will set you free" (v. 32) parallels "if therefore the Son sets you free" (v. 36), so that Jesus the Son of God the Father (v. 38) is the truth revealed in Jesus' word, i.e., Jesus as the Word. Moreover again, "my word has no room in you" (ὁ λόγος ὁ ἐμὸς οὐ χωρεῖ ἐν ὑμῖν – v. 37) antithetically parallels Jesus' abiding in disciples (14:20, 23; 15:4, 5) just as Jesus' abiding in disciples is paralleled by the abiding of his words (ῥήματα) in them (15:7; cf. 15:3: "you are already clean on account of the word [τὸν λόγον] that I have spoken to you"). Once again an association between Jesus and his word, or words, is so close that we can legitimately think of an identification. When he speaks his word, or words, he speaks himself – not in the emphatic sense that he himself speaks but in the sense that his identity as the Word provides the subject matter of his speech.

In 8:38 Jesus says, "The things that I have seen alongside the [= 'my'] Father I am speaking (λαλῶ), and you therefore are doing the things that you have heard from alongside the [= 'your'] father [the Devil – 8:44[97]]." You would expect doing to be paired with seeing and speaking to be paired with hearing (cf. 12:50 to a certain extent), but here it is vice versa so as to highlight Jesus' speaking. And what he speaks, i.e., the things he has seen alongside the Father, echoes the Word's being with God in the beginning (1:1–2).

John 8:39–47 offers a series of references to Jesus' speech. He says, "I have spoken to you the truth which I heard from alongside God" (v. 40). The last phrase reflects as often in John the Word's having been with God and having come into the world as the Word full of truth.[98] Just as Jesus is the truth he is also the Word speaking it. He goes on to ask the Jews, "Why do you not understand my speech (τὴν λαλιάν)?" and answers his own question, "Because you are not able to hear my word (τὸν λόγον τὸν ἐμόν)" (v. 43). So the truth equates with Jesus' speech, which equates in turn with his word.[99] That he has heard the truth from alongside God does not forestall its equation with himself (to the contrary, see 14:6), so that as the truth he is the subject matter of what he heard from alongside God and has now spoken to humankind. Unlike those who can-

---

[96] Of course, John 15:9–10 speaks of abiding in Jesus' love yet we do not say that he himself is love (though see 1 John 4:8: "God is love"). John does not name Jesus "Love," however, whereas he does name Jesus "Word."

[97] Conjecturing a corruption in John's text, which originally made Cain the Jews' father, are N. A. Dahl ("Der Erstgeborene Satans und der Vater des Teufels [Polyk. 7 1 und Joh 8 44]," in *Apophoreta* [BZNW 30; Berlin: Töpelmann, 1964], 70–85, esp. 76–79) and G. Reim ("Joh. 8.44 – Gotteskinder/Teufelskinder. Wie antijudaistisch ist 'Die wohl antijudaistischste Äusserung des NT'?" *NTS* 30 [1984]: 619–24).

[98] See also John 6:46; 7:29; 8:26; 9:16, 33; 10:18; 15:15; 16:27; 17:7, 8; cf. 17:5 and Rev 2:28.

[99] Barrett distinguishes between λαλιάν as audible speech and λόγον as a message (*John*, 348). But see 4:41–42.

not hear Jesus' word "the one who is of God does hear the words (τὰ ῥήματα) of God" (v. 47). So Jesus' speech and word, already equated with the truth which he himself is, equates also with the words of God. He is God's words as well as his own word, for as the Word he was God in the beginning.

Jesus' λόγος crops up again in 8:51–52: "Amen, amen I say to you, if anyone keeps my word, by no means will that person ever see death.... If anyone keeps my word, by no means will that person ever taste death." These statements correspond to 5:24: "Amen, amen I say to you that the person hearing my word and believing the one who sent me ... has transferred out of death into life." The correspondence indicates the synonymity of keeping Jesus' word, hearing it, and believing the Father who sent Jesus as the Word in whom is life (1:4; cf. 1 John 1:1: "what we have heard ... concerning the Word of life").

John 8:51–52 may represent a development of the saying recorded in Mark 9:1: "Amen I say to you that there are certain people standing here who will by no means taste death until they see God's rule having come with power" (similarly the parallels in Matt 16:28 and Luke 9:27).[100] If it does, John's adding a double reference to the keeping of Jesus' word exhibits all the more an emphasis on Word-Christology. In 8:55 Jesus turns around to say that he keeps his Father's word (τὸν λόγον). But according to 14:23–24 the Father's word is Jesus' word, or words: "If anyone loves me, that person will keep my word (τὸν λόγον μου) .... The person who does not love me does not keep my words (τοὺς λόγους μου), and the word (ὁ λόγος) that you hear is not mine but the Father's who sent me."

So in keeping the Father's word Jesus keeps the word that he passes on to his disciples, the word of life that negates death. Keeping that word means carrying out his function as the Word whom the Prologue describes as containing the light of life.[101] And it is in keeping Jesus' word to go wash in the Pool of Siloam that the man born blind receives sight so as to see the light of life (9:1–12). John translates Siloam as "Sent One" to call attention to Jesus as the Word whom God sent into the world from his preexistent location alongside God.

According to 10:19–21 the words of Jesus cause a division in his audience: "Again a division occurred among the Jews because of these words (τοὺς λόγους τούτους). And many of them were saying, 'He has a demon and is raving. Why do you hear him?' Others were saying, 'These are not the words (ταῦτα τὰ ῥήματα) of a demoniac. A demon cannot open a blind man's eyes, can it?'" By now John's audience know that "these words" are the words of the Word who was with God and was God, quite the opposite of a demon-possessed man. Verses 1–18 contain the words referred to. In them Jesus says he is the good shepherd who calls (φωνεῖ) his own sheep by name, whose voice (φωνή)

---

[100] See B. Lindars, "Discourse and Tradition: The Use of the Sayings of Jesus in the Discourses of the Fourth Gospel," *JSNT* 13 (1981): 95–96.

[101] Against Harnack, "Ueber das Verhältnis," 207.

his sheep hear and recognize, and who has other sheep that will hear his voice. And Jesus says he is the door of the sheep for their entrance into salvation and life, the noble shepherd who at his Father's command lays down his life for the sheep, and the one who knows God as his Father and is known by God. In other words, Jesus is again the subject matter of his words.

Dialogue with the Jews continues in 10:34–36: "Jesus answered them, 'Is it not written in your law, "I said, 'You are gods'" [Ps 82:6]? If he called (εἶπεν) those ones "gods" to whom the word of God became (ὁ λόγος τοῦ θεοῦ ἐγένετο) – and the Scripture cannot be broken – are you saying in reference to him whom the Father sanctified and sent into the world, "You are blaspheming," because I said, "I am God's Son"?'" Who were the ones to whom the word of God "became"? Several answers have been offered: the nation of Israel, Israel's judges, individuals who ascended to heaven, and angels.[102] What was the word of God that "became" to them? The law, or heavenly revelations, or the preexistent Logos.[103] When did the word of God "become" to them? In the OT period. And what is the nature of Jesus' argument? Most commentators answer that the argument is *a fortiori*: if God called those ones "gods" to whom the word of God became, how much more appropriate it is for him whom the Father sanctified and sent into the world to call himself God's Son. H. N. Ridderbos argues, however, that no *a fortiori* is needed; the argument consists only in the point that if certain ones were called gods in the OT, then Jesus is not blaspheming by calling himself God's Son.[104] A few commentators toy with the possibility of an allusion to Jesus as the Word of God but decide that since Jesus did not come on the scene in the OT period such an allusion could at most constitute a secondary meaning.[105]

---

[102] See M. J. J. Menken, "The Use of the Septuagint in Three Quotations in John: Jn 10,34; 12,38; 19,24," in *The Scriptures in the Gospels* (ed. C. M. Tuckett; BETL 131; Leuven: Leuven University Press, 1997), 370–82; J. H. Neyrey, "'I Said: You Are Gods': Psalm 82:6 and John 10," *JBL* 108 (1989): 647–63.

[103] For the preexistent Logos, see A. T. Hanson, "John's Citation of Psalm LXXXII," *NTS* 11 (1964–65): 158–62; idem, "John's Citation of Psalm LXXXII Reconsidered," *NTS* 13 (1966–67): 363–67; idem, *Prophetic Gospel*, 144–49; M. Hengel, "Die Schriftauslegung des 4. Evangeliums auf dem Hintergrund der urchristlichen Exegese," *Jahrbuch für Biblische Theologie* 4 (1989): 260–63 (with references to earlier literature).

[104] H. N. Ridderbos, *The Gospel according to John* (Grand Rapids: Eerdmans, 1997), 374–75. See also R. Jungkuntz, "An Approach to the Exegesis of John 10:34–36," *CTM* 35 (1964): 556–58.

[105] See J. S. Suh, *The Glory in the Gospel* (Oxford, Ohio: M. P. Publications, 1995), 117–21; M. E. Boismard, "Jésus, le Prophète par excellence, d'après Jean 10, 24–39," in *Neues Testament und Kirche* (ed. J. Gnilka; Freiburg: Herder, 1974), 171; R. E. Brown, *The Gospel according to John* (AB 29–29A; Garden City, N.Y.: Doubleday, 1970), 1:809–10; B. G. Schuchard, *Scripture within Scripture* (SBLDS 133; Atlanta: Scholars Press, 1992), 59–70; A. Obermann, *Die christologische Erfüllung der Schrift im Johannesevangelium* (WUNT 2/83; Tübingen: Mohr-Siebeck, 1996), 178–85, 380–87; and Hanson's discussions, cited above. Though Jesus *bore* the preexistent Logos, Hanson does not think that Jesus *was* the preexistent Logos that came to Israel at Sinai. Perhaps it should be said here that despite Moses' writing about Jesus (1:45; 5:45–46), 1:17 draws enough of a contrast between the giving of the law through Moses

Now in John 10:36 the aorist verbs ἡγίασεν ("sanctified") and ἀπέστειλεν ("sent") refer without question to Jesus' earthly ministry (cf. his use in the Synoptics of the aorist ἦλθον, "I came," for that ministry[106]). We have good reason, then, to take the aorist verb εγένετο ("became") as having the same referent just as this very same verb did in 1:14, "and the Word became (ἐγένετο) flesh and tabernacled among us," and 1:17, "Grace and truth became (ἐγένετο) through Jesus Christ." "The Word of God" in 10:35 is thus a direct and exclusive reference to Jesus as God's Word; and the ones "to whom the Word of God became" are Jesus' contemporaries, much as in 10:10 he said, "I came [ἦλθον] that they ['the sheep'] might have life," and as in 1:11 "he came [ἦλθεν] to his own, and his own did not receive him." For John's synonymous use of ἐγένετο and ἦλθεν see 1:6–7. The use in 10:35 of ἐγένετο instead of ἦλθεν is due to the OT formula אל יהוה דבר ויהי, "the word of Yahweh became to," which in the LXX comes out as καὶ ἐγένετό/ἐγενήθη λόγος/ῥῆμα κυρίου πρός (cf. Luke 3:2: ἐγένετο ῥῆμα θεοῦ ἐπὶ Ἰωάννην). M. J. J. Menken notes that in John 10:35 "the word of God" replaces "the word of the Lord" in the OT formula because John uses κύριος usually for Jesus and for God only in 12:13, 38 in dependence on the OT.[107] We might add that the Prologue's association and identification of the Word with God contribute to the replacement.

All in all, then, Jesus treats Ps 82:6 not as a historical statement about anybody in OT times but as a predictive prophecy fulfilled by his coming to his contemporaries, called "gods" by that text because Jesus has appeared on the scene to them and has done so as the Word of God. The fulfillment demonstrates the unbreakability of Scripture and falsifies the charge of blasphemy. The law can in fact be broken by disobedience. According to 7:23 failure to perform circumcision on the Sabbath (if the Sabbath falls on the eighth day after birth, it is understood) would count as a breaking of "the law of Moses," just as 5:18 speaks of breaking the Sabbath. The verb for breaking (λύω) is the same as that used in 10:35. Similarly in Matt 5:19 this verb occurs for breaking "one of these least commandments" of "the law." Moreover, the compound form of the verb (καταλύω) stands in Matt 5:17–18 as an antonym to πληρόω, "fulfill," and in parallel with γίνομαι, "come to pass," which in turn contrasts with παρέρχομαι, "pass away." Therefore in John 10:34–36 the unbreakability of Scripture

---

and the coming of grace and truth through Jesus Christ to forestall a unification of these events through a double reference in 10:34–35. The denials in 1:18 that anyone has ever seen God and in 6:32 that Moses gave the bread from heaven undermine further such a double reference, as they do also a correlation in 10:34–35 between Jesus as the Word of God and Jesus as a prophet like Moses (Deut 18:15). Jesus as the Word of the Prologue makes better Johannine sense. See the following discussion.

[106] See E. Arens, *The ΗΛΘΟΝ-Sayings in the Synoptic Tradition* (OBO 10; Göttingen: Vandenhoeck & Ruprecht, 1976).

[107] Menken, "Use of the Septuagint," 372. See the concordance for John's many uses of κύριος for Jesus.

fits a scheme of prediction and fulfillment better than it fits a historical reference. Jesus' statements in 5:39, "You search the Scriptures ... and those are the
ones testifying concerning me," and 46, "For that one [Moses] wrote concerning me," have prepared John's audience to understand the OT quotation and its
interpretation at 10:35–36 in terms of Word-Christology.[108] And numerous
further passages will confirm this understanding: 12:37–41 ("in order that the
word of Isaiah the prophet might be fulfilled .... These things Isaiah said because he saw his [Jesus'] glory [defined in 1:14 as the glory of the incarnate
Word] and spoke about him" [cf. 12:34: "We have heard from the law that the
Christ abides forever"]); 13:18 ("but in order that the Scripture might be fulfilled..."); 15:25 ("But in order that the word written in their law might be fulfilled..."); 19:24 ("in order that the Scripture might be fulfilled, which says..."),
36–37 ("For these things happened in order that the Scripture might be fulfilled
.... And again another Scripture says..."); 20:9 ("For they did not yet know the
Scripture that it is necessary for him to rise from the dead"). Three or four of
these passages cite the Psalms as 10:34 does. Since in the Prologue the Word
not only was with God and came from God but also was God we could even
think that in 10:35–36 "the Word of God" means both the Word spoken by God
(τοῦ θεοῦ as a subjective genitive) and the Word who was God (τοῦ θεοῦ as a
genitive of apposition).

It might be objected against the foregoing interpretation that if it were correct
Jesus would be quoted as saying, "If he called you [not 'those ones'] gods ...."
But the expression "those ones" includes more people than Jesus' immediate
audience, who have just taken up stones with which to stone him (10:31–33); for
again in reference to 1:11 "he came to his own, and his own did not receive him."
His immediate audience falls short of making up the entirety of "his own," and as
recently as 9:39–41 he has used the third person plural alongside the second person plural in reference to his audience. Therefore the objection would fail.

It might also be objected that nowhere in John does Jesus say outright, "I
am the Word of God," as he does say outright, "I am God's Son" (10:36). But
nowhere in John or the Synoptics does Jesus say, "I am the Son of Man," yet
everybody understands that at least the textual Jesus (if not the historical
Jesus) uses that phrase for himself some of the time (if not all the time – for
instances in John, see 1:51; 3:13, 14; 5:27; 6:27, 53, 62; 8:28; 9:35; 12:23, 34
[twice]; 13:31). So this objection too would fail to disprove that Jesus was the

---

[108] On the need to take account of a prophetically predictive implication in the statement,
"The scripture cannot be broken," see Hanson, "John's Citation of Psalm LXXXII," 161; idem,
Prophetic Gospel, 145–46, in dependence on Jungkuntz, "An Approach to the Exegesis of
John 10.34–36," 556–65. In private conversation M. Silva suggested to me that Jesus' calling
the Scripture "your law" evoked a reference to its unbreakability, but Silva admitted that law-
breaking as a violation of the law would make no sense in this passage. The aorists εἶπα, "I
said," and εἶπεν, "he said [in the sense of 'called']," refer of course to God's speaking in the
past what is recorded in Ps 82:6.

Word of God that came to those whom the law called gods, i.e., Jesus' contemporaries.

Commentators often note that after the Prologue "the Word" does not appear
absolutely in John. Therefore it might be objected once again that in 10:35 the
addition of the phrase "of God" to "the word" prohibits an equation of "the
word of God" there with "the Word" in the Prologue.[109] But the phrase "in the
beginning" made it inappropriate in the Prologue that "of God" should be
added; for "the word of God" connotes a message and in the beginning there
was not anyone to whom a message could be addressed. Once all things have
come into existence through the Word (1:3), however, and especially after the
Word has entered the world by being made flesh (1:14), "the Word of God" becomes a meaningful designation of Jesus as God's message to humankind.
Hence the absoluteness of "the Word" in John's Prologue puts no roadblock in
the way of taking "the Word of God" in 10:35 as a designation of Jesus just as
that very phrase indubitably designates him in Rev 19:13 (cf. "the Word of
life" – nonabsolute – in 1 John 1:1).

Already in the Prologue, moreover, the equation of the Word with God makes
the Word prospectively God's Word in effect though not in phraseology as does
also the Word's being the unique one who "exegeted" God (1:1, 18). Those who
think that John presents Jesus as Wisdom incarnate despite failing ever to use
the word "wisdom," much less to identify Jesus as Wisdom, should have no
trouble accepting that the Word who was *with* God and *was* God is the Word *of*
God (cf. Ign., *Magn.* 8:2). If Jesus appears as the Word of God in John 10:35 we
should dismiss the oft-repeated statement that after the Prologue λόγος ceases
to apply to Jesus.[110]

According to 11:28–29 Mary heard that Jesus the teacher was calling her. The
verb for calling, φωνεῖ, refers to Jesus' voice. As one of his sheep Mary recognized that voice as her shepherd's (even though it was relayed to her by Martha).
Mary got up quickly and started going to him. On arrival at the tomb of her
brother Lazarus, Jesus said to his Father, "I spoke on account of the crowd
standing around in order that they may believe that you sent me" (11:42). Jesus'
speaking aims to elicit people's believing just as according to John's Prologue
the Word came into the world to elicit people's believing in his name (1:9–12).
Then Jesus "shouted with a loud voice (φωνῇ μεγάλῃ ἐκραύγασεν), 'Lazarus,
come out!'" In 12:17 a back-reference to this shout underlines Jesus' voice: "he
called (ἐφώνησεν) Lazarus." As usual, Jesus' word was performative, for Lazarus came out of the tomb, as to be expected from 5:25: "Amen, amen I say to

---

[109] Cf. G. Strecker, *Theology of the New Testament* (New York: Walter de Gruyter, 2000),
473.

[110] For an especially clear example of such a statement, see H. J. Holtzmann, *Evangelium,
Briefe und Offenbarung des Johannes* (2d ed.; HKNT 4; Freiburg im Bresgau: Mohr-Siebeck,
1893), 8–9.

you that an hour is coming and now is when the dead will hear the voice of the Son of God and the ones having heard will live" (cf. Ezek 37:1–14, where Yahweh's word brings life to the dead). The verb for Jesus' shouting, κραυγάζω, occurs only nine times in the NT, six of them in John. It emphasizes the loudness of Jesus' voice, and that loudness stresses the power and authority of his word, his power and authority *as* the Word of God (cf. Rev 1:10). Through Jesus' speaking on account of the crowd standing around and through his shouting with a loud voice so as to raise Lazarus from the dead, Martha saw "the glory of God" (11:40) in accordance with the beholding of the glory of the incarnate Word, glory as of the unique one from alongside the Father (1:14).

In John 12:27 Jesus asks, "And what should I say (εἴπω)?" and in 12:36 he declares, "These things I have spoken (ἐλάλησεν)." His intervening words, then, are framed by formal references to his speaking. The next section containing Jesus' words is likewise framed by such references: "But Jesus shouted and said (ἔκραξεν καὶ εἶπεν)" (12:44); "In reference to the things that I speak (λαλῶ), according as the Father has spoken (εἴρηκεν) to me, thus I speak (λαλῶ)" (12:50). So Jesus' loud voice corresponds to the Father's thunder-like voice in intervening verses (12:28–29) – naturally, since Jesus is the Word *of God* (10:35–36).

In 12:47–48 Jesus says he is not judging the person who hears his words (ῥημάτων) but does not keep them; rather, the word (ὁ λόγος) which he has spoken (ἐλάλησα) will "at the last day" judge the person who fails to receive his words (ῥήματα), which failure equates with rejecting him (12:48) and with failure to receive Jesus the Word (1:11). The demonstrative pronoun ἐκεῖνος refers back to and lays emphasis on "the word which I have spoken." Earlier, Jesus said the Father "has given all judgment to the Son" (5:22; see also 5:27, 30; 8:16), so that – although Jesus presently judges no one (see also 8:15) because he came not to judge the world but to save the world (12:47; see also 3:17) – he will be the self-spoken Word that judges unbelievers at the last day (see also Rev 19:11–16 for Jesus as "the Word of God" coming in judgment).

Jesus' word is his Father's in addition to his own, as he himself said, "I did not speak (ἐλάλησα) from myself; rather, the Father who sent me – he has given me a commandment in reference to what I should say (εἴπω) and what I should speak (λαλήσω). And I know that his commandment is eternal life. Therefore in reference to the things that I speak, according as the Father has spoken to me, thus I speak" (12:49–50). Since life is in the Word (1:4) and Jesus is both "the life" (11:25; 14:6), "the Word of life" (1 John 1:1), and "life eternal" (1 John 5:20), the statement that the Father's commandment is eternal life implies that Jesus is that commandment in the same sense that he is the words that make up the Word.[111]

---

[111] Carson comments aptly, "Jesus' speech is a reflection of his person. Not only is what Jesus

Mark 8:38 (par. Matt 16:27 and Luke 9:26) records Jesus' saying, "For whoever is ashamed of me and my words (τοὺς ἐμοὺς λόγους) in this adulterous and sinful generation – the Son of Man will also be ashamed of him whenever he comes in the glory of his Father with the holy angels." If John has developed Jesus' statements in John 12:47–50 out of that synoptic saying we can see an expansion of the earlier reference to Jesus' words. ῥήματα has replaced λόγους, and the plural λόγους has changed to the singular λόγος. Being ashamed of Jesus' words has changed to rejecting him and not receiving his words, for his identity lies in his words. And in line with Word-Christology Jesus' speaking what the Father commanded him enlarges the verbal element.

In 13:13–14 Jesus commends the disciples' calling him "Teacher" (ὁ διδάσκαλος), affirms that he is in fact their teacher, and then calls himself "Teacher" (cf. 20:16, where Mary Magdalene calls Jesus "Rabbouni," which John takes care to translate as "Teacher" and notes that she recognized Jesus by hearing him call her by name, as in 10:1–5, 16, 27 the good shepherd calls his sheep by name and they recognize his voice). Not surprisingly, then, Jesus goes on to speak continually of his word, words (the plural of both λόγος and ῥῆμα), commandment, and commandments, and of his speaking qua speaking (13:34; 14:15, 21, 23–26, 28–30; 15:3, 7, 10, 12, 17, 20). As to Jesus' "new commandment that you love one another according as I loved you, that you also love one another" (13:34), it builds on the OT commandment that the synoptic Jesus quoted, "You shall love your neighbor as [you love] yourself" (Mark 12:31, 33; Matt 5:43; 19:19; 22:29; Luke 10:27). As the Word who is God, Jesus gives as his own a commandment that replaces God's commandment in the Mosaic law.[112]

Jesus asks, "Do you not believe that I [am] in the Father and the Father is in me? The words (ῥήματα) that I say (λέγω) to you I do not speak (λαλῶ) from myself, but the Father abiding in me does his works. Believe me that I [am] in the Father and the Father [is] in me. But if not, believe because of the works themselves" (14:10–11). As in the Prologue the Word was with God, in the Father's bosom, so here Jesus' words arise out of the mutual indwelling of him

---

says just what the Father has told him to say, but he himself is the Word of God, God's self-expression (1:1)" (*John*, 453). See also R. Kysar, *John* (ACNT; Minneapolis: Augsburg, 1986), 204 ("chapters 1–12 end … much as they started – with the claim that Jesus is the Word of God"), and Harris, *Prologue and Gospel*, 164 ("his [Jesus'] present speech is identical with the speech of God, and exactly reproduces what his Father has commanded him to say"). Contrast Harnack, "Ueber das Verhältmis," 206–8. Harnack thinks so diachronically in terms of sources that he underestimates the interrelatedness of John's Prologue with the rest of the Fourth Gospel.

[112] The switching from λόγον to λόγους and back to λόγος undermines the statement of Barrett, "It is shown at 14.23 f. that a distinction should be drawn between *word* (singular) and *words* (plural). The former means the divine message brought by Jesus taken as a whole, the latter is nearer in meaning to ἐντολαί, precepts" (*John*, 505). B. Lindars comes closer to the mark in writing that the plural ἐντολαί "refers to the manifold applications of the one commandment to love one another (compare 15.10 and 12)" (*The Gospel of John* [NCB; London: Oliphants, 1972], 477).

and the Father. Also, the conjoining of Jesus' words and the Father's works highlights the performative power of the words. *Just as the works are visible words, then, the words are audible works.* And so much is Jesus the Word that even after his going back to the Father, the Holy Spirit will teach the disciples all things and remind them of all that Jesus told them (14:26). Thus in the interests of Word-Christology the Holy Spirit's teaching the disciples what *they* should say, according to the Synoptics (Mark 13:11 par. Matt 10:1–20 and Luke 12:11–12), is exchanged in John for the Holy Spirit's reminding them of what *Jesus* said. Not only what Jesus said in the past but also what as the glorified Word he will yet say: "the Spirit of truth will guide you into all the truth, for he will not speak from himself but will speak *as many things as he will hear* and will announce to you the coming things.... he will *take [them] from me* and announce [them] to you" (John 16:13–15).[113]

According to 15:3 the disciples are clean because of the word (λόγον) that Jesus has spoken to them. According to 13:5, 10 they are clean because they have been washed with water, and 1 John 1:7, 9 speak of Jesus' blood as cleansing believers from all sin. Our minds turn naturally to John 19:34: "with his spear one of the soldiers pierced his [Jesus'] side and immediately there came out blood and water." So the word because of which the disciples are clean lines up with the cleansing blood and water of the Word-made-flesh (1:14).

The abiding of Jesus' words (ῥήματα) in the disciples (15:7) parallels the abiding of Jesus himself in them (15:4, 5) because as the Word he is his words.[114] "The word" (τοῦ λόγου) that Jesus "has spoken" to the disciples and that they are to "remember" is a word about his lordship over them: "A slave is not greater than his master [= 13:16]. If they have persecuted me they will persecute you too. If they have kept my word (λόγον) they will keep yours too" (15:20, the last statement being ironic, of course). We have already seen that keeping Jesus' word means hearing it, i.e., hearing him as the Word, and believing the one who sent him (5:24; 8:51). It looks as though the saying in 15:20 grew out of the one recorded in Matt 10:24–25: "A disciple is not above the teacher, neither a slave above his master. [It is] sufficient for the disciple that he become as his teacher and [that] the slave [become] as his master." If the Johannine saying did grow out of the Matthean one John's addition of Jesus' word is notable. Again that word is paired with Jesus' works so as to make his speech visible and his works audible: "If I had not come and spoken (ἐλάλησα) to them they would not have had sin.... If I had not done the works among them that no one else had done they would not have had sin" (15:22,

---

[113] Cf. Käsemann, *Testament of Jesus*, 46: "John ... identified the Spirit with the voice of Jesus which in the form of the Paraclete [on earth] continues to speak from heaven to the disciples when he himself [Jesus] is no longer with them"; see also Potterie, *La vérité*, 2:362–63.

[114] See Brown, *John*, 2:662: "Jesus and his revelation are virtually interchangeable, for he is incarnate revelation."

24). And in 15:25 "the word" (ὁ λόγος) written in the Jews' law and hated by them ("They hated me without a cause" – Pss 35:19; 69:5) is Jesus, written in the law as the "me" who is hated by his unbelieving contemporaries (cf. John 1:45; 2:17; 10:34–35; 12:14, 16).

John 16:1 starts with a warning that the disciples should not be "scandalized," i.e., "led to apostatize": "These things I have spoken (λελάληκα) to you that you should not be led to apostatize" (cf. Mark 13:23). The text could have read only, "You should not be led to apostatize," much as in Mark 13:5 (par. Matt 24:4 and Luke 21:8): "Beware lest anyone lead you astray." But no, the emphasis in John falls on Jesus' speaking; and there follows a cornucopia of references to his speaking: "But these things I have spoken to you ... I told you. But these things I did not tell you from the beginning .... however, because I have spoken these things to you .... however, I am telling you the truth .... I have yet many things to tell you .... What is this that he is saying to us? ... What is this that he is saying to us? ... what he speaks .... he said to them .... I said .... Amen, amen I say to you .... Amen, amen I say to you .... I have spoken these things to you in figures. An hour is coming when I will no longer speak to you in figures; rather, I will report (ἀπαγγελῶ) plainly to you concerning the Father.... Behold, now you are speaking plainly and you are not saying anything figurative.... These things I have spoken to you .... Jesus spoke these things" (16:4, 6, 7, 12, 17, 18, 19, 20, 23, 25, 29, 33; 17:1). Where in the Synoptics do we find anything even approaching such a magnification of Jesus' words? Surely this magnification develops out of John's portrayal of Jesus as the Word.

In prayer Jesus tells his Father that the disciples have kept the Father's word (λόγον – 17:6). This keeping of the Father's word amounts to hearing Jesus as the Word (see 5:24; 8:51 with the foregoing comments). "All things whatever that the Father has given [to Jesus]" (17:7) equate with "the words" (τὰ ῥήματα) that the Father has given him and that the disciples have received (17:8). The disciples have received these words in that they have come to know truly that Jesus came forth from the Father and in that they have believed the Father sent him (17:8 again).

Jesus says, "I am speaking (λαλῶ) these things in the world" (17:13) and "I have given them your word (λόγον)" (17:14). The latter statement parallels the one in 17:8 that Jesus has given the disciples the words that the Father has given him. Since these words in 17:8 equate with the word that in 17:14 is not from the world, in giving believers the Father's word Jesus gave himself as the Word that is not from the world. Jesus' having come forth from the Father and the disciples' having received Jesus' words echo similar statements in the Prologue concerning the Word. Thus "your [the Father's] word" (ὁ λόγος ὁ σός) in which according to 17:17 believers are sanctified and which is truth is Jesus himself, who earlier called himself the truth, whom the Prologue described as "the true light" and as "full of ... truth," and who says here that he is sanctifying himself on behalf of believers (1:1–18; 11:25; 14:6; 17:17, 19).[115] The ἐν before τῇ ἀληθείᾳ might be taken as instrumental ("*by* the truth") but a christological reference favors a locative ἐν, "in the truth," so as to link sanctification in the word with abiding in Christ (15:1 ff.). Believers, then, are sanctified in the Father's word because they abide in the self-sanctified Christ, who is that Word.[116]

The statement that the Father's word is truth seems to quote Ps 119:142: "And your law is truth." But the substitution of λόγος for the law reflects the Word-Christology of John (cf. the multiple interchanges of "word" and "truth" in 8:31–55; also 1 John 1:8, 10: "If we were to say that we have no sin, ... the truth is not in us.... if we were to say that we have not sinned, ... his word [λόγος, previously described as having been with the Father and manifested to us – 1:1–2] is not in us"). We may then at least ask whether in John 17:20 "their word" (τοῦ λόγου αὐτῶν) might allude to Jesus himself insofar as God has given Jesus as his word to the disciples and in that Jesus has given himself as God's word to them, so that he is now their word too, the subject matter of their word on account of which others will believe in Jesus.[117]

In the account of Jesus' arrest he takes the initiative by saying, "Whom do you seek?" (18:4, 7). It is his *saying*, "I am," that causes the arresting band to go backward and fall to the ground (18:5–6). And it is his *word*, "If then you seek me, let these go," that allows the band to arrest him and effects the salvation of his disciples (18:8). There results a fulfillment of Jesus' earlier "word that he spoke" (ὁ λόγος ὃν εἶπεν): "In reference to those whom you [the Father] have given me, I lost not even one of them" (18:9; cf. 6:39). Is Jesus himself this spoken word as well as the speaker of it? Probably yes, because he is the doer of the action (not losing one of those that the Father has given him) of which he spoke. See also 18:32 with 3:14; 8:28; and esp. 12:32–33 for the fulfillment of another word (λόγος) of Jesus in which he plays the central role.

In Mark 14:60–62 par. Matt 26:62–64 Jesus does not answer the testimony given against him before the Sanhedrin though he does answer the high priest's question whether he is the Christ, the Son of the Blessed One. Luke 22:66–70 keeps Jesus' answer to the high priest's question about his identity but drops the

---

[115] Cf. N. Turner, *Grammatical Insights into the New Testament* (Edinburgh: T. & T. Clark, 1965), 8–11; M.C. Tenney, "The Gospel of John," in *Expositor's Bible Commentary* (Regency Reference Library; Grand Rapids: Zondervan, 1981), 9:165; Obermann, *Die christologische Erfüllung,* 381–82; Van den Bussche, *Le discours d'adieu de Jésus,* 149; and against G.H. Clark, who takes "your word" as "the Scripture" (*The Johannine Logos* [Nutley, N.J.: Presbyterian and Reformed, 1972], 55).

[116] Cf. 15:3 and see the foregoing comments on 10:34–35 against drawing a sharp distinction between the absolute and nonabsolute uses of λόγος in John.

[117] Cf. H. Schlier, *Das Ende der Zeit: Exegetische Aufsätze und Vorträge III* (Freiburg: Herder, 1971), 18: "Der Geist, aber auch die Jünger sind Zeugen Jesu. Natürlich nicht nebeneinander, sondern so, dass sie durch ihn und er durch sie Jesus in seiner Wahrheit verkünden. In deiser Weise setzt der Jünger Wort das Wort Jesu, und das ist Gottes Wort, fort, vgl. 15,20; 17,20."

antagonistic testimony and therefore Jesus' nonanswer to it. John 18:19 likewise drops that testimony and Jesus' nonanswer but reserves till later the question about his identity and changes the high priest's question into one about Jesus' disciples (literally, "learners") and "teaching," i.e., Jesus' verbal ministry. The Word answers in terms of his words: "I have spoken openly (παρρησίᾳ λελάληκα) to the world. I always taught in synagogue and in the temple, where all the Jews come together; and in secret I spoke not one thing (ἐλάλησα οὐδέν)" (18:20).[118] What a sharp contrast with the so-called messianic secret and the private explanations of the mysteries of God's kingdom in the Synoptics![119] Strikingly and with the principal exception of the Upper Room Discourse Jesus does not instruct his disciples privately in John (4:31–38; 6:66–71; and 11:1–16 hardly consisting of theological instruction, and 6:60–65 having a mixed audience of believers and unbelievers). Even the Upper Room Discourse may not offer a true or entire exception, for there Jesus often instructs the disciples from a standpoint subsequent to his glorification (see, e.g., 12:31: "Now has the Son of Man been glorified") even though that event has not yet happened.[120] So 18:20 encapsulates Jesus' whole ministry as a public Word. And a good Word it was: "If I have spoken badly (κακῶς), testify regarding the bad. But if well (καλῶς), why are you hitting me?" (18:23). A feisty Word too: "Why do you ask me? Ask the ones who have heard what I said (ἐλάλησα) to them. Behold, these people know the things that I said (εἶπον)" (18:21). So far from taciturnity is this Word that a servant standing by gives him a slap (18:22).

To Pilate's amazement in Mark 15:3–5 par. Matt 27:12–14 Jesus does not answer one thing in response to the many accusations brought against him. Similarly in Luke 23:9–10 Herod Antipas questions Jesus "in many words" (ἐν λόγοις ἱκανοῖς) but Jesus answers not one thing. In John 18:33–38a, by contrast, he engages in a fullscale dialogue with Pilate, one that starts with a question of Jesus' identity, "Are you the king of the Jews?" and ends with Jesus' answer, "You are saying that I am a king. I have been born for this purpose and I have come into the world for this purpose, that I might testify to the truth. Everyone who is of the truth hears my voice." With his voice Jesus testified to himself as the Word who is himself the truth (see 1:9–10 for the Word's coming into the world).

---

[118] Cf. Isa 45:19 LXX: οὐκ ἐν κρυφῇ λελάληκα οὐδὲ ἐν τόπῳ γῆς σκοτεινῷ.... ἐγώ εἰμι ἐγώ εἰμι κύριος λαλῶν δικαιοσύνην καὶ ἀναγγέλων ἀλήθειαν, "I have not spoken in secret nor in a dark place of [the] earth.... I am, I am [the] Lord, speaking righteousness and announcing truth."

[119] Cf. W. Klassen, "Παρρησία in the Johannine Corpus," in *Friendship, Flattery, and Frankness of Speech* (ed. J. T. Fitzgerald; NovTSup 82; Leiden: E. J. Brill, 1996), 243.

[120] See the whole of C. Hoegen-Rohls's *Der nachösterliche Johannes* (WUNT 2/84; Tübingen: Mohr [Siebeck], 1996) and K. Scholtissek's "Abschied und Neue Gegenwart: Exegetische und theologische Reflexionen zur johanneischen Abschiedsrede 13,31–17,26," *ETL* 75 (1999): 341–45, with references to other earlier literature on this phenomenon.

When Pilate, terrified by the Jews' statement that Jesus has made himself God's Son, asks Jesus, "Where are you from?" Jesus temporarily refuses to give him an answer (19:7–9). Why? Because in view of Pilate's fear, to answer this question would be to save himself against his statement that he would lay down his life on his own initiative (10:17–18). But as soon as Pilate says, "You are not speaking (λαλεῖς) to me, are you? Do you not know that I have authority to release you and [that] I have authority to crucify you?" Jesus goes back into the word-business: "You would not have authority ..." (19:10–11). According to John's Prologue it is the Word who has authority (1:12). With characteristically Johannine irony Pilate heeds "these words" of Jesus' enemies rather than accepting Jesus' words or Jesus as the Word of truth who has spoken to him only to hear Pilate ask, "What is truth?" (19:13; cf. 18:38).

In contrast with the Synoptics the two angels sitting in the tomb of Jesus do not announce to Mary Magdalene his resurrection, nor does she recognize the risen Jesus by sight; rather, by hearing him call her name (cf. 10:3–5, 14, 16). Only then can she announce to the disciples, "I have seen the Lord," whereas earlier she had mistakenly supposed and reported a transfer of Jesus' corpse (20:1–18). Contrast Matt 28:17, "And having seen him they ['the eleven disciples'] worshiped him, but some doubted," and Luke 24:30–31, 35, "taking the bread he blessed [it] and having broken [it] he started giving [it] to them, and their eyes were opened and they recognized him.... he was known by them in the breaking of the bread," and 34, "the Lord has really risen and appeared to Simon." In the Synoptics sight and bread-breaking effect belief in Jesus' resurrection; in John it is his word that does so, as highlighted by the unnecessary and stylistically awkward placement of the editorial note, "And he told her [Mary] these things," right after a direct quotation of her statement, "I have seen the Lord." The note renews attention to Jesus' word as the trigger of her belief.[121]

---

[121] A number of commentators interpret 20:8, "Then, therefore, the other disciple ... saw and believed," as meaning that the beloved disciple believed in Jesus' resurrection because he saw the graveclothes Jesus had left behind. But the very next two verses say that "they [Peter and the beloved disciple] did not understand the Scripture that he must rise from [the] dead" and "therefore they went away to their homes" (vv. 9–10). The conjunctive "for" (γάρ) at the start of v. 9 goes so far as to make their lack of understanding the reason for the beloved disciple's seeing and believing! We already know what he saw. What then did he believe? Not that Jesus had risen from the dead, which would not comport with the causal lack of scriptural understanding that Jesus must rise from the dead; rather, the earlier report of Mary Magdalene that Jesus' corpse must have been transferred to another location unknown to her and them (vv. 1–2). To counter that the beloved disciple believed Jesus had risen and that this belief "was grounded simply upon what he had seen at the tomb," not additionally on Scripture (so Barrett, *John*, 564), makes nonsense of the conjunctive "for," as though the beloved disciple believed in Jesus' resurrection *because of* scriptural ignorance as well as seeing the graveclothes. Believing in a transfer of Jesus' corpse because of scriptural ignorance, however, makes good sense. The differences between seeing and believing here and seeing and believing in vv. 24–29 are two: (1) There Thomas hears a true

In Luke 24:36–43 Jesus' word, "Peace to you," only provokes a fright that is overcome by the sight of his hands and feet, flesh and bones, and of his eating fish. But in John 20:19–23 Jesus' very same word, "Peace to you," lends joy to the sight of him. John doubles this word of greeting and emphasizes it further with two immediate, unnecessary back references to it ("and having said this" [twice]). Then Jesus pronounces the Great Commission, breathes on the disciples, and bestows the Holy Spirit by saying, "Receive the Holy Spirit." Thomas's following insistence on seeing Jesus' scars leads Jesus to beatify those who believe without seeing. For though the sight of Jesus as risen is granted to Thomas, it is Jesus' word, or Jesus as the Word, that generates believing. And in 21:1–14 the disciples do not recognize Jesus by sight. It is his fulfilled word that draws recognition: "And he said to them, 'Cast the net on the right side of the boat and you will find [fish].' Therefore they cast [it on the right side] and they were no longer able to haul it in because of the multitude of fish. Therefore that disciple whom Jesus loved says to Peter, 'It is the Lord.'" [122]

Throughout the Gospel of John, then, Jesus the Word gives voice to the words that God his Father gave him to speak. But here a problem emerges. "The word" (ὁ λόγος) does not mean "the speaker" (ὁ λέγων), but "what is spoken" (τὸ λεγόμενον). [123] Therefore how can Jesus as a speaker be considered the Word that is spoken? By now the answer should be obvious: the words that the Father has given him to speak deal almost entirely with Jesus himself, nearly to the exclusion of the theme of God's kingdom which dominates the

---

report that Jesus has risen; here the beloved disciple hears a false report that Jesus' corpse has been transferred. (2) There Thomas sees Jesus' risen body complete with the scars of crucifixion; here the beloved disciple sees only graveclothes in an otherwise empty tomb. These differences bar the way to inferring from the later verses that here the beloved disciple believes Jesus has risen. Brown describes as "trite" a belief in the transfer of Jesus' corpse (*John*, 2:987). But not only is this description narratively myopic; it also overlooks inferior believing elsewhere in John (see 2:23–25; 8:31–38; 11:42–43; cf. 6:66). And saying that the ignorance of Scripture contradicts the beloved disciple's believing because the ignorance comes from a source with which the evangelist disagrees (so R. Schnackenburg, *The Gospel according to St John, Volume Three: Commentary on Chapters 13–21* [Herder's Theological Commentary on the New Testament; New York: Crossroad, 1982], 312–13) makes hash of the narrative, raises a question why the evangelist included something contradictorily disagreeable without revising it, and leaves the "for"-clause without anything to explain in the present text (so that Schnackenburg resorts to suggesting an original explanation of unbelief in Jesus' resurrection on the part of Mary Magdalene and Peter despite their having inspected the empty tomb). But even under the view that at the empty tomb the beloved disciple already came to believe in Jesus' resurrection vv. 24–29 devalue a belief that is based on seeing rather than hearing.

[122] Cf. 1 John 1:1, where hearing precedes seeing and observing, is complemented by the Word of life as the subject matter of what is heard, and together with that Word chiastically frames the references to seeing and observing. Similarly 1 John 1:2–3 starts with a reference to "the life," which has just been associated with "the Word," moves to the visible manifestation of the life and back to the preexistent state of being "with the Father" from the beginning (cf. John 1:1), reverts to being manifested and seen, but rests finally on being proclaimed and heard.

[123] Alford, *Greek Testament*, 1:678.

Synoptics, so that not only has the synoptic proclaimer become the Johannine proclaimed. *The proclaimer and the proclaimed have also become one and the same.* In John, Jesus is what *is* spoken even as he *does* the speaking.[124] The voice of the Father which twice in the Synoptics sounds from an open but distant heaven to identify Jesus as his beloved Son[125] changes in John to the voice of Jesus the incarnate Word speaking on earth many, many times to identify *himself* as the Son whom God the Father loves[126] and who speaks the words of God.[127]

---

[124] So also K. Berger, *Im Anfang war Johannes* (Stuttgart: Quell, 1997), 128: "Weil Jesus selbst 'das Wort' ist, sind alle seine Worte und Taten nichts anderes als Selbstauslegung des eigensten Wortes das Schöpfers selbst…. Wer Gottes Wort in sich trägt, der kann nur von Gott und von sich reden" (cf. p. 132); J. Blank, *Das Evangelium Johannes* (Geistliche Schriftlesung 4; Düsseldorf: Patmos, 1981), 4/1 b: 32: "im Johannesevangelium das Wort, das Jesus spricht, nicht irgendwelche 'Gegenstände' zum Inhalt hat, sondern ein Wort ist, das stets um die Bedeutung Jesu selber kreist; *ein Wort, in welchem Jesus selbst der zentrale Inhalt ist*; ein Wort also, in welchem fortgesetzt Jesus sich selbst auslegt und die Bedeutung seiner selbst erschliesst. Darum ist Jesu Wort auch in einem qualifizierten Sinn das Wort *Jesu*. Es ist das 'Wort des fleischgewordenen Wortes selbst', wie die Kirchenväter sagen" (italics original); idem, *Krisis* (Freiburg im Bresgau: Lambertus, 1964), 129, echoed by Kammler, *Christologie und Eschatologie*, 127–28. Others make the same point (neglected by Harnack, "Ueber das Verhältnis," 206–8) but without noting the christological subject matter of the spoken Word: "The Logos is, indeed, spoken, but he also speaks" (R. C. H. Lenski, *The Interpretation of St. John's Gospel* [Columbus, Ohio: Wartburg, 1942], 30); "the work of Jesus the Word (λόγος) is done through words (ῥήματα)" (C. K. Barrett, "The Parallels between Acts and John," in *Exploring the Gospel of John* [ed. R. A. Culpepper and C. C. Black; Louisville, Ky.: Westminster John Knox, 1996], 171); "as he [Jesus] speaks the word he is the Word" (C. H. Dodd in an oral statement reported by G. R. Beasley-Murray, *John* [WBC 36; Waco, Tex.: Word, 1987], 10); "Ses paroles (λόγοι, ῥήματα) et la Parole de Dieu sont si indiscernables qu'à moins de percevoir celle-ci en celles-là, il faut renoncer à les comprendre…. avec quelle force Jésus s'identifie avec son message" (Braun, *Les Grandes Traditions d'Israël*, 140–41).

[125] Mark 1:11 (par. Matt 3:17 and Luke 3:22); 9:7 (par. Matt 17:5 and Luke 9:35).

[126] John 3:35; 10:17; 15:9; 17:23, 24, 26.

[127] F. Godet asks what sense it makes for the Word to have existed in the beginning, i.e., before the coming into existence of creatures to whom God could communicate through the Word (*Commentary on the Gospel of John* [New York: Funk & Wagnalls, 1886], 1:246–48). The sense is that John writes retrospectively from his own standpoint and that of the incarnation and prospectively from the standpoint of the preexistent Word. Otherwise λόγος has to be taken in the noncommunicative sense of "unarticulated reason," unlikely here, or in the sense of "plan" (so J. Ashton, "The Transformation of Wisdom: A Study of the Prologue of John's Gospel," *NTS* 32 [1986]: 172–75). "Plan" fails to connect with the divine exegete in 1:18 as well as with Jesus' speech, voice, word, words, testimony, commandment, and commandments throughout the rest of John. Nor does a presentation of Jesus as Wisdom in terms of the Word link up very illuminatingly with those Johannine emphases. A presentation of Jesus as the Word in opposition to Wisdom offers a more illuminating possibility.

Addendum I: The Transfiguration of Jesus
according to John:
Jesus as the Heard Word

It is not my present purpose to discuss in detail the origin of John's Word-Christology or to offer a full explanation of its origin. But following is a suggestion that may provide at least a partial explanation. John's portrayal of Jesus as the Word who according to Peter has "the words of eternal life" (6:68) and who says, "The one hearing my word and believing him who sent me has eternal life" (5.24), recalls the voice of God that came to Peter, James, and John at the transfiguration: "Hear him" (Mark 9:7 par. Matt 17:5 and Luke 9:35). This voice also pronounced Jesus to be God's "beloved Son" just as John repeatedly portrays Jesus as the Son of God and as such the supreme object of God's love.[128] Furthermore, John portrays this supreme object of God's love as the "only" (μονογενής) Son of God just as at the close of the transfiguration the disciples see Jesus "only" (μόνον). Earlier the divine voice had come "out of the cloud" just as in John 12:28–29 the voice of the Father came "out of the sky/heaven," so that some were saying "it had thundered." According to Matt 17:2 Jesus' face shone "like the sun and his garments became white as the light." So also in John, Jesus the Word is "the light of the world" (8:12; 9:5), metaphorically equivalent to the sun (11:9; see also 3:19 [twice], 20, 21; 12:35, 36, 46 and esp. 1:4, 5, 7, 8, 9 for an association of the Word with light; cf. Rev 1:16). This Word who is the light has "glory," and people "beheld his glory" (1:14; 2:11; 8:54; 12:41; 17:5, 22, 24) just as according to Luke 9:32 "Peter and the ones with him … saw his [Jesus'] glory." The three tabernacles suggested by Peter but rejected by God at the transfiguration reduce to one divinely sanctioned tabernacle in John 1:14: "And the Word [who is 'the only God' – 1:18] became flesh and tabernacled among us," so that "grace and truth came through Jesus Christ" in contrast with the giving of "the law through Moses" (1:16), who along with Elijah at the transfiguration talked with Jesus about "his exodus … in Jerusalem" (Luke 9:31), where according to John 19:33–36 Jesus died as the true Passover in recollection of the first Passover at the exodus in Moses' time. Under the view that John knew and used the Synoptics or that he used tradition that made its way into the Synoptics it looks as though John may have developed his Word-Christology and much else related to it out of the transfiguration of Jesus.

---

[128] John 1:34, 49; 3:16, 17, 18, 35, 36 [twice]; 5:19 [twice], 20, 21, 22, 23 [twice], 25, 26; 6:40; 8:36; 10:17, 36; 11:4, 27; 14:13, 23; 15:9, 10; 17:1 [twice], 23, 24, 26; 19:7; 20:31.

Addendum II: In Defense of "Exegesis" in John 1:18

The text critical questions in John 1:18 need not detain us (one variant reading puts the definite article before "unique one" and another variant reading additionally has "Son" instead of "God"), but the verb ἐξηγήσατο demands our attention. I. de la Potterie has argued that the semantic associations of this verb in John differ from those of the same verb when it is used elsewhere in the sense of exegesis and that for lack of an expressed accusative of direct object and for lack elsewhere of a personal object where the verb has to do with exegesis, here the verb does not have to do with exegesis; rather, with leading or showing the way. Thus after coming out of the Father's bosom and by returning into it Jesus has opened the way for us and leads us with himself into the Father's bosom (cf. 14:6).[129]

But Potterie's own discussion puts on display a variety of semantic associations where ἐξηγέομαι has the sense of exegesis, so that the difference of those associations in John does not demand a different sense for the verb. In the Greek language, moreover, objects often have to be supplied from the context. John's omission of an object lets all the stress fall on exegesis as such.[130] And even Potterie's interpretation requires an ellipsis, viz., either the ellipsis of a genitive object for the ones *of* whom the unique one is the leader or the ellipsis of a dative object for the ones *to* whom a way is shown.[131] The expression of a personal object in the accusative might have left a misimpression that the verb has to do with governing. As it is, several factors favor that ἐξηγήσατο means "has exegeted" with "the Father," just mentioned, to be inferred as the object of exegesis: (1) nobody's ever having seen God in the first part of 1:18; (2) the preceding identification of the unique one as "the Word"; and (3) the special use of ἐξηγέομαι for priests', soothsayers', and deities' imparting information about divine secrets.[132]

It is another question whether to gain a typically Johannine double entendre we should add the meaning of leadership into the Father's bosom.[133] But several considerations militate against construing εἰς τόν κόλπον τοῦ πατρός with

---

[129] I. de la Potterie, "'C'est lui qui a ouvert la voie': La finale du prologue johannique," *Bib* 69 (1988): 340–70; cf. idem, *La vérité,* 1:213–28; also M. E. Boismard, *St. John's Prologue* [London: Blackfriars, 1957], 67, 70; L. Devillers, "Exégèse et théologie de Jean I, 18," *Revue Thomiste* 89 [1989]: 181–217.

[130] H. Gese, *Essays on Biblical Theology* (Minneapolis: Augsburg, 1981), 186; M. Theobald, *Die Fleischwerdung des Logos* (NTAbh nf 20; Münster: Aschendorff, 1988), 261–62.

[131] LSJ, s.v. ἐξηγέομαι I 3–4.

[132] Harris, *Prologue and Gospel,* 109–15; C. Spicq, "ἐξηγέομαι," *TLNT* 2:21–23.

[133] See Robert, "La double intention," 435–41; idem, "Le mot final du prologue johannique: A propos d'un article récent," *Revue Thomiste* 89 (1989): 279–88; idem, "Un précédent platonicien à l'équivoque de Jean 1, 18," *Revue Thomiste* 90 (1990): 634–39; W. Bindemann, "Der Johannesprolog: Ein Versuch, ihn zu verstehen," *NovT* 37 (1995): 330–54.

ἐκεῖνος ἐξηγήσατο ("that one has led [us] into the bosom of the Father") – as a result of which construal ὁ ὤν, "the one existing," would stand absolute in allusion to Exod 3:14 LXX and in anticipation of Jesus' ἐγὼ εἰμί, "I am," later in John – rather than traditionally with ὁ ὤν ("the one existing in the bosom of the Father"): (1) In the nontraditional construal εἰς and ἐξ- conflict with each other. You would expect εἰσηγήσατο rather than ἐξηγήσατο to go with εἰς τὸν κόλπον τοῦ πατρός. (2) ἐκεῖνος is interruptive. You would expect it to precede rather than follow the εἰς-phrase, which by telling where is adverbial. For in 1:33; 2:21; 5:11, 37; 8:44; 12:48; 13:25, 30; 15:26; 20:15, 16 ἐκεῖνος precedes an adverbial expression connected with the verb for which ἐκεῖνος acts as a subject. The only exceptions appear in 5:46; 7:45; 9:12; 20:13; and not as in 1:18 none of these exceptions offer a possibility of taking the adverbial expression with a preceding verbal expression. (3) The sense of direction in εἰς with the verb of being in 1:18 corresponds with the sense of direction in πρός with the verb of being in 1:1, where the πρός-phrase describes the relation to God the Father of the Word who was God, whereas to take the εἰς-phrase in 1:18 with ἐξηγήσατο would divorce that phrase from the Word and thus spoil the parallelistic *inclusio* with 1:1.

The unusualness of exegeting a person should not trouble us. John regularly uses language in unusual ways.[134] Right within the Prologue, for example, John's side-by-side distinguishing of the Word from God and equating of the Word with God provide an obvious example. Jesus' later statement, "The one having seen me has seen the Father" (14:9), provides another example of unusual language; and that example links nicely with Jesus as the one who exegetes the Father. Furthermore, ἐξηγέομαι does appear elsewhere in the sense of exegeting a person: ἐξηγούμενοι τὸν ποιητόν, "exegeting the poet [viz., Homer]" (Plato, *Cratylus* 407b).[135]

---

[134] See the whole of Petersen's *Sociology of Light*.

[135] See further G. H. Østenstad, *Patterns of Redemption in the Fourth Gospel* (Studies in the Bible and Early Christianity 38; Lewiston, N.Y.: Mellen, 1998), 85–93, 290–91; also Obermann, *Die christologische Erfüllung*, 338–40. Obermann notes that Jesus' being the way to the Father in 14:6 lies much more distant from 1:18 than does Jesus' being the Word in 1:1–17.

18. The Sense and Syntax of John 3:14–17
With Special Reference to the Use of
οὕτως … ὥστε in John 3:16

Introduction

According to popular understanding, John 3:16 means that God loved the world so much that he gave his only Son (and so on).[1] Indeed, some scholarly commentaries and translations reflect that very understanding: "For God loved the world so much that he gave his only-begotten Son" (Schnackenburg).[2] "Yes, God loved the world so much that He gave the only Son" (Brown).[3] "God loved the world so much that he gave his only Son" (NEB). "God loved the people of this world so much that he gave his only Son" (CEV). "For God loved the world so greatly that he gave the only Son" (Beasley-Murray).[4] "The 'so' (*houtōs*) is an adverb of degree which points toward the clause which follows and here serves to express the idea of infinity, a love that is limitless, that is fully adequate" (Turner and Mantey).[5] "The Greek construction … emphasizes the intensity of the love" (Carson).[6] Central to this understanding is a treatment of οὕτως as expressing a high degree of divine love ("so much") and of ὥστε as introducing its result ("that").

But does οὕτως indicate high degree in such a construction? Some standard lexicons and translations of various Greek texts say that it does. For example, we read in BDAG, s.v. οὕτω/ οὕτως 3, "marker of a relatively high degree, *so*, before adj. and adv. (Soph., Aristoph. et al.)…. Before a verb *so intensely*" (cf. LSJ, s.v. οὕτως III 1: "to such an extent, so much, so very, so exclusively," with a long list of representative passages following).

---

[1] Literally translated, the text reads "the only Son," but the definite article sometimes carries the force of a weak possessive (here, "his").

[2] R. Schnackenburg, *The Gospel according to St John* (HTCNT; New York: Herder, 1968), 1:398.

[3] R.E. Brown, *The Gospel according to John (I–XII)* (AB 29; Garden City, N.Y.: Doubleday, 1966), 129.

[4] G.R. Beasley-Murray, *John* (WBC 36; Waco: Word, 1987), 44.

[5] G.A. Turner and J.R. Mantey, *The Gospel according to John* (The Evangelical Commentary on the Bible 4; Grand Rapids: Eerdmans, n.d.), 98.

[6] D.A. Carson, *The Gospel according to John* (Grand Rapids: Eerdmans, 1991), 204.

We do not dispute that apart from ὥστε, οὕτως may indicate a high degree when modifying adjectives, adverbs, and adverbial phrases; but we do wish to cast doubt on that possibility when οὕτως modifies a finite verb and occurs in combination with a ὥστε that is followed by another finite verb, as in John 3:16.[7] Positively, we argue that in such circumstances οὕτως means "in this way" as a matter of manner other than high degree and that in John 3:16 and numerous other texts ὥστε introduces an addition that restates or supplements something previously referenced by οὕτως.[8]

Our argument begins by offering some philological considerations.We then test these considerations in the light of actual usage of οὕτως ... ὥστε where each word in this combination is construed with a finite verb. Since the construction appears nowhere in the NT besides John 3:16 our investigation extends to occurrences in other literature. To keep the discussion in bounds, selections come from passages in Demosthenes, Josephus, Philo, and Epictetus cited in lexicons for the meaning of high degree or translated with that understanding in the Loeb Classical Library.[9] Next we take up all Johannine instances of οὕτως without ὥστε, as the latter appears only in John 3:16. Probably no one would propose a οὕτως of high degree in any of these instances; so our discussion there shifts to the question whether John uses οὕτως retrospectively or prospectively. Finally, lexical conclusions lead to an interpretation of John 3:16 and its context.

Philological Considerations

ὡς means "as, like, so" in an adverbial sense. It answers the question, "How?" Used as a suffix, ὡς adds its meaning to that of the stem to which it is attached. For example, since the stem κακ- means "bad," κακῶς means "as bad, bad-like, bad-so" in relation to a verb, a verbal, an adjective, or another adverb. In better English, it means "badly." Likewise, since the stem of the pronoun οὗτος means

---

[7] "We" includes my coauthor of this essay, viz., Russell W. Howell.

[8] We have also canvassed occurrences of οὕτως ... ὥστε in which ὥστε is followed by an infinitive and have reached similar conclusions. Such a construction appears in Acts 14:1, but it is doubtful that anyone would understand the construction to indicate a high degree. The text means either that Paul and Barnabas spoke in some unspecified way that caused a large multitude to believe or in view of the usually backward reference of οὕτως that Paul and Barnabas spoke "boldly" in Iconium as they had in Psidian Antioch with the result of multitudinous belief (13:46).

[9] We used the TLG database and Silver Mountain Software to limit our survey to οὕτως and ὥστε combined with no more than twenty intervening words. Conspicuously missing are passages from the LXX. But it contains none that meet our criteria of construing finite verbs with both οὕτως and ὥστε and of being cited in a standard lexicon for high degree or rendered that way in a standard English translation such as Sir Lancelot C. L. Brenton's *The Septuagint with Apocrypha: Greek and English* (Regency Reference Library; Grand Rapids: Zondervan, n.d.; originally published by Samuel Bagster & Sons, London, 1851).

"this," the adverb οὕτως means "like this, this-ly, thus"; i.e., it responds to the question, "How?" with the answer, "In this way." The context defines what this way is; for as a demonstrative pronominal stem, οὑτ- requires a referent.

ὥστε consists of ὡς and τε, "and." Since τε is postpositive, ὥστε means "and so." When used in combination with a preceding οὕτως, the ὡσ- of ὥστε echoes the -ως of οὕτως; and the -τε of ὥστε indicates an addition to whatever adverbial thought οὕτως has referenced.

Though οὕτως like οὗτος may sometimes be used prospectively, most often it is used retrospectively. Furthermore, since the -τε of ὥστε indicates an addition (N.B. the meaning "and"),[10] in combination with a following ὥστε the adverb οὕτως would seem to reference an adverbial thought preceding at least the ὥστε-clause or -phrase and usually if not always the preceding οὕτως as well. For otherwise, what follows ὥστε could not make an addition to a previously mentioned adverbial thought.[11] And because τε is a coordinate conjunction ὥστε introduces something of a parallelism – synthetic if the following offers, say, a consequence or another example of what οὕτως has recently referenced; synonymous if what follows ὥστε restates in other words the earlier referent of οὕτως. The upshot is that since ὥστε, "and so," introduces a kind of parallelistic addition to some previously mentioned adverbial thought, οὕτως can hardly qualify a following ὥστε so as to produce the combined meaning, "so much that." For then the meaning of -τε, indicative of an addition, is lost; and the ὡσ- of ὥστε becomes redundant of the -ως in οὕτως

Occurrences of οὕτω(ς) ... ὥστε in Selected Literature outside the New Testament

But idiom does not always follow philology; so now we take up some texts to see whether or not actual usage strays from the philological considerations we have adduced. Against standard lexicons and translations we attempt to prove that it does not, that in these texts it is more natural to see in οὕτως a reference to some adverbial thought preceding the ὥστε-clause, and to recognize in ὥστε

---

[10] Of course, it might be objected that -τε has lost its force (cf. *A Lexicon Abridged from Liddell and Scott's Greek-English Lexicon* [17th ed.; Boston: Ginn & Heath, 1880], s.v. τε II: "in Ep. and Ion., τε is attached to Relatives, without altering their sense, as ὥστε, ὅσος τε, etc., which is to be explained from the fact that the Relative Pronouns were originally Demonstratives, and required to be joined by a Conjunction: afterwards when they gained a relative force the Conjunction was retained as a mere affix, as in ὥστε, οἷός τε, ἐφ᾽ ᾧτε." Whether or not we translate τε in such cases, however, the fact remains that what follows ὥστε adds a thought rather than filling out an incomplete thought.

[11] In John 3:16, then, the referent of οὕτως must precede since the following statement, "God loved the world," is not itself referenced by οὕτως; rather, it elucidates an earlier statement that is referenced by οὕτως (cf. H. W. Hollander, *Joseph as an Ethical Model in the Testaments of the Twelve Patriarchs* [Leiden: E. J. Brill, 1981], 21, on καὶ οὕτως).

the introduction to an addition somehow parallel to the earlier referent of οὕτως, than to take οὕτως and ὥστε closely together as an idiom meaning "so much that":[12]

Demosthenes 2.26 (cited by LSJ): The LCL translates, "And are you so [οὕτως] unintelligent, men of Athens, as [ὥστε] to hope that the same policy that has brought our state from success to failure will raise us from failure to success?" But Demosthenes has already detailed the Athenians' lack of intelligence (see §§ 22–25), so that the οὕτως-clause refers back to that discussion in terms of unintelligence as such, not in terms of a high degree of unintelligence; and the ὥστε-clause adds a further item of unintelligence (ὥστε … ἐλπίζετε). A better translation would read, "Are you then unintelligent in this way [just described] … and so do you hope …?"

Josephus, *Ant.* 8.7.7 § 206: "And in this way [οὕτως, i.e., by acting as a supervisor – so an earlier statement] he [Jeroboam] provided for the works [of building walls for the defense of Jerusalem], and so [ὥστε] the king [Solomon] approved him and as a reward gave him command over the tribe of Joseph" (against the LCL: "And so well did he supervise the work that the king marked him with his approval…"; N.B. that the Greek text has nothing corresponding to "well" in this translation).

Josephus, *Ant.* 9.5.1 § 98: The LCL translates, "And he was so far [οὕτως] out of his mind that [ὥστε] he forced the people to go up to the highest parts of the mountains and worship strange gods." But "far" has no basis in the Greek text, and the preceding sentences say that "Joram did not let a day go by without de-

---

[12] There are other ways to express in Greek the meaning "so much that," e.g., λίαν … ὡς (as in Josephus, *Ant.* 8.7.6 § 201: "Pharao loved him so much that [λίαν ἠγάπα, ὡς] he gave him in marriage his own wife's sister" [LCL]); λίαν with οὕτως (as in Dionysius Halicarnassus, *Is.* 8–9, where λίαν [twice] is needed to add a note of intensity that would otherwise be missing in οὕτως … ὥστε: "I should have wished … that in this way Hagnotheus did not have so exceedingly shameful a passion for money as to plot against the property of others" [properly taking λίαν with πρὸς χρήματ' ἔχειν αἰσχρῶς]; cf. Matt 8:28: "exceedingly violent, and so no one could go past the road," i.e., "so exceedingly violent that no one could…" [NASB]); πολύ … ὥστε (as in Philo, *Qu. in Gen.* 1.32: "differing much from ours, so that…," i.e., "differing so much from ours that…"; Strabo 13.1.18: "It is on the headland and runs far [πολύ] out towards Asia…, so that the passage across to Asia from it is no more than forty stadia" [LCL; i.e., "runs so far out … that"]; 16.1.18: "it can furnish so large [πολύ] a military force that…" [LCL; but more literally, since πολύ modifies the verb, not the direct object: "it so much provides also the military force that…"]; Dio Chrysostom 36.6: "there are some [towers] which stand quite [πολύ] apart…, so that you would not surmise…" [LCL; i.e., "stand so much apart … that…"]; 52.5: "yet [being] far removed [πολὺ δὲ ἀπέχοντα] from the rascality of to-day, in consequence of which [ὥστε] he might seem truly ancient" [LCL; i.e., "yet being so much removed … that…"]; cf. Dionysius Halicarnassus 3.21.7; 5.36.3; Strabo 15.2.6; 17.1.45); and τοσοῦτον (neuter accusative singular in an adverbial sense) … ὥστε (as in Sophocles, *Ant.* 453–55: "Nor did I suppose your proclamations to have so much strength that [σθένειν τοσοῦτον … ὥστ'] you, mortal dung, could overrun the gods' unwritten and sure laws"; cf. Matt 15:33). In this last combination τόσσον or τοσόνδε might be substituted for τοσοῦτον (see Sophocles, *Aj.* 1335; cf. Homer, *Il.* 6.450–55; 22.424–26). The foregoing citations are only exemplary, of course.

vising some new form of impiety and violation of his country's traditions" and that by taking half-measures to crush a revolt of the Idumeans he "gained nothing at all, for they all revolted from him, including those who inhabited ... Labina." Therefore οὕτως refers back to Joram's religious and political madness ("in this way [just described] he was out of his mind"), and the ὥστε-clause adds a further piece of evidence for that same madness in the forcing of pagan worship on the people ("and so he forced the people...").

Josephus, *Ant.* 9.12.3 § 255: The LCL translates, "But so [οὕτως] stupid and unmindful of his own good was this king [Achaz] that [ὥστε] not even when he was at war with the Syrians did he cease to worship their gods, but, on the contrary, continued to reverence them as if they would grant him victory." This translation assumes that οὕτως refers forward and intensively to Achaz's stupidity and unmindfulness of his own good in worshipping the Syrian gods when he was warring against the Syrians. But the preceding context details Achaz's stupidity and unmindfulness of his own good in taking as much gold as was in the royal treasuries and the silver that was in God's temple and the first votive offerings and giving them to the Assyrian king in payment for his attacks on Syria (particularly, Damascus) and northern Israel. The descriptions "stupid" (ἀνόητος) and "unmindful of his own good" (τοῦ συμφέροντος ἀσυλλόγιστος) are especially suitable to Achaz's stripping of his own treasuries as well as of the silver and votive offerings associated with the temple for payment to the Assyrian king. οὕτως refers back to these actions, then; and ὥστε, "and so," introduces an addition to the aforementioned stupidity and unmindfulness, viz., the worship of Syrian gods.

Josephus, *Ant.* 13.10.6 § 295: The LCL translates, "And Jonathan in particular inflamed his anger, and so [οὕτως] worked upon him that [ὥστε] he brought him to join the Sadducean party and desert the Pharisees." In this translation, "so ... that" may or may not be taken in terms of high degree. But against the possibility of high degree, Jonathan has just suggested that Hyrcanus employ a test to determine if a slanderous remark made by Eleazar was uttered with the Pharisees' approval. When the Pharisees fail this test Hyrcanus becomes suspicious and switches from them to the Sadducees. Therefore the following translation becomes preferable: "And, most of all, Jonathan spurred him against [the Pharisees] and managed [him] in this way [οὕτως, i.e., by way of suggesting that the Pharisees were up to no good], and so [ὥστε] he joined the party of the Sadducees, falling away from the Pharisees."

Philo, *Det.* 87: "But at that time the Archetype was formless in this way [οὕτως, i.e., by way of being invisible because the human soul on which the Deity was stamped was likewise invisible], and so [ὥστε] even His image was invisible" (against the LCL: "... so devoid of visible form that even His image could not be seen" – a translation that veers toward the redundancy of saying that lack of visibility makes something invisible).

Philo, *Agr.* 41: "In this way [οὕτως, i.e., by way of doing what is best for the flock even though doing it is unpleasant – see § 40, lines 39–40], then, shepherding has been thought worthy and beneficial, and so [ὥστε] the poetic kind are accustomed to call kings 'shepherds of peoples'" (against the LCL: "So full of dignity and benefit has the shepherds' task been held to be, that poets are wont to give kings the title of 'shepherds of peoples'"; N.B. that nothing in the Greek text underlies "full of").

Philo, *Agr.* 50: "In this way [οὕτως, i.e., by way of preventing a scattering – see § 49] shepherding is indeed a good thing, and so [ὥστε] not only to kings and wise men and perfectly cleansed souls but also to God the Governor of All it is rightly attributed" (against the LCL: "Indeed, so good a thing is shepherding that …").

Philo, *Her.* 83: "And according to Moses, in this way [οὕτως, i.e., by way of the aforementioned inward presence despite bodily absence or separation] a friend is near, and so [ὥστε] he does not differ from a soul" (against the LCL: "And in Moses' view a friend is so near that he differs not a whit from one's own soul").

Philo, *Congr.* 168: The LCL translates, "So holy is this unleavened bakemeat, that the oracles ordain that twelve unleavened loaves … be set forth on the golden table in the inmost shrine." By context, however, degree of holiness is not in view. Philo has been saying that "yearning and desire and love of the good" give sweetness to bitter toil. Then he makes the point by allegorizing the bread of presence: "This unleavened sweetmeat is holy in this way [οὕτως, i.e., by way of producing 'benefit' through 'the bread of affliction'], and so [ὥστε] it is set forth …."

Philo, *Congr.* 177: "In this way [οὕτως, i.e., by way of divine discipline as showing God's love – so Prov 3:11–12], then, rebuke and admonition are thought [to be] good, and so [ὥστε] through it confession to God becomes kinship [with him]" (against the LCL: "… are counted so excellent a thing, that they turn our acknowledgement of God into kinship with him").

Philo, *Somn.* 1.203: "For in this way [οὕτως, i.e., by way of similarity to the foulness with which the changeful disease of leprosy is regarded] certain people have considered the art of variegation an unimportant and obscure matter, and so [ὥστε] they have relegated it to weavers" (against the LCL: "For the art of variegation has been looked upon by some as so obscure and paltry a matter that they have relegated it to weavers"). (Philo proceeds to put a high valuation on variety.)

Philo, *Abr.* 31: The LCL reads, "So highly [οὕτως] does Moses extol the lover of virtue that [ὥστε] when he gives his [Noah's] genealogy he does not, as he usually does in other cases, make a list of his grandfathers, great-grandfathers and ancestors…, but of certain virtues." But the Greek text provides no justification for "highly." The translation should read, "In this way [i.e., by way of presenting the seventh day as 'the dominant mind' that triumphs over the five physical senses and joins speech to produce virtues – so the preceding context]

Moses extols the lover of virtue, and so when he gives his genealogy he does not....”

Philo, *Mos.* 1.234: Again, the LCL reads, “For the two [Israelite spies] who gave a highly favorable account were so [οὕτως] outweighed by the ten who said the opposite that [ὥστε] the latter brought over the whole multitude.” But Philo has just said that “courage confined to few is lost to sight, when timidity has the superiority of numbers.” A more plausible translation therefore reads, “For the two ... were outweighed in this way [i.e., by way of the larger number of timid spies]..., and so the latter [i.e., the timid ones] brought over the whole multitude.”

Philo, *Spec.* 2.87: Yet again, the LCL reads, “For some of the rich are so [οὕτως] poor-spirited that [ὥστε] when adversity overtakes them, they are as mournful and depressed as if they had been robbed of their whole substance.” But Philo has just spoken about rich people who resent “some loss” or “involuntary injury” as though it were “some strange and alien misfortune.” Hence the translation should read, “For some of the rich are poor-spirited in this way [i.e., by way of the just-mentioned resentment], and so when adversity overtakes them....”

Philo, *Prob.* 131: “Indeed, cocks are in this way [οὕτως, i.e., by way of exemplifying gallantry and endurance according to the preceding context] accustomed to struggle with a fondness for danger, and so [ὥστε] ... they continue [fighting] until death” (against the LCL: “Thus cocks are wont to fight with such intrepidity that rather than yield and withdraw, though outdone in strength yet not outdone in courage they continue fighting till they die”).

Philo, *Legat.* 157: “Rather, he [Augustus Caesar] hallowed our interests in this way [οὕτως, i.e., by way of neither ejecting the Jews from Rome nor taking away their Roman citizenship nor harming their places of prayer nor prohibiting their assembly for instructions in the laws nor opposing the firstfruit-offerings – again according to the preceding context], and so [ὥστε] ... he adorned our temple” (against the LCL: “Indeed so religiously did he respect our interests that supported by wellnigh his whole household he adorned our temple”). The ὥστε-clause adds a parallelistic positive to the earlier negatives referenced by οὕτως.

Philo, *Legat.* 163: “In this way [οὕτως, i.e., by way of calling the emperor Gaius ‘God’ so as to flatter him to their own advantage] the title of God is revered among them, and so [ὥστε] they have distributed it both to the ibises and venomous snakes and many other ferocious wild beasts” (against the LCL: “How much reverence is paid by them to the title of God is shown by their having allowed it to be shared by the indigenous ibises and...”). Apart from the translation of οὕτως ... ὥστε a correct understanding of this passage demands recognition of Philo’s biting sarcasm about the Alexandrians’ loose use of “God” for wild life as well as for Gaius the emperor.

According to Epictetus 1.11.1–5 et seqq. the philosopher asks an official how (πῶς...;) it is going with his family life. “Wretchedly,” the official answers. “In what way?” (τίνα τρόπον;), asks Epictetus, “For surely men do not marry and make children for themselves just for this, that they may be wretched, but rather that they [may be] happy!" The answer comes back, "Yet I feel thus [οὕτως] wretched about the [= 'my'] little children, and so [ὥστε] recently, when my little daughter was ill and seemed to be in danger, I did not stay even to be alongside her while she was ill but, taking flight, I departed till someone informed me, 'She is well.'" The LCL translates this last statement intensively: "I feel so wretched, that... I could not bear even to...." But there is nothing in the Greek text to justify "could," and the conversation goes on to deal with the questions whether the father had acted "rightly" (ὀρθῶς) or "naturally" (φυσικῶς) and whether there is a difference between acting in those ways. So the discussion does not have to do with intensity but with right versus wrong and with the natural versus the un-natural. That is to say, πῶς...; and τίνα τρόπον; make οὕτως refer to family-related wretchedness as such, not to it as intense; and the use of ὀρθῶς and φυσι-κῶς in the following discussion shows that it is not a high degree of family-re-lated wretchedness that Epictetus calls erroneous (twice he uses ἁμαρτάνω) but family-related wretchedness in and of itself that merits such a description.

Epictetus 4.11.19: "but it [the body of Socrates] was pleasing and sweet in this way [οὕτως, referring back to the statement that Socrates' body 'shone, gleamed, radiated' (ἔστιλβεν)], and so [ὥστε] the handsomest and highest-born loved him and longed to recline beside him rather than beside the comeliest" (against the LCL: "why, it was so attractive and sweet that...").

οὕτως by Itself in Johannine Literature

Now we try to determine the likelihood of a retrospective οὕτως in John 3:16:
"Thus is everyone begotten by the Spirit" (John 3:8): οὕτως refers back to the wind's blowing where it wants, and so on.
"Thus it is necessary for the Son of Man to be lifted up" (John 3:14): οὕτως refers back to Moses' lifting up the serpent in the wilderness.
"Jesus... was sitting thus at the well" (John 4:6): οὕτως refers back to his being wearied from a journey.
"Thus also the Son makes alive whomever he wills" (John 5:21): οὕτως refers back to the Father's raising the dead and making them alive.
"Thus also he has given to the Son to have life in himself" (John 5:26): οὕτως refers back to the Father's having life in himself.
"Never has a human being spoken thus" (John 7:46): οὕτως refers back to the manner of Jesus' speaking in earlier verses (33b–34, 36c–f, 37c–38).
"If we [the chief priests and the Pharisees] were to leave him thus" (John 11:48): οὕτως refers back to Jesus' performing many signs.
"Thus I speak" (John 12:50): οὕτως refers back to the Father's having spoken to Jesus.

"Therefore that [disciple], reclining thus on Jesus' chest" (John 13:25): οὕτως refers back to the beloved disciple's reclining in Jesus' bosom according to v. 23. Because of the intervening material in v. 24, the reclining is repeated in v. 25, with a typically Johannine use of synonymous expression, to make clear the referent of οὕτως.[13]

"Thus I do" (John 14:31): οὕτως refers back to the Father's commanding Jesus.

"Thus neither [can] you" (John 15:4): οὕτως refers back to the impossibility of a branch's bearing fruit of itself unless it abides in the vine.

"Do you answer the high priest thus?" (John 18:22): οὕτως refers back to Jesus' answer to the high priest in vv. 20–21.

"After those things Jesus manifested himself again to the disciples at the Sea of Tiberias, and he manifested [himself] thus" (John 21:1): this verse presents the only possible prospective use of οὕτως in John's Gospel. Its difference from the retrospective uses in chs. 1–20 might be considered an argument for different authorship of ch. 21 or, if there was no shift in authorship but a later addition of ch. 21, the prospective use may have arisen out of the interval of time that separated the writing of the last chapter from that of the preceding chapters. But apart from the questions of authorship and later addition we need to ask whether the οὕτως in 21:1 really does look forward. Instead, "thus" may refer back to Jesus' manifestation as a "self"-manifestation (so that the ἑαυτόν of v. 1a does not have to be repeated in v. 1b), as a further manifestation ("again" – v. 1a), and as a manifestation "at the Sea of Tiberias" (v. 1a). Following verses spell out the details, of course; but the normally retrospective use of οὕτως is sustainable by a reference to the features already mentioned in v. 1a. Even if not, this verse would present the sole prospective use among thirteen occurrences (excluding the one in 3:16) scattered throughout John's Gospel.

Let us bracket out further questions of authorship but bring into play occurrences of οὕτως in 1 John and the book of Revelation on the grounds of generally recognized connections that have caused many to think at least of a Johannine school (οὕτως not occurring in 2–3 John):

Whether or not οὕτως belongs to the original text of 1 John 2:6 (see the text critical apparatus), the reference is clearly backward: "just as that one walked, he also [ought] to walk thus."

1 John 4:8b–10, "God is love.... he loved us and sent his Son [as] a propitiation for our sins," provides the back-reference for οὕτως in 1 John 4:11: "Beloved, if God loved us thus."

"Thus you have also [people] holding the teaching of the Nicolaitans likewise" (Rev 2:15): οὕτως refers back to having people who hold the teaching of Balaam.

---

[13] Incidentally, οὕτως is omitted in ℵ A D W Θ Ψ *f*¹ 565 579 700 892 1241 *pm* lat sy sa pbo bo.

"The one who overcomes will thus be clothed in white garments" (Rev 3:5): οὕτως refers back to Jesus' promise of walking with him in white (v. 4). Or if οὕτως modifies νικῶν rather than περιβαλεῖται ("The one who thus overcomes") we have a back reference to the keeping of garments unsoiled (v. 4 again). Or perhaps we should accept the *v.l.* οὗτος (ℵ¹ Majority Text) instead of οὕτως (ℵ* A C 1006 2329 2344 2351 *al* latt sy co).

In Rev 3:16 οὕτως does not mean "thus" in the sense of "therefore," and it hardly looks forward to the μέλλω-clause as describing the way Jesus is about to vomit the Laodicean church out of his mouth. Rather, οὕτως belongs to the ὅτι clause and refers back to Jesus' statements, "I know your works, that you are neither cold nor hot. Would that you were cold or hot!" We should therefore translate v. 16 as follows: "Because you are thus lukewarm and neither hot nor cold ...." The hyperbaton that shoves οὕτως ahead of ὅτι in the Greek text emphasizes the way in which the lack of heat and cold has produced lukewarmness.

In Rev 9:17 οὕτως may be thought to refer to the following detailed description: "And thus I saw the horses in the vision and the ones sitting on them having breastplates, fiery and hyacinthine and sulphurous [in color]; and the horses' heads [were] like lions' heads, and out of their mouths proceed fire and smoke and sulphur." But οὕτως may equally well be thought to refer to the preceding indication that the horsemen numbered two hundred million. Favoring this latter construal is the emphasis put on the number of the horsemen right after their number is given and just before the καὶ οὕτως-clause: "I heard their number" (v. 16b).

"Thus he must be killed" (Rev 11:5): οὕτως refers back to the just-mentioned devouring fire.

Rev 16:18: "So very great an earthquake such as [οἷος ... τηλικοῦτος σεισμὸς οὕτω μέγας] has not occurred since human beings came to be on the earth." The overloaded Greek phrase defies word-for-word translation into even remotely natural English. Suffice it to say that the notion of high degree comes from τηλικ- in τηλικοῦτος and that οὕτω μέγας means "great in the way just described," viz., "such as has not occurred since human beings came to be on the earth."

"Thus with violence will Babylon, the great city, be thrown down" (Rev 18:21): οὕτως does not refer forward to ὁρμήματι ("with violence ... down"), but back to the statement earlier in v. 21: "And a strong angel took up a stone like a large millstone and threw [it] into the sea."

Lexical Conclusions

Although οὕτως like οὗτος may occasionally refer forward it usually refers backward and does so in Johannine literature nearly always, perhaps absolutely always. Furthermore, in combination with ὥστε, οὕτως regularly refers to something expressed prior to the ὥστε-clause and itself expresses a manner other than one of high degree. ὥστε in turn adds something more or less parallel to the earlier referent of οὕτως.

Interpretive Outcome

On the one hand, then, the statement in John 3:16, "for in this way God loved the world," means that God loved the world by way of determining (the δεῖ of scriptural and therefore divine necessitation) that the Son of Man be lifted up just as Moses lifted up the serpent in the wilderness (v. 14) and refers to Jesus' crucifixion, portrayed as usual in John as an exaltation.[14] On the other hand, the statement, "And so he [God] gave the only Son," likewise refers to Jesus' crucifixion (cf. 1 John 4:7–12, esp. 9–10) but presents a main clause to be paired with the earlier main clause, "in this way must the Son of Man be lifted up" (see our concluding layout). These two main clauses form the bases of a compound overall declaration (vv. 14–16a and 16b–17), each of whose halves is complex because of subordinate clauses attached to the main clauses. Since the second half deals with a carrying out of the determination stated in the first half we are encouraged to look for parallelism between the two halves. If we can discover parallelism it will fall right in line with the parallelistic style so evident and universally recognized elsewhere in John that it needs no elaboration here.

Let us search for parallelism, then – first, parallelism of thought. We have just noted that in compressed form v. 16b, "And so he gave the only Son," parallels the thought of v. 14, "And just as Moses lifted up the serpent in the wilderness, in this way must the Son of Man be lifted up." Because of this parallel we should treat ὥστε as introducing a restatement of v. 14 rather than a result of v. 16a ("for in this way God loved the world").[15] In expanded form v. 16c, "in

---

[14] The comparison with Moses' lifting up the serpent rules out the incarnation as a referent alongside crucifixion (against E. Haenchen, *A Commentary on the Gospel of John, Chapters 1–6* [Hermeneia; Philadelphia: Fortress, 1984], 205. On δεῖ as indicating scriptural necessity, see R. H. Gundry, *Mark* (Grand Rapids: Eerdmans, 1993), 446. Here in John 3:14 the allusion to Moses' lifting up the serpent in the wilderness (Num 21:9) supports the connotation of scriptural necessity.

[15] Since ὥστε appears nowhere else in Johannine literature we cite a typical example from Paul of ὥστε used to introduce a restatement, viz., 1 Cor 3:17: "And so [ὥστε] neither is the

order that everyone believing in him (εἰς αὐτόν) might not perish; rather, might have life eternal," parallels the thought and indeed almost all the wording of v. 15, "in order that everyone believing in him (ἐν αὐτῷ) might have life eternal," but probably with the difference that the "in him" of v. 16c goes with "everyone believing" rather than as in v. 15 with "might have life eternal."[16] And again in expanded form v. 17, "for God did not send the Son into the world in order that he might judge the world; rather, in order that the world might be saved through him," parallels the thought of v. 16a, "for in this way God loved the world."

Not only do we discover parallelism of thought. We also discover parallelism of structure. The leading statement in v. 16b opens with ὥστε just as the leading statement in v. 14 opens with καθώς and continues with οὕτως). The leading statement in v. 16b features "the only Son" just as the leading statement in v. 14 features "the Son of Man." Both leading statements are followed by a ἵνα-clause in which the subject is the same substantival participle (πᾶς ὁ πιστεύων – vv. 15 and 16c). And the closing statement in each half of the overall declaration is attached with the postpositive γάρ (vv. 16a and 17). Each γάρ is preceded by an adverb containing the diphthong ου (οὕτως and οὐ). And both of the closing statements feature ὁ θεός, "God," and τὸν κόσμον, "the world."

The οὕτως in v. 16a summarizes the way God loved the world as set out in detail by v. 14 (the determination that the Son of Man be lifted up just as Moses lifted up the serpent in the wilderness), so that v. 16a is considerably shorter than its match in v. 14. Inversely, the greater length of v. 16b as compared with its match in v. 15 is due to the addition of "might not perish," which in turn requires the further addition, "rather" (ἀλλʼ). These additions set up a contrast between perishing and having eternal life and thereby prepare for the further contrast in v. 17 between judging the world and the world's being saved. Thus the greater length of v. 17 as compared with its match in v. 16a is due to the ad-

---

planter anything nor [is] the irrigator anything, but God, who causes growth, [is everything]." These clauses restate the thought of vv. 5–6: "What then is Apollos? And what is Paul? Servants through whom you believed, even as the Lord gave to each one. I planted, Apollos irrigated, but God caused growth."

[16] On the other hand ἐν and εἰς were often interchanged. The two prepositional phrases appear in close proximity and in the same position within their respective clauses. That position favors a connection with "everyone believing" over a connection with "might have life eternal." And John likes to say things twice over. Therefore we just might consider ἐν αὐτῷ synonymous with εἰς αὐτόν. We also have to consider in v. 15 the strongly attested *v.l.* εἰς αὐτόν (ℵ 086 *f*[1] 33 205 565 it[a,fc] Gregory-Nyssa[vid] Cyril[ms]), which if adopted would create an exact correspondence with the comparable part of v. 16c. The exactness of this correspondence arouses a suspicion that some scribe was set on improving John's parallelism, however, though one could argue to the contrary (but probably less well) that some scribe changed εἰς αὐτόν to ἐν αὐτῷ for avoidance of monotony. For life in Christ see 1:4; 5:26; 1 John 5:11 (cf. John 5:39; 6:53; 1 John 3:15).

dition of "not… in order that he might judge the world," which again requires the further addition, "rather" (ἀλλ'). These additions produce another parallel, one contained in the second half of the overall declaration and featuring "rather" (ἀλλ') at the juncture in each pair of contrasts (cf. the double use of οὕτως in the first half of the overall declaration – vv. 14b, 16a).

"And just as Moses lifted up the serpent in the wilderness" provides a referent for "in this way must the Son of Man be lifted up." "In order that everyone believing might have in him life eternal" tells the purpose of the Son of Man's being lifted up. "For in this way God loved the world" supplies a reason for the necessity that the Son of Man be lifted up like the Mosaic serpent for the purpose of believers' having life eternal. That is to say, the γάρ-clause undergirds the whole of the preceding, not just the immediately preceding ἵνα-clause. "In this way" refers particularly to the necessity that the Son of Man be lifted up just as Moses lifted up the serpent in the wilderness, and "God loved the world" refers particularly to every believer's having in the Son of Man life eternal. The present indicative of δεῖ, "must," reflects the standpoint of Jesus, for whom being lifted up lay in the future, so that its necessity was ongoing at the time of speaking. The aorist indicative of ἔδωκεν, "gave," reflects the standpoint of John the evangelist, for whom God's giving the only Son lay in the past (cf. the use of this same verb for the crucifixion in 6:32–33, 51: "my Father gives you the true bread from heaven; for the bread of God is the one coming down out of heaven and giving life to the world…. and the bread that I will give for the world's life is my flesh").

Likewise, "in order that everyone believing in him might not perish; rather, might have life eternal" tells the purpose of God's giving the only Son. And "for God did not send the Son [and so on]" supplies a reason for God's giving the only Son in order that believers might not perish but have life eternal. That is to say, this γάρ-clause too undergirds the whole of the preceding (beginning with v. 16b), not just the immediately preceding ἵνα-clause. God's sending the only Son refers particularly to God's giving the Son, and the saving rather than judging of the world refers particularly to every believer's not perishing but having life eternal.

In conclusion, we may set forth in its original Greek the parallelistic structure of John 3:14–17 and then in English translation the grammatical structure of this same passage:

John 3:14–17 Treated as a Parallelistic Compound Sentence
(or as a Pair of Parallel Sentences)

Necessitation (3:14–16a)   Execution (3:16b–17)

καὶ καθὼς Μωϋσῆς ὕψωσεν
τὸν ὄφιν ἐν τῇ ἐρήμῳ

                               ὥστε τὸν υἱὸν τὸν μονογενῆ ἔδωκεν

οὕτως ὑψωθῆναι δεῖ τὸν υἱὸν
τοῦ ἀνθρώπου

ἵνα πᾶς ὁ πιστεύων ἐν αὐτῷ   ἵνα πᾶς ὁ πιστεύων εἰς αὐτὸν μὴ
                                        ἀπόληται

ἔχῃ ζωὴν αἰώνιον   ἀλλ' ἔχῃ ζωὴν αἰώνιον

                                    οὐ γὰρ ἀπέστειλεν ὁ θεὸς τὸν υἱὸν

                                    εἰς τὸν κόσμον

οὕτως γὰρ ἠγάπησεν ὁ
θεὸς τὸν κόσμον   ἵνα κρίνῃ τὸν κόσμον

                                    ἀλλ' ἵνα σωθῇ ὁ κόσμος δι' αὐτοῦ

Main Clauses (Unindented) and
Subordinate Clauses (Indented) in John 3:14–17

And just as Moses lifted up the serpent in the wilderness,
in this way must the Son of Man be lifted up
    in order that everyone believing might have in him life eternal,
        for in this way God loved the world;

and so God gave the only Son
    in order that everyone believing in him might not perish;
        rather, might have life eternal,
      for God did not send the Son into the world
    in order that he might judge the world;
        rather, in order that the world might be saved through him.

19. Angelomorphic Christology
in the Book of Revelation

Of late, interest in angelomorphic Christology has revived.[1] Because explicitly angelomorphic Christology appears more prominently in early Christian literature postdating the NT than in the NT itself, more attention has gone to that later literature.[2] To discover such Christology in the NT scholars have extrapolated backwards by inferring an angelomorphic Christology that stayed more or less underground in the NT but subsequently surfaced into full view. The OT and later Jewish literature are also adduced to support an underground Christology of this sort in the NT. For example, the portrayal of Melchizedek as a heavenly being in 11QMelch is combined with Melchizedek-Christology in Hebrews to infer the presence there of an underlying angelomorphic Christology (but *deeply* underlying, because Heb 1:4–14 emphatically distinguishes Jesus as a son from angels, who are much inferior). Similarly, an angelic identification of the "one like a son of man" in Dan 7:13 is put together with Son-of-Man Christology in the NT, and especially with the use for Jesus in Rev 1:7, 13; 14:14 of phraseol-

---

[1] See C. Rowland, "A Man Clothed in Linen: Daniel 10:6 ff. and Jewish Angelology," *JSNT* 24 (1985): 100, for "angelomorphic" as avoiding the categorization of Christ as a creature instead of deity (contrast the creaturely implication of "angelic"). A. F. Segal presents an example of recent interest in angelomorphic Christology and offers a brief history of such interest ("The Risen Christ and the Angelic Mediator Figures in Light of Qumran," in *Jesus and the Dead Sea Scrolls* [ed. J. H. Charlesworth; ABRL; New York: Doubleday, 1992], 302–28). See also H. Ulfgard, "In Quest of the Elevated Jesus: Reflections on the Angelomorphic Christology of the Book of Revelation within Its Jewish Setting," in *The New Testament as Reception* (ed. M. Müller and H. Tronier; JSNTSup 230; Sheffield: Sheffield Academic Press, 2002), 120–30.

[2] A partial bibliography: W. Lueken, *Michael* (Göttingen: Vandenhoeck & Ruprecht, 1898); J. Barbel, *Christos Angelos* (Bonn: P. Hanstein, 1941); M. Werner, *The Formation of Christian Dogma* (New York: Harper, 1957), 120–61; J. Daniélou, *The Theology of Jewish Christianity* (London: Darton, Longman and Todd/Chicago: Henry Regnery, 1964), 119–27; R. N. Longenecker, *The Christology of Early Jewish Christianity* (SBT 2/17; London: SCM, 1970), 26–32; C. H. Talbert, "The Myth of a Descending-Ascending Redeemer in Mediterranean Antiquity," *NTS* 22 (1976): 430–35; R. Lorenz, *Arius judaizaus?* (Forschungen zur Kirchen- und Dogmengeschichte 31; Göttingen: Vandenhoeck & Ruprecht, 1980), 141–79; L. W. Hurtado, *One God, One Lord* (Philadelphia: Fortress, 1988), 71–92; M. Mach, *Entwicklungsstadien des jüdischen Engelglaubens in vorrabbinischer Zeit* (TSAJ 34; Tübingen: Mohr [Siebeck], 1992), 287–91; E. Testa, *The Faith of the Mother Church* (Studium Biblicum Franciscanum, Collectio Minor 32; Jerusalem: Franciscan, 1992), 31–34; M. Barker, *The Great Angel: A Study of Israel's Second God* (Louisville: Westminster/John Knox, 1992), 190–232.

ogy from Dan 7:13 and from the description of a man-like but angelic figure in Daniel 10, to infer an angelomorphic portrayal of Jesus even though the term ἄγ-γελος, "angel, messenger," does not appear for him there.[3] Again similarly, the celebration of Christ's authority in Rev 12:10 after the victory over Satan of Michael and his angels is used to equate Christ with Michael, an archangel.[4]

With hardly any exception, however, the revival of interest in angelomorphic Christology has neglected the only passages in the NT where ἄγγελος may well apply to Jesus. These passages are found in the book of Revelation. Surprise at the recent neglect of them comes not only from the possibility of their using ἄγ-γελος for Jesus but also from the fact that older commentators – beginning with Victorinus and continuing up through the likes of Augustine, Andreas, Bede, Calovius, Vitringa, J. Gill, E. W. Hengstenberg, and E. B. Elliott (to name a few)[5] – quite often gave these passages a Jesuanic interpretation. Perhaps the time has come to reconsider it, perhaps even to revive it.

Pride of place belongs to Revelation 10 because there the evidence for a Jesuanic identification of the angel who dominates the passage has proved so strong (and will prove stronger than heretofore recognized) that even a few recent commentators have dared to adopt the identification.[6] The description of this angel as "clothed with a cloud" recalls 1:7, which said that Jesus "is coming with the clouds,"[7] so that the angel's "coming down out of heaven" (again 10:1) looks very like the second coming of Jesus from the "opened heaven" (19:11–16; see also 18:1 and 20:1 with the discussion below, and cf. the use of καταβαίνω for his first coming from heaven in John 3:13; 6:33, 38, 41, 42, 50, 51, 58[8]). The shift from "clouds" (plural – 1:7) to "a cloud" (singular – 10:1)

---

[3] C. Rowland, "The Vision of the Risen Christ in Rev. 1, 13 ff.: The Debt of an Early Christology to an Aspect of Jewish Angelology," *JTS* ns 31 (1980): 111; idem, "A Man Clothed in Linen," 99–110; A. Y. Collins in J. J. Collins, *Daniel* (Hermeneia; Minneapolis: Fortress, 1993), 102, 104–5.

[4] For this last exegesis see J. J. Collins, "The Son of Man and the Saints of the Most High in the Book of Daniel," *JBL* 93 (1974): 65–66. Collins' argument has its weaknesses, however: (1) he speaks about the awarding of the kingdom to Christ, but the biblical text about the taking place (ἐγένετο) of Christ's authority; (2) the immediately preceding part of the biblical text parallelistically speaks about the taking place of "salvation and power and the kingdom of our God," yet no one would equate God with Michael.

[5] See esp. the dialogue carried on with these and other older commentators by H. A. W. Meyer, *Critical and Exegetical Handbook to the Revelation of John* (New York: Funk & Wagnalls, 1887), and H. Alford, *The Greek Testament* (4th ed.; London: Rivingtons/Cambridge: Deighton, Bell, and Co., 1871).

[6] H. Kraft, *Die Offenbarung des Johannes* (HNT 16a; Tübingen: Mohr [Siebeck], 1974), 147; J. P. M. Sweet, *Revelation* (Philadelphia: Westminster, 1979), 176; M. Barker, *The Great Angel*, 76; G. K. Beale, *The Book of Revelation* (NIGTC; Grand Rapids: Eerdmans/Carlisle, UK: Paternoster, 1999), 522–26. Beale emphasizes OT background..

[7] See also Mark 13:26; 14:62; Matt 24:30; 26:64; Luke 21:27; Acts 1:9–11; cf. Dan 7:13; 1 Thess 4:17.

[8] In view of John 3:13 ("And no one has ascended into heaven except the one having descended out of heaven, [viz.,] the Son of Man"), the ascending and descending of angels on the

need not imply a difference in personal identity. The plural appears in Mark 13:26; Matt 24:30 but the singular in the parallel Luke 21:27; the plural in 1 Thess 4:17 for the clouds in which the saints are caught up at the Parousia but the singular in Rev 11:12 for the cloud in which the two witnesses, probably standing for the saints, ascend into heaven at the end, and the singular again in Acts 1:9–11 for the cloud in which Jesus was taken up at his ascension – and he will come back "in the same manner." The well-known use of clouds as a theophanic symbol[9] combines with the present angel's being "clothed" with a cloud to support his deification. That is to say, he wears the divine majesty that elsewhere in Revelation is worn only by Jesus in addition to God.[10] That the sitter on a cloud in Rev 14:14–16 carries the description "one like a son of man" and that this description comes from the very text, Dan 7:13, which supplies phraseology for Jesus' return in Rev 1:7a as well as elsewhere (Mark 13:26; 14:62; Matt 24:30; 26:64; Luke 21:27) favors an identification of the angel in 10:1 and his coming down out of heaven with Jesus, the one like a son of man, and with his coming down out of heaven at the Parousia (cf. also the use of Dan 7:9, 13 for Jesus in Rev 1:13–14).

The rainbow on the head of this angel recalls the rainbow arching over the throne of God in Rev 4:3 (cf. Ezek 1:26–28). Since Jesus occupies the throne of God (3:21; 22:1, 3), its rainbow signifies him as well as God and thereby identifies the angel with Jesus.[11]

ὡς ὁ ἥλιος, "as the sun," describes the angel's face (πρόσωπον). This description recalls the description in 1:16 of Jesus' face (ὄψις, a synonym of πρόσωπον): ὡς ὁ ἥλιος φαίνει ἐν τῇ δυνάμει αὐτοῦ, "as the sun shines in its power" (cf. 21:23; 22:5; Matt 17:2). We may well think that in 10:1 John omits φαίνει κτλ out of an expectation that his audience will supply it by memory of 1:16, just as the first ὡς-phrase in 1:15 is meant to be supplied in 2:18 (see the following paragraph and footnote here). John's describing the faces of Jesus and the angel with the same simile favors an identification of the angel with Jesus.

Son of Man (John 1:51) presupposes his prior descent and ascent. See R. Schnackenburg, "'Der Vater, der mich gesandt hat': Zur johanneische Christologie," *Anfänge der Christologie* (ed. C. Breytenbach and H. Paulsen; Göttingen: Vandenhoeck & Ruprecht, 1991), 284–85, on the close interrelationship of Johannine Son-of-Man Christology with descent from heaven and ascent to heaven.

[9] See numerous references in R. H. Gundry, *Mark* (Grand Rapids: Eerdmans, 1993), 460, 745, 785–86.

[10] See 1:12–16; 5:11–14; 7:9–17; 11:15–18; 12:10; 19:11–16; 21:22–22:5. The use of clouds for taking up the two witnesses and the saints in Rev 11:12; 1 Thess 4:17 does not weaken this theophanic implication; rather, it indicates a divine reception of the witnessing saints.

[11] R. C. H. Lenski objects to a correlation with 4:3 on the ground that there the rainbow is large enough to encircle God's throne whereas the rainbow here rests only on the angel's head (cf. *Apoc. Abr.* 11:3; *The Interpretation of St. John's Revelation* [Columbus: Wartburg, 1943], 312). This objection presumes what needs proof, viz., that John means to convey information about size.

The description of the angel's feet (here including the legs; cf. Dan 10:6) ὡς στῦλοι πυρός, "as pillars of fire," recalls the description in 1:15; 2:18 of Jesus' feet, ὅμοιοι χαλκολιβάνῳ ὡς ἐν καμίνῳ πεπυρωμένης, "like burnished bronze, fired as in a furnace,"[12] only with a shift from burnished bronze to pillars (the elements of feet and fire remaining the same) for an allusion to the pillar of fire (doubled to match a pair of feet) by which Yahweh led Israel from bondage in Egypt (Exod 13:21–22; 14:19, 24). Again the correspondence favors an identification of the angel with Jesus.

The angel has in his hand a scroll. This scroll looks very like the scroll that Jesus took in 5:1–8;5, "Hand" appears in both 5:1 (by the implication of τὴν δεξιάν – cf. 1:16, 17; 10:5; 13:16) and 10:2, 8, 10, though because of the taking in 5:2, 7–8 the scroll has shifted from the hand of God to Jesus' hand.[13] Jesus took the scroll to open it (5:2, 3, 4, 5, 9); and now that he has opened it by opening the seven seals that kept it closed (6:1, 2, 5, 7, 9, 12; 8:1) John describes it as "opened" (ἠνεῳγμένον – perfect tense; 10:2, 8). Though this description contrasts with the earlier description "sealed" (κατεσφραγισμένον – likewise perfect tense; 5:1), the contrast does not prove a difference between the two scrolls (despite statements to this effect by numerous commentators). On the contrary! Inasmuch as Jesus has opened all seven seals between chs. 5 and 10, the opened state of the scroll in ch. 10 favors the identity of this scroll with the formerly sealed one which in ch. 5 Jesus took to open. N.B. that opening the *scroll* in 5:2, 3, 4, 5 merges into opening its *seals* in 5:5, 9; 6:1, 3, 5, 7, 9, 12; 8:1, so that the opening of the seals has produced an opened scroll.[14]

---

[12] The ὡς-phrase is missing in 2:18 but is almost certainly meant to be supplied by the memory of 1:15.

[13] A. Y. Collins sets out further parallels between chs. 5 and 10 but comes to a different conclusion regarding the scrolls (*The Combat Myth* [HDR 9; Missoula: Scholars Press, 1976], 21).

[14] This merger comes out most clearly in the compound phrase, "to open the scroll and its seven seals" (5:5), and spoils the argument of Alford that the scroll of ch. 10 must differ from that of ch. 5 because the earlier scroll has not been opened, but only its seals, whereas the present scroll has been opened (*The Greek Testament*, 4: 654). Some commentators attribute the opened state of this scroll to John's borrowing from Ezek 2:10, not to Jesus' having opened the scroll of ch. 5, and thereby free themselves to distinguish the present scroll from the earlier one (see, e.g., I. T. Beckwith, *The Apocalypse of John* [New York: Macmillan, 1922], 580). To be sure, John's eating the scroll in 10:8–11 borrows from Ezek 2:8–3:11. But there the scroll appears as still closed when Ezekiel is told to eat it, and then it is opened as he watches, whereas here the scroll appears as already opened some time before John is told to eat it. This difference favors that the already opened state of the scroll in Revelation 10 derives from Rev 6:1–17; 8:1–5, not from Ezek 2:10. It might be argued that the recommissioning of John (10:11: "You must prophesy again") after he has eaten the scroll requires that it has to do with following materials as distinct from preceding materials related to a different earlier scroll (cf. A. Y. Collins, *The Combat Myth*, 26–32). But the symbolism of eating so as to prophesy, as in Ezek 2:8–3:11, is satisfied by understanding the further prophesying to deal with the same process that the past prophesying has dealt with, i.e., the process by which Jesus takes his rightful possession of the world. The sameness of the process eliminates any need to distinguish between scrolls. Naturally, equation of the scrolls in chs. 5 and 10 invalidates the many attempts to specify the tex-

The use of βιβλαρίδιον for the scroll of 10:2 ℵ* A C² P 1 2351 al (cf. βιβλιδάριον [ℵ¹] C* 1006 1611 1841 2053 2344 al; βιβλάριον 2329 pc), 8 ℵ P 1
2344 2351 al (cf. βιβλιδάριον Majority Text; βιβλάριον 2329), 9 Aᶜ C P 1 2351
al (cf. βιβλιδάριον Majority Text; βιβλάριον A* 2329), 10 A C 2344 2351 Majority Textᴬ (cf. βιβλιδάριον 1006 1611 1841 2053 al; βιβλίδιον P⁴⁷ pc) does
not block an equation with the βιβλίον of 5:1, 2, 3, 4, 5, 7, 8, 9; for both βιβλαρίδιον and βιβλίον are diminutives of the same word βίβλος. Thus βιβλαρίδιον does not have to refer to a scroll smaller than the one referenced by βιβλίον. Furthermore, John's interchanging of βίβλος and βιβλίον for one and the
same "scroll of life" shows that for him a diminutive form of this word need not
have any distinguishing function (see 3:5; 13:8 P⁴⁷ℵ 1611 1854 2344 al; 20:15
for the βίβλος of life; 13:8 C; 17:8; 20:12; 21:27 for the βιβλίον of life; cf. the
interchanging of πρόβατον with the diminutives ἀρνίον and προβάτιον in
John 21:15, 16, 17 [including v.ll.]). Furthermore again, 10:2 P⁴⁷ᵛⁱᵈ Majority
Text gig vgᵐˢˢ Vic Tyc Prim, 8 A C 1006 1611 1841 1854 2053 pc lat, 9 P⁴⁷ ℵ
1006 1841 1854 2053 pc latt, 10 ℵ 1854 Majority Textᴷ lat read βιβλίον for the
scroll of ch. 10 just as in ch. 5.

The angel's placement of his right foot on the sea and of his left on the land
(10:2, 5, 8) symbolizes his taking possession of the whole world (cf. 5:13; 7:1,
2, 3; 10:6; 12:12; 14:7; 16:2–3; 21:1), even that part of it harboring the chaotic
forces of evil (the sea; cf. 5:13; 13:1; 21:1), as rightfully his (for placing one's
feet on something as owning and possessing it see Gen 13:17; Deut 1:36; 11:25;
Josh 1:1–9, esp. v. 3; 4:9; Zech 14:4; Acts 7:5). That John mentions this element
of his vision no fewer than three times puts great emphasis on the possession-
taking. Because the angel has opened the scroll, which is a title deed to the
world,[15] the angel can take possession. Jesus' taking the scroll in ch. 5 indicated

---

tual boundaries of the scroll in ch. 5 as, say, 6:1–8:5 or 6:1–11:19, and those of the scroll in ch. 10
as, say, 11:1–13 or 12:1–22:5.

[15] When at first no one is found worthy to take the scroll and open its seals, John weeps because the evil forces that have usurped control will persecute the saints so long as the rightful
owner does not take possession. The scroll should be viewed as a title deed, then, not as a book
of destiny in which future events are inscribed. With the opening of each seal certain events
take place, to be sure. But these events do not make up the contents of the scroll, for it is not
open for the reading of its contents till all seven seals are opened. Nor is any reading said to be
done on the opening of each seal, or even after all seven seals have been opened (contrast *1
En.* 81:1–3; 93:1–3; 103:1–2; 106:19–107:1, the sealing in heaven at 108:7 B C having prevented
a reading on earth without prevention of a reading by heavenly angels). The opening of the
seals does not *reveal* events; it *causes* events just as conversely the sealing up of the seven
thunders in 10:3b–4 does not conceal events so much as it keeps them from taking place (the
equivalent in John's Apocalypse of the shortening of the great tribulation in the so-called Little
Apocalypse [Mark 13:19–20 par. Matt 24:21–22]) and just as the command that John "not seal
up the words of the prophecy of this scroll" (22:10) has the purpose not of ensuring their publication but of ensuring their fulfillment (as likewise in the OT the very speaking or acting out of
prophetic words ensured, indeed contributed to, their own fulfillment [L. Dürr, *Die Wertung des
göttlichen Wortes im Alten Testament und im antiken Orient* (MVAG [E.V.] 42/1; Leipzig: Hin-

rightful ownership (so the implication of the question, "Who is *worthy* to open the scroll and loosen its seals?" and of the statements, "And no one was able... to open the scroll or look [inside] it," "no one was found worthy," "Behold, the lion... has conquered to open the scroll and its seven seals," and "Worthy are you to take the scroll and open its seals" [5:2, 3, 4, 5, 9]). But rightful ownership was one thing. Taking possession is another. The events triggered by Jesus' opening of the seven seals enabled him to seize his property, the world, from those forces of evil who had usurped control over it, so that "the kingdom of the world has become [the kingdom] of our Lord and of his Christ" (11:15). This possession-taking confirms the identification of the scroll as a title deed and equates the angel who puts his feet on the world's two constituent parts, sea and land, with Jesus the Christ, who with his Lord now establishes his rule over the world.

The loudness of the angel's voice tends toward the same equation (see n. 30), and "as a lion roars" recalls the portrayal of Jesus as a conquering lion (5:5; cf. Joel 4[3]:16; Amos 3:8; 2 Esd 11:37; 12:31–32).[16] The use of ὡς-phrases for comparisons of Jesus' loud voice in 1:10 and 4:1 (with the blast of a trumpet), 1:15 (with the sound of many waters), and 14:2 (with the sound of many waters and of loud thunder – for the voice of the Lamb plus the 144,000 "with him"[17]) combines with the present ὥσπερ-phrase to provide minor support for an identification of the angel with Jesus (cf. occurrences of ὡς-phrases in other descriptions of Jesus [1:14 (three times), 15, 16; 2:18, 27; 3:3; 5:6; 16:15], though ὡς-phrases describe voices other than his in 6:1; 19:6 [three times; but in both passages for a collective voice, Jesus' voice being the only one of a lone individual described as loud as this or that] and also draw other comparisons quite unrelated to Jesus [passim]).

Though sometimes thought to rule out an identification with Jesus,[18] the angel's raising his right hand to heaven and swearing by the ever-living Creator (10:5–6; cf. Dan 12:7) suits well the element of subordination to God in Johannine Christology (cf. the implication of "our Lord and his Christ" in 11:15).[19]

---

richs, 1938)]). The very next clause, "for the time is near" (contrast the sealing for secrecy in Dan 12:9 because the time of the end lies at a temporal distance from Daniel), has to do with fulfillment (see 1:1, 3), not with publication (cf. T. Holtz, *Die Christologie der Apokalypse des Johannes* [2d ed.; TU 85; Berlin: Akademie, 1971], 35–36; against A. Y. Collins, *The Combat Myth*, 24–25, though Collins does take note that deeds are to be included among legal documents sealed in the ancient world [p. 22; cf. Jer 32:9–15]).

[16] Comparisons with lions' teeth and heads at 9:8, 17 use λέων in the plural. The singular in a comparison with the mouth of a lion (so 13:2) draws on Dan 7:4 and parodies Jesus (see the whole of 12:18–13:18 for a Satanic trinity).

[17] The Lamb is "standing," not seated on his throne (14:1), and a new song is sung "before the throne and before the four living creatures and before the elders" (14:3). Therefore the 144,000's standing with the Lamb (14:1) seems to imply that his and their voices are one.

[18] R. H. Mounce, *The Book of Revelation* (2d ed.; NICNT; Grand Rapids: Eerdmans, 1998), 201.

[19] See Rev 1:1, 6; 2:26; 3:2, 12; John 5:19–20, 30; 7:16; 10:29. After noting the parallel be-

According to Deut 32:40 God lifts his hand to heaven and says, i.e., swears, "As I live forever…"; and in Heb 6:13 God even swears by himself, so that neither swearing itself nor swearing by God implies less than deity in the swearer. The fact that earlier in Revelation John has referred four times to the right hand of Jesus (1:16, 17, 20; 2:1), the only exception being the right hand of God his Father (5:1, 7), also lends some support to an identification of the angel with Jesus. In view of the many parallels in Johannine Christology between Jesus the Son and God his Father (in Revelation, for example, they share the same throne, kingdom, and authority – 3:21; 5:13; 6:16; 7:9–11, 15–17; 11:15; 12:5, 10; 20:6; 22:1, 3), the two earlier references to God's right hand add to this support.[20]

The angel's instruction to John that he eat the scroll draws on Ezek 2:8–3:3 (cf. Jer 15:16). In that passage God gives the instruction. It seems likely, then, that in Rev 10:9–11 the same instruction is given by none less than the divine angel-messenger, viz., Jesus.

If the "voice from heaven" (10:4, 8) is the voice of God, as seems likely (cf. 6:6; 9:13; 11:12; 14:13; 16:1, 17; and esp. 18:4), we have a hint of the ange-lomorphic Christ in the plural of λέγουσιν, "they say," at 10:11. For elsewhere in Revelation Christ is constantly paired with God.[21] It would therefore make good sense to identify the "they" who recommission John as the angelomorphic Christ, who has just spoken to him (10:9), and God, who spoke to John just before the angel did (10:4, 8). After all, it was Christ through whom God gave John his original commission to prophesy (see 1:11 with 1:1–2[22]).

How then do John's other descriptions of the angel fit an identification with Jesus? It has been argued that John's describing the angel as ἄλλος (10:1) fore-stalls an identification with Jesus because ἄλλος means "another of the same kind" whereas Jesus would be ἕτερος, "another of a different kind," i.e., a divine angel and therefore one who is uniquely superior.[23] But the distinction be-

---

tween Rev 10:5–6 and Dan 12:7 R.H. Charles draws an equation between the man in Dan 12:7 and the man-like Gabriel in Dan 8:15–16 and suggests that John's describing the angel in Rev 10:1 as strong plays on the similarity between גבריאל ("Gabriel") and גבור ("strong man"; *A Critical and Exegetical Commentary on the Revelation of St. John* [ICC; Edinburgh: T. & T. Clark, 1920], 1:258–59). Since John never mentions Gabriel, however, even though he does mention Michael (Rev 12:7), such a play would hardly prove an identification of the angel with Gabriel rather than with Jesus. Even if an anonymous allusion to the angel Gabriel were to be accepted it might represent an identification of Jesus with the angel Gabriel just as *Herm. Sim.* 8.3.3 with 9.12.78 may represent an identification of Jesus with the angel Michael.

[20] The imprint of the mark of the Beast on the right hand of his worshippers has yet to appear (13:16); and inasmuch as the Beast parodies Christ, that later reference hardly damages a reference to the right hand of Christ in John's mention of the angel's right hand.

[21] See 1:1–2, 4–6, 9; 2:28; 3:2, 5, 12, 14, 21; 4:11 with 5:9–14; 6:16–17; 7:9–17; 11:15; 12:10, 17; 14:4, 10, 12; 20:4, 6; 21:22–23; 22:1, 3 et passim in the Gospel of John.

[22] See the comments below on the angel in 1:1–2.

[23] See, e.g., R.L. Thomas, *Revelation 1–7* (Chicago: Moody, 1992), 467 (though with reference to the same expression in 7:2–3).

tween ἄλλος and ἕτερος does not hold.[24] ἕτερος appears nowhere in Revelation, and ἄλλος sometimes means "another of a different kind": a red horse as opposed to a white one (6:2, 4), an angel ascending from the East and having the seal of the living God as differentiated from four angels standing at the four corners of the earth and holding its four winds (7:1–2), and an angel standing at the heavenly altar as distinct from seven angels who stand before God and to whom seven trumpets were given (8:2–3). Though both signs qualify as great and heavenly the "other (ἄλλο) sign" of the great dragon, the ancient serpent called the Devil and Satan, surely differs in kind from the sign of the woman who bears the messianic child (12:1, 3, 9) as does also the "other (ἄλλο) sign," again heavenly and great, of the seven angels having the seven last plagues of God's wrath (15:1). The "other (ἄλλο) beast" of 13:11 differs from the beast of 13:1 by coming up out of the earth and having two horns rather than coming up out of the sea and having ten horns. The description of the "other (ἄλλο) scroll" as the scroll "of life" containing the names of the saints seems to put it in a category different from that of "the scrolls," apparently the scrolls containing a record of human beings' "deeds" (20:12). To stay within the Johannine corpus for one further example but with respect to ἕτερος, the "other (ἑτέρα) Scripture" of John 19:37 surely does not differ in kind from the Scripture of John 19:36.[25] Though ἄλλος calls attention to similarity, then (otherwise why use the word at all?), distinctions are not ruled out. Thus in 10:1 ἄλλον calls attention to similarity with regard to angelhood but does not rule out a uniquely superior kind of angelhood.

John's description of the angel as "strong" (10:1) does not favor a Jesuanic identification, but neither does it disfavor that identification. Some have argued contrariwise that the description of angels as "strong" also in 5:2 and 18:21 does disfavor it because the angel in 5:2 differs from Jesus the Lion and Lamb, the parallel with 10:1 then favoring a similar differentiation there. But reasons will come to light below for identifying the strong angel of 18:21 with Jesus, and in any case 18:8 describes as "strong" the Lord God who judges Babylon. If the description "strong" does not cancel out other reasons to see the Lord God as superior to beings similarly described neither does this same description of the angel in ch. 10 cancel out the reasons just canvassed for seeing him as superior to the angel similarly described in 5:2. That the two angels differ from each other, in fact, is supported by the one angel's never even touching the scroll in ch. 5 (the scroll is passed from God to Jesus) whereas the other angel is holding the scroll in ch. 10.[26]

[24] BDAG, s.v. ἄλλος 2a, ἕτερος 1bγ.
[25] Cf. R. H. Gundry, "On True and False Disciples in Matthew 8.8–22," *NTS* 40 (1994): 433–41; idem, "In Defense of the Church in Matthew as a *Corpus Mixtum*," *ZNW* 91 (2000): 153–65.
[26] Against Alford, *The Greek Testament*, 4:649.

It might also be argued that an interpretation of the angel's descent from heaven in terms of the second coming puts that coming too early in the book of Revelation. But the fullest description of that coming, i.e., the description in 19:11–16, has been anticipated already in 1:7. And within the main body of the book prior to 19:11–16 the sixth seal has brought things to the verge of the end (cf. 6:12 with Mark 13:24–27 par. Matt 24:29–31) and the seventh seal to the end itself (so the meaning of a half hour's silence in heaven, the casting of fire to earth from the heavenly altar, and the peals of thunder, rumblings, flashes of lightning, and earthquake – accompaniments of the Parousia like those of the theophany at Sinai [cf. 8:1–5 with Exod 19:16–19; 20:18; 24:15–18; Judg 5:4–5; Heb 12:18–19]) just as the seventh trumpet and the seventh bowl will bring things to the end itself, the Parousia (11:15–19: "The kingdom of the world has become [the kingdom] of our Lord and of his Christ.... you [Lord God Almighty] have taken your great power and reigned [ἐβασίλευσας, an inceptive aorist: 'begun to reign'] .... and your wrath has come and the time of the dead to be judged and to give reward to your servants the prophets [et al.]," plus an opening of the heavenly temple, a display of the ark of the covenant, flashes of lightning, rumblings, peals of thunder, an earthquake, and a great hailstorm; 16:17–20: "It has happened!" plus flashes of lightning, rumblings, peals of thunder, a great earthquake, the fall of Babylon and of the cities of the nations, the disappearance of every island and mountain, and a great hailstorm; see also 11:11–13; 14:14–20 for other anticipations of the end). So there is no problem of order in understanding the angel's descent at 10:1 in terms of the second coming.

An angel in some respects reminiscent of the one in ch. 10 appears at 18:1–3. The description ἄλλον, "another," has already been found uninimical to a christological identification. "Coming down out of heaven" links up with the same phrase in 10:1, where we found ample reason to make an identification of the angel with Jesus. Just as there the angel's descent to take possession of sea and land represented what Jesus will do at the second coming, so here too the angel's descent represents what Jesus will do at the second coming, i.e., preside over the fall of Babylon, which the angel proceeds to announce (see also the comments below on the descent of an angel from heaven in 20:1–3 to seize the Dragon and throw him into the abyss; cf. the throwing of the Dragon's Beast and False Prophet, the latter also a beast according to 13:11–12, into the lake of fire at the second coming [19:20]).

The greatness of this angel's authority (ἔχοντα ἐξουσίαν μεγάλην – 18:1) likewise suits the authority of God's Christ in 12:10, an authority which there relates to the downfall of the Dragon, Devil, or Satan just as in 20:1 the angel coming down out of heaven will throw the Dragon, Devil, or Satan into the abyss. The Beast who suffered a mortal wound but lived (or came to life [13:1–10, 12, 14; 17:8, 11]) – i.e., the second person of the unholy trinity of

Dragon, Beast, and False Prophet – stands over against Christ the Lamb, who died and came to life (1:5, 18; 2:8; 5:6), the Second Person of the Holy Trinity. Therefore the description of the angel's authority as "great" in 18:1 combines with the description of the Beast's authority as "great" in 13:2 (cf. 13:4, 5, 7, 12) and with the lack of this description for anyone else's authority in Revelation (see 2:26; 6:8; 9:3 [twice], 10, 19; 11:6 [twice]; 17:12, 13; 20:6; 22:14) to favor an identification of the angel having great authority in 18:1 with Jesus the Lamb, messianic counterpart to the Beast having great authority in 13:2.

The enlightenment of the earth with the glory of this angel anticipates the enlightenment of the new Jerusalem, which like the angel comes down out of heaven to the earth (21:1–4), with the glory of God and of Jesus the Lamb (21:23–25; 22:4–5; cf. Ezek 43:2) to further the identification of the angel with Jesus.[27] The strength of the angel's voice tends toward this identification (see n. 30 and 10:3). Because of the frequent pairing of God and Jesus throughout Revelation[28] the pairing of the angel, who announces that Babylon has fallen (18:1–3), with God, who calls his people out of Babylon and describes in detail the fall of Babylon (18:4–20), yet again points to an identification of the angel with Jesus.[29]

At 18:21 a "strong angel" appears, as earlier in 5:2; 10:1. Just recently 18:8 has described "the Lord God who judges her [Babylon]" as "strong." This description-cum-action of the Lord God parallels that of the strong angel who in 18:21 picks up a large millstone and throws it into the sea as a sign of Babylon's judgment. The parallel suggests an identification of the strong angel with Jesus inasmuch as this angel and his activity are paired with God and God's activity in accordance with Johannine Christology and 10:1–11; 18:13, where additional considerations favored the identification.[30]

---

[27] For Jesus as the light of the world in Johannine literature see also John 1:4–5, 7–9; 3:19–21; 8:12; 9:5; 11:9–10; 12:35–36, 46; and for the glory of Jesus, Rev 5:12–13; 15:3–4 et passim in the Gospel of John.

[28] See n. 21.

[29] It might be objected that the order elsewhere in Revelation, viz., God–Jesus, militates against a present identification, which would reverse that order. But 20:4 presents a clear case of the reverse order (cf. also 1:1), so that the objection would fail.

[30] The strong angel in 5:2 seems to differ from Jesus. But since ch. 5 acknowledgedly portrays Jesus as both a lion and a lamb, perhaps – just perhaps – we should allow the possibility of an identification between him and this strong angel proclaiming "with a loud voice, 'Who is worthy to open the scroll and loosen its seals?'" Jesus is the only one to have earlier spoken with a loud voice (1:10); and apart from the loud voice of crowds in 5:12; 6:9; 7:10; 11:15; 12:10; 19:1 (cf. 14:2) the individual speakers with a loud voice in 7:2; 8:13; 10:3; 11:12 (cf. 4:1 with 1:1); 14:6; 16:1, 17; 18:2 *v.l.*; 19:17; 21:3 are either certainly or conceivably to be identified with Jesus. The matter remains in doubt, however, because the speakers with a loud voice can hardly be identified with Jesus at least in 14:7, 9, 15, 19. Nevertheless, the loud voice of the strong angel in 10:1; 18:21 agrees with the same in 1:10; 4:1 (with 1:1); 11:12, where little or no doubt exists that Jesus is speaking. Just as deity as well as less-than-deity is described as strong, so the voice of deity as well as that of less-than-deity may be described as loud, so that

Since in 18:21–24 an angel *not* called "another" to distinguish him from the last-mentioned angel in 18:1 announces the fall of Babylon just as did that angel, we should probably equate these angels and thus identify the one in 18:21 with Jesus because of the evidence for such an identification in 18:1–3. The parallel between descriptions of the present angel as "strong" (ἰσχυρός) and of the earlier angel's voice as likewise "strong" supports this argument, especially as everywhere else in Revelation (and this twenty times!) voices are said to be "loud" (μεγάλη) but not "strong."[31] Perhaps εἷς, attached in 18:21 to ἄγγελος and meaning "one," is designed to equate these angels. The usual translation is "an," and one should not dispute the possibility of this translation. But its propriety may be questioned here (cf. John 7:21; 8:41; 10:16; 11:49, 50; 18:14, 22; 20:7). If the angel of 18:21 is to be identified with Jesus, the use of εἷς likewise agreeing in gender, case, and number with a noun in 8:13; 9:13; 19:17 and only in these passages so far as Revelation is concerned suggests that in them too an adventurous identification should be made between Jesus and the eagle crying with a loud voice as it flies in midheaven, the voice from the four horns of the golden altar before God (cf. the comments below on 8:3–5), and the angel standing in the sun, respectively.[32]

As in 10:1–7; 18:1–3 the angel's coming down out of heaven to take possession of sea and land and to preside over the fall of Babylon represented what Jesus will do at the second coming, so too in 20:1–3 the angel's coming down out of heaven to bind Satan and throw him into the abyss represents what Jesus will do at the second coming. "Having the key of the abyss" recalls Jesus' having "the keys of death and of hades" in 1:8 (cf. 3:7–8). In 9:1 a fallen star seems to represent the angel of the abyss, probably Satan (9:11). His being given (ἐδόθη, probably a "divine passive") the key of the shaft of the abyss parodies Jesus' having keys and thus favors an identification of the angel having the key of the abyss with Jesus.[33] It would also seem to take no less a figure than Jesus to

---

the loudness of the angel's voice in 10:1; 18:21 should in no way inhibit the recognition of a divine angel Jesus as distinct from creatures less-than-divine though they too have loud voices.

[31] See 1:10; 5:2, 12; 6:10; 7:2, 10; 8:13; 10:3; 11:12, 15; 12:10; 14:7, 9, 15, 18; 16:1, 17; 19:1, 17; 21:3 (cf. 14:2).

[32] For several reasons the standing of "one angel ... in the sun" (ἕνα ἄγγελον ... ἐν τῷ ἡλίῳ) in 19:17 may slightly favor an identification with Jesus: (1) Jesus' face shone like the sun in 1:16; (2) the angel who for other reasons may be identified with him in 7:2 (see the discussion below) ascends from the rising of the sun; (3) the angelomorphic Christ of 10:1 has a face like the sun; (4) the light of the Lamb as well as of God eliminates any need of the sun for the new Jerusalem (21:23; 22:5); and (5) the very frequency of Jesus' association with the sun adds some support. See the foregoing discussion for the loudness of the angel's voice. On the other hand, "in the sun" may merely indicate a position that all the birds of prey can see just as the loudness indicates a voice they all can hear (cf. 8:13; 14:6–7).

[33] See M. S. Moore, "Jesus Christ: 'Superstar' (Revelation xxii 16b)," *NovT* 24 (1982): 82–91, for a possible contrast between Jesus as the bright and morning star and Satan as a fallen star, with stars indicating angels or deities.

seize the Dragon, Devil, or Satan, bind him, throw him into the abyss, and lock him up there for a thousand years (cf. Matt 12:29; John 12:31; *1 En.* 10:4–6; 10:11–12). Michael and his angels succeeded only in throwing the Dragon and his angels down to earth, where the Dragon and his angels were then able to vent their wrath (12:7–17). The angel's sealing the abyss in 20:3 recalls the multiple earlier associations of Jesus with seals (5:1–2, 5, 9; 6:1, 3, 5, 7, 9, 12; 7:2 [according to the interpretation offered below]; 8:1; cf. 7:4–8 for the seal of God, with whom Revelation often pairs Jesus) and thus offers further support for an equation of the two.[34]

The business of sealing figures in 7:2–3 also. There John sees "another angel," distinct from the angels holding the four winds (see the foregoing discussion of 10:1 for ἄλλον, "another"). This angel is not coming down out of heaven as in 10:1; 18:1; 20:1. Hence the passage does not initially allude to the second coming. It is too early for that: the four winds have yet to blow during the hour of testing which is coming on the whole inhabited earth. Rather, the angel is "going up (ἀναβαίνοντα, 'ascending') from [the] rising of [the] sun [i.e., the East]" to supervise the sealing of the 144,000, about whom John *hears* as such but whom he then *sees* to be the innumerable company of saved people just as he *heard* about a lion whom he then *saw* to be a lamb (cf. 7:4, 9 with 5:5–6), and thus make them able to withstand those winds of judgment (cf. 6:17, "because the great day of their [God's and the Lamb's] wrath has come, and who is able to stand?" and 7:9, which answers the question of ability to stand: "a large crowd [of the saved] ... standing before the throne and before the Lamb"). Especially in Johannine theology Jesus' ascension had the purpose of completing the work of salvation (John 3:13; 6:62; 20:17; cf. the theme of Jesus' being lifted up in John 3:14; 8:28; 12:32, 34); and from a standpoint on Patmos the ascension took place in the East, where the sun rises (cf. the association of Jesus' resurrection, which makes up one element in the Johannine Jesus' glorification/

---

[34] In 9:11 the double naming of the king over the demonic locusts as "Abaddon," Hebrew for "Destruction," and "Apollyon," Greek for "Destroyer," seems to parody the inscription on Jesus' cross, "The King of the Jews," written in Hebrew, Latin, and Greek (John 19:20) but with Latin omitted to concentrate attention on the pun regarding Nero's (and Domitian's?) claim to be Apollo, whose name sounds like "Apollyon" (cf. Aeschylus, *Ag.* 1082–83, 1085–86). A contrast thus emerges between this king as a destroyer and Jesus as the king who saves from destruction (see the use of ἀπόλλυμι in John 3:16; 6:27, 39; 10:10, 28; 11:50; 17:12; 18:9). But since Rev 9:11 describes the king over the demonic locusts also as "the angel of the abyss," the antithetic parallel with King Jesus may suggest that Jesus too is an angel, a heavenly and divine one. Strangely, Mounce favors an equation of the angels in 9:11 and 20:1 (*Revelation*, 351). But how can we think that the destroying angel of the abyss, who leads the demonic locusts, equates with the angel who stops the nefarious activity of Satan? Mounce goes on to argue that the recurring "I saw" of 19:11, 17, 19; 20:1, 4, 11 (missed by Mounce), 12; 21:1 (plus 21:2, 22, we might add) produces a succession of events, one following another, so that recapitulation is unlikely. Certainly a back reference to the first coming is unlikely, as Mounce is concerned to argue, but not a reference to a further aspect of the second coming.

lifting up/ascension, with sunrise in John 20:1 [Mary comes to his tomb "while it is still dark" in contrast with Mark 16:1; Matt 28:1; Luke 24:1, so that the risen Jesus' appearance to her makes a sunrise (he is "the light of the world" [John 8:12; 9:5; 12:46], i.e., the sun [John 11:9])] and in John 21:4 [where the risen Jesus' appearance correlates again with sunrise]; see once more his association with the sun in Rev 1:16; 21:23; 22:5 [and 10:1; 19:17 under the foregoing interpretations]). That the angel is ascending even though the 144,000 are to be sealed on earth points to Jesus' ascension as the means by which the saved are guaranteed their safety from divine judgment.[35]

"Having [the] seal of [the] living God" anticipates 20:1–3 (cf. the association of seal and God with Jesus in John 3:31–34). According to John 6:27 God has sealed Jesus. If the foregoing interpretation of Rev 20:1–3 is correct the angelomorphic Christ has the power of sealing there. In that passage sealing is linked with "shutting" by means of "the key of the abyss"; and according to 1:18 it is Christ who has the keys of death and of hades. Similarly in 3:7–8 he has "the key of David" and "shuts and no one opens" as well as "opens and no one shuts" (again cf. the parody in 9:1–11 of a fallen star's being given the key of the abyss and opening it, and see n. 30 for a discussion of the angel's loud voice). The angel's referring to "our God" does not rule out an identification with Jesus but favors it, for God is the God of Jesus according to 2:7 (1006 1611 1841 2050 2053 2351 Majority Text[K] latt sy[h] co); 3:2, 12 (three times); 11:15 and the God of Jesus along with his disciples according to John 20:17 (in connection with the ascension as here: "but go tell my brothers and say to them, 'I am going up… to my God and your God'").[36]

Another angel now comes and stands at the altar of incense (8:3–5; again see the foregoing discussion of ἄλλος, "another"). As can be told from the preceding phrase "in heaven" (8:1) and from the subsequent throwing of fire "to the earth" (8:5), this altar belongs to the heavenly sanctuary (so 9:13). It is appropriate that the angelic ascent of 7:23 eventuates in an angelic coming (ἦλθεν) to heaven, and thus the text gives some initial encouragement to think again of Jesus' heavenly ascent and arrival. Standing at the altar echoes Amos 9:1, where Yahweh stands at the altar. Both here and there the one who stands plays a judgmental role, and Jesus often stands in for Yahweh. Moreover, John has described Jesus as girded with a golden girdle (1:13). The twenty-four elders had golden crowns and golden bowls full of incense "which are the prayers of the

---

[35] Notably, commentators labor over the meaning of the East but pay little or no attention to the angel's going up.

[36] Against Thomas, *Revelation 1–7*, 467. See J. Gill, *An Exposition of the New Testament* (London: George Keith, 1776), 5:504: "for who but he [Jesus Christ] should have the privyseal of heaven … and who could speak in such an authoritative manner to the four angels … and who should seal the servants of the Lord, but he who has them in his hands, and keeps them by his power, so that none of these shall perish?"

saints" (4:4; 5:8). The elders cast their crowns before the throne of God and the Lamb, and here the incense of the saints' prayers is given to the angel (8:3). The parallels in the use of "golden" and between the casting of crowns and the giving of incense favor an identification of the angel with Jesus the Lamb, and praying in his name (John 14:13–14; 15:16; 16:23–24, 26) correlates with the angelomorphic Jesus' offering up the prayers of the saints. Since no one comes to the Father except through Jesus (John 14:6) and Jesus is the saints' advocate with the Father (1 John 2:1; cf. John 17) it would seem according to Johannine theology that only Jesus could offer up the saints' prayers, as here.[37]

The angel's taking a censer, filling it with fire from the altar, and throwing it to the earth represent vindictive judgment on persecutors of the saints in answer to the saints' prayers (cf. 6:9–11), a judgment such as elsewhere in Revelation Jesus inflicts on those persecutors (see above all 19:11–16 with 19:1–10, 17–21 but also 12:10–12; 17:1–18:24, esp. 17:6 with 17:14). Furthermore, the peals of thunder, rumblings, flashes of lightning, and earthquake that accompany the fiery judgment look like the accompaniments of the seventh trumpet, when "the mystery of God has been finished" (10:7), and of the seventh bowl, when "it has happened"; and as under the present seventh seal again the thunder, lightning, and earthquake seem to draw a parallel between God's descent at Sinai and Jesus' descent at the second coming (cf. 8:1–5; 11:15–19; 16:17–21 with Exod 19:16–20).[38]

John identifies the speaker in 22:6 as "one of the seven angels who had the seven bowls" and who said that he would "show" (δείξω) John "the bride, the wife of the Lamb" (21:9). In 22:6 this speaker refers to God's "angel" as one

---

[37] Cf. the mediatorial role of angels in Tob 12:15; *1 En.* 8:4 with 9:1–11; 15:1–2; 16:2; 89:76; 104:1; *T. Levi* 3:5–6; *3 Bar.* 11–17. Alford objects that since in Rev 5:6 the twenty-four elders holding the golden bowls full of incense do not equate with Jesus, neither does the angel with the golden censer (*The Greek Testament*, 4:632). This objection overlooks other possibilities, e.g., that the twenty-four elders represent the saints themselves in their prayers for deliverance from persecution (cf. the 12 + 12 of the gates and foundations, inscribed with the names of the patriarchs and apostles respectively, in the new Jerusalem [22:12–14]), the present angel functioning as the Christ-Advocate who mediates those prayers to God.

[38] In 14:14 the figure like a son of man sitting on a white cloud and wearing a golden crown on his head (cf. the golden censer of the angel in 8:3–5) most likely represents Jesus in terms of Dan 7:13, used also in Rev 1:7, 13. The description of the angel in 14:15 as "another" may then imply that the figure like a son of man is to be considered angelic. But this argument is weak in that "another" may relate rather to the angels in 14:6, 8, 9, 10 (cf. A.P. Van Schaik, " "Αλλος ἄγγελος in Apk 14," in *L'Apocalypse johannique et l'Apocalyptique dans la Nouveau Testament* [ed. J. Lambrecht; BETL 53; Gembloux: J. Duculot/Leuven: Leuven University Press, 1980], 217–25). Since the other angel in 14:15 came out of the temple and differs from Jesus the figure like a son of man, the further other angel also coming out of the temple in 14:17 is probably not Jesus either. But in 14:18 the yet further other angel who comes out of the altar and has authority over the fire must equate with the "other angel" in 8:3–5 who stood at the altar, offered incense with the prayers of the saints, and threw fire to the earth – and whom we have identified with Jesus. Thus Jesus the altar-angel who has fire-power gives a subordinate angel who comes out of the temple an order to sickle in judgment the ripe grapes representing wicked people.

whom God "sent (ἀπέστειλεν) to show (δεῖξαι) to his servants the things which must happen soon." According to 1:1 God gave Jesus Christ a revelation "to show to his servants the things which must happen soon." Furthermore, in 1:1 God signified the revelation by "sending (ἀποστείλας) [it] through his angel to his servant John."[39] The parallel between God's giving a revelation to Jesus Christ to show to his servants, on the one hand, and signifying it by sending it through his angel to his servant John, on the other hand, favors that God's angel is none other than Jesus Christ, especially since the very next verse says that John testified the Word of God and the testimony of Jesus Christ. This understanding is further supported by the chiasm that results from it: (a) the revelation of Jesus Christ (subjective genitive in the Greek text); (b) the revelation which God gave; (b') the Word of God (subjective genitive, equivalent in meaning to "which God gave"); (a') the testimony of Jesus Christ (subjective genitive). God's servant John then writes down the revelation, Word, or testimony for the rest of God's servants. The parallel with 22:6 (cf. "the words of the prophecy" and the "keeping" [τηρέω] of them in both 1:3 and 22:7) then favors that in 22:6 the angel sent to show God's servants the things which must happen soon is none other than Jesus Christ, God's angel of sent revelation also in 1: 1.[40]

Is the angel who speaks in 22:6 and whom 21:9 identified as one of the seven angels who had the seven bowls – is this angel speaking about himself in 22:6 when he speaks about the angel whom God sent? If so, Jesus is the seventh angel. Favoring such an identification is the following of the statement, "And behold, I am coming soon" (22:7), without any indication of a change in speakers just as in 22:12 the "I" who is "coming soon" appears to be the angel speaking to John in 22:10 and ever since 21:9 (see also 22:1, 6). For it is surely Jesus who is coming soon (22:20: "The one testifying these things says, 'Yes, I am coming soon.' Amen! Come, Lord Jesus"). Also favoring an identification of the angel who speaks in 22:6 with the angel about whom he speaks is the parallel between the description of the angel spoken about as sent "to show" God's servants "the things which must happen soon" and the description in 22:8 of the angel who has been and is speaking as "showing" John "these things." Yet again favoring this identification is the parallel between the description of the speaking angel's words as "faithful and true," Jesus' description of himself in 3:14 as

---

[39] On the ground that according to 22:16 Jesus sent his angel "to testify these things" we might regard Jesus as the subject of "signified" in 1:1 and as the one who "sent" the revelation "through his servant John." As a matter of fact, however, it is Jesus who first appears to John with a revelation (1:9 ff.). God is the dominant subject in 1:1a; Jesus Christ has been referenced only in the genitive and dative. "His angel" whom the Lord God has sent to show the things which must happen soon refers indubitably to God's angel. And elsewhere in Revelation servants (δοῦλοι) belong predominantly to God (so 7:3; 10:7; 11:18; 15:3; 19:1–2, 5; 22:3, 6) rather than to Jesus (so only 2:20 and possibly 22:3).

[40] See Ulfgard, "In Quest of the Elevated Jesus," 122–24.

"the faithful and true testifier," and John's description of the returning Jesus in 19:11 as "faithful and true."

On the other hand, it may seem questionable that the angel uses the third person ("his angel") rather than the first ("me") if he is speaking about himself. Moreover, the speaking angel's refusal of John's falling down and worshiping him (22:8–9) disagrees with the falling down and worshiping of Jesus and Jesus' acceptance of those actions in 5:8–14; 7:9–12 (cf. 15:3–5). (Yet John's falling down before the angel to worship him even though in 19:10 he was corrected by the angel "for the same ill-advised act"[41] suggests that John could think of Christ as an angel worthy of worship.) And the angel who in 19:9 (see 17:1, 7 for the angelic identity) tells John, as here, not to worship him seems to distinguish himself from Jesus not merely by referring to Jesus in the third person but also by including himself among those who "hold" (ἐχόντων) the testimony of Jesus (19:10), an expression which elsewhere describes Jesus' followers (6:9; 12:17). Moreover again, the Jesus of Revelation, the ruler of the kings of the earth (1:5), the King of kings and Lord of lords (19:16), who sits on God's throne with God (3:21; 22:1, 3), would hardly describe himself as a fellow servant with John, with John's brothers the prophets, and with the ones "who keep the words of this book." Consequently, just as the unintroduced "I" of Jesus in 22:18 differs from the speakers in 22:17, who ask him to come, so also the unintroduced "I" of Jesus in 22:7 differs from the speaker in 22:6. And there turn out to be two angels, the angelomorphic Jesus spoken about and sent by God in 22:6b and the angelic speaker in 22:6a, 8c, 10, respectively.

How should one respond to such exegetical data as seem to display angelomorphic Christology in the book of Revelation? Though no attempt has heretofore been made to set them out with such detail as in the present essay, their older expositions have usually been met by a response perhaps best stated by H. Alford:

Throughout the book [of Revelation] ... angels are the ministers of the divine purposes, and the carriers out of the apocalyptic course of procedure, but are every where distinct from the divine Persons themselves. In order to this their delegated ministry, they are invested with such symbols and such delegated attributes as beseem in each case the particular object in view: but no apparent fitness of such symbolical investiture to the divine character should induce us to break through the distinction.[42]

As seen above, however, not only the descriptions but also the activities of certain angels in the book of Revelation match those of Jesus Christ. But for the term ἄγγελος and the nonhuman and nondivine meaning of its usual English translation "angel," whereas it truly means a messenger of any kind, an equation

---

[41] Mounce, *Revelation*, 391.

[42] Alford, *The Greek Testament*, 4:649; cf. M. E. Boring, *Revelation* (Interpretation; Louisville: John Knox, 1989), 139; J. D. G. Dunn, *Christology in the Making* (2d ed.; London: SCM, 1989), 156.

of these angels with Jesus would probably meet with little resistance. To sharpen the point one could easily substitute Jesus' name for ἄγγελος, though not in the case of other angels appearing in the book. Now according to 22:16 "I Jesus sent my angel to testify these things," and the "I" who "testifies" in 22:18 seems to be Jesus "the one testifying these things" in 22:20 and saying, "Yes, I am coming soon." Therefore it is probably best to understand the angels who look and act like him as his angel in the same sense that in the OT Yahweh has an angel, i.e., not as a messenger distinct from Jesus or Yahweh but as Jesus or Yahweh in the form of a messenger (cf. Dunn's succinct statement: "'the angel of Yahweh' is simply a way of speaking about Yahweh himself,"[43] as can be told from the identification of Yahweh's angel with Yahweh).[44]

The great variety of Christologies in Revelation makes the presence there of angelomorphic Christology unsurprising; and the role of Yahweh's angel in the Exodus-narrative and later Jewish literature concerning it[45] combines with the prominence of Exodus-typology throughout Revelation[46] and with the prominence of angelology elsewhere in apocalyptic literature to provide multiple impetuses for an angelomorphic Christology in Revelation comparable to angelomorphic theology in the OT and later Judaism. Inasmuch as such Christology provides an angelic connection for the saints on earth with God in heaven, a further impetus may be found in the felt need of such a connection, a need due to the original audience's having suffered ostracism from Jewish synagogues, Greco-Roman civic life and culture, the Roman government and its agents (with the threat of emperor-worship), and the rich and powerful provincial elite.[47] Given the possibility of these impetuses and the probably late date for Revelation as compared with most other books of the NT, one should be reticent to treat this angelomorphic Christology as a low and primitive sort that maintained a literarily secret existence for the most part until Revelation brought it out of the closet.[48] It still seems likely that Christology started with Jesus' talking and

---

[43] Dunn, *Christology in the Making*, 150; cf. J. Ashton, *Studying John* (Oxford: Clarendon), 71–89, for angel-of-the-Lord Christology in the Gospel of John.

[44] See, e.g., Gen 16:7–13; 21:17–18; 22:15–16; 31:11–13; Exod 3:2–4:17; Judg 6:11–27; Acts 7:30–34; cf. Acts 23:11 with 27:23. Sometimes the texts oscillate between God and the angel of God rather than between Yahweh and Yahweh's angel.

[45] Though not without opposition in later Jewish literature; see J. Fossom, "Kyrios Jesus as the Angel of the Lord in Jude 5–7," *NTS* 33 (1987): 234–37, for the evidence.

[46] See, e.g., 1:5–6 and 5:9–10 with 5:10; also 7:1–17; 8:5; 12:1–17; 15:2–4; 18:4 and, of course, parallels of detail with the ten plagues that fell on Egypt.

[47] Cf. A. Y. Collins, *Crisis and Catharsis* (Philadelphia: Westminster, 1984); idem, "The Revelation of John: An Apocalyptic Response to a Social Crisis," *CurTM* 8 (1981): 4–12.

[48] Against Longenecker, *The Christology of Early Jewish Christianity*, 32; Hurtado, *One God, One Lord*, 82. In particular, whether Gal 4:14 represents angelomorphic Christology hinges on whether the parallelism in ὡς ἄγγελον θεοῦ ..., ὡς Χριστὸν Ἰησοῦν is synonymous or progressive. The anarthrousness of ἄγγελον favors progressive parallelism ("as an angel of God..., and [what is more] as Christ Jesus") and therefore undermines support for early angelomorphic

acting out of a sense that God was his Father in a distinctive way[49] and proceeded with the effect of the resurrection on Jesus' first disciples. But though a later development, the angelomorphic Christology in Revelation may well have contributed to the even later Christology in the Fourth Gospel of Jesus as the one sent from heaven and returning there.[50]

Addendum: A Rejoinder to Peter R. Carrell
and Adela Yarbro Collins

It is disappointing that P. R. Carrell, though accepting angelomorphic Christology elsewhere in the Apocalypse, rejects an identification of the angel in ch. 10 with Jesus.[51] According to Carrell, "Gundry ... overlooks the point that against the wider context of glorious angels, the angel in Apc. 10.1 is not unusual and thus there is no need to press the resemblance to the conclusion that the angel is Jesus."[52] But Carrell himself overlooks an astonishingly large number of items: (1) that the angel in ch. 10 has an opened scroll in his hand; (2) that in ch. 5 Jesus the Lamb took a seven-sealed scroll from the hand of God; (3) that between chs. 5 and 10 Jesus has loosened all the seals of the scroll so as to open it; (4) that the interchange between opening it, loosening its seals, and opening its seals in 5:2, 4–5, 9; 6:1, 3, 5, 7, 9, 12; 8:1 equates the loosening of the seals with the opening of the scroll; (5) that the vocalic reduplication of the perfect participle ἠνεῳγμένον no fewer than three times – first with η, second with ε, and third with ω – and the repetition of this participial form in 10:2, 8 make it hard to miss an emphasis on Jesus' having opened the scroll as a consequence of loosening its seals; (6) that the interchange between βιβλίον and βιβλαρίδιον in 10:2, 8, 9, 10 (cf. the interchange of βίβλος and βιβλίον elsewhere in the Apocalypse, for which see 3:5; 13:8; 17:8; 20:12; 21:27) subverts any argument from βιβ-

---

Christology. Though in Dan 7:13 "one like a son of man" may refer to an angel (see, e.g., J.J. Collins, *The Apocalyptic Vision of the Book of Daniel* [HSM 16; Missoula: Scholars Press, 1977], 123–52); idem, *Daniel*, 305–6, 310, 313–19; H. Sahlin, "Wie wurde ursprünglich die Benennung 'Der Menschensohn' verstanden?" *ST* 37 [1983]: 147–79), the shift in the canonical Gospels and Acts from the comparative "one like ..." to a straightforward "the Son of Man" veers away from angelomorphic Christology. Only the comparative expression implies an angel.

[49] So, correctly, W. Michaelis, *Zur Engelchristologie im Urchristentum* (Gegenwartsfragen Biblischer Theologie 1: Basel: Henrich Majer, 1941), 5–12, though Michaelis's negativism toward angelomorphic Christology goes to an extreme.

[50] Cf. U.B. Müller, *Menschenwerdung des Gottessohnes* (SBS 140; Stuttart: KBW, 1990): 62–67, 80–83 (though without reference to Revelation). On Jesus as the sent one in John see J.-A. Bühner, *Der Gesandte und sein Weg im 4. Evangelium* (WUNT 2/2; Tübingen: Mohr [Siebeck], 1977).

[51] P. R. Carrell, *Jesus and the Angels* (SNTSMS 95; Cambridge: Cambridge University Press, 1997), 131–38.

[52] Ibid., 137 n. 36.

λαρίδιον that the scroll in ch. 10 differs from the one in ch. 5, where only βιβ-λίον occurs; (7) that according to ch. 5 only Jesus is worthy to take and open the scroll by loosening-opening its seals; (8) that the events which took place during the course of Jesus' opening the seals of the scroll have led to his taking possession of the world as represented not only by the opened state of the scroll but also by the planting of the angel's feet on sea and land; (9) that the reversal of the usual order of land first and then sea (5:13; 7:1–3; 12:12; 14:7) stresses a subjugation of the powers of chaos, represented by the sea, such as only Jesus can accomplish and such as occurs elsewhere in Revelation only at the Parousia; (10) that the mention of standing on sea and land no fewer than three times in ch. 10 adds to this stress; and (11) that the comparison of the angel's feet to pillars of fire recalls the divine theophany that led Israel in the wilderness (cf. the Exodus-theme that runs throughout the Apocalypse).

Also against Carrell, the angel's being "clothed" with a cloud does not describe a mode of transport so much as it tells something about the angel himself. It makes for a theophany insofar as the Apocalypse portrays Jesus, here in angelic form, as divine (cf. the angel of Yahweh in the OT). That 10:1 uses a different word for "face" (πρόσωπον) from the one for Jesus' face in 1:16 (ὄψις) poses no problem for angelomorphic Christology in ch. 10; for John the Seer often uses synonyms without distinction in meaning (see, e.g., μαστοί and στήθη for breasts in 1:13 and 15:6; "the ruler [ἄρχων] of the kings of the earth" and "the King (βασιλεύς) of kings" in 1:5; 17:14; 19:16; "the alpha and the omega," "the first and the last," and "the beginning and the end" in 1:8, 17; 2:8; 21:6; 22:13; "white garments," "white robes," "washed robes," "clean white linen," and "clean bright linen" in 3:5, 18; 4:4; 6:11; 7:9, 13, 14; 19:8, 14; 22:14; "the Devil," "Satan," "the serpent," and "the dragon" in 2:9, 10; 12:3, 4, 7, 9, 12–17; 13:2, 4, 11; 20:2, 7, 10; and "forty-two months" and "1,260 days" in 11:2, 3; 12:6; 13:5; cf. the well-known penchant for synonyms in the Gospel of John[53]); and the comparison of both Jesus' face and the angel's face to the sun favors an identification of the angel with Jesus. As to John's falling at Jesus' feet in 1:17 but not at the angel's feet in ch. 10, John finds himself already within arm's length of Jesus at 1:17 ("and he put his right hand on me"), so that proximity makes natural a knee-jerk reaction (pun intended), whereas in ch. 10 John sees a cosmic figure astride sea and land at a distance, so that John has to "go" (ὕπαγε – v. 8), i.e., "go away" (ἀπῆλθα – v. 9; note again the use of synonyms), to take the opened scroll out of the angel's hand.

The use in ch. 10 of βιβλίον as well as βιβλαρίδιον for a scroll small enough to be eaten by John shows that here βιβλίον is not to be taken as a faded diminutive; so there is no need to consider βιβλίον in ch. 5 as a faded diminutive referring to a

---

[53] Examples: ἀμνός, ἀρνίον, and πρόβατον, πλοῖον and πλιοάριον, βόσκω and ποι-μαίνω, ἀγαπάω and φιλέω, ἑλκύω and σύρω, ἀληθής and ἀληθινός, and so on.

larger scroll (cf. the use of βιβλίον in Deut 24:1, 3 LXX; Matt 19:7 for a bill of divorce with the dimensions of the bill of divorce discovered among the Dead Sea Scrolls, 4 3/8" x 8 5/8" [Mur 19]; see also Herodotus, *Hist.* 1.123–24, for a βιβ-λίον so small as to allow concealment in the belly of a hare and to contain material that occupies only half a page of Greek text in the Loeb edition, which features tiny pages to begin with; and 3.128, for many βιβλία the contents of which consist of only a single statement each). The anarthrousness of the opened scroll in 10:2 is due to the scroll's having been unopened as yet in ch. 5, not to the introduction of a different scroll in ch. 10.[54]

Like Carrell, A. Y. Collins agrees with me on the presence of angelomorphic Christology in the book of Revelation but rejects a christological identification of the angel in Revelation 10.[55] Readers may infer Collins' additional criticisms of the identification from the further part of this rejoinder. A subtraction of references to the Fourth Gospel would make little difference to my argument because those references are always supplementary to evidence gleaned from the book of Revelation itself. Though the differences between this book and the Fourth Gospel are great, the existence of links, which Collins acknowledges, would seem to justify their use in a supplementary role. To argue further that the links are far more numerous, close, and therefore perhaps less indirect than generally recognized would strengthen the argument, but that avenue has been well probed by J. Frey in an appendix to the revised, German edition of M. Hengel's book on the Johannine question.[56]

I do *not* assume that "the use of similar images for two entities implies the equation of the two entities."[57] Rather, I explicitly take into account that ὡς-phrases apply to others than Jesus as well as to him, and likewise with respect to the description "strong," to dying and coming back to life, to having great authority, to having keys, to showing things to John, to the description "faithful and true," to leonine traits, and to speaking with a loud voice. I accept the burden of proving that similarities of image are close, striking, clustered, and frequent enough to favor an equation.

As noted above, the description of the angel in ch. 10 as "clothed" with a cloud favors theophanic symbolism over miraculous transport. For "clothed with a cloud" does not describe a mode of transport but tells something about the angel himself, as do also the associated descriptions of him as strong and having a rainbow over his head, a face like the sun, and feet like pillars of fire.

---

[54] The treatment of Revelation 10 by L. T. Stuckenbruck shares many of the deficiencies of Carrell's (*Angel Veneration and Christology* [WUNT 2/70; Tübingen: Mohr (Siebeck), 1995], 229–32). For general background see W. Horbury, *Jewish Messianism and the Cult of Christ* (London: SCM, 1998), 119–217.

[55] A. Y. Collins, "Response to E. Janzen and R. Gundry" (paper presented at the annual meeting of the SBL, Chicago, 19–22 November 1994), 3–6.

[56] M. Hengel, *Die johanneische Frage* (WUNT 2/67; Tübingen: Mohr, 1993).

[57] Collins, "Response," 4.

Furthermore, the use elsewhere of clouds to make someone invisible can have no relevance here, for John speaks of *seeing* the angel clothed with a cloud.[58] Moreover, passages such as Revelation 11, 1 Thessalonians 4, and Acts 1 use clouds to envelop those who are taken *up* and *out of* view, whereas John speaks here of a coming *down* and *into* view.

Puzzling is the argument that 1:7 refers to the future but ch. 10 to an event in the past, i.e., a segment of the process through which John received revelation.[59] Throughout the Apocalypse the mechanics of having received revelation in the past are intertwined with the contents of revelation concerning the future. Take ch. 11, for instance, where John's measuring the temple, altar, and worshipers in the past is bound up with predictions of the future. So the angel's predicting no more delay and commissioning John to prophesy again hardly negate a representation of the Parousia in the angel's descent, especially if the prophesying again is recapitulative, as Collins seems to agree in saying that "the visions associated with the scroll of chapter 5 describe the same imaginative historical or eschatological process as those associated with the scroll of chapter 10."[60] And especially if he has been portrayed as an angel, i.e., a messenger, it should not seem strange for Jesus to deliver a message about the end after descending in a way that portrays the end. If we do not give a parousianic interpretation to the descent of this angel, described in terms reminiscent of Jesus' description, and to the putting of the angel's right foot on the sea and left foot on the land as indicative of Jesus' finally taking possession of the world, these details lose much of their significance, or at least much of their impact. The loss is too high an interpretive price to pay.

As to the relation of the visions of seals and trumpets to the opening of the scroll, ch. 10 does not speak of an opening of the scroll but of the scroll as *already* opened, so that we can hardly miss the emphasis on completion of the action in the past. Furthermore and again as noted above, the perfect participle appears *twice* to emphasize the scroll's state of openness. In the second place, the written contents of the scroll of ch. 5 were not revealed and read when the scroll was being opened seal by seal. Instead, events took place that led to Jesus' taking possession of the world. The fully opened state of the scroll represents that possession-taking, as does also the planting of feet on sea and land. The trumpets do not represent intervening events but similar, concurrent events to those of the seals; and like them they come to a climax in the Parousia.

To distinguish the βιβλίον of ch. 5 from the βιβλαρίδιον of ch. 10 Collins bypasses the use in 10:8 of βιβλίον for the βιβλαρίδιον of 10:2, 9, 10 and, though recognizing the diminutive *form* of βιβλίον in ch. 5, twice denies it a diminutive

---

[58] Against Collins, "Response," 4.
[59] So Collins, "Response," 5.
[60] Collins, "Response," 5.

meaning.[61] But evidence cited above shows unquestionably the diminutive meaning to have been still alive, and everybody recognizes John's aforementioned penchant for using synonyms without a distinction in meaning. *If* a greater emphasis on smallness attaches to βιβλαρίδιον than to βιβλίον, I suggest that when the angel is directly in view, as in vv. 2, 9, and 10, βιβλαρίδιον is used to highlight his comparatively large size (standing astride sea and land implies gigantic stature), but when the angel is only indirectly referred to, as in v. 8, John reverts to the βιβλίον of ch. 5. In any case, how can βιβλίον fail to carry a diminutive meaning in ch. 10 when βιβλίον alternates with βιβλαρίδιον, which by common consent does carry a diminutive meaning? And if βιβλίον carries a diminutive meaning in ch. 10 why can it not do so in ch. 5 too? The interchange in ch. 10 subverts a distinction between scrolls. And the interchange of βίβλος and βιβλίον elsewhere in Revelation has at least the significance of showing John capable of using cognates from the root βιβλ- without a shift in reference.

The question whether John and others of his time had the same understanding that modern scholars do of the angel of Yahweh is just that – a question, not a problem for the angelomorphic interpretation unless a difference in understandings can be demonstrated. Against identifying the messenger of Jesus with John in 22:16 stands the fact that nowhere else does Revelation call John a messenger (ἄγγελος). That Jesus is speaking directly to a plural audience is not in question, but a plural audience does not favor his talking about John over his talking about an angel.

---

[61] Collins, "Response," 5–6.

20. The New Jerusalem: People as Place, Not Place for People

Symbolic language fills the book of Revelation as it fills other apocalyptic literature. We may therefore presume that the description of the new Jerusalem in Rev 21:1–22:5 deals in symbolism. Our presumption is rewarded when we read of the city's coming down out of heaven, stretching out and up to unheard-of dimensions, having gates that each consist of a single pearl, being paved with gold that can be seen through, and so on. Such language invites symbolic interpretation, whatever the nature – whether concrete or abstract – of the reality so described.

But the new Jerusalem is a very large symbol. Its description occupies a whole chapter or more. Therefore we may rightfully expect that the details of the description contribute small, individual symbols to the large, overall symbol even as contemporary interpreters of Jesus' parables have come to understand that although we must resist allegorism, the longer the story that constitutes a narratival parable the more likely it is that some details of the parable have their own significance within the overall meaning.[1]

A symbolic interpretation of the new Jerusalem will be a hypothesis, for any interpretation of any text is a hypothesis. The proofs of an interpretive hypothesis lie first in its power to bring the text to life, to make it understandable why the author took the time and trouble to write the text and to a lesser degree why its first audience thought enough of it at least not to throw it away. Then those proofs lie in the power of the interpretive hypothesis to explain the data of the text coherently yet completely, naturally yet deeply, with a minimum of strain yet a maximum of detail, with what mathematicians call "elegance" – a blend of simplicity and richness. Without simplicity and naturalness the suspicion will arise that the interpretation is being foisted on the text. Without richness and detail the suspicion will arise that the interpretation does not penetrate the text. The following interpretation will therefore need to satisfy these criteria.

---

[1] See, e.g., G. Caird, *The Language and Imagery of the Bible* (Philadelphia: Westminster, 1980), 160–67; J. Drury, "The Sower, the Vineyard, and the Place of Allegory in the Interpretation of Mark's Parables," *JTS* ns 24 (1973): 367–79; H.-J. Klauck, *Allegorie und Allegorese in synoptischen Gleichnistexten* (NTAbh nf 13; Münster: Aschendorff, 1978); C. E. Carlston, "Parable and Allegory Revisited: An Interpretive Review," *CBQ* 43 (1981): 228–42.

I will state an old interpretation and identify some deficiencies in its presentations to date. Then I will identify my lines of approach to it, refine it, and relate it to the text first with regard to the overall symbol, then with regard to the individual symbols. Finally I will take up objections that might be lodged against the interpretation and draw a conclusion.

The new Jerusalem symbolizes the saints. That is the old interpretation.[2] But it has not been applied very thoroughly and consistently to the details of John's description of the new Jerusalem. It has not been tied very closely to the situation of the audience for whom he wrote the book of Revelation. And it has not been carried out to the extent of denying that the city even partly symbolizes the place where the saints will dwell forever.

In an attempt to make up somewhat for these omissions let us set aside source critical questions, e.g., the question of a Jewish source and the question of an original distinction between a millennial city and an eternal city, and take the text as its stands. Although those questions are important in their own right we must presume that the text as it stands had a meaning for the author and his first audience. We want to discover that meaning.

The path to discovery lies along the line of historical-grammatical interpretation, which assumes that the language of the biblical text, including its symbolic language, grows out of and speaks to the historical situation of the writer and his audience. To take a nonreferential view of language, particularly of symbolic language, may open up possibilities of contemporary interest and deconstructive play but it blocks the path to historical understanding. Our pursuit of historical understanding therefore requires that we stick to the line of referential language in trying to interpret the new Jerusalem.

Jewish traditions concerning a renewal of Jerusalem and concerning a heavenly Jerusalem have often led commentators on Revelation to think that John christianizes those traditions in describing the final abode of the saints.[3] He not only christianizes those traditions, however; he also transforms Jerusalem into a symbol of the saints themselves. To be sure, a city – like a region or a country or even the whole world – may mean both its inhabitants and their dwelling place. But John is not describing the eternal dwelling place of the saints. He is describing *them*, and them *alone*. Does this hypothesis have the power to enliven the text and give it an elegant explanation?

---

[2] See esp. D. Mathewson, *A New Heaven and a New Earth* (JSNTSup 238; Sheffield: Sheffield Academic Press, 2003); P. Lee, *The New Jerusalem in the Book of Revelation* (WUNT 2/129; Tübingen: Mohr Siebeck, 2001), 267–304; W. W. Reader, *Die Stadt Gottes in der Johannesapokalypse* (Ph.D. Diss., University of Göttingen, 1971); R. J. McKelvey, *The New Temple* (New York: Oxford University Press, 1969), 167–76; W. Thüsing, "Die Vision des 'Neuen Jerusalem' (Apk 21, 1–22, 5) als Verheissung und Gottesverkündigung," *TTZ* 77 (1968): 17–34; T. Holtz, *Die Christologie der Apokalypse des Johannes* (TU 85; Berlin: Akademie, 1962), 191–95.

[3] See also the monograph by Lee, *The New Jerusalem*, passim.

Let us refine the hypothesis and start exploring the text so as to make possible an answer to the question. The new Jerusalem is a dwelling place, to be sure. But it is God's dwelling place in the saints rather than their dwelling place on earth. The new earth – the whole of it so far as we can tell, not just a localized city no matter what megalopolitan size it might attain – is the saints' dwelling place. Revelation 21:1–22:5 does not *describe* the new earth, however. It only *mentions* the new earth. What it describes is the new *city*: Jerusalem.

Quite early in his book John gave a hint that his readers were to regard the new Jerusalem as personal rather than topographical. At 3:12 he presented Christ's promise to write on the overcomer – i.e., on the professing believer who proves to be genuine – the name of the new Jerusalem as well as the name of God and his own (i.e., Christ's) new name. In other words, Christ identifies the new Jerusalem with the person who overcomes much as he identifies his own person and that of God his Father with the overcomer.[4]

Another hint appeared in 20:9, where "the beloved city" of the millennium stood in parallel with "the camp of the saints." To come against this city or camp, Gog and Magog had to spread out "over the breadth of the earth." So the city did not seem to be confined to one spot. It consisted of the saints themselves wherever on earth they lived.

In 21:2–3, 9b–10, however, the earlier hints turn into a virtually explicit personal identification of the new Jerusalem with the saints. In this passage John first compares the city to a bride adorned for her husband and then calls the city "the bride, the wife of the Lamb."[5] We already know from 19:7–8 that the Lamb's bride is the saints, arrayed in their righteous acts. The repeated description of the bride-wife as "made ready" also unites these two passages. Confirmation comes from 22:17, where the bride will join the Spirit in saying, "Come," which is the prayer of the suffering saints, "Amen, come, Lord Jesus" (22:20). Therefore the city = the bride-wife = the saints, whose dwelling place John has already introduced. That dwelling place is the earthly part of the new universe (21:1), down to which part they descend to take up their abode (21:2).[6]

---

[4] Cf. the oneness of God, Christ, and believers in John 14–15, 17, which at the least may come from the same Johannine school out of which came Revelation.

[5] That is to say, a simile ("like a bride") evolves into a metaphor ("the bride"; cf. similar evolutions in 15:2; 21:11, 18). As said by G. R. Osborne, "there is no significant change in meaning" (*Revelation* [Baker Exegetical Commentary on the New Testament; Grand Rapids: Baker, 2002], 747). It is therefore hard to understand why he thinks it "unlikely that there is a complete identity of the city with the saints." One might have thought that the similarity in meaning would make the difference between simile and metaphor irrelevant to the question whether the new Jerusalem represents the saints, their eternal abode, or both them and their abode. For a representation of the saints see G. K. Beale, *The Book of Revelation* (NIGTC; Grand Rapids: Eerdmans, 1999), 1066, 1070–71 et passim.

[6] The descent of the new Jerusalem and its equation with the saints disagree with the astral

On his side, God takes up his abode with the saints (21:3). The presence of his tabernacle with them means that just as he made Israel his abode, so he will make the saints, who are the church, his abode.[7] The better textual tradition (A et al.) reads the plural "peoples" (λαοί) in 21:3, apparently to emphasize the internationality of the church, made up as it is of the redeemed from heathen nations as well as from Israel. As peoples, the church will be God's city. Thus the description of the city is a description of them. More particularly, it is a description of them that contrasts with their state of affliction under the beast. What the city is is what they will be, and what they will be is the happy opposite of what they are about to suffer under the beast.[8]

What then is this happy opposite? The answer to this question will not only describe the saints in their eternal, perfected state. It will also confirm the identification of the new Jerusalem with them. The fit between the new Jerusalem and the saints will provide the confirmation, and the completeness of that fit will leave nothing left over that would require the new Jerusalem to represent anything more than the saints themselves.

The new Jerusalem is holy (21:2). The cowardly, unbelieving, and abominable, murderers, immoral people, sorcerers, idolaters, and liars will not be part of it (21:8, 27; 22:15). Thus John portrays the perfected saints as a holy city, not so much purged individually of those sins that need confession and the advocacy of Jesus Christ the righteous one,[9] but purged collectively of those non-overcomers who avoided persecution by accommodating themselves to the world and thus incurred the judgment Christ threatened in his messages to the seven churches (Revelation 2–3). The list of evil people probably does not refer to non-Christians in general, whose fate was described in 20:11–15; rather, to professing Christians who in time of persecution turned out to be false. Their cowardice made them shrink back from persecution. Their unbelief made them unfaithful to Christ and the church. To save their necks they participated in the vile practices of non-Christians and murderously betrayed their fellow Christians to the persecuting authorities, practiced the sexual immorality and magic that went along with idolatry, and denied the truth of the gospel in life and word by accepting the big lie of the beast (Revelation 13).

---

interpretation of B. J. Malina (*On the Genre and Message of Revelation* [Peabody, Mass.: Hendrickson, 1995], 238–44) and B. J. Malina and J. J. Pilch (*Social-Science Commentary on the Book of Revelation* [Minneapolis: Fortress, 2000], 243–53).

[7] Against Osborne, who thinks of the new Jerusalem as "a place ... where God 'dwells' with his people" as well as God's people with whom he dwells (*Revelation*, 733; also against R. Bauckham, *The Theology of the Book of Revelation* [New Testament Theology; Cambridge: Cambridge University Press, 1993], 132–36, and – apparently – C. Deutsch, "Transformation of Symbols: The New Jerusalem in Rv 21 1–22 5," *ZNW* 78 [1987]: 106–26).

[8] Cf. 1 John 3:2, which does not have to do with suffering and its reversal, however.

[9] So 1 John 1:9; 2:1.

John also portrays the city as new (21:2). As newly resurrected, that is to say, the saints will belong to the new earth and the new earth will belong to them. At the present time some of them suffer dispossession because of their Christian life and witness. "I know your tribulation and poverty," Jesus said to the church at Smyrna (2:9). He probably meant the persecution that caused them poverty. This kind of persecution will become worse (cf. esp. 13:16–17). In the new earth, by contrast, the saints will be the landholders: "But you are rich" (the very next statement that Jesus made to the church at Smyrna) anticipates everlasting earthly wealth. We should not spiritualize the statement by making it refer to a heavenly inheritance, for the descent of the new Jerusalem out of heaven makes it quite clear that the book of Revelation promises eternal life on the new earth, not ethereal life in the new heaven. By putting the newness of the descending Jerusalem in conjunction with the newness of the earth John promises a redistribution of property, an exclusive redistribution of property to the saints. It does not require Marxist inclinations to see the liveliness of the text (so understood) in the sociological setting of Christian believers dispossessed through persecution.[10]

The new Jerusalem descends out of heaven from God (21:2). This descent means that at the dawn of the new creation the saints, who do not belong among those repeatedly called "the earth-dwellers" in Revelation but who are enrolled in heaven in the Lamb's book of life, will come from their place of heavenly origin in God to take possession of their property, the new earth. In accordance with the widespread ancient notion of the heavenly city, or city of the gods, commentators usually interpret this part of the description as an indication that the saints' eternal dwelling place already exists as the heavenly Jerusalem. But though the adjective "new" contrasts this Jerusalem with the present earthly one, it also disfavors an already existing prototypical city. For such a city would have to belong to the presently existing old heaven, yet the new Jerusalem descends out of the new heaven after the old one has passed away. Furthermore, if the new Jerusalem is the perfected peoples of God, its coming down simply follows the Johannine pattern of descent from heaven to take possession of the earth.

This pattern appeared, for example, in Rev 10:1–3. There a strong angel "comes down out of heaven" and takes over sea and land by planting his pillar-like feet of fire on them. Likewise in Rev 18:1 an angel having great authority and illuminating the earth with his glory "comes down out of heaven" to announce that Babylon has fallen. And in Rev 20:1 an angel who has the key of the abyss (cf. the keys of death and of hell that Christ has in 1:18) "comes down out of heaven" to bind the dragon Satan. Similarly, then, the coming down of the

---

[10] True, the church at Laodicea is rich in worldly wealth. But their spiritual poverty calls their salvation into such serious question, perhaps to the point of denial (cf. 3:17–20), that their worldly wealth does not undermine our taking the wealth of the new Jerusalem as compensatory for the poverty of persecuted true believers like those at Smyrna.

new Jerusalem represents the saints' coming down at the dawn of the new creation to take possession of an earth no longer dominated by Babylon, no longer ravaged by Satan.

Sheer happiness characterizes the city, a happiness unadulterated by tears, pain, or death – elements in the old creation that have peculiar poignancy for those facing persecution to the death by the beast (21:4; cf. 7:12–17 above all, but also 2:13; 6:9–11; 11:1–13; 12:1–13:18; 14:13). Let us pay more attention to the absolute security of the new Jerusalem, however. The city is perched on a mountain so huge and high that no invading army could possibly gain a foothold on it (21:10). The city wall is so thick and high – 144 cubits thick and naturally as high as the city itself, it would appear, since 144 cubits would not at all be high in comparison with the city's height of 12,000 stadia – the city-wall is so thick and high that no invading army could breach or scale it even if they were able to gain a foothold on the mountain (21:12a). Standing guard at each gate is an angel, more than a match for any invader (21:12b). Twelve mammoth stones interspersed between the gates support the wall (21:14a). John is not describing an eternally secure place. He is describing eternally secure peoples. Neither Satan nor demons nor beast nor false prophet nor evil men will be able to touch the city of God, which is his saints. To troubled saints John promises total absence of anxiety over persecution such as looms on the horizon of the old earth.

The huge dimensions of the city do not mean that it has to be large to hold all the saints so much as they mean that all the saints, whom the city represents, will amount to an astronomically high number. Twelve thousand stadia long, wide, and high (21:16) the city is reminiscent of the twelve thousand from each of the twelve tribes of Israel, especially since the cubical shape of the city makes twelve edges of twelve thousand stadia each, coming to a total of 144,000, just as in the case of the Israelites (7:1–8; 14:1–5). In ch. 7 John heard about Israelites but when he actually saw them they turned out to be an innumerable company of the redeemed from all nations, tribes, and languages (vv. 9–17) just as he had earlier heard about a lion but saw it to be a lamb (ch. 5). So also the multiplied twelve thousands of stadia, though numbered, represent the innumerability of the saints. Sufferers naturally tend to think of themselves as few, often as alone. John aims to lift the suffering saints out of their sense of isolation by pointing to the immense number of the redeemed.[11]

As is well known, the cubical shape of the city matches the shape of the holy of holies in the tabernacle and temple (1 Kgs 6:20) and means that the perfected saints will be God's most sacred dwelling place, the inmost room of his

---

[11] Since in ch. 7 the Israelites are not the saved of the OT but the international church of the NT, the names of the Israelite tribes inscribed on the pearly gates of the new Jerusalem do not stand for the saved of the OT but for the NT church of the apostles, whose names are correspondingly inscribed on the twelve foundation stones of the new Jerusalem.

new creation, the ultimate in-group of people who are presently outsiders because they have come out of Babylon so as not to share in her sins (see Rev 18:4).[12] For the encouragement of these outsiders their coming cubical shape turns things outside in. Thus the whole of the city has the glory of God because the whole of the city is the holy of holies, filled with the glory of his presence.[13]

Now at outs with the world, the saints are suffering poverty. So in addition to the promise already given of landed property (the new earth) John promises the saints incalculable wealth of precious stones and precious metal. Again we should resist the temptation to spiritualize and should give the text a materialistic reading agreeable with the earthly locale of the new Jerusalem and with the saints' need of a compensation appropriate to their present material poverty. Such a reading may sound crass to those of us whose intellectual ears Plato has attuned to the abstract music of the spheres (and, ironically, whose physical bodies now enjoy more phenomenal comforts than he could ever have imagined), but historical-grammatical sensitivity drives us to that reading. And the strong OT emphasis on material prosperity in the time of salvation combines with the OT flavor of Revelation to support it (see, e.g., Isa 60:9, 17; 61:6).[14]

The wall of the city is made of jasper, the gates of pearls, the foundation stones of different gems, the city of pure gold, even its streets of pure gold. The city's wealth means the saints' wealth.[15] The harlot Babylon too was adorned with material wealth of gold and gems and pearls (17:4). But the gems of the new Jerusalem are crystal clear, her pearls white, her gold like pure glass, like transparent glass (21:11, 18, 21). In other words the eternal wealth of the saints will be untainted and perfectly pure of Babylonian selfishness, greed, dishonesty, and oppression. The wealth will be pure of such evils because the saints themselves, whom this bejeweled city of gold symbolizes, will be pure of such evils.

And just as the city is God's tabernacle, he and the Lamb are the temple of the city (21:22). Ordinarily God dwells in the temple and the temple is located in the city. Here he and the Lamb are the temple, so that the city, since it is the cubically shaped holy of holies, is located in the temple – a striking reversal

---

[12] Cf. John 8:23; 15:18–19; 17:14, 16.

[13] Cf. Gal 2:9; 1 Cor 3:16–17; 6:19–20; 2 Cor 6:16–7:1; Eph 2:19–22; 1 Tim 3:15; Heb 3:1–6; 1 Pet 2:4–10; 4:17 on the church as a temple; also 1QS 5:5–6; 8:4–10; 9:3–6 on the community at Qumran as a temple; and for discussion, McKelvey, *New Temple,* 46–53, 92–139.

[14] Contrast the nonmaterialistic interpretation of Lee, *The New Jerusalem,* 285–86.

[15] Since the nonovercomers in 3:17–18 were materially wealthy in this world, the "gold refined by fire" that Christ advised them to buy may stand for spiritual wealth. On the other hand, that text may imply not present spiritual wealth in place of present material wealth but future material wealth in place of present material wealth. For white garments, which there stand parallel with refined gold, had recently carried a futuristic (and apparently materialistic as well as symbolic) reference in 3:5; and the shame of nakedness (also in 3:17–18) seemed to have in view the Last Judgment, not the present time.

which means that the saints will dwell in God and the Lamb just as God and the Lamb will dwell in them. We can see the correctness of this deduction by glancing at 3:12, where in reference to "the new Jerusalem" Christ promises to make overcomers pillars "in the temple of my God," which in view of 21:22 we should read as "the temple that *is* my God" (a genitive of apposition).[16]

We might compare the reciprocal indwelling of God, the Lamb, and the saints in the *futuristic* eschatology of the new Jerusalem with the reciprocal indwelling of God, his Son, and believers in the *realized* eschatology of John 14–17. Similarly we might contrast the *eternal* daylight of the new Jerusalem with not having the light in oneself at the *present* time according to John 11:10. The thought is at least as much that the light of life will shine *in* the saints as that they will walk in its light..

By the same token the river of the water of life (22:2) does not flow beside the city or even through it from outer source to outer destination as in old Babylon. Rather, it wells up within the city, coming from the throne of God and the Lamb, who indwell the cubical city of superlative holiness just as the pillar-like city of 3:12 indwells God and the Lamb.[17] And suitably to the size of the city, i.e., to the huge number of the saints, the fountain mentioned in 21:6 has swollen to a river; and the single tree of life in the Garden of Eden, mentioned earlier at 2:7, has multiplied into a plurality of specimens lining the river and yielding fruit every month, i.e., without seasonal interruption. Plenty of water for plenty of trees to supply plenty of life for all the saints no matter how large their number and no matter how many they will be and no matter how tenuous their present lives and livelihoods. Even the leaves of the tree will be used as a poultice for the healing of the nations of redeemed peoples who make up the new Jerusalem. John promises eternal good health for their resurrected bodies – preventative medicine to the utmost (cf. 20:4–6).

But what should we make of elements in the text that seem to distinguish the new Jerusalem from the saints?[18] The city cannot be the bride, the church, can it, because 21:2 *compares* the city to a bride ("prepared as a bride adorned for her husband")? More accurately, however, 21:2 does not compare the city itself to a bride. It compares the *preparation* of the city to the adornment of a bride for her husband. This comparison leads naturally and without contradiction to an identification of the city itself with the bride, the Lamb's wife, several verses later (21:9).

---

[16] Cf. 4Q403 1 i 38–46, where – as noted by D.C. Allison ("4 Q403 Fragm. 1, Col. I, 38–46 and the Revelation to John," *RevQ* 12 [1986]: 409–14) – various parts of the temple are portrayed as living beings, though not as human beings.

[17] Cf. John 4:14b; 7:38.

[18] See esp. E. S. Fiorenza, *Priester für Gott* (NTAbh nf 7; Münster: Aschendorff, 1972), 348–50, echoed by Osborne, *Revelation*, 733, and D. E. Aune, *Revelation 17–22* (WBC 52C; Nashville: Thomas Nelson, 1998), 1122, 1170–75.

But how can the saints be the city when 21:7 says they will inherit it? On the contrary 21:7 says they will inherit "these things," which more naturally refers to the "all things" made new in 21:5, to inherit which things the saints come down *as* the new Jerusalem.

Above all, however, does not the portrayal of the new Jerusalem as a place through whose light the nations will walk and into which the kings of the earth will bring the glory and honor of the nations (21:24–26) point to a city that is the saints' residence rather than the saints themselves? Does not this passage even reflect the sometimes millennial notion of Jerusalem as capital city of the world and as occupied by regathered Israel while the Gentiles live outside? Perhaps so originally, but not in the present context of Revelation. For here the unbelieving nations and kings of the earth have met their doom in the lake of fire. The ones who were redeemed from those nations have now become the nations of the new earth. And because they rule it (22:5) they have become the new kings of the earth, all of them, whole nations of kings. The political side of the promise here complements the economic side.

To be outside the city, then, is not to be outside it on earth. It means to be on earth not at all; rather, in the lake of fire. For the city is the saints, the royalized nations of the redeemed who populate the whole of the new earth. There is no room for anyone else. Just as the plural noun "peoples" shifted in reference from unbelievers (7:9; cf. 5:9) to the saints (21:3), so also the plural noun "nations" has made the same shift.[19] As nations of kings rather than kings of nations the saints have finally fulfilled God's original commission to "be fruitful and multiply and fill the earth and subdue it and rule over... every living thing that moves on the earth" (Gen 1:28). As often in apocalyptic literature, *Endzeit* recaptures *Urzeit*.

"Bring into it [i.e., into the city]" is spatial language but the meaning is non-spatial just as the dimensions of the city are spatial but their meaning nonspatial. So it is false to infer that "bring into it" means that kings and nations dwell outside and come and go just as it is false to infer that the city covers 144,000,000 square stadia of earth but not the whole earth or that the 144,000 Israelites do not encompass the innumerable multitude. The meaning of "bring into it" has to do with the glory and honor of the saintly nations of kings that make up the city, not with unsaintly traffic from countryside into city. John immediately adds 21:27 to guard against a misunderstanding of the latter sort: "and there will not enter into it anything unclean or anyone who practices abomination and lying but only those who are written in the Lamb's book of life." To enter the city is to help make it up – and there is nothing about leaving it once the glory and honor have been brought in. To the contrary see 3:12 again: the overcomer "will not go outside any more."[20]

---

[19] Cf. L. Thompson's "soft boundaries" in "The Mythic Unity of the Apocalypse," *SBL Seminar Papers, 1985* (SBLSP 24; Atlanta: Scholars Press, 1985), 21–24.

[20] The foregoing paragraph should be set against interpretations of Rev 21:1–22:5 tending

Nothing is left over in John's description of the new Jerusalem that would require our enlarging the referent of the symbol. We may therefore conclude with fair assurance that John wanted his Christian audience, who had barely begun to suffer the severity of persecution that he expected to come on them, to see in the new Jerusalem not their future dwelling place but – what was even more heartening – their future selves and state.

Addendum: Abiding in the Temple of the New Jerusalem

The statement in Rev 21:22 that "the Lord God, the Almighty, and the Lamb are its [the new Jerusalem's] temple" is reminiscent of the identification with Jesus' "body" of the temple he said he would "raise in three days" if the Jews destroyed it (John 2:18–22). The reminiscence gains strength from the designation of Jesus as "the Lamb" in Rev 21:22. For *not* as in the Synoptics, Jesus drives out the sheep and oxen when in John 2:14–16 he cleanses the temple after the Baptist's designating him "the Lamb of God that takes away the world's sin," so that those sacrificial animals are no longer needed (John 1:29, 36).[21] And Jesus' calling the temple "my Father's house" (John 2:16) means that John's identifying the temple with Jesus' body amounts to an identification of Jesus' body with the house of his Father – naturally since by definition a temple is the house, the dwelling place, of deity; and God the Father indwells Jesus his Son (John 14:10).[22]

"My Father's house" appears once elsewhere in John's Gospel – at 14:2: "In my Father's house are many abodes." If John is his own best interpreter Jesus is referring to himself or more specifically to his own body. Now σῶμα, "body,"

---

toward universal salvation (see, e.g., Thüsing, "Vision," 22–23 n. 12, 33; Fiorenza, *Priester,* 359; to a certain degree R. J. Bauckham, *The Climax of Prophecy* [Edinburgh: T&T Clark, 1993], 238–337; and to a lesser degree D. Mathewson, "The Destiny of the Nations in Revelation 21:1–22:5: A Reconsideration," *TynBul* 53 [2002]: 121–42). For further criticism of the universalistic interpretation and for citations of others who take that interpretation see Beale, *Revelation,* 1094–1103, and E. J. Schnabel, "John and the Future of the Nations," *BBR* 12 (2002): 243–71.

[21] It might be objected that Rev 21:22 uses ἀρνίον for "Lamb" whereas John 1:29, 36 uses ἀμνός. But John the evangelist likes to use synonyms. For example ἀρνίον and πρόβατον too occur for lambs and sheep in John 2:14, 15; 10:1, 2, 3 (twice), 4, 7, 8, 11, 12 (twice), 13, 15, 16, 26, 27; 21:16, 17 (or προβάτιον as well in 21:16 B C565 *pc* and 21:17 A B C565 *pc*; see also above, p. 395). Therefore the evangelist's ἀμνός in 1:29, 36 is easily equivalent to ἀρνίον in Rev 21:22.

[22] It might be objected that for "house" John 14:2 uses οἰκία whereas John 2:16 uses οἶκος. But again John's liking to use synonyms undermines the objection. Without any distinction in meaning οἰκία occurs also in 4:53; 8:35; 11:31; 12:3 and οἶκος also in 2:17; 11:20. Moreover, the use of οἶκος in 2:16 may be determined by anticipation of its use in the very next verse, where in a quotation it reflects the LXX of Ps 68:10.

connotes a corpse when associated with death, and several features of John 2:14–22 do associate Jesus' σῶμα with death: (1) "Zeal for your house will *consume* me" (v. 17); (2) "*Destroy* this temple" (v. 19); and (3) "When therefore he was raised *from the dead* his disciples remembered that he had said this" (v. 22). Additionally John refers twice to Jesus' σῶμα in the account of Jesus' burial (19:38, 40).

If then Jesus' body is initially the temple consisting of his corpse but a corpse then raised from the dead in three days (cf. the portrayal of Jesus in Rev 5:6 as the Lamb that had been "slain," as evidenced by the scars of crucifixion [see also John 20:24–29], yet "standing" in resurrection as opposed to lying on an altar), the many abodes located in his Father's house are located in his slain-but-raised body. There believers in God and in Jesus abide just as God the Father abides there. And he prepared "a place" for those believers by laying down his life on his own authority and by taking it up again likewise (10:17–18; cf. 2:19, "in three days *I* will raise it," Jesus' practically insisting on getting arrested in 18:2–11, and Pilate's lack of inherent authority over Jesus according to 19:11). As does the Father's house, "a place" (τόπον) also refers to Jesus' slain-but-raised body; for alongside its general meaning it carries in certain contexts a temple-reference: "in Jerusalem is the *place* where it is necessary to worship" (John 4:20); "the Romans will come and take away both our *place* and our nation" (John 11:48). With the location of the many abodes in the Father's house/temple/place of Jesus' slain-but-raised body we may compare the requirement of eating his flesh and drinking his blood in 6:51–58. And of course *the abodes in that body of his relate to the theme of abiding in him according to 15:1–9 and 1 John passim*, so that the Father's house connotes also a family dwelling, a household, in agreement with being "born from above" (3:3–7) and Jesus' calling believers "children" (τέκνα in 1:12; 11:52 and τεκνίον in 13:33), not to detail the constant talk of "Father" and "Son."

The description of the abodes as "many" links up with the innumerability of the redeemed (Rev 7:9), with the "nations" of saved people who make up the new Jerusalem whose temple God and the Lamb are (Rev 21:22), and with the emphasis in John's Gospel on Jesus as the Lamb of God who takes away the sin "of the world" (1:29) and as the good shepherd who has "other sheep… not of this fold" that he must bring (10:16; cf. John's emphasis on the large crowd that acclaims Jesus at the triumphal entry, a crowd so large that the Pharisees ex-claim in frustration and disgust, "Look! The *world* has gone after him"). And the many abodes exist in his Father's house, i.e., in his body, "because" he goes to prepare a place for believers by laying down his life and taking it again.[23]

---

[23] Here I take "but if not, I would have told you" (14:2) as parenthetical, so that ὅτι is causal: "In my Father's house are many abodes … because I am going to prepare a place for you" (so also A. R. Kerr, *The Temple of Jesus' Body* [JSNTSup 220; Sheffield: Sheffield Academic Press, 2002], 276). See commentaries for alternative views.

Jesus' going (πορεύομαι) means his journeying to the Father via crucifixion and resurrection, for this journey has the Father as its destination (see the use of πορεύομαι in 14:12, 28; 16:7, 28). So Jesus' work of preparation reaches completion not until he ascends to the Father on the first Easter Sunday, as he said to Mary Magdalene on the morning of that very day: "go to my brothers and tell them, 'I am ascending to my Father and your Father and [to] my God and your God'" (20:17). The work of preparation then complete, Jesus can come again to receive believers – "to himself" (14:3) because he himself is their abiding-place. "Again" implies an earlier coming of Jesus, at the incarnation of the Word, as mentioned repeatedly in John.[24]

But from Jesus' and the disciples' standpoint, exactly when will he come again? The answer appears in 20:19 ("Jesus *came* and stood in the midst of the disciples and said to them, 'Peace to you'"), 24 ("Thomas... was not with them when Jesus *came*"), 26 ("And after eight days ... Jesus *comes*"); and 21:13 ("Jesus *comes*"). *Among NT writers John alone uses the verb "come" (ἔρχομαι) for the recently risen Jesus.* All the others talk only about Jesus' appearing to the disciples and about their seeing him. In the first instance, then, he comes again right after his crucifixion, resurrection, and ascension in order that his disciples may abide in him. So also in 14:18: "I will not leave you orphans, I am *coming* to you." And just as believers take up their abodes in him, the Father and he will come to the believer and make their abode with the believer (14:23).[25] Shades of Revelation 21–22 where, as noted above, God and the Lamb will dwell in the saints inasmuch as the saints, the new Jerusalem, are the tabernacle where God will dwell just as they will dwell in God and the Lamb inasmuch as the cubically shaped city consisting of the saints will be the holy of holies, located in the temple consisting of God and the Lamb.

But there is a still future coming of Jesus in John's Gospel. Chapter 21, verses 22–23 record that after he had come again several times the risen Jesus said, "If I want him [the beloved disciple] to abide [i.e., stay alive] *till I come*, what is that to you [Peter]? Follow me." So Jesus' comings right after his glorification to receive believers into their abodes in the temple of his own body, which is "the Father's house" – those comings anticipated his coming yet in the future. In the book of Revelation, then, John the seer writes about Jesus, "Be-

---

[24] For theologically freighted mentions see 1:9, 11; 3:2, 19, 31 [twice] et passim.

[25] H.-J. Klauck draws attention to the difference between παρά ("with, alongside"), used in 14:23, and ἐν ("in"; "Himmlisches Haus und irdische Bleibe: Eschatologische Metaphorik in Antike und Christentum," *NTS* 50 [2004]: 25). The latter, he says, connotes "Innerlichkeit" and the former, "Präsenz, Anwesenheit, Gemeinschaft." But little or nothing should be made of the difference between these prepositions. For not only does John like to use synonyms without distinction in meaning but also in 14:20 Jesus uses ἐν for his dwelling in believers: "I [am] in the Father, and you [are] in me, and *I am in you*." So being "in" and "with" mean the same thing (cf. Jesus' saying in 14:3 that he "will receive" (παραλήμψομαι) believers to himself that they may abide "in" (ἐν) him.

hold, he *is coming* with clouds, and every eye will see him, even those who pierced him" (1:7). And he quotes Jesus: "Yes, I *am coming* quickly" (22:20a). The Christian response is, "Amen! *Come*, Lord Jesus" (Rev 22:20b).

Before that yet future coming the command to abide in Jesus carries the note of perseverance as opposed to apostasy, as in John 15:6: "If anyone does not abide in me he is thrown out as a branch [is thrown out] and dries up, and people gather them and throw [them] into the fire, and they are burned up" (cf. the apostasy of many of Jesus' disciples in John 6:60–71). But after that yet future coming, abiding in Jesus changes from perseverance into permanence. For Rev 3:12 quotes Jesus as saying, "The one who wins the victory [i.e., who proves to be a true believer by persevering] – I will make him a pillar in the temple of my God [i.e., in Jesus' slain-and-raised body] and he will never go out anymore [Of course not, because pillars don't walk! Cf. the caryatids in the porch of the Erechtheum on the Acropolis in Athens], and I will write on him the name of my God and the name of the city of my God, the new Jerusalem [made up of the saints]…, and my new name." Meanwhile, by abiding in Jesus believers are already where he is, in heaven with God the Father just as the Father and Jesus abide in believers on earth: "in order that where I am you too may be."[26]

---

[26] The foregoing interpretation of John 14:2–3 shares a number of points with Kerr's *The Temple of Jesus' Body*; J. McCaffrey's *The House with Many Rooms* (AnBib 114; Rome: Pontifical Biblical Institute, 1988); J. H. Neyrey's "Spaces and Places, Whence and Whither, Homes and Rooms: 'Territoriality' in the Fourth Gospel," *BTB* 32 (2002): 65–66, 68–69; and F. F. Segovia's *The Farewell of the Word* (Minneapolis: Fortress, 1991), 82–84; but they do not interrelate the passage with passages in the book of Revelation. The foregoing interpretation also represents some significant revisions of my interpretation in "'In my Father's House are many *Monai*' (John 14:2)," *ZNW* 58 (1967): 68–72. See Klauck, "Himmlisches Haus und irdische Bleibe," 20–27, for a particularly rich bibliography.

Indexes

1. Ancient Sources

2:5–7	101	6:45–8:26	75
2:9, 10	94	7:1–23	47
2:12, 13, 14	79	7:3–4	71
2:15	90	7:6	189
2:19–20	335	7:6–13	199
2:27	77	7:8–9	134
3:1	94	7:11	71
3:1–6	101	7:19–23	189
3:3, 5	94	7:23	71
3:6	101	7:24–30	338
3:11	108	7:25, 26	94
3:14	90	7:31	71, 78
3:16	72	7:31–37	70
3:16–19	91	7:34	71
3:17–19	71	8:1–10	70
3:20–21	90, 91	8:22	94
3:27	312	8:22–26	70, 75
3:29	102	8:23	94
Ch. 4	92	8:27–31	7
4:1–2	79, 94	8:29	72
4:1–32	131	8:31	80
4:8	46, 113	8:32	81
4:10	94	8:32–33	72
4:11	83, 94	8:33	59
4:11–12	82, 83	8:34–38	46
4:13–20	94	8:35	78, 297
4:15, 16, 18	331	8:38	142, 327, 352
4:20	46, 113, 331	9:1	72, 297, 346
4:26–29	77	9:2	72, 91
4:29	304	9:5	72
4:33–34	94	9:7	108, 303, 359, 360
5:1–20	90	9:14–16	83
5:2	94	9:14–27	90
5:7	108	9:17	94
5:8, 15, 16	94	9:21	83, 89, 94
5:18	90, 94	9:22–24	83
5:19	90	9:24	94
5:22, 25, 33, 35, 36	94	9:25	96
5:37	72	9:25–27	83, 84
5:41	71, 89	9:26–27	89
6:4	331	9:28	83
6:7–11	91	9:30–32	80
6:7–13	131	9:32	84, 328
6:9	158	9:33–37	131
6:12	80	9:35	329
6:18	119	9:37	338
6:27	96	9:41	7, 138
6:30	80, 81	9:42	9
6:30–31	80	9:42–48	131
6:34	81, 82	Ch. 10	92
6:35–44	70	10:1	81, 94, 95
6:39	96	10:1–34	95
6:45–56	70	10:13–45	92

6:66	340, 358	8:26	345
6:66–71	356	8:26–30	344
6:68	327, 339, 341, 360	8:28	323, 330, 349, 355,
6:71	343		388
7:5	6	8:29	323
7:7	329, 341	8:31	327
7:11–17	341	8:31–32	344
7:14	323	8:31–38	344, 345, 358
7:14–17	330	8:31–55	355
7:15	341	8:32	345
7:16	323, 382	8:35	408
7:16–18	331	8:36	345, 360
7:17	323	8:37	327, 345
7:21	387	8:38	331, 345
7:26	341	8:39–47	345
7:27	322	8:40	331, 345
7:27–28	334	8:41	387
7:28	323, 330, 341	8:42	323
7:28–29	142, 323, 334	8:42–44	331
7:29	345	8:43	327, 331, 345
7:32	342, 348	8:44	317, 344, 345, 362
7:33–34	370	8:47	327, 328, 346
7:35	323	8:51	327, 329, 331, 353,
7:36	327, 342, 370		354
7:37	330	8:51–52	328, 346
7:37–38	370	8:52	327, 329, 331
7:37–39	6, 11, 180, 318,	8:54	343, 360
	336, 341, 342	8:55	142, 327, 346
7:38	9, 406	8:58	8, 9, 336
7:40	327, 331, 342	8:59	109
7:40–43	342	9:1–12	346
7:40–44	322	9:2	323
7:44–46	342	9:3	9
7:45	362	9:5	360, 386, 389
7:45–52	322	9:8–9	336
7:46	342, 370	9:9	99
7:50	109	9:12	362
7:51	312	9:13–41	328
8:12	8, 336, 337, 360,	9:16	345
	386, 389	9:17	322
8:12–20	342	9:22	322
8:13	329	9:33	345
8:14	323, 329, 334	9:35	337, 349
8:15	340, 351	9:35–39	9
8:16	351	9:37	337
8:18	329, 334	9:39	320
8:19	142	9:39–41	349
8:20	323, 327, 341, 342	9:41	320
8:21	328	10:1	408
8:23	343, 405	10:1–5	352
8:24	9, 328, 343, 344	10:1–18	346
8:25	343, 344	10:2	408
8:25–30	331	10:3	329, 331, 408

2. Modern Authors

3. Selected Topics

454   *Indexes*

Wissenschaftliche Untersuchungen zum Neuen Testament

Alphabetical Index of the First and Second Series

Bolyki, János: Jesu Tischgemeinschaften. 1997.
Volume II/96.
Bosman, Philip: Conscience in Philo and Paul.
2003. *Volume II/166.*
Bovon, François: Studies in Early Christianity.
2003. *Volume 161.*
Brocke, Christoph vom: Thessaloniki – Stadt
des Kassander und Gemeinde des Paulus.
2001. *Volume II/125.*
Brunson, Andrew: Psalm 118 in the Gospel of
John. 2003. *Volume II/158.*
Büchli, Jörg: Der Poimandres – ein paganisier-
tes Evangelium. 1987. *Volume II/27.*
Bühner, Jan A.: Der Gesandte und sein Weg im
4. Evangelium. 1977. *Volume II/2.*
Burchard, Christoph: Untersuchungen zu
Joseph und Aseneth. 1965. *Volume 8.*
– Studien zur Theologie, Sprache und Umwelt
des Neuen Testaments. Ed. von D. Sänger.
1998. *Volume 107.*
Burnett, Richard: Karl Barth's Theological
Exegesis. 2001. *Volume II/145.*
Byron, John: Slavery Metaphors in Early
Judaism and Pauline Christianity. 2003.
Volume II/162.
Byrskog, Samuel: Story as History – History as
Story. 2000. *Volume 123.*
Cancik, Hubert (Ed.): Markus-Philologie. 1984.
Volume 33.
Capes, David B.: Old Testament Yaweh Texts in
Paul's Christology. 1992. *Volume II/47.*
Caragounis, Chrys C.: The Development of
Greek and the New Testament. 2004.
Volume 167.
– The Son of Man. 1986. *Volume 38.*
– see *Fridrichsen, Anton.*
Carleton Paget, James: The Epistle of Barnabas.
1994. *Volume II/64.*
Carson, D.A., O'Brien, Peter T. and *Mark
Seifrid* (Ed.): Justification and Variegated
Nomism.
Volume 1: The Complexities of Second
Temple Judaism. 2001. *Volume II/140.*
Volume 2: The Paradoxes of Paul. 2004.
Volume II/181.
Ciampa, Roy E.: The Presence and Function of
Scripture in Galatians 1 and 2. 1998.
Volume II/102.
Classen, Carl Joachim: Rhetorical Criticsm of
the New Testament. 2000. *Volume 128.*
Colpe, Carsten: Iranier – Aramäer – Hebräer –
Hellenen. 2003. *Volume 154.*
Crump, David: Jesus the Intercessor. 1992.
Volume II/49.
Dahl, Nils Alstrup: Studies in Ephesians. 2000.
Volume 131.

Deines, Roland: Die Gerechtigkeit der Tora im
Reich des Messias. 2004. *Volume 177.*
– Jüdische Steingefäße und pharisäische
Frömmigkeit. 1993. *Volume II/52.*
– Die Pharisäer. 1997. *Volume 101.*
– and *Karl-Wilhelm Niebuhr (Ed.):* Philo und
das Neue Testament. 2004. *Volume 172.*
Dettwiler, Andreas and *Jean Zumstein (Ed.):*
Kreuzestheologie im Neuen Testament.
2002. *Volume 151.*
Dickson, John P.: Mission-Commitment in
Ancient Judaism and in the Pauline
Communities. 2003. *Volume II/159.*
Dietzfelbinger, Christian: Der Abschied des
Kommenden. 1997. *Volume 95.*
*Dimitrov, Ivan Z., James D.G. Dunn, Ulrich
Luz* and *Karl-Wilhelm Niebuhr* (Ed.): Das
Alte Testament als christliche Bibel in
orthodoxer und westlicher Sicht. 2004.
Volume 174.
Dobbeler, Axel von: Glaube als Teilhabe. 1987.
Volume II/22.
Du Toit, David S.: Theios Anthropos. 1997.
Volume II/91
Dübbers, Michael: Christologie und Existenz im
Kolosserbrief. 2005. *Volume II/191.*
Dunn, James D.G. (Ed.): Jews and Christians.
1992. *Volume 66.*
– Paul and the Mosaic Law. 1996. *Volume 89.*
– see *Dimitrov, Ivan Z.*
Dunn, James D.G., Hans Klein, Ulrich Luz and
Vasile Mihoc (Ed.): Auslegung der Bibel in
orthodoxer und westlicher Perspektive. 2000.
Volume 130.
Ebel, Eva: Die Attraktivität früher christlicher
Gemeinden. 2004. *Volume II/178.*
Ebertz, Michael N.: Das Charisma des Gekreu-
zigten. 1987. *Volume 45.*
Eckstein, Hans-Joachim: Der Begriff Syneidesis
bei Paulus. 1983. *Volume II/10.*
– Verheißung und Gesetz. 1996. *Volume 86.*
Ego, Beate: Im Himmel wie auf Erden. 1989.
Volume II/34
Ego, Beate, Armin Lange and Peter Pilhofer
(Ed.): Gemeinde ohne Tempel – Community
without Temple. 1999. *Volume 118.*
Eisen, Ute E.: see *Paulsen, Henning.*
Ellis, E. Earle: Prophecy and Hermeneutic in
Early Christianity. 1978. *Volume 18.*
– The Old Testament in Early Christianity.
1991. *Volume 54.*
Endo, Masanobu: Creation and Christology.
2002. *Volume 149.*
Ennulat, Andreas: Die 'Minor Agreements'.
1994. *Volume II/62.*
Ensor, Peter W.: Jesus and His 'Works'. 1996.
Volume II/85.

Eskola, Timo: Messiah and the Throne. 2001. *Volume II/142.*
- Theodicy and Predestination in Pauline Soteriology. 1998. *Volume II/100.*

Fatehi, Mehrdad: The Spirit's Relation to the Risen Lord in Paul. 2000. *Volume II/128.*

Feldmeier, Reinhard: Die Krisis des Gottessohnes. 1987. *Volume II/21.*
- Die Christen als Fremde. 1992. *Volume 64.*

Feldmeier, Reinhard and *Ulrich Heckel* (Ed.): Die Heiden. 1994. *Volume 70.*

Fletcher-Louis, Crispin H.T.: Luke-Acts: Angels, Christology and Soteriology. 1997. *Volume II/94.*

Förster, Niclas: Marcus Magus. 1999. *Volume 114.*

Forbes, Christopher Brian: Prophecy and Inspired Speech in Early Christianity and its Hellenistic Environment. 1995. *Volume II/75.*

Fornberg, Tord: see *Fridrichsen, Anton.*

Fossum, Jarl E.: The Name of God and the Angel of the Lord. 1985. *Volume 36.*

Foster, Paul: Community, Law and Mission in Matthew's Gospel. *Volume II/177.*

Fotopoulos, John: Food Offered to Idols in Roman Corinth. 2003. *Volume II/151.*

Frenschkowski, Marco: Offenbarung und Epiphanie. Volume 1 1995. *Volume II/79* – Volume 2 1997. *Volume II/80.*

Frey, Jörg: Eugen Drewermann und die biblische Exegese. 1995. *Volume II/71.*
- Die johanneische Eschatologie. Volume I. 1997. *Volume 96.* – Volume II. 1998. *Volume 110.*
- Volume III. 2000. *Volume 117.*

Frey, Jörg and *Udo Schnelle (Ed.):* Kontexte des Johannesevangeliums. 2004. *Volume 175.*

Freyne, Sean: Galilee and Gospel. 2000. *Volume 125.*

Fridrichsen, Anton: Exegetical Writings. Edited by C.C. Caragounis and T. Fornberg. 1994. *Volume 76.*

Garlington, Don B.: 'The Obedience of Faith'. 1991. *Volume II/38.*
- Faith, Obedience, and Perseverance. 1994. *Volume 79.*

Garnet, Paul: Salvation and Atonement in the Qumran Scrolls. 1977. *Volume II/3.*

Gese, Michael: Das Vermächtnis des Apostels. 1997. *Volume II/99.*

Gheorghita, Radu: The Role of the Septuagint in Hebrews. 2003. *Volume II/160.*

Gräbe, Petrus J.: The Power of God in Paul's Letters. 2000. *Volume II/123.*

Gräßer, Erich: Der Alte Bund im Neuen. 1985. *Volume 35.*
- Forschungen zur Apostelgeschichte. 2001. *Volume 137.*

Green, Joel B.: The Death of Jesus. 1988. *Volume II/33.*

Gregory, Andrew: The Reception of Luke and Acts in the Period before Irenaeus. 2003. *Volume II/169.*

Gundry, Robert H.: The Old is Better. 2005. *Volume 178.*

Gundry Volf, Judith M.: Paul and Perseverance. 1990. *Volume II/37.*

Hafemann, Scott J.: Suffering and the Spirit. 1986. *Volume II/19.*
- Paul, Moses, and the History of Israel. 1995. *Volume 81.*

Hahn, Johannes (Ed.). Zerstörungen des Jerusalemer Tempels. 2002. *Volume 147.*

Hannah, Darrel D.: Michael and Christ. 1999. *Volume II/109.*

Hamid-Khani, Saeed: Relevation and Concealment of Christ. 2000. *Volume II/120.*

Harrison; James R.: Paul's Language of Grace in Its Graeco-Roman Context. 2003. *Volume II/172.*

Hartman, Lars: Text-Centered New Testament Studies. Ed. von D. Hellholm. 1997. *Volume 102.*

Hartog, Paul: Polycarp and the New Testament. 2001. *Volume II/134.*

Heckel, Theo K.: Der Innere Mensch. 1993. *Volume II/53.*
- Vom Evangelium des Markus zum viergestaltigen Evangelium. 1999. *Volume 120.*

Heckel, Ulrich: Kraft in Schwachheit. 1993. *Volume II/56.*
- Der Segen im Neuen Testament. 2002. *Volume 150.*
- see *Feldmeier, Reinhard.*
- see *Hengel, Martin.*

Heiligenthal, Roman: Werke als Zeichen. 1983. *Volume II/9.*

Hellholm, D.: see *Hartman, Lars.*

Hemer, Colin J.: The Book of Acts in the Setting of Hellenistic History. 1989. *Volume 49.*

Hengel, Martin: Judentum und Hellenismus. 1969, ³1988. *Volume 10.*
- Die johanneische Frage. 1993. *Volume 67.*
- Judaica et Hellenistica. Kleine Schriften I. 1996. *Volume 90.*
- Judaica, Hellenistica et Christiana. Kleine Schriften II. 1999. *Volume 109.*
- Paulus und Jakobus. Kleine Schriften III. 2002. *Volume 141.*

Hengel, Martin and *Ulrich Heckel* (Ed.): Paulus und das antike Judentum. 1991. *Volume 58.*

Hengel, Martin and *Hermut Löhr* (Ed.): Schriftauslegung im antiken Judentum und im Urchristentum. 1994. *Volume 73.*

Hengel, Martin and *Anna Maria Schwemer:* Paulus zwischen Damaskus und Antiochien. 1998. *Volume 108.*

– Der messianische Anspruch Jesu und die Anfänge der Christologie. 2001. *Volume 138.*

Hengel, Martin and *Anna Maria Schwemer* (Ed.): Königsherrschaft Gottes und himmlischer Kult. 1991. *Volume 55.*

– Die Septuaginta. 1994. *Volume 72.*

Hengel, Martin; Siegfried Mittmann and *Anna Maria Schwemer* (Ed.): La Cité de Dieu / Die Stadt Gottes. 2000. *Volume 129.*

Herrenbrück, Fritz: Jesus und die Zöllner. 1990. *Volume II/41.*

Herzer, Jens: Paulus oder Petrus? 1998. *Volume 103.*

Hoegen-Rohls, Christina: Der nachösterliche Johannes. 1996. *Volume II/84.*

Hofius, Otfried: Katapausis. 1970. *Volume 11.*

– Der Vorhang vor dem Thron Gottes. 1972. *Volume 14.*

– Der Christushymnus Philipper 2,6-11. 1976, ²1991. *Volume 17.*

– Paulusstudien. 1989, ²1994. *Volume 51.*

– Neutestamentliche Studien. 2000. *Volume 132.*

– Paulusstudien II. 2002. *Volume 143.*

Hofius, Otfried and *Hans-Christian Kammler:* Johannesstudien. 1996. *Volume 88.*

Holtz, Traugott: Geschichte und Theologie des Urchristentums. 1991. *Volume 57.*

Hommel, Hildebrecht: Sebasmata. Volume 1 1983. *Volume 31* – Volume 2 1984. *Volume 32.*

Hvalvik, Reidar: The Struggle for Scripture and Covenant. 1996. *Volume II/82.*

Johns, Loren L.: The Lamb Christology of the Apocalypse of John. 2003. *Volume II/167.*

Joubert, Stephan: Paul as Benefactor. 2000. *Volume II/124.*

Jungbauer, Harry: „Ehre Vater und Mutter". 2002. *Volume II/146.*

Kähler, Christoph: Jesu Gleichnisse als Poesie und Therapie. 1995. *Volume 78.*

Kamlah, Ehrhard: Die Form der katalogischen Paränese im Neuen Testament. 1964. *Volume 7.*

Kammler, Hans-Christian: Christologie und Eschatologie. 2000. *Volume 126.*

– Kreuz und Weisheit. 2003. *Volume 159.*

– see *Hofius, Otfried.*

Kelhoffer, James A.: The Diet of John the Baptist. 2005. *Volume 176.*

– Miracle and Mission. 1999. *Volume II/112.*

Kieffer, René and *Jan Bergman (Ed.):* La Main de Dieu / Die Hand Gottes. 1997. *Volume 94.*

Kim, Seyoon: The Origin of Paul's Gospel. 1981, ²1984. *Volume II/4.*

– Paul and the New Perspective. 2002. *Volume 140.*

– "The 'Son of Man'" as the Son of God. 1983. *Volume 30.*

Klauck, Hans-Josef: Religion und Gesellschaft im frühen Christentum. 2003. *Volume 152.*

Klein, Hans: see *Dunn, James D.G..*

Kleinknecht, Karl Th.: Der leidende Gerechtfertigte. 1984, ²1988. *Volume II/13.*

Klinghardt, Matthias: Gesetz und Volk Gottes. 1988. *Volume II/32.*

Koch, Michael: Drachenkampf und Sonnenfrau. 2004. *Volume II/184.*

Koch, Stefan: Rechtliche Regelung von Konflikten im frühen Christentum. 2004. *Volume II/174.*

Köhler, Wolf-Dietrich: Rezeption des Matthäusevangeliums in der Zeit vor Irenäus. 1987. *Volume II/24.*

Köhn, Andreas: Der Neutestamentler Ernst Lohmeyer. 2004. *Volume II/180.*

Kooten, George H. van: Cosmic Christology in Paul and the Pauline School. 2003. *Volume II/171.*

Korn, Manfred: Die Geschichte Jesu in veränderter Zeit. 1993. *Volume II/51.*

Koskenniemi, Erkki: Apollonios von Tyana in der neutestamentlichen Exegese. 1994. *Volume II/61.*

Kraus, Thomas J.: Sprache, Stil und historischer Ort des zweiten Petrusbriefes. 2001. *Volume II/136.*

Kraus, Wolfgang: Das Volk Gottes. 1996. *Volume 85.*

– and *Karl-Wilhelm Niebuhr* (Ed.): Frühjudentum und Neues Testament im Horizont Biblischer Theologie. 2003. *Volume 162.*

– see *Walter, Nikolaus.*

Kreplin, Matthias: Das Selbstverständnis Jesu. 2001. *Volume II/141.*

Kuhn, Karl G.: Achtzehngebet und Vaterunser und der Reim. 1950. *Volume 1.*

Kvalbein, Hans: see *Ådna, Jostein.*

Kwon, Yon-Gyong: Eschatology in Galatians. 2004. *Volume II/183.*

Laansma, Jon: I Will Give You Rest. 1997. *Volume II/98.*

Labahn, Michael: Offenbarung in Zeichen und Wort. 2000. *Volume II/117.*

Lambers-Petry, Doris: see *Tomson, Peter J.*

Lange, Armin: see *Ego, Beate.*

Lampe, Peter: Die stadtrömischen Christen in den ersten beiden Jahrhunderten. 1987, ²1989. *Volume II/18.*

Landmesser, Christof: Wahrheit als Grundbegriff neutestamentlicher Wissenschaft. 1999. *Volume 113.*

– Jüngerberufung und Zuwendung zu Gott. 2000. *Volume 133.*

Lau, Andrew: Manifest in Flesh. 1996. *Volume II/86.*

Lawrence, Louise: An Ethnography of the Gospel of Matthew. 2003. *Volume II/165.*

Lee, Aquila H.I.: From Messiah to Preexistent Son. 2005. *Volume II/192.*

Lee, Pilchan: The New Jerusalem in the Book of Relevation. 2000. *Volume II/129.*

Lichtenberger, Hermann: see *Avemarie, Friedrich.*

Lichtenberger, Hermann: Das Ich Adams und das Ich der Menschheit. 2004. *Volume 164.*

Lierman, John: The New Testament Moses. 2004. *Volume II/173.*

Lieu, Samuel N.C.: Manichaeism in the Later Roman Empire and Medieval China. ²1992. *Volume 63.*

Lindgård, Fredrik: Paul's Line of Thought in 2 Corinthians 4:16-5:10. 2004. *Volume II/189.*

Loader, William R.G.: Jesus' Attitude Towards the Law. 1997. *Volume II/97.*

Löhr, Gebhard: Verherrlichung Gottes durch Philosophie. 1997. *Volume 97.*

Löhr, Hermut: Studien zum frühchristlichen und frühjüdischen Gebet. 2003. *Volume160.*

– : see *Hengel, Martin.*

Löhr, Winrich Alfried: Basilides und seine Schule. 1995. *Volume 83.*

Luomanen, Petri: Entering the Kingdom of Heaven. 1998. *Volume II/101.*

Luz, Ulrich: see *Dunn, James D.G.*

Mackay, Ian D.: John's Raltionship with Mark. 2004. *Volume II/182.*

Maier, Gerhard: Mensch und freier Wille. 1971. *Volume 12.*

– Die Johannesoffenbarung und die Kirche. 1981. *Volume 25.*

Markschies, Christoph: Valentinus Gnosticus? 1992. *Volume 65.*

Marshall, Peter: Enmity in Corinth: Social Conventions in Paul's Relations with the Corinthians. 1987. *Volume II/23.*

Mayer, Annemarie: Sprache der Einheit im Epheserbrief und in der Ökumene. 2002. *Volume II/150.*

McDonough, Sean M.: YHWH at Patmos: Rev. 1:4 in its Hellenistic and Early Jewish Setting. 1999. *Volume II/107.*

McGlynn, Moyna: Divine Judgement and Divine Benevolence in the Book of Wisdom. 2001. *Volume II/139.*

Meade, David G.: Pseudonymity and Canon. 1986. *Volume 39.*

Meadors, Edward P.: Jesus the Messianic Herald of Salvation. 1995. *Volume II/72.*

Meißner, Stefan: Die Heimholung des Ketzers. 1996. *Volume II/87.*

Mell, Ulrich: Die „anderen" Winzer. 1994. *Volume 77.*

Mengel, Berthold: Studien zum Philipperbrief. 1982. *Volume II/8.*

Merkel, Helmut: Die Widersprüche zwischen den Evangelien. 1971. *Volume 13.*

Merklein, Helmut: Studien zu Jesus und Paulus. Volume 1 1987. *Volume 43.* – Volume 2 1998. *Volume 105.*

Metzdorf, Christina: Die Tempelaktion Jesu. 2003. *Volume II/168.*

Metzler, Karin: Der griechische Begriff des Verzeihens. 1991. *Volume II/44.*

Metzner, Rainer: Die Rezeption des Matthäusevangeliums im 1. Petrusbrief. 1995. *Volume II/74.*

– Das Verständnis der Sünde im Johannesevangelium. 2000. *Volume 122.*

Mihoc, Vasile: see *Dunn, James D.G..*

Mineshige, Kiyoshi: Besitzverzicht und Almosen bei Lukas. 2003. *Volume II/163.*

Mittmann, Siegfried: see *Hengel, Martin.*

Mittmann-Richert, Ulrike: Magnifikat und Benediktus. *1996. Volume II/90.*

Mußner, Franz: Jesus von Nazareth im Umfeld Israels und der Urkirche. Ed. von M. Theobald. 1998. *Volume 111.*

Niebuhr, Karl-Wilhelm: Gesetz und Paränese. 1987. *Volume II/28.*

– Heidenapostel aus Israel. 1992. *Volume 62.*

– see *Deines, Roland*

– see *Dimitrov, Ivan Z.*

– see *Kraus, Wolfgang*

Nielsen, Anders E.: "Until it is Fullfilled". 2000. *Volume 126.*

Nissen, Andreas: Gott und der Nächste im antiken Judentum. 1974. *Volume 15.*

Noack, Christian: Gottesbewußtsein. 2000. *Volume II/116.*

Noormann, Rolf: Irenäus als Paulusinterpret. 1994. *Volume II/66.*

Novakovic, Lidija: Messiah, the Healer of the Sick. 2003. *Volume II/170.*

Obermann, Andreas: Die christologische Erfüllung der Schrift im Johannesevangelium. 1996. *Volume II/83.*

Öhler, Markus: Barnabas. 2003. *Volume 156.*

Okure, Teresa: The Johannine Approach to
Mission. 1988. *Volume II/31.*

Onuki, Takashi: Heil und Erlösung. 2004.
Volume 165.

Oropeza, B. J.: Paul and Apostasy. 2000.
Volume II/115.

Ostmeyer, Karl-Heinrich: Taufe und Typos.
2000. *Volume II/118.*

Paulsen, Henning: Studien zur Literatur und
Geschichte des frühen Christentums. Ed. von
Ute E. Eisen. 1997. *Volume 99.*

Pao, David W.: Acts and the Isaianic New
Exodus. 2000. *Volume II/130.*

Park, Eung Chun: The Mission Discourse in
Matthew's Interpretation. 1995.
Volume II/81.

Park, Joseph S.: Conceptions of Afterlife in
Jewish Insriptions. 2000. *Volume II/121.*

Pate, C. Marvin: The Reverse of the Curse.
2000. *Volume II/114.*

Peres, Imre: Griechische Grabinschriften und
neutestamentliche Eschatologie. 2003.
Volume 157.

Philonenko, Marc (Ed.): Le Trône de Dieu.
1993. *Volume 69.*

Pilhofer, Peter: Presbyteron Kreitton. 1990.
Volume II/39.

– Philippi. Volume 1 1995. *Volume 87.* –
Volume 2 2000. *Volume 119.*

– Die frühen Christen und ihre Welt. 2002.
Volume 145.

– see *Ego, Beate.*

Plümacher, Eckhard: Geschichte und Geschich-
ten. Aufsätze zur Apostelgeschichte und zu
den Johannesakten. Herausgegeben von Jens
Schröter und Ralph Brucker. 2004.
Volume 170.

Pöhlmann, Wolfgang: Der Verlorene Sohn und
das Haus. 1993. *Volume 68.*

Pokorný, Petr and *Josef B. Souček:* Bibelausle-
gung als Theologie. 1997. *Volume 100.*

Pokorný, Petr and *Jan Roskovec* (Ed.):
Philosophical Hermeneutics and Biblical
Exegesis. 2002. *Volume 153.*

Porter, Stanley E.: The Paul of Acts. 1999.
Volume 115.

Prieur, Alexander: Die Verkündigung der
Gottesherrschaft. 1996. *Volume II/89.*

Probst, Hermann: Paulus und der Brief. 1991.
Volume II/45.

Räisänen, Heikki: Paul and the Law. 1983,
²1987. *Volume 29.*

Rehkopf, Friedrich: Die lukanische Sonderquel-
le. 1959. *Volume 5.*

Rein, Matthias: Die Heilung des Blindgeborenen
(Joh 9). 1995. *Volume II/73.*

Reinmuth, Eckart: Pseudo-Philo und Lukas.
1994. *Volume 74.*

Reiser, Marius: Syntax und Stil des Markusevangeliums. 1984. *Volume II/11.*

Rhodes, James N.: The Epistle of Barnabas
and the Deuteronomic Tradition. 2004.
Volume II/188.

Richards, E. Randolph: The Secretary in the
Letters of Paul. 1991. *Volume II/42.*

Riesner, Rainer: Jesus als Lehrer. 1981, ³1988.
Volume II/7.

– Die Frühzeit des Apostels Paulus. 1994.
Volume 71.

Rissi, Mathias: Die Theologie des Hebräerbriefs.
1987. *Volume 41.*

Roskovec, Jan: see *Pokorný, Petr.*

Röhser, Günter: Metaphorik und Personifikation
der Sünde. 1987. *Volume II/25.*

Rose, Christian: Die Wolke der Zeugen. 1994.
Volume II/60.

Rothschild, Clare K.: Luke Acts and the
Rhetoric of History. 2004. *Volume II/175.*

Rüegger, Hans-Ulrich: Verstehen, was Markus
erzählt. 2002. *Volume II/155.*

Rüger, Hans Peter: Die Weisheitsschrift aus der
Kairoer Geniza. 1991. *Volume 53.*

Sänger, Dieter: Antikes Judentum und die
Mysterien. 1980. *Volume II/5.*

– Die Verkündigung des Gekreuzigten und
Israel. 1994. *Volume 75.*

– see *Burchard, Christoph*

Salier, Willis Hedley: The Rhetorical Impact of
the Sēmeia in the Gospel of John. 2004.
Volume II/186.

Salzmann, Jorg Christian: Lehren und
Ermahnen. 1994. *Volume II/59.*

Sandnes, Karl Olav: Paul – One of the
Prophets? 1991. *Volume II/43.*

Sato, Migaku: Q und Prophetie. 1988.
Volume II/29.

Schäfer, Ruth: Paulus bis zum Apostelkonzil.
2004. *Volume II/179.*

Schaper, Joachim: Eschatology in the Greek
Psalter. 1995. *Volume II/76.*

Schimanowski, Gottfried: Die himmlische
Liturgie in der Apokalypse des Johannes.
2002. *Volume II/154.*

– Weisheit und Messias. 1985. *Volume II/17.*

Schlichting, Günter: Ein jüdisches Leben Jesu.
1982. *Volume 24.*

Schnabel, Eckhard J.: Law and Wisdom from
Ben Sira to Paul. 1985. *Volume II/16.*

Schnelle, Udo: see *Frey, Jörg.*

Schutter, William L.: Hermeneutic and
Composition in I Peter. 1989. *Volume II/30.*

Schwartz, Daniel R.: Studies in the Jewish Background of Christianity. 1992. *Volume 60.*

Schwemer, Anna Maria: see *Hengel, Martin*

Scott, James M.: Adoption as Sons of God. 1992. *Volume II/48.*

– Paul and the Nations. 1995. *Volume 84.*

Shum, Shiu-Lun: Paul's Use of Isaiah in Romans. 2002. *Volume II/156.*

Siegert, Folker: Drei hellenistisch-jüdische Predigten. Teil I 1980. *Volume 20* – Teil II 1992. *Volume 61.*

– Nag-Hammadi-Register. 1982. *Volume 26.*

– Argumentation bei Paulus. 1985. *Volume 34.*

– Philon von Alexandrien. 1988. *Volume 46.*

Simon, Marcel: Le christianisme antique et son contexte religieux I/II. 1981. *Volume 23.*

Snodgrass, Klyne: The Parable of the Wicked Tenants. 1983. *Volume 27.*

Söding, Thomas: Das Wort vom Kreuz. 1997. *Volume 93.*

– see *Thüsing, Wilhelm.*

Sommer, Urs: Die Passionsgeschichte des Markusevangeliums. 1993. *Volume II/58.*

Souček, Josef B.: see *Pokorný, Petr.*

Spangenberg, Volker: Herrlichkeit des Neuen Bundes. 1993. *Volume II/55.*

Spanje, T.E. van: Inconsistency in Paul? 1999. *Volume II/110.*

Speyer, Wolfgang: Frühes Christentum im antiken Strahlungsfeld. Volume I: 1989. *Volume 50.*

– Volume II: 1999. *Volume 116.*

Stadelmann, Helge: Ben Sira als Schriftgelehrter. 1980. *Volume II/6.*

Stenschke, Christoph W.: Luke's Portrait of Gentiles Prior to Their Coming to Faith. *Volume II/108.*

Sterck-Degueldre, Jean-Pierre: Eine Frau namens Lydia. 2004. *Volume II/176.*

Stettler, Christian: Der Kolosserhymnus. 2000. *Volume II/131.*

Stettler, Hanna: Die Christologie der Pastoralbriefe. 1998. *Volume II/105.*

Stökl Ben Ezra, Daniel: The Impact of Yom Kippur on Early Christianity. 2003. *Volume 163.*

Strobel, August: Die Stunde der Wahrheit. 1980. *Volume 21.*

Stroumsa, Guy G.: Barbarian Philosophy. 1999. *Volume 112.*

Stuckenbruck, Loren T.: Angel Veneration and Christology. 1995. *Volume II/70.*

Stuhlmacher, Peter (Ed.): Das Evangelium und die Evangelien. 1983. *Volume 28.*

– Biblische Theologie und Evangelium. 2002. *Volume 146.*

Sung, Chong-Hyon: Vergebung der Sünden. 1993. *Volume II/57.*

Tajra, Harry W.: The Trial of St. Paul. 1989. *Volume II/35.*

– The Martyrdom of St.Paul. 1994. *Volume II/67.*

Theißen, Gerd: Studien zur Soziologie des Urchristentums. 1979, ³1989. *Volume 19.*

Theobald, Michael: Studien zum Römerbrief. 2001. *Volume 136.*

Theobald, Michael: see *Mußner, Franz.*

Thornton, Claus-Jürgen: Der Zeuge des Zeugen. 1991. *Volume 56.*

Thüsing, Wilhelm: Studien zur neutestamentlichen Theologie. Ed. von Thomas Söding. 1995. *Volume 82.*

Thurén, Lauri: Derhethorizing Paul. 2000. *Volume 124.*

Tolmie, D. Francois: Persuading the Galatians. 2005. *Volume II/190.*

Tomson, Peter J. and *Doris Lambers-Petry* (Ed.): The Image of the Judaeo-Christians in Ancient Jewish and Christian Literature. 2003. *Volume 158.*

Trebilco, Paul: The Early Christians in Ephesus from Paul to Ignatius. 2004. *Volume 166.*

Treloar, Geoffrey R.: Lightfoot the Historian. 1998. *Volume II/103.*

Tsuji, Manabu: Glaube zwischen Vollkommenheit und Verweltlichung. 1997. *Volume II/93*

Twelftree, Graham H.: Jesus the Exorcist. 1993. *Volume II/54.*

Urban, Christina: Das Menschenbild nach dem Johannesevangelium. 2001. *Volume II/137.*

Visotzky, Burton L.: Fathers of the World. 1995. *Volume 80.*

Vollenweider, Samuel: Horizonte neutestamentlicher Christologie. 2002. *Volume 144.*

Vos, Johan S.: Die Kunst der Argumentation bei Paulus. 2002. *Volume 149.*

Wagener, Ulrike: Die Ordnung des „Hauses Gottes". 1994. *Volume II/65.*

Wahlen, Clinton: Jesus and the Impurity of Spirits in the Synoptic Gospels. 2004. *Volume II/185.*

Walker, Donald D.: Paul's Offer of Leniency (2 Cor 10:1). 2002. *Volume II/152.*

Walter, Nikolaus: Praeparatio Evangelica. Ed. von Wolfgang Kraus und Florian Wilk. 1997. *Volume 98.*

Wander, Bernd: Gottesfürchtige und Sympathisanten. 1998. *Volume 104.*

Watts, Rikki: Isaiah's New Exodus and Mark. 1997. *Volume II/88.*

Wedderburn, A.J.M.: Baptism and Resurrection. 1987. *Volume 44.*

Wegner, Uwe: Der Hauptmann von Kafarnaum. 1985. *Volume II/14.*

Weissenrieder, Annette: Images of Illness in the Gospel of Luke. 2003. Volume II/164.

Welck, Christian: Erzählte ‚Zeichen'. 1994. *Volume II/69.*

Wiarda, Timothy: Peter in the Gospels . 2000. *Volume II/127.*

Wilk, Florian: see *Walter, Nikolaus.*

Williams, Catrin H.: I am He. 2000. *Volume II/113.*

Wilson, Walter T.: Love without Pretense. 1991. *Volume II/46.*

Wischmeyer, Oda: Von Ben Sira zu Paulus. 2004. *Volume 173.*

Wisdom, Jeffrey: Blessing for the Nations and the Curse of the Law. 2001. *Volume II/133.*

Wucherpfennig, Ansgar: Heracleon Philologus. 2002. *Volume 142.*

Yeung, Maureen: Faith in Jesus and Paul. 2002. *Volume II/147.*

Zimmermann, Alfred E.: Die urchristlichen Lehrer. 1984, [2]1988. *Volume II/12.*

Zimmermann, Johannes: Messianische Texte aus Qumran. 1998. *Volume II/104.*

Zimmermann, Ruben: Christologie der Bilder im Johannesevangelium. 2004. *Volume 171.*

– Geschlechtermetaphorik und Gottesverhältnis. 2001. *Volume II/122.*

Zumstein, Jean: see *Dettwiler, Andreas*

Zwiep, Arie W.: Judas and the Choice of Matthias. 2004. *Volume II/187.*

For a complete catalogue please write to the publisher
Mohr Siebeck • P.O. Box 2030 • D–72010 Tübingen/Germany
Up-to-date information on the internet at www.mohr.de